MW01627535

SARGENT WHISTLER & VENETIAN GLASS

American Artists and the Magic of Murano

EDITED BY

Crawford Alexander Mann III.

WITH CONTRIBUTIONS BY

Sheldon Barr
Melody Barnett Deusner
Diana Jocelyn Greenwold
Stephanie Mayer Heydt
Crawford Alexander Mann III.
Brittany Emens Strupp

Smithsonian American Art Museum
Washington, DC
in association with Princeton University Press
Princeton and Oxford

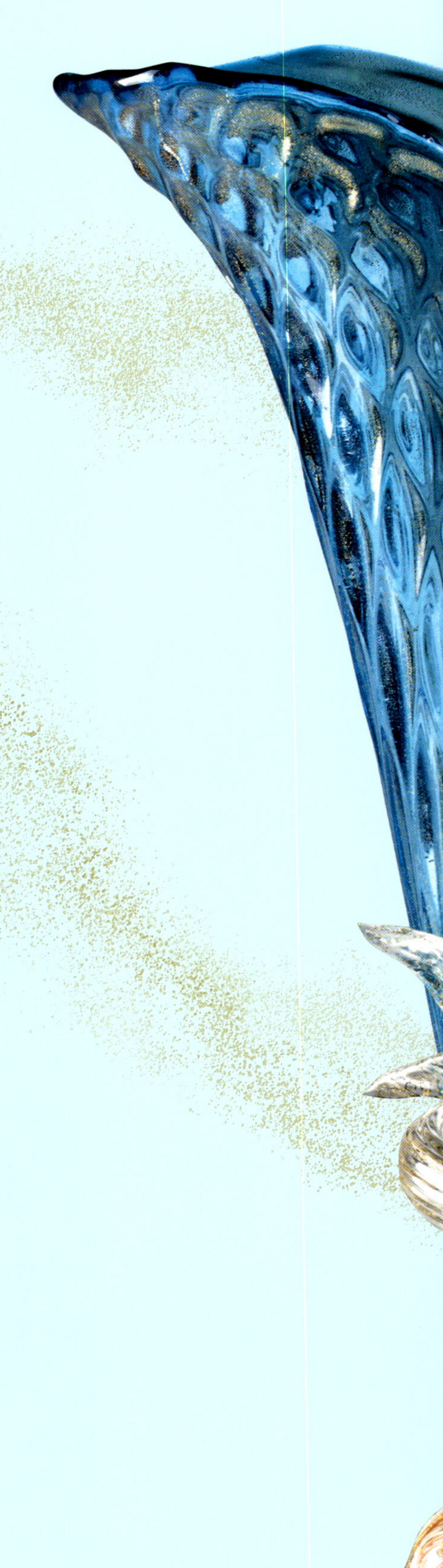

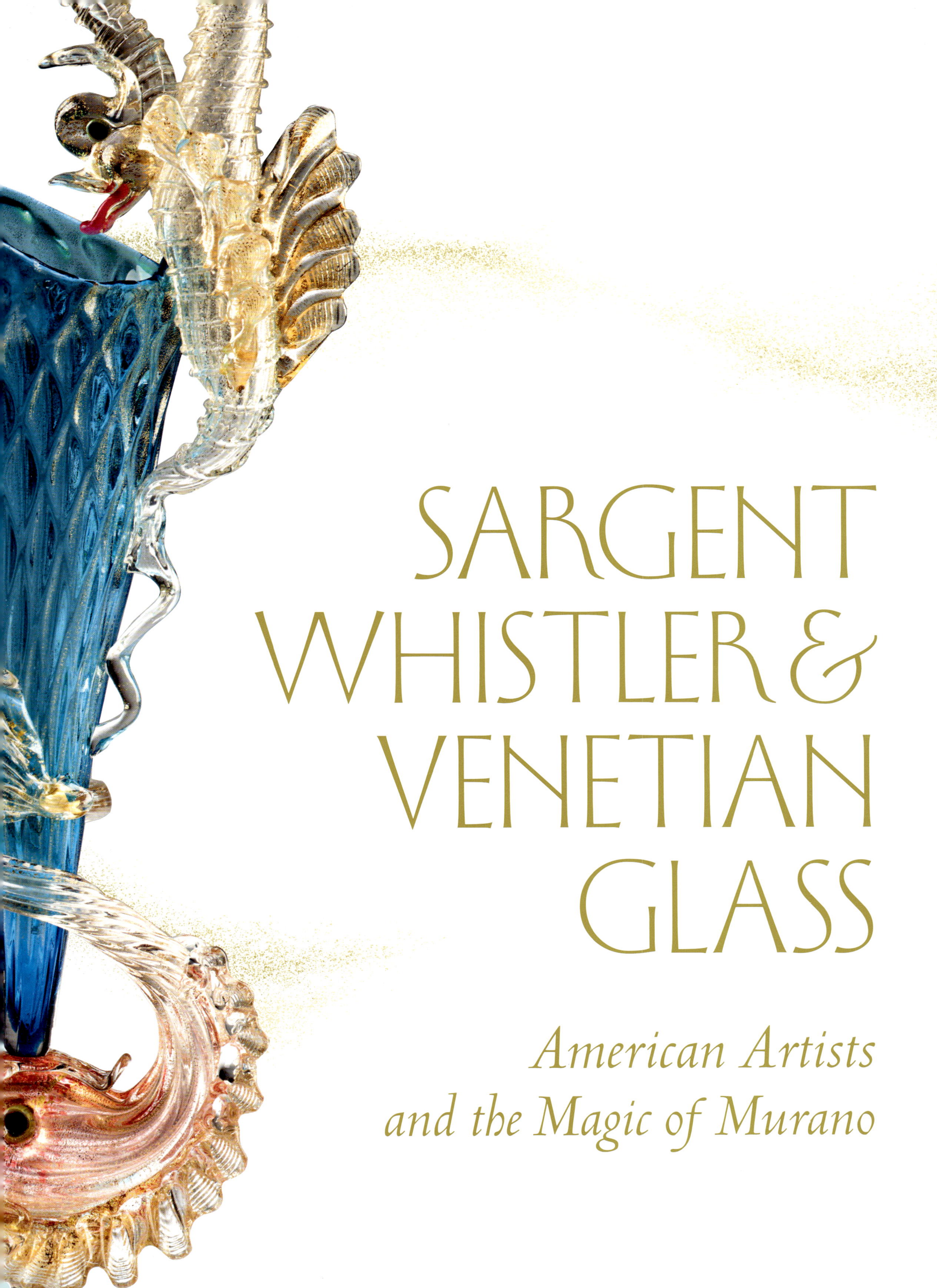

SARGENT WHISTLER & VENETIAN GLASS

American Artists and the Magic of Murano

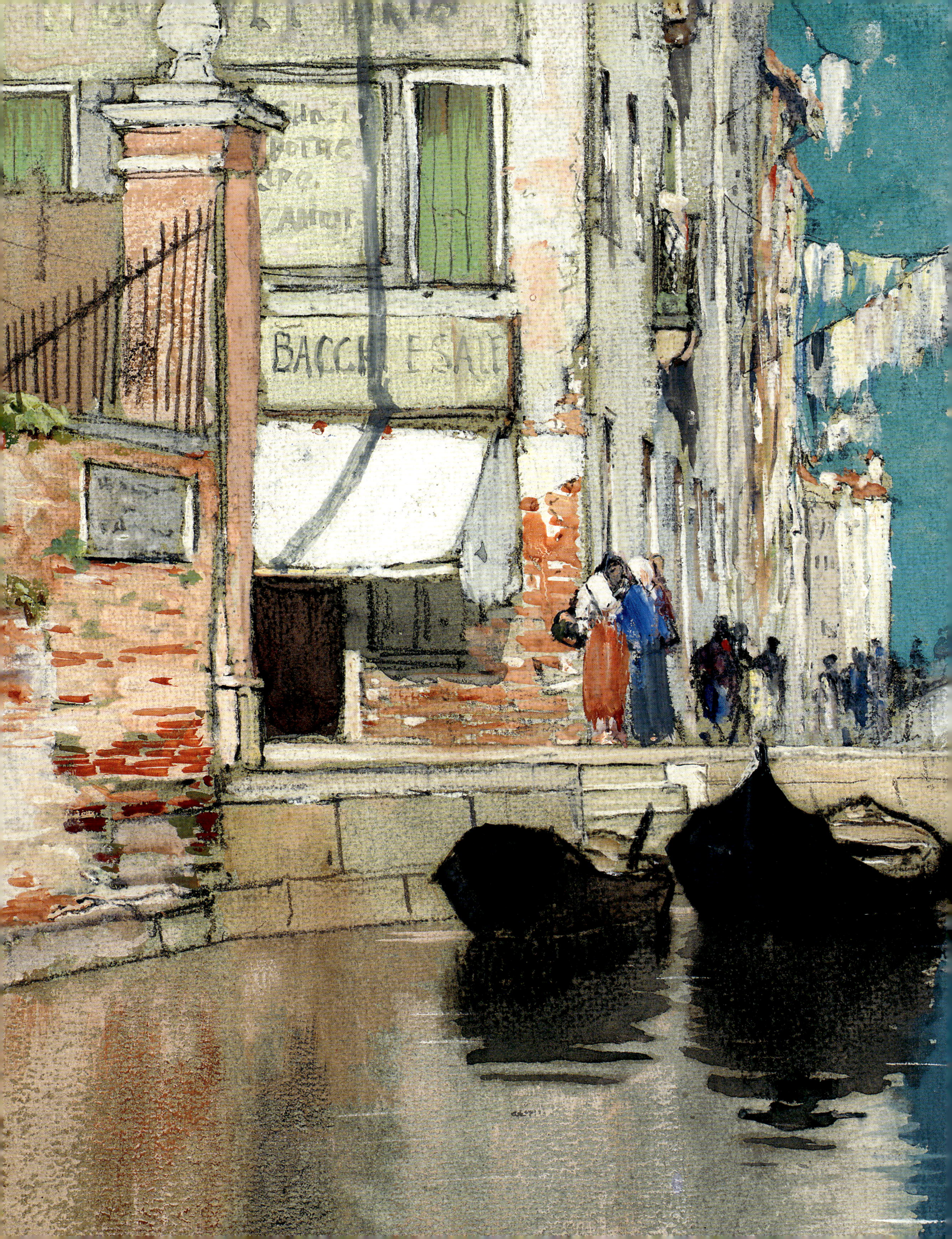

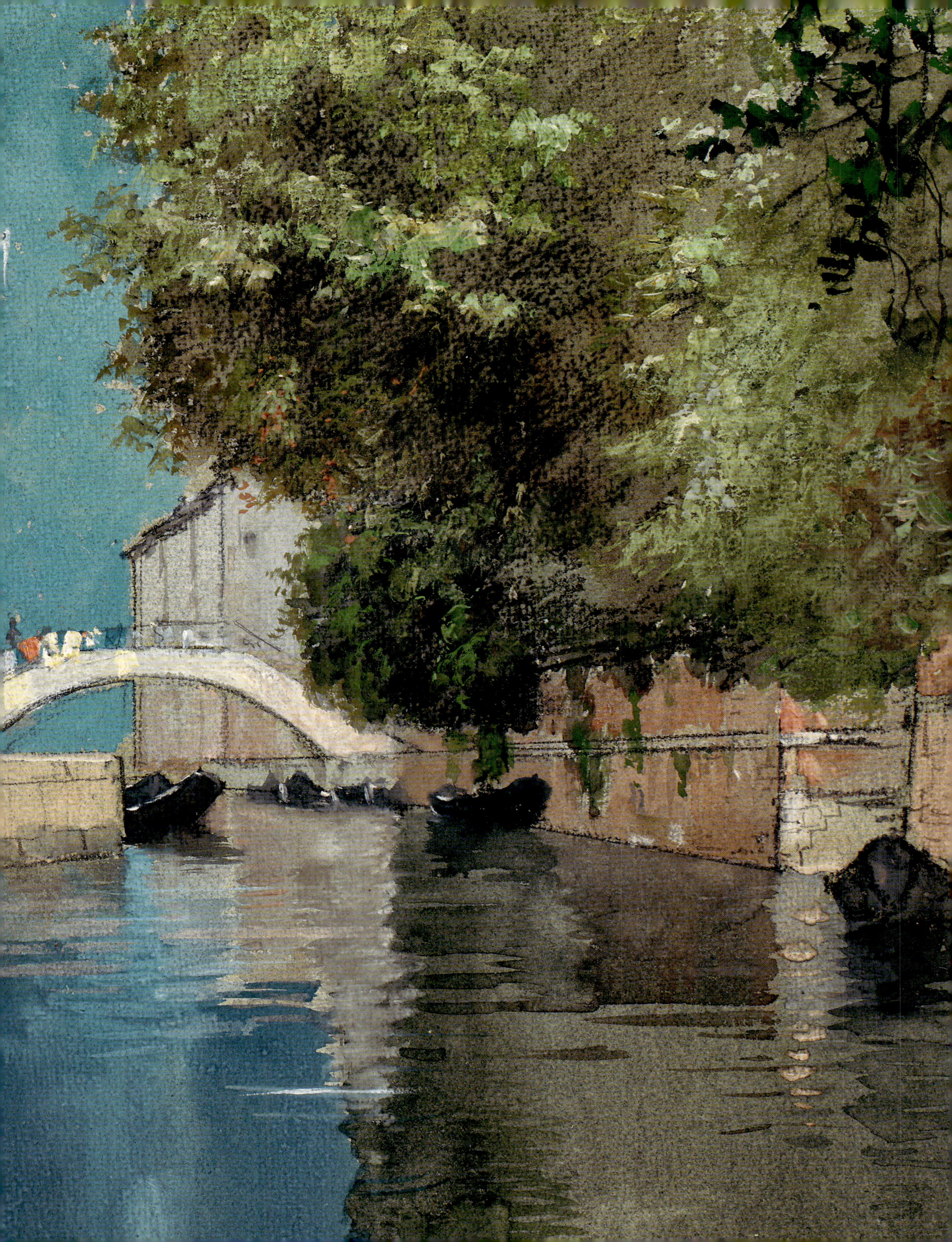

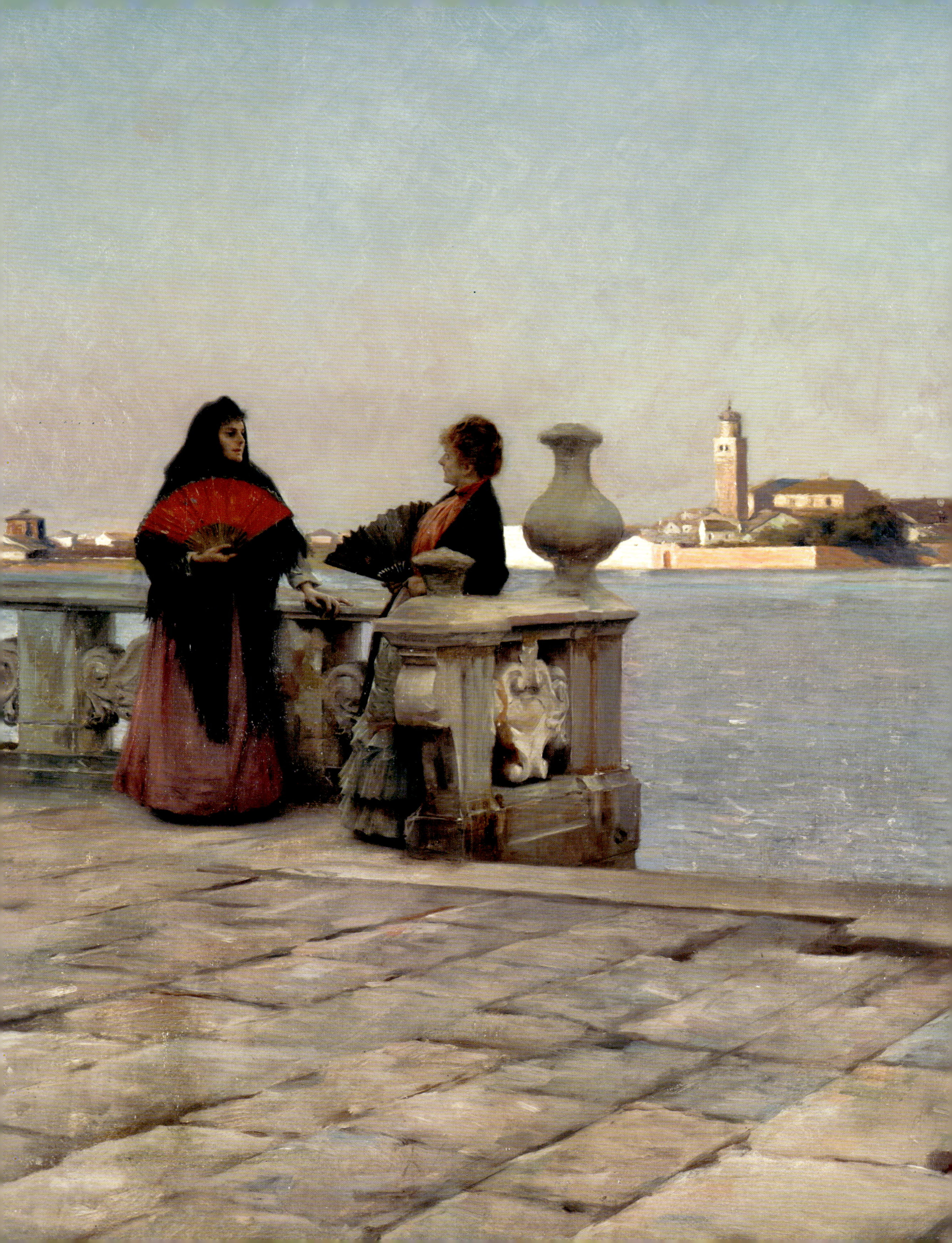

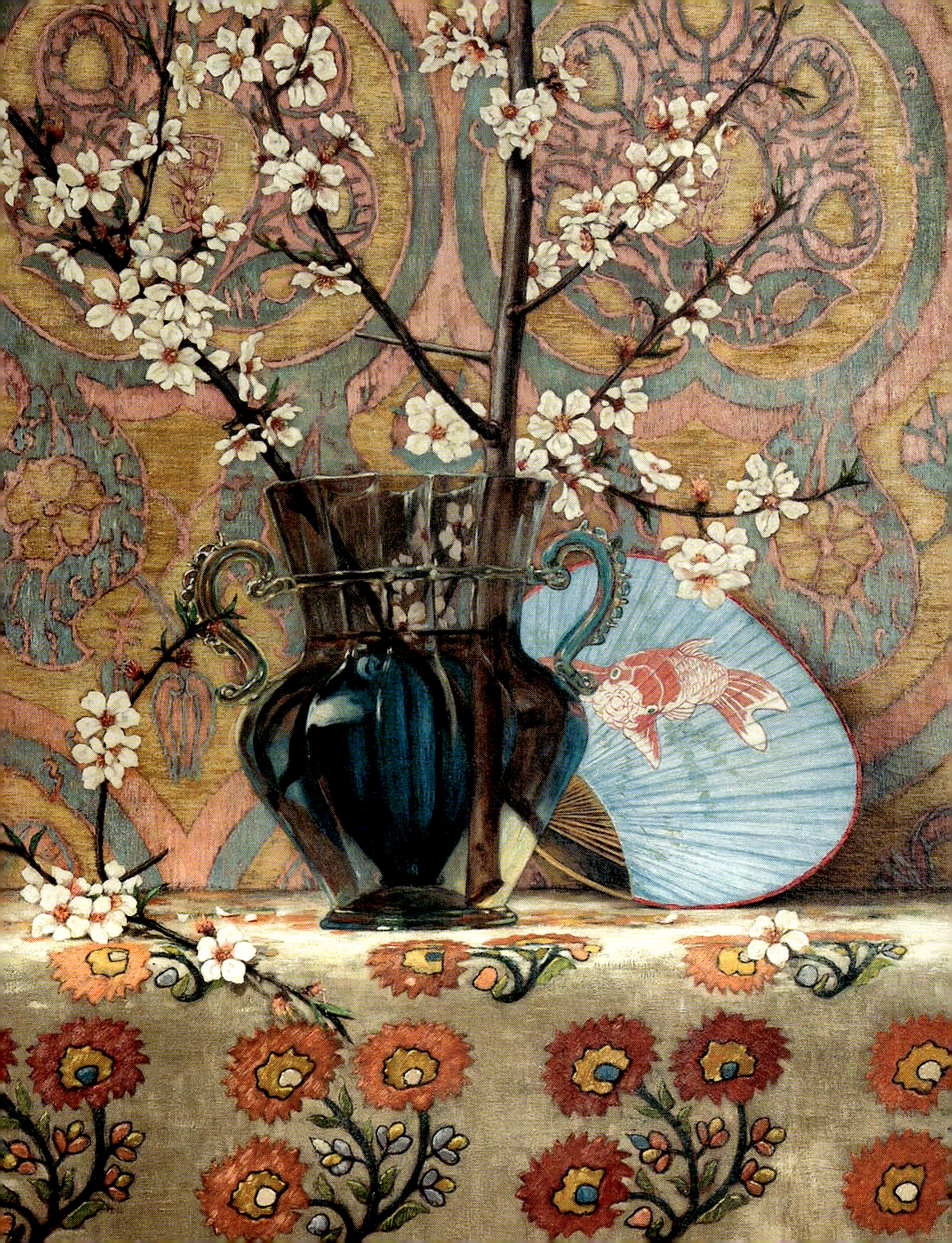

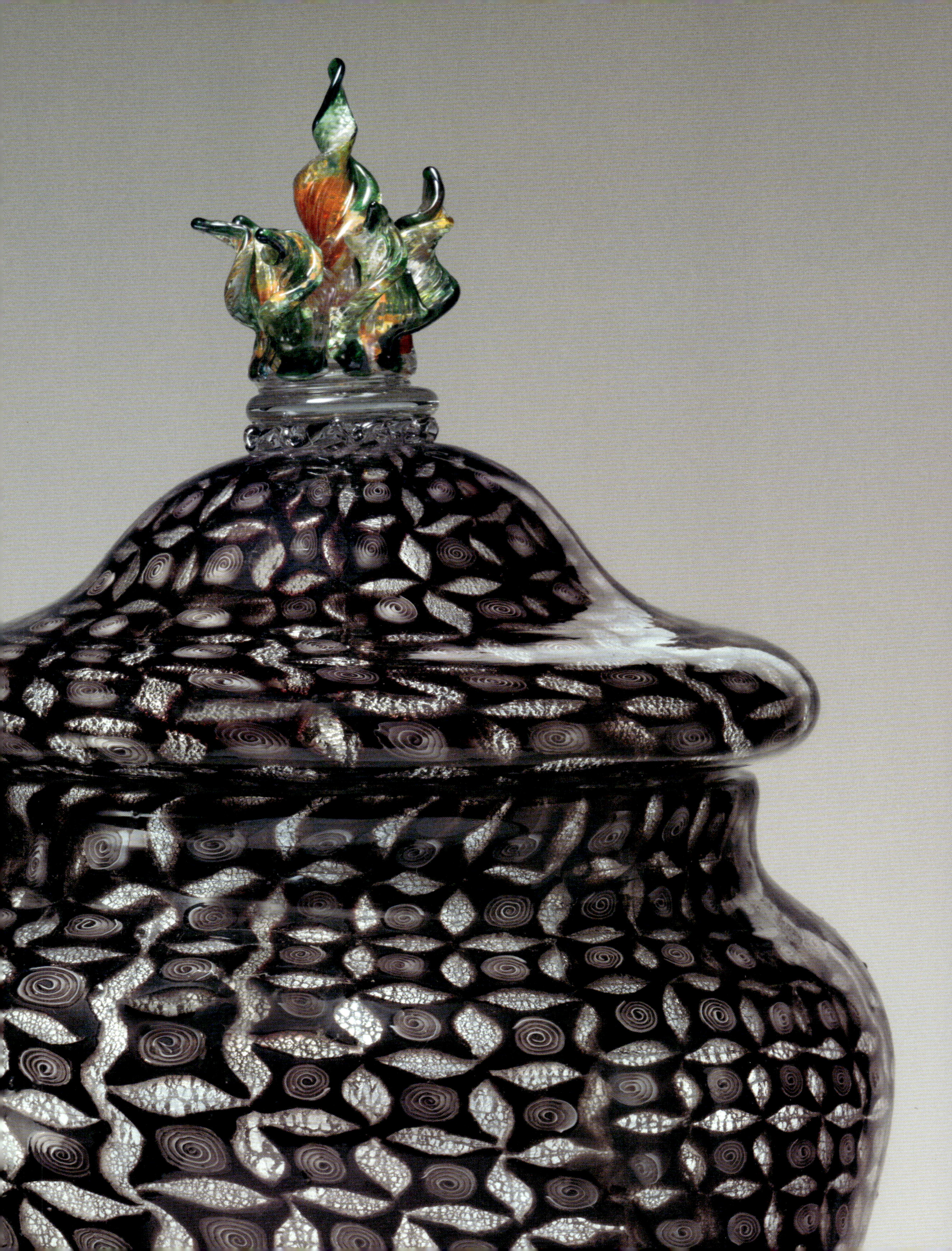

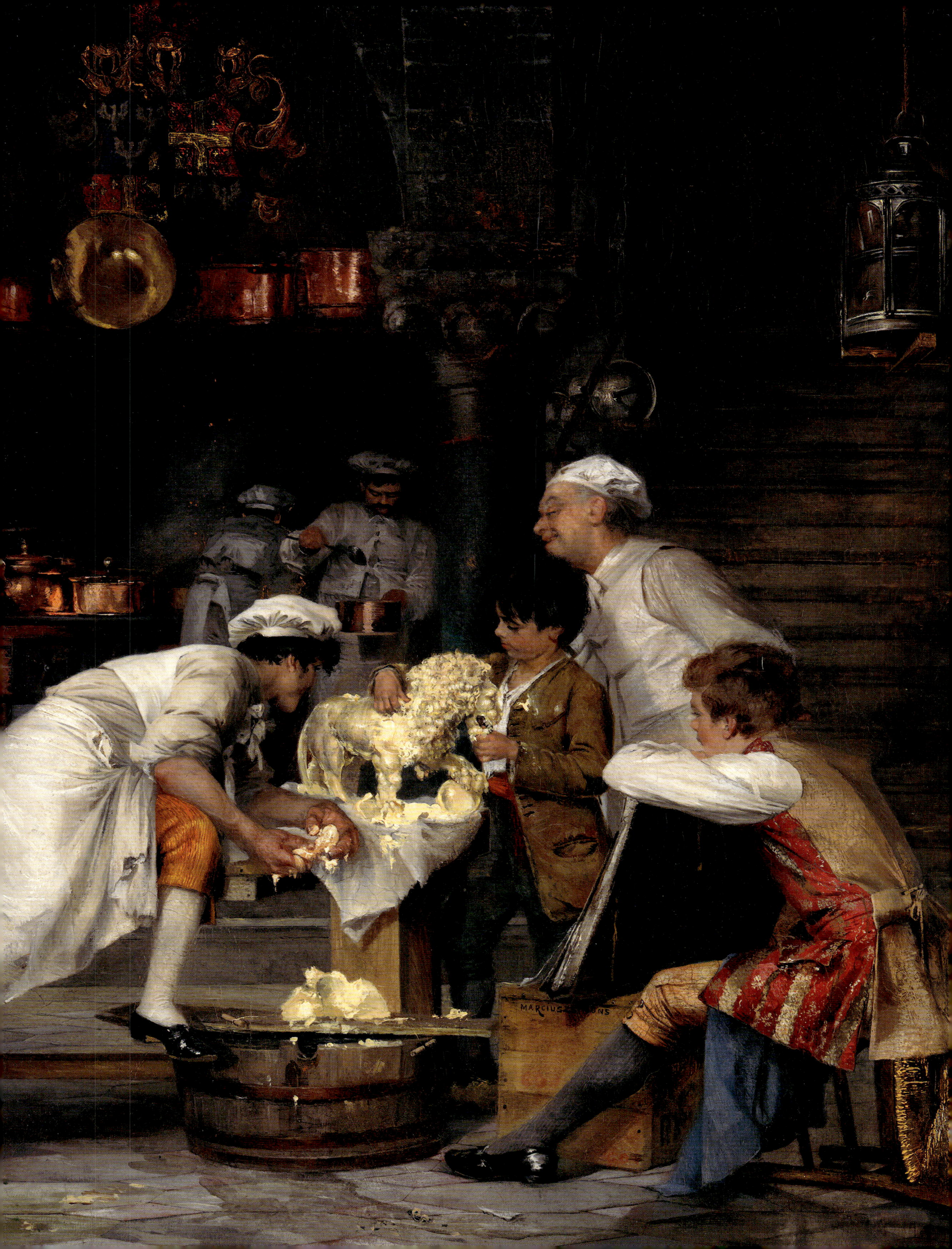

Sargent, Whistler, and Venetian Glass: American Artists and the Magic of Murano
is organized by the Smithsonian American Art Museum.

Generous support has been provided by:

The Gladys Krieble Delmas Foundation
Embassy of Italy in Washington, DC
Raymond J. and Margaret Horowitz Endowment
Janet and William Ellery James
William R. Kenan Jr. Endowment Fund
Maureen and Gene Kim
The Lunder Foundation—Peter and Paula Lunder Family
Lucy S. Rhame
Holly and Nick Ruffin
Smithsonian Scholarly Studies Awards
Rick and Lucille Spagnuolo
Myra and Harold Weiss

The accompanying catalogue is supported in part by Jane Joel Knox.

In-kind support has been provided by Christie's.

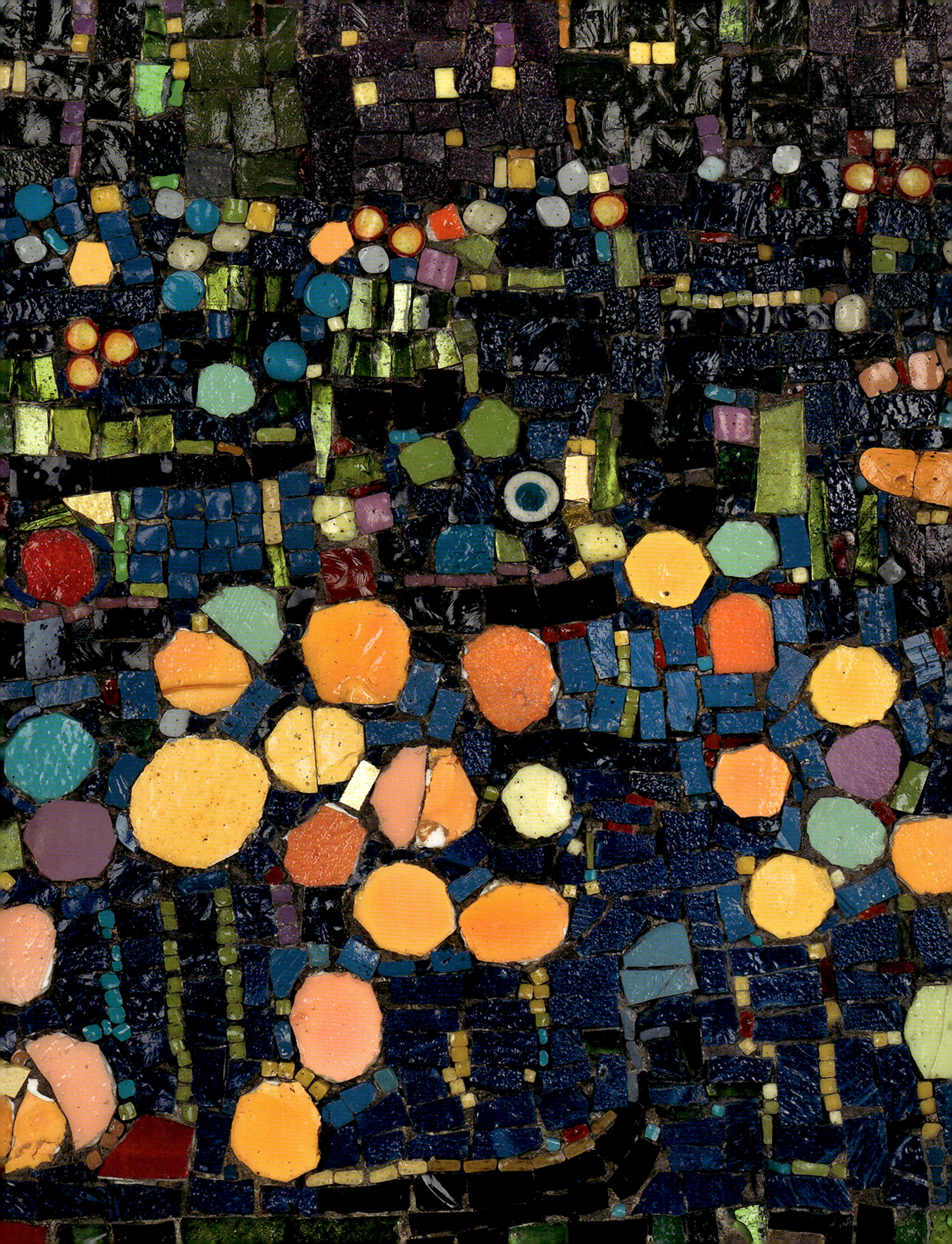

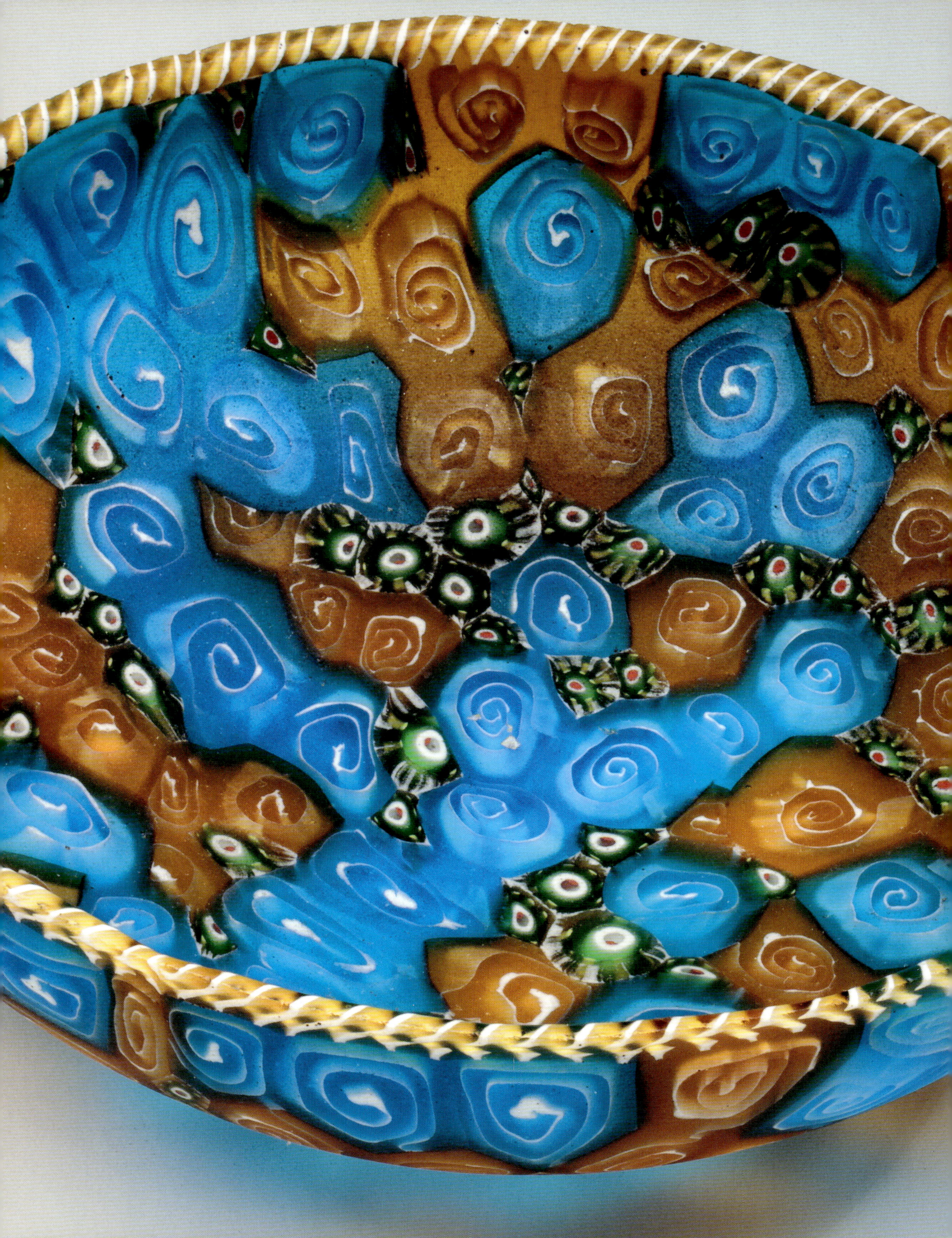

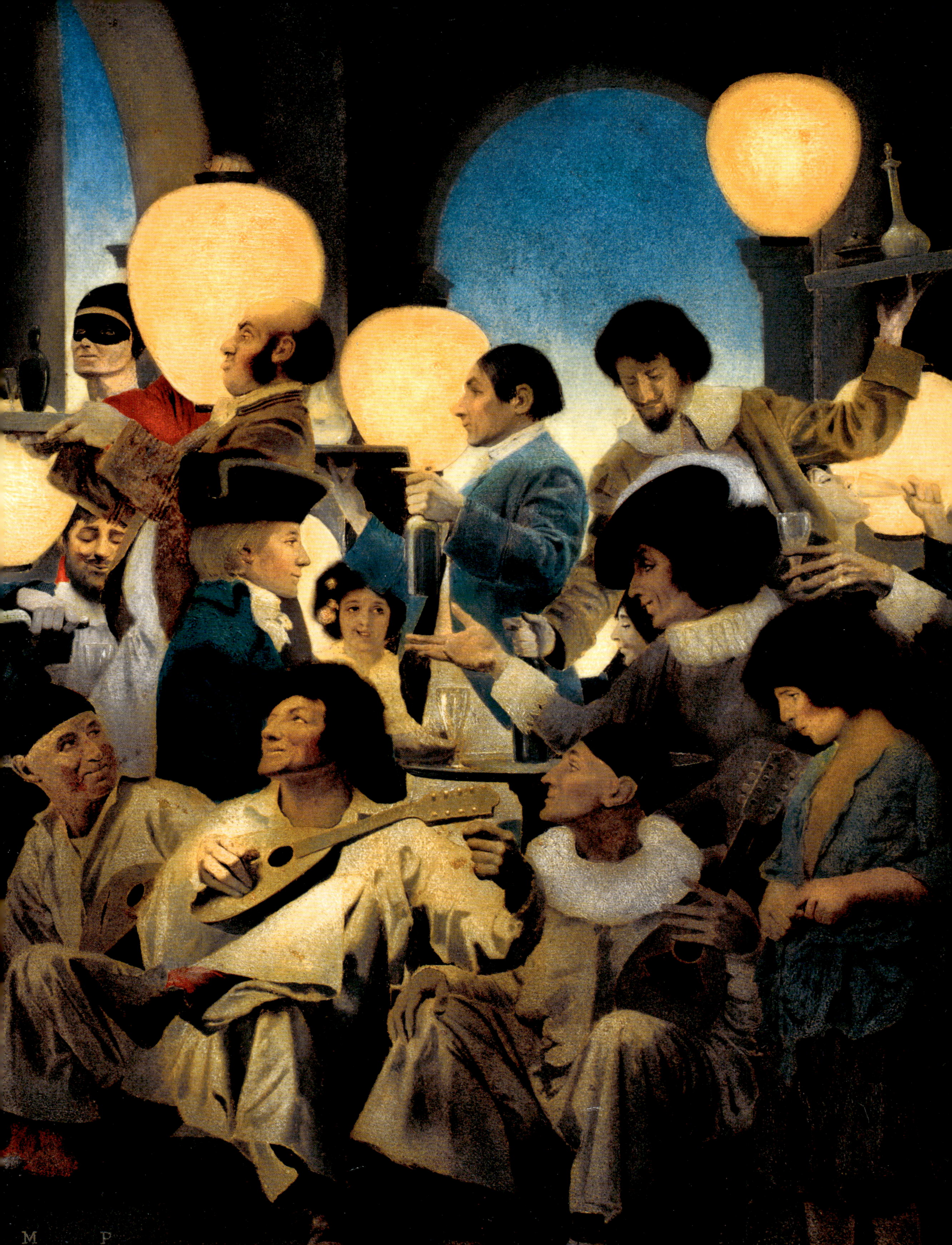

Contents

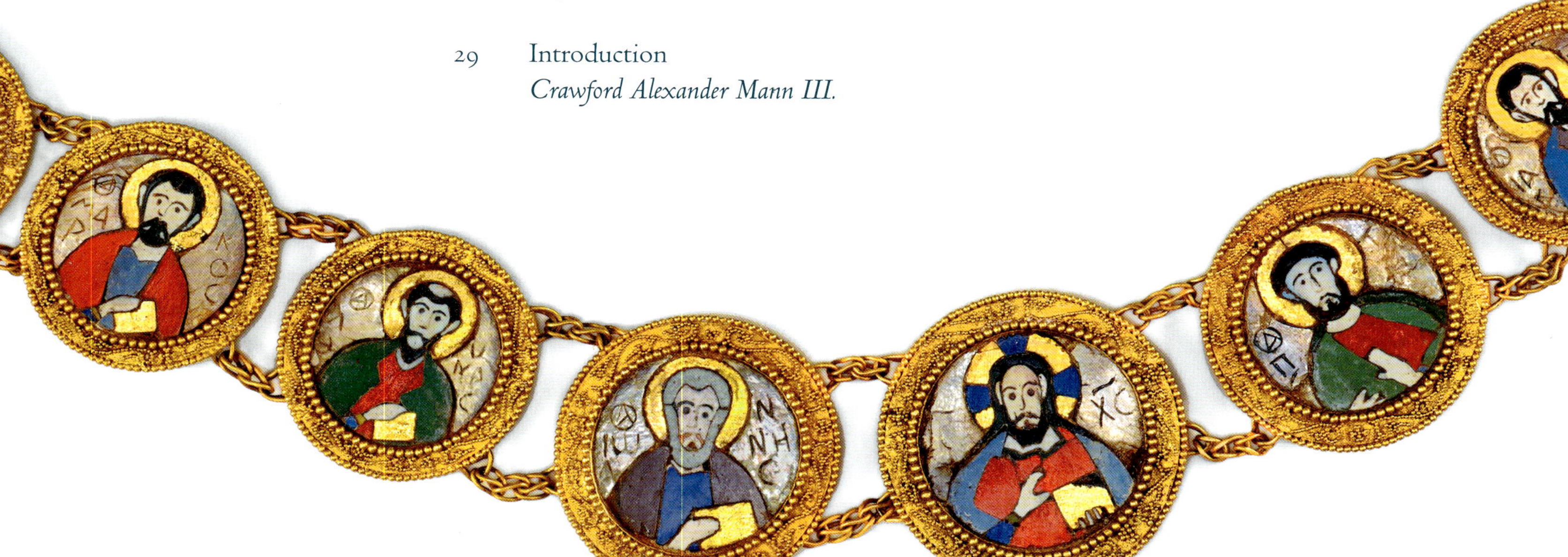

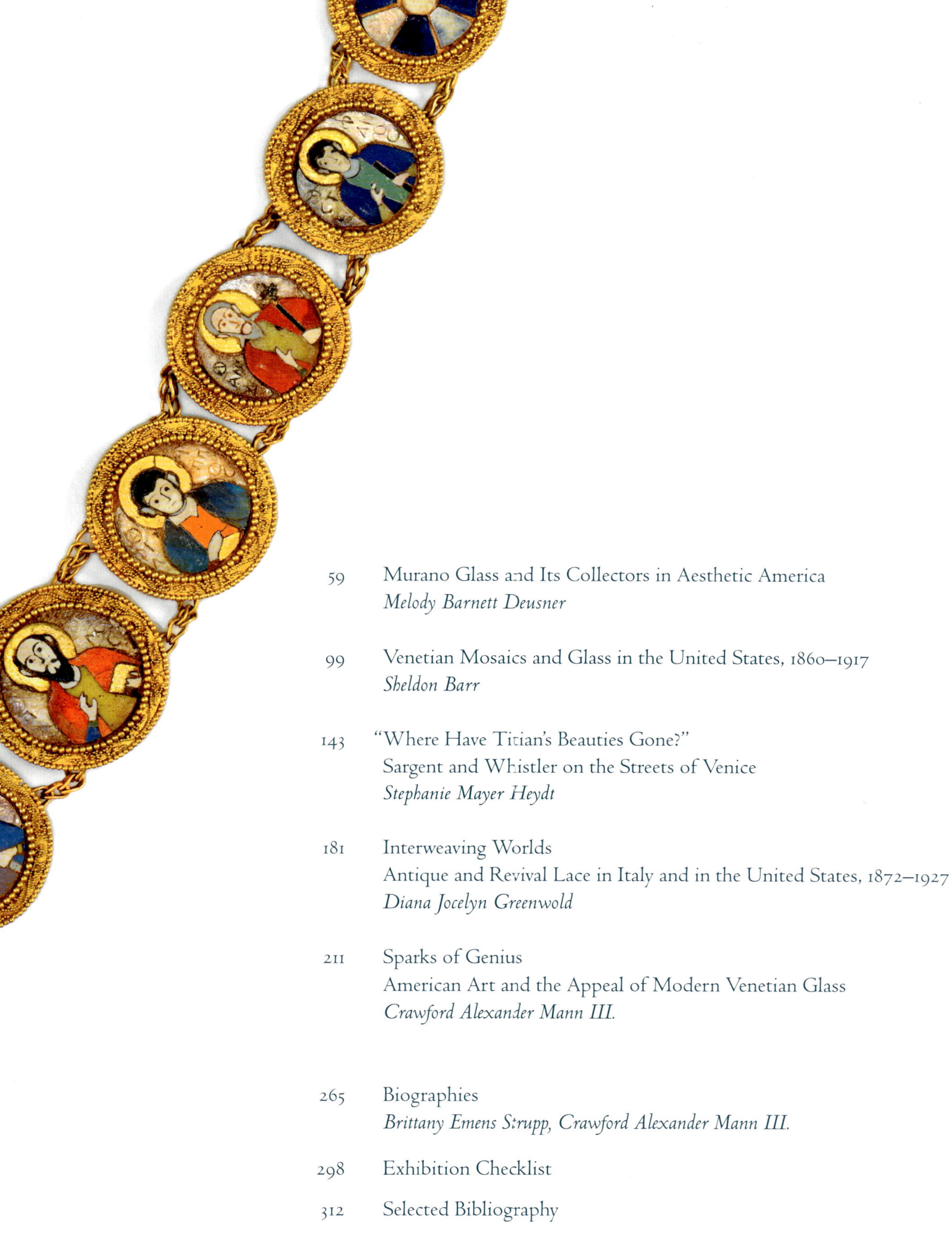

Lenders to the Exhibition

Albany Institute of History & Art
Michael and Jean Antonello Family Foundation
Art Bridges
The Art Institute of Chicago
The Baltimore Museum of Art
Bowdoin College Museum of Art
Brooklyn Museum
Iris & B. Gerald Cantor Center for Visual Arts at Stanford University
Chrysler Museum of Art
Cincinnati Art Museum
Clark Art Institute
Cooper Hewitt, Smithsonian Design Museum
The Corning Museum of Glass
Vincent and Kako Crisci
Fry Fine Art Gallery
Mary Anne Goley
Illinois State Museum
Darrel C. Karl
Jane Joel Knox
Lucas Museum of Narrative Art
David Mamet and Rebecca Pidgeon
McGuigan Collection
The Metropolitan Museum of Art
Minneapolis Institute of Art
Museum of Art, Rhode Island School of Design
Museum of Fine Arts, Boston
Museum of the City of New York
National Anthropological Archives, Smithsonian Institution
National Gallery of Art, Washington, DC
National Museum of American Illustration and American Illustrators Gallery
The National Museum of Women in the Arts
The New York Public Library
North Carolina Museum of Art
The Phillips Collection
Lisa and Michael Sandman
Smithsonian American Art Museum
Stanford University Libraries, Department of Special Collections
Toledo Museum of Art
US Senate Collection
The Walters Art Museum
Williams College Museum of Art
Woodmere Art Museum
The Estate of Robert and Linda Wueste
and generous private lenders

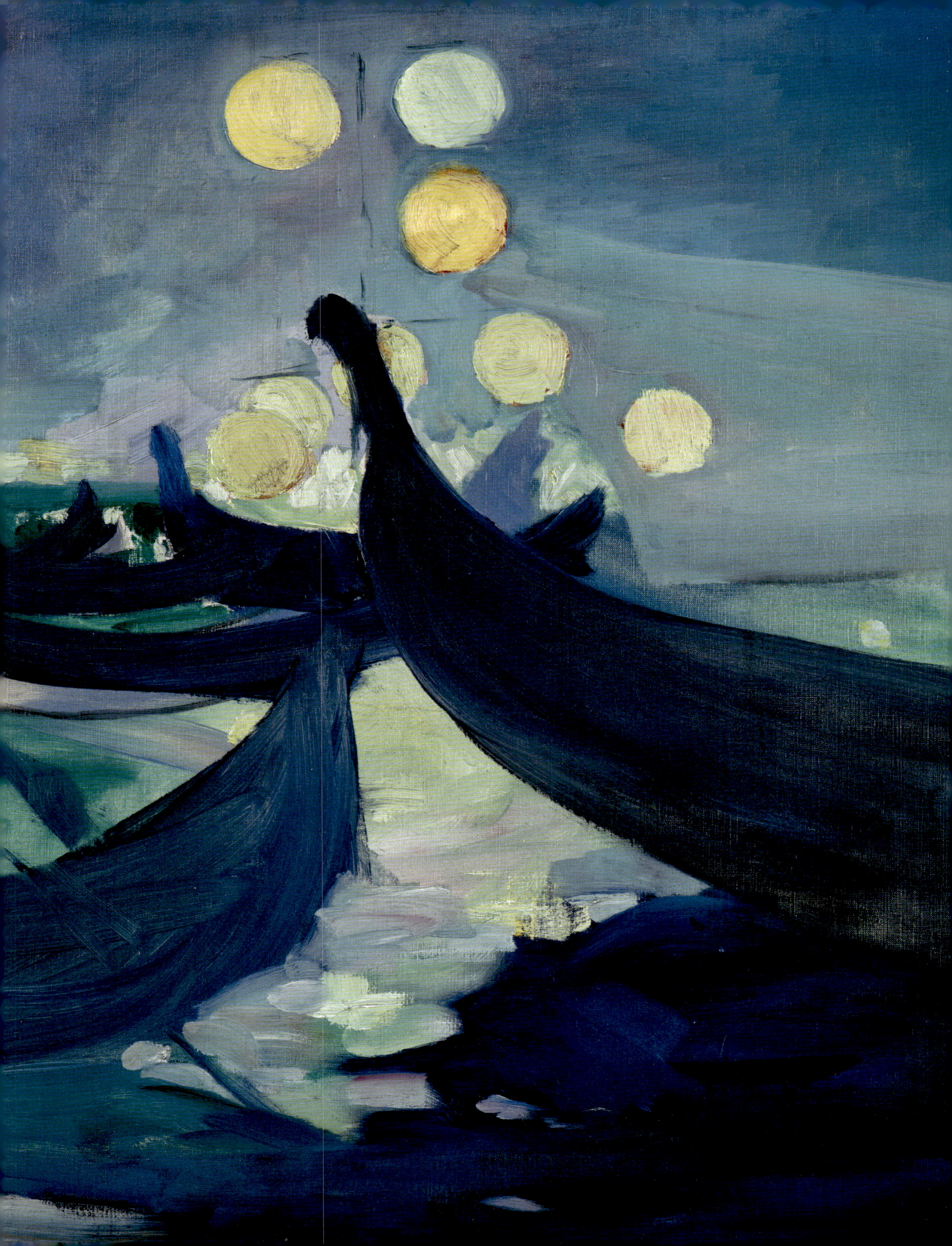

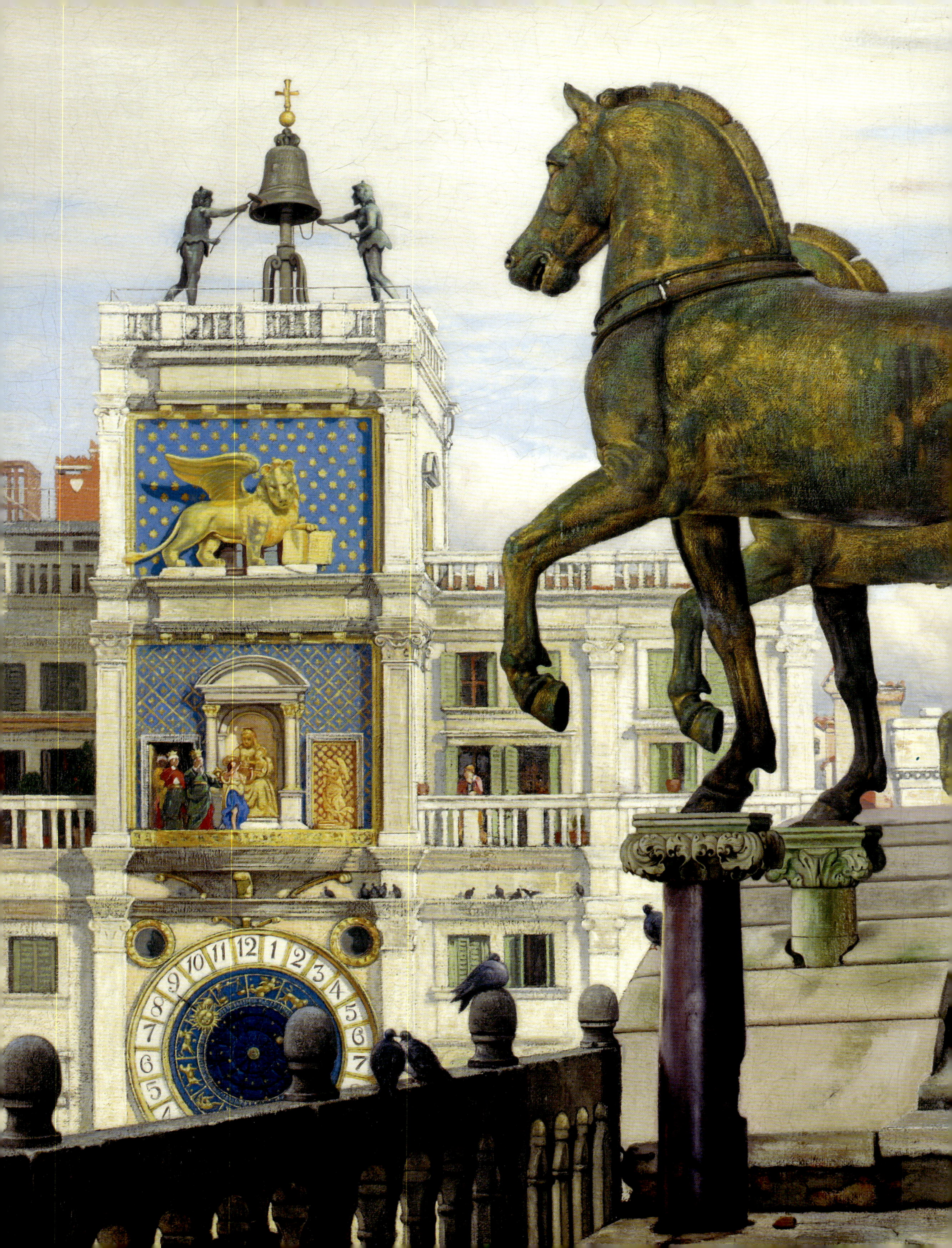

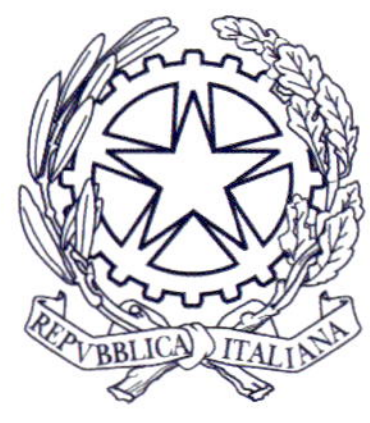

Embassy of Italy
Washington

Sargent, Whistler, and Venetian Glass: American Artists and the Magic of Murano recognizes glassmaking as a source of inspiration for top American artists—a creative exchange that influenced culture, society, and ideologies on both sides of the Atlantic.

For centuries, Venice was the heart of a thriving maritime empire whose wealth and power nurtured the most talented artists of the era and sparked unparalleled creativity. Today, Venice is a modern and vibrant city, open to the world and to the future, retaining its strong entrepreneurial culture and its support for artistic innovation.

Venice discovered the art of glassmaking from southwestern Asia and gradually refined it into a world-renowned industry. In 1291, the glass artisans and factories moved from Venice to Murano, a small island in the Venetian lagoon. To this day, Murano glass manufacture—an expression of art and highest quality craftsmanship—has deservedly kept its place in the spotlight, evolving and adapting, while respectfully preserving ties to its ancient traditions.

Sargent, Whistler, and Venetian Glass: American Artists and the Magic of Murano features more than 140 exquisite works, including ornate handblown glass objects by the main glassmakers of Murano and marvelous paintings and prints by dozens of American artists. Together they offer insight into the artistic dialogue across the Atlantic from the Italian Risorgimento to World War I, between the young American nation and a newly unified Italy. This cross-cultural exchange continues today at the Venice Biennale and through innumerable contacts between artists, intellectuals, and diverse members of society.

This spectacular exhibition, together with its scholarly catalogue, testify to the strong cooperation between several great cultural institutions in Italy and the United States: the Smithsonian American Art Museum, the Amon Carter Museum of American Art in Fort Worth, TX, and the Ca' Pesaro Galleria Internazionale d'Arte Moderna in Venice. Their collaborations strengthen the deep bonds of friendship between our countries. It is, therefore, only fitting that this initiative form an integral part of the celebrations marking 160 years of diplomatic relations between Italy and the United States.

Reading this book and visiting the exhibition will be enriching experiences, fostering knowledge and appreciation of the strong cultural ties our countries proudly share.

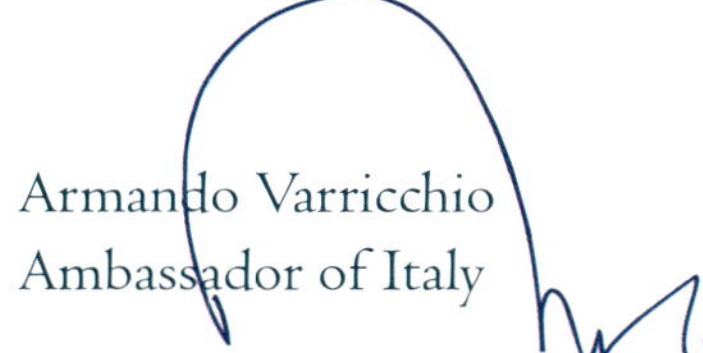

Armando Varricchio
Ambassador of Italy

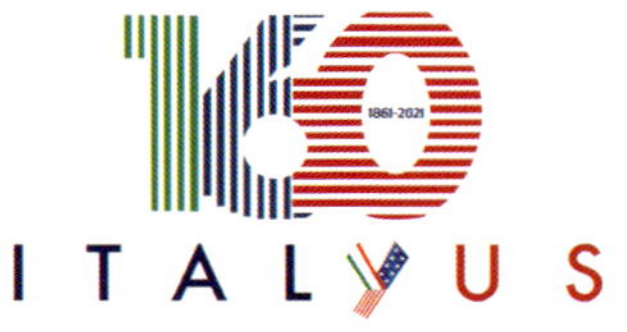

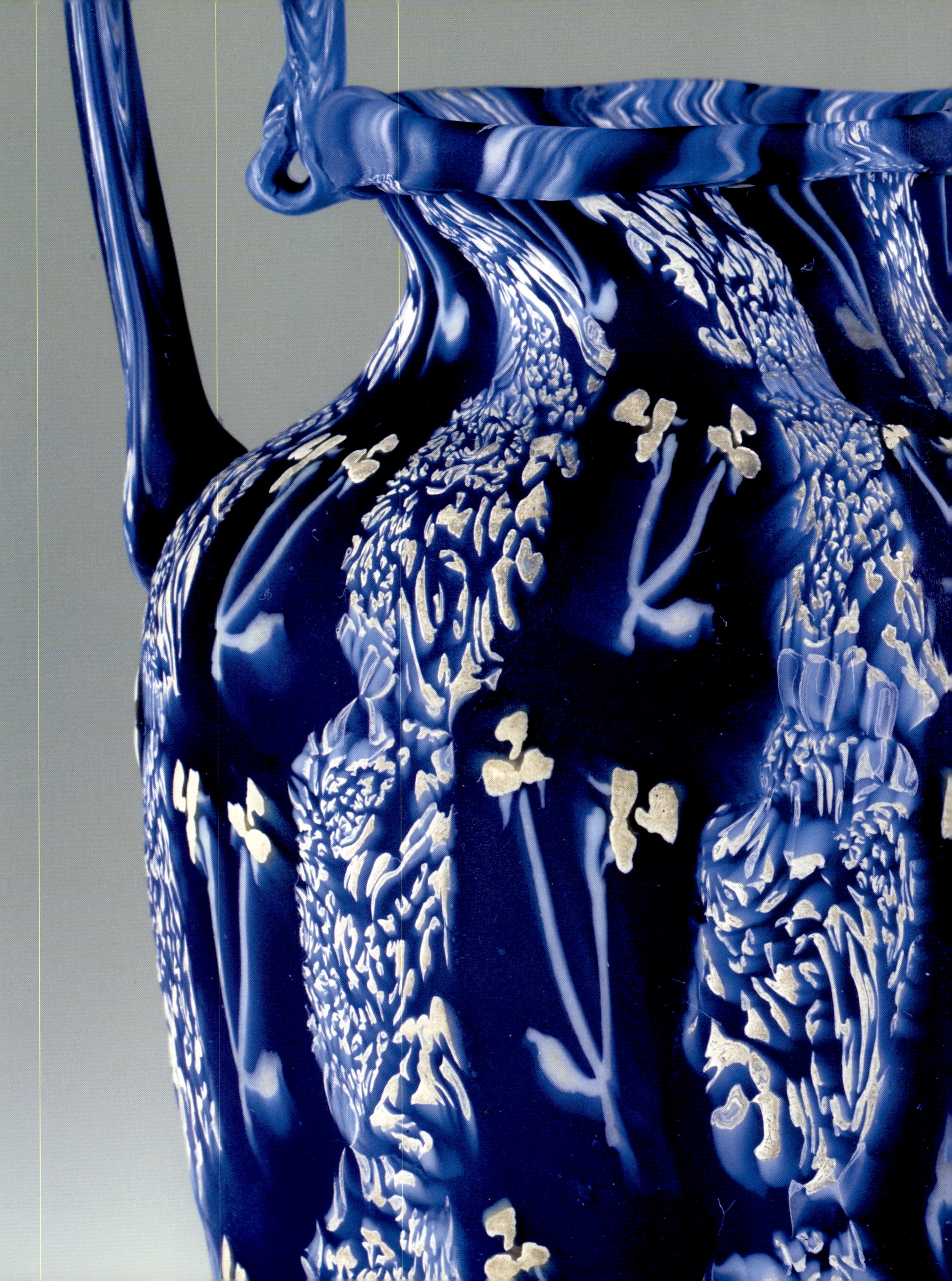

Director's Foreword

Between 1860 and 1915, the renowned glassmaking industry on the Venetian island of Murano experienced intense growth. This Venetian glass revival coincided with a surge in Venice's popularity as a destination for American tourists, many of whom visited the glass furnaces and eagerly collected ornate handblown goblets decorated with flowers, dragons, and sea creatures. Venetian glass was more than a grand tour souvenir; these were museum-quality works of fine art. Collector interest led to frequent depictions of Italian glassmakers and glass objects by prominent American artists of that era, including John Singer Sargent, James McNeill Whistler, and Robert Frederick Blum. Bearing witness to this esteem for Murano and its craftspeople are hundreds of examples of modern Venetian art glass donated to the United States' oldest museums during their founding decades, including the National Collection of Fine Arts, the predecessor of today's Smithsonian American Art Museum (SAAM).

Despite this prestige, shifts in tastes later denigrated Venetian revival glass as derivative or kitsch, and these once-prized artworks were relegated to attics, museum vaults, and antiques stores. In this exhibition and book, SAAM reunites these exquisitely crafted objects with paintings, etchings, and drawings from the same milieu, thereby recovering and explaining their past significance. Our project demonstrates that this dynamic transatlantic cross-pollination had a lasting impact on American art, literature, and education, as well as period concepts of gender and social class.

Our show grows from seven years of research by Crawford Alexander Mann III., investigations that began before he became SAAM's curator of prints and drawings in 2017. Building on his expertise in artistic exchange between Italy and the United States and his curiosity about how travel and migration shape culture, Mann has been on a treasure hunt for Venetian glass in archives, books, and museum collections. In SAAM's storage warehouse he identified nine specimens among the vast assortment of paintings, antiquities, and decorative arts donated in 1929 by John Gellatly—pieces whose singularity and complexity are comparable to the choicest works in Murano's Museo del Vetro and at the Corning Museum of Glass. We present these alongside cousins from Stanford University's Cantor Center for Visual Arts, the Metropolitan Museum of Art, and other notable collections—all acquired more than a century ago.

To reveal these transatlantic influences, this show juxtaposes these works of Italian glass with specific paintings and prints by Sargent, Whistler, and three dozen of their contemporaries. International travel was central to these artists' practice, and their experiences of Venice followed established patterns, including visits to glass factories. References to Venice and glass subsequently became a common thread in their work. Though glittery colors and flamboyant sculptural flourishes made Venetian glass seem frivolous to later eyes, these objects originally connoted appreciation for beauty, respect for history and science, and, on a societal level, commitment to political self-determination and economic individualism. Every day I work at a desk that embodies these ideals. A model of the desk, covered with tiny replicas of Venetian glass, appears in a charming diorama that belonged to John Gellatly (see p. 61). The full-sized desk, highly carved and replete with secret drawers and panels, was commissioned in Italy by Gellatly, who donated a rich collection to the museum, including Venetian glass. Gellatly's collection expresses these period values, and when Murano's products and their makers appear in works of fine art, they reinforce these statements of identity, or, in some cases, critique and challenge them.

This exhibition continues SAAM's commitment to exploring American art and its global connections, fostering inclusive conversations approaching US history and culture from fresh points of view. As a nexus for commerce among Asia, Africa, and Europe, Venice enjoys the nickname the "Crossroads of the World," and international tourism has nurtured its distinctive artistic traditions, including excellence in lace- and glassmaking. Today Washington, DC, is also a cultural crossroads, home to embassies, think tanks, universities, tech firms, research hospitals, and museums, with a global mosaic of languages, cuisines, and customs among its residents. As this exhibition shares past stories of travel, exchange, and influence, it invites reflection on the present-day circulation of artworks and material goods and on their sometimes unnamed creators.

As cochair of the Smithsonian American Women's History Initiative, I am especially proud of this project's attention to female agency: as artists, tastemakers, collectors, and philanthropists. Although our title artists, Sargent and Whistler, were among the most prolific of their generation to explore Venice, their reputations should not overshadow the talents of Ellen Day Hale, Bertha Evelyn Jaques, and Mabel Pugh—women featured here and meriting monographic exhibitions. Furthermore, the essays in this volume describe the arts patronage of Isabella Stewart Gardner, Jane Lathrop Stanford, and Florence Colgate Speranza, each of whom facilitated exchange between the United States and Italy. This show thus considers the grand tour through a variety of new lenses, correcting the historical canon. We disrupt hierarchies of gender and of market value and reframe familiar images of the Rialto Bridge and the Doge's Palace among forgotten stories and new discoveries.

On behalf of SAAM and its visitors, I thank the lenders to this groundbreaking exhibition. I also recognize the following individuals, foundations, and corporations for their support: Christie's, the Gladys Krieble Delmas Foundation, the Raymond J. and Margaret Horowitz Endowment, Janet and William Ellery James, the William R. Kenan Jr. Endowment Fund, Maureen and Jim Kim, the Lunder Foundation—Peter and Paula Lunder Family, Lucy S. Rhame, Holly and Nick Ruffin, Smithsonian Scholarly Studies Awards, Rick and Lucille Spagnuolo, and Myra and Harold Weiss. The exhibition catalogue has benefited from the generosity of Jane Joel Knox. I am also grateful to His Excellency Armando Varricchio, Ambassador of Italy to the United States, and the staff of the Embassy of Italy in Washington, DC, for their contributions to this project.

Furthermore, I thank our tour partners. Few institutions more closely share SAAM's mission than the Amon Carter Museum of American Art in Fort Worth, Texas. It is always a pleasure to work with my friend and colleague, director Andrew J. Walker, and curators Margaret Adler and Spencer Wigmore. By contrast, exhibitions about historic American art do not frequently travel overseas, so it is an honor to collaborate with Gabriella Belli, director of the Fondazione Musei Civici di Venezia, and Elisabetta Barisoni, head of the Ca' Pesaro Galleria Internazionale d'Arte Moderna, to bring this exhibition "home" to Venice and welcome new voices to our global conversations.

Most of all, I thank and applaud SAAM's staff. I salute Alex Mann for his insightful devotion to the topic and for his diligent research that has added a new and compelling chapter in American art and the grand tour story that has long fascinated us. The production of an international traveling loan exhibition and accompanying book are achievements that stretch energy and ingenuity in the best of times. However, this project reached its most intense production phases just as the COVID-19 pandemic triggered unimaginable changes to our daily lives, workplaces, and finances. Despite the transition to telework and struggles with anxiety, frustration, and grief, this team has maintained its commitment to Smithsonian standards of academic excellence and top-quality design, sharing in the conviction that art museums provide beautiful and educational experiences that lift our spirits and brighten our planet's darkest hours. In that regard, this show testifies not only to the talents of Sargent, Whistler, their colleagues, and the glassmakers of Murano, but also to the brilliance and resilience of SAAM's staff, with whom I am humbled to work.

The sacrifices and isolation of 2020 and 2021 deepen appreciation for the joy of travel and connection, be it firsthand or imagined. In that spirit, I present *Sargent, Whistler, and Venetian Glass* as a rich and rewarding journey, a magical gondola ride with an international circle of friends and unforgettable works of art.

Stephanie Stebich
The Margaret and Terry Stent Director
Smithsonian American Art Museum

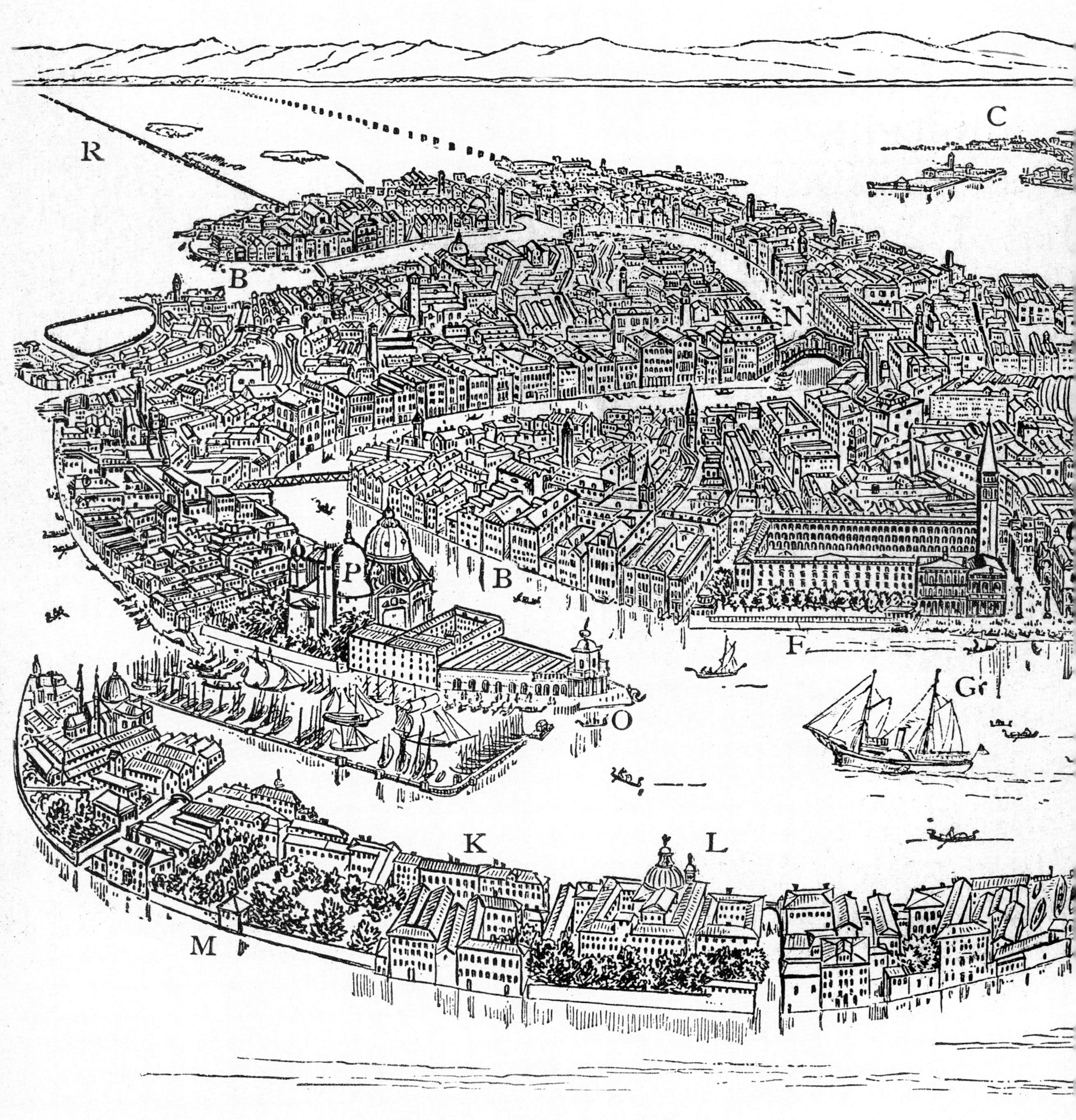
R
C
B
N
P
B
F
G
O
K
L
M

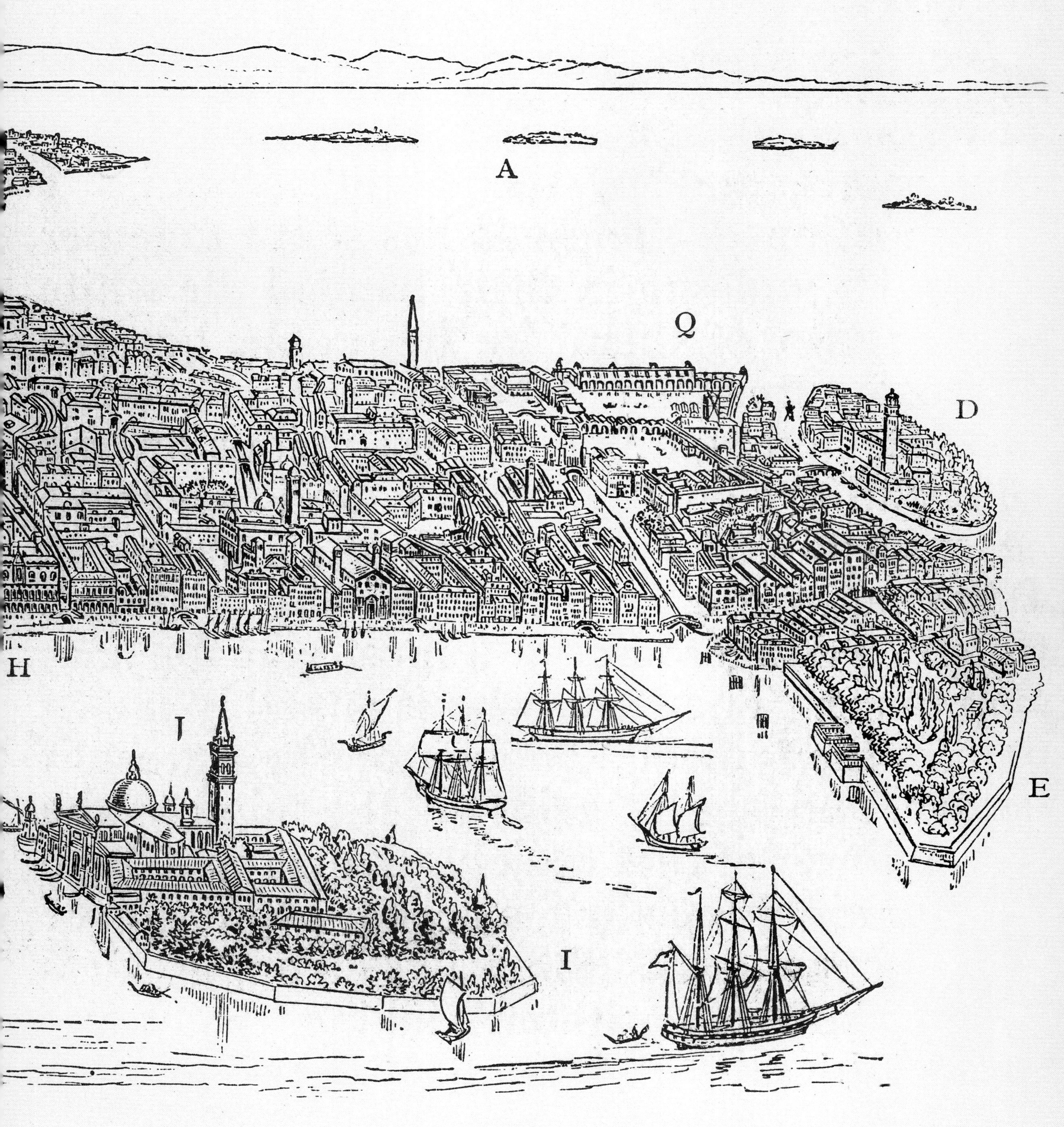

BIRD'S-EYE VIEW OF VENICE.

A, Lagoon — B, Grand Canal — C, Murano — D, Island of S. Pietro — E, Public Gardens — F, Place of St. Mark — G, Campanile — H, Ducal Palace and St. Mark's — I, Island of S. Giorgio Maggiore — J, S. Giorgio Maggiore — K, Canal of the Guidecca — L, SS. Redentore — M, Island of the Guidecca — N, Bridge of the Rialto — O, Custom-house — P, S. Maria della Saluta — Q, Arsenal — R, Railroad.

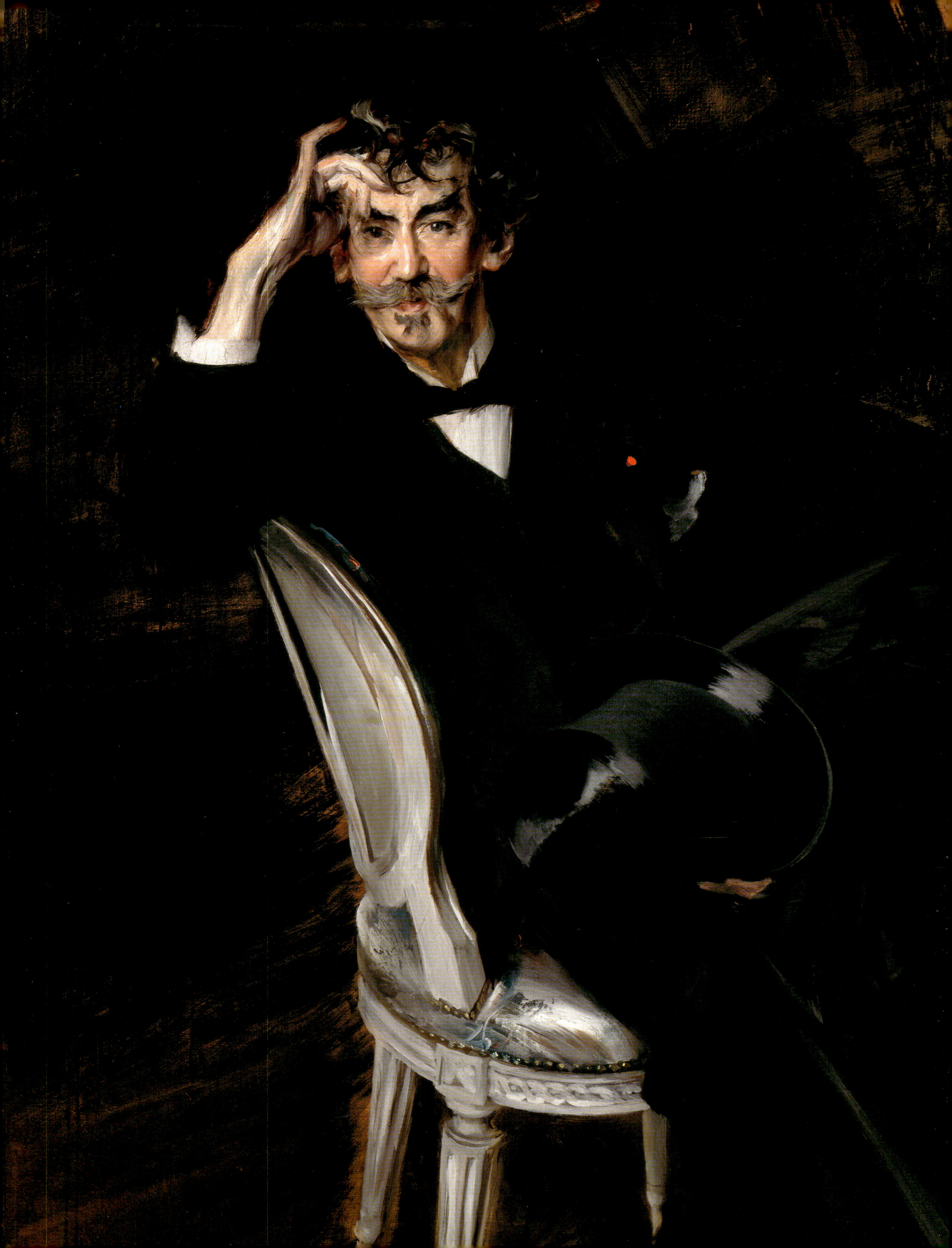

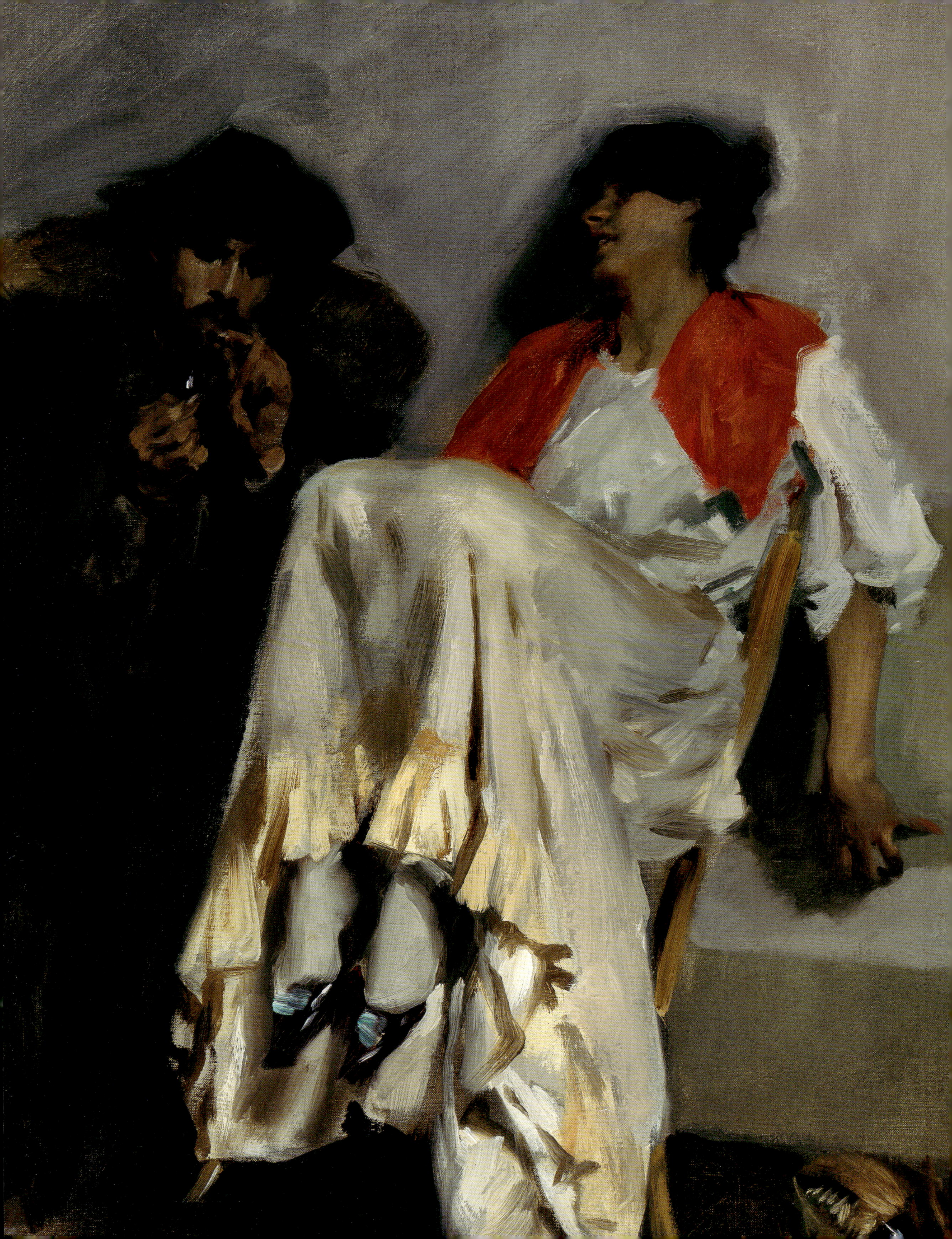

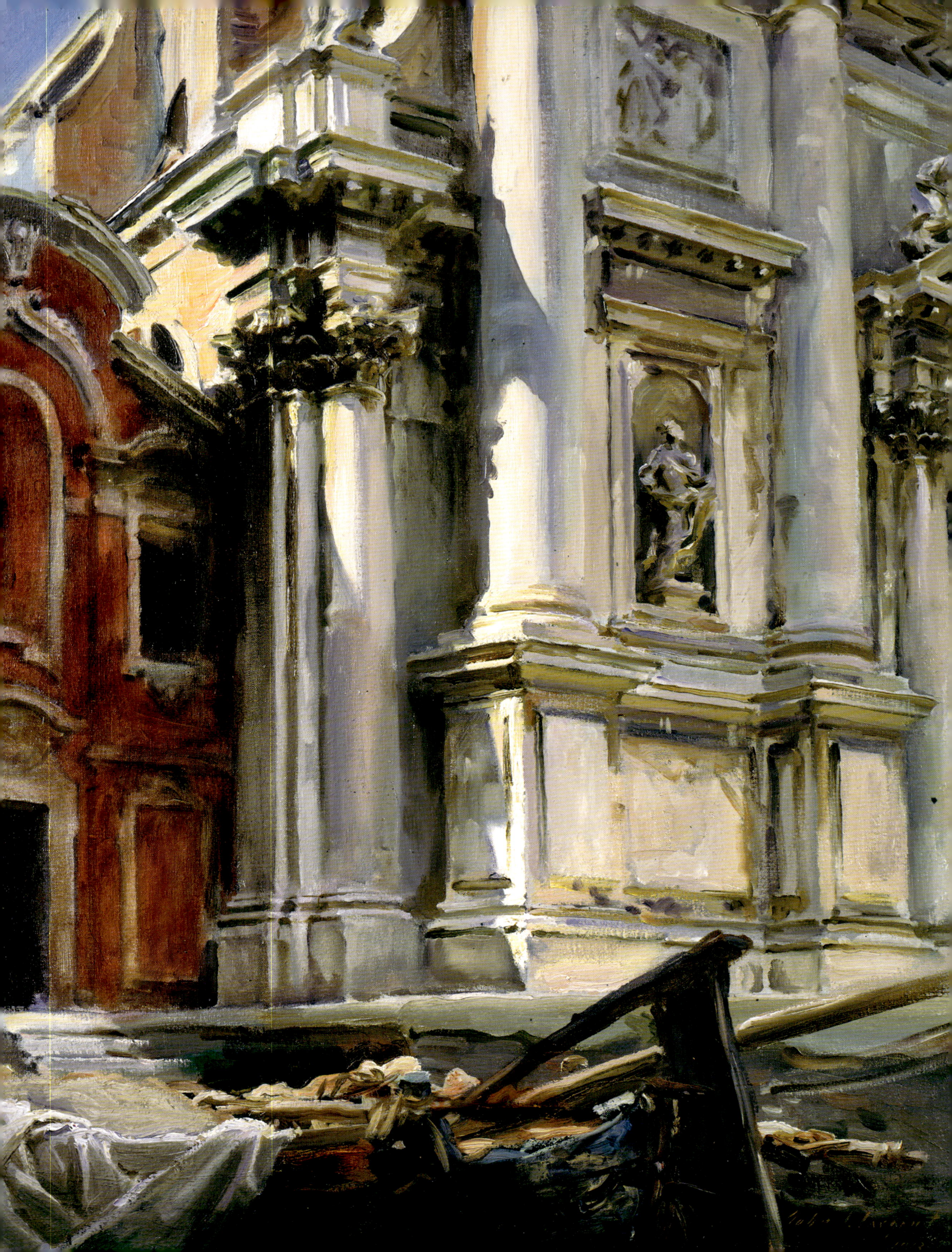

Introduction

John Singer Sargent passed the fall of 1882 in Venice creating some of his most striking works, including the monumental painting *A Venetian Woman* (CAT. 1-1). Viewing the life-size picture some thirty years later, when it still hung in Venice at the Palazzo Barbaro, he purportedly announced, "I have never painted a better head."[1] Was this a boast about the workmanship of this particular painting? Or was it praise for the dark-haired coquette, a model who appears in a half dozen of his works? Sargent may have planned this audacious piece for exhibition at the Paris Salon, as he did with his other large-scale celebrations of female confidence and beauty from the early 1880s, *El Jaleo* and *Portrait of Madame X (Madame Pierre Gautreau)*. However, *A Venetian Woman* was not completed on schedule and remained in Venice with the Curtis family, his art-loving cousins and frequent hosts.[2] Inside their fifteenth-century Grand Canal mansion, it summarized Sargent's experiences of Venice and the charms that drew many American artists, tourists, and expatriates (like the Curtises) to the enchanted, floating city. These included its attractive citizens and magnificent architecture, the sense of intrigue that filled its gloomy alleys and palaces, and Venice's fame as an artistic training ground for color, seen here in the model's aubergine shawl and her fanlike bundle of blue glass rods. The long, thin glass canes are soon to be cut and polished into beads, one of Venice's chief exports in the nineteenth century, a staple of trade in Asia and Africa and with Native communities in North America. Cradling her cluster of canes, Sargent's model poses as a *cernitrice*, a sorter employed to group them by color, a task done as piecework labor outside the bead factories by women throughout the islands.[3] Within the painting the glass *canne* punctuate the dark background to reference the Venetian setting with a single accessory, while compositionally their vertical sweep transforms the model's body into a slender bouquet, crowned by her seductive stare.

These glass props within Sargent's largest Venetian painting illustrate the importance of the glass industry to Venice's economy, society, and artistic character during the late nineteenth century. Venetian glass also appears in the work

John Singer Sargent, *Corner of the Church of San Stae* (detail), 1913; **see p. 256**

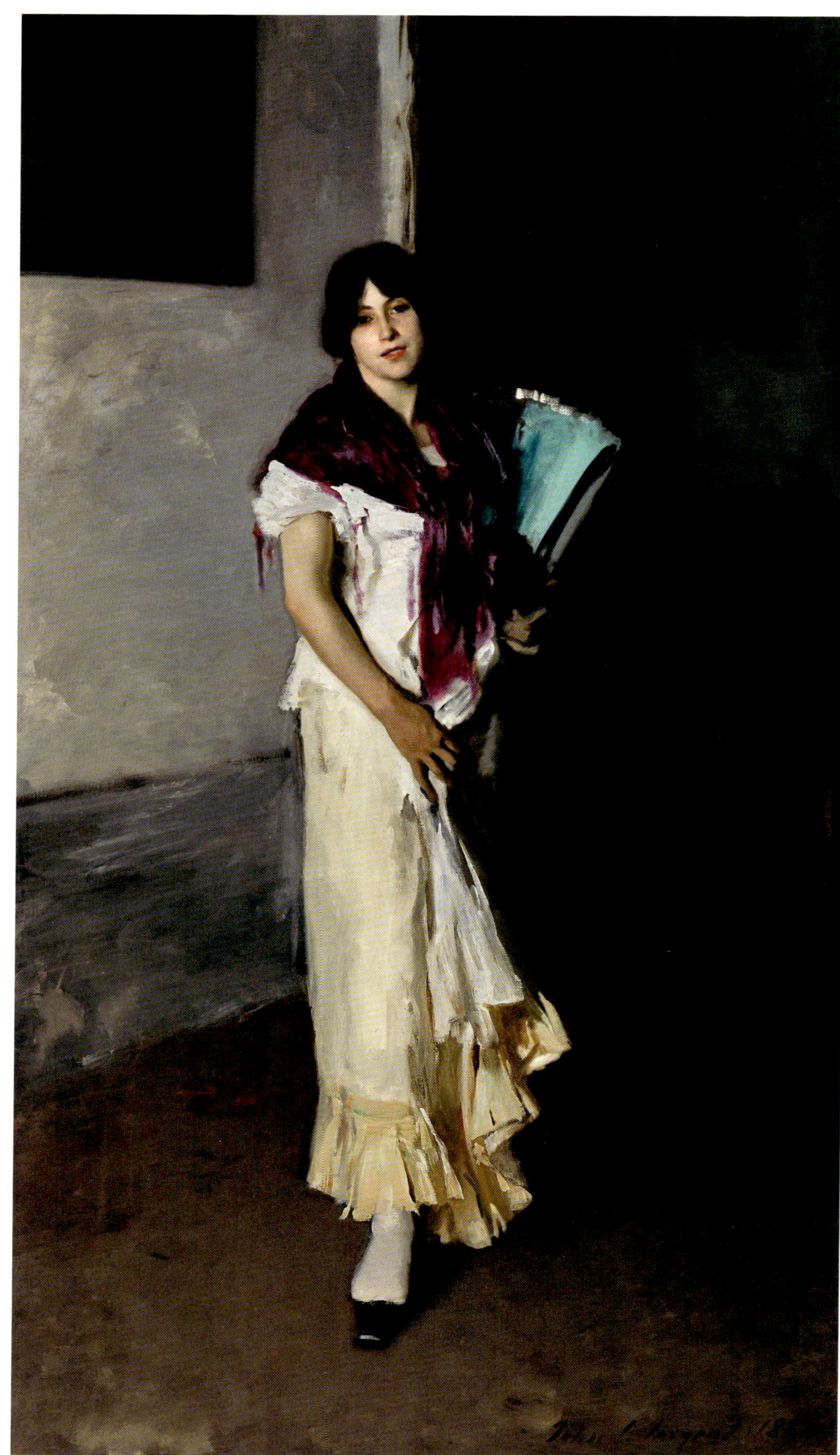

✲ CAT. 1-1
John Singer Sargent,
A Venetian Woman,
1882, oil on canvas,
93 ¾ × 52 ⅜ in., Cincinnati
Art Museum, The Edwin and
Virginia Irwin Memorial

of James McNeill Whistler, who enjoyed a magnificently productive fourteen months in Venice from 1879 to 1880, overlapping briefly with his younger compatriot, Sargent. Female beadworkers populate many of the prints and pastel drawings Whistler made as he ventured beyond famous landmarks such as St. Mark's Square and the Rialto Market and into side streets and less familiar canals, as seen in *The Venetian Mast* (CAT. 1-2).[4] Here the cluster of loitering locals in the foreground includes several seated women whose hunched posture bespeaks their occupation: they are *impiraresse,* bead stringers, with trays of finished *perline* to be separated by size and color into strands of equal weight—the last stage in the production process. Their activity is a reminder that although Venice's Mediterranean empire had long fallen, the glass industry continued to connect the island city to far corners of the globe. Like the winged Lion of St. Mark atop the pole in the center of the street, glass beads were conspicuous symbols of Venice, unrelated to generically Italian motifs of classical architecture and mythological statues. Through these details Whistler provides just enough visual clues to confirm that this is not Florence, Rome, Naples, nor another grand tour destination; it can only be, in Thomas Mann's words, "the most improbable of cities."[5]

☆ CAT. 1-2
James McNeill Whistler, *The Venetian Mast (First Venice Set)*, 1879–80, etching and drypoint on paper, 13 7/16 × 6 7/16 in., The Baltimore Museum of Art, Garrett Collection

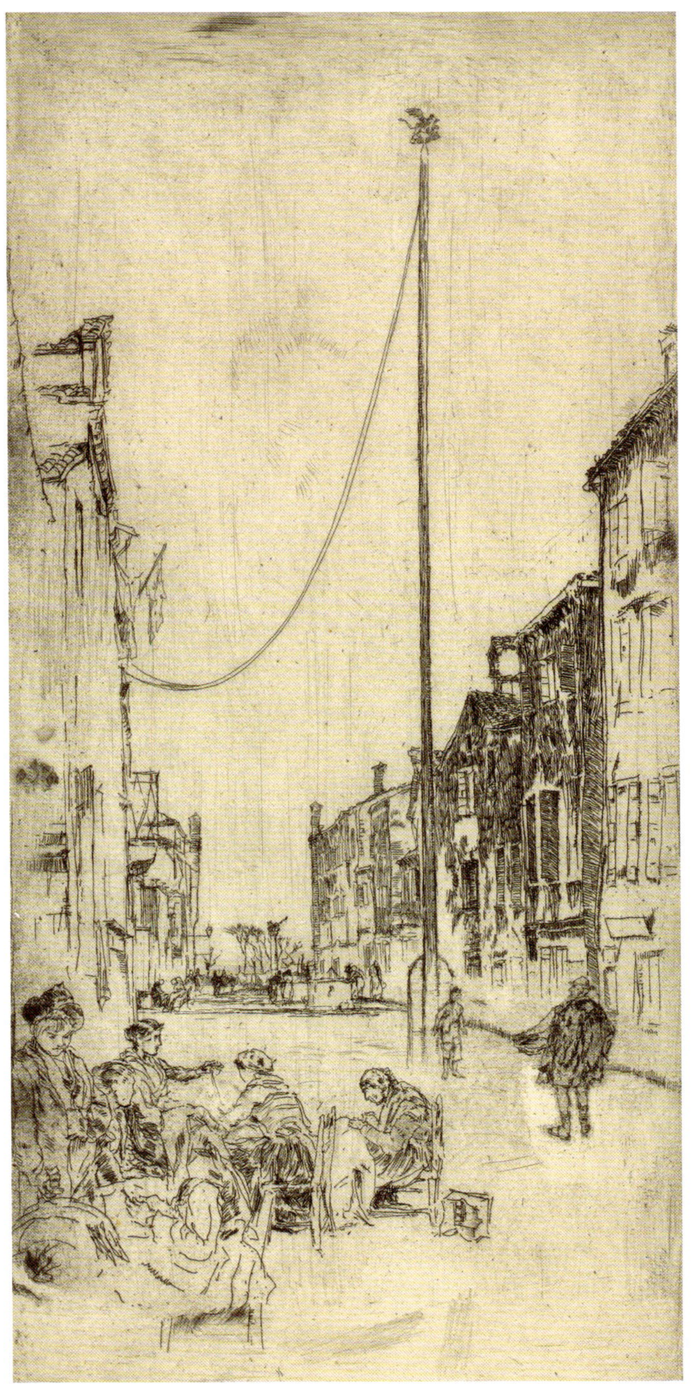

Many foreign visitors completed their Venetian itineraries with firsthand tours of the glass factories, housed mostly on the adjacent island of Murano. Here they enjoyed rare access to an industry once famed for secretive practices and carefully guarded glass paste formulas. When Charles Frederic Ulrich painted this fiery spectacle, his work found an eager audience; it was immediately purchased for the Metropolitan Museum of Art and soon published as a photogravure (CAT. 1-3), the newest form of high-quality art reproduction technology. It depicts a half dozen craftsmen occupying stations around a circular furnace, with the nearest showing off a large, lacy-stemmed goblet to a group of young ladies. A lidded goblet once owned by Providence, Rhode Island, collector William Ames exemplifies this eye-catching and distinctively Venetian category of glassware, featuring symmetrical serpent-shaped wings flanking its stem and a tiny swan serving as a playful finial (CAT. 1-4). Such tourist-friendly luxury objects were appreciated for both their beauty and their difficulty of creation, and provocative patterns, shapes, or zoomorphic ornaments made each handblown piece unique and exuberant

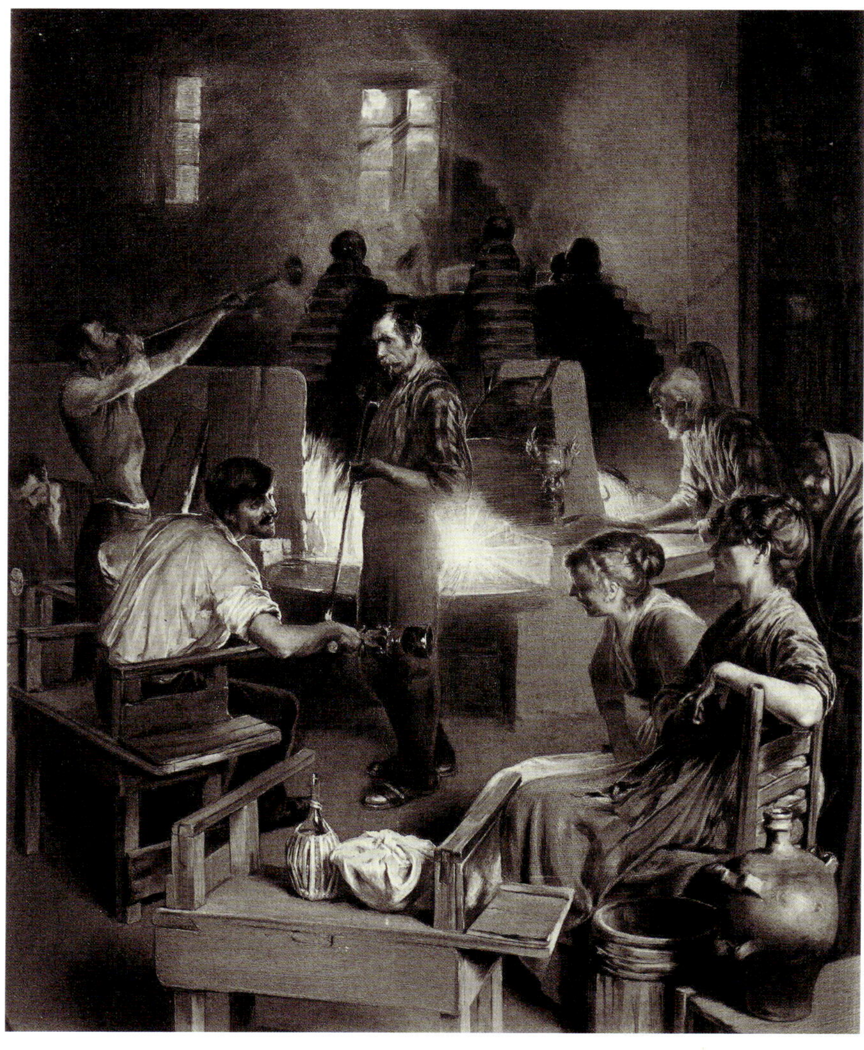

☆ CAT. 1-3
Charles Frederic Ulrich, designer, Goupil & Co., printmaker, *Glass Blowers*, 1887, printed 1890, photogravure on paper, 10 15/16 × 8 3/4 in., Private collection

in the eyes of souvenir seekers. Thus, while the photogravure of Ulrich's painting successfully captures the drama of the workers' movement and radiance of the fires, its publishers could leave to viewers' imagination the glassware's colors and details: Murano's hallmark style was widely known to period audiences.

Amid burgeoning glass production, Sargent, Whistler, and their followers created artworks that redefined how Americans remembered and imagined Venice's light, colors, pageantry, and other charms. Scholars have observed the presence of bead stringers, glassblowers, and fellow artisans within acclaimed pictures from this period, but no exhibition has yet explored this body of paintings, prints, and glass together.[6] By surveying the island city's artistic output and inventive spirit broadly, this study exposes moments of dialogue between Venice's fine and decorative arts communities. It offers new perspectives on the oeuvre of many leading American artists of the late nineteenth century, while also contributing to the ongoing reappraisal of the sophistication of Venetian glass. Far too often academic conversations on fine art and glass are separate, and in museums, curatorial divisions—between pictorial and decorative art, between European and American art—make these intertwined stories difficult to assess. Reconnecting these threads and reuniting a diverse assortment of Venetian-made objects, this assemblage of

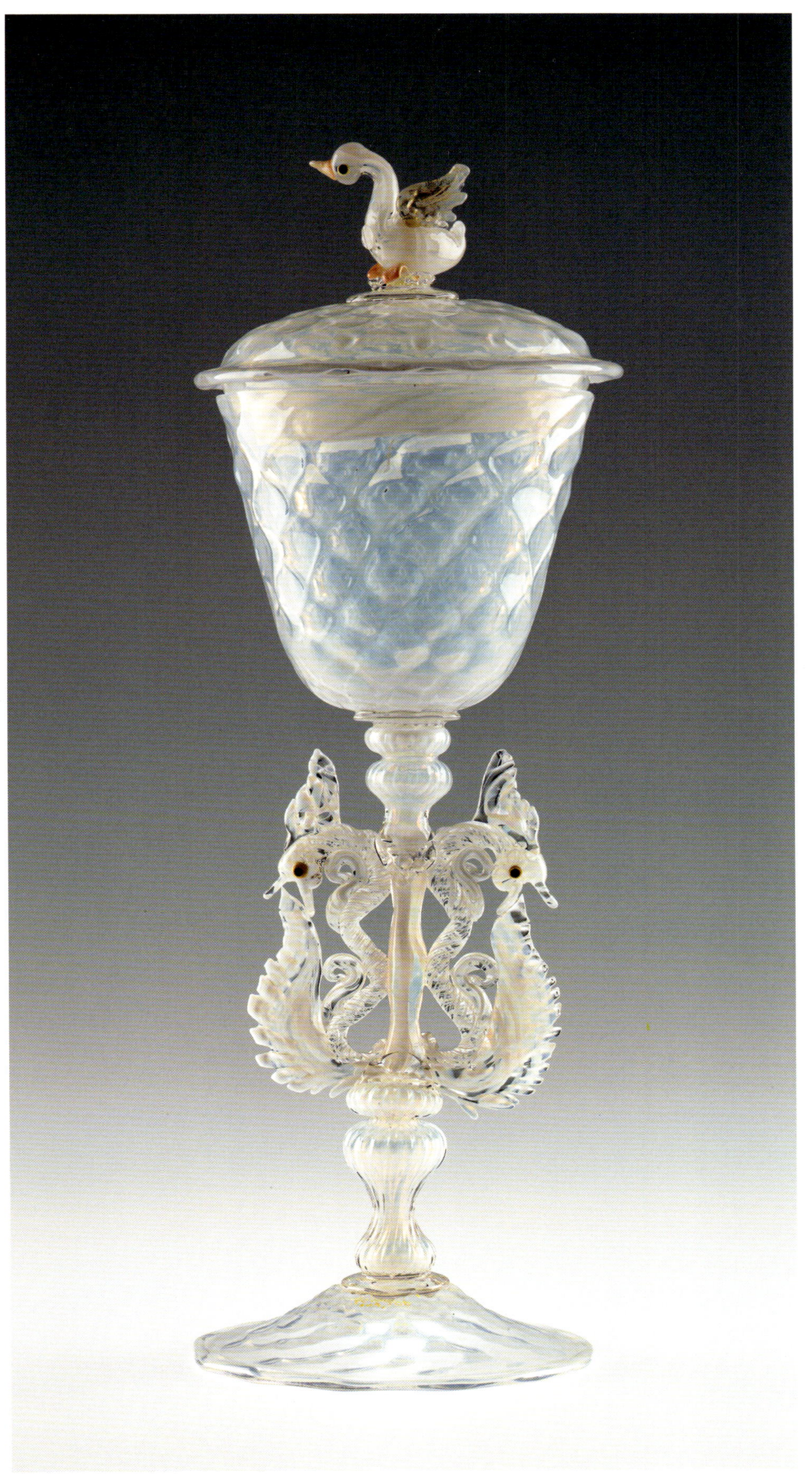

☆ CAT. 1-4

Venice and Murano Glass and Mosaic Company Ltd. (Salviati & Co.) or Fratelli Barovier, Opalescent Glass Lidded Pokal with Serpent Stem, ca. 1870s–90s, blown and applied hot-worked glass, 14 × 4 3/16 in. diam., RISD Museum, Gift of Mrs. Frank Mauran and John O. Ames

case studies unveils important and previously overlooked parallels of style, patronage, and critical fortunes. Examinations of collecting patterns and instances of cross-media influence reveal the ways in which the glass industry inspired Venice's increasingly international communities of painters and printmakers. This book also investigates links between Murano's manufacturing and related craft exports, such as lace. Finally, it uncovers and analyzes echoes of the vogue for Venice and Venetian glass that were created on American soil.

SCOPE

This project considers the period from roughly 1865 to 1915, an era of change and recovery in the political, economic, and cultural position of Venice and in the fortunes of its glass industry. These years saw American taste dramatically shift from relative ambivalence toward Venetian glass as exotic souvenirs to high regard as symbols of creativity and modernity. Luxury glass from Murano as well as rival *façon de Venise* glassware from the Low Countries, Bohemia, Germany, and France were owned by colonists already in the early 1600s, as archaeological excavations in Jamestown, Virginia, demonstrate.[7] Nonetheless, Murano's limited operations and minimal tourist appeal initially confined experience of these objects to patrician contexts. This corresponded to the Venetian Republic's severe decline in wealth and power between its sixteenth-century peak as a naval empire and its conquest by Napoleon Bonaparte and subsequent control by Austria.[8] Visitors to Murano in the early nineteenth century therefore encountered glass primarily through beadmakers, who supplied glass trinkets not widely regarded as works of art. Mark Twain and others lamented the glass factories' near extinction during these decades of political impotence and economic depression for northern Italy, with Twain describing the Queen of the Seas in the 1860s as "decayed, forlorn, poverty-stricken, and commerceless—forgotten and utterly insignificant."[9] However, changes were underway; concurrent with Italian unification, the famous furnaces began a renaissance of production. By the turn of the twentieth century, Venice was again an active center for trade and manufacturing, boasting restored leadership in the field of glassmaking, particularly mosaics and ornate blown glass vessels, as well as beads. New generations of Muranese artisans created complex and colorful goblets and bowls based on historical forms and techniques, and ornamental glass regained its coveted status amid a surge in the city's popularity as a destination for tourists, artists, and art collectors.

Though its nexus was an island of less than one square mile, this Venetian glass revival was an international phenomenon, with many of its greatest achievements and accolades occurring far from Murano. This book addresses one facet of a global vogue for Italian glass around the turn of the twentieth century: its allure and influence in the United States. Venetian glass was marketed and admired worldwide, from Austria and France to Australia and Argentina, but the character of and motives behind its appeal varied from country to country. Americans were not its largest consumers or importers by volume or sales, but their enthusiasm for Venice and for Venetian vases, bowls, mosaics, and beads marks a discrete and colorful episode within histories of the grand tour and art buying. Why did Venetian glass resonate so strongly on the opposite side of the

✲ CAT. 1-5
Walter Launt Palmer, *Interior San Marco*, 1902, gouache on composition board, 24 × 17 in., Albany Institute of History & Art, Bequest of J. Townsend Lansing

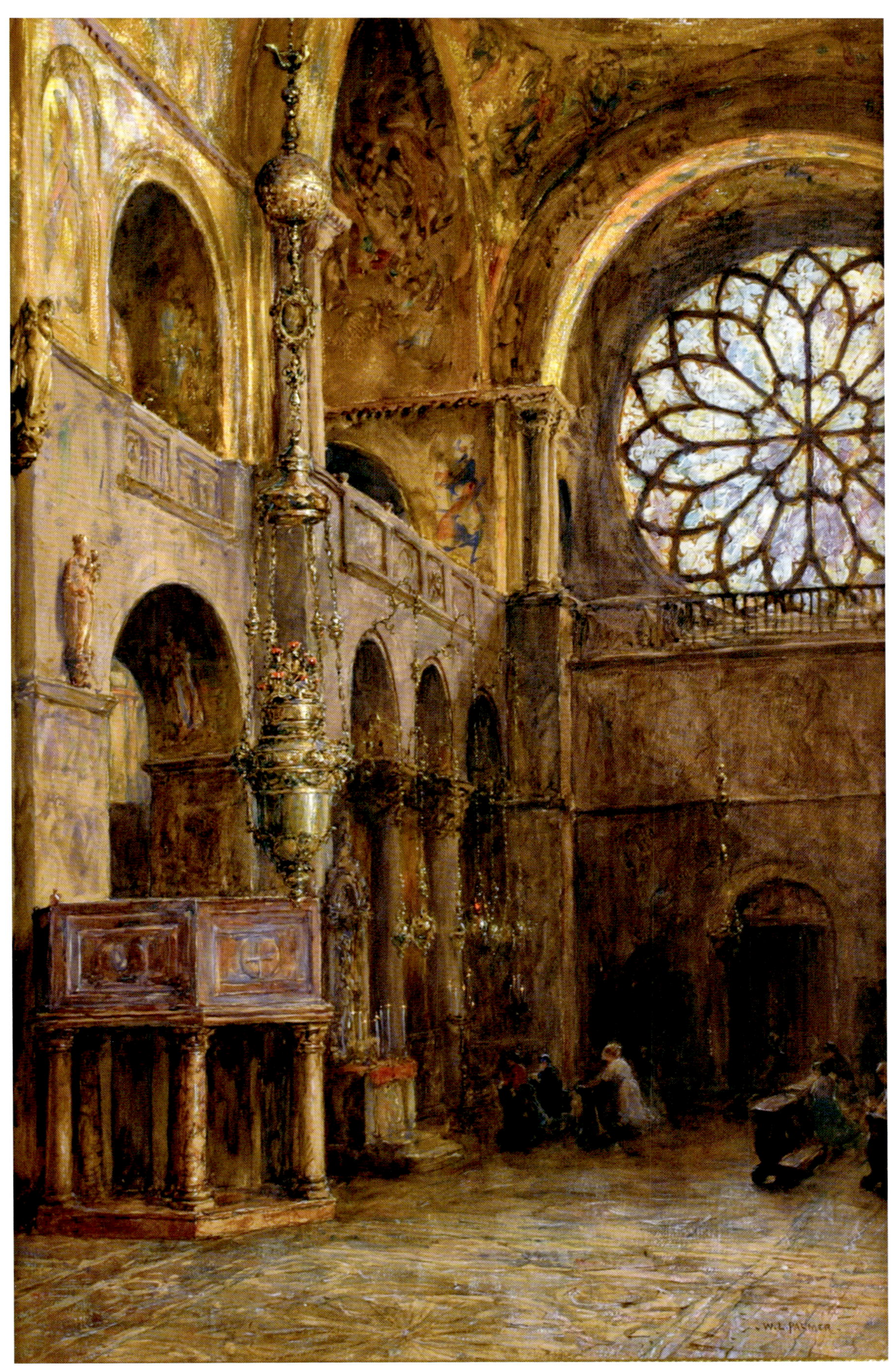

Atlantic? Who were the leading tastemakers contributing to its popularity? Where did Americans learn about and purchase these works? What role did Venetian glass and kindred forms of old-world artisanship play in tourism to increasingly modern Italy? And finally, how did American artists and collectors use Venetian glass and other tangible emblems of Venice to express their own cultural and political values?

The revival era in Murano glassmaking began with the founding in 1859 of a new workshop to produce mosaic glass tiles, under the administration of lawyer-turned-entrepreneur Antonio Salviati, and the opening of the Museo Civico Vetrario (today's Glass Museum) on Murano in 1861.[10] Foreign appreciation for Venice's artistic heritage no doubt sparked some of these early initiatives, including John Ruskin's architectural commentary *The Stones of Venice* (1851–53) and perhaps more directly, George Sand's 1838 historical novel *The Master Mosaic-Workers,* a tale of rivalry among teams of designers in the sixteenth century charged with creating the gold-drenched interior of St. Mark's Basilica. Sand invents names and personalities for the anonymous artisans who created one of Venice's chief attractions, adding cameo appearances by Titian and Jacopo Tintoretto, who express admiration for the glassworkers' aesthetic instincts. Her fictional exchange between painters and mosaic makers directed fresh attention in the late nineteenth century to this widely lauded Venetian artistic practice, spurring civic-sponsored projects to restore the mosaics in St. Mark's and other churches.[11] Soon after, American painters like Sargent, Robert Frederick Blum, and Walter Launt Palmer paid homage to the Byzantine basilica's polychrome patterned floors and sparkling ceilings in watercolors, prints, and oil paintings (CAT. 1-5). Meanwhile, equally vibrant new specimens of Venetian mosaic-inlaid furniture and elaborate mosaic pictorial works, including portraits, received acclaim at world's fairs, from the Great London Exposition of 1862 to the Louisiana Purchase Exposition in St. Louis in 1904. To meet growing demand, Venetian designers and craftspeople invented new means of transporting and installing large-scale architectural designs, and they developed a library of more than seventeen thousand colors of glass tiles.[12] Achieving rapid international success, this mosaic revival paved the way for the people of Murano to reassert their skills in other dimensions of glassmaking.

In 1866—the same year that Venice joined the newly unified Kingdom of Italy—Salviati's operations expanded to include *vetri artistici* (artistic blown glass). While commissions for mosaics were generally for churches and civic structures, these domestically sized and affordable blown glass creations won the attention of middle- and upper-class consumers, including many Americans. To best observe the dialogue between the Venetian glass revival and American art, this study addresses glass made principally between the 1870s, when American artists and tourists began to take note of the new fires in Venetian furnaces, and the 1910s, when Italy's entry into World War I disrupted trade and tourism, and when critics and collectors lost interest in Murano's signature styles. Nonetheless, many of the forms, patterns, and features of revival-era glass remain in production today, and Murano glassmaking dynasties—such as the Seguso, Barovier, and Moretti families—continue to produce fine objects and new generations of artists.

While this project surveys many aspects of the glass industry, primary attention is given to luxury blown vessels and mosaics—the two categories most widely advertised as fine art. Arbiters of etiquette and decorating commended the elegance and affordability of such "modern" Italian glass in books and popular magazines; in 1879 *Scribner's* magazine advised, "Among dinner-table adornments, I know of nothing more beautiful and seductive to the housekeeper than the modern glass, now imported in quantities, and at prices within the reach of a moderate purse."[13] Citing their individuality, delicacy, and historical references, promoters of the Venetian revival successfully branded these prized yet accessible commodities as symbols of refinement, ingenuity, virtue, and freedom.

Paradoxically, however, beads were the earliest specimens of Venetian glass to be collected by American museums—not as fine art but as subjects of ethnographic study. Beads from Venice and other glassmaking centers had been traded with American Indians since the fifteenth century, most famously in connection with the displacement of Lenape peoples from Manhattan Island by the Dutch in the early 1600s.[14] By the 1870s, anthropologists from the Smithsonian Institution were conducting archaeological excavations and removing beads and bead-decorated objects from sites formerly inhabited by Native communities.[15] Museums also purchased modern Venetian glass beads directly from Murano for reference in sorting, identifying, and dating the works in their custody.[16] These were often acquired in the form of sample cards (CAT. 1-6) from bead trading firms, such as New York's Stephen A. Frost & Son. The cards provided a catalogue of the newest colors and patterns from Murano, though anthropologists expressed little interest in the aesthetic properties of beads and their artistic reuse by American Indians.[17] Connoisseurs thus held beads in less esteem than blown glass from Murano, but canes and beads nonetheless contributed to Venice's reputation, particularly when they appeared in the hands of Sargent's beautiful Italian *impiraresse* and models.

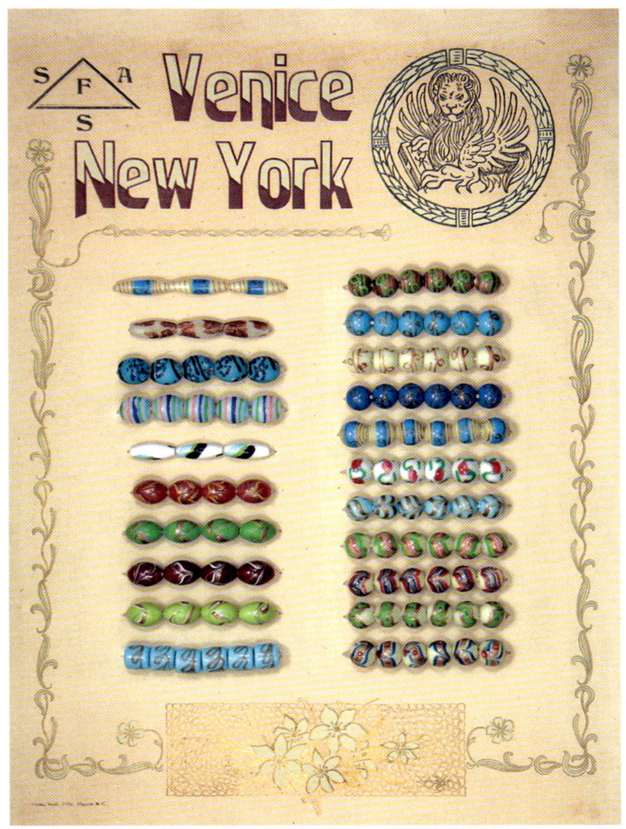

✲ CAT. 1-6
Attributed to Società Veneziana per l'Industria delle Conterie (SVC), Stephen A. Frost & Son, Sample Card with Flameworked Beads, late 19th century–1904, 107 flameworked glass beads mounted to printed card, 13 1/2 × 18 in., Illinois State Museum, Gift of Dan Frost

Utilitarian glass objects, down to the common wine bottle, also carried distinctive Venetian associations. "These [glass]workers have given a word to the language," reported Mary Sherwood after visiting Murano in 1869. "Why is *fiasco* a synonym for failure? Because, essaying to make a goblet, the workman sometimes fails, and burying his long tube again in the glowing furnace, he petulantly says 'Fiasco,' and makes, not a goblet, but a flask."[18] The traveler gives a firsthand account to a curious etymological anecdote: a double meaning that speaks to the difficulty of glassmaking and the suspense of each production, hovering until the final moments of creation on the brink of destiny as a museum-worthy treasure or a generic jug. The glassworkers were loath to waste vessels that did not meet expectations, and their castoffs figure in high

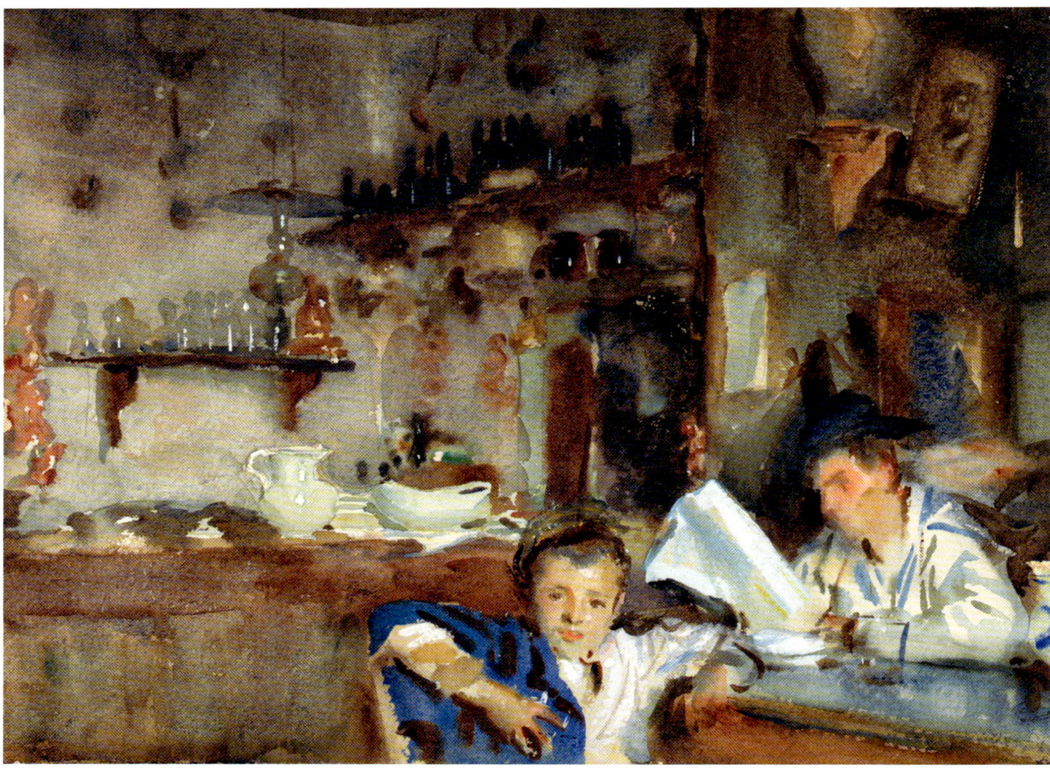

Fig. 1-1
John Singer Sargent,
***A Venetian Trattoria (Venetian Interior)*,**
ca. 1902–3, watercolor and graphite on paper, 9 13/16 × 13 7/8 in., Philadelphia Museum of Art, John G. Johnson Collection, cat. 1079

and low corners of Venetian society and throughout depictions of Venice by American artists. In this context, the dark wine bottles on upper shelves in Sargent's *A Venetian Trattoria* (Fig. 1-1) suggest a range of artistic and enological pleasures that a visitor might encounter, amplifying the atmosphere of abundance in this working-class café. Dots of light sparkle on the adjacent row of transparent *fiaschi* and subtly define two glass cups in use by the man and boy in the foreground, showcasing the artist's mastery of watercolor painting. Although bottles, mirrors, lighting fixtures, furniture, glass for optical instruments, and sheet glass were important segments of the islands' economy, these contributed less to the cultural mystique of Venetian glass in the United States. Healthy output from American factories obviated demand for many categories of utilitarian glass, and the Murano furnaces received widest attention for their decorative and luxury goods.[19]

In the early twentieth century, the popularity and prestige of revival glass began to wane. New mechanical advances in glassmaking challenged the Venetian tradition of creating ornate and singular handcrafted articles. In the United States, American-made works by designers like Louis Comfort Tiffany and Frederick Carder gained a wider share of the top-tier market. Moreover, changing aesthetic tastes made historical references and extreme technical complexity, hallmarks of revival-era glass, not virtues but flaws.[20] American museums, meanwhile, became custodians of large collections of modern Venetian glass amid the field's declining cachet. With great enthusiasm, art historian and critic James Jackson Jarves gave around three hundred pieces to New York's Metropolitan Museum of Art in 1881 and praised these objects' commitment to form over function. He wrote:

> *The highest aim of the Venetian artist was to overlook prosaic utility entirely in his glass; to invent something so bizarre, ethereal, light, imaginative, or so splendid, fascinating, and original in combinations of colors and design, as to captivate both the senses and understanding, and lead them rejoicing into far-away regions of the possibilities of an ideal existence.*[21]

For Jarves, the decorative extravagance of Venetian glassware was as deliciously intoxicating as a visit to the island city where such whimsies were made, itself a fantastical water-bound maze amid palaces and churches everywhere adorned with Gothic stone carvings, precious marble veneers, or mosaics. However, more temperate tastes ruled by 1914, when William Ames's descendants gave his collection to the art museum at the Rhode Island School of Design, a similar donation of roughly two hundred specimens. Despite its scale and quality, museum director Louis Earle Rowe was less adulatory. In announcing the gift, he apologized for the gratuitous flourishes of works like its gilt and enamel-decorated goblet (CAT. 1-7), featuring a green bowl painted in a scale pattern (typical of the sixteenth century) and a spiky rococo stem whose twisting glass vines, flowers, and pinched *morise* protrusions defy easy handling. Rowe said:

> *With a facile material at hand the tendency was in the direction of over-decoration. Flower and animal forms received plastic shape until in some cases the vases have lost their original purpose.*[22]

Challenged by streamlined machine age and art deco styles, Venetian revival glass surrendered its place of honor in museum displays, as disdain for flamboyant patterns and intricate embellishments obscured its experimental forms, technical achievements, and nuanced relations with historical works of art. In this spirit, a 1958 exhibition surveying Venetian glass at the Corning Museum of Glass entirely omitted nineteenth-century pieces with the dismissal that they "displayed great virtuosity but often little else."[23] Today collectors and curators have again taken interest in their innovations and aesthetic properties, and fine examples can be viewed at Corning, the Metropolitan Museum of Art, the Toledo Museum of Art, the Chrysler Museum of Art, and other institutions with distinguished survey collections of glass. Through colloquia and publications, notably those organized by Corning and the Istituto Veneto di Scienze, Lettere ed Arti, a global conversation among scholars about these works is growing.[24]

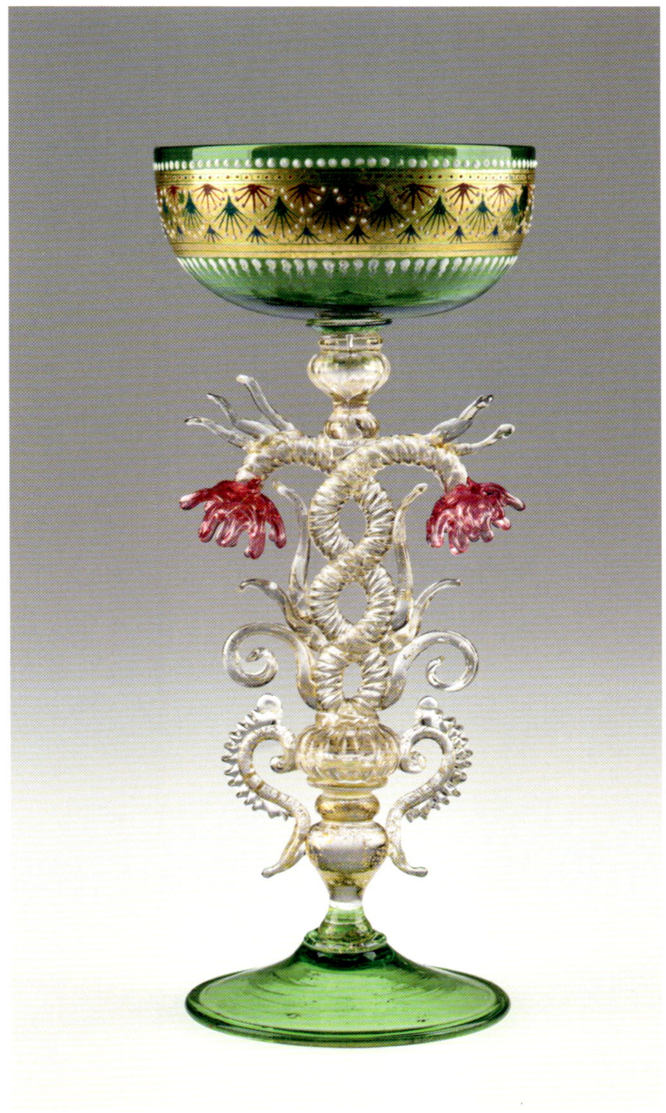

☆ CAT. 1-7
Attributed to Fratelli Toso, Goblet with Twisted Floral Stem, ca. 1900–1903, blown, gilded, enameled, and applied hot-worked glass, 7 ⅞ × 3 ⅜ in. diam., RISD Museum, Gift of Mrs. Frank Mauran and John O. Ames

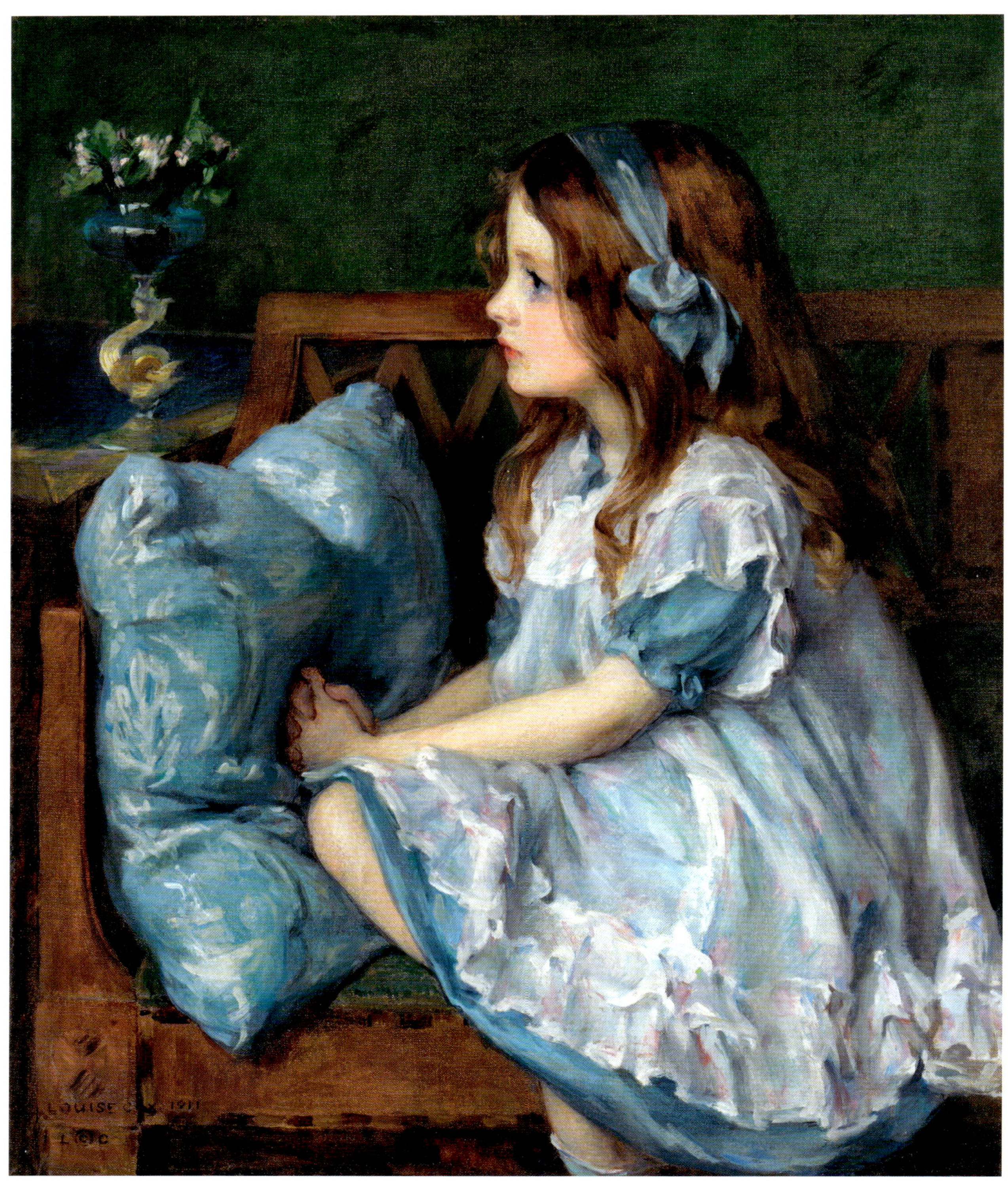

✡ CAT. 1-8

Louise Cox, *May Flowers*, 1911, oil on canvas, 24 ⅛ × 20 ⅛ in., Smithsonian American Art Museum, Gift of William T. Evans

Gilded Age America's fascination with Murano glass is evident in the 1911 painting *May Flowers* (CAT. 1-8). Here Louise Cox depicts a young girl seated in profile on a cushioned Regency bench and contemplating a small vase and bouquet on an adjacent table. All elements of the picture are in harmony: the delicacy of the flowers is echoed in the child's ruffled dress; in the ribbons in her long, wavy hair; and in the artist's soft, impressionistic paint strokes. Completing the ensemble is the vase, identifiable as Venetian by its flameworked stem in the form of a sea serpent, which faces the child with its tail raised to support a wide blue bowl. This rich yet transparent blue and the shimmering, gold-flecked stem bespeak Murano's famed mastery of color, while the playful monster is a virtuoso production, a Renaissance-era motif popular during the revival because of its sculptural complexity and historic associations. Larger and more elaborate variations on this design might feature multiple animal forms, flowers, colorful accents, textured surfaces, and other delicate, whimsical embellishments. Manufacturers and connoisseurs employed an evocative lexicon of Italian adjectives to describe the available shades and patterns of glass: *fenicio, scavo, metalliformi, calcedonio, zanfirico,* and more.[25]

We find an array of these features on a twenty-inch-tall vase (CAT. 1-9) once owned by American financier John Gellatly, whose passion for glass is discussed in this volume's opening essay by Melody Barnett Deusner. With its ribbed, trumpet-shaped bowl towering over a rainbow ensemble of applied flameworked forms—a trio of dolphins and chrysanthemums—a vase like Gellatly's could easily serve as a foyer or parlor centerpiece, commanding attention and exhibiting its owner's fine taste. Likewise, though barely a third of its height and lacking glass flowers, the squat posy vase in Cox's painting is similarly eye-catching and competes with its leafy contents to charm the child. It also demands admiration from this picture's target audience: sophisticated viewers who appreciate its handblown and hand-sculpted form. Deusner's essay provides an extended account of the foundations of glass's attraction for collectors like Gellatly and Isabella Stewart Gardner as well as artists like Cox, who followed principles popularized by Charles Locke Eastlake, Jarves, Whistler, and other contributors to the Anglo-American Aesthetic movement.

May Flowers, with its miniature still life of a Venetian vase, also raises the question of how such glass arrived in American homes and collections, the topic of this volume's next chapter, which reconstructs the mechanics of this market. Here glass historian Sheldon Barr traces the origins of Murano's revival and how Italian manufacturers sought patronage from governments and wealthy art lovers like Gellatly, as well as those of more modest means. Though

☆ CAT. 1-9
Attributed to Compagnia di Venezia e Murano (CVM), Vase with Dolphins and Flowers, ca. 1880s–90s, blown and applied hot-worked glass, 20 ½ × 8 ⅛ in. diam., Smithsonian American Art Museum, Gift of John Gellatly

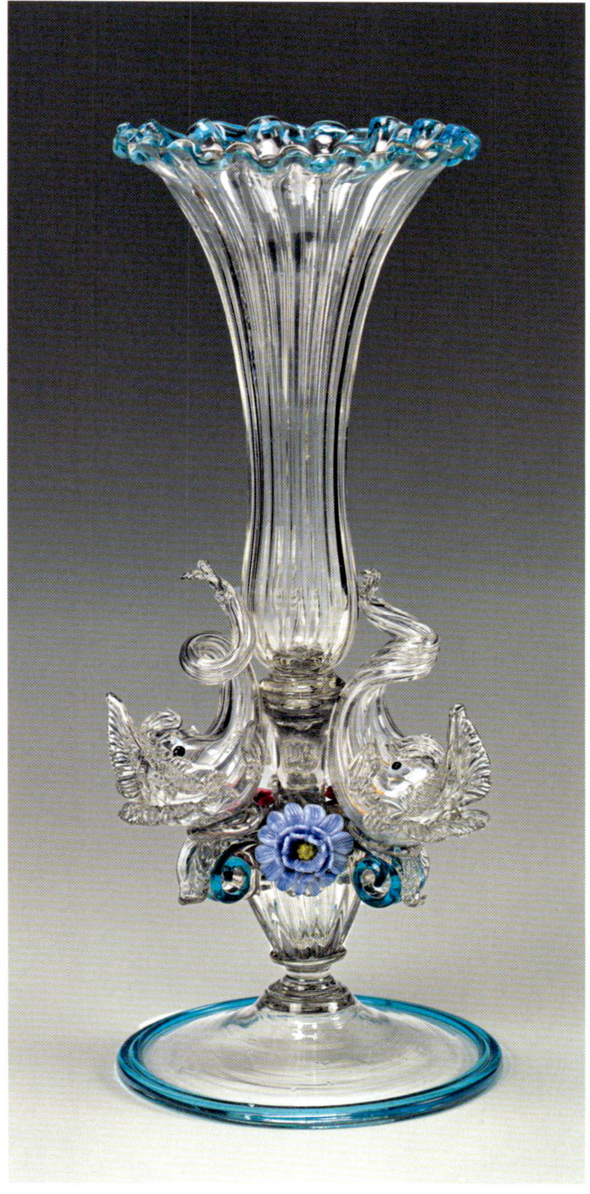

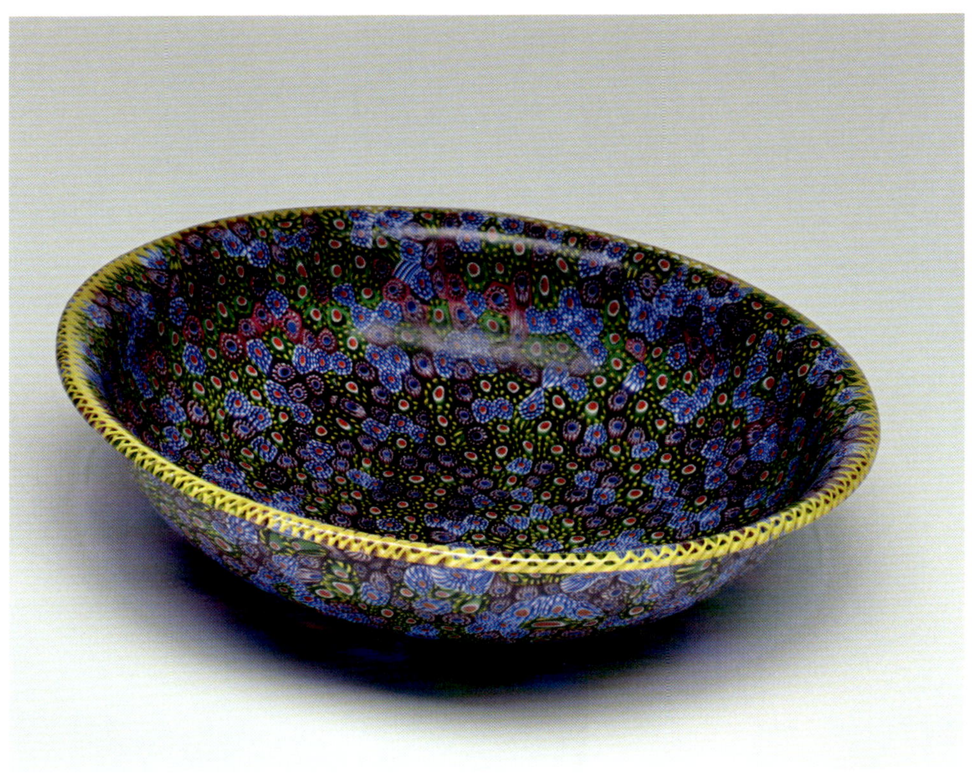

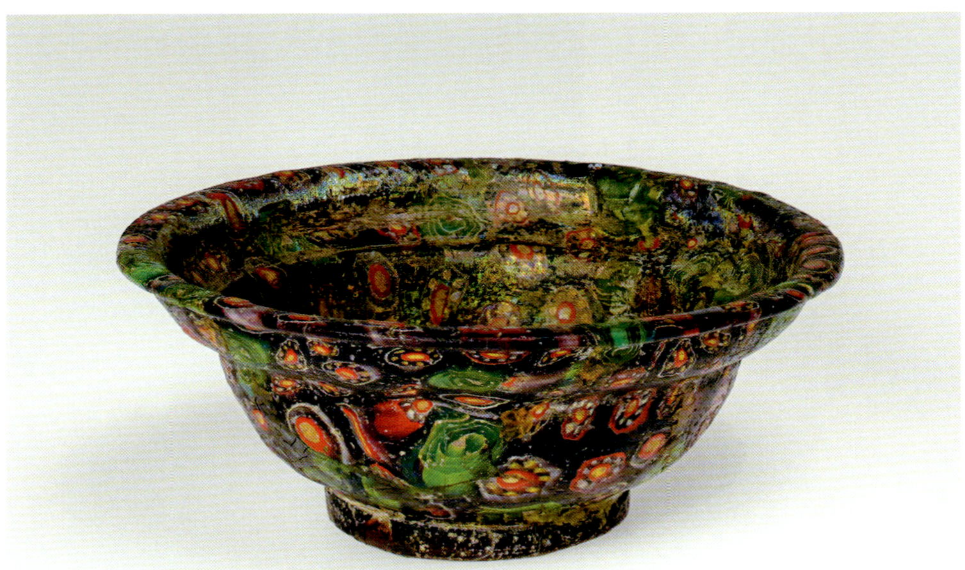

☆ CAT. 1-10

Venice and Murano Glass and Mosaic Company Ltd. (Salviati & Co.) or Compagnia di Venezia e Murano (CVM), Ancient Roman–Style Mosaic Glass Bowl, ca. 1875–80, hot-worked and slumped mosaic glass with applied glass rim, 1 ⅞ × 6 13/16 in. diam., The Walters Art Museum, Acquired by Henry Walters

☆ CAT. 1-11

Unidentified artist, Roman Empire, Mosaic Glass Patella Cup, 1st century BCE–2nd century CE, slumped, polished, and applied mosaic glass, 1 ½ × 3 ⅝ in. diam., Smithsonian American Art Museum, Gift of John Gellatly

some Americans, such as Gardner and her husband, Jack, purchased Venetian glass while vacationing in Venice, most first experienced these delicate treasures through articles in popular magazines, displays in department stores, and presentations at world's fairs. Barr describes the array of promotional efforts organized beginning in the 1860s by Murano's burgeoning firms as they collaborated and competed to expand the audience for a diverse range of recognizably Venetian-made creations. These included blown works like the dolphin-stemmed vase in Cox's painting and others imitating ancient Mediterranean glassware in shape and technique, such as the yellow-rimmed mosaic glass bowl (CAT. 1-10) originally owned by Baltimore collector Henry Walters. This was crafted through the fusion of circular slices of multicolored glass canes, repopularizing the delightfully irregular *millefiori* (or "thousand flowers") patterns known from equally coveted specimens from Roman Empire–era archaeological sites (CAT. 1-11). As they replicated antique vessels and pushed the physical potential of the medium to new heights, Salviati and his rivals operated within a shifting market and strove to understand and influence the American appetite for their wares. Barr's essay surveys this network of promoters and suppliers to illuminate some of the key artists, agents, and strategies that brought Murano's merchandise to the United States.

Whether encountered in museums, shops, fairs, or fine parlors, Venetian glassware was inseparable in the eyes of American collectors from its famous place of origin. Views of Venice provided a visual context for these objects, sometimes topographical and documentary in their detail, or perhaps more poetic or fanciful. Stephanie Mayer Heydt's chapter traces these perspectives and possibilities through images of bead stringers and other working-class women by three of the most prolific American artists who found inspiration in Venice: Sargent, Whistler, and Blum. As a group, their paintings and prints capture changes to the city's fortunes in the 1870s and 1880s, notably the glassmaking revival and the parallel expansion of sister craft industries, particularly lacemaking on the Venetian island of Burano. However, the artists approach similar subjects with unique styles (ranging from ethereal to precise) and varying curiosity and intimacy. The experiences and attitudes of each grand tourist differed, Heydt explains, while assessing degrees of idealization in these depictions of modern life. Close comparison exposes tensions between US artists' hunt for handsome subjects and the economic realities of post-Risorgimento Italy.

Just as the Italian glassmakers successfully marketed their fine handcrafted products to enthusiastic US patrons, other Venetian craft

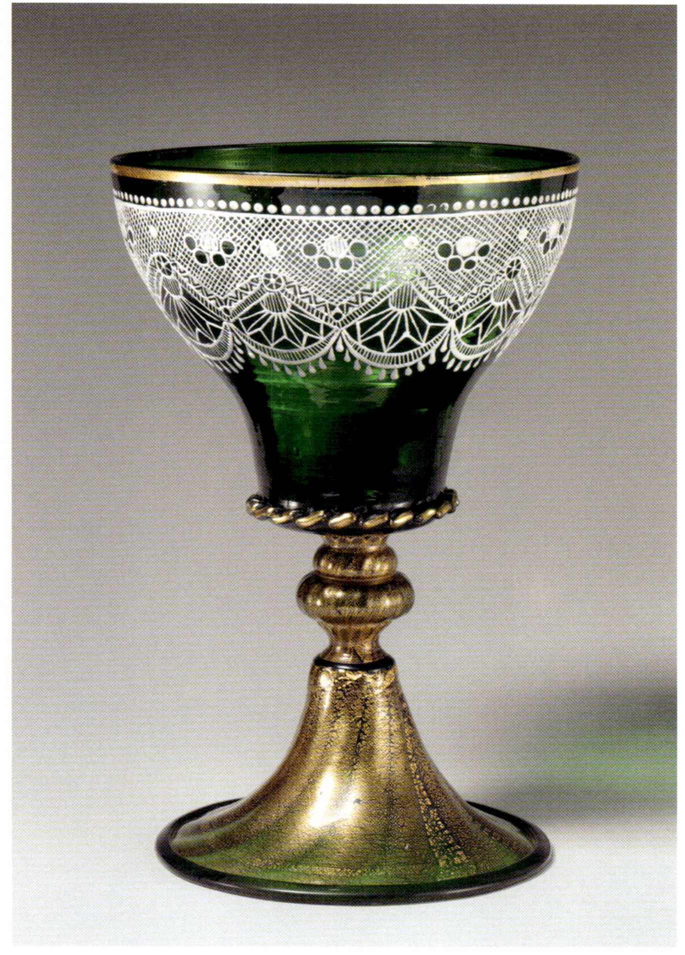

✫ CAT. 1-12
Società Anonima per Azioni Salviati & C., Goblet with Lace Design, ca. 1870s, blown, enameled, and gilded glass, 7 ¾ × 4 ⅞ in. diam., The Metropolitan Museum of Art, Gift of James Jackson Jarves

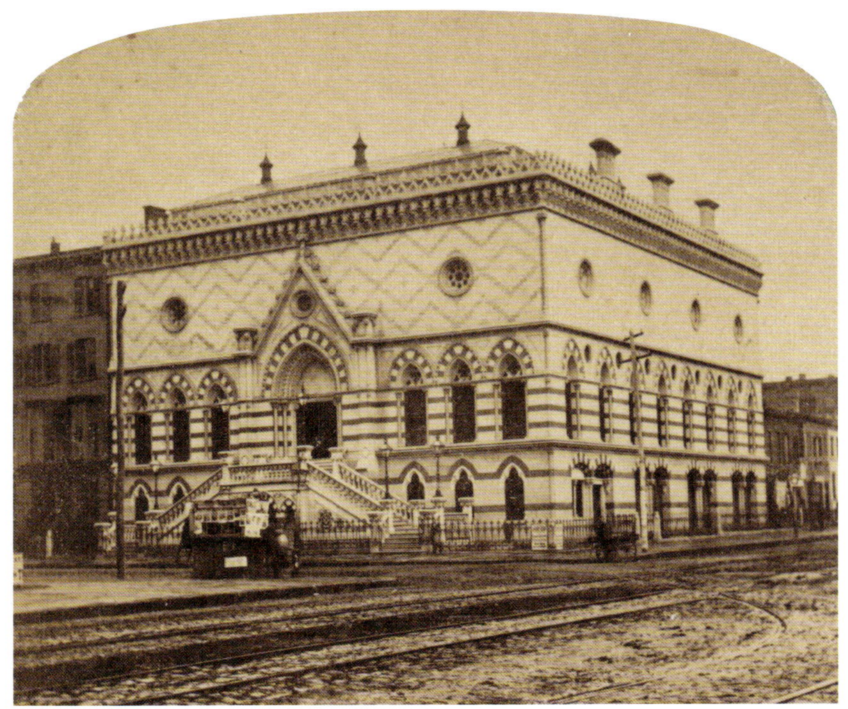

Fig. 1-2
National Academy of Design, ca. 1865–95, albumen print on stereograph card, 3 ½ × 7 in., Library of Congress, Prints and Photographs Division

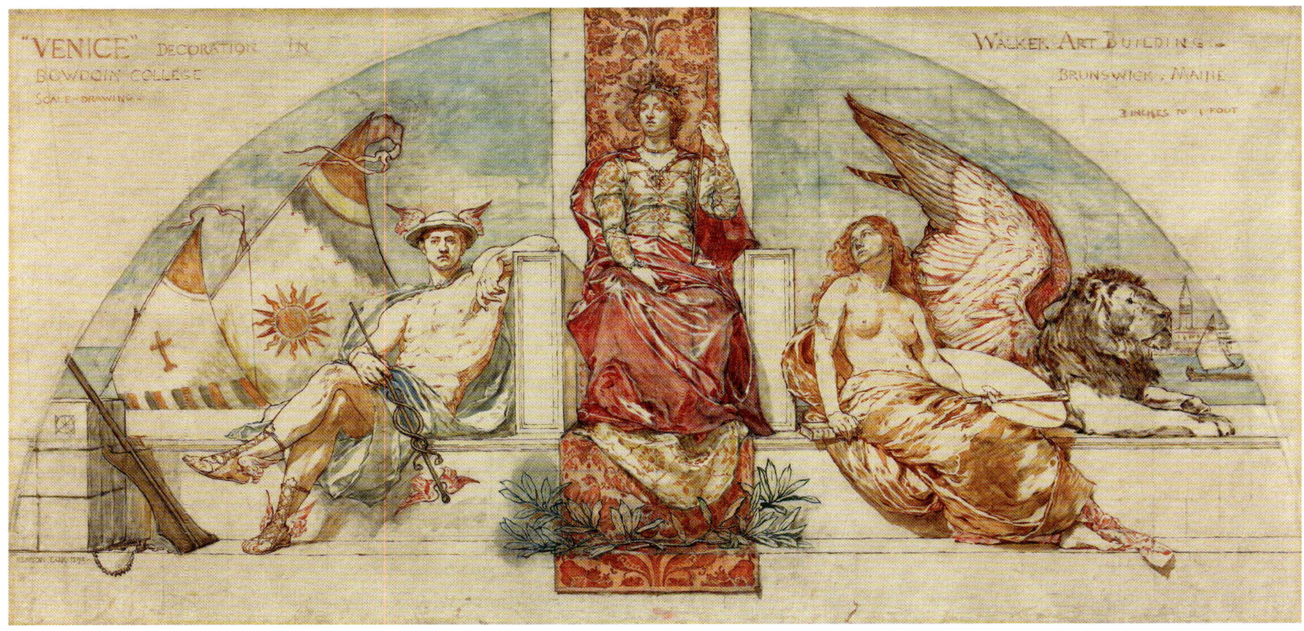

✲ CAT. 1-13
Kenyon Cox, Study for *Venice*, 1894, oil and graphite on canvas, 29 ⅝ × 59 ⅝ in., Bowdoin College Museum of Art, Brunswick, Maine, Gift of Colonel Leonard Cox, Mrs. Caroline Cox Lansing, and Mr. Allyn Cox

traditions looked to their past renown for economic stimulus and new audiences. A green and gold goblet with painted lace patterns (CAT. 1-12), acquired by Jarves in the late 1870s, reveals that Murano designers took inspiration from the Burano lace revival for decorative elements, no doubt aware that glass and lace would appear side by side in the shops around St. Mark's Square and in displays of contemporary Italian design at international expositions. Connections and parallels between these movements run deeper, and Diana Jocelyn Greenwold's chapter explores the twofold resonance of Venetian lace in the US Gilded Age: as collectible objects and as an inspiration for art making across the Atlantic. As in the case of artistic glass, connoisseurs bought examples of Burano lace among other treasures, demonstrating a broad appreciation for the arts of Italy. For example, Gardner assembled Venetian paintings, prints, furniture, glass, and an especially fine assortment of lace, all displayed in her Boston mansion-museum that she modeled after a Venetian palazzo. Greenwold's essay further explores the nuances of gender identity in this field, discussing the appeal of highly skilled women's work to collectors and to an enterprise called the Scuola d'Industrie Italiane in New York City, where Italian immigrant women studied to become lacemakers. Here the legacy of Venetian craftsmanship offered newcomers to the United States an opportunity to earn respect and to improve their social standing.

This volume returns to the fine arts and literature in its final chapter, considering Venice and its glass within the context of American political and cultural values. Venice intrigued tourists, artists, and collectors from the United States through its blend of past artistic excellence and present-day potential, in which historical architecture and artifacts actively nurtured new generations of Italian genius. Independence and unification fueled the glass revival and other forms of art making, setting a stage, in Americans' eyes, for a second Renaissance. Could the United States achieve similar artistic success? Louise Cox considered the relationship between these nations early in her career when training at New York's National Academy of Design, housed at that time in an 1865 Venetian Gothic Revival edifice modeled on the Doge's Palace (Fig. 1-2), which she described in her memoirs as "my youthful ideal of architectural perfection."[26] This building served as a professional womb for Cox and countless American artists, inspiring them to think of Venice not as a crumbling relic, but as a crossroads of the past and future. Her husband, painter Kenyon Cox, later created a mural for Bowdoin College, an allegory of *Venice* as one of four great European cities contributing to civilization and the arts. His painted study for the lunette (CAT. 1-13), executed in 1894, depicts Venice enthroned in elegant embroidered robes, handsome Mercury to her right, with ships and pearls symbolizing commerce, and a muse of painting opposite, posing with a majestic Lion of St. Mark.[27] This presentation shows no sign of the poverty and ruin that had characterized the city a few decades earlier; approaching the dawn of the twentieth century, she is once again rich and proud, welcoming business and the arts.[28] This essay outlines new post-romantic conceptions and stereotypes of Venice and describes how its glass industry further encouraged Americans to look to the lagoons of northern Italy for inspiration in their own pursuit of technological and cultural leadership.

Kenyon Cox, Study for *Venice* (detail), 1894; see p. 44

Thus, through discussion of Whistler, Sargent, and selected colleagues and patrons, this book offers fresh insights on the Venetian glass revival and on the American grand tour. Its goal is not to provide a balanced or comprehensive narrative of artistic tourism to Venice and Murano.[29] Likewise, its selection of glass objects and related decorative arts does not systematically represent the bounty of styles and types created by Murano's glassmakers of the nineteenth century. Instead it relies on patterns in collecting and taste, using specimens known to have been acquired by Americans during this period, either as souvenirs or through secondary markets. Provenance guides these choices, drawing attention to the strong holdings of a select group of museums. This approach explores Venice in reverse through its material culture, rather than diaries and anecdotes of travel. It then asks what glass, mosaics, and lace, as well as paintings and prints, reveal about the city within the context of American homes and museums.

"[Glass] neither rusts nor decays," observed Jarves, as he argued for the merits of this medium. "Moths can not consume it, nor time alter its shape or dim its beauty. It is always the same frolicsome, fascinating, suggestive, imperishable object."[30] Nonetheless, as this study discusses, many of these treasures have passed through American hands but are now lost—some destroyed by storms, earthquakes, or neglect, and others simply discarded by generations who did not value their forms, workmanship, and remarkable histories of intercontinental circulation. As Venice faces growing threats to its survival from climate change and mass tourism, this project provides a fresh step in the ongoing journey to understand its many unique contributions to the history of art and to preserve these stories for the future.

Crawford Alexander Mann III.
Curator of Prints and Drawings
Smithsonian American Art Museum

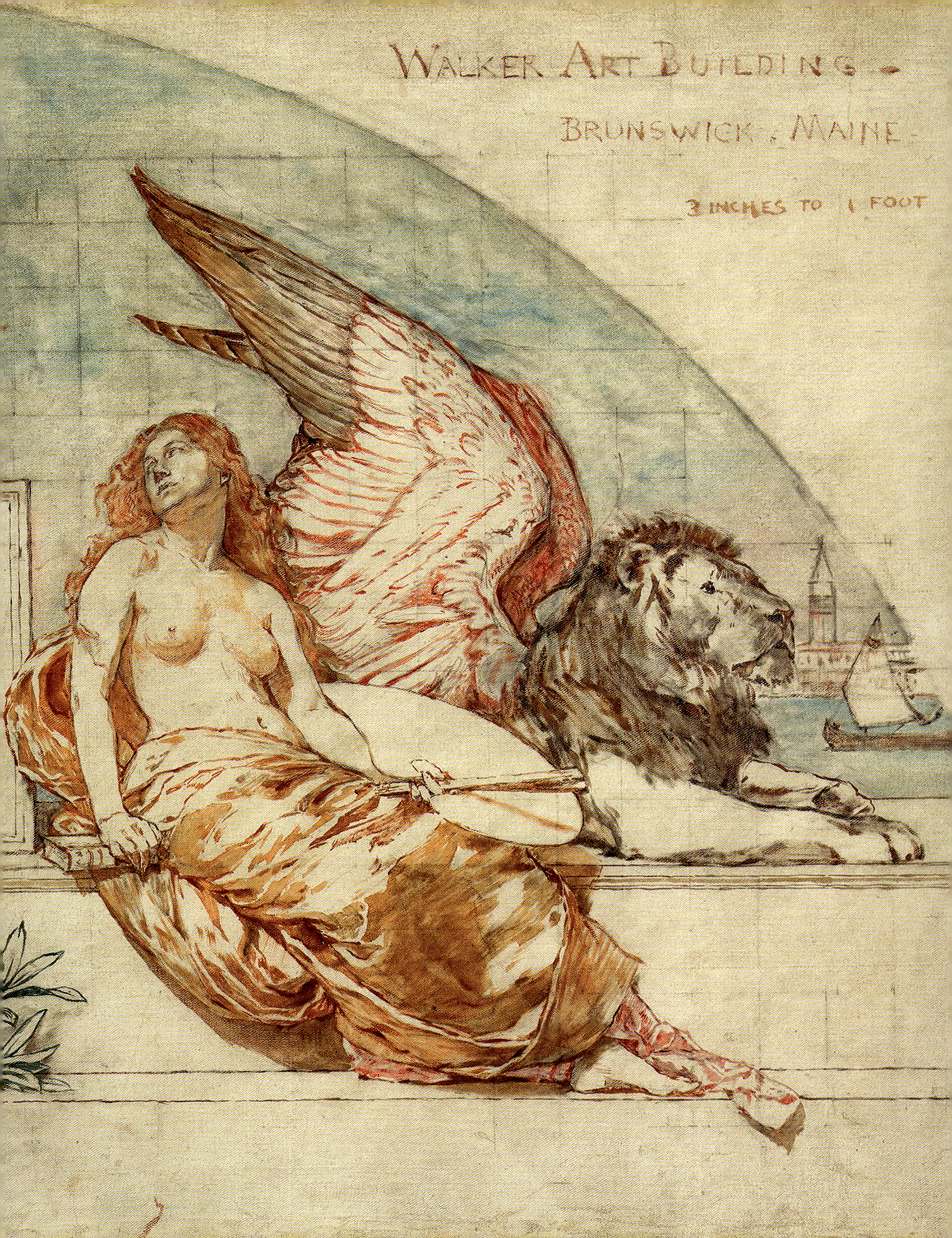
WALKER ART BUILDING
BRUNSWICK : MAINE
3 INCHES TO 1 FOOT

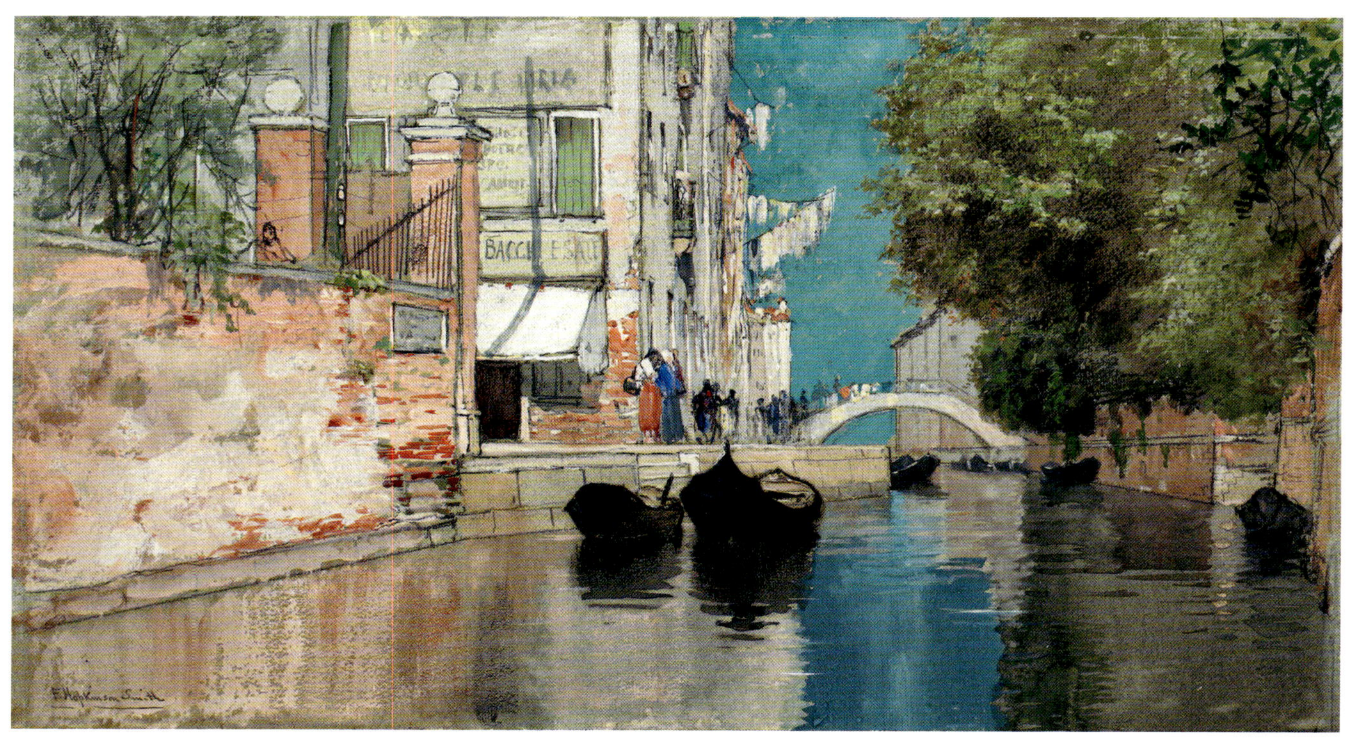

☆ CAT. 1-14
Francis Hopkinson Smith, *On the Way to the Public Garden*, ca. 1895, opaque watercolor and pastel over graphite on paper, 14 ½ × 24 ¾ in., Smithsonian American Art Museum, Gift of Laura Dreyfus Barney and Natalie Clifford Barney in memory of their mother, Alice Pike Barney

☆ CAT. 1-15
Robert Frederick Blum, *Canal in Venice, San Trovaso Quarter*, ca. 1885, oil on canvas, 34 × 23 ⅛ in., Smithsonian American Art Museum, Gift of William T. Evans

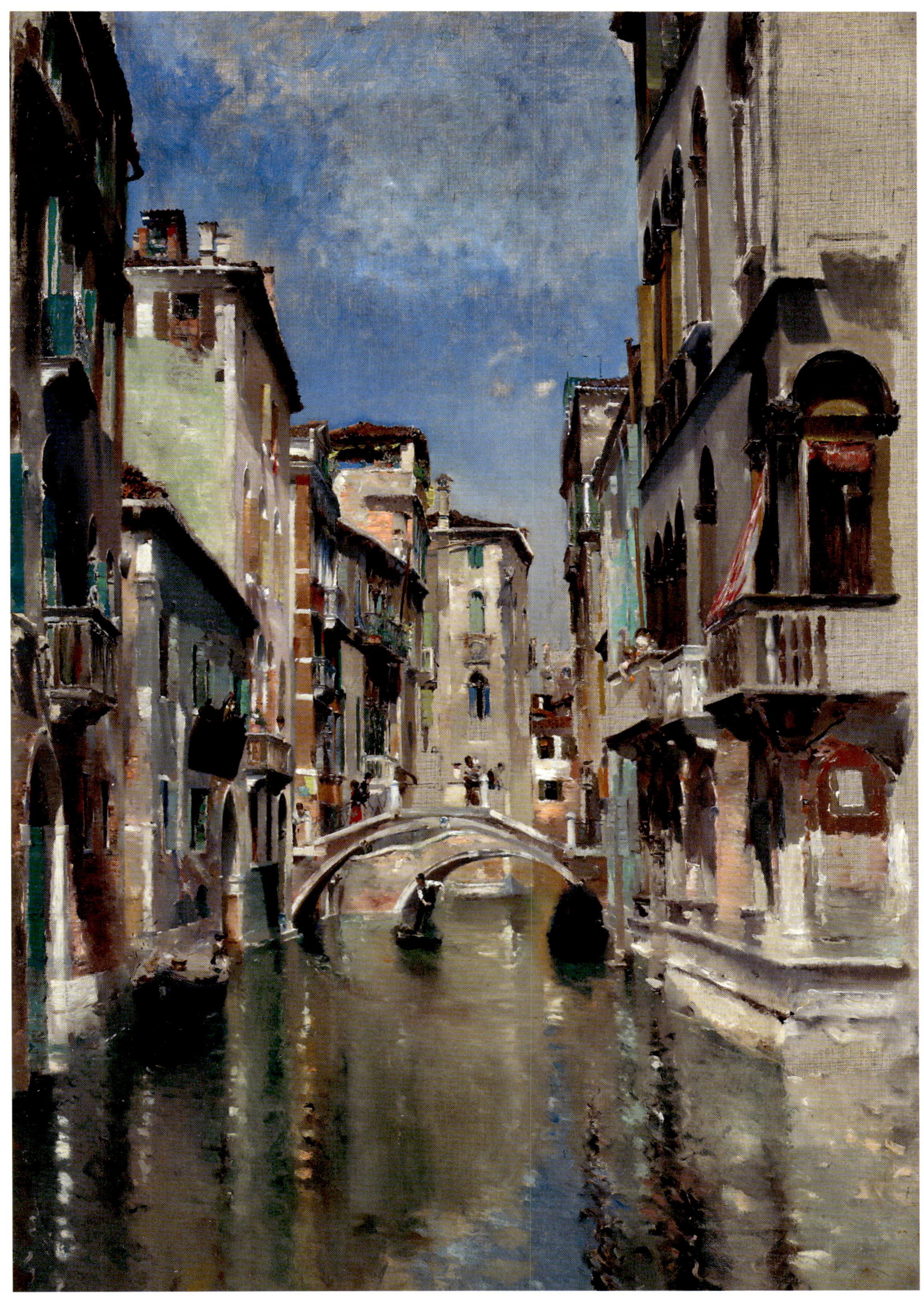

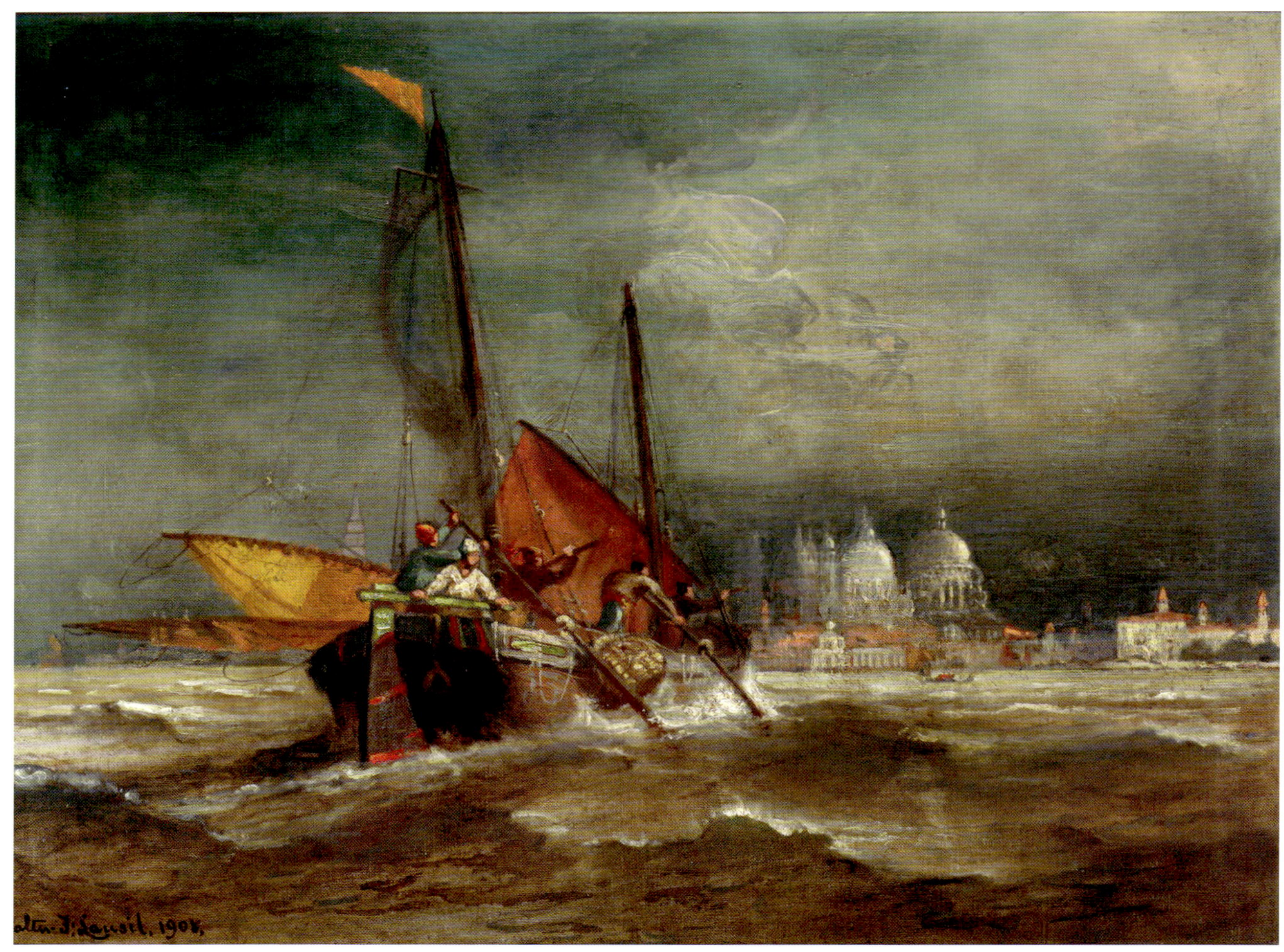

✡ CAT. 1-16

Walter Franklin Lansil,
***The Coming Storm*, 1908,**
oil on canvas, 22 × 29 in.,
Fry Fine Art Gallery

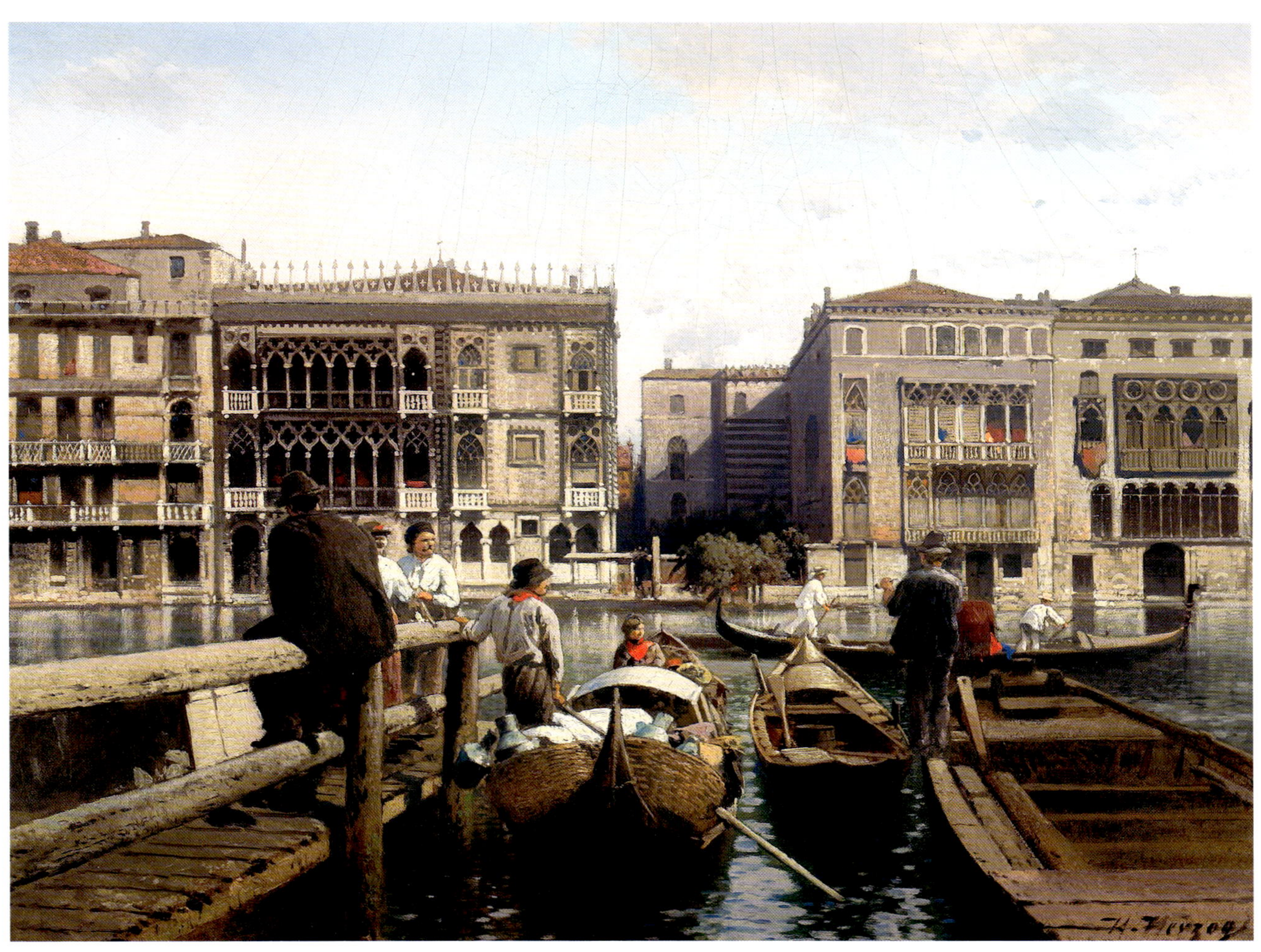

✡ CAT. 1-17

Hermann Herzog, *Along the Grand Canal, Venice*, ca. 1890s, oil on canvas, 23 ½ × 30 ½ in., Woodmere Art Museum, Bequest of Charles Knox Smith

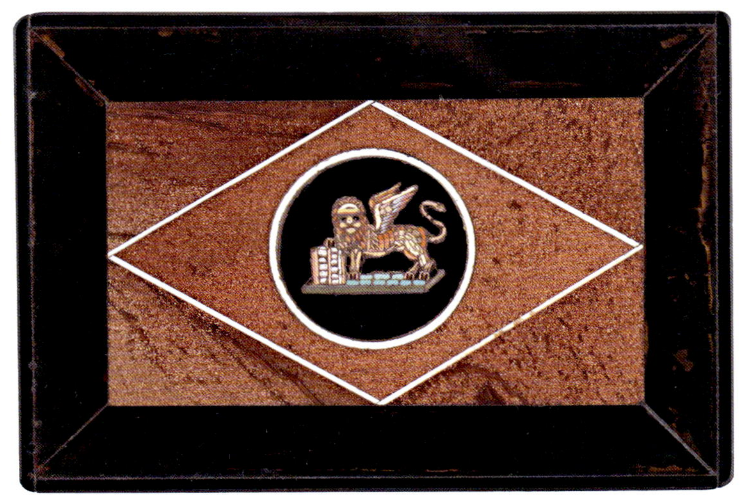

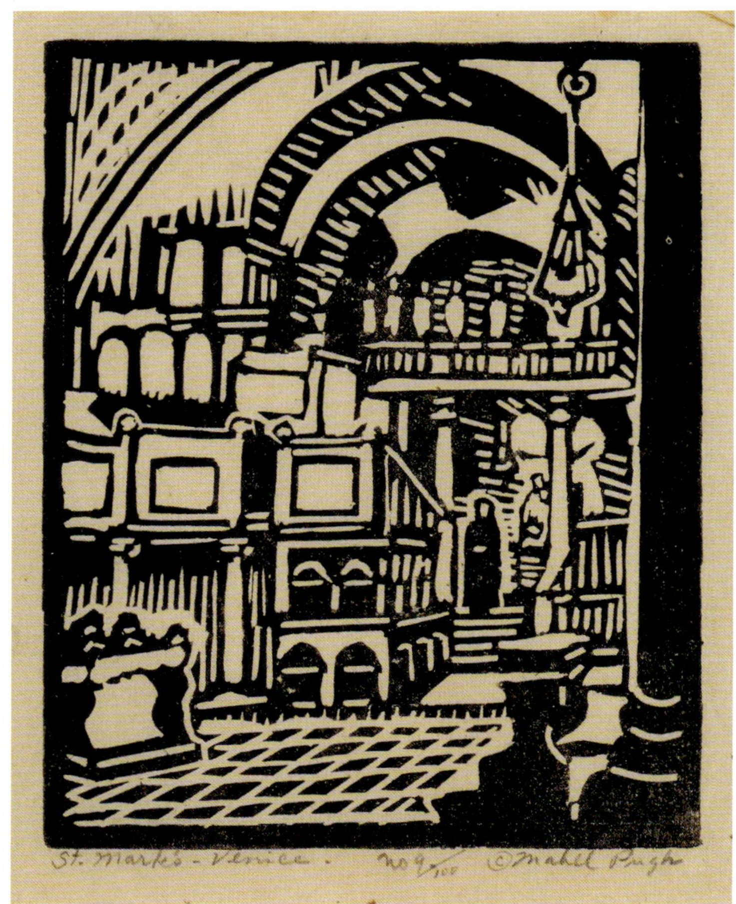

☆ CAT. 1-18
Possibly Studio del Mosaico Vaticano, Micromosaic with Lion of St. Mark, ca. 1860–84, glass micromosaic, 2 ¾ × 4 × 11/16 in., Iris & B. Gerald Cantor Center for Visual Arts at Stanford University, Stanford Family Collections

☆ CAT. 1-19
Mabel Pugh, *St. Mark's, Venice*, ca. 1923–26, linoleum cut on paper, 5 ¼ × 4 ⅛ in., Smithsonian American Art Museum, Transfer from the North Carolina Museum of Art (Gift of the Artist, 1977)

☆ CAT. 1-20
Mabel Pugh, *Near the Rialto, Venice*, ca. 1923–26, linoleum cut on paper, 9 ½ × 7 ⅜ in., Smithsonian American Art Museum, Transfer from the North Carolina Museum of Art (Gift of the Artist, 1977)

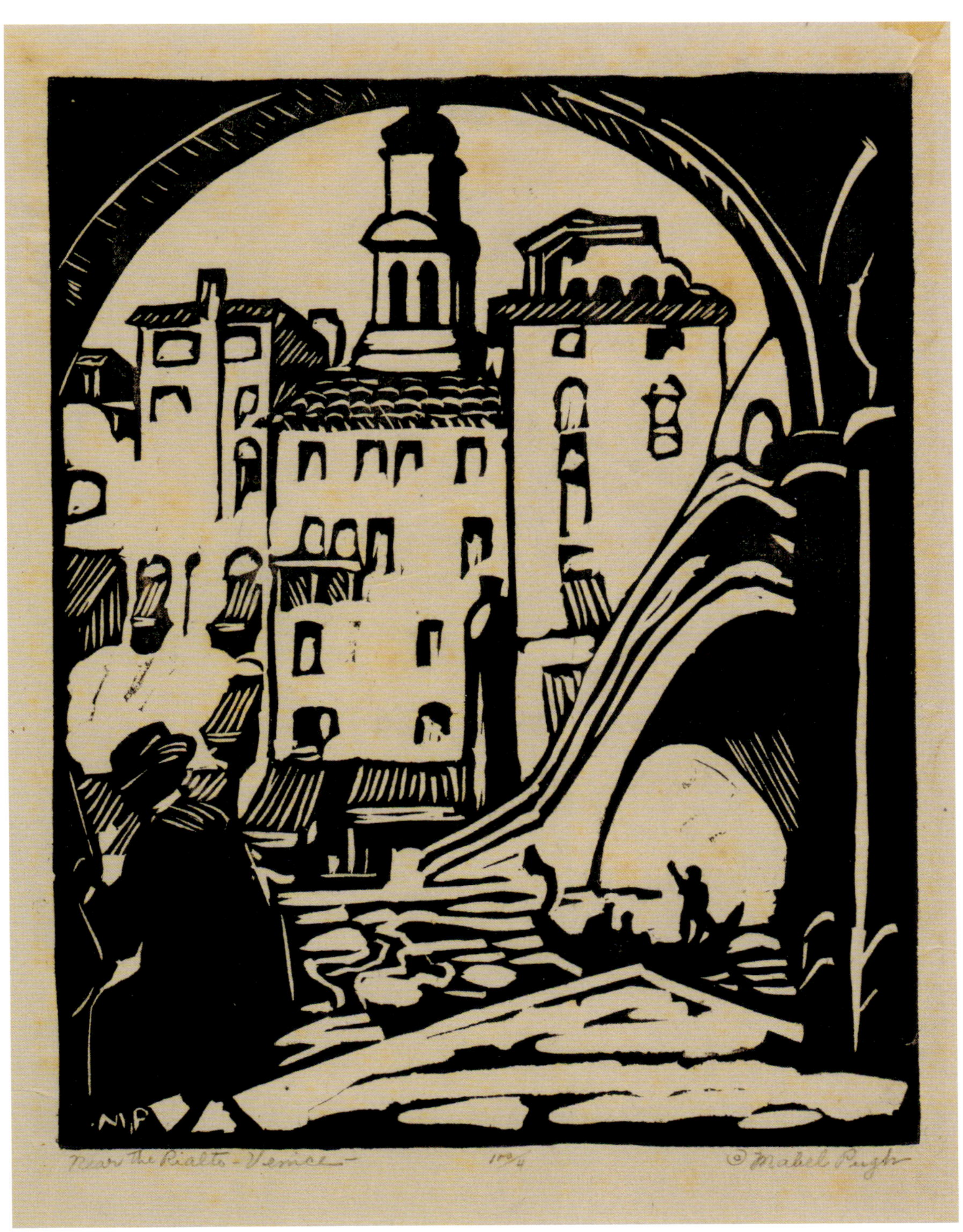
Near the Rialto - Venice -
© Mabel Pugh

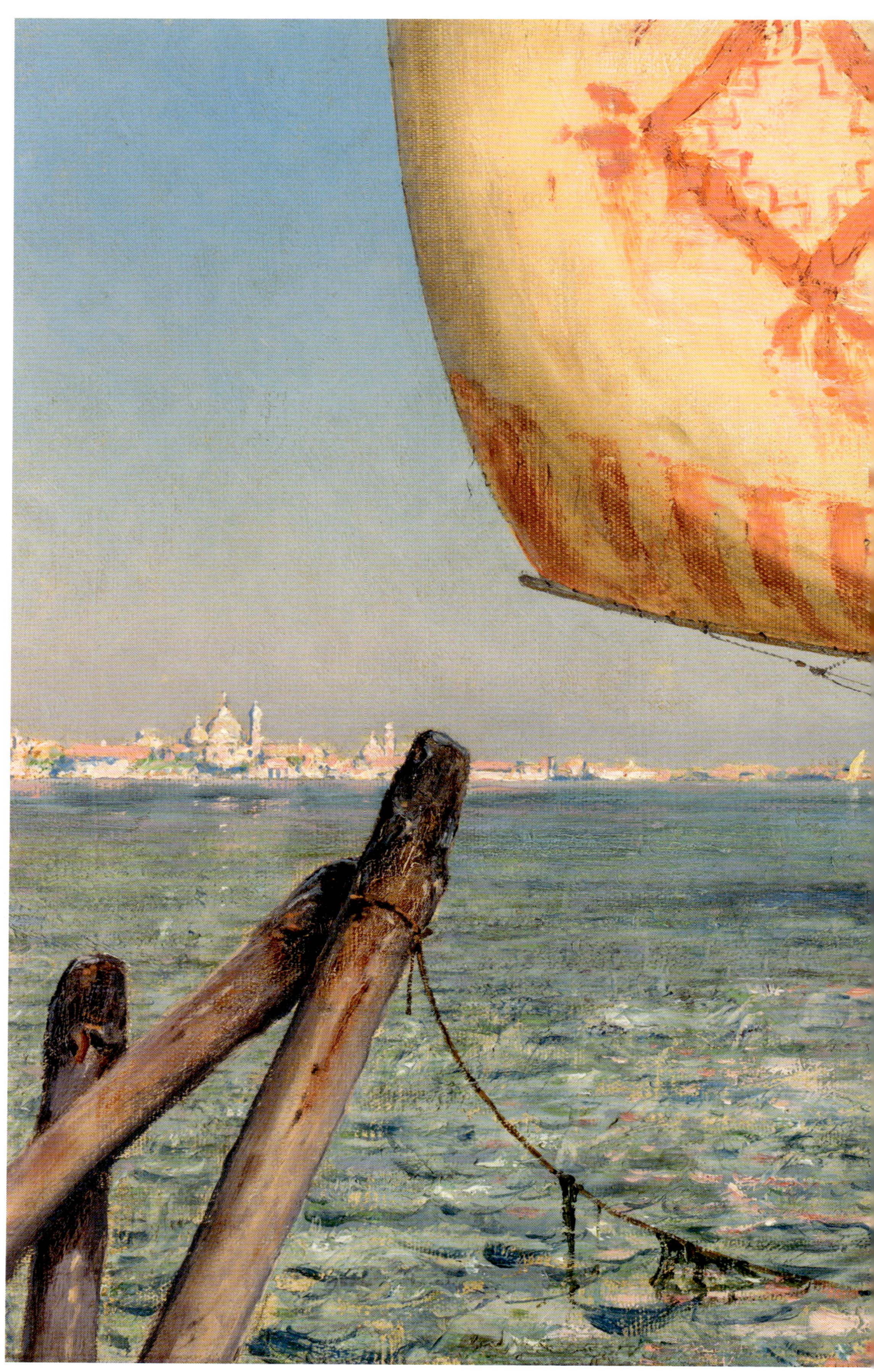

✡ CAT. 1-21
Walter Launt Palmer,
Wing and Wing,
1890, oil on canvas,
18 × 27 in.,
Private collection

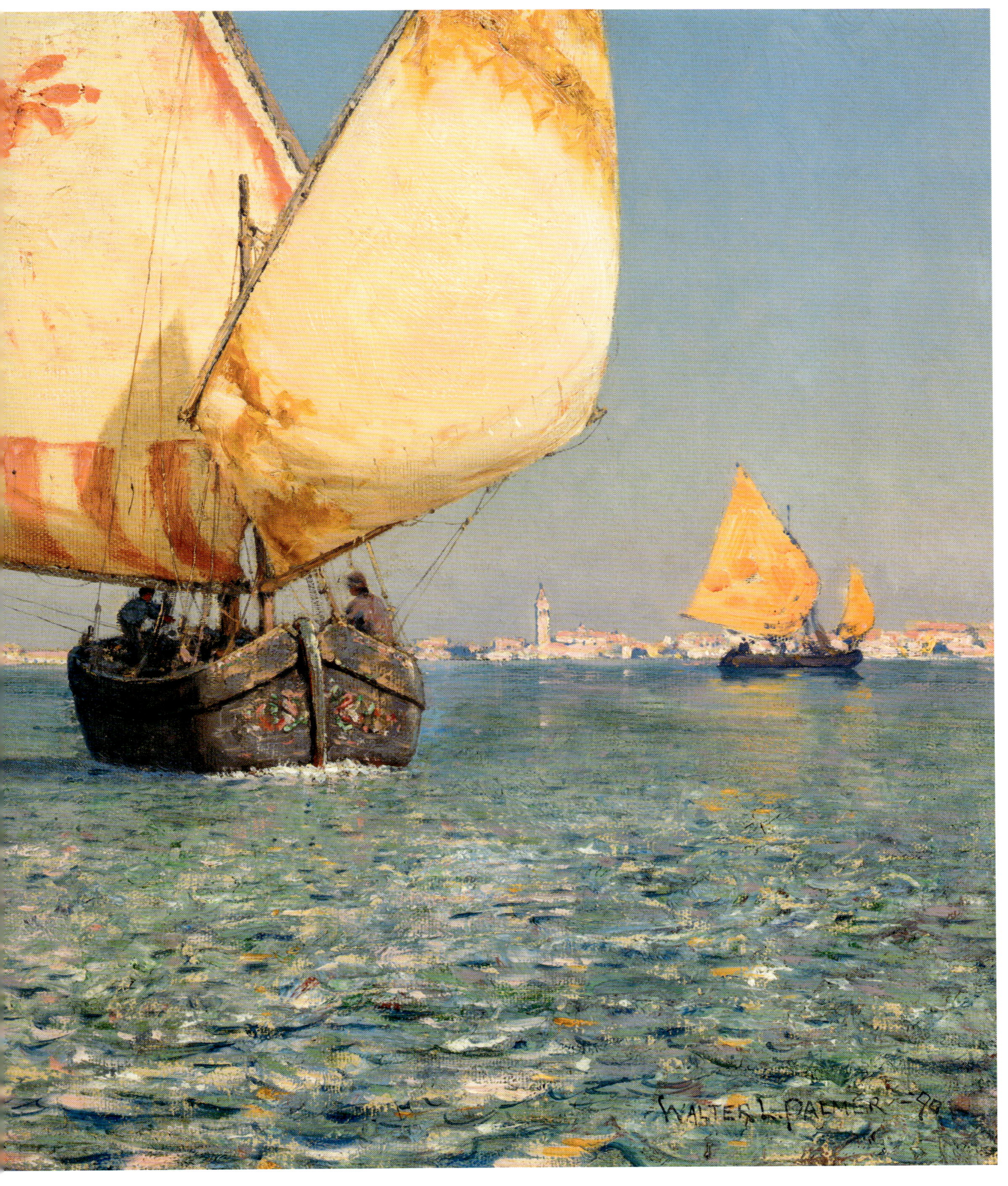
WALTER L. PALMER

NOTES

1 Richard Ormond and Elaine Kilmurray, *John Singer Sargent: Figures and Landscapes, 1874–1882* (New Haven, CT: Yale University Press, 2006), 316–17, 336.

2 Accounts of the nineteenth-century expatriate community in Venice include Hugh Honour and John Fleming, *The Venetian Hours of Henry James, Whistler and Sargent* (Boston: Bulfinch, 1991); Elizabeth Anne McCauley et al., *Gondola Days: Isabella Stewart Gardner and the Palazzo Barbaro Circle* (Boston: Isabella Stewart Gardner Museum, 2004); Warren Adelson et al., *Sargent's Venice* (New Haven, CT: Yale University Press, 2006); Ormond and Kilmurray, *John Singer Sargent: Figures and Landscapes, 1874–1882*, 307–85; Richard Ormond and Elaine Kilmurray, *John Singer Sargent: Venetian Figures and Landscapes, 1898–1913* (New Haven, CT: Yale University Press, 2009), 21–61; and Hanne Borchmeyer, *Das amerikanische Künstlermilieu in Venedig: Von 1880 bis zur Gegenwart* (Berlin: Akademie, 2013).

3 On the manufacture of beads in Venice, see Anna Bellavitis, Nadia Maria Filippini, and Maria Teresa Sega, eds., *Perle e Impiraperle: Un Lavoro di Donne a Venezia tra '800 e '900* (Venice: Arsenale, 1990); and Giovanni Sarpellon, *Venetian Murrine and Beads* (Venice: Fondazione Musei Civici di Venezia, 2018).

4 For extended accounts of Whistler's activities and art making in Venice, see Margaret F. MacDonald, *Palaces in the Night: Whistler in Venice* (Berkeley: University of California Press, 2001); and Eric Denker, *Whistler and His Circle in Venice* (London: Merrell, 2003).

5 "die unwahrscheinlichste der Städte" in Thomas Mann, *Der Tod in Venedig: Novelle* (Berlin: S. Fischer, 1925), 41. Translation by author.

6 The exception is the 1992 exhibition *The Lure of Italy*, which displayed an assortment of souvenir decorative arts, illustrated as an appendix in the catalogue with limited discussion. See Theodore E. Stebbins Jr., *The Lure of Italy: American Artists and the Italian Experience, 1760–1914* (Boston: Museum of Fine Arts, Boston, 1992), 445–50.

7 John L. Cotter and J. Paul Hudson, *New Discoveries at Jamestown: Site of the First Successful English Settlement in America* (Washington, DC: US Government Printing Office, 1957), 45.

8 See Margaretta M. Lovell, *Venice: The American View, 1860–1920* (San Francisco: Fine Arts Museums of San Francisco, 1984), 11–16. The Napoleonic Wars have often been presented as an endpoint in Venetian history, leading to a dearth of scholarship on nineteenth-century Venice and its artistic products. John Julius Norwich provides what he calls "the whole story of Venice," a rich survey beginning with the city's settlement that cuts off abruptly with the fall of the republic in 1797. Norwich, *A History of Venice* (New York: Vintage Books, 1989), xxiv. Recent studies of this period note and correct this gap, including Borchmeyer, *Das amerikanische Künstlermilieu in Venedig*, 42–59; and R. J. B. Bosworth, *Italian Venice: A History* (New Haven, CT: Yale University Press, 2014).

9 Mark Twain, *The Innocents Abroad; or, The New Pilgrim's Progress* (Hartford, CT: American Publishing, 1869), 221.

10 Surveys of the history of the Venetian glass revival, introducing its chief products and innovations, include Reino Liefkes, "Antonio Salviati and the Nineteenth-Century Renaissance of Venetian Glass," *Burlington Magazine* 136, no. 1094 (May 1994): 283–90; Sheldon Barr, *Venetian Glass: Confections in Glass, 1855–1914* (New York: Harry N. Abrams, 1998); and Rosa Barovier Mentasti, ed., *Exquisite Glass Ornaments: The Nineteenth-Century Murano Glass Revival in the de Boos-Smith Collection* (Venice: Marsilio, 2010).

11 Sand's novel was translated and published serially in the leading American art magazine *The Crayon* (January–September 1856). See Henry F. Majewski, "George Sand's Aesthetic Dream: Artists and Artisans in *Les Maîtres Mosaïstes*," in *Transposing Art into Texts in French Romantic Literature* (Chapel Hill: University of North Carolina Press, 2002), 62–76; and Nicole Savy and Pierre-Marc de Biasi, "Du modèle à l'artiste," *Magazine Littéraire* 431 (May 2004): 53–55. On the restoration of St. Mark's Basilica, see Charles Yriarte, "Les Restaurations de Saint-Marc de Venise," *Revue des Deux Mondes* 38, no. 4 (April 15, 1880): 827–56; and Sheldon Barr, *Venetian Glass Mosaics 1860–1917* (Woodbridge, UK: Antique Collectors' Club, 2008), 9–12.

12 Sophia Bompiani, "Ancient Mosaics in the Churches of Rome," *Ladies' Repository: A Monthly Periodical, Devoted to Literature, Arts, and Religion* 4, no. 2 (August 1876): 139.

13 Sacharissa [Constance Cary Harrison?], "Decoration of the Dinner Table," *Scribner's Monthly* 18, no. 3 (July 1879): 463.

14 See Peter Francis Jr., "The Beads That Did *Not* Buy Manhattan Island," *Beads* 22 (2010): 41–51.

15 Smithsonian annual reports describe individual beads taken from sites in New York, Florida, Pennsylvania, and California, demonstrating the worldwide circulation of glass beads long before the Venetian glass revival. See Samuel Stehman Haldeman, "Beads," in *Report upon United States Geographical Surveys West of the One Hundredth Meridian*, vol. 7, *Archaeology* (Washington, DC: Government Printing Office, 1879), 270.

16 "The Smithsonian Institution has recently secured a collection of about five hundred varieties of modern Venetian beads.... Interesting examples occur in the Cesnola and Egyptian collections of the Metropolitan Museum, New York." Haldeman, "Beads," 270–71. See

also Haldeman, "On a Polychrome Bead from Florida," in *Annual Report of the Board of Regents of the Smithsonian Institution* (Washington, DC: Government Printing Office, 1878), 304–5.

17 The international circulation and multiple lives of Venetian glass beads invite study of intersections between the fields of art and anthropology that extend beyond the scope of this book.

18 Mary Elizabeth Wilson Sherwood, "Venice," *Galaxy* 14, no. 5 (November 1872): 671. This oft-repeated root story for foreign usage of "fiasco" is reported as early as 1858 in German in "Theater, Kunst und Literatur," *Neu-Wien*, August 8, 1858, 4; and in English in 1864 in "Fiasco," *Notes and Queries* 146 (October 15, 1864): 306.

19 Throughout these decades, Murano's newspaper, *La Voce di Murano*, reported diligently on the state of glassmaking in other countries to help improve local operations and expand their market share. See Marco Verità and Sandro Zecchin, "Industrial and Artistic Glass Production in Murano: Late 19th–Middle 20th Centuries," in *Study Days on Venetian Glass: The Origins of Modern Glass Art in Venice and Europe, about 1900*, ed. Rosa Barovier Mentasti and Cristina Tonini (Venice: Istituto Veneto di Scienze, Lettere ed Arti, 2017), 21–32.

20 See Barovier Mentasti, ed., *Exquisite Glass Ornaments*. For a broader survey of glassmaking trends, see Hugh Tait, ed., *Five Thousand Years of Glass* (London: British Museum, 1991).

21 James Jackson Jarves, "Ancient and Modern Venetian Glass of Murano," *Harper's New Monthly Magazine* 64, no. 380 (January 1882): 186.

22 Louis Earle Rowe, "The Ames Collection of Venetian Glass," *Bulletin of the Rhode Island School of Design* 2, no. 4 (October 1914): 7.

23 Paul N. Perrot, *Three Great Centuries of Venetian Glass: A Special Exhibition 1958* (Corning, NY: Corning Museum of Glass, 1958), 26.

24 Nineteenth-century Venetian glass was a focal point for the Annual Seminar on Glass at the Corning Museum of Glass in 2003 and 2004, and those video recordings are available at the museum's Rakow Research Library. The annual Study Days on Venetian Glass at the Istituto Veneto di Scienze, Lettere ed Arti addressed this era in 2015 and published the proceedings; see Rosa Barovier Mentasti and Cristina Tonini, *Study Days on Venetian Glass: The Birth of the Great Museum: The Glassworks Collections between the Renaissance and Revival* (Venice: Istituto Veneto di Scienze, Lettere ed Arti, 2016). In 2018 the Glass Art Society held its annual conference in Venice, featuring speakers on this category of glassmaking.

25 These and other common terms are defined in this volume's glass glossary, p. 129.

26 Louise Howland King Cox and Richard Murray, "Louise Cox at the Art Students League: A Memoir," *Archives of American Art Journal* 27, no. 1 (1987): 12.

27 Cox's "pearls" cite the glass bead industry. This may be through mistranslation or misunderstanding (in Italian, beads are called *perle* or *perline*, and the French word is *perles*) or through Venice's reputation for producing imitation pearls made of opaque white glass, commonly known as "Venetian pearls" among anglophone haberdashers. See "Mock Pearls," *New York Times*, December 28, 1873, 2: "The Venetian pearls are generally vitreous, and little likely to deceive, yet they are sold by thousands of boxes, throughout Europe, Asia, and the New World."

28 See H. Barbara Weinberg, "American 'High' Renaissance: Bowdoin's Walker Art Building and Its Murals," in *The Italian Presence in American Art, 1860–1920*, ed. Irma B. Jaffe (New York: Fordham University Press, 1992), 121–32.

29 Useful introductions to the canon of Venetian grand tour pictures include Lovell, *Venice: The American View*; and Erica E. Hirshler, "'Gondola Days': American Painters in Venice," in Stebbins, *Lure of Italy*, 112–28.

30 Jarves, "Ancient and Modern Venetian Glass of Murano," 186.

MURANO GLASS

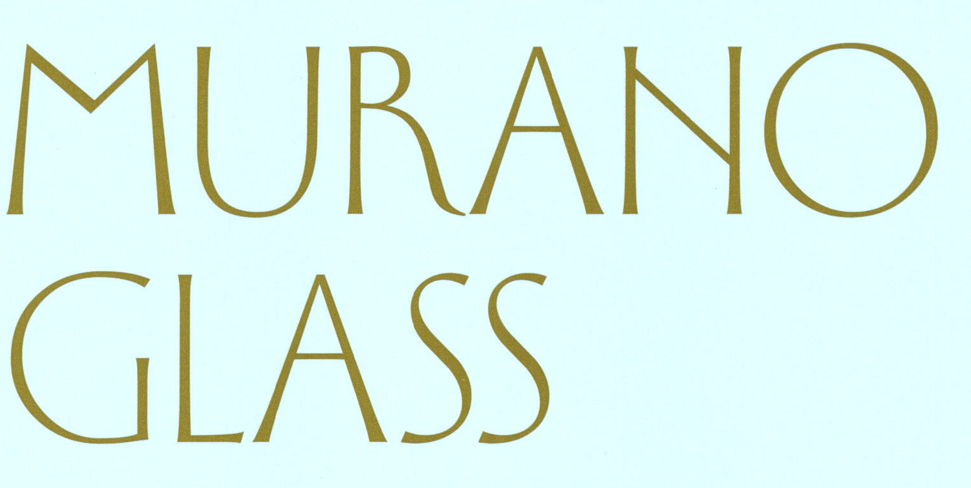

and Its Collectors in Aesthetic America

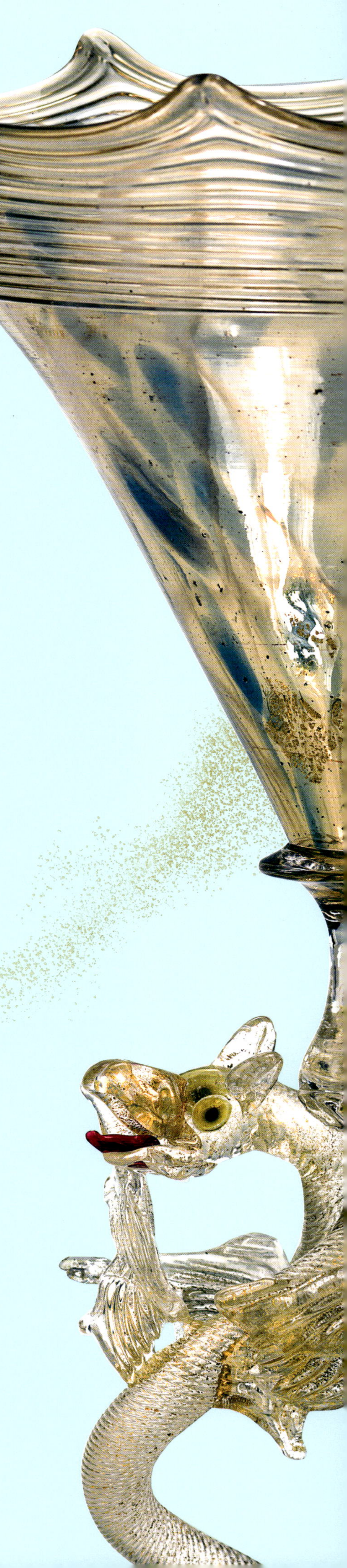

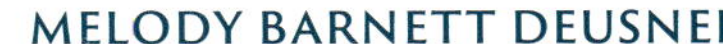
MELODY BARNETT DEUSNER

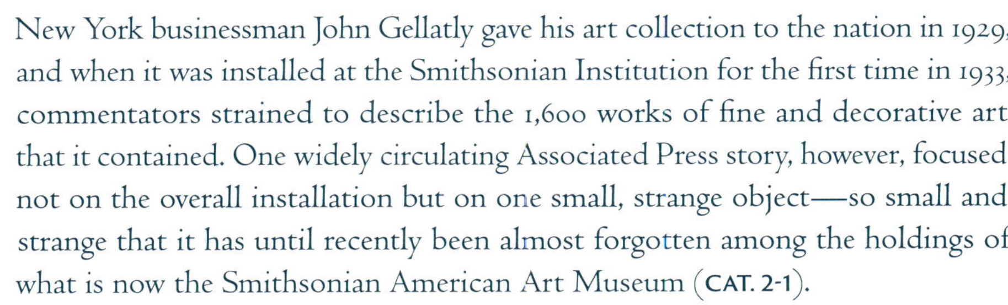

New York businessman John Gellatly gave his art collection to the nation in 1929, and when it was installed at the Smithsonian Institution for the first time in 1933, commentators strained to describe the 1,600 works of fine and decorative art that it contained. One widely circulating Associated Press story, however, focused not on the overall installation but on one small, strange object—so small and strange that it has until recently been almost forgotten among the holdings of what is now the Smithsonian American Art Museum (CAT. 2-1).

Newspapers at the time described it as "an icon-like concoction of cigar boxes, broken glass and beads, braids, and knick-knacks from the 5 and 10 cent store" assembled by Gellatly's butler-turned-curator, Ralph Seymour, in an attempt to salvage the fragments of "an exquisite old bottle of fifteenth-century iridescent glass" that "was broken beyond repair." The diorama, originally installed in a case with Venetian glass pillars, also includes tiny reproductions of a carved desk, American painter Abbott Thayer's *Stevenson Memorial* (see p. 84), and "the case of rare glasses that Gellatly often sat fingering late into the night." It was, readers were told, "an exact miniature of Gellatly's favorite corner, and each object in it may still be recognized by a keen observer as a copy of something in the collection."[1]

Seymour's tribute to Gellatly comes down to us—along with Thayer's original painting and the artifacts of ancient and modern glass that Gellatly once carefully placed in front of it (CAT. 2-2)—because his gift stipulated that the entire collection must remain intact. Hence the surprising survival of an important survey collection of Italian glass, including antique vessels and previously under-researched specimens of nineteenth-century Venetian art glass, within a museum today devoted to American art. This book offers a new opportunity to explore the history of these delicate, colorful vessels and the fantasies that attached to them—and to Venice more broadly—in the nineteenth and early twentieth centuries.

Preceding pages:
Salviati Dott. Antonio, Conical Goblet with Entwined Serpents Stem (detail), ca. 1880s; **see p. 70**

Why was historical glass so important to Gellatly that it both anchored his favorite collecting corner and constituted a considerable portion of his gift? Significantly, Gellatly was not alone; his bequest came fairly late in a series of efforts by other donors to place Venetian glass among the founding acquisitions of art museums in the United States. This process, begun in the 1870s and 1880s, often involved transforming or transporting what had been private domestic collections into publicly accessible institutions, where they became permanent exemplars of value, enshrined as national cultural patrimony.

This essay considers the role played by Venetian glass in these private-public collections and begins by examining a set of ideas circulating during the late-nineteenth-century cultural moment in which they were first assembled—ideas associated with the Anglo-American Aesthetic movement in art, design, and interior decoration. Among other things, this loosely defined "movement" proposed that domestic spaces (indeed, rooms in general) might be thought of as compositions to be artfully coordinated and arranged, just as a painter might choose and place colors and forms on a canvas "for art's sake" rather than to communicate a particular story, message, or moral. And the Aesthetic movement inspired many art collectors to think of their holdings in turn as harmonious wholes worth preserving in perpetuity—an idea that had far-reaching consequences for American museums. What, after all, were these museums intended to promote and preserve, and how were their contents to be arranged? Were they shrines to unique masterpieces? Instructional archives for aspiring craftsmen and ambitious industrialists? These were unsettled debates at the turn of the century, and they raised fundamental questions about art, money, and power in the United States and about the relationship of the country to the rest of the world, in the past and in the present. The Venetian art glass that found its way into American museum collections offers a lens through which we can understand some of these changing ideas about art and design and how American museums evolved.

VENETIAN GLASS AND THE AESTHETIC MOVEMENT

As Victorians and Gilded Age Americans looked out upon a world increasingly defined by mass-produced goods, modern materials, and a consumerist landscape that seemed somehow both infinitely variable and flattened into predictability, English artist and critic John Ruskin directed their attention to what appeared to be a more authentic and rewarding past. His observations inspired generations of artists and craftsmen to rethink their relationship to labor and its products. In his book *The Stones of Venice* (1851–53), Ruskin examined the foundations and evolution of medieval Venetian architecture "stone by stone" in order to make a case for the inventiveness of spiritually motivated art that had been created before the onset of the more humanistically oriented Italian Renaissance.[2] His immediate goal was to highlight what he felt were the underappreciated pleasures of Gothic Venetian design, including "fancifulness," "love of variety," and "love of richness."[3] More broadly, however, he sought to use Venice in its heyday—which he saw as a commercial island republic not unlike his own mid-nineteenth-century London—as a case study for helping

☼ CAT. 2-1
Ralph Seymour, Miniature Diorama of John Gellatly Collection, ca. 1924–29, wood, fabric, glass, and other materials, 11 ⅞ × 12 ¼ × 6 in. (open), Smithsonian American Art Museum, Gift of John Gellatly

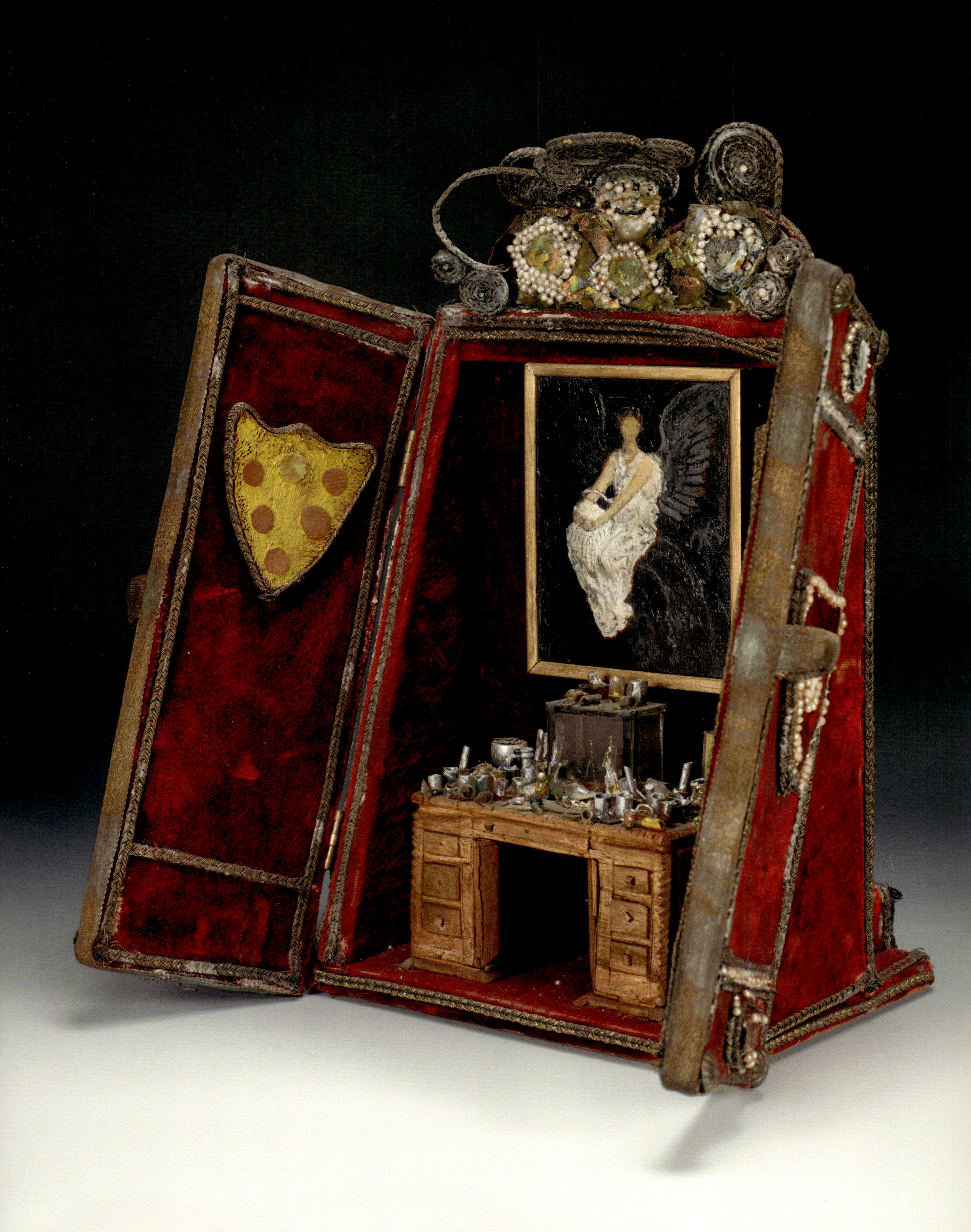

his contemporaries develop an eye and appetite for something better than imitative, uninspired, mechanically reproduced designs. Among other examples, Ruskin cited medieval Venetian glass as a model of craftsmanship that prized idiosyncratic creativity over thoughtless uniformity. "[T]he old Venetian cared not a whit whether his edges were sharp or not," he told his readers, "but he invented a new design for every glass that he made, and never moulded a handle or a lip without a new fancy in it."[4] In this way, Ruskin showed his readers how to appreciate art and architecture that was both functional and beautiful: how to locate and trace the visual evidence of craftsmen setting out to solve specific problems and taking evident joy in their work.

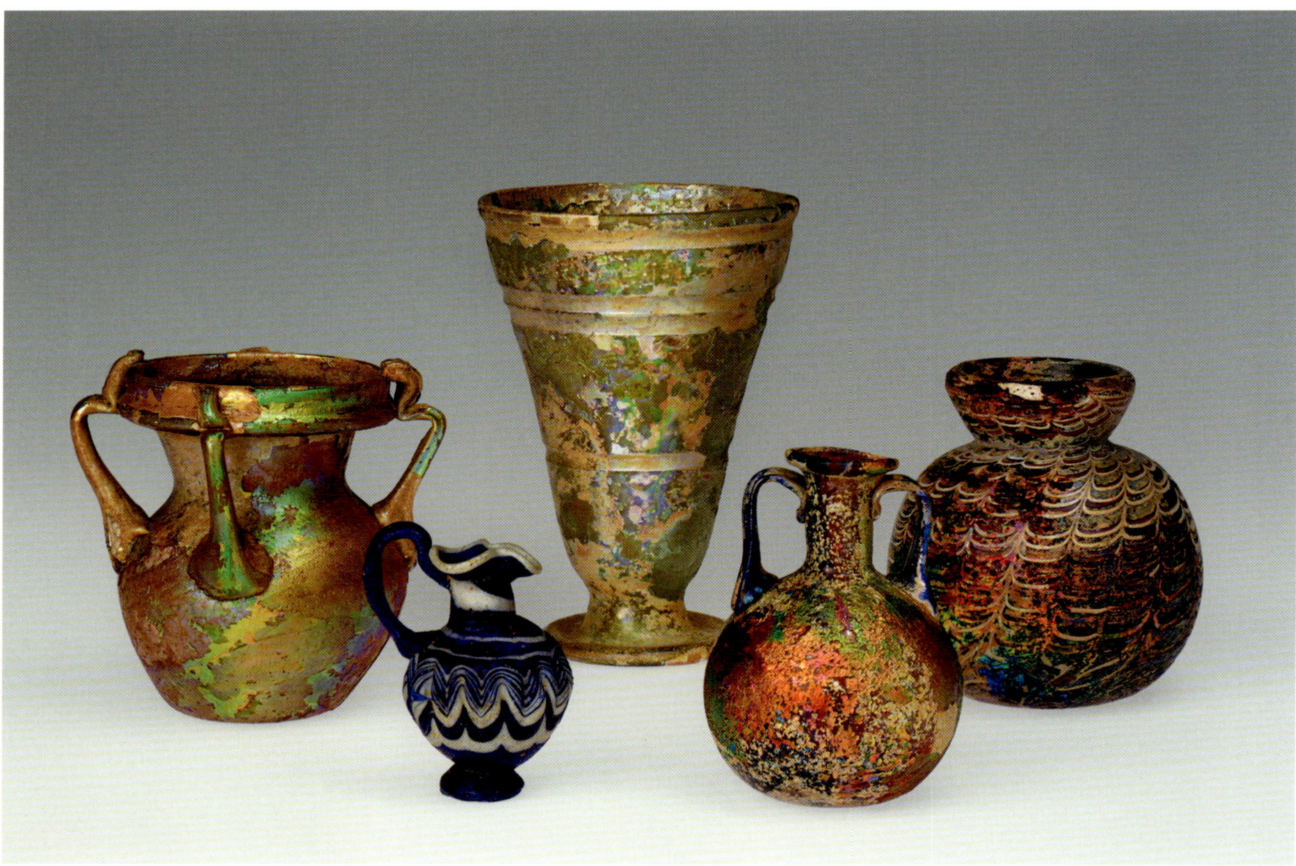

✲ CAT. 2-2
Ancient Mediterranean vessels, 6th c. BCE–4th c. CE, glass (various techniques), 2 ⅝ to 4 ⅞ in. tall, Smithsonian American Art Museum, Gifts of John Gellatly

Ruskin's preference for old, handmade, and thoughtfully constructed objects spurred householders to think more carefully about the things they acquired. By the mid-1860s, British artists furnishing their studio-homes to cultivate comfort, culture, and sales were becoming standard-bearers for an eclecticism built of such ingredients as "carved oak furniture, sculptured fireplaces in wood and stone, tapestry, majolica ware, Venetian glass, and bric-a-brac in its costliest and choicest forms"—a mode of decorating that built up entire rooms out of well-crafted, decorative objects whether they were made recently or long ago, locally or half a world away.[5] The transatlantic art press celebrated these so-called "artistic" spaces as exemplars of what could be accomplished if one followed one's own tastes rather than the dictates of professional upholsterers, and thereby helped

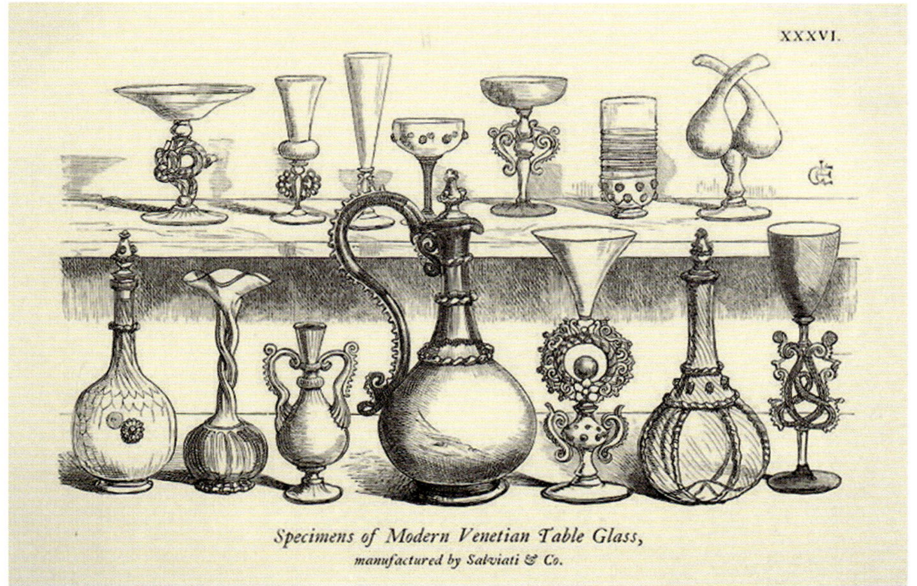

Fig. 2-1
Charles Locke Eastlake, *Specimens of Modern Venetian Table Glass, manufactured by Salviati & Co.*, from Eastlake, *Hints on Household Taste* (Longmans, Green, 2nd edition, 1869)

against the material's fundamentally ductile properties. At the same time, part of the pleasure that Eastlake and some of his contemporaries took in Salviati's glass was in its optimistic testimony that craft traditions of the past, handed down through generations of Muranese glassblowers, were not irrecoverably lost nor necessarily at odds with the modern industrial present: they could be recovered and even perhaps improved upon. As American art critic and collector James Jackson Jarves put it, Salviati and his assistants brought the "superior technical processes and chemistry of the nineteenth century" to bear on the "graceful, elegant, and varied form[s]" of old Venetian glass as well as on the new designs and shapes they were pioneering. Venetian glass, then, appealed to decorators and collectors through its distinct potential to close the gap between the past and the present.[10]

But this was not the only work that Venetian glass performed. Both Eastlake and Harriet Prescott Spofford, who further popularized and commercialized Eastlake's ideas in the United States, emphasized the educational power of furniture and bric-a-brac within the home. These objects shaped the taste of its inhabitants, encouraging them to make or to buy things with a deeper historical awareness and sensitivity to the relationship between form and function. Eastlake promoted a modernized medieval style of furniture design (called "Gothic") in which function largely dictated form: sturdy, blocky shapes with shallow-carved ornament that celebrated the essentially architectural character of furniture as a series of vertical, horizontal, and diagonal panels and planks. In her book *Art Decoration Applied to Furniture* (1877), Spofford explained how to decorate with Eastlake's Gothic (Fig. 2-2), among other styles, showing her readers how to arrange furniture and bric-a-brac (including china, majolica, and Venetian glass) to maximize their beauty and utility. Beyond this, however, she wanted her readers to understand the history of the craft traditions that produced the objects in their homes because she believed that the study of decorative arts was "as important...as the study of politics" and that "the story of furniture" was "the story of the [human] race." The selection of one's furniture and bric-a-brac, then, was no trivial matter. "The private home is at the foundation of the public state, subtle and unimagined influences moulding the men who mould the state."[11]

Thus far we have been discussing the ideas and expectations that attached to Venetian glass from the 1850s to the 1870s, first in England and subsequently in the United States. But to what degree were consumers able to see these objects for themselves? One Boston reviewer of Eastlake complained in 1872 that "Nine Americans in ten can possibly have no practical acquaintance" with and in fact "know little and care little about the parquetry floors, medieval metal work, door-knockers, and coal-scuttles, inlaid decorations, and old Venetian glass" that were the province of England's leisured and moneyed classes.[12] But the 1870s gradually brought increasing opportunities for Americans to see and judge for themselves the effects of Eastlake-inspired Gothic-style furniture, as well as those of the new textile, wallpaper, and stained glass designs produced by the London firm of Morris & Company. In the spirit of Ruskin and Eastlake, William Morris and his band of artist-designers sought to turn revived craft traditions toward the

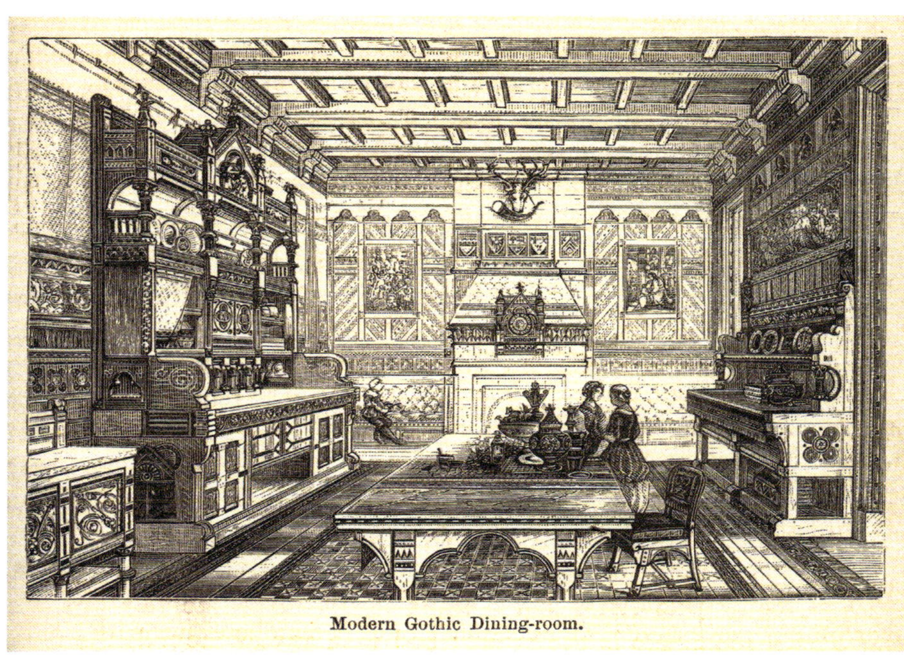

Fig. 2-2
***Modern Gothic Dining-room*, from Harriet Prescott Spofford, *Art Decoration Applied to Furniture* (Harper and Brothers, 1877)**

decoration of modern homes. At events such as the Cincinnati Industrial Exposition of 1873, Americans who lived far from the coastal cities had the opportunity to inspect these objects in person.[13] Morris sent to its inaugural Household Art display a stained glass window by Edward Burne-Jones and samples of the firm's early wallpapers (Fig. 2-3).[14] The whole ensemble "makes a brilliant and attractive display, and one that will long hold the visitor over the beautiful form of an old vase or a piece of Venetian glass," wrote one critic for whom the vases, pitchers, and flagons loaned by private collectors coordinated harmoniously with the Morris papers and Tiffany silver offered for sale at the fair.[15]

At precisely the same moment, the London-based Scottish decorator and designer Daniel Cottier was setting up a new gallery-showroom in New York to meet a rising American demand for high-quality furnishings. Objects for sale, one contemporary tells us, included the "best English decoration by [Lawrence] Alma-Tadema; stained glass reproductions of the old English style; and choice Venetian jars and vases."[16] But no one played a greater role in promoting Cottier's than the art critic Clarence Cook. In his *Scribner's* columns and subsequent book, *The House Beautiful* (1878), Cook lauded Cottier's displays as setting a new standard for artistic home decoration. He rhapsodized over the Venetian vessels that featured so prominently at Cottier's showroom as works of art in and of themselves, giving us a sense of how they might have looked in a high-end, late-nineteenth-century home before the adoption of electric light:

> *The mysteries of the tinting of these things of beauty are to us unfathomable; but, next to the colors of evening clouds and jewels, they appear to us about the most beautiful and wonderful in color of any thing in the world, and we could spend hours, or even days, in looking at one against the light, at another by gas-light, or at the flicker of a third in a shadowy corner.*[17]

Fig. 2-3
Morris & Co., *Daisy*, designed 1864, block-printed wallpaper, 27 × 21 ½ in., The Metropolitan Museum of Art, Purchase, Edward C. Moore Jr. Gift, 1923, 23.163.4b

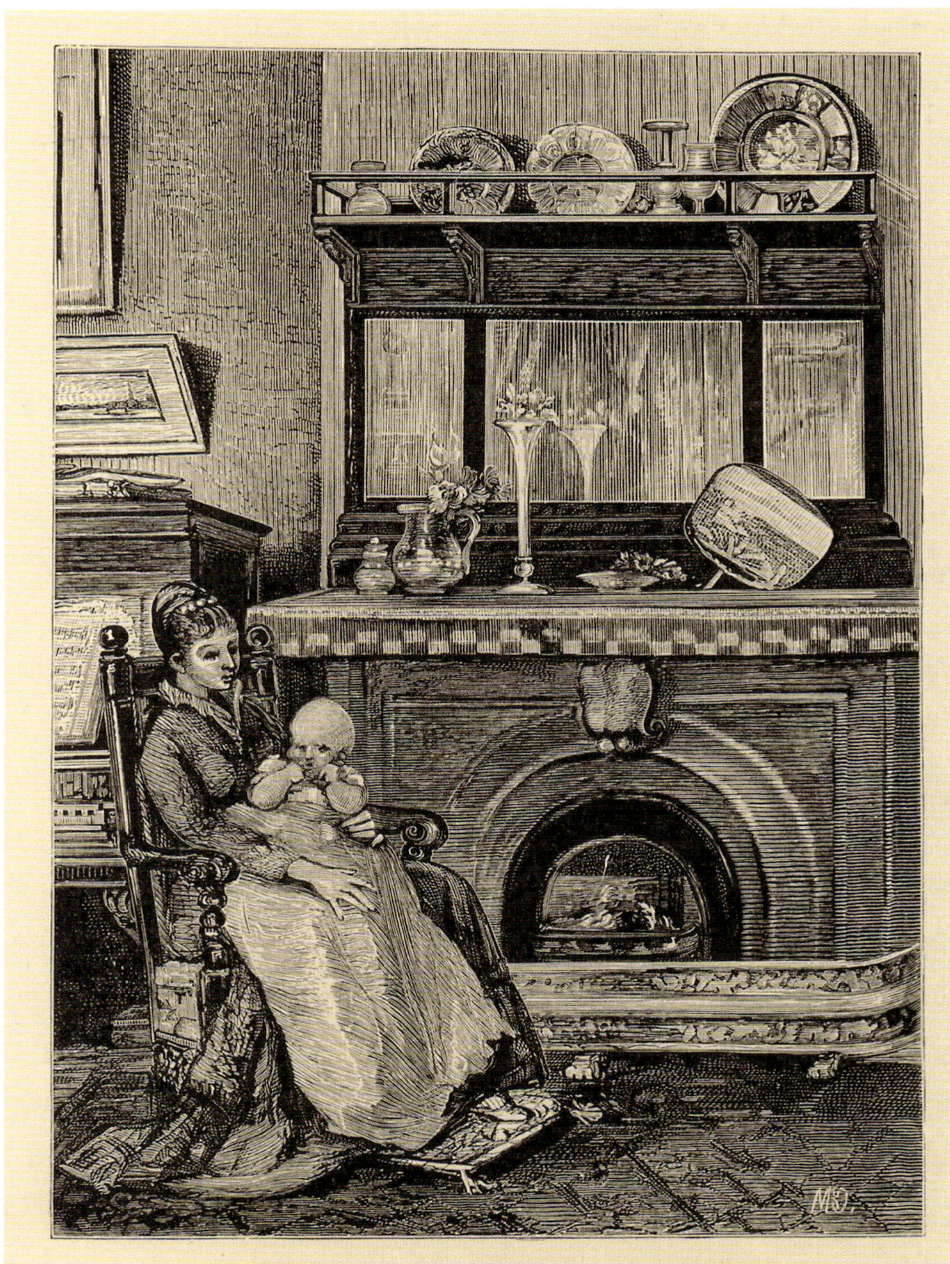

An Every-day Mantel-piece, Simply Treated.
No. 45.

✡ CAT. 2-4
Maria Oakey Dewing, designer; Henry Marsh, engraver; *An Every-day Mantel-piece, Simply Treated*, wood engraving on paper, from Clarence Cook, *The House Beautiful*, (Scribner, Armstrong, 1878)

Cook here evokes both the optical and the tactile pleasures of handling these fragile glass creations, while accompanying illustrations, whether in periodicals or books, helped readers envision such fine objects within their homes. For example, a tall, trumpet-shaped Venetian glass vase is the elegant centerpiece of Maria Oakey Dewing's domestic print *An Every-day Mantel-piece, Simply Treated* (CAT. 2-4), in which a woman and child rock before a hearth displaying a painted fan and an assortment of distinctively shaped and patterned plates, jugs, and jars. Other illustrations provide more explicit vignettes of tasteful décor, such as Francis Lathrop's print of a piece of furniture from Cottier's, a *Hanging Shelf and Cabinet* that functioned as a showcase for Venetian glass and other valuable objects (Fig. 2-4). But these were not included as mere cabinet filler: Cook insisted that it was the artistic effect of the "color of the pots and the bits of glass that are arranged on the shelves" that mattered more than the furniture itself.[18]

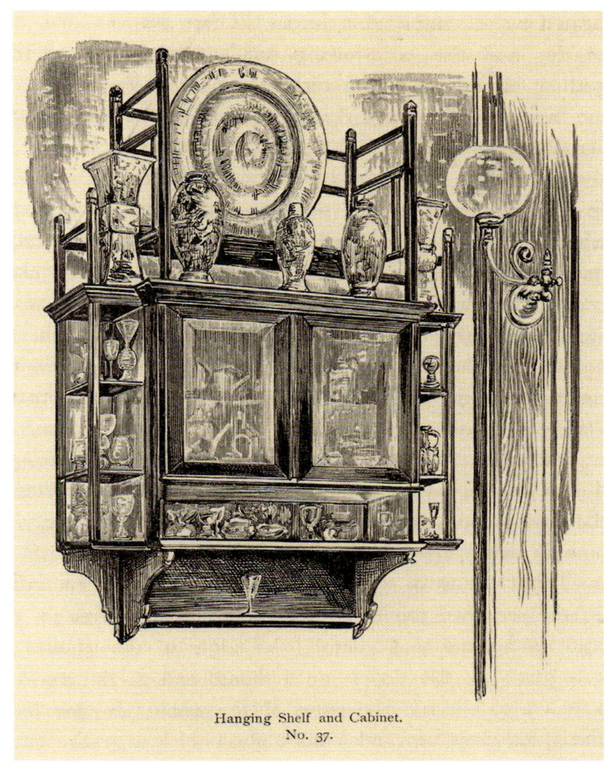

Fig. 2-4
Francis Lathrop, *Hanging Shelf and Cabinet*, wood engraving on paper, from Clarence Cook, *The House Beautiful* (Scribner, Armstrong, 1878)

Venetian glass at Cottier's is celebrated here less for its historical associations or educational value than as raw material, notes of color to be arranged within an interior. Paintings, too, were being sold and exhibited at Cottier's, in a separate gallery space and interspersed among the home goods for sale, and some of these represented a distinct aesthetic shift toward decorative compositions among some American and international artists. In 1875, the painter John La Farge organized a special exhibition at Cottier's to highlight recent decorative paintings by artists whose non-narrative pictures were not receiving adequate attention at the National Academy of Design's annual shows. Among La Farge's artists, Maria Oakey Dewing, who had contributed drawings of Cottier displays to Cook's columns, showed a (now lost) still life painting of azaleas in a Venetian vase she had borrowed from an American collector. The vessel, which may have closely resembled this goblet (CAT. 2-5), featured "colors as delicate and shifting as those of a soap-bubble" with "a shape as slender as the stem of a water-lily. . . . A little serpent of gold-colored glass twists about the base of the stem, the whole thing forming one of the most exquisite of these exquisite fragile Venetian baubles."[19] This exhibition reveals the degree to which shoppers were gradually being encouraged to think of pictures, furniture, and bric-a-brac as elements to arrange in creating domestic "compositions," as well as the integration of Venetian glass objects and decorative American paintings within the same spaces and collections.

When writers on bric-a-brac hunting and the creation of "artistic" domestic interiors in the 1860s and 1870s discussed glass made on Murano, they vacillated between approaching the vessels as historical artifacts, as fragile art glass for decorative display, and as fashionable wares for actual use as "table glass." By 1870, the *Art Journal* was predicting that soon any table would be considered "incomplete" if it failed to display "some of the fantastic forms, and ruby, opal, or other delicate hues, of Murano glass."[20] *Harper's Bazaar* tantalized readers with

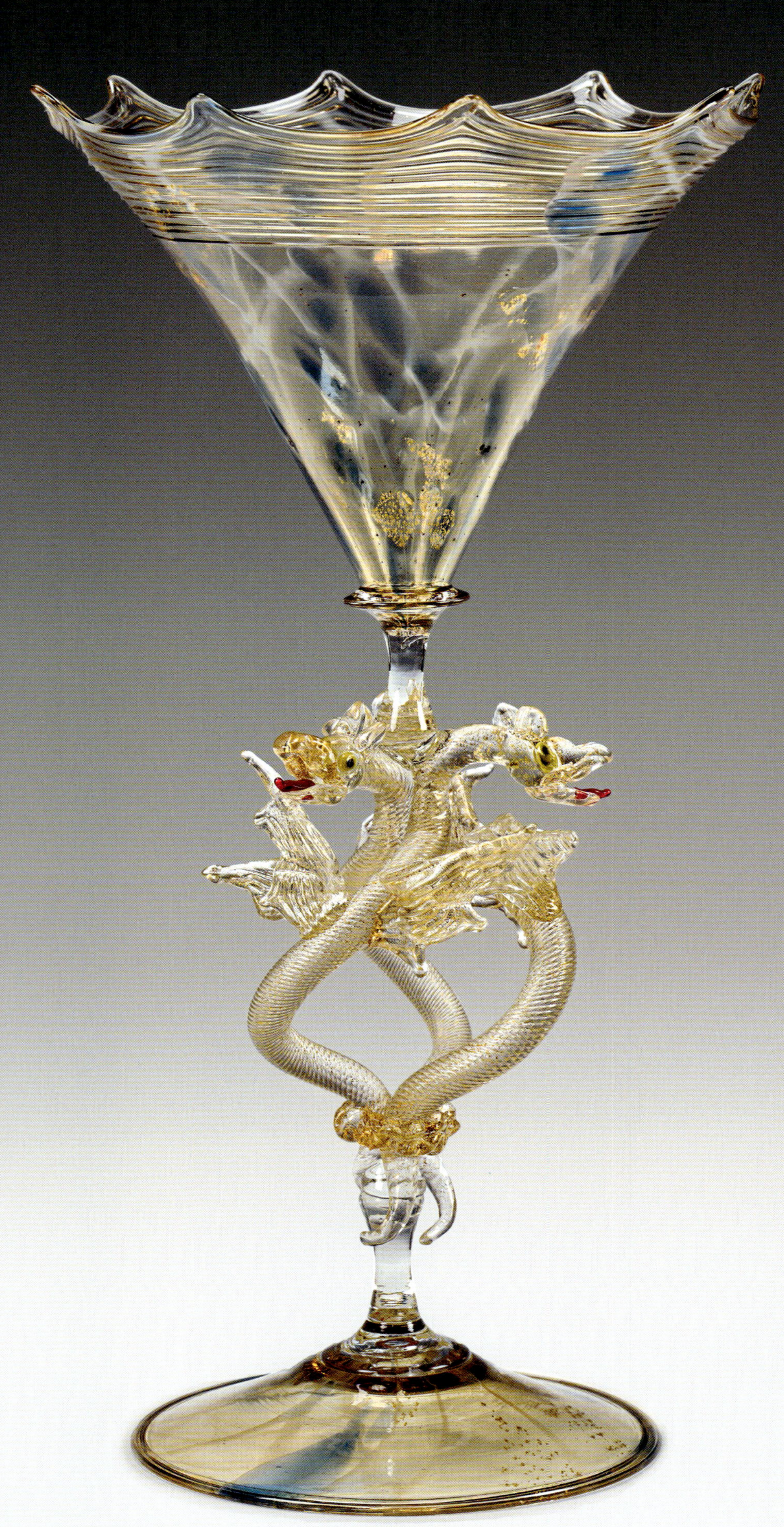

a description of the Salviati glass available for purchase at New York's Tiffany & Co. in 1872.[21] "For those who delight in color is the rare Venetian glass of pale blue or dark scarlet in vases of unique design, and goblets for hock or sherry that seem to have gold ground into them. Finger-bowls of Venetian glass are in harlequin sets, in pairs, or else all different."[22]

✡ CAT. 2-5
Salviati Dott. Antonio, Conical Goblet with Entwined Serpents Stem, ca. 1880s, blown and applied hot-worked glass, 12 ⅜ × 6 ⅜ in. diam., Smithsonian American Art Museum, Gift of John Gellatly

Returning to the Conical Goblet (CAT. 2-5), it is clear that the spiraling necks of the dragons and delicate undulations of the lip of such an "exquisite fragile Venetian bauble" would render it more effective as a glass sculpture than as a functional drinking glass. And so we begin to sense a tension arising in the mid-1870s between those who saw the value of Venetian glass as essentially beautiful *and* utilitarian, and those who increasingly felt its purely aesthetic properties ought to be cultivated on their own, without demand for functionality. James Jackson Jarves, in describing the glass collection he gave to the Metropolitan Museum of Art in 1881 for *Harper's Monthly,* underscored its instructional capacity for improving American manufactures and taste. But he wrote even more passionately of the intense yet temporary pleasures these objects evoked. Sounding like an American Walter Pater, he told his readers, "The Venetian workman" of old

> *despised use, threw it to the winds, as a motive of work. Hence Venetian is unlike all other glass. Its highest merit and greatest value consist in its virtually being incapable of being used for other purposes than to administer to the human craving for beauty, perfection, the supreme aesthetic ideal of the moment, restless, ever-changing, and never-satisfied, because beauty is rooted in the infinite.*[23]

He illustrated these rarified pursuits with examples from his donated collection (Fig. 2-5), such as attenuated wine glasses copying sixteenth- and seventeenth-century models, twelve to fourteen inches tall, with various "complicated," "fanciful," and boldly impractical stems.

Perhaps it should not surprise us, then, that James McNeill Whistler, the best-known pioneer of an "art for art's sake" approach to painting and decoration at this time, would choose to illustrate some of these key ideas by charting the artistic evolution of a drinking vessel as a form. In his "Ten O'Clock" lecture of 1885, Whistler outlined a history of art in which the first artist traced designs on a decorative gourd, followed by others who perfected the earthenware vessel, the choice goblet, and finally the "masterpiece." With each iteration, the people drank from the cup "not from choice, not from a consciousness that it was beautiful, but because . . . there was none other!" This situation provided, for a time, a perfect marriage between what the artist wanted and what the people needed, until the people discovered that equally functional things could be made cheaper and with less art, and utility took over as the chief driver of a debased mass aesthetics.[24] Indeed,

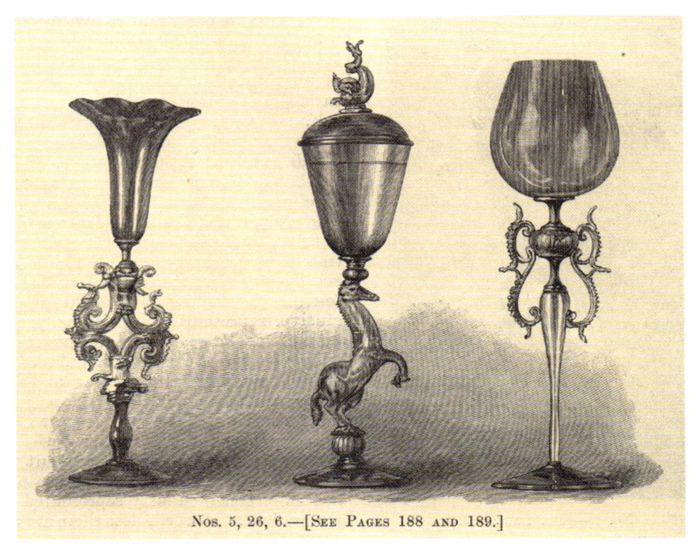

Fig. 2-5
Illustration from James Jackson Jarves, "Ancient and Modern Venetian Glass of Murano," *Harper's New Monthly Magazine*, January 1882

a distinctly English desire for utility and economy was frequently blamed for the decline of its native glassware, which was often used as a foil against which to praise the inventive and artistic qualities of the new Salviati designs.[25] The first scholarly books on glass, catalogues of holdings at the British Museum and South Kensington Museum, confirmed these laments by describing the technical sophistication and luxurious character of earlier periods, particularly glass from imperial Rome and Renaissance Venice. These richly illustrated volumes reinforced the ideas articulated by Whistler, Cook, Ruskin, and other critics, ultimately serving as pattern-books for contemporary Murano glassmakers and as shopping lists for Americans eager to express aesthetic sophistication and for their local public collections to rival the museums of London.[26]

VENETIAN GLASS AND AESTHETICISM IN AMERICAN PRIVATE—PUBLIC COLLECTIONS

Against this backdrop, American collectors and, ultimately, donors were exposed to Venetian glass in its complex and sometimes contradictory ancient and modern, utilitarian and decorative, attainable and aspirational, real and represented aspects. John L. "Jack" and Isabella Stewart Gardner of Boston, Leland and Jane Lathrop Stanford of San Francisco, and John and Edith Rogers Gellatly of New York witnessed its rising popularity in the 1870s and 1880s and had the opportunity to inspect Venetian antiques as well as Salviati's modern creations in person in New York, London, Venice, and elsewhere. They all agreed that Venetian glass should be included and celebrated within their collections and, eventually, that their private collections should be preserved in some way as public museums. But they did not all see precisely the same things when they held these delicate vessels up to the light. Examining the roles that glass played within these collections helps us understand some of the key forms American art institutions could take at the turn of the century and shows the far-reaching impact of each art patron's personal tastes.

ISABELLA STEWART GARDNER: "C'EST MON PLAISIR"

Isabella Stewart Gardner's fascination with Venice would eventually inspire her to construct a Boston mansion, Fenway Court (1901–3), which one period observer described as "not merely a building in the Italian style, but actually a building that might, down to the last brick of it, have been transported from the Grand Canal."[27] Inscribed over the doorway of her house museum was her motto, "C'est mon plaisir" ("It's my pleasure," in French), both the gracious expression of a welcoming host and a declaration of the personal pleasures (rather than strict educational concerns) that guided the assemblage of art and furniture within.[28]

Scholars have argued that we should understand Gardner's collecting within the context of the Aesthetic movement, and indeed, by the time Gardner took her first of nine trips to Venice in 1884, she had already met Whistler at a Grosvenor Gallery reception in London in 1879.[29] The newly established Grosvenor offered what La Farge was seeking in New York—institutional support for artists wrestling with the question of what painting for its own sake

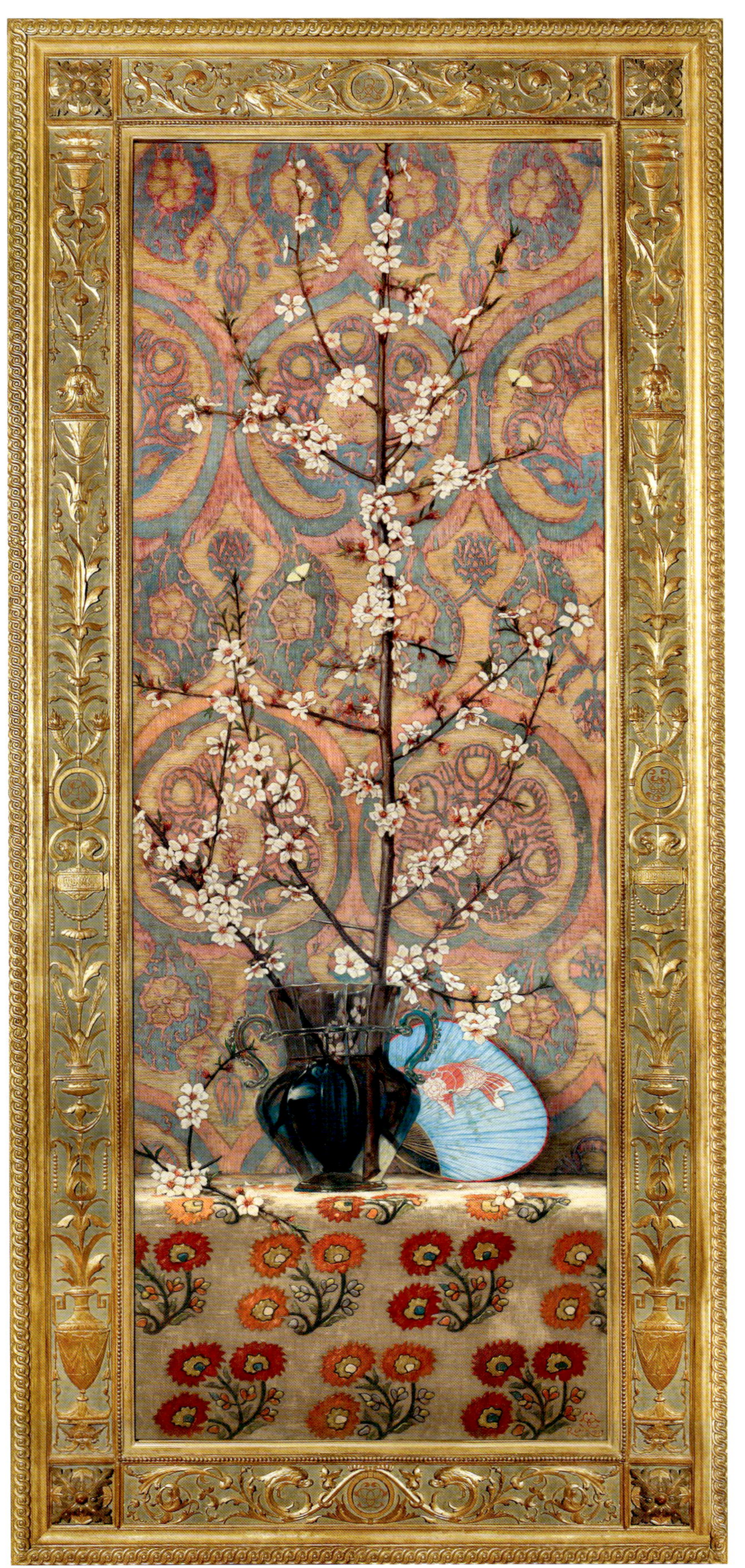

☆ CAT. 2-6
Charles Caryl Coleman, *Still Life with Peach Blossoms*, 1877, oil on canvas, 71 ½ × 25 ¼ in., Art Bridges

might look like.[30] At the 1879 Grosvenor exhibition, Gardner would have seen a painting by her countryman Charles Caryl Coleman, whose still lifes played with variations of blossoming branches, embroidered textiles, and vessels drawn from his collection of bric-a-brac. Consider his *Still Life with Peach Blossoms* (**CAT. 2-6**), in which the flowering branch stretches rhythmically across the canvas, flanked by a Japanese paper fan and anchored by a Salviati-style glass amphora.[31] Like Maria Oakey Dewing's azalea painting, Coleman's paintings were both collectable *and* offered lessons in collectorship, incorporating decorative objects of the type that could also be purchased and demonstrating how to arrange them within a domestic space-as-composition.

Back in Boston in 1882, Gardner dined with Oscar Wilde as he was embarking on his American lecture tour.[32] Wilde, too, used Venetian glass as a point of reference in explaining Aesthetic movement ideas. "In its primary aspect a painting has no more spiritual message than an exquisite fragment of Venetian glass," he announced. "It is a certain inventive and creative handling of line and color which touches the soul—something entirely independent of anything poetical in the subject—something satisfying in itself."[33]

Gardner carried these experiences with her on her biennial summer journeys to Venice, first as a member and eventually as host of the artistic and literary Palazzo Barbaro circle. The Gardners initially visited their New England friends Ariana and Daniel Sargent Curtis in Venice in 1884, when the Curtises were renting the fifteenth-century Venetian palace on the Grand Canal. In 1890, the Gardners began renting the Palazzo Barbaro themselves, where they hosted artists (Frank Duveneck, John Singer Sargent), writers (Robert Browning, Vernon Lee, Henry James), and others.[34] The main salon of this palazzo, later documented by Walter Gay in 1902 (**CAT. 2-7**), served as a grand but time-worn stage set against which its residents and guests lingered and socialized. Its undulating plaster walls and ceilings, gilt furniture, and massive canvases by Venetian old masters like Sebastiano Ricci and Giovanni Battista Piazzetta provided silent, elegant testimony that the creative efforts of these modern makers (and their patrons) revivified and continued those of the Barbaro's Renaissance and baroque past.

The Gardners spent their Venetian days drifting in gondolas, listening to music, conversing with guests, sightseeing, and shopping for bric-a-brac, an experience evoked by Julius LeBlanc Stewart's painting *Sotoportego del Magazen* (**CAT. 2-8**). Here a vendor has strategically positioned herself at a choke point in the busy streets near the Rialto Bridge, a shadowy passage among the neighborhood's shops in which her table of trinkets sparkles to tempt passing tourists. Under such impulses, the Gardners took up bric-a-brac hunting in earnest in the 1890s. What began as a pastime of Jack's—Isabella reportedly preferring to spend her time in churches looking at pictures—eventually became an activity that consumed them both.[35] Frequently, they compelled the "antiquity men" to come to them.[36]

The Gardners' purchases were destined for the new Boston home they were planning in the mid-1890s. But in 1897, before returning to Venice once again, Isabella proposed instead the construction of a house *museum*, a decision that added fuel to and enlarged the importance of the Gardners' pursuit of architectural

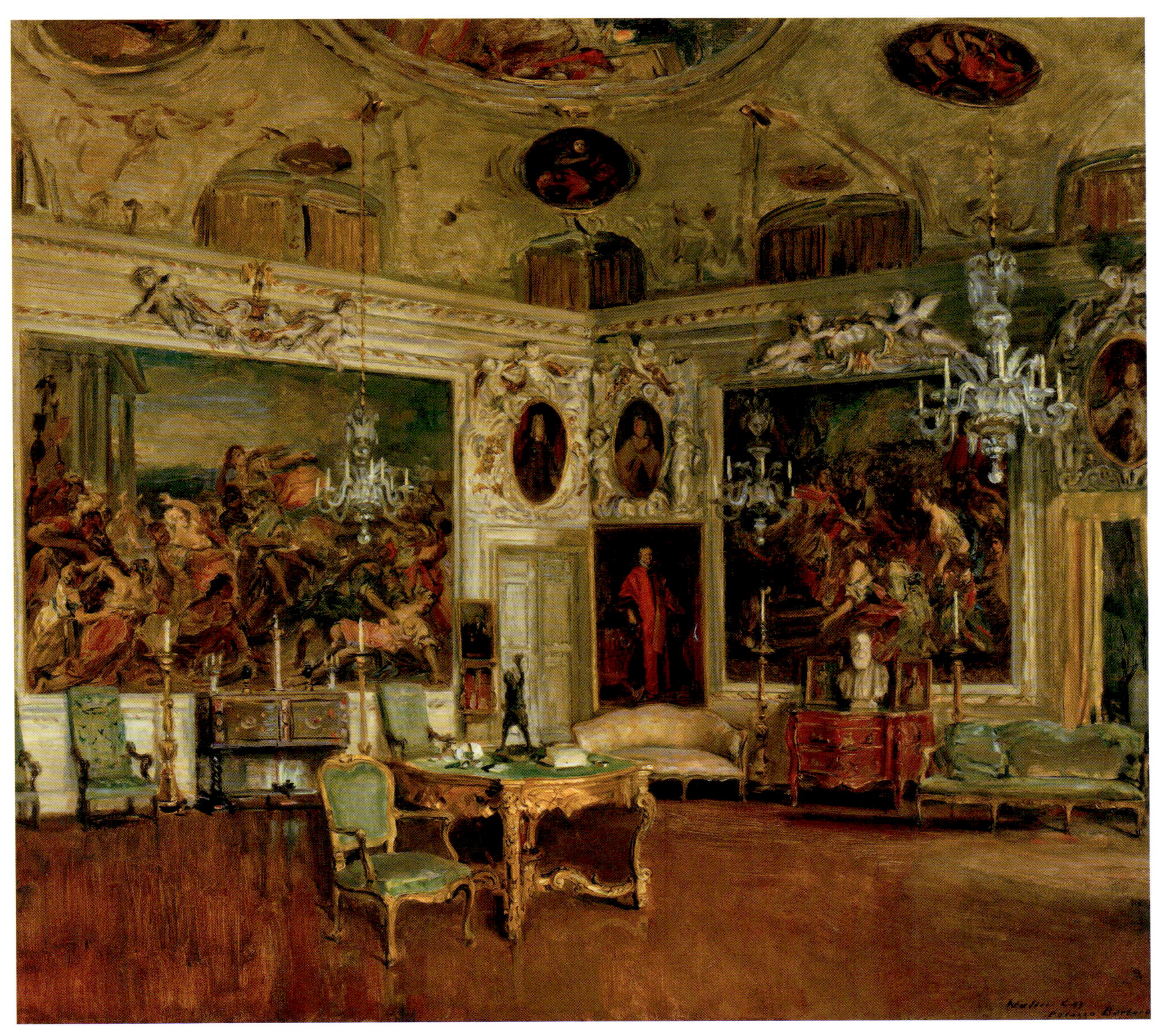

✡ CAT. 2-7
Walter Gay, *Interior of Palazzo Barbaro, Venice*, 1902, oil on canvas, 35 ⅝ × 39 ½ in., Museum of Fine Arts, Boston, The Hayden Collection—Charles Henry Hayden Fund

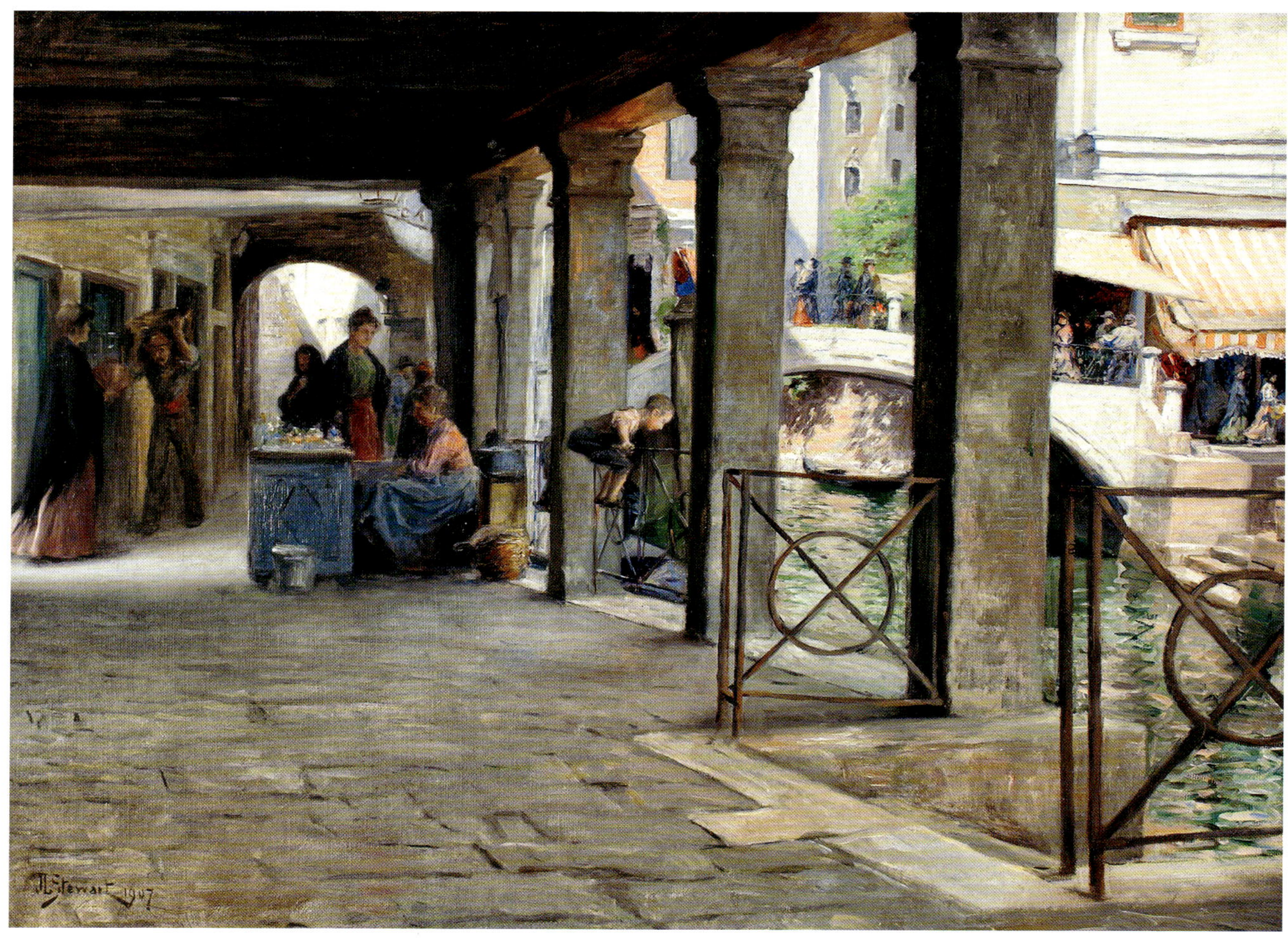

✲ CAT. 2-8

Julius LeBlanc Stewart, *Venetian Market Scene (Sotoportego del Magazen)*, 1907, oil on canvas, 21 ½ × 28 ¾ in., Michael and Jean Antonello Family Foundation

fragments, furniture, mirrors, and glass for the interlinked private-public project.[37] As part of this buying spree, in September 1897, Isabella purchased an eighteenth-century Venetian glass bottle decorated with floral enamel, while Jack secured two modern Venetian vases; the following month Isabella added two specimens of Renaissance Venetian glass from Gaetano Pepe of Naples.[38] Eventually, Isabella would install this glassware in the Titian Room of Fenway Court (Fig. 2-6), placing every object here, as she did in each room, to create visually harmonious, symbolically resonant, and personally meaningful associations. The room remains anchored by Titian's *Rape of Europa* (1562), which includes representations of the four elements (air, water, earth, and fire), painted by a Venetian who lived within sight of the great glass furnaces of Murano.[39] Placing the bulk of her Venetian glass in this room highlighted its elemental transformations. Visitors today experience these rooms-as-compositions just as she arranged them.

Significantly, Gardner did not set out to create period rooms, which would have provided a frozen glimpse of a particular moment in art and design history. Her Venetian objects in fact evoke something more subtle and social. Elizabeth Anne McCauley characterizes them as "intimate, ambiance-enhancing objects that fill out the mood of a room rather than form its centerpiece."[40] In this sense, we might also see these Venetian bottles, vases, and glasses as evocations of the lively social spirit of dinners, parties, and conversations at the Gardners' Palazzo Barbaro, Katharine and Arthur Bronson's Casa Alvisi, and other expatriate American salons. In his *Italian Hours* of 1909, Henry James vividly described the experience of "polyglot talk, artful *bibite*, artful cigarettes," and a graceful hostess (in this case, the Gardners' friend Katharine de Kay Bronson) who could cause guests and "delicate tobacco and little gilded glasses to circulate, without ever leaving her sofa cushions or intermitting her good-nature."[41] The set of eight tiny gilded Venetian glass tumblers that Isabella eventually installed in the Titian Room at Fenway Court reminds us of the material's role as conduit for personal as well as historical and artistic associations.[42] Her museum, while not a duplication of the Palazzo Barbaro, placed Venetian glass within the context of a seemingly magical place where the paintings of Titian and Sargent, the words of Ruskin and James, and the tastes of Renaissance princes and Gilded Age industrialists mingle in an aesthetic and social harmony orchestrated by Gardner herself.

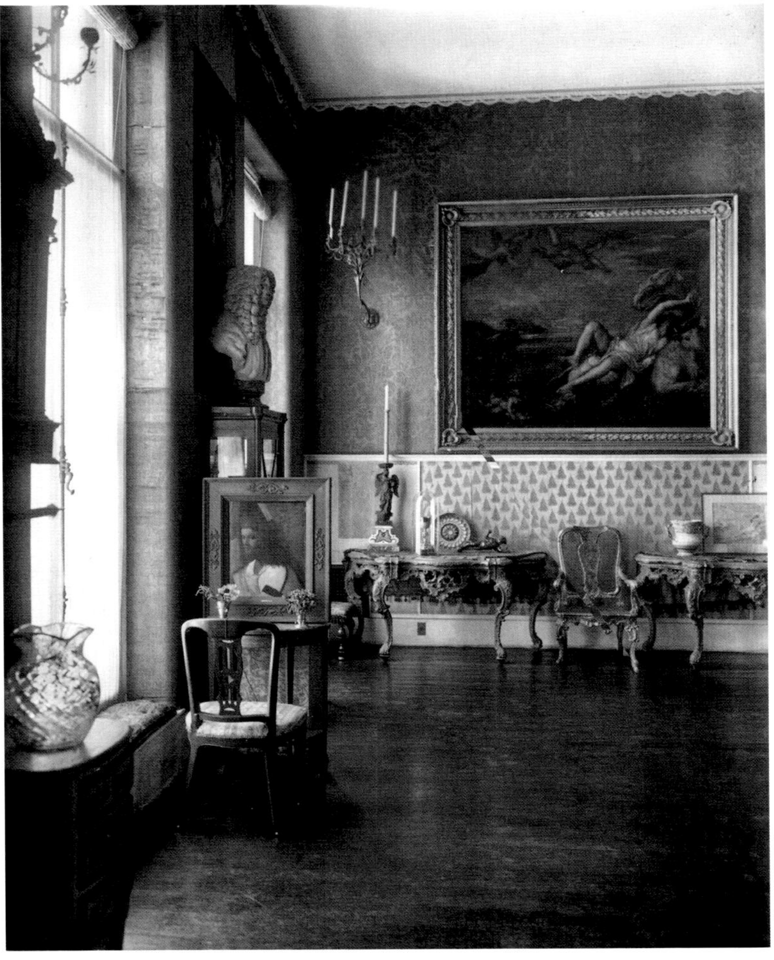

Fig. 2-6
Thomas E. Marr and Son, *Titian Room*, 1926, glass plate negative, Isabella Stewart Gardner Museum, Boston

COLLECTING THE WORLD: THE STANFORDS' UNIVERSITY MUSEUM

In contrast to Isabella Gardner's conception of a museum as a shrine to *son plaisir*, Leland and Jane Stanford founded their encyclopedic art institution within a university context and with dual educational and memorial aims.[43] Funded by Leland's career heading the transcontinental Central Pacific Railroad, their acquisitions were first made with home use in mind. Whether purchasing contemporary European sculpture at the Philadelphia Centennial Exhibition (1876) or commissioning custom furniture from premier firms, the Stanfords participated in a period trend among wealthy Americans of gathering a global array of goods and sorting them into thematic rooms within their homes.[44] This was yet another extension of Aesthetic movement ideas about intentional and personally expressive decorating and served as the governing principle within their grandest dwelling, their Pottier & Stymus–decorated mansion in San Francisco (1875–76). When President Benjamin Harrison toured the American West in 1891, the Stanfords held a dinner in his honor, at which the lavish table decorations included objects of Venetian glass.[45]

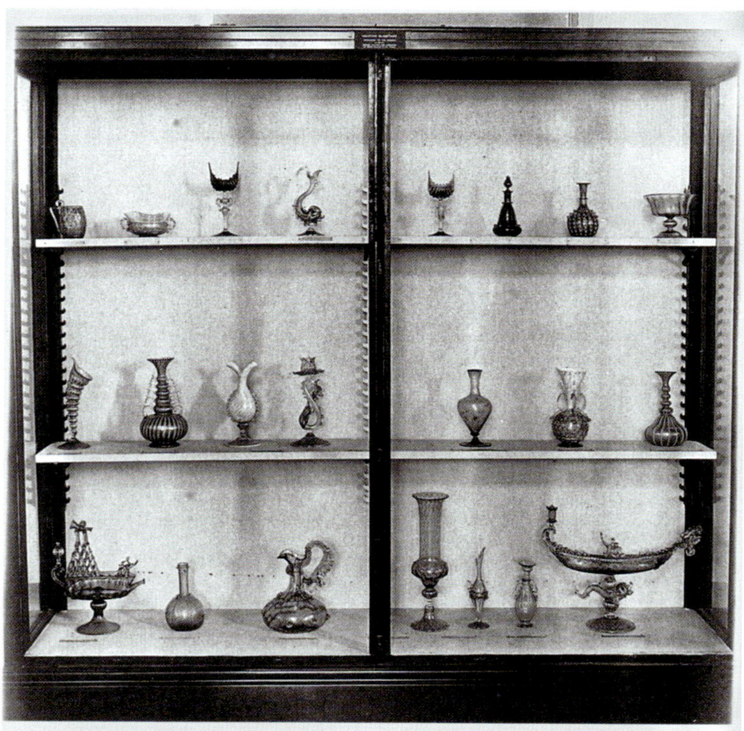

Fig. 2-7
Stanford Museum glass display case, Stanford University Libraries, Department of Special Collections and University Archives

What role would these objects have played within the Stanfords' domestic scheme? Drawing from Diana Strazdes's perceptive analysis of the mansion, we learn of its orientation toward public display and of the message communicated by its artistic holdings and décor, from its Roman floor mosaics to its painted allegorical lunettes: "What harnesses time, connects the continents, benefits agriculture and industry, and brings culture? It is the railroad, the business that created the mansion."[46] The suite of rooms embodied not only the railroad's near-boundless extension beyond California, but also the capital and connections necessary to bring the world's goods to the state, which Leland Stanford also led as governor (1862–63) and US senator (1885–93).[47] Demonstrating the successful transportation of delicate Venetian vessels wrought by breath and fire from glassworks to banquet table, then, involved more than mere conspicuous consumption.

Venetian glass acquired new shades of public and personal significance for the Stanfords in the 1880s. In 1883, they took their precocious son, Leland Jr., to visit the Salviati factory on Murano and secured a lampworked glass bead for him as a souvenir.[48] But after he was struck down by typhoid fever the following year in Florence, their Italian idylls became the stuff of haunting memories. In 1885, the grieving parents founded the namesake university in their son's honor and launched plans for a world-class museum within it. Carol Osborne usefully frames their efforts within the larger wave of museum building in the 1870s and 1880s. Donors to these fledgling institutions often sought to fill them out quickly yet with some guarantee of quality, and so they gravitated to collections that had already been assembled by others. Some of railroad magnate Henry Gurdon Marquand's early donations to the Metropolitan Museum had followed this pattern, including the ancient and modern glass collections formed by the Frenchman Jules Charvet, which Marquand donated in multiple installments in the early 1880s.

Such was the strategy Jane Stanford used in stocking the new university museum.[49] Yet the Muranese ware she secured for it in the early 1900s came by a different path. Honoring her family's love of Venice and the Stanfords' conception of themselves as central to the cultivation of education and culture in the United States, she commissioned the reconstituted Salviati firm to create mosaic decorations for the exterior of the museum and the interior of the campus chapel dedicated to the memory of her husband, who had died in 1893.[50] After visiting the work site, the firm's new partners offered a donation of a historical survey of Venetian glassmaking, comprising hundreds of objects for the museum's collection. Even a single case of these items (Fig. 2-7) indicates the variety of forms and techniques represented by this assemblage, a savvy gift designed to benefit the university, the Stanfords, and the firm itself.

Personal motivations ran deep in the establishment of this institution, which was at that time the largest privately owned museum building in the world.[51] But in contrast to the spaces of the Gardner museum, Venetian glass is displayed here in a manner that encouraged visitors to inspect its development systematically. The social and utilitarian values of these goblets and vases are displaced by their roles as historical specimens within the context of an ambitious, world- and history-spanning museum, funded by the profits from Leland Stanford's time- and space-spanning technologies.

GELLATLY, GLASS, AND THE AMERICAN RENAISSANCE

While Gardner and Stanford have been extensively studied, details of John Gellatly's life, homes, and purchases are rather difficult to pin down. This is surprising, given that his gift was once expected to constitute a separate Gellatly Gallery within the Smithsonian, comparable to the Freer Gallery of Art on the National Mall.[52] As collecting priorities and tastes shifted, many treasures among this eclectic ensemble vanished into the museum's vaults. However, their significance, and that of Gellatly himself, demands fresh consideration. Gellatly once stated that his goal as a collector was "to prove that the great American Renaissance 1860–1910 holds its own and in much surpasses the European Renaissance."[53] He was not alone in viewing the United States as the natural descendant and continuation of Western culture, of "the best which has been thought and said in the world," in Matthew Arnold's famous phrasing.[54] World's fairs hosted in Chicago, St. Louis, and San Francisco at the turn of the century explicitly promoted this idea by erecting enormous temporary buildings, monuments, and statuary in a mix of ancient Greek and Roman and Italian Renaissance styles. But Gellatly's conception of the American Renaissance was distinctive and idiosyncratic and resulted in the formation of a private-then-public collection that

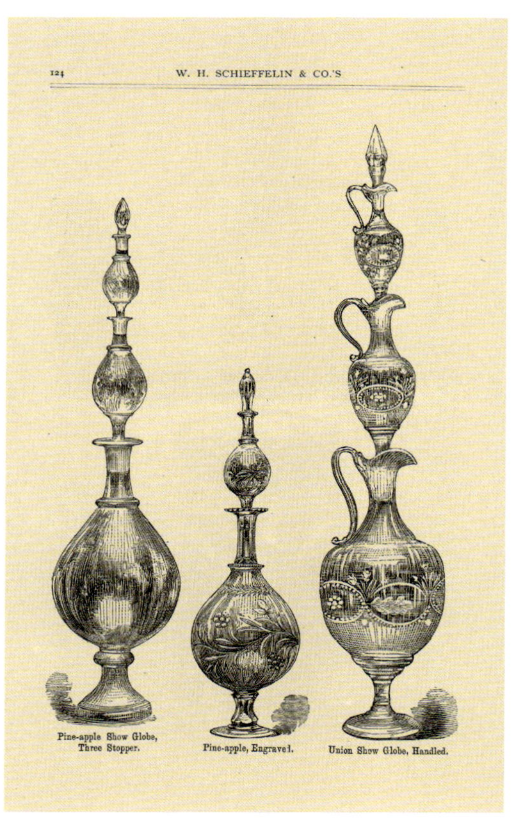
124 W. H. SCHIEFFELIN & CO.'S

Pine-apple Show Globe, Three Stopper.

Pine-apple, Engraved.

Union Show Globe, Handled.

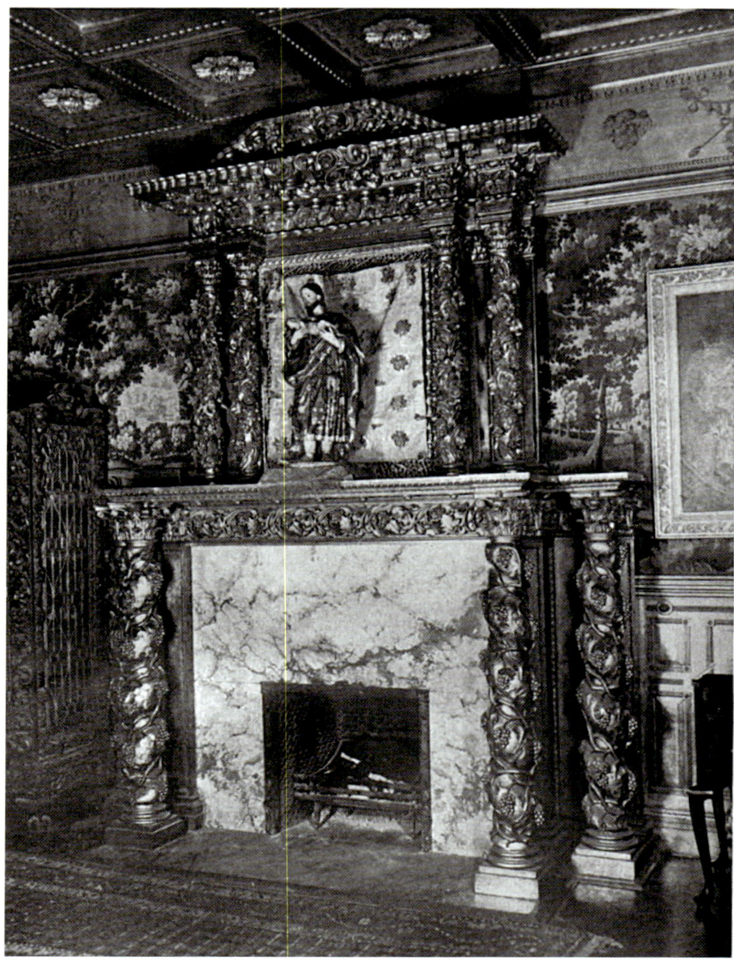

Fig. 2-8
***Show Globes*, from *General Prices Current of Foreign and Domestic Drugs, Medicines, Chemicals* (W. H. Schieffelin, 1876)**

Fig. 2-9
"Fireplace showing Spanish Statue of Saint Joseph and old Carved and Gilded Spanish Woodwork from Mexico. From the town house of John Gellatly, Esq.," from William Lauren Harris, "Spanish Furniture: What We Really Know about It," *Good Furniture*, January 1919

is split between American paintings, some on frequent display at the Smithsonian, and a diverse mix of objects, including an enormous collection of historical and modern glass, now rarely exhibited.

Orphaned at a young age, Gellatly was raised by an uncle and entered the family business as a teenager, working as a clerk and then a salesman for the international pharmaceutical wholesaling firm of W. H. Schieffelin & Co.[55] At the age of twenty-three, he co-organized a charitable exhibition at the Brooklyn Academy of Music, collaborating with leading figures in the New York art world in what may have been his debut as a connoisseur.[56] The artist Bruce Crane later recalled meeting Gellatly around 1882, when the budding collector was living in a room off Gramercy Park. "Now and then at that time, [Gellatly] occasionally purchased a small canvas[,] but they were never framed because he said he could not afford it."[57]

Despite these evidentiary gaps, there is one thing we can say with certainty about Gellatly's early professional life at Schieffelin. As the *American Journal of Pharmacy* put it in 1871, "Almost everything we handle is made of glass."[58] In pharmaceutical trade publications, specialists defined best practices for shipping, storing, displaying, and selling chemicals in non-reactive containers; debated the relative merits of earthenware versus glass bottles; and worked to determine which varieties of colored glass—black, blue, red, yellow, amber—were best suited to blocking out light rays while still revealing the contents within.[59] This practical need for glass knowledge brought drug manufacturers and merchants within the realm of art in surprising ways, as when the *Paint, Oil and Drug Review* summarized a lecture on decorative stained glass for its readers, or when the *American Chemical Journal* included "the beautiful products of the revived glass industry of Murano . . . under Salviati" in its "Brief Review of the Most Important Changes in the Industrial Applications of Chemistry within the Last Few Years."[60] Schieffelin's catalogues featured illustrations of engraved and cut-glass "show globes" (Fig. 2-8), decorative bottles, and other apothecary furnishings. They sold paints, enameled window glass, and patent medicines, packaged in a variety of colored glass bottles.[61] The trade also required skills in exhibition design; Schieffelin was applauded in the early 1880s for its *materia medica* displays in which drugs were arranged in uniform bottles among flowers and other decorations. Gellatly was responsible for creating some of these exhibits, and Schieffelin donations formed a foundational part of the Smithsonian Institution's *materia medica* collections as installed over the east entrance of the Arts and Industries Building.[62]

By 1884, Gellatly had left pharmaceuticals for insurance and real estate.[63] Fittingly, he took a leadership position in the New York Architectural League, where he organized winter loan exhibitions demonstrating recent achievements in decorative painting and design. The 1887 display, for example, included Tiffany glass and pictures by Americans Will Hicok Low, Edwin Howland Blashfield, Thomas Wilmer Dewing, John La Farge, and Frederick Stuart Church. Critics admired the committee's "judicious selecting, inviting, and borrowing" of these harmoniously arranged objects.[64] (Salviati's firm may not have participated until the early twentieth century, but examples of Venetian wood carving, ironwork, tooled leather, and mosaics were regular features of the League's displays.[65]) Loans from Gellatly's own collection in this period indicate a preference for these decorative painters, a taste that he shared with his wife, Edith Rogers, from their marriage in 1886 until her death in 1913. The resources she inherited from her father and uncle, and those Gellatly in turn inherited from her, substantially underwrote his collecting.[66]

Critic Annie Nathan Meyer cited Gellatly in 1905 as a praiseworthy example of a collector who was truly "living with" his artworks rather than amassing them for show or sale, but who and what did a guest to the townhouse at 34 West 57th Street see?[67] One visitor, art critic Mary L. Alexander, recalled being warmly welcomed to the home by Gellatly and described him as he would eventually be captured in a portrait by Irving Ramsey Wiles (CAT. 2-9): "a most picturesque gentleman with flowing white hair and dressed immaculately in white flannels." As he led her through his living spaces and picture gallery, she was "struck by the unusual beauty of the paintings and their settings."[68] Period photographs accompanying two profiles of Gellatly in the magazine *Good Furniture* offer a glimpse into these private precincts. In this photograph of his dining room (Fig. 2-9), we see a transatlantic array of salvaged fragments Gellatly combined to create a lived-in composition, including carved and gilded Spanish woodwork from Mexico, for which he tried out multiple American paintings as the centerpiece. (Ultimately, he settled on a Spanish polychrome wood figure of St. Joseph.) He assembled these rooms through both purchases and commissions:

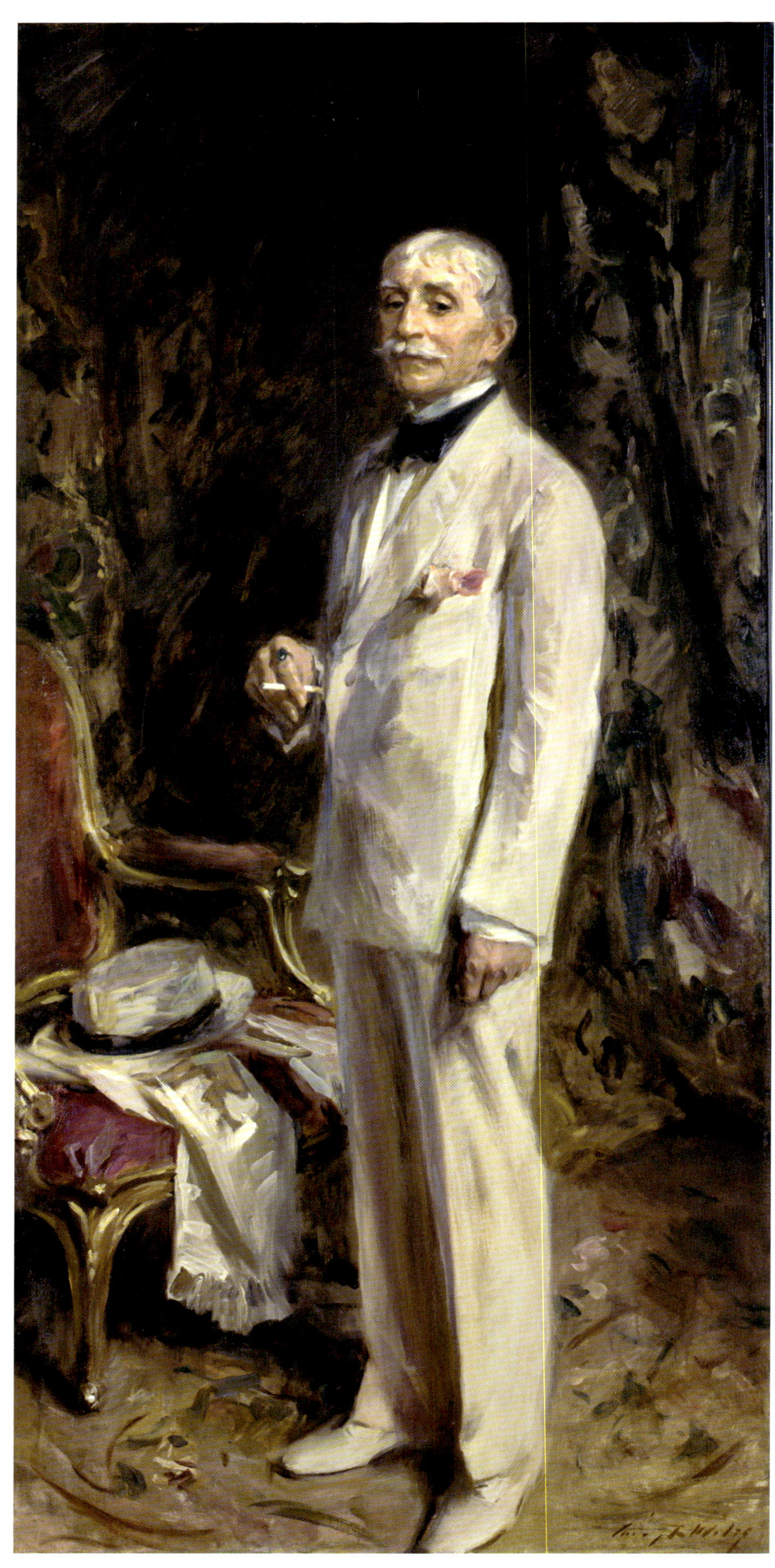

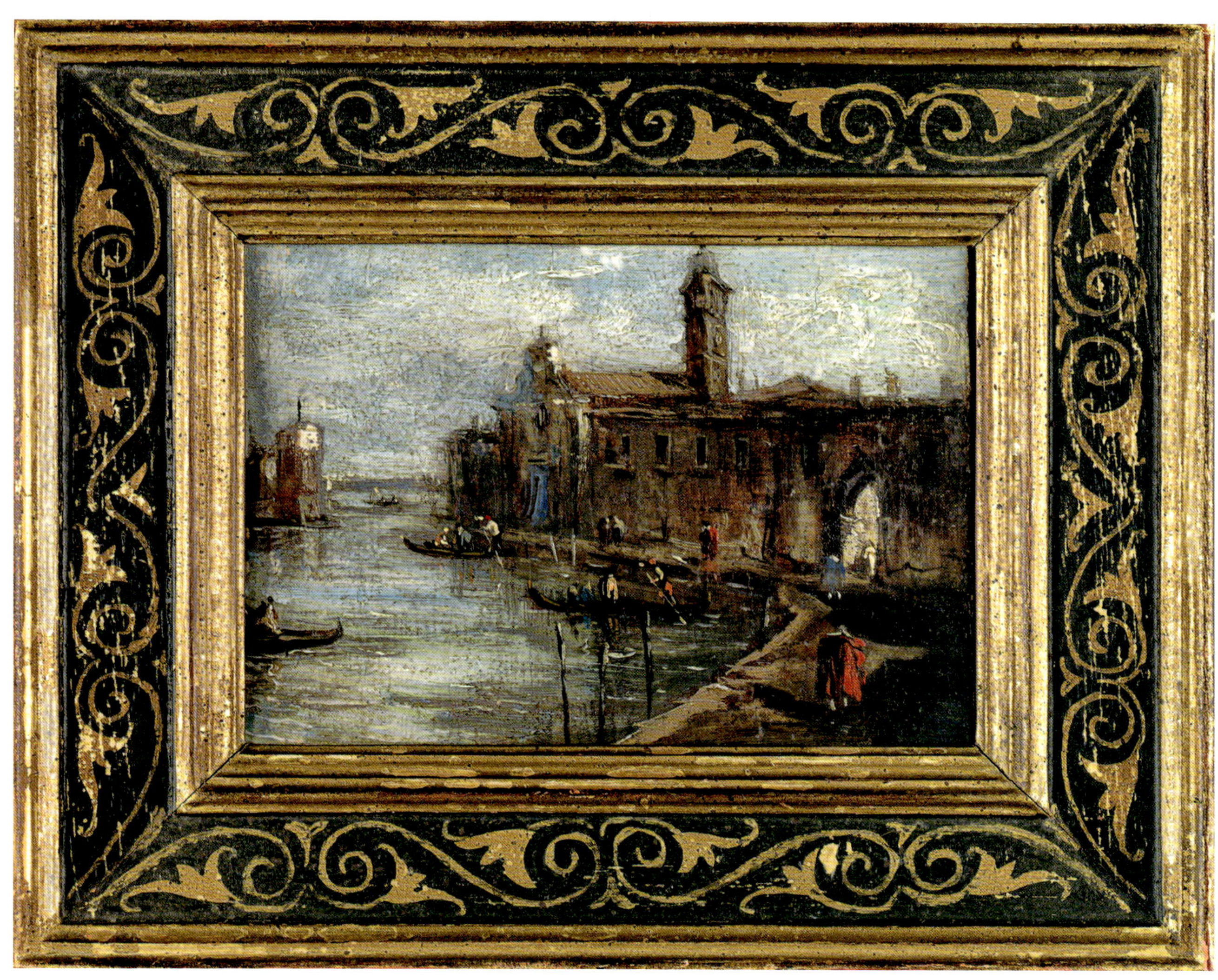

✡ CAT. 2-9
Irving Ramsay Wiles, *John Gellatly*, 1930–32, oil on canvas, 79 × 38 3/8 in., Smithsonian American Art Museum, Gift of the artist

✡ CAT. 2-10
Follower of Francesco Guardi, *Canal in Venice*, 18th century, oil on canvas in gilded and painted wood frame by M. Grieve Co. (ca. 1924), 5 7/8 × 7 1/8 in. overall, Smithsonian American Art Museum, Gift of John Gellatly

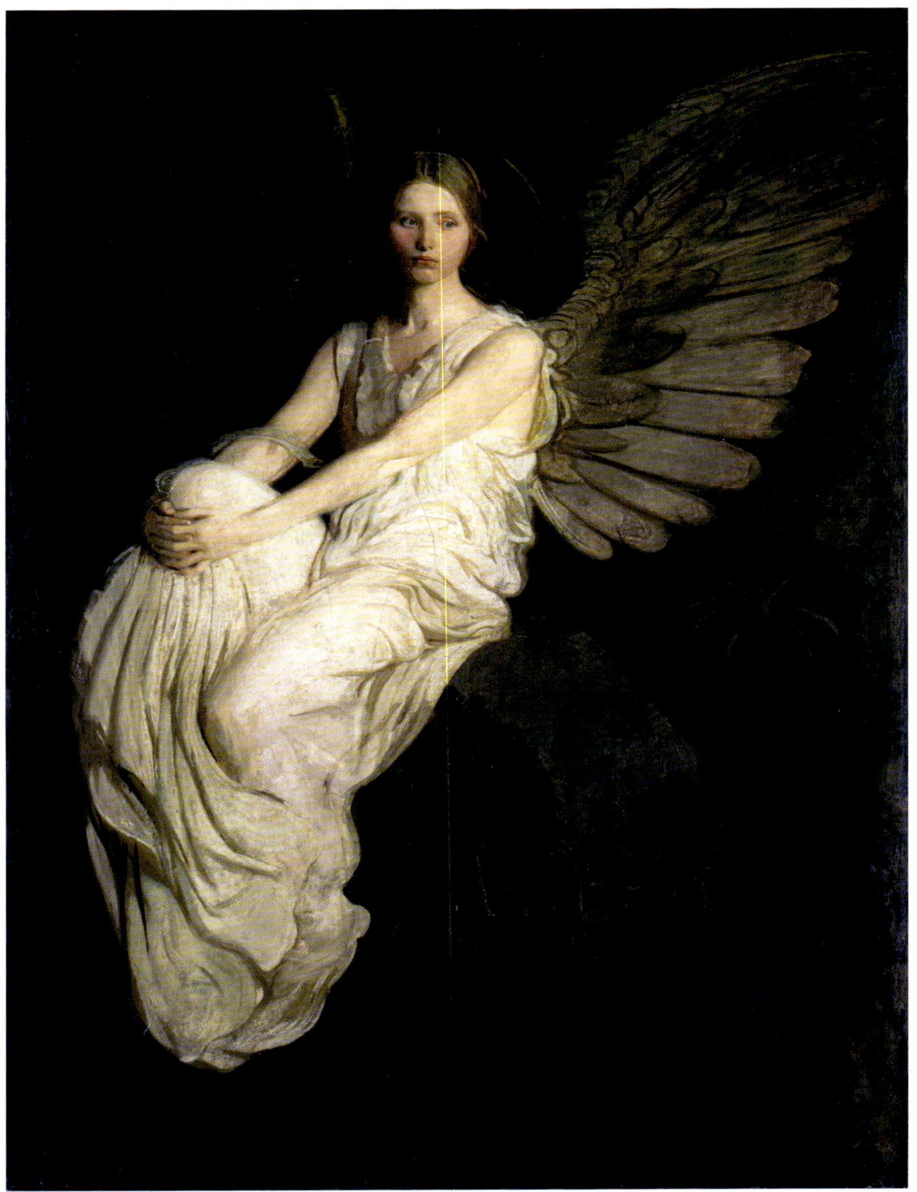

Fig. 2-10
Abbott Handerson Thayer, *Stevenson Memorial*, 1903, oil on canvas, 81 ⅝ × 60 ⅛ in., Smithsonian American Art Museum, Gift of John Gellatly, 1929.6.127

when he could not find the furniture or frames he desired, he ordered them custom-built to match his interior. For example, a small panel painting of a Venetian canal, church, and gondoliers (CAT. 2-10), perhaps optimistically purchased as the work of Francesco Guardi, features a 1920s frame by M. Grieve Co. in a Renaissance Venetian style, painted with stylized gilt foliage designs. The effect of the whole, *Good Furniture* tells us, was that of "a well-defined and satisfactory arrangement of sculpture, wood carvings and furniture together with a great variety of miscellaneous but beautiful works of art"—a harmonious arrangement that served as proof that Gellatly's taste was deeper and more authentic than money could buy. "A Morgan or an Altman, though they expended millions of their gold were yet unable to secure the harmony and delicate balance of every detail displayed in the decorations of Mr. Gellatly's house."[69]

Gellatly's picture collection was particularly rich in works by American Aesthetic movement painters such as Thomas Wilmer Dewing and Frederick Stuart

Church, as well as artists in whose canvases decorative effects often predominated, including Albert Pinkham Ryder and Childe Hassam. But no artist found greater representation here than the New York– and New Hampshire–based aesthetic painter Abbott Handerson Thayer, from whom Gellatly would eventually acquire at least twenty-three pictures. Thayer's friends and family spent countless hours posing for these meditations on modern angels and Madonnas. His *Stevenson Memorial* (Fig. 2-10), a mournful tribute to Scottish author Robert Louis Stevenson, took many years and many forms, beginning as a portrait of Thayer's three children and evolving into an allegorical depiction of his housekeeper Bessie Price as an angel perched on a rocky outcropping.[70] Like a Renaissance artist commanding a workshop of apprentices, Thayer worked with students and studio assistants to copy and rework details until he achieved what he felt was the most essential and ideal compositional balance. This picture served as the centerpiece of Gellatly's favorite collecting corner, according to Ralph Seymour and his diorama.

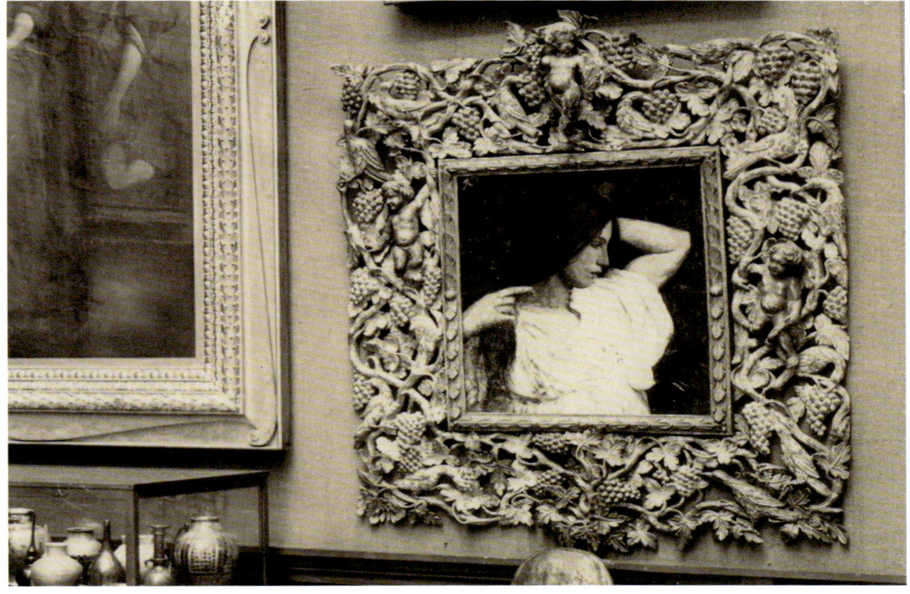

Fig. 2-11
Abbott Handerson Thayer, *Girl Arranging Her Hair*, 1918–19, oil on canvas in Sansovino-style, gilded wood frame (Venice, 16th c.), Smithsonian American Art Museum, Gift of John Gellatly

But Gellatly's investment in Thayer extended beyond commissions and purchases. He frequently sent the artist Renaissance-era (or -style) frames for the dual purpose of raising the sales value of Thayer's pictures and of dictating a specific direction for the artist's work.[71] According to Seymour, the original carved "Sansovino-style" frame for Thayer's *Girl Arranging Her Hair* (Fig. 2-11) came from Venice, and one suspects the patron's involvement behind several Thayer paintings still presented in old master–style frames today.[72] Gellatly also invited friends to see Thayer's pictures in progress on the walls of his home gallery, a sensory experience that enhanced their appeal. According to Mary Alexander, "The general atmosphere of the place was one to make the artistic pulse beat faster."[73] Gellatly, then, quite literally framed Thayer within the context of an "American Renaissance."[74]

Indeed, Gellatly's approach to art collecting was largely comparative, a perspective he adopted as a participant in New York's private social club exhibition circuit and as an acquaintance of Charles Lang Freer, noted collector of Asian and American art. The Union League Club set a new precedent for combining objects of various media and origins into tonally sympathetic displays. In 1890, for instance, the club placed foreign and American watercolors alongside cases of ancient and modern artistic glass, including Salviati wares.[75] Freer, too, encouraged Gellatly to think comparatively, writing a series of letters that invited him to compare the paintings of Thomas Wilmer Dewing with those of Whistler, who "unite[s] the art of the Occident with that of the Orient."[76] Artists like Thayer and Dewing who could (or had to) depend on these patrons for purchases often invited or thematized comparative looking in their pictures. Dewing's *Portrait of a Lady* (Fig. 2-12) is a representative artifact of this distinctive cultural, social, and economic environment in which the iridescent tones of antique glassware sometimes supplied part of the comparative equation.

In 1924, as Gellatly began to explore options for donating his collection, he expanded it so prodigiously with purchases of old master paintings, Italian woodcarvings, and Chinese glassware that his townhome could no longer contain them. He rented six rooms in New York's Heckscher Building and transferred most of his holdings to them, rearranging their contents into harmonious displays. The miniature glass vessels that crowd the desktop in Seymour's diorama suggest this profusion of objects as well as the clear delight Gellatly took in handling them and using them as the material from which to construct stimulating comparative installations. He sought a museum that would promise to retain his holdings, as he stipulated, "complete as collected by me without alteration or addition."[77] After negotiations with Columbia University fell apart, the gift was accepted by the Smithsonian in 1929. To prove what his favorite American artists had achieved, Gellatly explained regarding his donation, "I have surrounded the paintings of the American Renaissance by master-pieces of the world's art of four thousand years or more, the art of the world is really assembled."[78] After his death in 1931, these objects were finally transferred to Washington, DC, and temporarily installed in the United States National Museum (now the Smithsonian's Natural History building) (Fig. 2-13) until a permanent home for them could be constructed. This display included an homage to Gellatly's presentation at home and at the Heckscher, as recorded by Seymour's toy-sized diorama, with specimens of glass presented atop his massive carved wooden desk and surrounded by handsomely framed paintings from Thayer, Dewing, and other leading American artists of the Aesthetic movement.

The eccentricities within Gellatly's collection—as well as its abundance and scale—posthumously landed his name in newspapers around the country and renewed calls among press, politicians, and the public for a dedicated federal art museum building, as the donor had hoped.[79] The attention may also have added momentum to an alternate plan by millionaire collector and former Secretary of the Treasury Andrew W. Mellon to eclipse Gellatly's glory with his own gift to the nation. In 1935 Mellon confirmed widespread rumors with a formal promise to donate his $100 million collection as the basis for a new National Gallery of Art, which opened in 1941. Showcasing exclusively old masters and historical works, it bore no family name on its neoclassical façade and offered

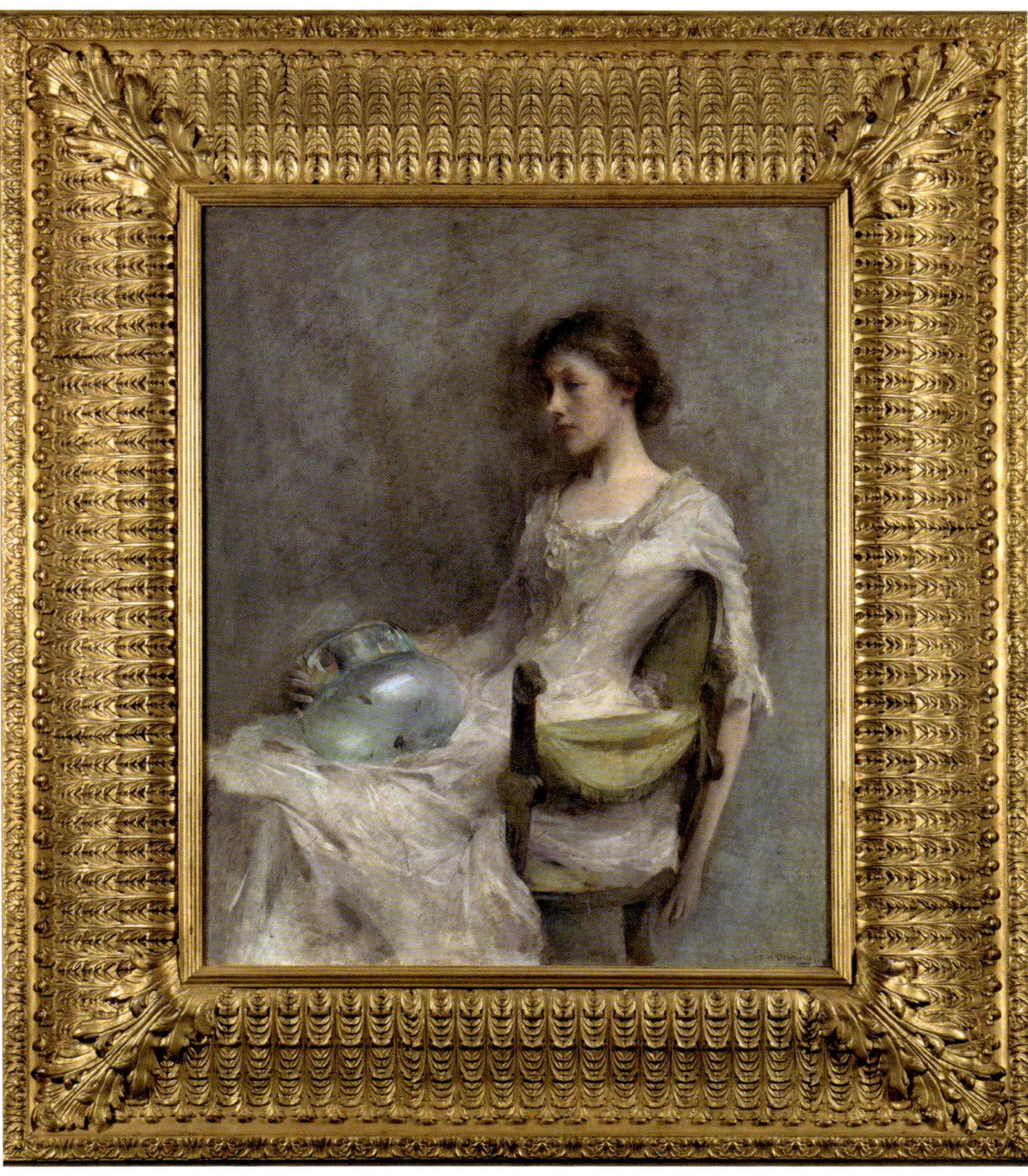

no insights into its benefactor's travels, tastes, or personality. In addition, Mellon's stipulations on standards of "quality" for its holdings and growth simultaneously excluded and critiqued the Aesthetic period mode of collecting, with its worldwide variety of bric-a-brac, juxtapositions across periods and cultures, and attention to living artists. Mellon's choice can be viewed as evidence that Thayer, Dewing, and Venetian glass were becoming less fashionable by the 1930s, although the Smithsonian still welcomed Gellatly's gift. However, as Carol Duncan posits, Mellon was also carefully crafting a legacy as a self-effacing "Good Citizen" museum-builder through deliberately impersonal art-buying to create a national collection governed by (and reinforcing) an established Western canon of prestige, authority, and market value.[80]

Meanwhile, across the National Mall at the Freer Gallery of Art, at the Isabella Stewart Gardner Museum in Boston, and in the Gellatly Collection at the Smithsonian American Art Museum, a donor's idiosyncratic presence

Fig. 2-12
Thomas Wilmer Dewing, *Portrait of a Lady*, 1898, oil on panel, 24 × 19 ¼ in., Private collection

Following pages:
Fig. 2-13
Gellatly Collection in the United States National Museum, June 1933, photograph, 8 in. × 10 in., Smithsonian Institution Archives

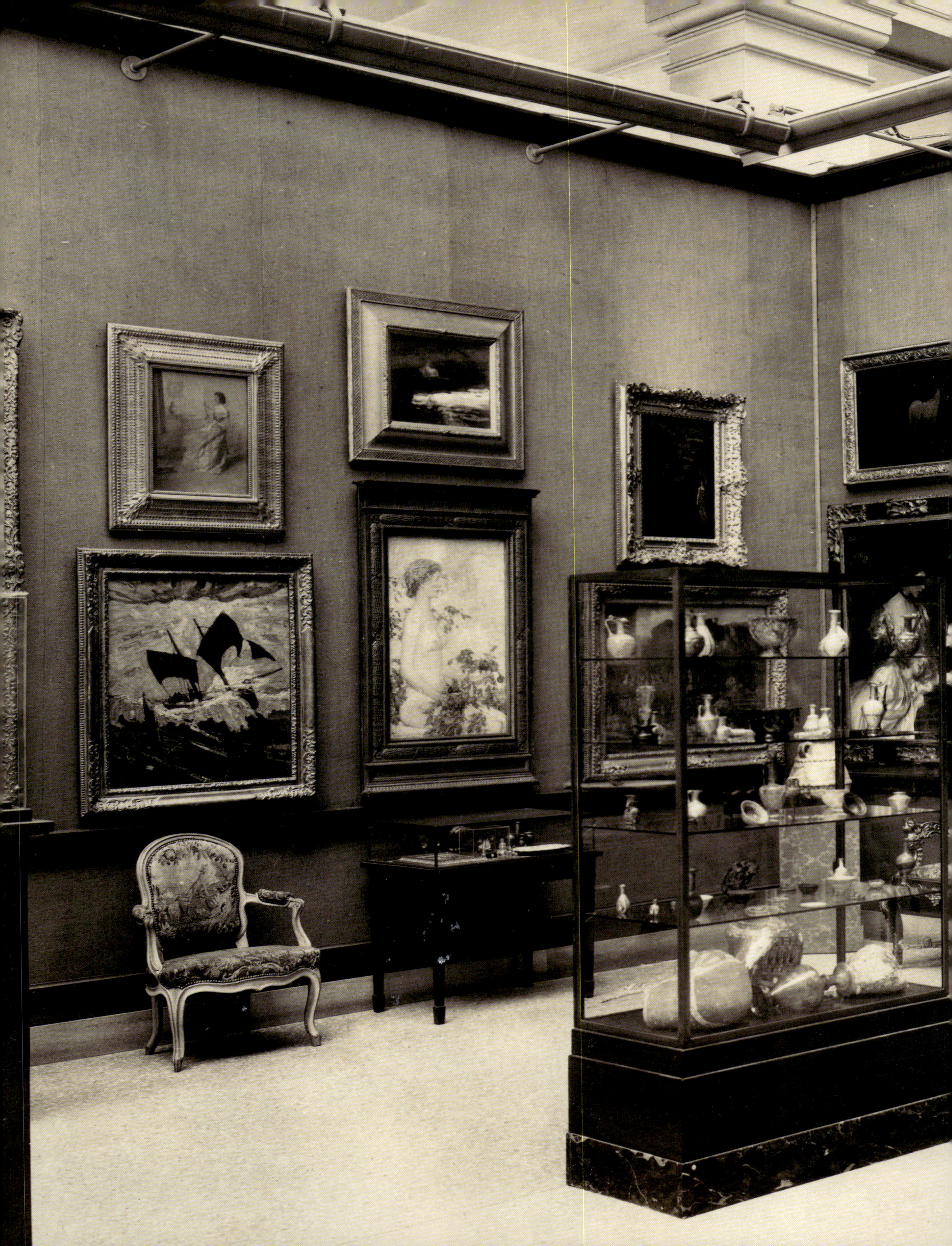

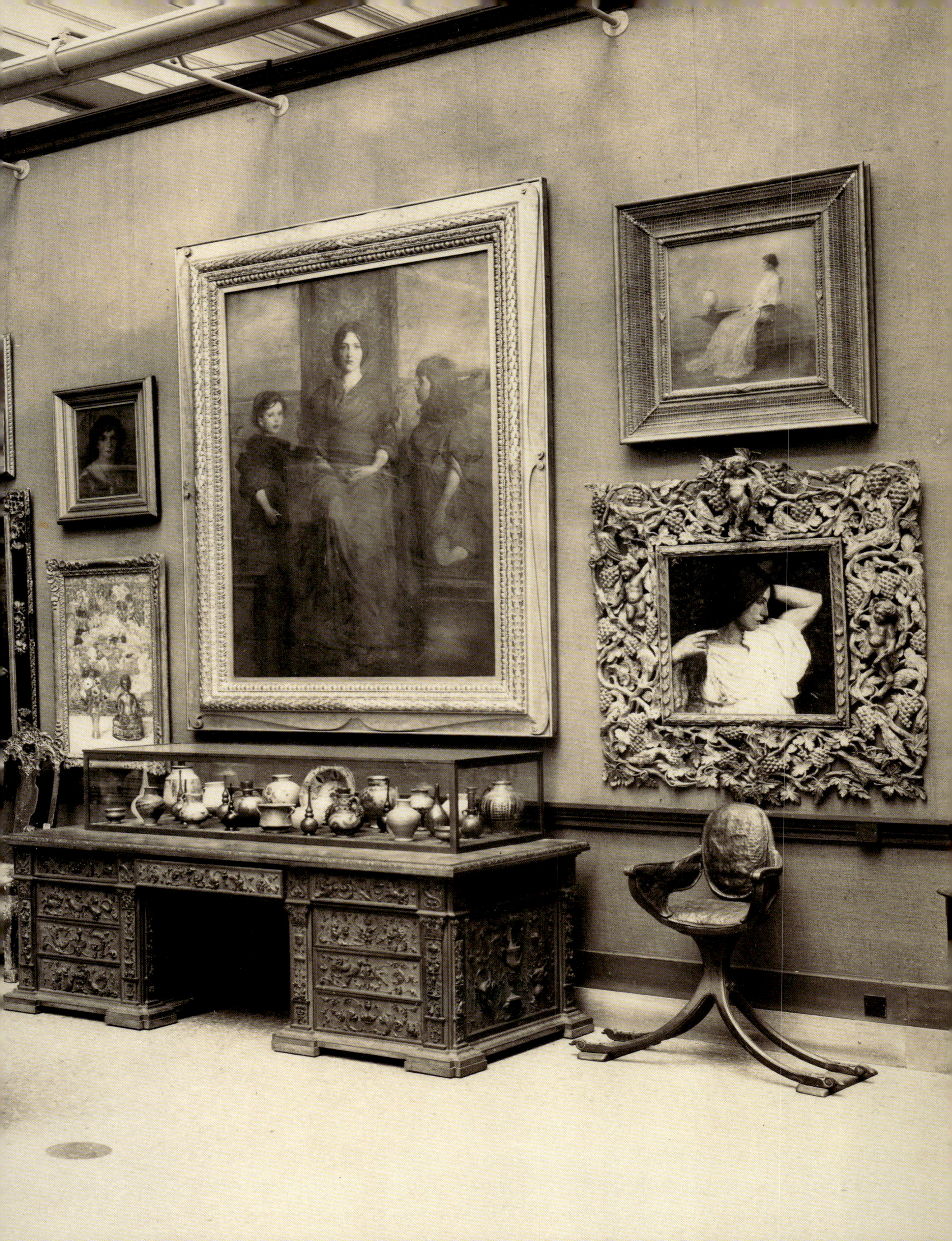

may still be felt, and restrictions against addition and subtraction remain in force. Are these museums time capsules of collectorship? Or is such a gift fated to become "a dead store-house representing merely the taste of the donor," as one of Gellatly's contemporaries worried?[81] At the Smithsonian American Art Museum, many objects remain in storage, including Ralph Seymour's woebegone *Diorama.* Is it the work of an "art joker," trying to fool viewers into thinking an assemblage of "gimcracks" is an actual masterpiece, as the Associated Press saw it in 1933?[82] Maybe—or perhaps not a joke at all, but an attempt to insert, in whatever form, an inescapable institutional reminder of what the collection's donor believed was its fundamental identity: a unified whole, selected and placed by Gellatly's own hands.

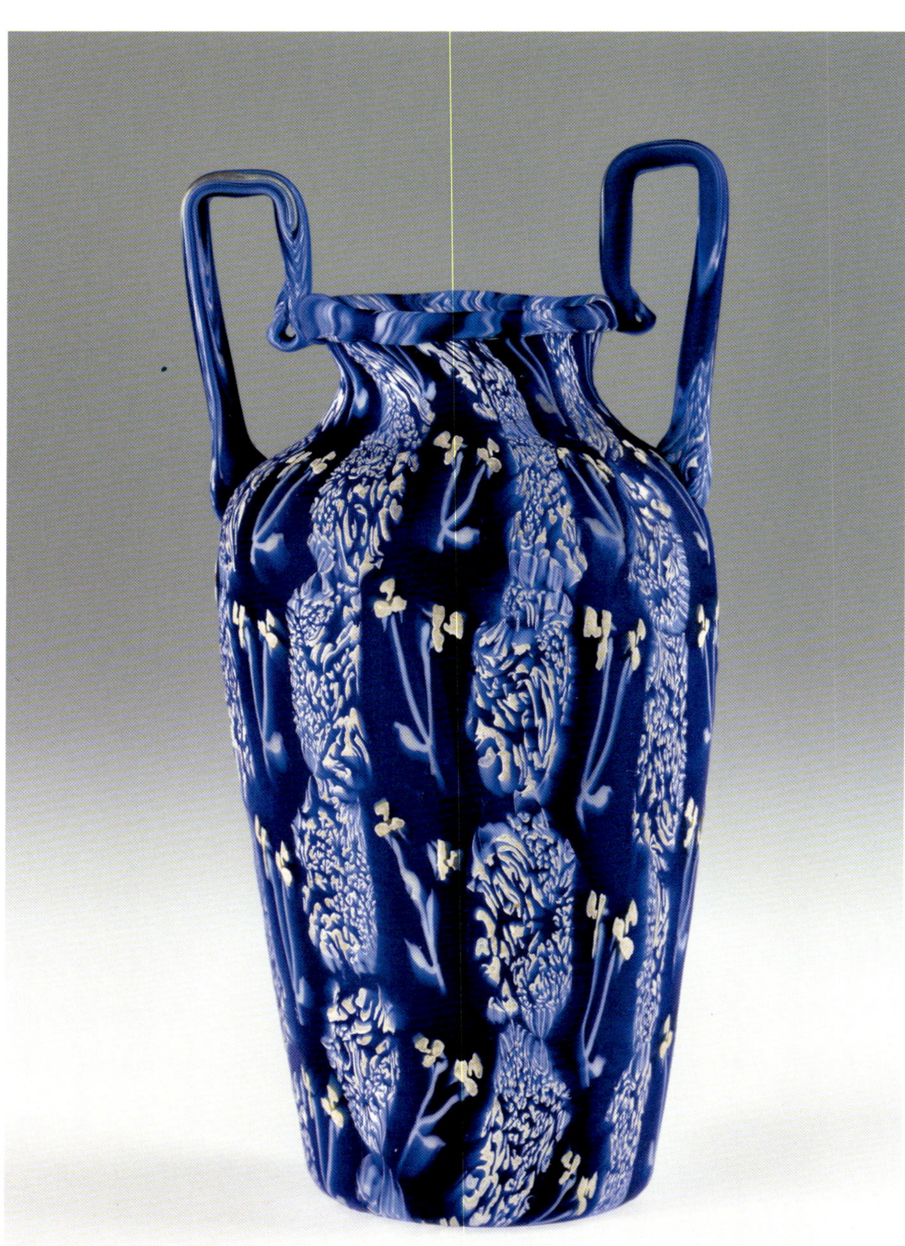

✡ CAT. 2-11
Fratelli Toso, Mosaic Glass Amphora, ca. 1880s–90s, blown and applied hot-worked, acid-etched glass, 6 5/16 × 3 1/8 in. diam., RISD Museum, Gift of Mrs. Frank Mauran and John O. Ames

✡ CAT. 2-12
Unidentified, Murano, Seventeenth Century–Style Goblet with Undulating Bowl, ca. 1870s–90s, blown and applied hot-worked glass, 7 5/8 × 4 3/8 in. diam., RISD Museum, Gift of Mrs. Frank Mauran and John O. Ames

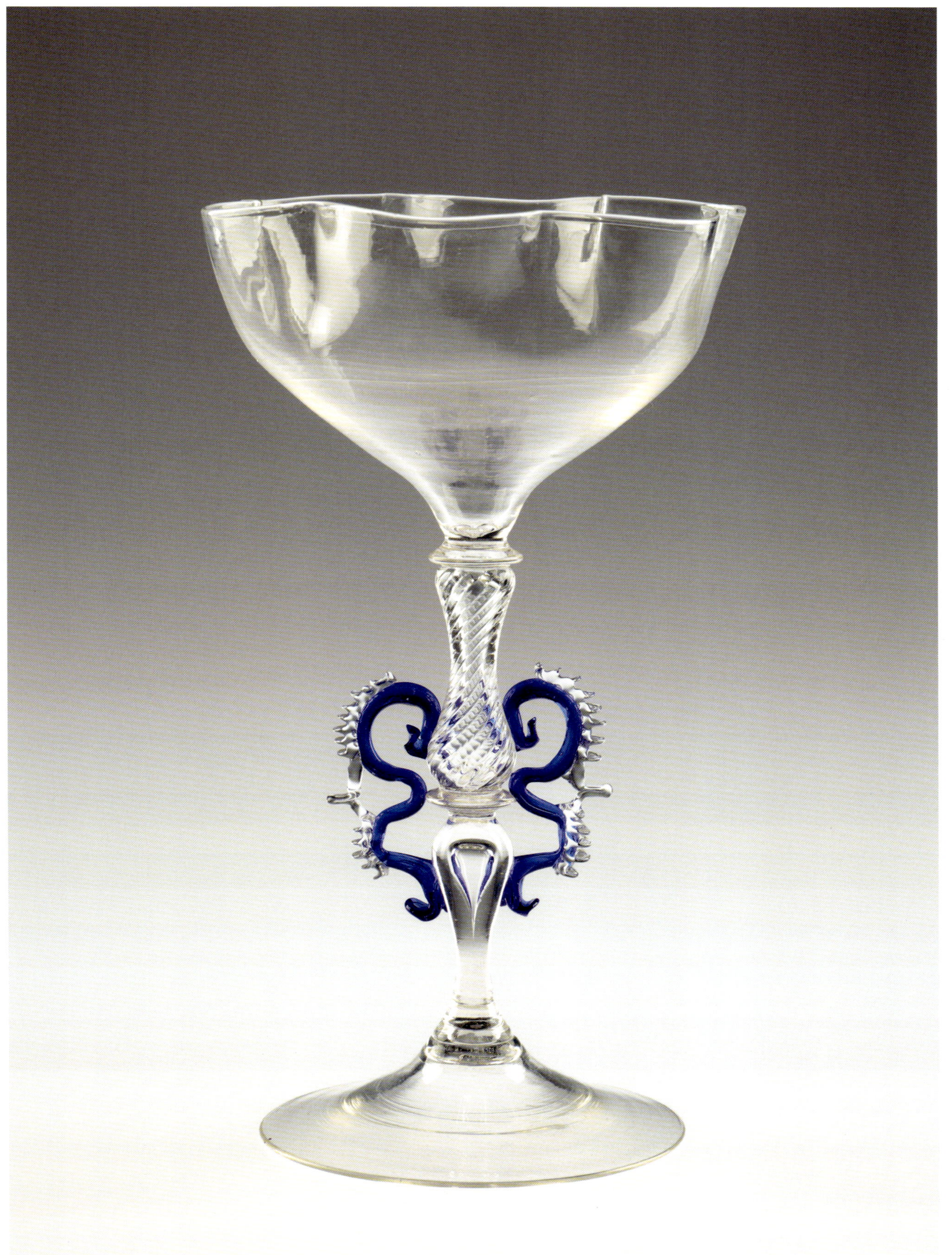

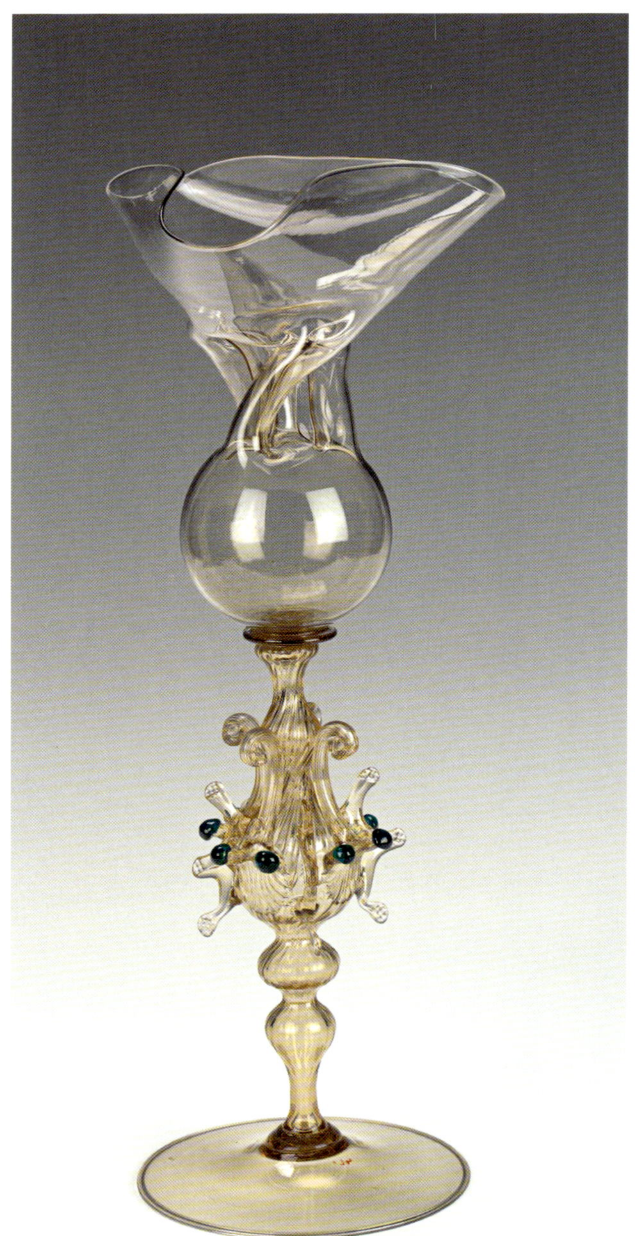

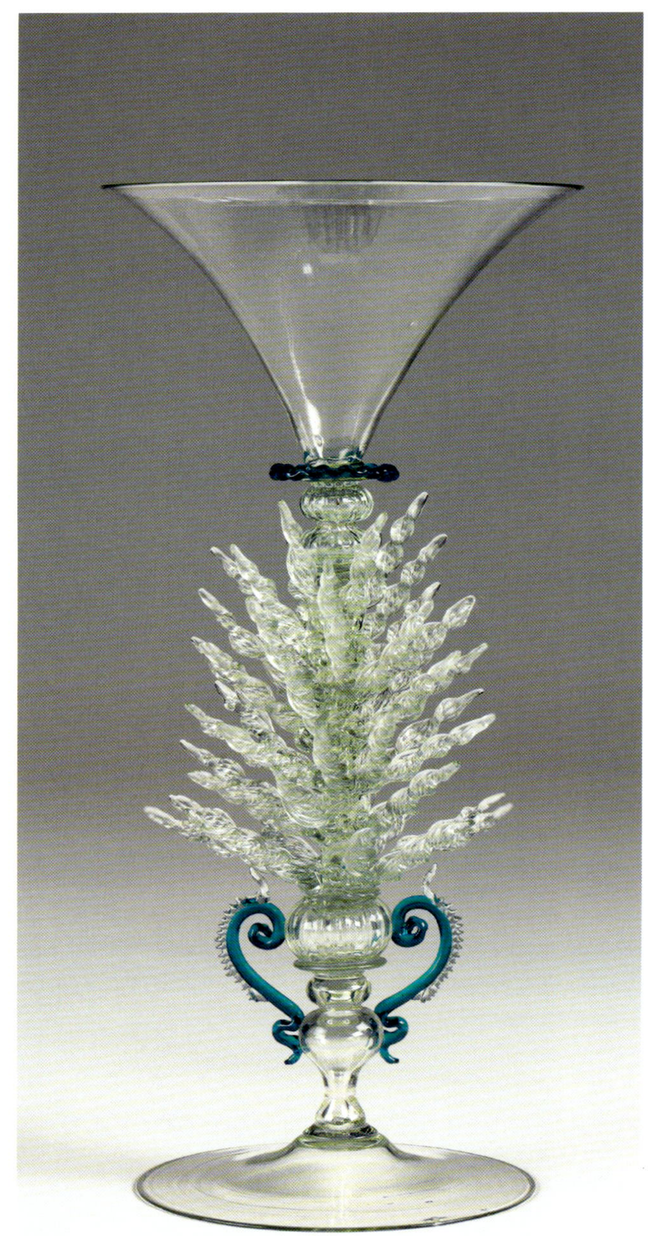

✲ CAT. 2-13

Compagnia di Venezia e Murano (CVM), Kuttrolf-Style Vase, ca. 1880s–90s, blown and applied hot-worked glass, 13 3/8 × 5 1/4 in. diam., Smithsonian American Art Museum, Gift of John Gellatly

✲ CAT. 2-14

Salviati Dott. Antonio, Goblet with Thorny Stem, ca. 1870s–90s, blown and applied hot-worked glass, 11 × 5 in. diam., Museum of the City of New York, Gift of the Estate of Miss Agnes Miles Carpenter, 1955

NOTES

1 "Art Joker Fools Critics," *Washington Post*, July 9, 1933, 2. It is difficult to distinguish Ralph Seymour's insights from the reporter's assumptions, but Seymour was quoted directly in other newspaper articles at the time of the collection's Smithsonian debut; see "Recluse's $4,000,000 Art Group on Display," *St. Louis Post-Dispatch*, July 6, 1933, 19.

2 John Ruskin, *The Stones of Venice*, vol. 1, *The Foundations* (London: Smith, Elder, 1851), vi.

3 Ruskin, *The Stones of Venice*, vol. 2, *The Sea-stories* (London: Smith, Elder, 1853), 154.

4 Ibid., 168. This passage was excerpted in "Venetian Glass," *Crayon* 2, no. 8 (August 22, 1855): 114; this magazine was one of many avenues for the circulation of Ruskin's ideas in the United States.

5 "The Round of the Studios," *Pall Mall Gazette* (London), April 6, 1865, 10.

6 Oscar Wilde, "The English Renaissance," in *Miscellanies* (London: Methuen, 1908), 270.

7 On Palmer's painting and the Nortons' home, see Karen Zukoswki, *Creating the Artful Home: The Aesthetic Movement* (Layton, UT: Gibbs Smith, 2006), 161.

8 Major Herbert Byng Hall, "Bric-a-Brac Hunting," *Belgravia* (UK) 2 (April 1867): 206; the columns were published as *The Adventures of a Bric-a-Brac Hunter* (London: Tinsley Brothers, 1868). See also "Modern Venetian Glass and Enamel Mosaics," *Cornhill Magazine* (UK) 19, no. 112 (April 1869): 459–68; also reprinted in Boston's *Every Saturday* 7, no. 175 (May 8, 1896): 601.

9 Salviati became known to America through mosaics first. For details about Salviati's efforts to promote his company in the United States, see Sheldon Barr's essay in this catalogue, pages 106–7.

10 For Eastlake, the Venetian glass revival marked "an important era in the history of industrial art. In no other direction that can be named—neither in the design of cabinet work, ceramic productions, or jewellry, have we moderns realised so nearly the tastes and excellences of a by-gone age." Eastlake, *Hints on Household Taste* (London: Longmans, Green, 1868), 230.

11 Harriet Prescott Spofford, *Art Decoration Applied to Furniture* (New York: Harper and Brothers, 1877), 232. On Spofford's role in creating an "aestheticized consumerism" in the United States, see Jonathan Freedman, *Professions of Taste: Henry James, British Aestheticism, and Commodity Culture* (Stanford, CA: Stanford University Press, 1990), 109.

12 "Current Literature: Hints on Household Taste," *Literary World* (Boston) 3, no. 7 (December 1, 1872): 97.

13 These were brought to Cincinnati by the efforts of Moncure Conway, an important conduit for Aesthetic movement ideas in America. See "Art Exhibition of 1873," *Church's Musical Visitor* 2, no. 11 (August 1873): 6; and Conway, "Correspondence. London Letter," *Cincinnati Commercial*, August 11, 1873, 1.

14 *Exhibition of Paintings, Engravings, Drawings, Aquarelles, and Works of Household Art in the Cincinnati Industrial Exposition* (Cincinnati, OH: Cincinnati Industrial Exposition, 1873), 48.

15 "The Cincinnati Exposition for 1873," *Church's Musical Visitor* 2, no. 12 (September 1873): 3.

16 "The Arts," *Appletons' Journal* 13, no. 320 (May 8, 1875): 600.

17 [Clarence Cook?], "Fine Arts: American Pictures at Cottier's," *New York Tribune*, May 17, 1875, 2; see also "Excellent Specimens of American Work," *Crockery Journal* 1 (May 13, 1875): 4.

18 Cook, "Beds and Tables, Stools and Candlesticks 4: Mantel-Pieces, Corner Cupboards, Hanging Shelves, Etc.," *Scribner's Monthly*, April 1876, 818–19.

19 "The Arts," *Appletons' Journal* 13, no. 316 (April 10, 1875): 473.

20 "Murano Table-Glass," *Art Journal* 104 (August 1870): 252; see also "Venetian Glass," *Observer* (London), August 2, 1868, 5.

21 Carol M. Osborne has discovered that Tiffany was stocking Salviati wares in his New York store by 1872, when Clover Adams commented on them in a letter; see Osborne, *Venetian Glass of the 1890s: Salviati at Stanford University* (London: Philip Wilson, 2002), 19.

22 "New York Fashions," *Harper's Bazaar*, August 3, 1872, 507. Tiffany & Co. is among the shops listed as providing information for this article.

23 James Jackson Jarves, "Ancient and Modern Venetian Glass of Murano," *Harper's New Monthly Magazine* 64, no. 380 (January 1882): 187.

24 James McNeill Whistler, *Mr. Whistler's Ten O'Clock*, originally delivered in 1885 (London: Chatto & Windus, 1888), 11–13.

25 See, for example, "Necessity versus Art," *Catholic World* 17, no. 100 (July 1873): 561.

26 Alexander Nesbitt, *Catalogue of the Collection of Glass Formed by Felix Slade, Esq. F.S.A.* (London: Wertheimer, Lea, 1871); and Nesbitt, *A Descriptive Catalogue of the Glass Vessels in the South Kensington Museum* (London: Chapman & Hall, 1878). See also Donald B. Harden, "Study and Research on Ancient Glass: Past and Future," *Journal of Glass Studies* 26 (1984): 9.

27 L.W.C., "Mrs. 'Jack' Gardner's Palace," *Daily Mail* (London), June 3, 1909, 6.

28 Elizabeth Anne McCauley, "A Sentimental Traveler: Isabella Stewart Gardner in Venice," in *Gondola Days: Isabella Stewart Gardner and the Palazzo Barbaro Circle*, ed. McCauley et al. (Boston: Isabella Stewart Gardner Museum, 2004), 33. For more on Isabella Stewart Gardner and her Boston museum, see Kathleen D. McCarthy, "Isabella Stewart Gardner and Fenway Court," in *Women's Culture: American Philanthropy and Art, 1830–1930* (Chicago: University of Chicago Press, 1991), 149–76; Wanda M. Corn, "Art Matronage in Post-Victorian America," 9–21, and Anne Higonnet, "Private Museums, Public Leadership: Isabella Stewart Gardner and the Art of Cultural Authority," 79–92, both in *Cultural Leadership in America: Art Matronage* *and Patronage* (Boston: Isabella Stewart Gardner Museum, 1997); and Higonnet, *A Museum of One's Own: Private Collecting, Public Gift* (Pittsburgh, PA: Periscope Publishing, 2009).

29 McCauley, "A Sentimental Traveler," 49n138; Alan Chong, "Henry James, Mrs. Gardner and Art," in *Henry James: Letters to Isabella Stewart Gardner*, ed. Rosella Mamoli Zorzi (London: Pushkin Press, 2009), 32.

30 On British aestheticism as an attempt to determine "what art might be, if it is not for the sake of anything else," see Elizabeth Prettejohn, *Art for Art's Sake: Aestheticism in Victorian Painting* (New Haven, CT: Yale University Press, 2007), 2.

31 On Coleman's use of Salviati glass in this and other compositions, see Adrienne Baxter Bell, "Charles Caryl Coleman on Capri," *Magazine Antiques* 165, no. 5 (November 2005): 138–47.

32 McCauley, "A Sentimental Traveler," 33.

33 Oscar Wilde, "The English Renaissance," a lecture delivered at Chickering Hall, New York, on January 9, as quoted in "The New Life," *Philadelphia Inquirer*, January 11, 1882, 7; and "Oscar Wilde's Lecture," *New York World*, January 16, 1882, 3. A slightly different version of this statement expresses a similar sentiment in Wilde's later publication of the lecture in *Miscellanies* (London: Methuen, 1908), 261. In Philadelphia, "a ewer of ultramarine Venetian glass of antique shape, containing water" was reportedly placed upon an ebonized table on the stage beside him; see "Wilde's Lecture," from *Philadelphia Press*, reprinted in *Atlanta Constitution*, January 21, 1882, 3.

34 McCauley, "A Sentimental Traveler," 16–17.

35 Louise Hall Tharp, *Mrs. Jack: A Biography of Isabella Stewart Gardner* (Boston: Little, Brown, 1965), 164.

36 Joseph Lindon Smith, writing from the Palazzo Barbaro in 1894, reported, "The Antiquity men were active, and Mrs. Jack had things sent in constantly for her approval and purchase. . . . Clerle sold her some fine things." Quoted in Chong, "Artistic Life in Venice," 102–3. The following year, John Gardner's diary recorded: "Went to Simonetti's, the antiquario. Selected chairs and stuffs which Mrs. G. purchased afterwards"; and "to Villegas and bought for Mrs. G. the things she had selected;" quoted in Tharp, *Mrs. Jack*, 185.

37 McCauley, "A Sentimental Traveler," 33; McCarthy, "Isabella Stewart Gardner and Fenway Court," 167.

38 Isabella Stewart Gardner Museum accession numbers C26n71, C26n14, C26n4, C26n52, and C26n28. See the museum's website, accessed August 19, 2020, https://www.gardnermuseum.org/experience/collection/12330.

39 Paul Hills, "Titian's Fire: Pyrotechnics and Representations in Sixteenth-Century Venice," *Oxford Art Journal* 30, no. 2 (2007): 185, 199.

40 McCauley, "A Sentimental Traveler," 34.

41 Henry James, *Italian Hours*, (Boston: Houghton, Mifflin, 1909), 111.

42 Isabella Stewart Gardner Museum accession number C26n63.1, set of eight gilded glass tumblers, late eighteenth century, Venice.

43 On the Stanfords' philanthropy, see Osborne, *Venetian Glass of the 1890s: Salviati at Stanford University*; Osborne, *Museum Builders in the West: The Stanfords as Collectors and Patrons of Art, 1870–1906* (Stanford, CA: Stanford University Museum of Art, 1986); Dianne Sachko Macleod, "Art and Activism," in *Enchanted Lives, Enchanted Objects: American Women Collectors and the Making of Culture, 1800–1940* (Berkeley: University of California Press, 2008), 93–133; and John Ott, "Missionary Work: Jane Stanford, Educational Philanthropy, and the Mission Revival," in *Manufacturing the Modern Patron in Victorian California: Cultural Philanthropy, Cultural Capital, and Social Authority* (Surrey, UK: Ashgate, 2014), 217–50.

44 Osborne, *Venetian Glass of the 1890s*, 25. On glass exhibits at the Philadelphia Centennial, including those inspired by Salviati's recent work, see Alice Cooney Frelinghuysen, "Aesthetic Forms in Ceramics and Glass," in *In Pursuit of Beauty: Americans and the Aesthetic Movement*, ed. Doreen Bolger Burke et al. (New York: Metropolitan Museum of Art, 1986), 237. Thematically organized interiors included homes designed for Henry Gurdon Marquand and the Vanderbilts; see, among others, Wayne Craven, *Gilded Mansions: Grand Architecture and High Society* (New York: W. W. Norton, 2009).

45 Mrs. Robert P. Porter, "Grace Bates' Struggle," *Washington Post*, September 20, 1891, 13.

46 Diana Strazdes, "The Millionaire's Palace: Leland Stanford's Commission for Pottier & Stymus in San Francisco," *Winterthur Portfolio* 36, no. 4 (Winter 2001): 237.

47 Ibid., 23–40.

48 Osborne, *Venetian Glass of the 1890s*, 21–22.

49 Osborne, *Museum Builders in the West*, 17.

50 For details about Jane Stanford's mosaic commissions for the Stanford Memorial Chapel, see Sheldon Barr's essay in this catalogue, pages 122–24.

51 Osborne, *Museum Builders in the West*, 15.

52 "House Votes to Exhibit Art in Smithsonian," *New York Herald Tribune*, May 30, 1929, 13.

53 Gellatly to Gari Melchers, Chairman, National Gallery of Arts Commission, 27 March 1929, Smithsonian American Art Museum registrar's files on John Gellatly (hereafter SAAM Gellatly files).

54 Matthew Arnold, *Culture and Anarchy: An Essay in Political and Social Criticism*, 2nd ed. (New York: Macmillan, 1875), x. For more on the American Renaissance, see especially David Carew Huntington, *The Quest for Unity: American Art between World's Fairs, 1876–1893* (Detroit, MI: Detroit Institute of Arts, 1983).

55 H. S. Livingston to Ruel P. Tolman, February 16, 1935, SAAM Gellatly files, Gellatly, John—life of; Susan Hobbs, "John Gellatly," *American National Biography Online* (2000).

56 "Baptist Home: Fair and Art Exhibition at the Academy," *Brooklyn Union*, October 25, 1876, 3; "Charity at the Academy," *Brooklyn Daily Eagle*, October 26, 1876, 2.

57 Bruce Crane to Ruel P. Tolman, 26 December 1936, SAAM Gellatly files, Correspondence A–Z, Folder C.

58 Robert Simpson, "On the Preservation of Pharmaceutical Apparatus from Breakage by Change of Temperature," *American Journal of Pharmacy* (May 1871): 196.

59 "Chemical Stone-Ware Manufacture," from *Chemist and Druggist*, reprinted in *American Journal of Pharmacy* (1861): 535–39; Hans M. Wilder, "Non-Actinic Glassware," *American Journal of Pharmacy* (February 1877): 59–61.

60 "Ancient and Modern Stained Glass," *Paint, Oil and Drug Review* 3 (January 1, 1885): 35, reporting on lecture of Charles Barnard at Chickering Hall, New York, "A Bit of Glass," which featured "a large number of fine specimens of stained glass which had been loaned for the occasion by several New York firms"; "Reviews and Reports," *American Chemical Journal* 2, no. 1 (April 1880): 62.

61 *General Prices Current of Foreign and Domestic Drugs, Medicines, Chemicals, Extracts, Pharmaceutical Preparations, Essential Oils, Sponges, Fancy Goods, Druggists' Sundries, Perfumery, Proprietary Articles, etc.* (New York: W. H. Schieffelin & Co., 1876). For more on Schieffelin, see "W. H. Schieffelin and Co.," in *The Successful Business Houses of New York* (New York: A. J. Clark, 1872), 59; W. H. Schieffelin & Co., *One Hundred Years of Business Life, 1794–1894* (1894); and Carl C. Dickey, *150 Years of Service to American Health* (New York: Schieffelin, 1944).

62 For the Smithsonian display, see "Washington," *Medical News* 40, no. 12 (March 25, 1882): 335–36; and "An Elegant Exhibition," *Washington Post*, September 11, 1883. See also the US National Museum Curators Annual Reports—Materia Medica, 1882, Smithsonian Institution Archives, accessed July 29, 2020, https://transcription.si.edu/project/8239. For Gellatly's arrangement of flowers in a materia medica exhibit, see "The Exhibition at Prospect Park Pavilion," *Niagara Falls Gazette*, September 20, 1882, 4.

63 Gellatly is listed as "real estate, 5 W 27th" street in *Trow's New York City Directory*, XCVIII (1884–85), 617.

64 "Third Annual Exhibition of the Architectural League," *Art Amateur* 18, no. 3 (February 1888): 56; "Architecture and Decoration. An Exhibition to Be Visited," *Town Topics: The Journal of Society* 18, no. 25 (December 22, 1887): 19.

65 Two examples of "ornamental work" by Dr. Salviati were listed in the catalogue of the league's 1905 exhibition, for instance; see *Yearbook of the Architectural League of New York* 20 (1905): 39.

66 See Bruce Crane to Ruel P. Tolman, 26 December 1936, photocopy in SAAM Gellatly files, Correspondence, Registrar; and Tolman, introduction to *Catalog of the American and European Paintings in the Gellatly Collection* (Washington, DC: Smithsonian Institution, 1945), 3–4.

67 Annie Nathan Meyer, "Collecting American Paintings," *The World's Work* 10, no. 3 (July 1905): 6388.

68 Mary L. Alexander, "The Week in Art Circles," *Cincinnati Enquirer*, July 16, 1933, 5.

69 "Seen in New York. Antique Objects of the Home Furnishing Arts and the Lessons They Teach," *Good Furniture* 8, no. 1 (January 1917): 15–16; and William Lauren Harris, "Spanish Furniture: What We Really Know about It," *Good Furniture* 12, no. 1 (January 1919): 24, 34.

70 The inscription, VAEA, designates Stevenson's Samoan burial site.

71 See, for example, Thayer's letters to Gellatly of 19 and 29 April, probably 1905, John Gellatly letters received from artists, 1887–1931, Box 1, Folder 9, Archives of American Art, Smithsonian Institution.

72 SAAM curatorial file for *Girl Arranging Her Hair* (folder 12). For other Renaissance style frames, see, for example, Thayer, *Margaret McKittrick*, ca. 1903, Newfields (Indianapolis Museum of Art), Gift of the Friends of American Art, acc. no. 25.312, accessed July 30, 2020, http://collection.imamuseum.org/artwork/56187/.

73 On artists and potential purchasers viewing Thayers at Gellatly's, see, among others, Gellatly to Thayer, 29 December 1917, Thayer Papers, Archives of American Art, Smithsonian Institution. On the experience of viewing Gellatly's home and gallery, see Alexander, "The Week in Art Circles."

74 See John Gellatly, "Thayer in the American Renaissance," *The Touchstone: The Arts and the American Art Student* 1, no. 6 (June/July 1921): 2.

75 See "The Union League Exhibition," *New York Tribune*, April 12, 1890, 4; Montague Marks, "My Note Book," *Art Amateur* 22, no. 6 (1890): 112.

76 Charles Lang Freer to Gellatly, 30 March 1904; see also Freer to Gellatly, 5 April 1904, both Charles Lang Freer Papers, Freer Gallery of Art, Smithsonian Institution.

77 Gellatly to Gari Melchers, Chairman, National Gallery of Arts Commission, 27 March 1929, SAAM Gellatly files.

78 Ibid.

79 Artist Ernest Peixotto particularly commended Gellatly's tastes and support for living artists, writing, "In the creation of his collection, a pursuit of beauty was the dominating preoccupation. His collecting was not to have and to hold but to have and to give." Peixotto, "A Tribute to John Gellatly," *New York Times*, November 22, 1931, 9.

80 Carol Duncan, "Something Eternal: The Donor Memorial," in *Civilizing Rituals: Inside Public Art Museums* (New York: Routledge, 1995), 72–101. I am grateful to Crawford Alexander Mann for his assistance with this history.

81 C. L. Borie Jr. of Zantzinger, Borie & Medary, to Gari Melchers, 9 April 1929, SAAM Gellatly files.

82 "5 and 10 Cent Store Gimcracks Given Place in Art Collection Exhibited at National Museum," *Star-Gazette* (Elmira, NY), July 13, 1933, 24.

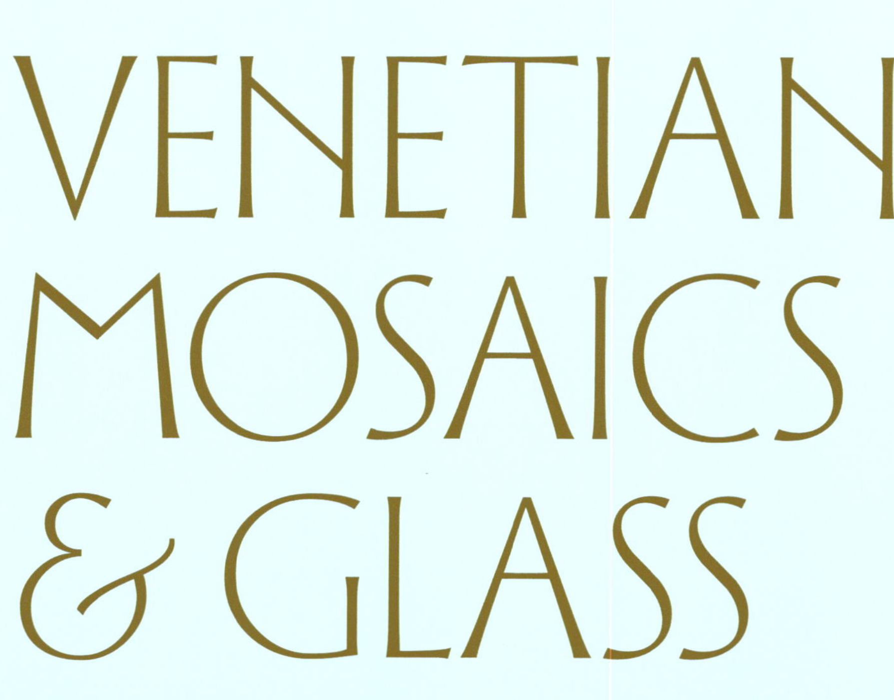

in the United States, 1860–1917

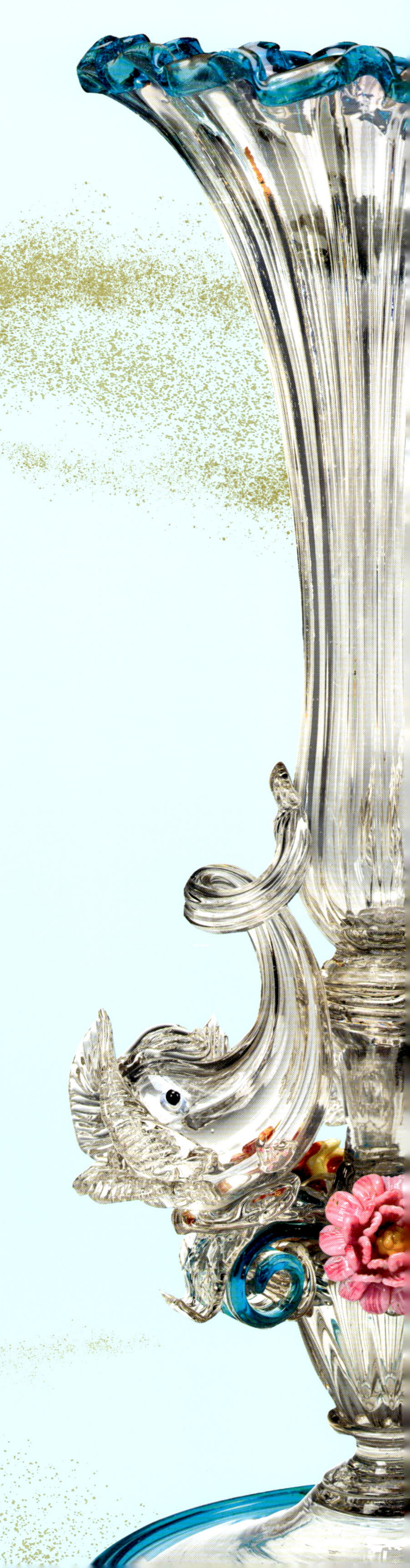

SHELDON BARR

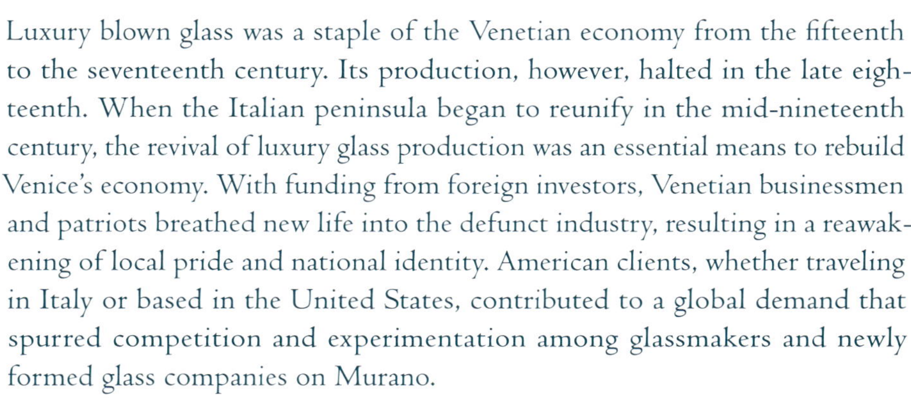

Luxury blown glass was a staple of the Venetian economy from the fifteenth to the seventeenth century. Its production, however, halted in the late eighteenth. When the Italian peninsula began to reunify in the mid-nineteenth century, the revival of luxury glass production was an essential means to rebuild Venice's economy. With funding from foreign investors, Venetian businessmen and patriots breathed new life into the defunct industry, resulting in a reawakening of local pride and national identity. American clients, whether traveling in Italy or based in the United States, contributed to a global demand that spurred competition and experimentation among glassmakers and newly formed glass companies on Murano.

EARLY HISTORY OF GLASS IN VENICE

In 697 CE, as the rest of Europe descended into the Dark Ages, the Republic of Venice was founded on a group of islands in a lagoon of the Adriatic Sea. Over time it evolved into a powerful seafaring nation. By the ninth century, the republic had established a lucrative relationship with mercantile centers in the eastern Mediterranean. By the fifteenth, an enormous quantity of merchandise was transported in both directions by Venice's armed galleys. Trade prospered, Venice grew rich, and the arts flourished.

In time, glassmakers from southwestern Asia migrated to Venice and set up small furnaces for the production of gilded and enameled glassware in the Islamic tradition. Venice later became Europe's leading glassmaking center and luxury glass an extremely important export commodity. Eventually glassmakers began to leave the overcrowded city and relocate to the nearby island of Murano. In 1291 Venice's Grand Council directed those remaining in Venice to extinguish their fires and join their comrades. Murano thus became the glassmakers' "gilded cage"; once there, they enjoyed great esteem but were forbidden by law to leave.

Preceding pages: Attributed to Compagnia di Venezia e Murano (CVM), Vase with Dolphins and Flowers (detail), ca. 1880s–90s; **see p. 41**

In the late fifteenth century, new Portuguese shipping routes around southern Africa ended Venice's trade monopoly with Asia. Despite increasing competition from other nations, Venice remained a center for art making and commerce.

On Murano, glassmakers continued to produce an amazing variety of luxury glass for the palaces of the European nobility and the mansions of the bourgeoisie. Demanding a high level of artistic and technical perfection from the sequestered glassmakers, the cultivated tastes of the Renaissance were satisfied with dazzling virtuosity.

However, by the eighteenth century, the republic had lost its traditional economic pillars—the spice trade and the shipbuilding industry. Lace, silk, and wool production also had declined. Still, luxury glassware remained highly desirable, and its manufacture persisted even as Venice's fortunes faded. With the economy in ruins and glassmaking the only viable industry, the draconian Grand Council was known to send assassins to hunt down glassmakers who emigrated, if the imprisonment of close relatives failed to bring them back to Murano.

In the latter 1700s, competing with burgeoning glass industries elsewhere in Europe, Venetian luxury glassware experienced a steep decline in popularity. Austere English and Bohemian crystal—a hard, brilliant kind of glass, often embellished with the "cold" techniques of engraving and wheel carving—had caught the fickle world's fancy.

Having lost its fortunes, Venice also forfeited power on the world stage. On May 12, 1797, the eleven-hundred-year-old republic surrendered its independence to Napoleon Bonaparte's fleet. Venice then endured a series of foreign occupations that culminated in Austria's taking control in 1814.

Seeking to destroy the Venetian glassmaking industry in favor of its Bohemian factories, Austria dealt the coup de grâce by enacting tariffs on both the import of required raw materials and the export of finished glassware. Double taxation rendered most glass manufacture profitless. After more than half a millennium, Venetian luxury glass production ended. Untold numbers of glassmakers migrated to other countries to find work. Nevertheless, part of the industry survived by fabricating utilitarian glassware for domestic consumption and glass beads that were essential bartering tools in colonial trade. Venetian beadmakers, working at small factories or at home, preserved two glassmaking techniques (*filigrana* and ***millefiori***) that might otherwise have been lost.[1] The successive foreign occupations lasted almost seventy years until a new optimism took hold.

SALVIATI AND THE GLASS REVIVAL

When the glass revival story began in the 1850s, Venice was in wretched condition. The long-depressed economy, the benign neglect of foreign dominion, and the more tangible destruction wrought by Austrian bombardment during Venice's failed 1848 revolt had all contributed to the crumbling state of the city's magnificent buildings.

Yet a fateful moment for the future of Venetian glass was at hand. In 1851 thirty-five-year-old Antonio Salviati, a lawyer of modest background from Vicenza, moved to Venice with his family. Italian writer Michele Lessona later romanticized Salviati's early impressions of the city:

He had the soul of an artist, and the wonders that filled his eyes in Venice each day took possession of his thoughts: he witnessed the decadence of the arts of glassmaking and mosaic, and was filled with the noble desire to bring them back to life.[2]

At that time the mosaic decoration of the eleventh-century St. Mark's Basilica was in danger of being lost due to the years of neglect. After visiting the thriving Fabbrica Vaticana dei Mosaici in Rome, Salviati returned to Venice determined to revive the lost arts of mosaic manufacture and glassmaking. He quickly found two equally inspired allies—Muranese abbot and glass historian Vincenzo Zanetti, who also desired to revitalize both skills, and Antonio Colleoni, a politically active pharmacist and future mayor of Murano who yearned to restore employment to the people of his island.[3]

Zanetti and Colleoni joined forces to persuade Salviati to abandon the legal profession and launch a business devoted to the manufacture of mosaics. Their persuasive powers triumphed in 1859, when Salviati founded a company he named Salviati Dott. Antonio fu Bartolomeo.[4]

That year the administrators of St. Mark's Basilica drew up a fifteen-year contract with the new Salviati company for the supply of ***smalti***, the glass used in mosaic production, for the restoration of damaged mosaics and, when deemed necessary, the manufacture of newly designed mosaics to replace those that had been lost beyond repair.

According to Conte de Castellane, "In 1859 it was impossible to restore the mosaics of the church of San Marco because the essential material, colored smalti, didn't exist."[5] Thus Salviati's initial task was the manufacture of a huge range of colored glass as well as metallic smalti to reconstitute the sparkling gold backgrounds for which the basilica was well-known. To this end, a showroom (Stabilimento Salviati)[6] and factory were set up in central Venice at Dorsoduro 731. Salviati hired the Roman mosaicist Enrico Podio as his art director and the visionary glass technician Lorenzo Radi, who had researched new colors for mosaic tesserae for twenty years.[7]

Radi is best remembered for rediscovering the formula for *calcedonio* glass (glass imitating banded agate, also known as chalcedony). By analyzing surviving Renaissance examples, he recovered the lost process in 1846. By adding a coloring agent made up of the salts of silver, iron, and copper to molten glass at specific intervals, Radi succeeded in reproducing the desired veined or striated appearance of the originals.[8] His patterns were cut into large pieces for floor tiles, and he also blew *calcedonio* into vessels imitating historical examples, as seen in the Cantor Arts Center's Chalcedony Glass Urn (CAT. 3-1), inspired by the ancient Greek cantharus form.

Concurrent with his work on the basilica, Salviati obtained the first of many foreign mosaic commissions. In 1860 Egypt's Muhammad Sa'id Pasha ordered monumental mosaics for the walls of a salon in his new palace at Mex, near Alexandria. One year later, he ordered a mosaic and tile pavement for the palace's dining hall. International projects and investment would become essential to the long-term growth and success of Salviati's enterprise and the glass revival overall.

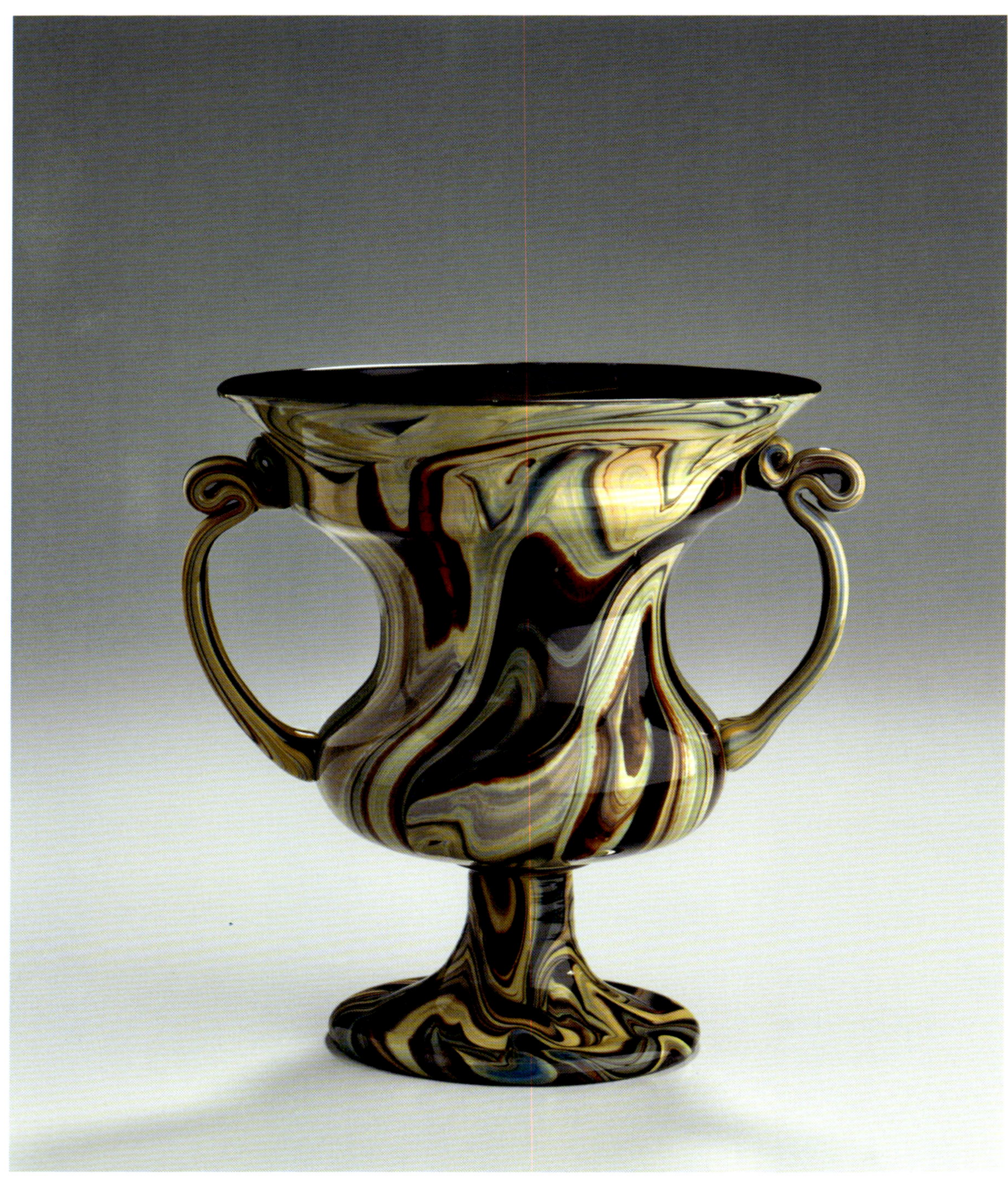

☆ CAT. 3-1

Artisti Barovier, Chalcedony Glass Urn, ca. 1890–1904, blown and applied hot-worked glass, 6 × 5 7/8 × 5 5/16 in., Iris & B. Gerald Cantor Center for Visual Arts at Stanford University, Gift of Erede Dr. A. Salviati & Co

In the autumn of 1860, Salviati met English archaeologist Sir Austen Henry Layard in Venice. Born in Italy, Layard was renowned for his leadership in excavating the ruins of Nineveh and Babylon. He then pursued a distinguished career in politics, serving two terms in Parliament. More importantly for Salviati, Layard was an unabashed lover of Venice and things Venetian and was extremely influential and exceedingly rich. The two men connected immediately.

With Layard's encouragement, Salviati chose the 1861 Esposizione Italiana Agraria, Industriale e Artistica in Florence, the first exhibition in the newly formed Kingdom of Italy, to introduce his firm's production. The jury awarded the company six gold medals for its debut, which consisted of sundry small items (jewel boxes, letter openers, etc.) and several examples of Radi's blown chalcedony glass. Two copies of Byzantine mosaics were also exhibited, publicizing the firm's successful work in St. Mark's and its readiness for new projects in architectural decoration.

Additional prestigious opportunities came in 1865, when Layard became chief adviser to Queen Victoria on artistic matters. As a member of the design committee for royal monuments to the late Prince Albert, Victoria's consort, Layard steered numerous commissions to Salviati Dott. Antonio fu Bartolomeo. These included the ecclesiastical mosaic decoration of the walls and portico of the Royal Mausoleum at Frogmore, near Windsor Castle, in 1862, followed by decorative mosaics for the Albert Memorial (Wolsey) Chapel at Windsor and the Albert Memorial in London's Kensington Gardens, as well as ecclesiastical mosaics in Westminster Abbey and St. Paul's Cathedral in London. These installations in conspicuous venues enhanced the reputation of the new company not only in Europe but also around the world.

During or shortly after his participation in the London International Exhibition of 1862, Salviati, probably at Layard's suggestion, opened a shop on Oxford Street in the capital for the sale of mosaics, tiles, Radi's blown chalcedony glass, and other wares with the aid of Baron Robert Amadeus Heath, the British vice-consul for Italy.[9]

In the wake of these successful international showcases, Zanetti, the director of Murano's Museo Civico Vetrario (now the Glass Museum),[10] organized the Prima Esposizione Vetreria (First Glasswork Exhibition) in November 1864. The stated purpose of this relatively modest exhibition was to stimulate financial investment in the glass industry and encourage young glassmakers to concentrate on the production of *artistic* blown glass as a supplement to the ongoing mass production of beads and utilitarian sheet glass in factories. In the guide to the exhibition, Salviati was praised for "founding a Venetian mosaic school and a ***stabilimento***, unique in Italy, . . . which brought employment to many young men and food to many families."[11] Most importantly for the revival of luxury glass, this exhibition resulted in the Glass Museum acquiring copies of sixteenth- and seventeenth-century blown glass Venetian vessels, which were made at the Fratelli Toso[12] glassworks by Giovanni Barovier, Giovanni Fuga, and their assistants.

Salviati, Zanetti, and Colleoni were certain that the revival of the Venetian blown glass industry would prove as great a success as had their revival of the mosaic industry. However, the realization of their ambitious project required spacious quarters capable of supporting larger furnaces, more technicians, and more glassmakers. Considerable investment was needed, and the three lacked the necessary funds. Layard disclosed that in 1866 Salviati was nearing bankruptcy and was not able to complete the mosaic work at the Wolsey Chapel or the Albert Memorial without an influx of capital.[13] So once again Salviati commissioned the glassblowers at the Fratelli Toso glassworks to create samples of the Venetian glass vessels that he, Zanetti, and Colleoni wanted to revive.

Salviati specified that the vessels be embellished with unmistakable Venetian characteristics, such as meticulously applied threading, ***fragole***, or ***morise***, and/or borders in colored glass.[14] *Morise*, as shown in this example from the Museum of the City of New York (CAT. 3-2), are small decorative protrusions created by pinching threads of molten glass to decorate a glass object, in this case, along the wings of a goblet. Salviati then took the vessels to London and presented them to Layard and Heath. Upon seeing the vessels, both became impassioned by the blown glass project. They and others like historian William Drake, William Fite, William Edward Quentell, Lachlan Mackintosh Rate, and Charles Sommers clubbed together to invest in the new venture.[15]

On March 20, 1866, after receiving financial pledges from the investors, Salviati telegraphed Zanetti and Colleoni from London and instructed them to go ahead with their plan to take over a former glasshouse in the courtyard of the twelfth-century Palazzo da Mula on Murano, assuring them the "money is in transit."[16] Glass technician Antonio Camozzo began laying down the new furnaces almost immediately. Even Colleoni is reputed to have lent a hand in their construction.

Thus the British-Venetian partnership, the Società Anonima per Azioni Salviati e Compania, was launched.[17] Its London showroom debuted that summer in the same Oxford Street shop that Salviati opened with Heath. According to a later article, Salviati went in search of descendants of the historic glassblowing families.

> *Firmly convinced that . . . art-genius is hereditary, [Salviati] looked through the 'golden books' of the old Republic, in which the names of the best masters were formerly entered, and then made inquiries in Venice and Murano, where at length he had the pleasure of discovering certain descendants of the two famous families of Radi and Bonvico, who were still connected with glass-making.*[18]

✡ CAT. 3-2
Attributed to Compagnia di Venezia e Murano (CVM), Seventeenth Century–Style Long-Stemmed Goblet, ca. 1900, blown and applied hot-worked glass, 11 × 5 in. diam., Museum of the City of New York, Gift of the Estate of Miss Agnes Miles Carpenter, 1955

Salviati found living members of three celebrated glassmaking families of the past—Seguso, Ongaro, and Barovier. He engaged them to instruct the intricacies of glassmaking to the often illiterate, young apprentices with whom he was compelled to fill the ranks of his new glassworks. Zanetti had founded the Scuola di Disegno Applicato all'Arte Vetraria on Murano in 1862,[19] and there the apprentices were instructed in the techniques of glassmaking—glassblowing, lampworking, decorating with enamels and gold leaf, engraving, grinding, and fusing. Finally, certain that literacy would improve their self-esteem and awaken pride in the great glassmaking heritage to which they were heir, Salviati established a free school where the young men could learn to read and write.

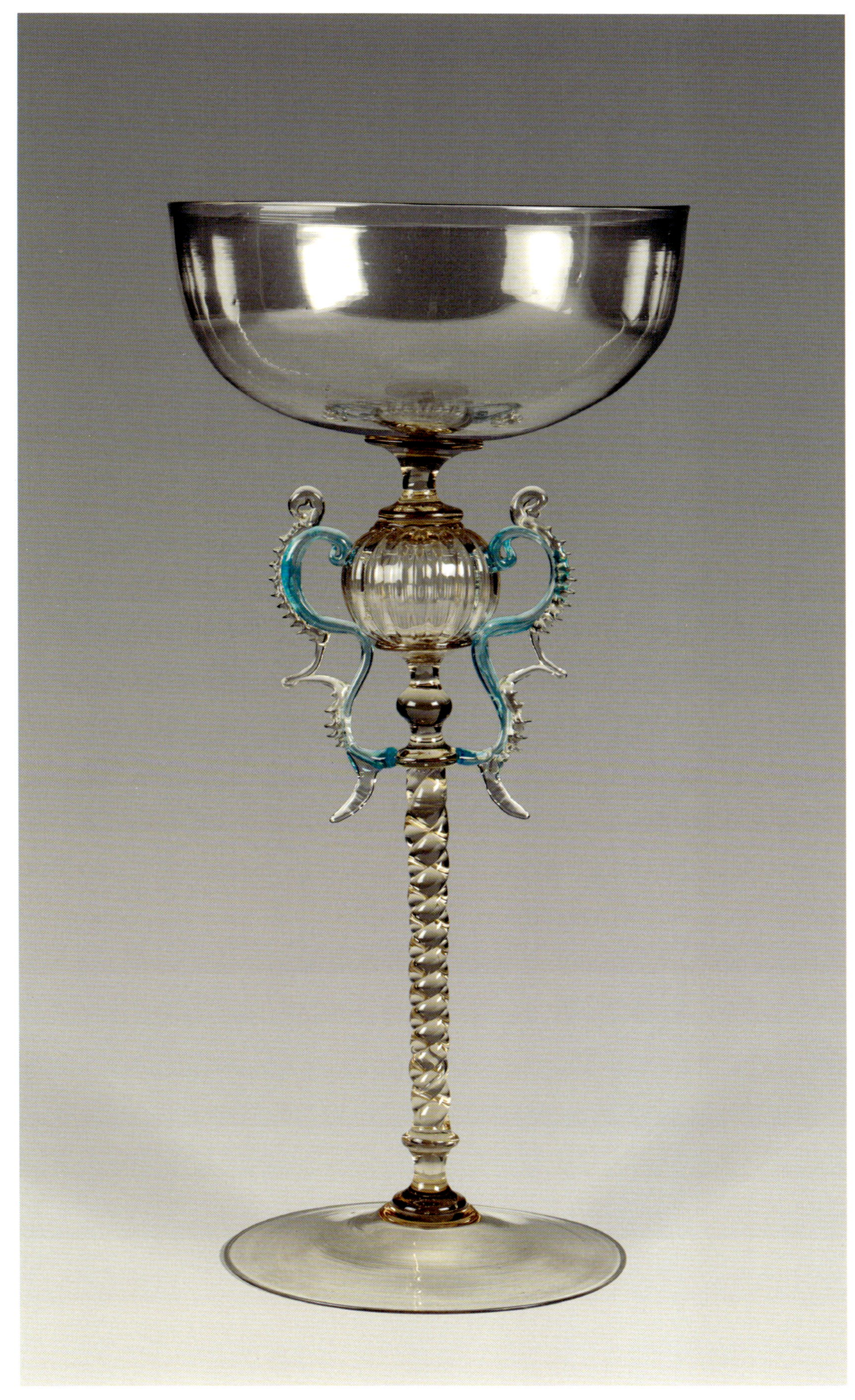

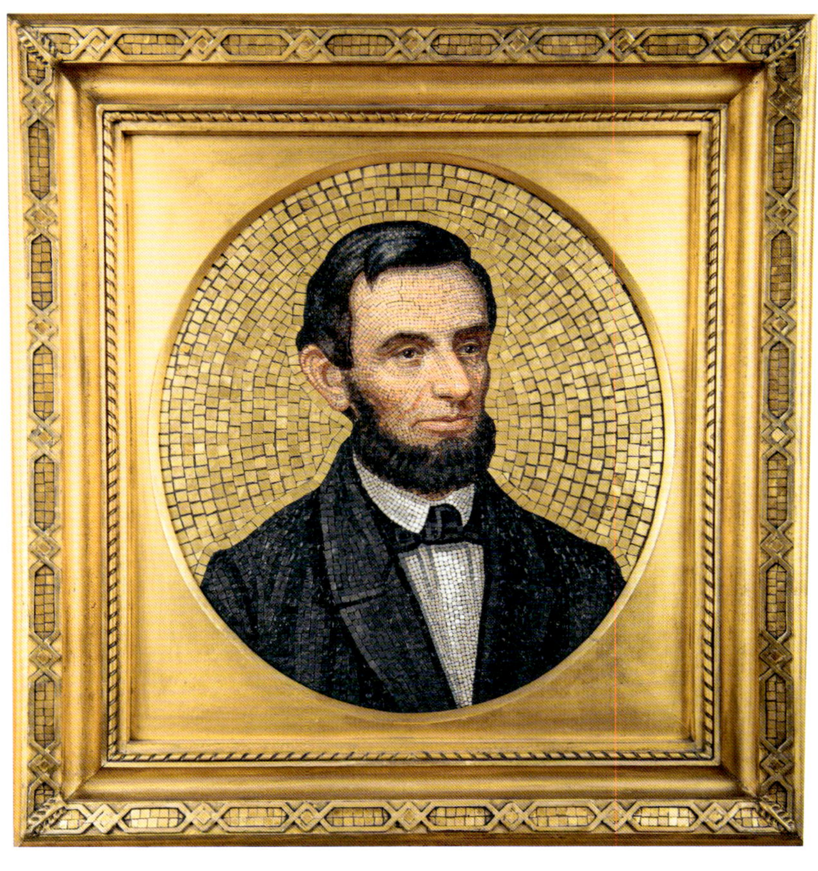

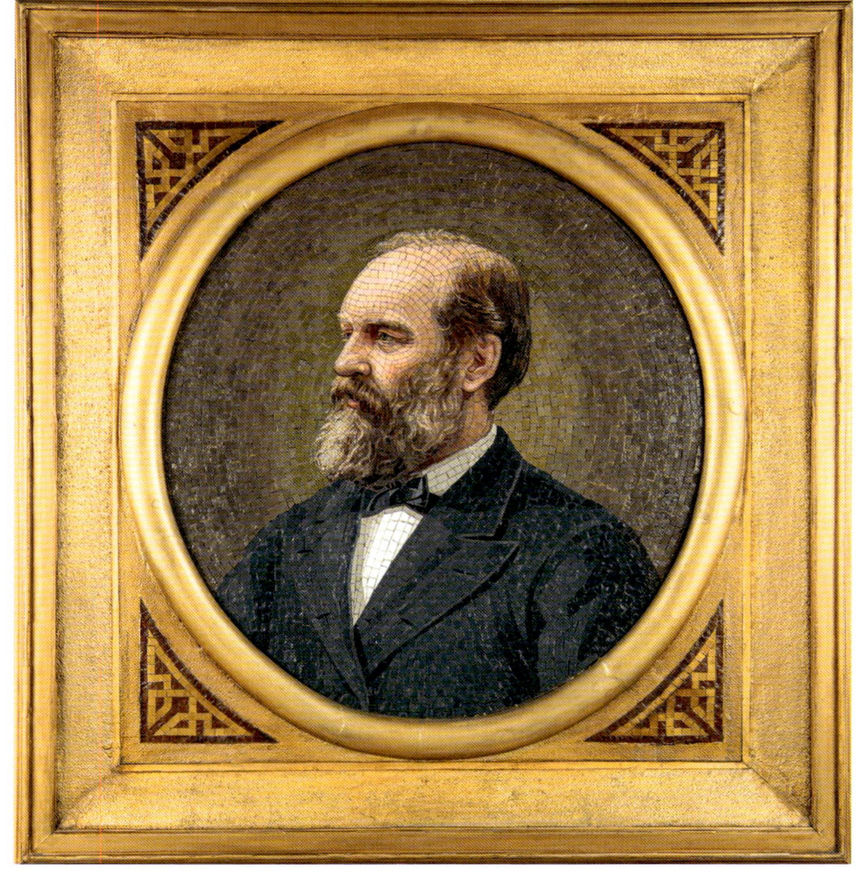

☆ CAT. 3-3
Salviati Dott. Antonio fu Bartolomeo, *Portrait of Abraham Lincoln*, 1866, glass mosaic tiles, 22 ¾ × 20 ¼ in., US Senate Collection

Fig. 3-1
Antonio Salviati, *James A. Garfield*, 1882, enamel mosaic, 25 × 23 in., US Senate Collection

For his mosaic production, Salviati discovered two talented glass technicians working on Murano—Vincenzo Moretti and Luigi dalla Venezia. Salviati hired them both for his new factory. Soon Moretti, assisted by dalla Venezia, took over the production of smalti from sixty-three-year-old Lorenzo Radi.[20] In this way, Salviati and his business partners cultivated glassmaking skills among young workers and spurred the revival of traditional Venetian techniques.

PROMOTING AND MARKETING VENETIAN LUXURY GLASS TO THE WORLD

In 1866, after almost seventy years of foreign domination, Venice underwent major political changes when the beleaguered Austrian Empire lost its war with the Kingdom of Italy. In a plebiscite, with Napoleon III as intermediary, the people of Venice overwhelmingly voted to join the five-year-old Kingdom of Italy. Unlike Austria, the new kingdom welcomed foreign investment. It also sought to expand its trade with the outside world. That year, in an effort to promote his mosaic business in the United States, Salviati presented a mosaic portrait of President Abraham Lincoln to the United States Senate (CAT. 3-3). Salviati, a professed admirer of Lincoln, described him as "one of the world's greatest heroes."[21] The portrait of Lincoln is set against a glittering oval Byzantine-style gold mosaic background, evoking portraits of saints and martyrs in medieval Orthodox Christian art in Constantinople and the mosaics in Venice's eleventh-century St. Mark's Basilica. Hoping to generate important mosaic commissions in the United States as he had done in Britain, Salviati had unfortunate timing. The US government lacked funds after the Civil War and did not commission glassworks from Venice.

Salviati tried this marketing tactic again in 1883, working through intermediaries to donate another mosaic portrait to the US government, this one of recently assassinated President James A. Garfield (Fig. 3-1). It was accepted by a concurrent resolution of Congress in May 1884[22] and joined Salviati's mosaic portrait of Lincoln in the collection of the Senate. This likeness has a slightly less formal, less rigid character, using smaller tesserae of glass in order to achieve more naturalistic representations of the sitter's flesh. Whereas the Lincoln portrait's gold mosaic backdrop conveys the grandeur of a Byzantine emperor or saint, Garfield's portrayal is more naturalistic and humanized, a shift in style that corresponds to a growing informality in painted portraiture in those same years. This time Salviati's strategy appears to have succeeded; the Church of St. Ignatius Loyola in New York City commissioned Salviati and company to manufacture three monumental mosaics for its baptistery chapel in time for the 1898 dedication of the church.[23]

Attempts to market Venetian glass abroad also continued through participation in organized exhibitions, each one presenting new technical and artistic achievements. Acting on behalf of Layard, Alessandro Castellani, the renowned Roman jeweler and antiquities collector, orchestrated the Società Anonima's participation in the 1867 Exposition Universelle in Paris.[24] Salviati's workers, from old maestri to young apprentices, did not let him down. Salviati brought more than five hundred blown glass objects to the exhibition.[25] Zanetti described them as follows:

There was an abundance of models in varied colors and forms; goblets, bowls, amphorae, cruets, vases, delicately tinted vessels with combinations of filigree and reticello, bands of enamel graffito, glittering with aventurine, ruby, aquamarine, opal, and with borders, flowers, butterflies, serpents, dolphins, swans, initials, masks.[26]

An illustration of Venetian glassware at the Paris exhibition (Fig. 3-2) conveys the elaborate styles and extraordinary variety already in production—even without the benefit of color. Many of these vessels were inspired by eighteenth-century Venetian prototypes, which in turn were based on seventeenth-century Bohemian models. Several have letters of the alphabet applied to the central medallion, suggesting that they were intended to serve as personalized gifts. The Smithsonian American Art Museum's **Fenicio** Goblet with Swans and Initial "S" Stem (CAT. 3-4) is one such example of the type of brilliantly colored luxury glass displayed. Another popular vessel, the one illustrated on the top row center, was produced for many years.[27] Apparently, the Paris exhibition was a success for the new company. Zanetti wrote, "Of the blown glass objects sent to Paris, none returned to Venice, rather there was an indescribable competition to purchase what was there and to order new pieces."[28]

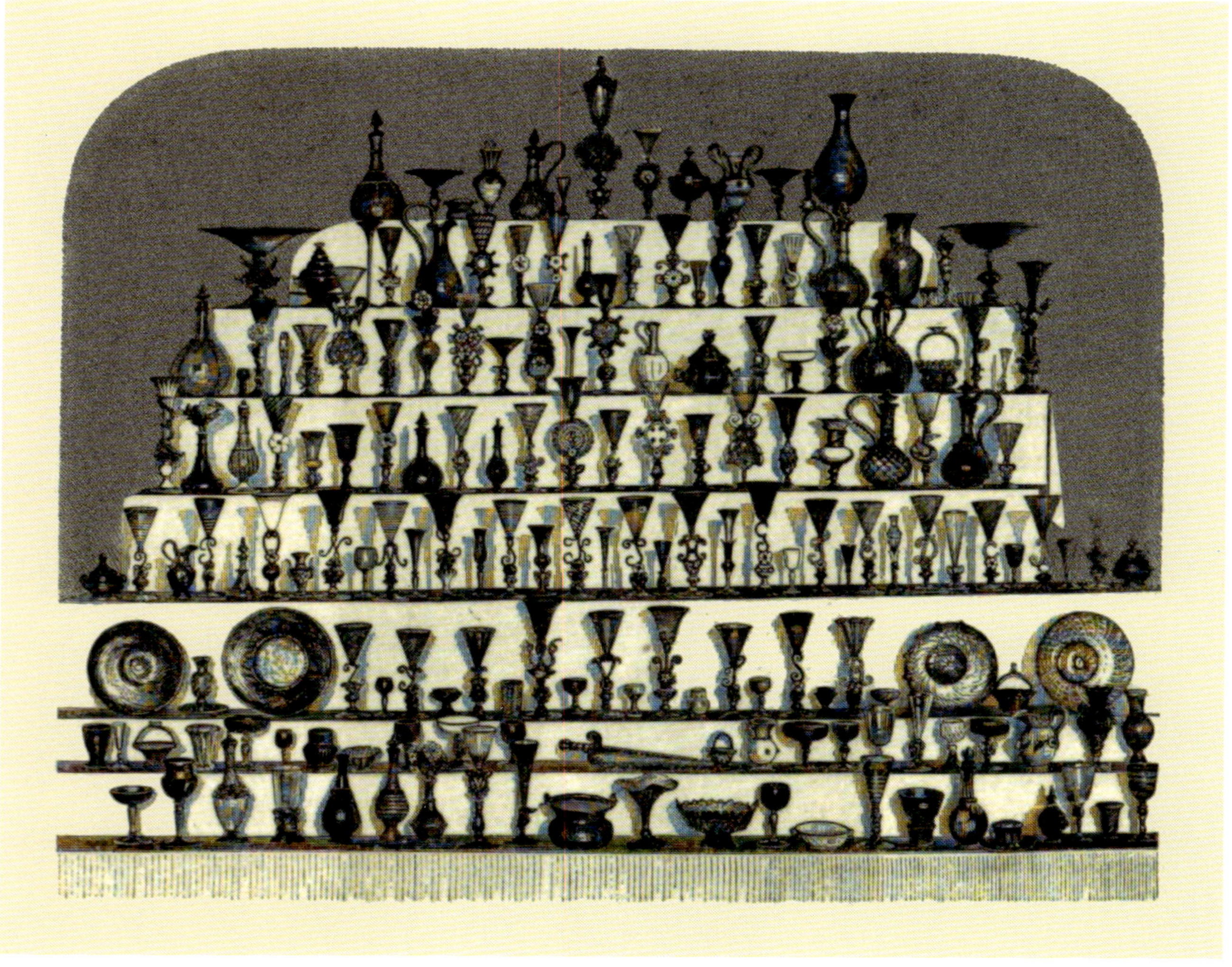

Fig. 3-2
Paris exhibition illustration from *L'Italia alla Esposizione Universaledi Parigi nel 1867* (Le Monnier, 1868)

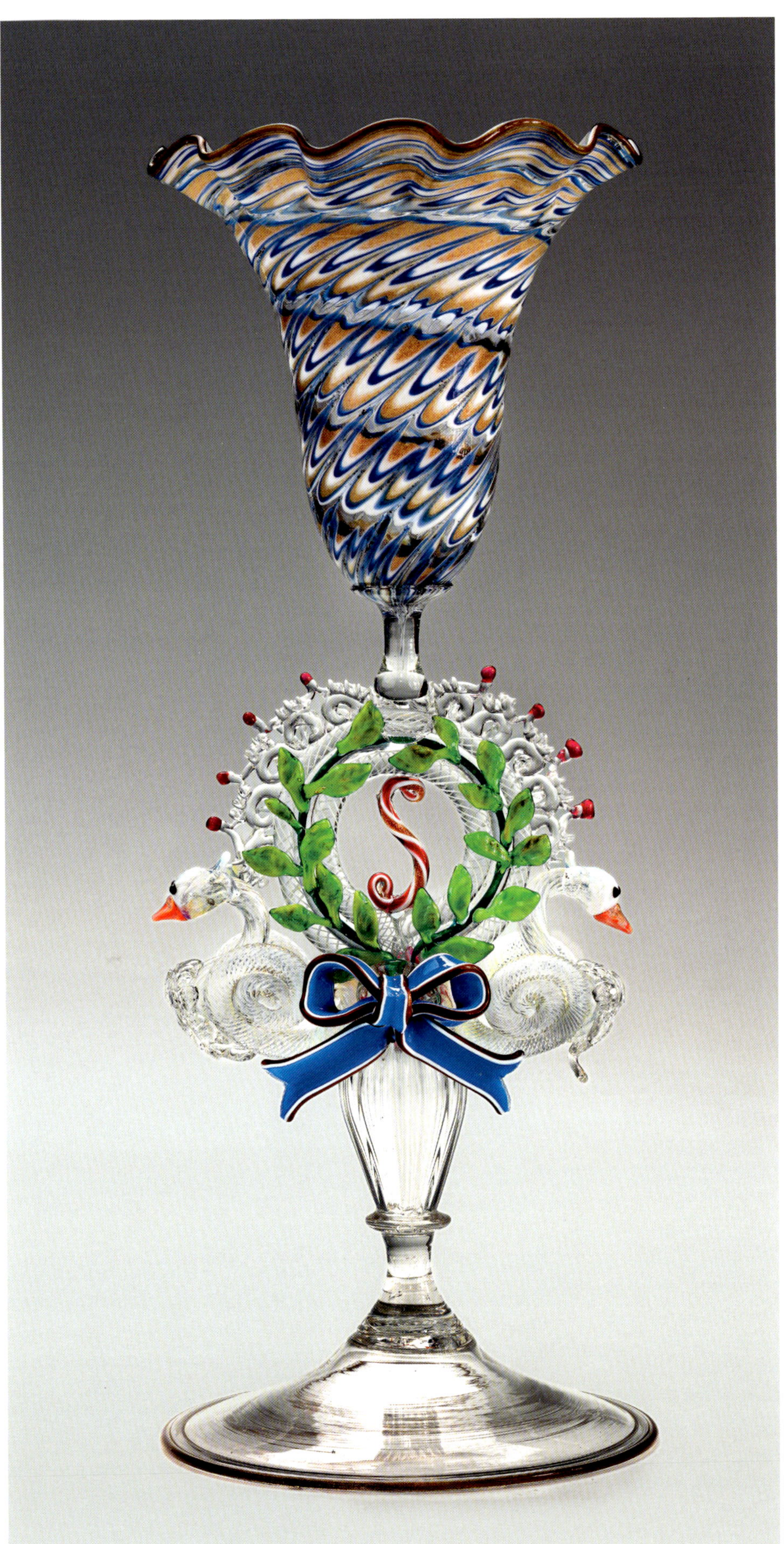

✡ CAT. 3-4
Società Anonima per Azioni Salviati & C., Fenicio Goblet with Swans and Initial "S" Stem, ca. 1870, blown and applied hot-worked glass, 12 ⅝ × 5 ⅛ in. diam., Smithsonian American Art Museum, Gift of John Gellatly

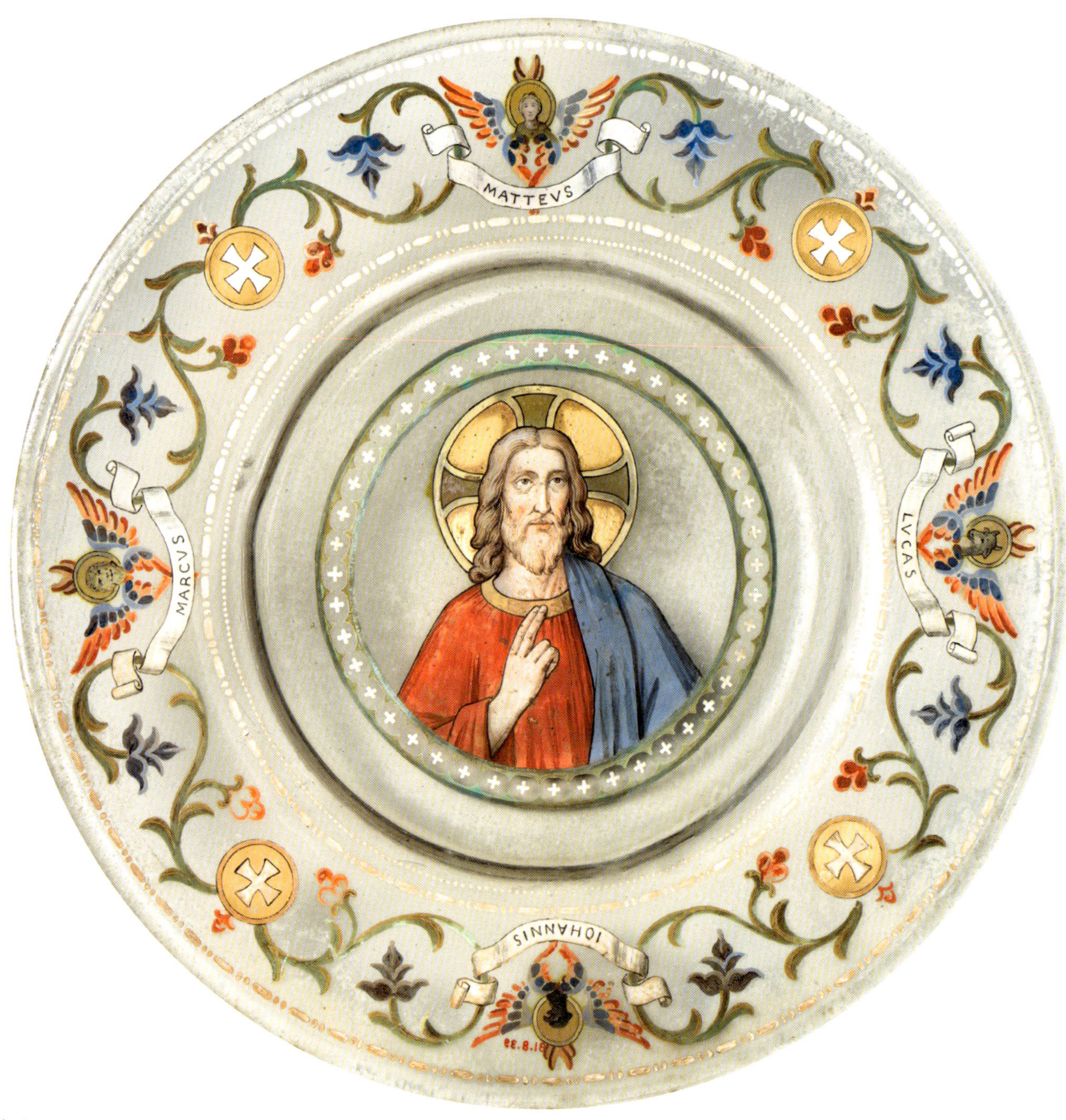

☆ CAT. 3-5

Società Anonima per Azioni Salviati & C., Renaissance-Style Dish with Christ and Four Evangelists, ca. 1870s, blown, enameled, and gilded glass, 2 ¾ × 18 ⅝ in. diam., The Metropolitan Museum of Art, Gift of James Jackson Jarves, 1881

At the 1867 Paris exhibition, Salviati met the enamelist Giuseppe Devers, who later played a major role in developing Salviati's gilded and enameled glassware. At that time, Devers, a native of Turin, was working as a ceramic decorator at the Sèvres factory. When Salviati saw his enameled pottery at the Paris fair, he realized that his compatriot's expertise could facilitate his reproduction of Murano's fifteenth-century gilded and enameled vessels. He persuaded Devers to come to Venice, where he established a school of enameling and gilding.[29] Devers mentored Leopoldo Bearzotti, who is identified in contemporary reviews as Salviati's enamelist. It is possible that Bearzotti painted the Renaissance-Style Dish with Christ and Four Evangelists now at the Metropolitan Museum of Art (CAT. 3-5).

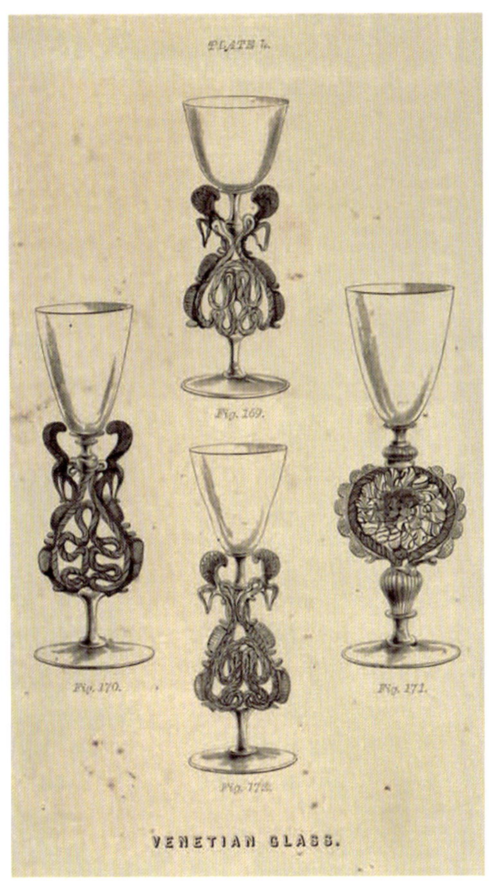

Fig. 3-3
***Venetian Glass*, from Alexander Nesbitt, *Catalogue of the Collection of Glass Formed by Felix Slade* (Wertheimer, Lea, 1871)**

The New York jewelry and silver firm of Tiffany & Co. also exhibited at the Paris fair and won the first award of merit for silver smithery ever presented to an American company by a foreign jury. Edward C. Moore, soon to become Tiffany & Co.'s chief designer, visited the Paris fair and was undoubtedly impressed by the Salviati display. In all probability, this led to Tiffany & Co.'s decision to sell Venetian glass in its Union Square, New York, store, which offered an extensive selection of imported European goods. Based on epistolary accounts from grand tourists, the Venetian glass available to consumers in the United States was of the highest quality, despite the challenges of shipping these fragile objects. For example, when Marian "Clover" Hooper Adams and her husband, economist Henry Adams, visited the Società Anonima's shop in Venice in October 1872, Marian wrote to her sister that there was little reason to purchase glass in Venice because "Tiffany had the pick."[30]

By 1870, in addition to supplying its shops in Venice and London, the Società Anonima furnished mosaics and blown glass to agents in other European cities. In the United States, San Francisco's Norton & Co. joined Tiffany & Co. as a Società Anonima agent.

Back in Italy, printed material was an important source of inspiration for Murano's glassblowers. One such publication was the 1871 *Catalogue of the Collection of Glass Formed by Felix Slade*, published by antiquarian Alexander Nesbitt in London.[31] Felix Slade had assembled his impressive holdings of "fragile Venetian beauties" (as he referred to them)[32] in the second quarter of the nineteenth century—years before Zanetti and Colleoni began their quest for Venetian glass in the 1860s. When the Glass Museum acquired a copy of Nesbitt's book in 1872, Muranese artists began to copy or find inspiration in Slade's Venetian vessels (Fig. 3-3).[33] Art glass based on forms from Nesbitt's book found an international audience, including a lidded pokal with serpent stem (see p. 33) and a seventeenth century–style goblet with a knotted stem (see p. 220), both acquired by Rhode Island collector William Ames and later donated to the Rhode Island School of Design Museum. Not surprisingly, the artisans used newly invented nineteenth-century techniques such as blown **aventurine** to create their "copies," thereby surpassing the complexity of Slade's antiques.

Thanks to Salviati's relentless pursuit of technical perfection and the young glassblowers' highly competitive spirit, they were able to transcend the technical skills of their ancestors and achieve an absolute mastery of their medium in a remarkably short time. In 1890 author Madeline A. Wallace-Dunlop proclaimed, "Venetian blown glass is now as nearly perfect as anything human can be."[34]

In 1871, while overseeing the installation of a "huge and dazzling chandelier" in the Quirinale, Italy's royal palace in Rome, Salviati purchased examples of locally excavated fragments of Roman glass.[35] On his return to Murano, he gave

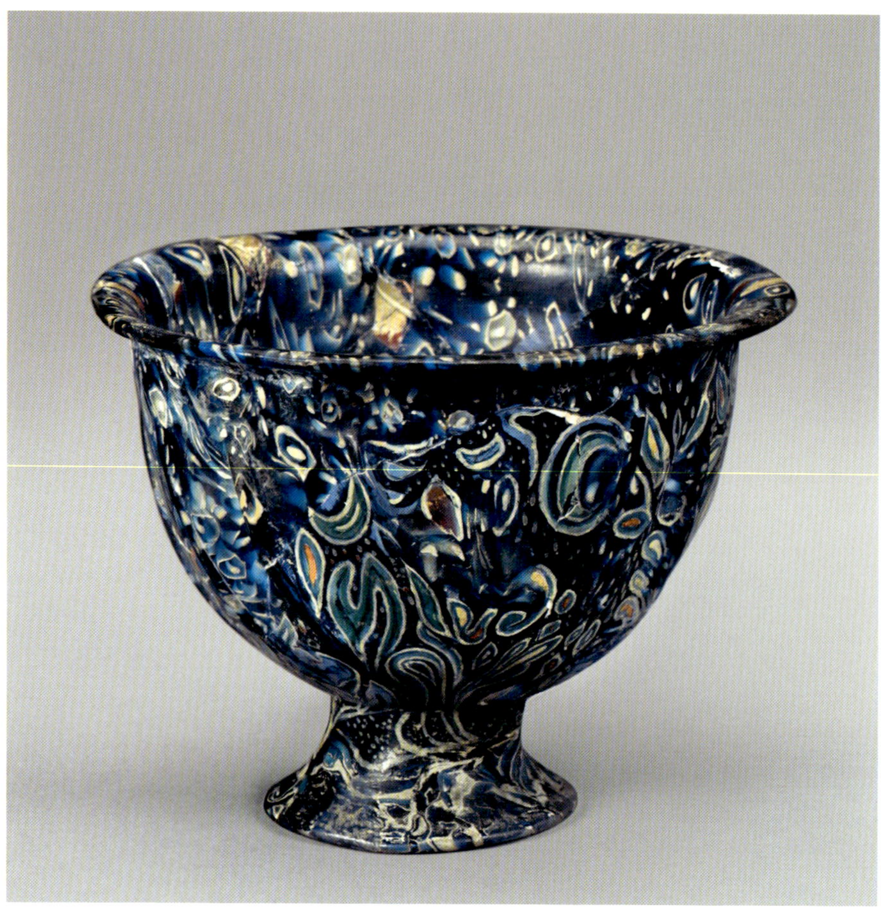

☆ CAT. 3-6
Unidentified, Roman Empire, Mosaic Glass Bowl, 1st century BCE–1st century CE, slumped, polished, and applied mosaic glass, 5 ⅛ × 6 ¾ in. diam., Smithsonian American Art Museum, Gift of John Gellatly

the ancient fragments (composed of fused ***murrhines***[36] and/or segments of canes) to Moretti and dalla Venezia. A Roman bowl from the Smithsonian American Art Museum (CAT. 3-6) illustrates this ancient style. The motivated duo soon succeeded in re-creating "spiral" and other types of Roman murrhines.[37] Before the advent of glassblowing (ca. 50 BCE), the non-blown casting or slumping technique was used to produce Roman glass vessels. This method, although not complicated, had not been employed for two thousand years in Europe and was entirely forgotten by the nineteenth century.

Later that year, the Società Anonima took part in the Esposizione Internazionale Marittima in Naples. At this fair, a new kind of blown glass, called *Pompeiian*, was introduced. Typical of nineteenth-century inventiveness, Pompeiian glass marries the fifteenth-century ***millefiori*** technique with ancient Roman–style components. Since the Pompeiian vessels were produced using

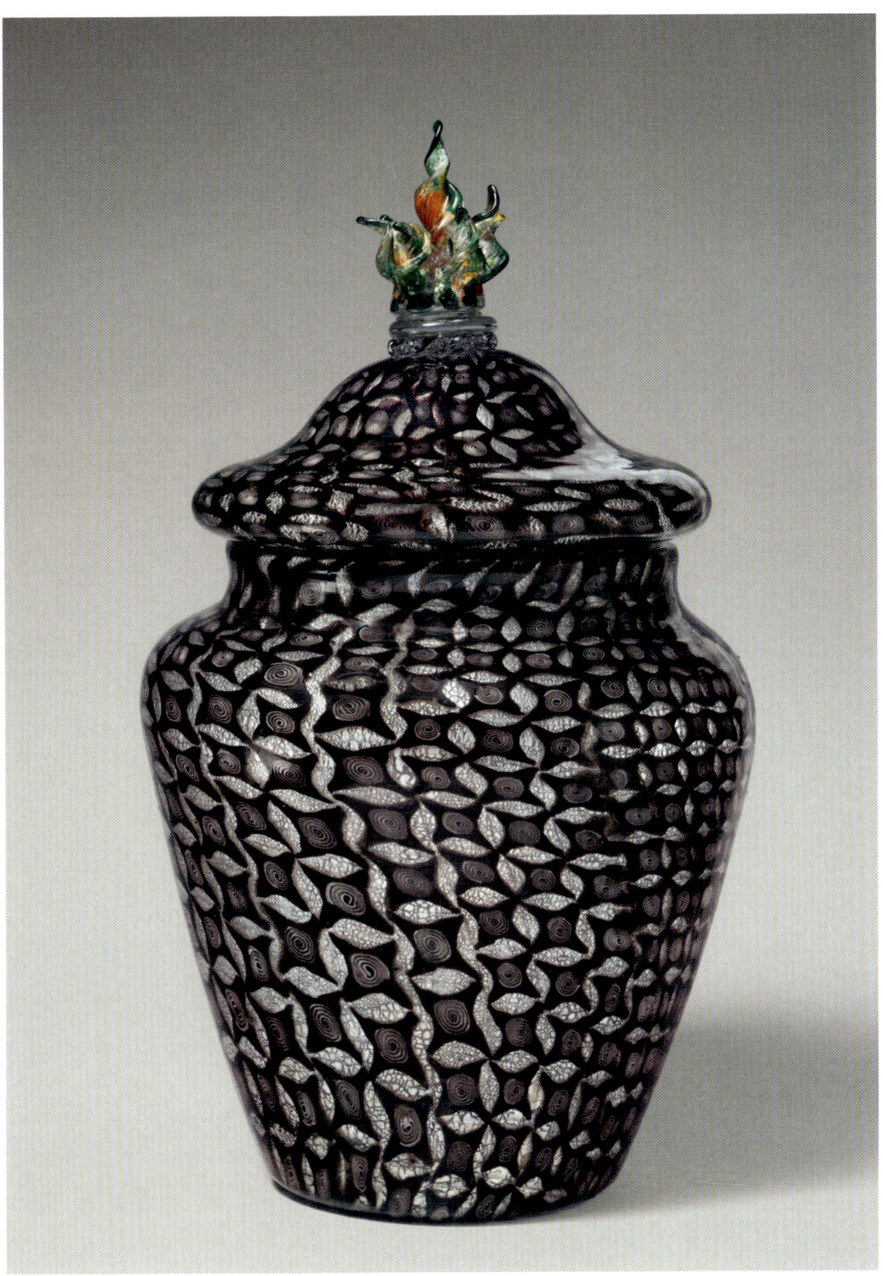

techniques and shapes different from ancient Roman examples, they cannot technically be regarded as revival pieces.

The Pompeiian vessels were described in 1871 as imitations of Greek and Roman glass. In reality, they were nothing like the Roman vessels in that they were blown, even though their murrhines were often credible copies of the antique. When the glassblowers chose not to copy ancient murrhines, such as in the Metropolitan Museum's funerary urn (CAT. 3-7), where square murrhines are enclosed with silver leaf, the vessels are simply referred to as vetro mosaico, or mosaic glass.

Before long, technical mastery and creativity were not limited to the elder maestri. Because they worked in close quarters, a lively competition soon developed among the young members of the Barovier and Seguso glassmaking dynasties. In 1875 seventeen-year-old Isidoro Seguso reproduced a celebrated tour de force of manual dexterity, the *Guggenheim Cup*. Revealing his equal glassmaking skills,

✡ CAT. 3-7
Venice and Murano Glass and Mosaic Company Ltd. (Salviati & Co.), Lidded Mosaic Glass Urn with Silver Leaf Design, ca. 1880, blown and applied hot-worked glass, 11 ¾ × 7 ¼ in. diam., The Metropolitan Museum of Art, Gift of James Jackson Jarves, 1881

twenty-three-year-old Giuseppe Barovier created a second copy within the year. Few glassmakers had the skill to create these extremely elaborate vessels, though a scant number survive, including ones at the Museum of the City of New York (CAT. 3-8). At that time, the seventeenth-century original (now lost) was in the collection of Michelangelo Guggenheim, a Venetian manufacturer of fine furniture.[38] To inspire the young glassmakers to equal or perhaps even surpass their forebears, Guggenheim lent pieces of antique Venetian glass to the Scuola di Disegno Applicato all'Arte Vetraria (the Murano Design School).

NEW DESIGNS IN VENETIAN GLASSMAKING

In the last quarter of the nineteenth century, designers in Europe and the United States were yielding to the attraction of the budding art nouveau style. However, in Venice the *stabilimenti* discouraged stylistic innovation while prizing technical perfection. The commercial success of Murano's historically inspired, exquisitely crafted glass objects was considered too important to jeopardize.

Salviati's blowers, however, weary of revival forms, capitalized on a Muranese tradition that had persisted for centuries—two free hours at the company furnace at the end of each day's work. There they experimented with new forms and color combinations. Their innovations, glass embellished with swans and dolphins and an occasional serpent, pleased Salviati and the public as well. The *New York Herald* explained in an 1875 article,

> *The workmen toil ten hours a day at the furnace mouth—eight hours for their masters, two for themselves. . . . During the two hours of recreation, which they may apply in study or in working overtime, which is paid separately, if one of the men produces a new idea all cluster round, suggest and criticize.*[39]

Not surprisingly, opposition to the new forms diminished as prosperity returned to the long-impoverished city. Slowly these new designs began to appear in contemporary catalogues alongside more traditional items.

It must have appeared to Layard that Salviati was encouraging his blowers to produce flamboyant glass showcasing their mastery of the art and, in so doing, was violating the original concept of the Anglo-Italian partnership. Layard, it must be noted, was much more than a mere investor. Despite the fact that he was not involved in the day-to-day operation of the firm, he was obsessed with what he believed to be its mission—the resurrection of lost and endangered Renaissance techniques and, that having been accomplished, the recovery of forgotten ancient ones as well. Innovation did not interest him. Salviati, on the other hand, was sympathetic to the frustrations of his workers and sensed a strong market for their new creations.

The same *New York Herald* article also described the organization of the Società Anonima's factory, reporting that the Palazzo da Mula had two furnaces, each with several glory holes. The Barovier family labored at one and the members of the Seguso clan at the other.[40] Both furnaces burned around the clock for ten months and were rebuilt in the summer months. The article effused:

✡ CAT. 3-8
Venice and Murano Glass and Mosaic Company Ltd. (Salviati & Co.), Replica of a Seventeenth-Century Lidded Pokal (*Guggenheim Cup*), ca. 1876–1880s, blown and applied hot-worked glass, 26 × 6 in. diam., Museum of the City of New York, Gift of the Estate of Miss Agnes Miles Carpenter

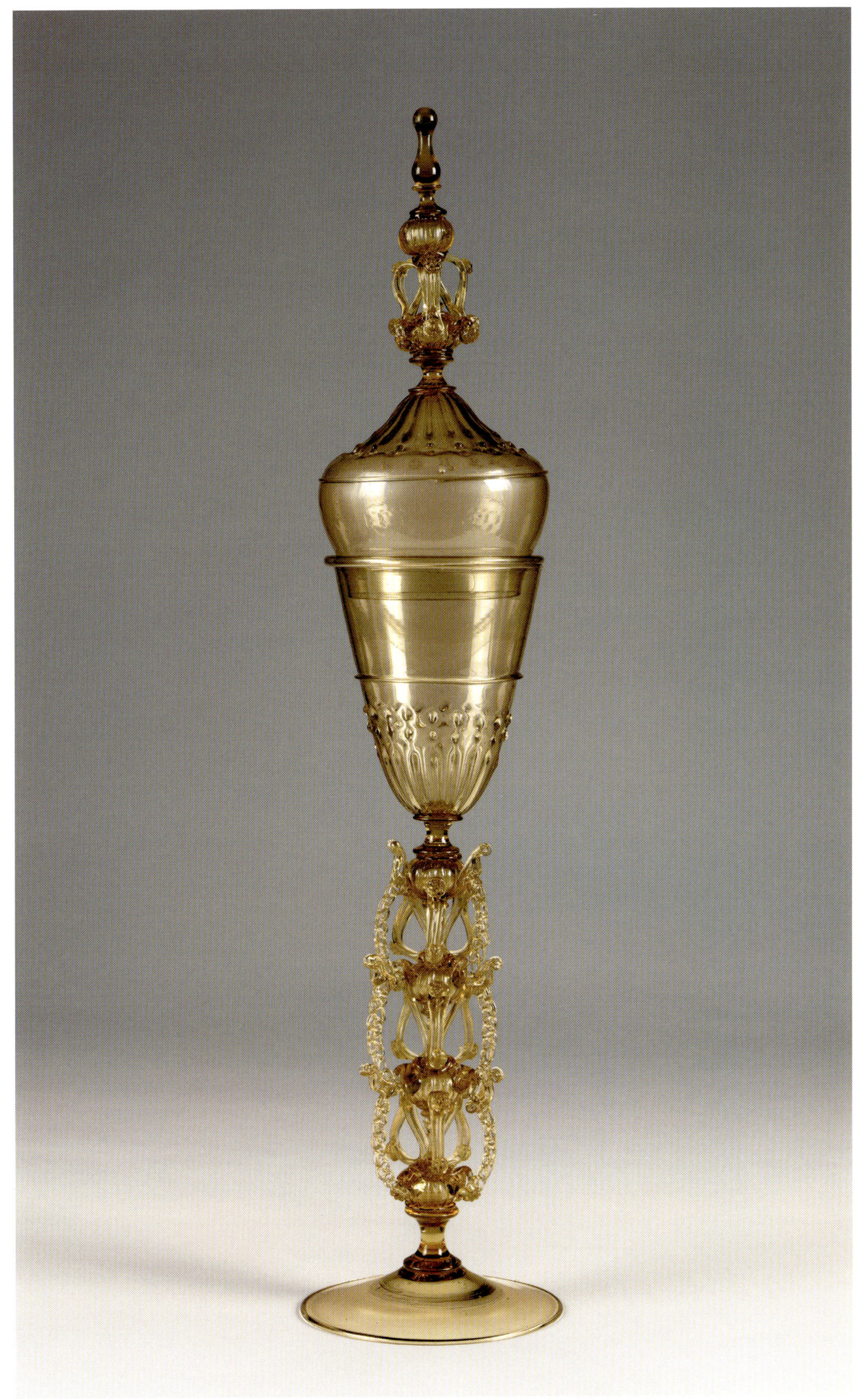

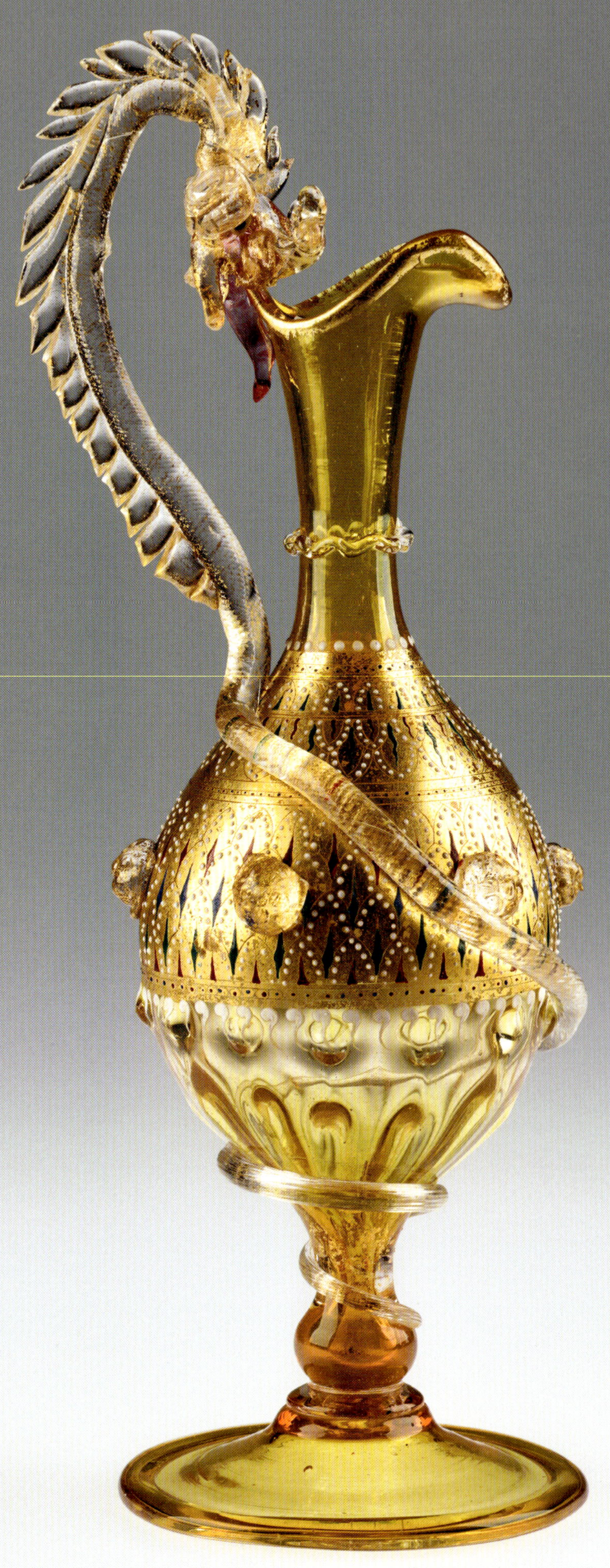

Once a year the furnaces are extinguished, and the men are sent to France, England, and Vienna to see the expositions and art treasures of each country. Any model that strikes their fancy they reproduce from memory on their return, and, of course, any model in drawing or any object that you set before them they copy unhesitatingly and without a flaw.[41]

A bit late, but with unbridled enthusiasm, Venice broke with its artistic traditions and, by incorporating forms and motifs from Japanese art and other cultures, joined the artistic quest most of Europe had been pursuing for decades. With their imaginations stimulated and glassmaking skills challenged, Murano's artisans, synthesizing what they had seen, began to create vessels embellished with exotic hybrid beasts. All the modern and recently recovered historic glassmaking techniques and colors were combined in new ways. A sinuous asymmetry, never before seen in Murano's glass, infiltrated the new production, and fabulous monsters such as imperial dragons of China and Japan began to appear. Venetian artists had created a new and significant body of work—the Venetian expression of the art nouveau style, which won instant popularity. This Ewer with Serpent Handle (CAT. 3-9) manifests the exuberance of Venetian art nouveau.

Commercial success notwithstanding, Salviati's partners were irritated by the fact that the credit for the firm's financial and artistic success always accrued to him. In addition, Layard is reported to have considered Salviati "financially untrustworthy."[42] Therefore, on December 6, 1872, the company's directors decided to anglicize the firm's name to the Venice and Murano Glass and Mosaic Company Ltd. (Salviati & Co.). Several months later, they dropped Salviati's name altogether.[43]

VENETIAN GLASS IN THE UNITED STATES

As part of its continuing marketing efforts in the United States, the Venice and Murano Glass and Mosaic Company Ltd. (hereafter referred to as CVM) took part in Philadelphia's Centennial Exhibition in 1876. Honoring the hundredth anniversary of the ratification of the Declaration of Independence, it hosted exhibitors from thirty-nine countries, including the Kingdom of Italy. James D. McCabe wrote in the catalogue, "Venice sent a number of exquisite examples of her glassware, and also some beautiful mosaics and corals. A prominent feature of this collection consisted of the handsome mirrors of all sizes, which were in the best style of Venetian workmanship."[44] (He did not disclose the names of the companies to which he referred.) It seems that Italy was focusing primarily on mass-produced products like mirrors with the sole objective of fostering their export to the United States.

The Centennial Exhibition inspired a string of fairs throughout the country, and the presence of Venetian glass at these events varied. For example, in the 1885 World's Industrial and Cotton Centennial Exposition in New Orleans, the Kingdom of Italy did not participate with a national pavilion as it had in Philadelphia. However, Italian retailers exhibited independently, and four of their entries in the exhibition's catalogue mention Venetian glass.[45] Subsequent fairs held in Atlanta, Georgia, in 1881 and 1895 were smaller with fewer European

✡ CAT. 3-9
Fratelli Barovier or Compagnia di Venezia e Murano (CVM), Ewer with Serpent Handle, ca. 1870s–90s, blown, gilded, enameled, and applied hot-worked glass, 9 11/16 × 4 in. diam., RISD Museum, Gift of Mrs. Frank Mauran and John O. Ames

exhibitors. Glass companies may have chosen not to participate at these smaller events, since the significant expenditure of money and labor would not have been productive.

COMPETITION SPURS INNOVATION

The expanding appreciation of Venetian glass created an opportunity for growth and may have exacerbated the differences between Salviati and his foreign backers. Ultimately, the partnership was dissolved in 1877. The British bought out Salviati and his son, Giulio. They kept the showrooms in Venice and London, the Palazzo da Mula glassworks on Murano, and all the stock on hand. Members of the Seguso family stayed with the English firm, while the Baroviers left with Salviati.

Consistent with his successful attempt to recover forgotten Renaissance styles and techniques, Layard also decided to resurrect ancient Roman ones. Consequently, before Salviati and his partners severed ties, their glass technicians (Moretti, dalla Venezia, and their collaborators, including Giovanni Barovier) succeeded in re-creating two early forms—Roman cast or slumped glass,[46] which originally dated to the two centuries surrounding the birth of Christ (CAT. 3-10), and "paleochristian" (early Christian) glass, known as *fondo d'oro* or gold glass, which was found in the Roman catacombs.[47] Layard's friend, Alessandro Castellani, is credited with having encouraged Salviati (while he and Layard were still associated) to attempt the recovery of both ancient techniques.[48]

✲ CAT. 3-10

Venice and Murano Glass and Mosaic Company Ltd. (Salviati & Co.) or Compagnia di Venezia e Murano (CVM), Ancient Roman–Style Striped Glass Bowl, ca. 1875–80, hot-worked and slumped glass with applied glass rim, 1 1/16 × 4 3/4 in. diam., Toledo Museum of Art, Gift of Edward Drummond Libbey

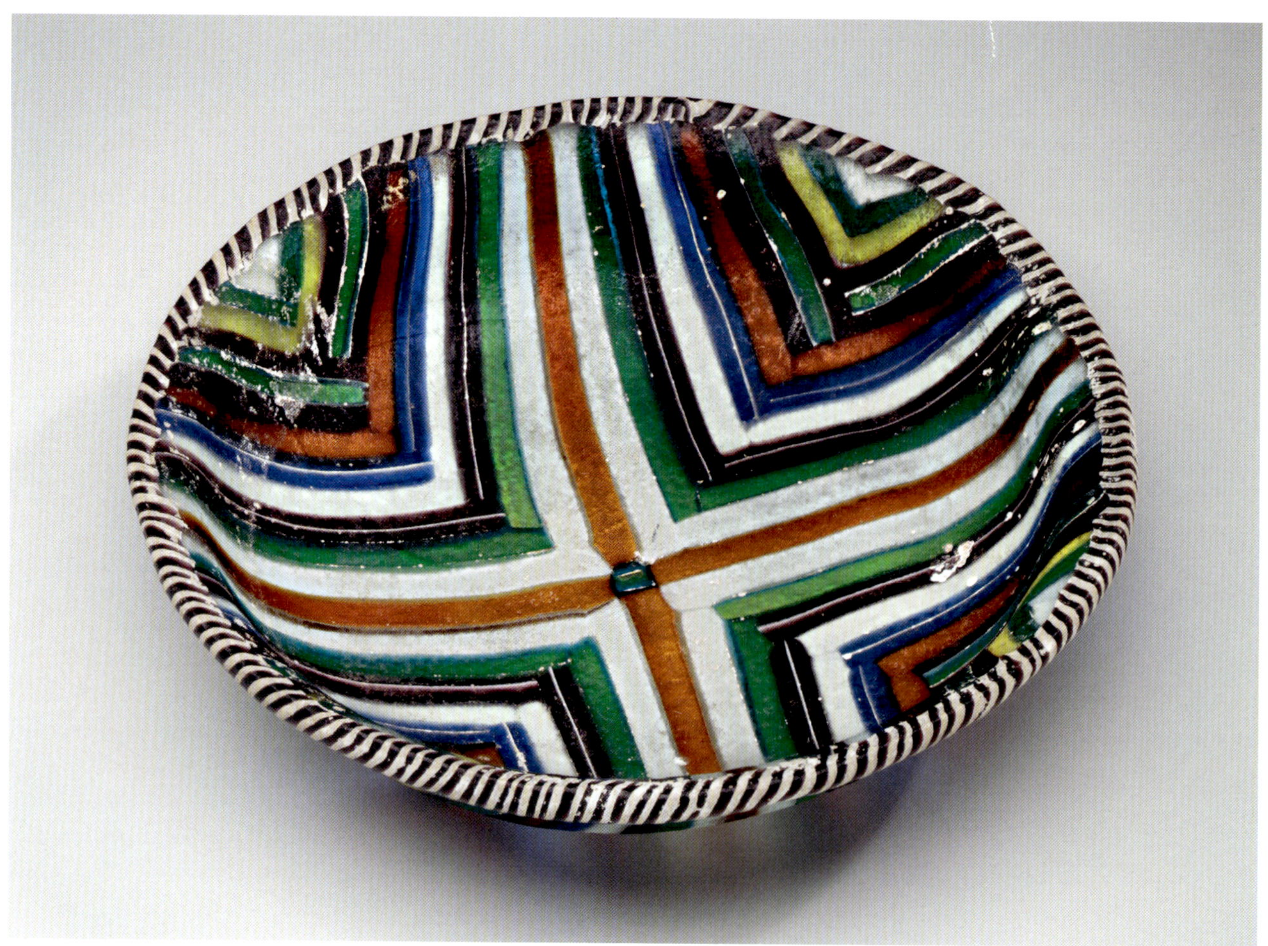

A scant eight months after the separation, the CVM and the new Salviati firm exhibited side by side in the Italian section of the 1878 Exposition Universelle in Paris. The companies had become instant archrivals and competed fiercely not only at this exhibition but also at all the others that followed. Both exhibited examples of mosaics, furniture with glass inlay, candelabra, sconces, mirrors, chandeliers, and blown glass vessels.

Since neither company had had sufficient time to develop an individual style, critics found their displays in Paris too much alike. The similarity was probably because the Segusos, working at the CVM, and the Baroviers, now at the Salviati Dott. Antonio furnace, continued to produce their traditional products for a time. Furthermore, the CVM kept all the stock on hand after buying out the Salviatis, including, we must assume, pieces created by the Baroviers.

The CVM exhibited forty-six examples of the Roman-style cast glass that frequently used the same Moretti/dalla Venezia murrhines used in their earlier Pompeiian pieces. The critics in Paris received them with ecstatic acclaim. All were sold, "purchased for handsome sums by the most eminent persons of knowledge, learning and wealth, and further copies had to be made for the demand far exceeded the quantities available."[49] A member of the Rothschild family purchased an example of cast glass for 4,500 lire, an enormous sum at the time.[50]

In Paris, Salviati also presented his firm's versions of ancient Roman glass. These vessels, made by the Baroviers, were ignored by the critics, probably due to their late arrival at the fair. Although the Baroviers' pieces were almost identical to the *vetro murrine* works by the CVM, they were blown and can be identified by the presence of a pontil mark. Examples were donated to the Glass Museum, where they can be seen today.[51]

The firm of Fratelli Toso, a rare participant at international expositions, exhibited a selection of blown glass for the first time since 1864. They were made by Giovanni Toso, a nephew of Gregorio Toso, one of the company's founders and its first manager. The maestro, formerly a student at the Murano Design School, presented reproductions of antique glass and a few items of his own design, most of which were donated to the Glass Museum after the exhibition ended.[52] The firm undoubtedly exhibited its signature production of candelabra and chandeliers, which it sold to the various Venetian *stabilimenti*, including Salviati's.

Tiffany & Co. also took part in the Paris exposition. Its jewelry won a gold medal, its silverware garnered the Grand Prix, and Charles Lewis Tiffany was appointed Chevalier de la Légion d'Honneur. Tiffany was probably alerted to his imminent award and attended the event in person.

Tiffany bought large quantities of modern Venetian glass in Paris to resell in his stores in the United States. His purchase included "Salviati's latest reproductions of the Venetian Glass of the sixteenth century," now dubbed ***soffiato***, and the firm's newly introduced iridescent *metalliformi* glass. Tiffany & Co. incorrectly advertised the *metalliformi* pieces in the *Art Interchange* as "Facsimiles of the Trojan iridescent bronze glass exhumed by Dr. [Heinrich] Schliemann."[53] Nevertheless, Salviati must have been delighted with Tiffany's purchase. To have his new company associated with one of the leading retailers of luxury goods in the United States was a dream come true.

Fig. 3-4
Salviati & Co., Verreries–Mosaïques, ca. 1920–24, printed postcard, Private collection

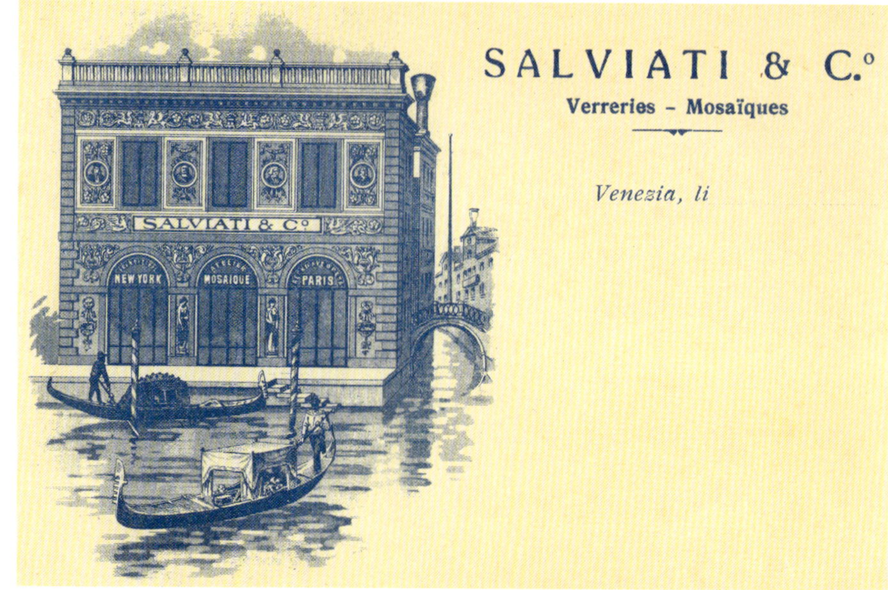

After the Paris expo, the CVM continued as Murano's largest glassmaking establishment with a permanent staff of forty or fifty people. Salviati opened a glass-blowing factory on Murano named Salviati Dott. Antonio and bought a smaller palazzo on the Grand Canal that he renovated into his own two-story showroom simply named Salviati e Compagnia. To attract the multitudes of Venice's tourists to his new location, he opened another showroom on St. Mark's Square and published postcards and pamphlets depicting this location and later canal-front headquarters for his growing glass empire (Fig. 3-4). In 1883 he launched a shop in Paris at 17, rue de la Paix, where he exhibited blown glass and mosaics.[54]

That same year, at age sixty-seven, Salviati decided to withdraw from the manufacturing division of the business. Because the Baroviers had been working semi-independently at the Murano works since 1878 (under the name of Fratelli Barovier), Salviati rented the premises to them and sold them all the glassmaking equipment. They continued to supply the Salviati shops and its agents with blown glass. They also agreed to keep the name of Salviati Dott. Antonio until 1895, when they changed it to Artisti Barovier.

In 1893 the CVM mounted an impressive display in Chicago at the World's Columbian Exhibition. On a fifteen-thousand-square-foot lot on the Midway Plaisance,[55] the firm erected a green and gold Venetian Gothic–style palazzo embellished with mosaics of its own manufacture. Inside, the company set up an exhibition furnace where blown glass was made and sold. Mosaic workers (many of them women) fabricated mosaics with smalti brought from Murano. Many of the firm's glassblowers, their assistants, and the mosaic workers had relocated to Chicago for the duration of the fair. Using raw materials and tools imported from Venice, they produced, according to a description by the fair's organizers,

> *Reproductions of the very best pieces now collected in the museums and treasuries of churches in Europe, art gems of world-wide celebrity, graffiti, murrhines, cameo glasses, diatretes, Christian plates, oriental, renaissance, filigree and lace works, etched and frosted glass, avventurina, sapphire, corniola, agate, topaz, jasper, onyx, amethyst, jacinth.*[56]

That is, they created the CVM's entire glass repertoire. As a result, the company was able to offer an additional savings to the American public. Since the objects were made in the United States, the 60 percent import duty to which they would have normally been subject was waived. An admission fee of twenty-five cents, refundable with a purchase, was charged. For this the CVM cited as precedent the Paris fair of 1889 wherein, "the rush of people was so great . . . that nobody could see anything, consequently they had been obliged . . . to charge an admittance fee."[57] On artistic merits, the glass made at the fair was far inferior to that produced on Murano itself, functioning merely as souvenirs of the event rather than fine art.[58]

At this point, the Venetian glass revival was no longer the hobby of men like Layard, but rather it had become the legitimate profession of artists, craftspeople, investors, and entrepreneurs as well as an extremely important source of income for the city in the lagoon.

COURTING AMERICAN COLLECTORS

In addition to their ambitious artistry and keen international marketing, Italian companies also courted American connoisseurs, many of whom had been beguiled by Venetian glass at expositions in the United States and American retailers such as Tiffany & Co. Some were lucky enough to have traveled to or lived in Venice, where they could see the furnaces and showrooms firsthand.

Many of the most influential went on to donate their collections of Venetian glass to major American museums or even to found their own. Here we consider two major collectors, James Jackson Jarves, who made an important donation of Venetian glass to the Metropolitan Museum of Art, and Jane Elizabeth Lathrop Stanford, whose private museum in Palo Alto, California, houses one of the most important Venetian glass collections in the country. These and other leading American collectors and their associated museums helped cement widespread appreciation for the artistic value of Venetian glass in the United States.

JAMES JACKSON JARVES

Massachusetts-born journalist James Jackson Jarves moved to Italy in 1851 and settled in Florence, where he began his career as a builder of art collections, focusing primarily on early Renaissance Italian artists. From 1880 to 1882, Jarves served as the vice-consul for the United States in Florence. Because his father, Deming Jarves, had founded the Boston and Sandwich Glass Company in Massachusetts in 1825,[59] James's interest in glass was likely inevitable. In Italy, he began accumulating Italian and Venetian glass of all periods with the help of Zanetti.

In 1881 Jarves attempted to sell his collection of 280 pieces of glass to New York's Metropolitan Museum of Art. When that failed, he decided to donate the entire glass collection to the museum.[60] The Met accepted the "Jarves Gift," as Jarves requested that it be known, on April 25, 1881.

Jarves had intended his collection to exhibit the history of Italian glassmaking. However, because it was assembled in a short period of time, growing from 50 to 280 pieces in a matter of months, the collection abounds in examples from the late nineteenth century obtained from both Salviati and the CVM.[61] Regarding his gift, Jarves admitted in *Harper's Monthly Magazine*,

> *Specimens of the two earlier periods [the early and later Renaissance] are not easily found now; consequently, the decadence and revival or modern period are more conspicuously represented than the ancient.*[62]

The Jarves Gift is undoubtedly the most important collection of Venetian glass in the United States. He assembled it in the formative years of the revival, and it contains several nineteenth-century masterpieces, such as Leopoldo Bearzotti's enameled goblet (see p. 43) and the mosaic glass funerary urn (see p. 113).

Jarves's promotion of Venetian glass did not end with his gift to the Met and the article in *Harper's.* When he learned of the American Exhibition of the Products, Arts, and Manufactures of Foreign Nations (1883–84) in Boston, he encouraged Italian firms to take part. Several did. As listed in the official catalogue, the firm of Doctor Antonio Salviati exhibited "artistic glass," consisting of blown glass, mirrors, candelabra, enameled and imitation antique glass, and ancient- and modern-style monumental mosaics, including its new portrait of US President James A. Garfield (see p. 106).

THE STANFORD FAMILY

In the early 1880s, California railroad magnate Leland Stanford, his wife Jane, and their son Leland Jr. visited Salviati's shop in Venice to purchase glass. They began a relationship with Maurizio Camerino, the firm's young, English-speaking director.[63] Sadly, a family tragedy sealed their friendship. As Camerino wrote in 1917,

> *I met Mr. and Mrs. Stanford and their son when they came to visit my business place and the glass works. I became a good friend of the Stanford family and was always with them during their stay in Venice. They went to Florence and it was there that their son fell ill and unfortunately died [on March 13, 1884]. Mr. and Mrs. Stanford called me at once to Florence and I assisted them in everything I could possibly do during their great misfortune.*[64]

In 1885 the bereaved Stanfords consoled themselves by founding the Leland Stanford Junior University on the grounds of their eight-thousand-acre horse farm in Palo Alto. They also built a museum focusing on his interests and bought collections of Greek antiquities and Cypriot pottery. Housed in a neoclassical building of reinforced concrete, it opened to the public in 1894.

When Leland Stanford Sr. died in 1893, financial complications postponed the groundbreaking of a Memorial Church planned as the focus of the university campus.[65] Soon after the 1899 groundbreaking, Jane Stanford returned to the Salviati shop in Venice and informed Camerino that she wished to embellish the church with mosaic decoration. Together they viewed the mosaics on the maritime facade of the Palazzo Barbarigo (the CVM's *stabilimento*) and went to Paris to view the Salviati mosaics on the ceiling of the *avant-foyer* of the Opéra. Jane Stanford had developed an interest in mosaics during an 1883 grand tour of Europe, which included visits to St. Mark's in Venice and Byzantine churches in Constantinople.[66]

In 1900 Jane Stanford returned to the Salviati shop in Venice. She discussed her church project with Camerino and asked him to create a mosaic copy of Cosimo Rosselli's *Last Supper* fresco in Rome's Sistine Chapel. Camerino obtained the special permission of Pope Leo XIII to reproduce the mosaic. Because it was made to be seen up close, it was executed in tesserae much finer than mosaics installed later. Two of the firm's artisans traveled with the mural to California and labored for months to assemble it behind the church's main altar.[67]

Delighted with the *Last Supper* mosaic, Jane Stanford met with Camerino in Florence in November to discuss a second but much larger mosaic for the exterior gable of the church. When the proposal was completed, Camerino met with her again, and she promptly approved the latest design. Except the *Last Supper*, all the mosaics in and on the church were designed by the Italian artist Antonio Ermolao Paoletti.[68]

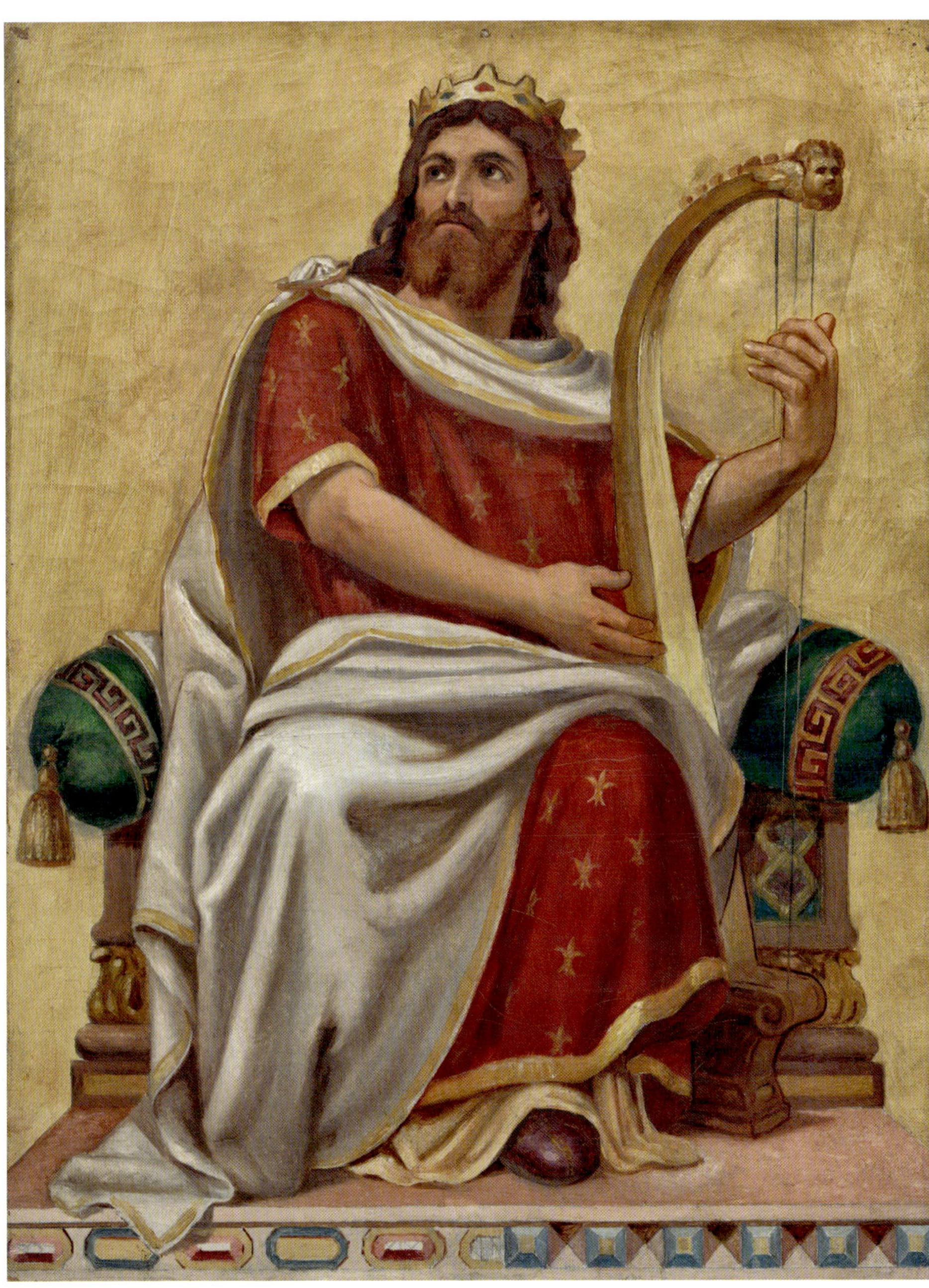

✲ CAT. 3-11

Attributed to Antonio Ermolao Paoletti, Study for *David* Mosaic in Stanford Memorial Chapel, ca. 1903–5, oil on canvas, 21 ½ × 16 ½ in., Stanford University Libraries, Department of Special Collections

In February of 1903 Camerino visited California for the first time. He brought Paoletti's plans for the eight rectangular allegoric mosaics for the facade of the museum and additional proposals for the church interior. Jane Stanford approved them all. Paoletti's study (**CAT. 3-11**) for the Byzantine-style mosaic of King David is preserved in the Stanford University Archives. Later in 1903, the firm donated about two hundred pieces of glass to the museum.

After his return to Venice, Camerino fulfilled his longtime ambition to own his own business and joined Salviati's son, Silvio, to establish a successor company, Erede Dr. A. Salviati & Co.[69] The firm kept the Salviati e Compagnia showroom and the branches and agents in other countries. It continued buying blown glass and mosaic smalti from Artisti Barovier and others, and its chandeliers and lamps from Fratelli Toso. The firm was immediately charged with completing the Stanford commission. It reportedly deferred all other mosaic work in order finish the project on time.[70]

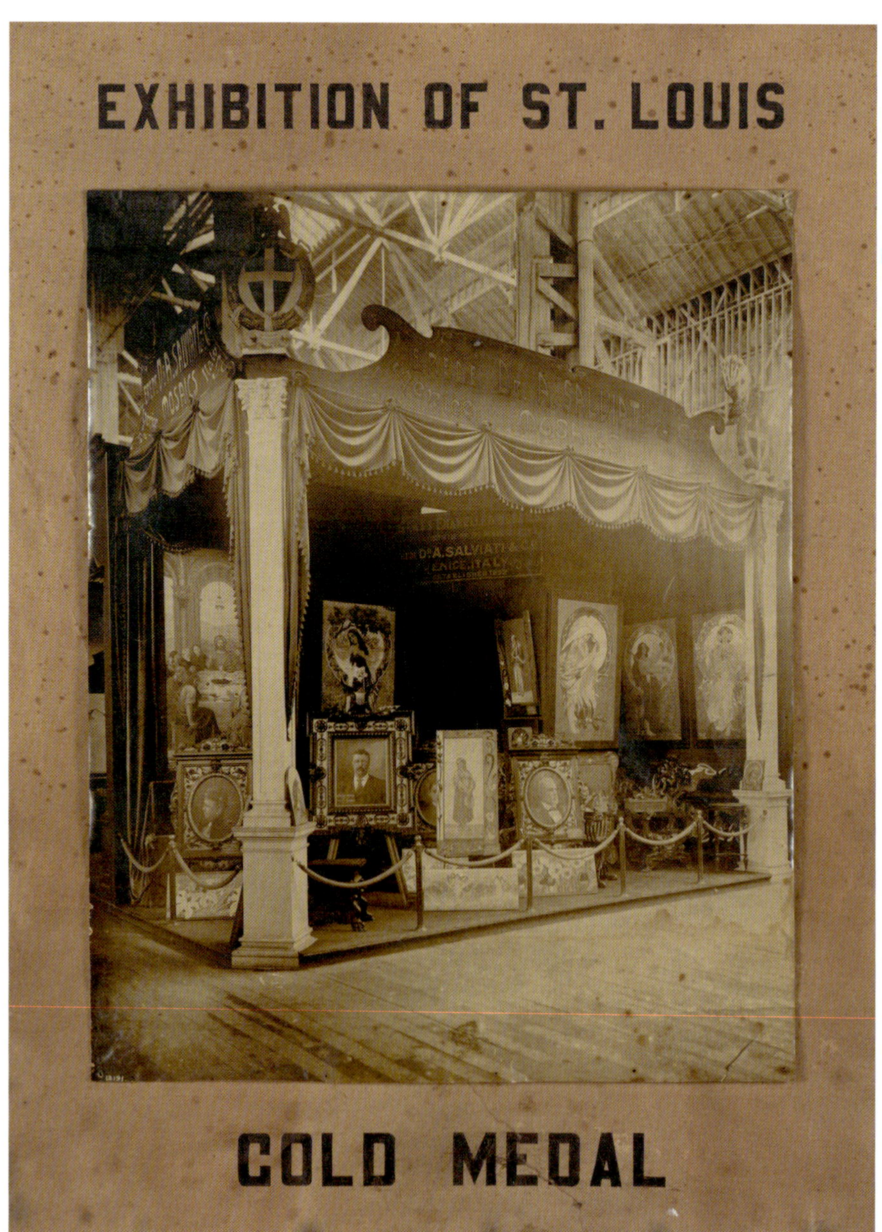

Fig. 3-5
Erede Dr. A. Salviati & Co. mosaics stall at the Louisiana Purchase Exposition, St. Louis, Missouri, 1904, gelatin silver print mounted on paper, 15 ¾ × 13 in., The Corning Museum of Glass, Rakow Research Library Special Collections

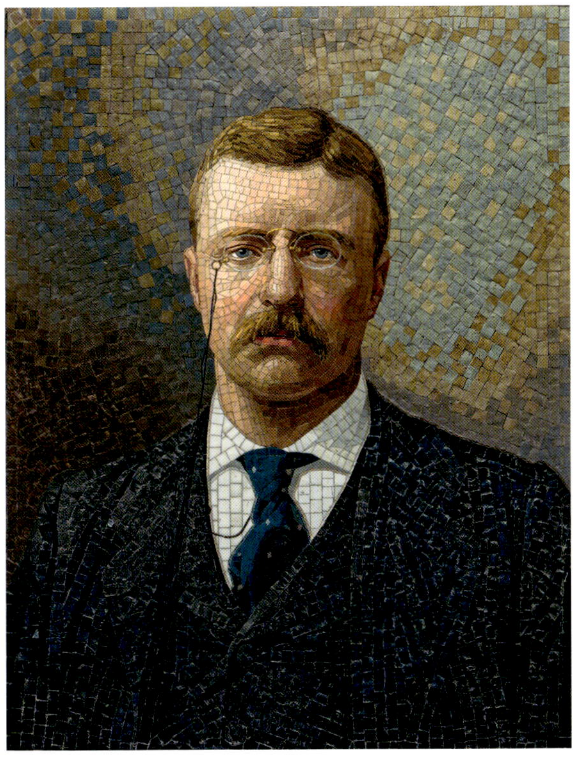

✡ CAT. 3-12
Erede Dr. A. Salviati & Co., ***Portrait of Theodore Roosevelt***, ca. 1904, glass mosaic tiles and cement, 24 ⅝ × 19 ⅛ in., The Corning Museum of Glass

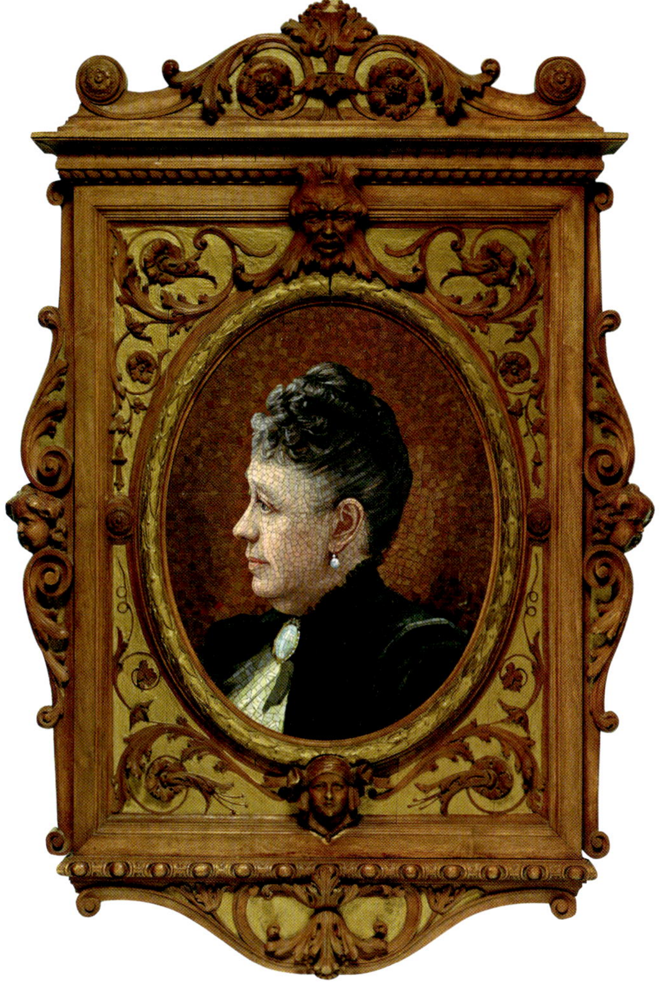

✡ CAT. 3-13
Dott. Antonio Salviati & C. or Erede Dr. A. Salviati & Co., ***Portrait of Jane Lathrop Stanford***, ca. 1902, glass mosaic tiles, 21 ½ × 16 ⅝ in., Iris and B. Gerald Cantor Center for Visual Arts at Stanford University, Gift of Erede Dr. A. Salviati & Co.

Despite the massive, ongoing commission, the company continued its promotion of mosaics in the United States by participating in the Louisiana Purchase Exposition in St. Louis, Missouri, in 1904. Erede Dr. A. Salviati set up two exhibits, one for blown glass, chandeliers, and mirrors, and the other for an extensive display of mosaics. A photograph of the Salviati booth for mosaics at this fair (Fig. 3-5) shows a portrait of US President Theodore Roosevelt (CAT. 3-12), three portraits of Stanford family members, including Jane (CAT. 3-13), three art nouveau Alphonse Mucha–style figures, and a religious panel.[71]

Attesting to the success of the Venetian glass revival, several rival Venetian companies exhibited. Francesco Toso Borella introduced a copy of the fifteenth-century enameled and gilded *Campanile Cup* (CAT. 3-14).[72] Fratelli Toso brought glass in the "modern art nouveau style," and the Testolini firm exhibited vessels purchased from or consigned by the CVM.

During the exposition, Camerino visited California for a second time to deliver additional designs for the church mosaics. Jane Stanford approved them

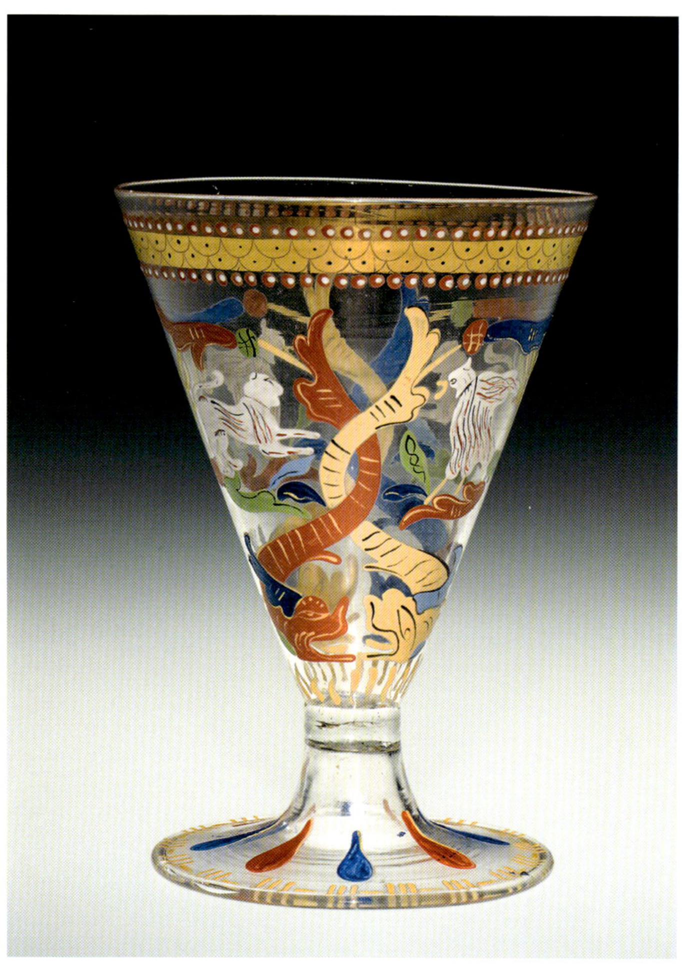

☆ CAT. 3-14
Compagnia di Venezia e Murano (CVM), Replica of a Renaissance Goblet (*Campanile Cup*), ca. 1903–12, blown, enameled, and gilded glass, 5 ⅝ × 4 ⅛ in. diam., The Corning Museum of Glass

all. When the Missouri show ended, Camerino donated eighty more blown glass vessels to the Stanford museum.[73] It is likely that Camerino decided to donate the *unsold* items to the museum. Leaving unsold items behind was not unusual for foreign exhibitors, given that the cost of shipping them back to their countries of origin was prohibitive. Camerino's gift is rich in rare types of glass such as *calcedonio*, ***smelze***, and ***scavo*** that were either sent to St. Louis in large numbers or did not appeal to the American public and therefore went unsold.

The Stanford museum's blown glass collection was exhibited in its Venetian Room, which was embellished with Venetian chandeliers and five mosaic portraits of the extended Stanford family, including Jane herself.[74] The church's mosaic installation was completed in 1905. In February of that year, Jane Stanford died mysteriously in Hawaiʻi.

On the morning of April 18, 1906, a powerful earthquake struck the San Francisco area. South of the city, the Stanford University complex was devastated. More than two-thirds of the museum collapsed, and much of its glass collection was destroyed. The recently completed church met a similar fate.

Original mosaic fragments, preserved in the Stanford University Archives and other collections, attest to the beauty of these decorations and the complexity of their iconographic program. For example, a triangular chunk now in the Corning Museum of Glass collection (CAT. 3-15), originally from the narthex, features two interlocking symbols, an alpha and an omega (the first and last letters of the Greek alphabet). In situ, it alternated with a Chi Rho, the first two letters in the Greek spelling of Christ. Compared to the figurative mosaics of the church, the two walls appeared purely ornamental, but they conveyed spiritual meaning. Most of the shattered mosaics were discarded, but this fragment, probably rescued by a souvenir hunter or a worker, has survived.

After a lengthy hesitation, the university trustees decided to restore the church. In November 1913, Camerino visited the university campus for the third time to assess the damage. The original cartoons for the mosaics were preserved in the Salviati workrooms in Venice, so identical replacement mosaics were ordered. With the signing of the contract, 170 more blown glass vessels were presented to the museum to replace those destroyed by the earthquake.

A total of 450 pieces of blown glass were given to Stanford in 1903, 1904, and 1913. Today 244 survive in the enlarged museum. This important collection provides a unique record of late nineteenth- and early twentieth-century Venetian glass production. It includes some of the finest extant examples of *calcedonio* and *smelze* (CAT. 3-16), as well as a group of superb mosaic glass vases and numerous examples of art nouveau glass embellished with fabulous creatures.[75] The production of the Barovier family dominates the collection, but vessels from Fratelli Toso and the CVM are also present.

The Stanford collection is probably the largest collection of nineteenth-century Venetian glass in the United States, but its importance is overshadowed by the Met's Jarves Gift. Most of Stanford's collection is not on view and is housed in an earthquake-proof steel safe in the museum's basement. The Met's collection had not been on view since a 1938 hurricane destroyed a good deal of it. In 2019 the Met's curator put several important Jarves Gift vessels on display.

THE LEGACY OF THE GLASS REVIVAL

Global events brought an abrupt hiatus to Venice's glass revival when Italy entered World War I on the side of France and Britain. Virtually on the front lines, Venice was shelled by the Austro-German army, and local industries came to a standstill. Many glass factories closed and relocated to Livorno or Naples. By this time, some of the individual glass artisans began working more independently of the Salviati and CVM marketing network, building their own name recognition. Both

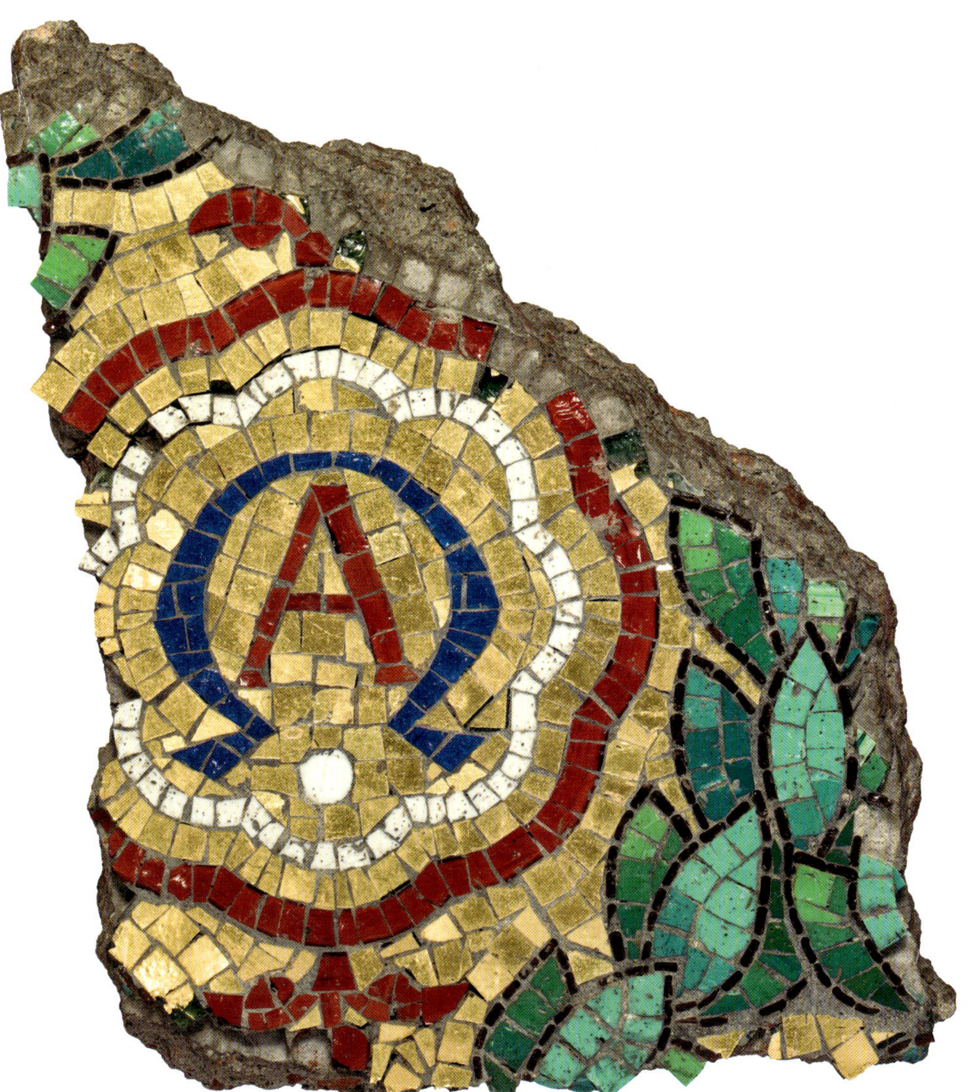

✡ CAT. 3-15
Erede Dr. A. Salviati & Co., Fragment from Stanford Memorial Church Mosaic Cycle, ca. 1903–5, glass mosaic tiles and cement on sandstone with gold foil, 11 7/16 × 9 ½ × 2 15/16 in., The Corning Museum of Glass, Gift of Sheldon Barr and Thomas Gardner

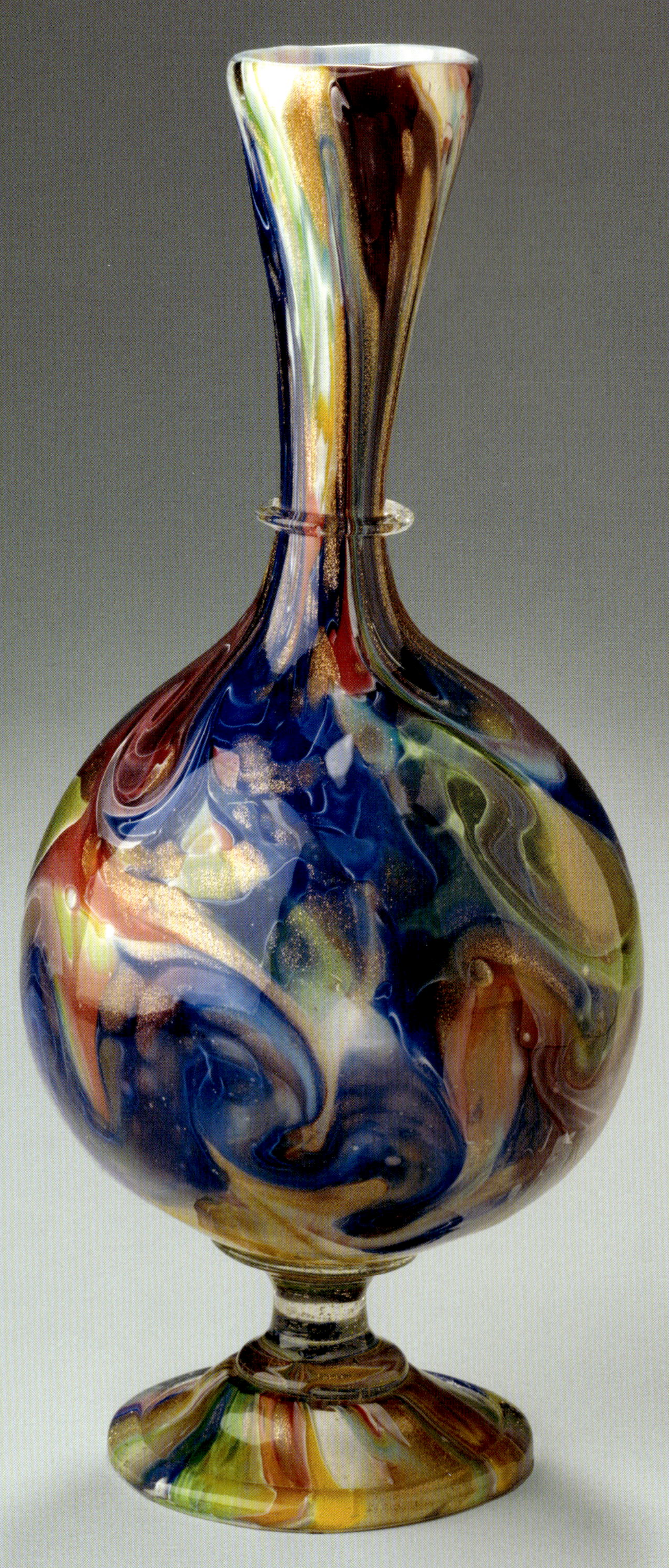

of the epoch's great entrepreneurial luminaries, Antonio Salviati and Sir Austen Henry Layard, had by this time died, along with their beneficial rivalry.

It is no exaggeration to say the Murano glass revival carried the glass industry into the modern epoch. In the course of a sixty-year period, the forgotten techniques of two millennia were recovered, and new ways of manipulating glass were invented and perfected.

In the 1930s, when Murano's glassmakers began producing a heavier, more sculptural glass, they were equipped with an unrivaled repertoire of technical expertise. American taste for Venetian glass followed these trends, and collecting continued. At the forefront of art glass production for many years, Murano's glass masters became icons for young ambitious glass artists, many of whom passed on centuries-old traditions and thus secured the survival of their craft for centuries to come.

GLOSSARY OF TERMS

Aventurine: Glass that imitates the aventurine mineral. Originating in 1400s Venice, aventurine glass includes gold, copper, or chromic oxide.

Fenicio: Italian for "Phoenician." A decorative technique in which the glass surface is brushed with a tool to produce a pattern of waves or festoons.

Fragole: Glass ornamentation in the shape of berries.

Millefiori: Italian for "thousand flowers." Glass made from slices of canes that are fused together to form distinctive flower patterns.

Morise: Small crests produced with pliers that glassmakers use to pinch applied glass decoration into a serrated pattern.

Murrhine: Discs cut from glass canes that are used to form designs in other glass works.

Scavo: Italian for "excavation." A process of acid etching and/or the hot fusing of a siliceous crust to the surface of a vessel to mimic the appearance of ancient, excavated glass.

Smalti: Italian for "enamel." The glass used in mosaic production, whether colored or metallic.

Smelze: A fused mass of glass of different colors, often including bits of aventurine.

Soffiato: Italian for "blown." Sixteenth-century-style glass that is extremely lightweight in very simple shapes and colors.

Stabilimento: A showroom or factory.

Vetro a fili: Italian for "glass with threads." Blown glass with patterns that form parallel lines, which are made from glass canes.

Vetro a retorti: Italian for "glass with twists." Blown glass with spiral patterns made from twisted canes. Sometimes called "zanfirico."

✲ CAT. 3-16
Artisti Barovier or Compagnia di Venezia e Murano (CVM), Smelze Glass Vase, ca. 1890–1904, blown and applied hot-worked glass, 9 ¾ × 3 ¾ in. diam., Iris & B. Gerald Cantor Center for Visual Arts at Stanford University, Gift of Erede Dr. A. Salviati & Co.

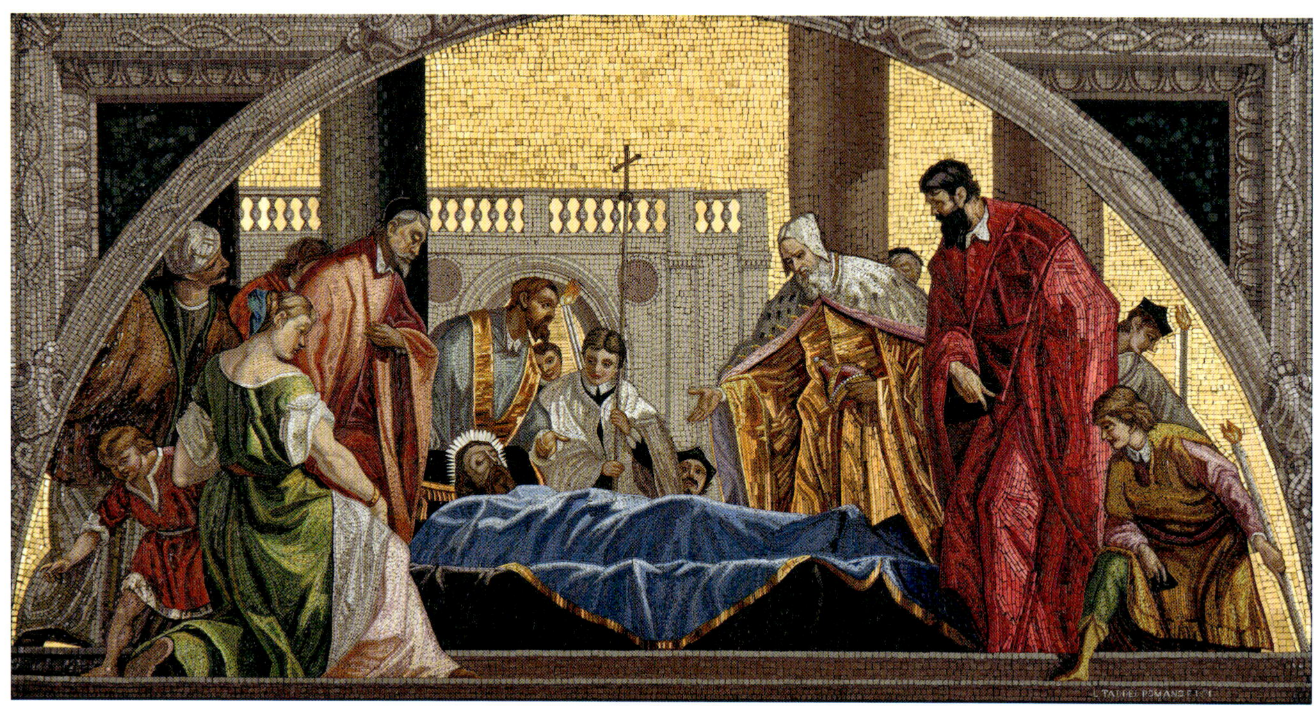

✲ CAT. 3-17
Luigi Taddei, ***St. Mark's Body Venerated by the Doge***, 1871, glass mosaic tiles, 16 × 32 in., Collection of Vincent and Kako Crisci

✲ CAT. 3-18
Società Anonima per Azioni Salviati & C., Replica in Glass of a Byzantine Chalice (*Chalice of Emperor Romanos II*), ca. 1870, blown, enameled, and gilded glass, 8 3/16 × 6 5/16 in. diam., The Walters Art Museum, Acquired by Henry Walters

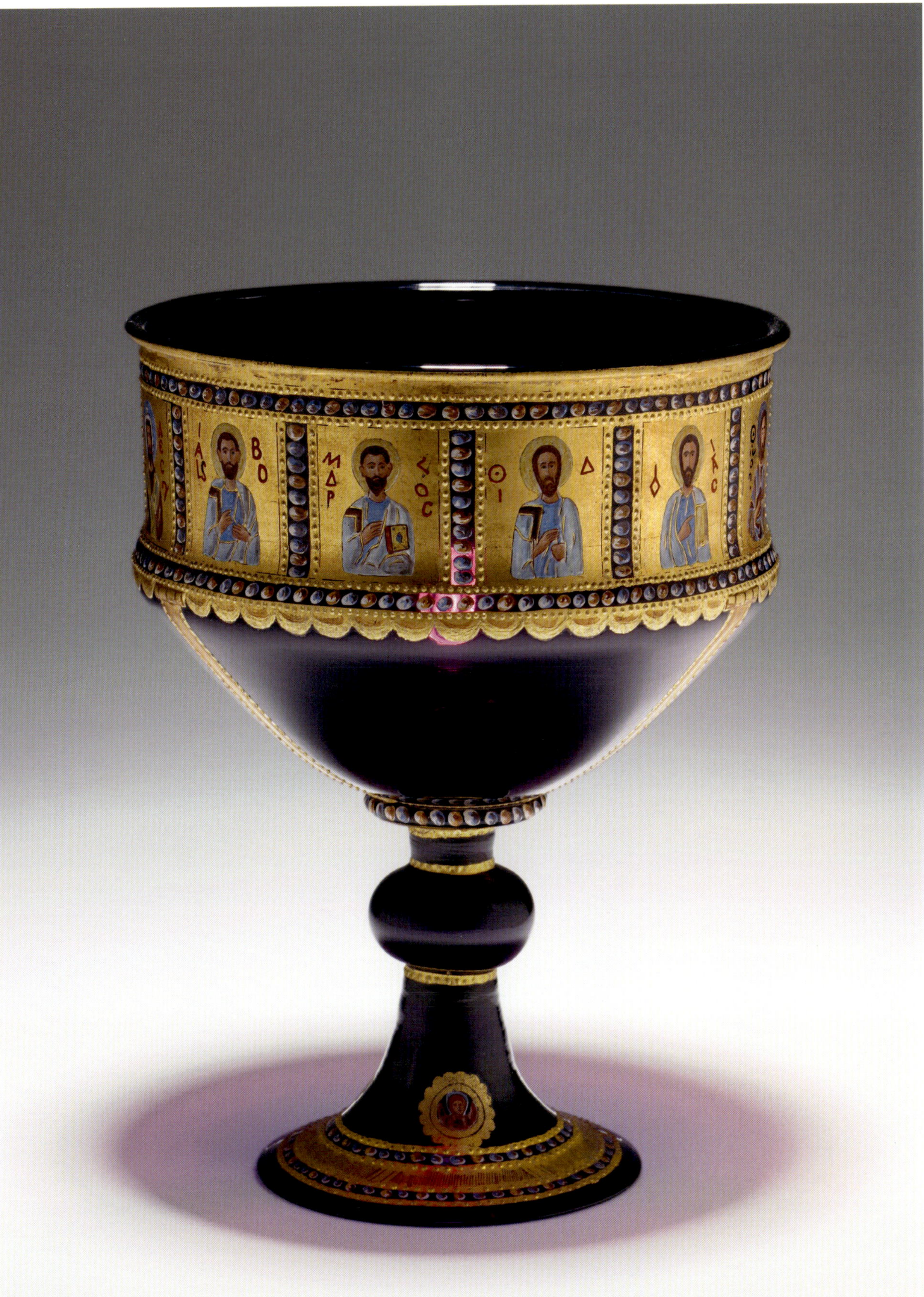

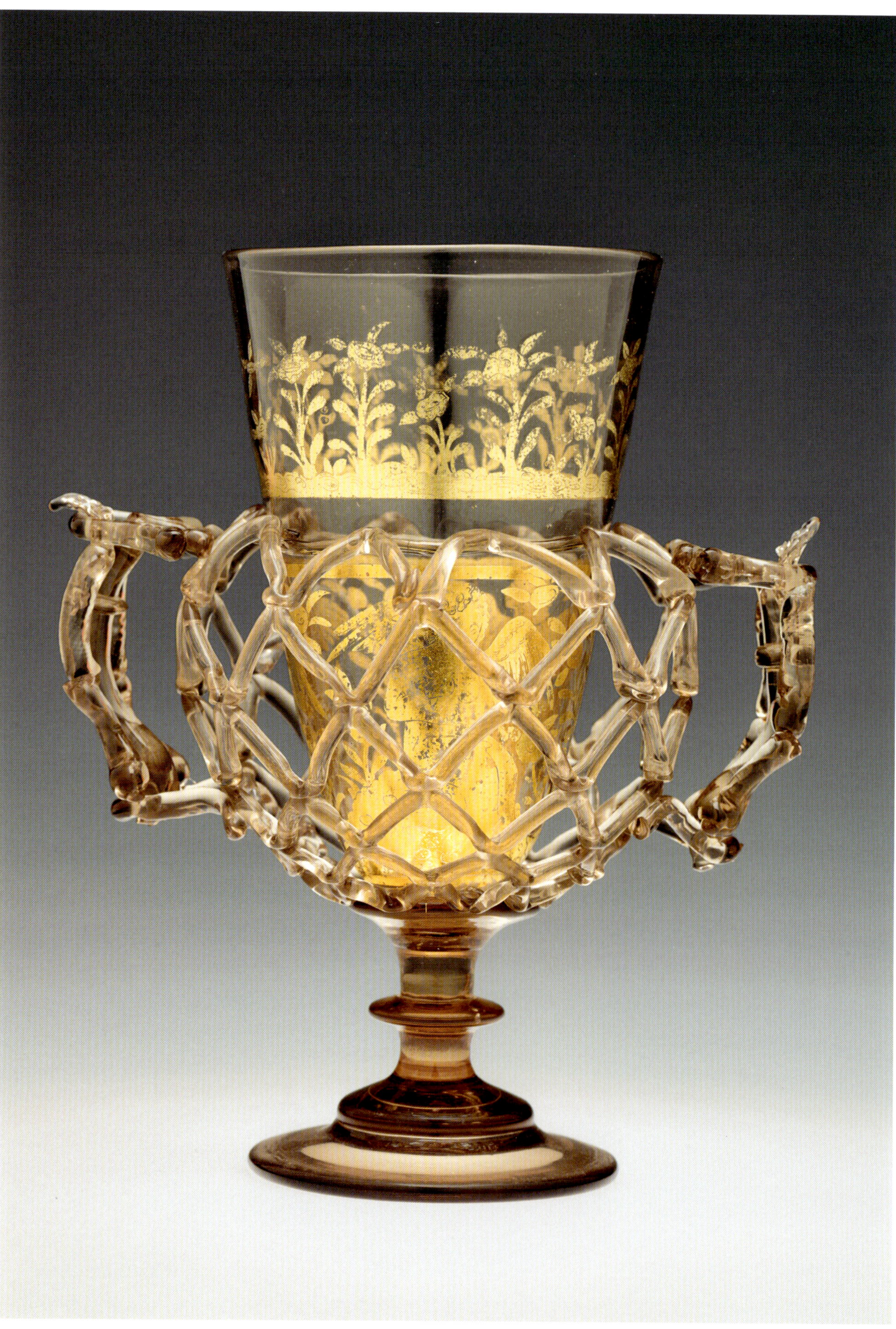

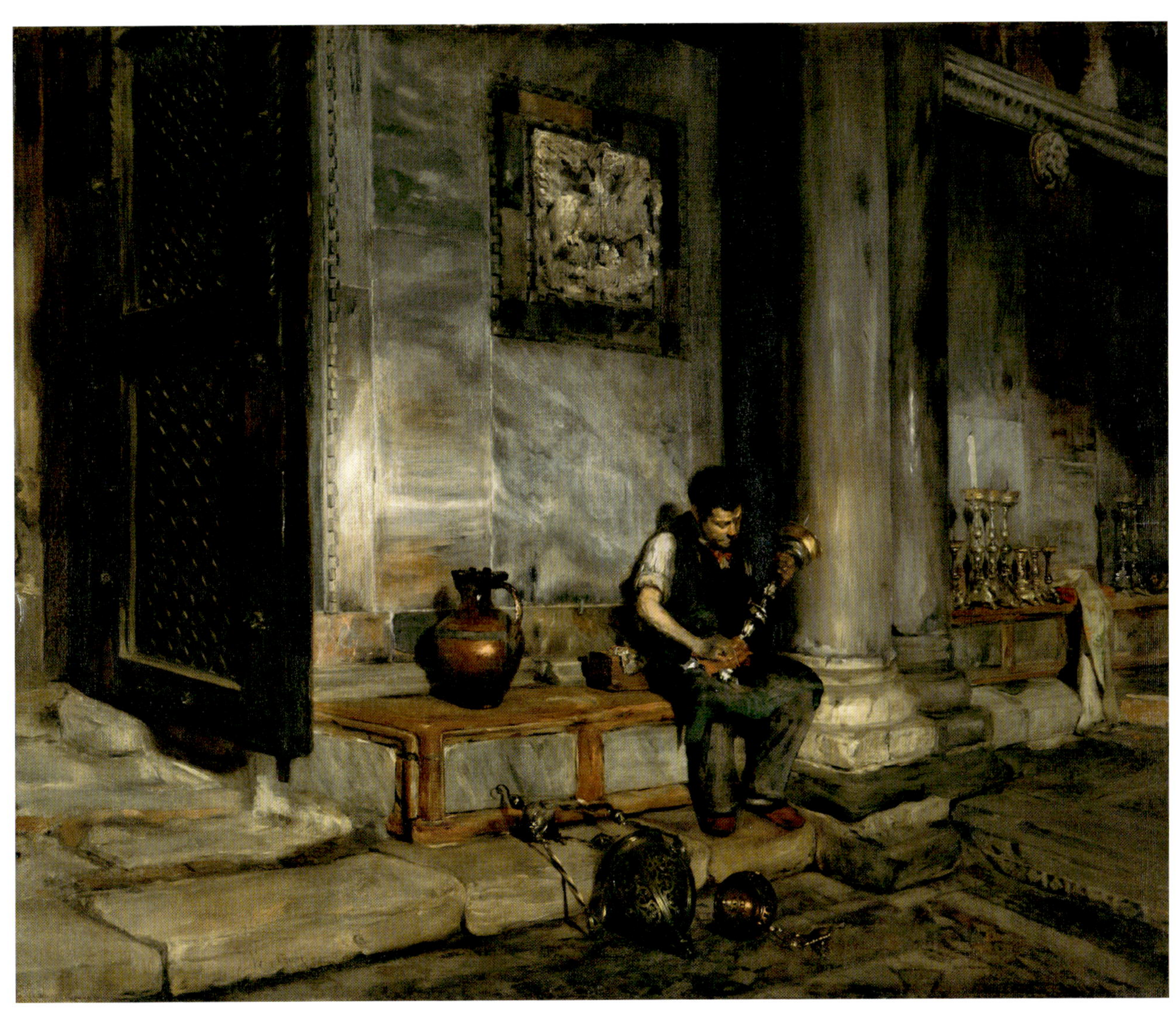

✡ CAT. 3-19
Compagnia di Venezia e Murano (CVM) or Salviati Dott. Antonio, Replica of an Ancient Roman Diatreta or Cage Cup (*Disch-Sangiorgi Cantharus*), ca. 1880s–90s, blown, gilded, and applied hot-worked glass, 7 × 6 3/16 in. diam., RISD Museum, Gift of Mrs. Frank Mauran and John O. Ames

✡ CAT. 3-20
William Merritt Chase, *In the Baptistry of St. Mark's, Venice*, 1878, oil on canvas, 33 ½ × 43 ½ in., North Carolina Museum of Art, Raleigh, Gift of Marcia Bishopric Gest in memory of Joseph Henry Gest and Henry Gest Jr.

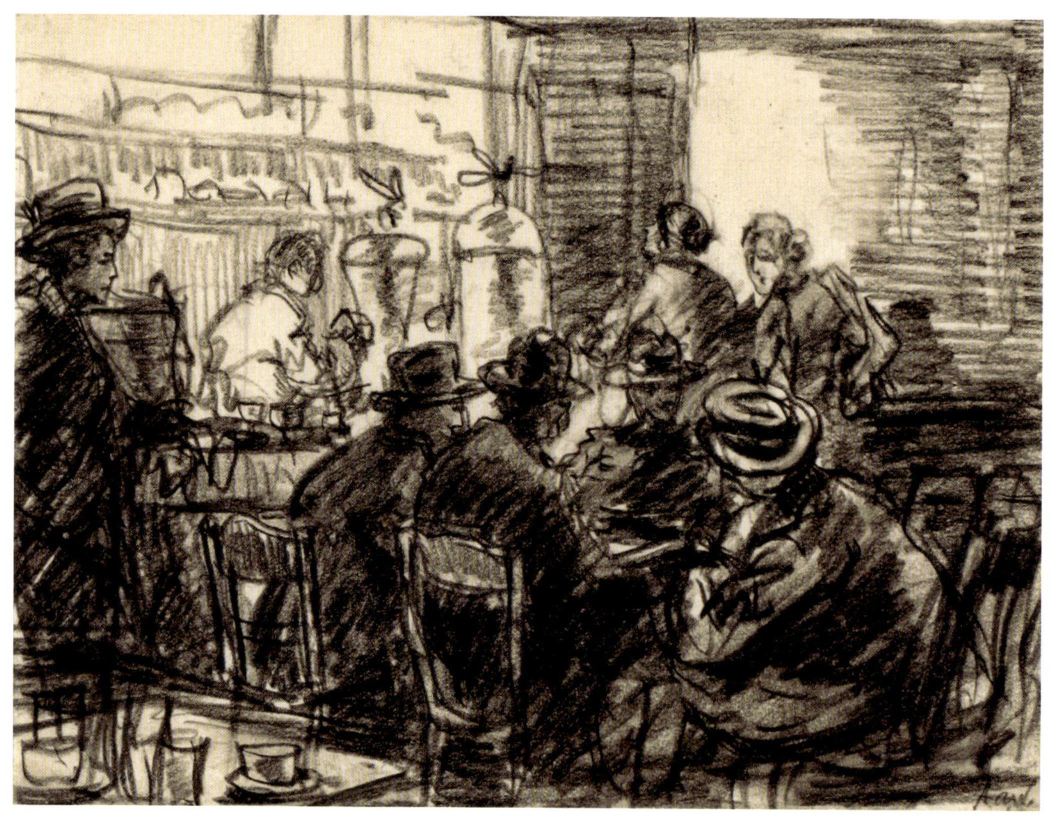

✲ CAT. 3-21

Herman Armour Webster, *To the Caffetteria—Capuccino's Time, Venice Zattere*, 1935, carbon pencil on paper, 5 ¼ × 7 in., Smithsonian American Art Museum, Gift of Moune G. H. Webster

✲ CAT. 3-22

James McNeill Whistler, *The Piazzetta* (*First Venice Set*), 1879–80, etching and drypoint on paper, 10 1/16 × 7 1/16 in., The Baltimore Museum of Art, Garrett Collection

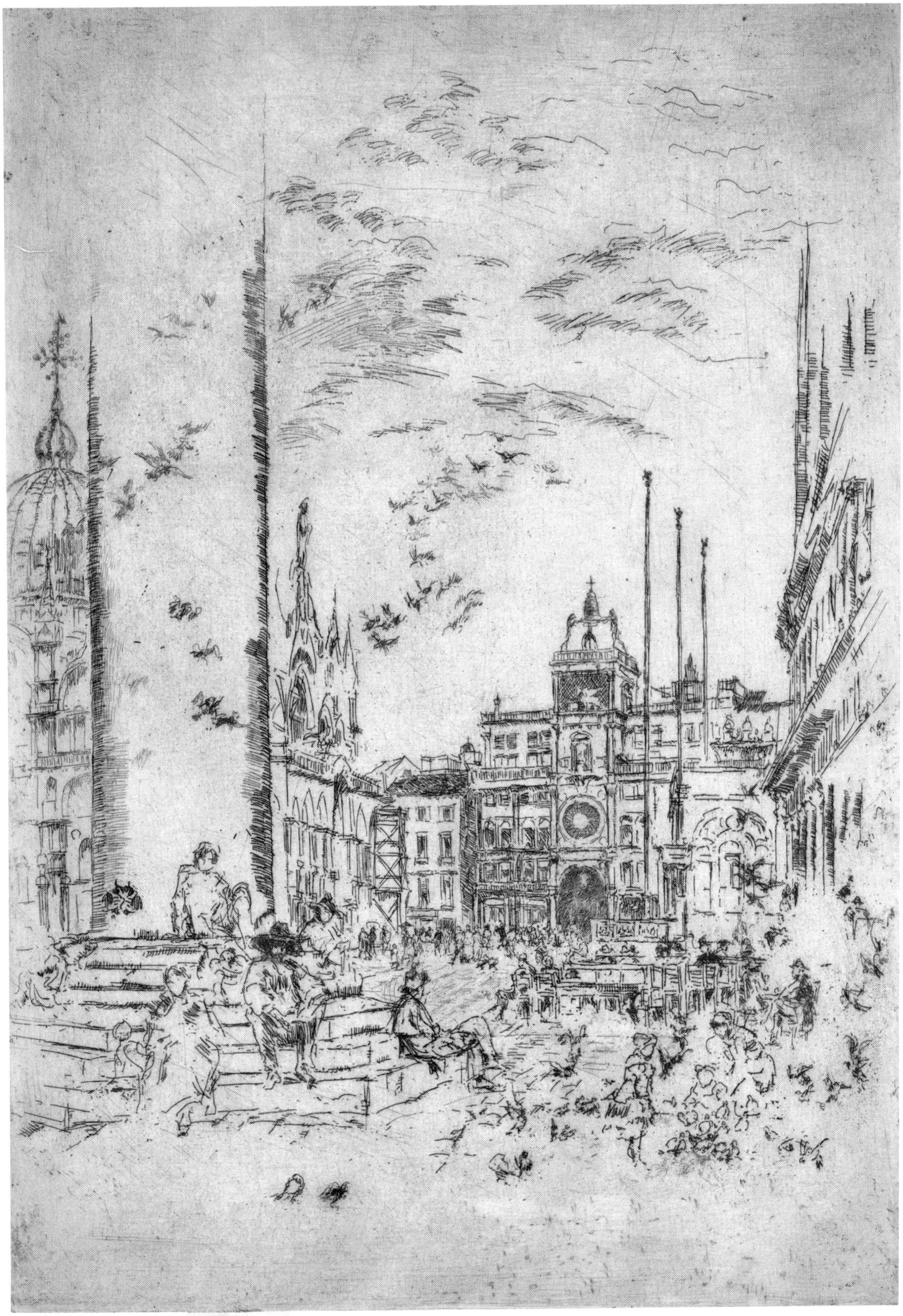

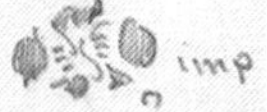
imp

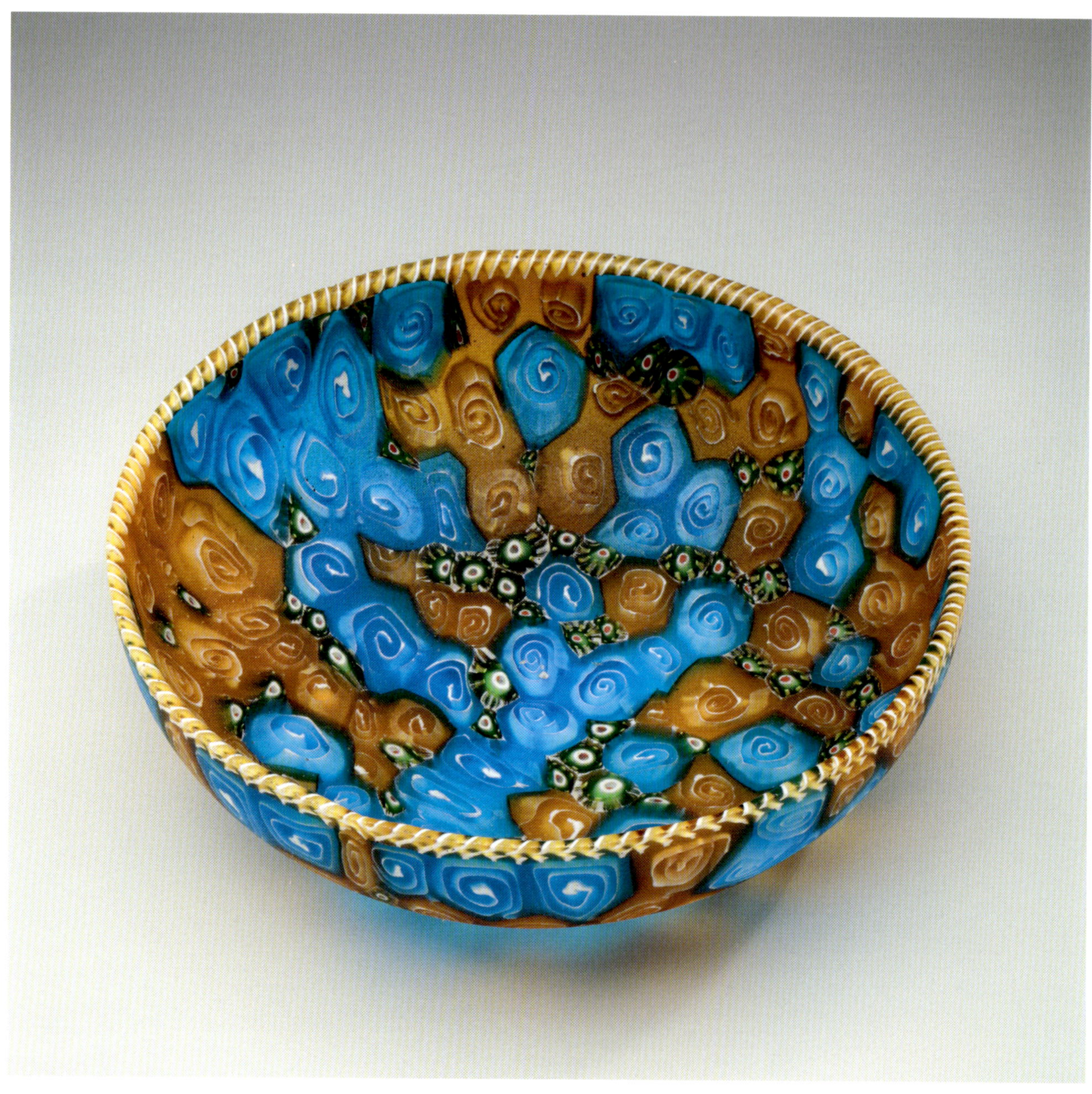

✡ CAT. 3-23

Venice and Murano Glass and Mosaic Company Ltd. (Salviati & Co.) or Compagnia di Venezia e Murano (CVM), Ancient Roman–Style Mosaic Glass Bowl, ca. 1875–80, hot-worked and slumped mosaic glass with applied glass rim, 2 × 5 ¾ in. diam., Toledo Museum of Art, Purchased with funds from the Libbey Endowment, Gift of Edward Drummond Libbey

✡ CAT. 3-24

Charles Caryl Coleman, *The Bronze Horses of San Marco, Venice*, 1876, oil on canvas, 40 ¼ × 32 ½ in., Minneapolis Institute of Art, Gift of the Regis Collection

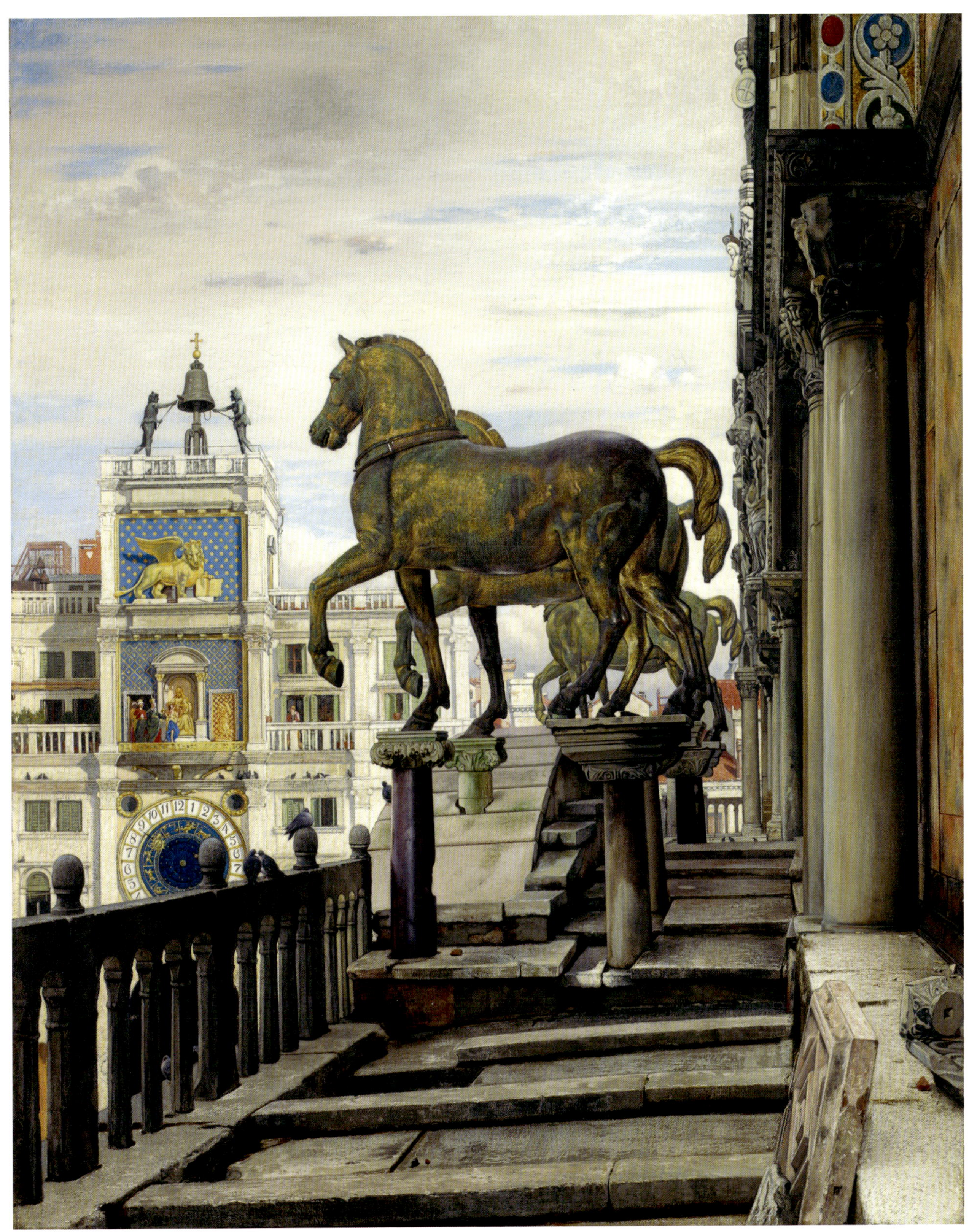

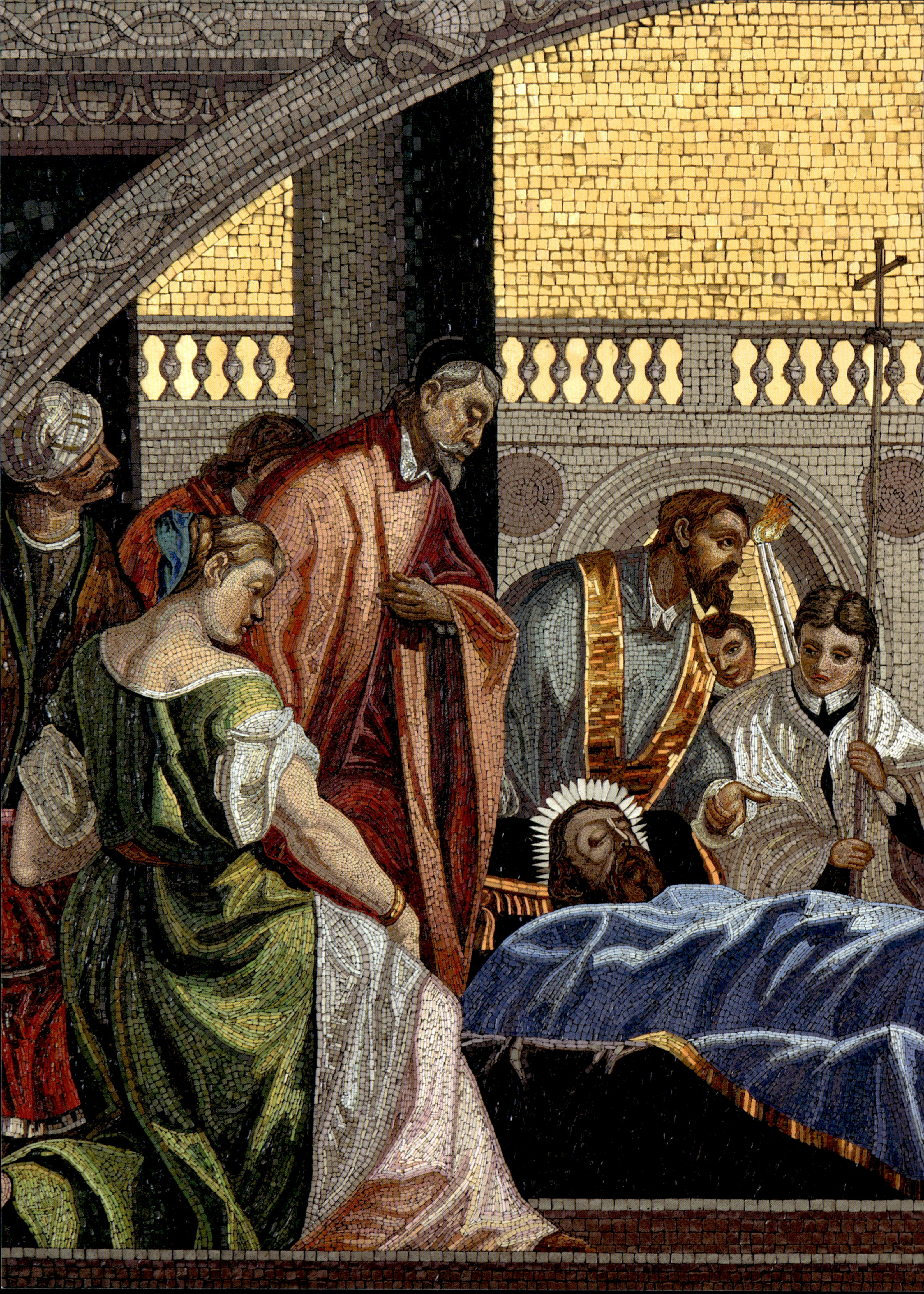

NOTES

1 Beadmakers kept two essential Venetian techniques, *filigrana* (filigree) and *millefiori*, alive by producing canes for beads at the glassmaker's lamp. Simple beads were produced using filigree canes alone. More complex beads were produced by applying extremely thin slices of millefiori cane to the surface of a nascent bead.

2 Michele Lessona, "Volere è potere, Vetri e Musaici di Antonio Salviati," in *L'Esposizione Italiana del 1884 in Torino* (Milan: Edoardo Sonzogno, 1884), 155.

3 Zanetti was ordained in 1850. Before entering the seminary, he worked in a factory producing glass canes for beads. Colleoni, a pharmacist by trade, arrived in Murano in 1841 and rented an existing pharmacy that he subsequently bought. He participated in the revolution of 1848 and later held a succession of political offices including first deputy of the commune of Murano. In 1866, after the Veneto region was liberated from Austrian domination, Colleoni was elected Murano's mayor for the first of nine terms. Aldo Bova, Attilia Dorigato, and Puccio Migliaccio, eds., *Vetri Artistici del Primo Ottocento: Museo del Vetro di Murano* (Venice: Marsilio, 2006), 159–60.

4 The phrase "fu Bartolomeo" is Venetian vernacular indicating that Antonio is the son of Bartolomeo Salviati, deceased.

5 Conte de Castellane, "Vetrerie e Mosaici di Venezia," in *L'Esposizione Universale del 1867 Illustrata*, ed. Francesco Ducuing (Milan: Edoardo Sonzogno, 1867), 1:298.

6 A *stabilimento* was a retail showroom, often of vast proportions, sometimes occupying an entire palazzo. Some light manufacturing, such as the cutting of smalti and the assembly of mosaics, might be carried out on upper floors.

7 Lorenzo Radi (1803–1874) was descended from a long line of glassmakers. In 1837 he began to experiment independently with colored smalti (for mosaics), and in 1840 he was awarded a gold medal by the Istituto Veneto di Scienze, Lettere ed Arti for the low-cost process he had invented for the manufacture of metallic (gold or silver) smalti. In 1860, while working at the Salviati firm, examples of his colored and metallic smalti and his blown chalcedony glass were presented to the Istituto Veneto. The Istituto declared Radi's smalti for Salviati superior to esteemed antique examples and awarded him the Grande Medaglia di Prima Classe on January 22, 1861. That year Radi donated a collection of his chalcedony glass vessels to Murano's Museo Civico Vetrario, where they can be seen today. Bova, Dorigato, and Migliaccio, *Vetri Artistici del Primo Ottocento*, 125–45.

8 Alexander Nesbitt, "Introduction," in *A Descriptive Catalogue of the Glass Vessels in the South Kensington Museum* (London: Chapman & Hall, 1878), xcii.

9 Madeline A. Wallace-Dunlop, "Modern Venetian Glass, and Its Manufacture," *Magazine of Art* 13 (April 1890): 207.

10 The Museo Civico Vetrario was founded in 1861 by Colleoni and Zanetti in the seventeenth-century Palazzo Giustinian on Murano. Its purpose was to collect documentation of glassmaking on the island and examples of antique Venetian glass.

11 *Prima Esposizione Vetraria Muranese Inaugurata nel 1864* (Venice: Antonio Clementi, 1864), xiii.

12 Pietro Toso and his six sons—Gregorio, Angelo, Ferdinando, Carlo, Liberato, and Giovanni—founded the Fratelli Toso glassworks on Murano in 1854. They initially made primarily utilitarian objects such as small bottles and flasks for pharmaceutical and domestic use. "The Great Murano Glass Masters: Fratelli Toso," *Glass of Venice* (blog), February 26, 2016, https://www.glassofvenice.com/blog/the-great-murano-glass-masters-fratelli-toso/.

13 Teresa Sladen, "The Mosaics," in *The Albert Memorial: The Prince Consort National Memorial: Its History, Contexts, and Conservation*, ed. Chris Brooks (New Haven, CT: Yale University Press, 2000), 294.

14 A letter from Salviati stating these requirements is preserved in the Glass Museum's archives. Reino Liefkes, "Salviati and the South Kensington Museum," in *The Colours of Murano in the XIX Century*, ed. Aldo Bova, Rossella Junck, and Puccio Migliaccio (Venice: Arsenale, 1999), 18.

15 Financial backers noted in Astone Gasparetto to N. Paul Perrot, director of the Corning Museum of Glass, Venice, 16 November 1966, The Juliette K. and Leonard S. Rakow Research Library of the Corning Museum of Glass, Corning, New York. Company directors (Drake, Layard, and Rate) are noted in Layard to Donald James Mackay, 6 October 1888, The Juliette K. and Leonard S. Rakow Research Library of the Corning Museum of Glass, Corning, New York, Gift of Sheldon Barr and Thomas Gardner.

16 The telegram is preserved in the Glass Museum's archives.

17 The name translates to "Corporation of the Stockholders of Salviati and Company," and its years of operation were 1866–72.

18 "Dr. Salviati's Glass-Works," *Chambers's Journal*, 4th ser., 19 (September 9, 1882): 576.

19 Wallace-Dunlop, "Modern Venetian Glass," 209.

20 G. A. Ronco, "Fra Vetri e Cristalli," in *Milano e L'Esposizione Italiana del 1881* (Milan: Fratelli Treves, 1881), 135.

21 Quoted in William Kloss and Diane K. Skvarla, *United States Senate Catalogue of Fine Art* (Washington, DC: US Government Printing Office, 2002), 260.

22 Kloss and Skvarla, *United States Senate Catalogue*, 162.

23 Sheldon Barr, *Venetian Glass Mosaics 1860–1917* (Woodbridge, UK: Antique Collectors' Club, 2008), 84–87.

24 Alessandro Castellani to Austin Henry Layard, Paris, March 1867, British Library, The General Correspondence of A. H. Layard during the Years 1861–69, Add MSS 38993, f. 381–82.

25 Francesco Dall'Ongaro, "L'Arte Applicata all'Industria: I Musaici e I Soffiati di Murano," in *L'Italia alla Esposizione Universale di Parigi nel 1867* (Paris: Simon Raçon; Florence: Le Monnier, 1868), 54.

Luigi Taddei, *St. Mark's Body Venerated by the Doge* (detail), 1871; **see p. 130**

26 Vincenzo Zanetti, "Parte Moderna: Vetri Soffiati di Lusso," in *Monografia Vetraria Veneziana e Muranese* (Venice: Antonelli, 1874), 75–76.

27 Examples of this design are preserved in London's Victoria and Albert Museum and the Corning Museum of Glass in Corning, New York.

28 Francesco Dall'Ongaro, "Ancora sui Soffiati di Murano e sull'Arte Vetraria in Genere," in *L'Italia alla Esposizione Universale di Parigi nel 1867* (Paris: Simon Raçon; Florence: Le Monnier, 1868), 308.

29 Giovanni Mariacher, "Introduction," in *Antonio Salviati e la Rinascita Ottocentesca del Vetro Artistico Veneziano* (Vicenza: Museo Civico di Palazzo Chiericati, 1982), 11.

30 Otto Friedrich, *Clover: The Tragic Love Story of Clover and Henry Adams and Their Brilliant Life in America's Golden Age* (New York: Simon and Schuster, 1979), 51.

31 In 1871 a limited edition of one hundred copies was printed in London by Wertheimer, Lea, and Company for private distribution.

32 Hugh Tait, *The Golden Age of Venetian Glass* (London: British Museum Publications, 1979), 7.

33 Rosa Barovier Mentasti, *Vetri di Murano dell'800* (Venice: Alfieri Editori, 1978), 13. Per Barovier Mentasti, other printed sources of inspiration included *Il Libro del Serenissimo Signore Principe Luigi d'Este*, an early seventeenth-century essay reproduced by the Museo Civico Vetrario in 1871; Achille Deville, *L'Histoire de l'Art de la Verrerie dans l'Antiquité* (Paris: Morel, 1873); Alexander Nesbitt, *A Descriptive Catalogue of the Glass Vessels in the South Kensington Museum*; and Raffaele Garrucci, *Vetri Ornati di Figure in Oro: Trovati nei Cimiteri Cristiani Primitivi di Roma* (Rome: Salviucci, 1858).

34 Wallace-Dunlop, "Modern Venetian Glass," 209.

35 Giovanni Sarpellon, *Miniature Masterpieces: Mosaic Glass, 1838–1924* (New York: Prestel, 1995), 94.

36 Although the term *murrhine* was not used in reference to glass until 1877, it is now the generic term for the disks (cut from canes) that are used in beads, cast or slumped glass, and blown millefiori (or "mosaic glass") production.

37 Sarpellon, *Miniature Masterpieces*, 45.

38 Guggenheim was a member of the Swiss family whose American branch attained great wealth and gained lasting fame in the world of collecting. Giovanni Mariacher, "Introduction," in *Antonio Salviati e la Rinascita Ottocentesca del Vetro Artistico Veneziano*, 11.

39 "Italian Industries," *New York Herald*, August 16, 1875.

40 Ibid.

41 Ibid.

42 Sladen, "The Mosaics," 301.

43 These name changes are confirmed to a degree by entries in *Kelly's Post Office London Directory* for the 30 St. James's Street address. From 1868 to 1869, only "Salviati & Co Ltd" is listed; from 1870 to 1872 both the "Venice & Murano Glass & Mosaic Co Ltd" and "Salviati & Co Ltd" are listed; and finally, the entries from 1873 onward list only the "Venice & Murano Glass & Mosaic Co Ltd."

44 James D. McCabe, *The Illustrated History of the Centennial Exhibition* (Philadelphia: National Publishing, 1876), 418–19.

45 Kenneth R. Speth, *1884—New Orleans—1885: The Great World's Fair* (2018), 154.

46 The glassmakers of ancient Rome produced large quantities of intricate non-blown vessels. Many survive today in whole or in part. Murrhines and/or ***vetro a fili*** or ***vetro a retorti*** cane segments were arranged on a marver (once a marble slab, later bronze) that was put into a furnace and slowly heated until the closely packed elements softened and fused together. The resulting mass was picked up and slumped over or pressed into a simple, usually plate- or cup-shaped form. Only occasionally was it manipulated into a specific shape. After cooling, the resulting object was polished to reveal the intricate and colorful patterns of the fused elements.

47 To create a gold glass vessel, a parison (a bubble of molten glass, usually of a contrasting color) is inflated over the flat underside of a vessel previously ornamented in *graffito* (scratched) gold leaf. In the Jewish catacombs of ancient Rome, broken-off undersides of these vessels were used to ornament the tombs. The designs were portraits, scenes of daily life, or Jewish symbols. By the third century, when the recently Christianized Romans adopted the Jewish custom of burying their dead, they also began to ornament their catacomb tombs with these gold glass objects, but, of course, they used Christian symbols.

48 In 1871 Salviati purchased shards of ancient Roman cast or slumped glass in Rome. Castellani donated his shards to the Murano museum in 1873. In 1876 British antiquarian Alexander Nesbitt donated more.

49 *Voce di Murano*, December 15, 1878; cited in Sarpellon, *Miniature Masterpieces*, 102.

50 "Vetraria: La Compagnia Venezia-Murano," in *L'Esposizione Italiana del 1881 in Milano Illustrata* (Milan: Sonzogno, 1881), 155.

51 Ibid.

52 Vincenzo Zanetti, "Correzione, Rettifiche e Giunte alla Guida di Murano," in *Guida di Murano e della Celebri Sue Fornaci Vetrarie* (Venice: Gaetano Longo, 1880), 38.

53 Tiffany's advertisement for Salviati's glass appeared in *Art Interchange*, October 16, 1878, ii; cited in Doreen Bolger Burke et al., *In Pursuit of Beauty: Americans and the Aesthetic Movement* (New York: Metropolitan Museum of Art, 1986), 473. Heinrich Schliemann was the German archaeologist and excavator of Troy, Mycenae, and Tiryns. He found no glass, iridescent or not, in what he believed to be Troy.

54 "Le Docteur Salviati," *Le Monde Illustré* (Paris), December 29, 1883, 416.

55 The mile-long Midway Plaisance was the section of the fair devoted to carnival-like rides, such as the Ice Railway and the famed Ferris Wheel, as well as "educational" displays. The CVM and the Libbey Glass Company of Toledo, Ohio, were located on the Midway opposite one another. Because both set up functioning demonstration furnaces and both charged an admission fee, they were classified as amusements.

56 *The Venice & Murano Exhibiting Co. of Venice, Italy, at the World's Columbian Exposition Chicago, Ill. 1893* (Chicago: W. B. Conkey, 1893), 3. The "very best pieces" mentioned in this quotation refer to the originals, not the CVM's reproductions.

57 Ibid., 2–3.

58 I have personally inspected these mosaics and blown glass.

59 Alice Cooney Frelinghuysen, "Aesthetic Forms in Ceramic and Glass," in Burke, *In Pursuit of Beauty*, 404–5.

60 Francis Steegmuller, *The Two Lives of James Jackson Jarves* (New Haven, CT: Yale University Press, 1951), 276–79.

61 Paul Hollister, "The Remarkable Glass Gift of James Jackson Jarves, A Collector in a Hurry," *Acorn: Journal of the Sandwich Glass Museum, the Sandwich Historical Society* 5 (1994): 8.

62 James Jackson Jarves, "Ancient and Modern Venetian Glass of Murano," *Harper's Monthly Magazine* 64, no. 380 (January 1882): 185.

63 Camerino began work at Salviati's Venetian shop in 1882 at age twenty-three. He eventually became its managing director and, later, its owner.

64 Willis Lincoln Hall, *Stanford Memorial Church: The Mosaics, the Windows, the Inscriptions* (Palo Alto, CA: Times, 1921), 30.

65 The cost of building the church was $600,000. Robert Scott Osborne, "A Unique American Church," *Munsey's Magazine* 31, no. 5 (August 1904): 710.

66 Stanford University, "Venetian Family Donates Historic Watercolors of Church Mosaics," news release, March 3, 1992, https://news.stanford.edu/pr/92/920303Arc2379.html.

67 Much of this information is excerpted from a letter from Camerino to Willis L. Hall on August 25, 1917. Hall, *Stanford Memorial Church*, 35.

68 In 1910 Erede Dr. A. Salviati & Co. commissioned Paoletti (1834–1912) to design a cycle of mosaics for the Church of St. Ignatius Loyola in New York City. Ultimately, fourteen Stations of the Cross embellished the north and south walls of the church, and three monumental mosaics were placed behind the main altar.

69 The name translates to Dr. A. Salviati's Heir and Company.

70 The mosaics were prefabricated in jigsaw-like sections in Murano, shipped to New York by sea, and transported to California by train.

71 Except for the three Stanford family portraits, all the mosaics, including the Theodore Roosevelt mosaic, were available for sale. The Roosevelt mosaic was not sold. It remained with the Camerino family for many years and was eventually acquired by the Corning Museum of Glass.

72 When the bell tower in St. Mark's Square in Venice collapsed on July 14, 1902, the Venetian authorities decided to rebuild it. While excavating the rubble, a fragment of a fifteenth-century beaker was discovered. It was richly decorated with multicolored enamels depicting allegorical motifs of plants and animals. The Venetian glassmaking firm of Francesco Toso Borella copied it and offered reproductions for sale at various subsequent expos, including the 1904 Louisiana Purchase Exposition.

73 See Carol M. Osborne, *Venetian Glass of the 1890s: Salviati at Stanford University* (London: Philip Wilson, 2002), 30.

74 In addition to the three mosaic portraits of the Stanfords exhibited at the Louisiana Purchase Exposition, two more mosaic portraits of Jane Stanford's brother, Charles Lathrop, and his wife were displayed in the Venetian Room.

75 Osborne, *Venetian Glass of the 1890s*, 39.

WHERE HAVE TITIAN'S BEAUTIES GONE?

Sargent and Whistler on the Streets of Venice

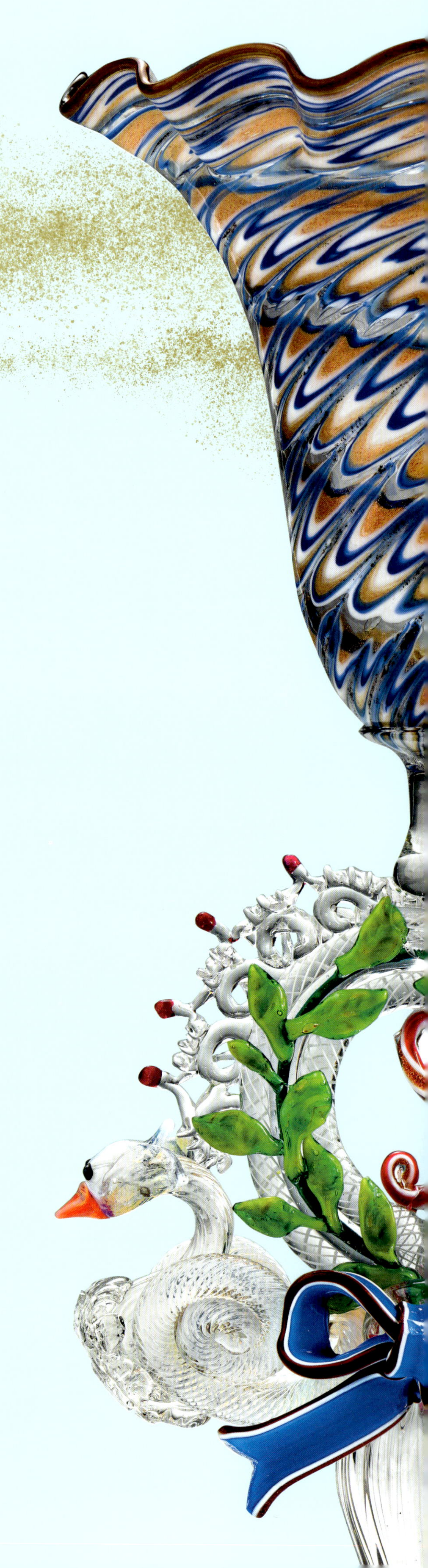

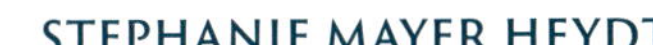
STEPHANIE MAYER HEYDT

It is not necessary to describe minutely, the general aspect of this most singular city, familiarized as it is to every one by prose, poetry (and much stuff which is neither), and by pencil, and brush.... The consequence is that no one enters Venice as a stranger; almost every feature of importance is already more or less known.[1]

—Sir Francis Palgrave, *Hand-book for Travellers in Northern Italy*, 1842

Venice was an exceptionally well-recorded place. Since the fifteenth century, the city had attracted the attention of the tourist. And with the influx of visitors came the requisite demand for mementos of its singular sights—St. Mark's Basilica and its piazza, the shops and stalls of the Rialto Bridge, scenic views across the Grand Canal, and, more generally, the city's setting amid the sparkling blue waters of the Adriatic Sea. Artists of all nationalities found their place in Venice, and by the last quarter of the nineteenth century, the American love affair with the city was well underway.[2]

Before the 1870s, Americans seeking artistic inspiration ranked Venice behind Rome and its antiquities. Though visitors, poets, writers, and artists always found their way to the city on the lagoon to experience its unique lifestyle, British and American travelers were gently warned by authorities such as Sir Francis Palgrave of the inconveniences and grittiness of a city diminished from its former glory.[3] Yet after the occupying Austrians retreated in 1866, foreign visitors not only came to Venice but lingered. For American artists, the intensifying fascination with Venice from 1870 onward corresponded with a waning interest in the moralizing and rigid neoclassicism inspired by sojourns in Rome. In the post-Civil War years, the bright coloration, bold brushwork, and bravura of the Venetian painters of the Renaissance had begun to appeal to a new generation of artists. Even the most avant-garde among the modern set could not help but find something to admire in the old Venetian masters. The American expatriate artist James McNeill Whistler, for example, admired the eighteenth-century Venetian scene painter Canaletto—not for his meticulous renderings of the city but rather for his application of color. "Canaletto,"

Preceding pages:
Società Anonima per Azioni Salviati & C., Fenicio Goblet with Swans and Initial "S" Stem (detail), ca. 1870; see p. 109

Whistler explained, "could paint a white building against a white cloud. That was enough to make any man great."[4]

According to the younger American artist Otto Henry Bacher, Whistler even scaled the walls in the Scuola di San Rocco for a better view of its renowned series by Jacopo Tintoretto. "He climbed up with great difficulty, in order to get a close look at the technique of that master, and was in great glee over it, perhaps because it coincided well with his own." Painters Paolo Veronese and Titian were, in Whistler's words, "great swells," though he found the Florentine painter Michelangelo Buonarroti "too much given to contortion."[5]

The city's wondrous views and its centuries of artworks on display in churches and palaces no doubt enticed the American artists who flocked there. For most, Venice inspired looking back to tradition; for others it became a place for innovation. Whistler and his younger contemporary, John Singer Sargent, came to Venice just as American artists were starting to take close notice of it. But rather than finding their place among the countless who, as Palgrave noted, "familiarized" the city "by prose, poetry (and much stuff which is neither), and by pencil, and brush," Whistler and Sargent found something new to portray that would, in time, reset the direction of American art for decades to come.

"CLEVERNESS SO GREAT": WHISTLER IN VENICE

By the time Whistler arrived in Venice in September of 1879, the city was teeming with artists. Whistler had retreated there from London, nearly broke and reeling from a bitter feud with the conservative English art critic, John Ruskin. Following

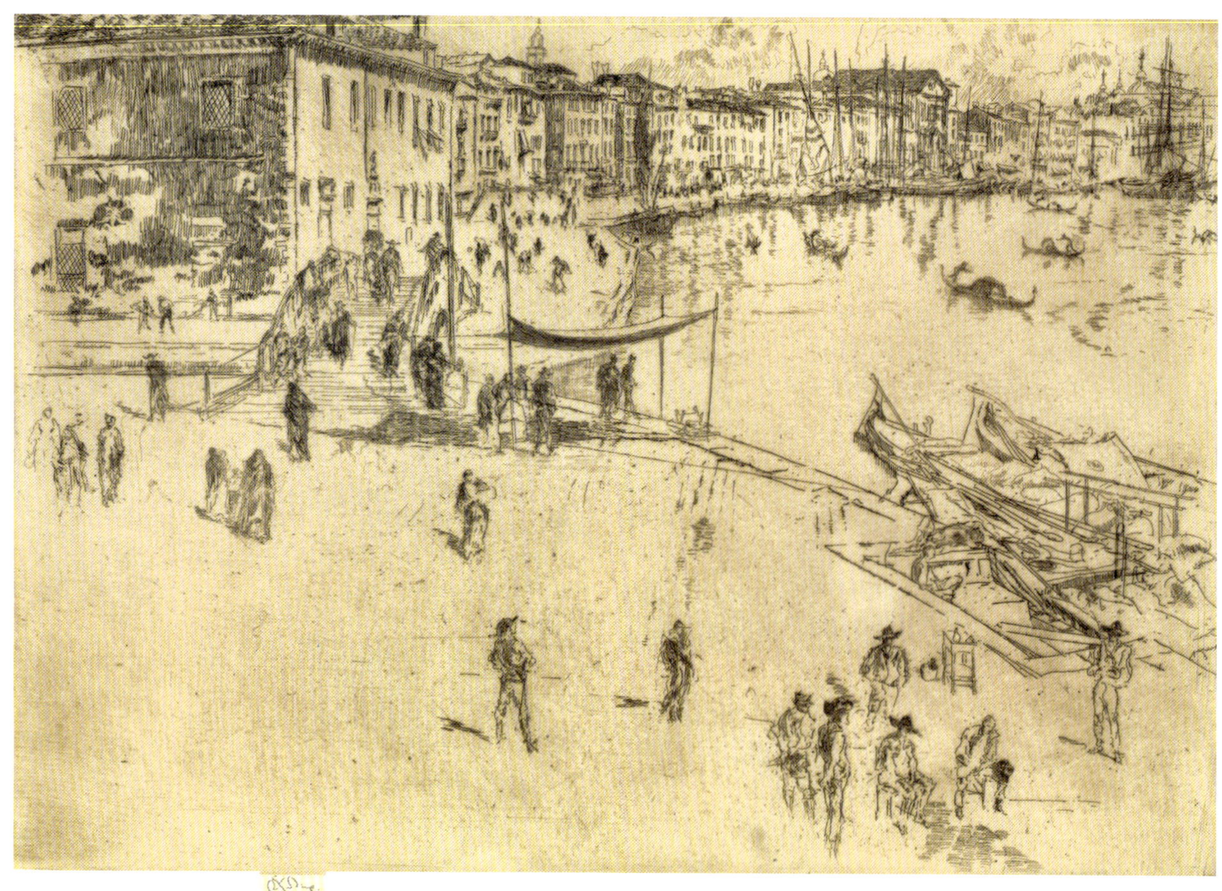

✲ CAT. 4-1
James McNeill Whistler, *The Riva, No. 2 (Second Venice Set)*, 1879–80, etching and drypoint on paper, 8 7/16 × 11 7/8 in., The Baltimore Museum of Art, The George A. Lucas Collection, purchased with funds from the State of Maryland, Laurence and Stella Bendann Fund, and contributions from individuals, foundations, and corporations throughout the Baltimore community

Ruskin's scathing critique of the American artist's daring paintings of London at night, Whistler sued for libel, extending the controversy over his unconventional approach to making art.[6] In Venice, Whistler's focus veered from exhibition-size painting to a suite of intimate, small-scale views rendered in print and pastel. He completed only three oil paintings in Venice but made more than fifty etchings and one hundred pastels during what became a fourteen-month-long stay.

Though a decidedly unconventional artist, in Venice Whistler set up his easel in all the expected places.[7] Like many before him, Whistler painted such well-known sites as St. Mark's Basilica and sketched sweeping views across the Grand Canal and the bustling promenade of the Riva degli Schiavoni. Yet his familiar views of these landmarks were anything but expected. In *Riva, No. 2* (CAT. 4-1), for example, Whistler devotes a good deal of the composition to empty space, clustering the buildings, boats, and people of this busy thoroughfare in the top and right quadrants of the picture. Compared to a similar view by the American artist Frank Duveneck, for example, who animated his scene of the same waterfront street with fishermen and beggar women, children and promenading tourists (CAT. 4-2), Whistler resists anecdote. Duveneck, who met Whistler in Venice, took clear compositional cues from the older, famous artist; he flattened his composition and dramatically raised the horizon line, compressing the scene into an aggressively vertical arrangement reminiscent of the other views of Venice by Whistler that no doubt he had seen.[8] Yet like many of the Americans working in Venice at that moment, Duveneck retained a narrative bent. His *Riva* recalls the picturesque traditions established by Canaletto in such works as *Riva degli Schiavoni, Venice (View on the Grand Canal)* (Fig. 4-1), where fishermen launch their boats into the lagoon, dogs scamper across the street, tradesmen gather for impromptu conversation, and other quaint vignettes of daily life unfold. Whistler's *Riva, No. 2*, by contrast, offers only a series of impressions, suggestions of activity and life on the street, but not specific enough to convey even the beginnings of a story.

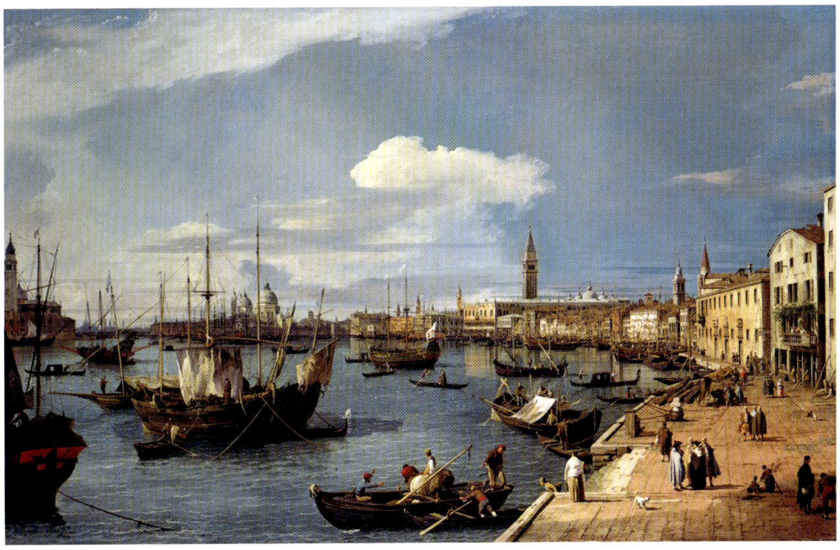

Fig. 4-1
Giovanni Antonio Canal (Canaletto), *Riva degli schiavoni, Venice (View on the Grand Canal)*, ca. 1734–35, oil on canvas, 49 11/16 × 80 5/16 in., Sir John Soane's Museum

Whistler entirely abandons all didactic pretense in his 1880 rendering of St. Mark's Basilica, perhaps the most pictured building in all of Venice. *Nocturne: Blue and Gold, St. Mark's, Venice* (Fig. 4-2) shows the iconic, late medieval landmark under the hazy veil of night. The far-right portal of the five-bay facade is jarringly cropped; a dazzling collection of bright dots, representing the flicker of gas lamps on the piazza, divert the viewer's gaze toward a curious void. A barely visible form of the piazza's famous clock tower, also shown in partial view, edges the far left of the composition. The most iconic of Venetian sites, the bell tower located just

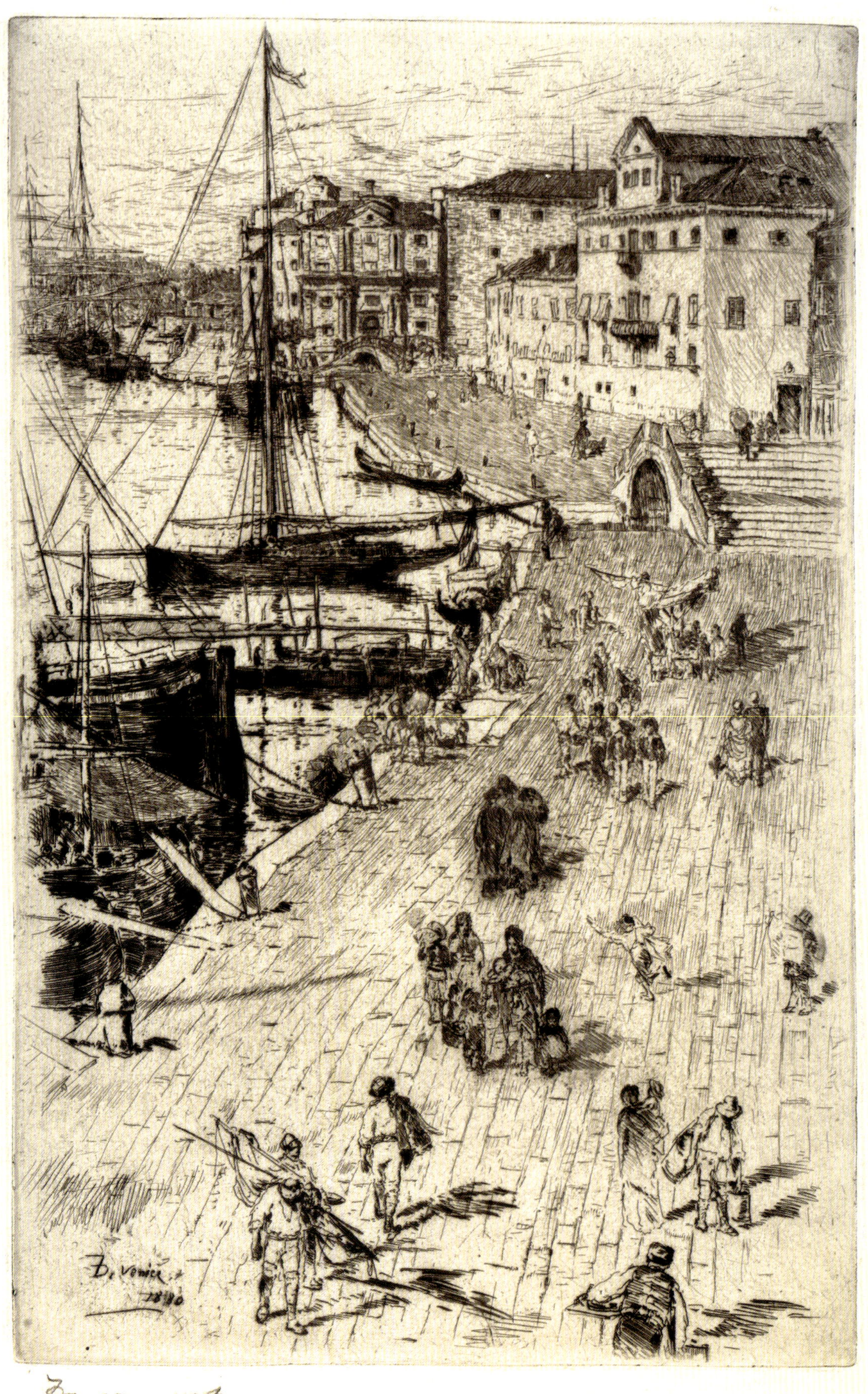
D. venice
1880

to the right of the basilica, is eliminated altogether. Whistler's picture stands in contrast to the highly articulated presentations of Venice's most famous public square by artists such as Canaletto,[9] as well as the many artists to follow through the centuries, including other American painters in Venice at that time.[10]

✡ CAT. 4-2
Frank Duveneck, *Riva degli Schiavoni, No. 2,* 1880, etching on paper, 13 ¼ × 8 ⅝ in., Smithsonian American Art Museum, Museum purchase

More than just a fresh take on an old subject, however, Whistler's subversion of detail in rendering this famously elaborate facade can also be understood as a jab against his old rival, Ruskin, who doted on the historic minutiae of St. Mark's and other sites in his widely read three-volume treatise on Venetian art and architecture, *The Stones of Venice* (1851–53).[11] Perhaps without coincidence, many sites Whistler selected for his Venetian work bear some relation to what Ruskin had discussed and pictured in his book. The American's determination to rework his adversary's impression of Venice may have provided one motivation to search for something new to show of the city. The city itself likely provided the rest.

Whistler had been sent to Venice for a short stay to create a portfolio of twelve etchings for the Fine Art Society of London, a strategically timed commission that mercifully removed the bankrupt artist from London following the embarrassment of the Ruskin affair. Yet as fall stretched into winter, Whistler had little to send back to London. To his investors he explained in January of 1880, terrible weather and poor health had interfered with his progress. But something profound, he wrote reassuringly, was in the works: "I have learned to know a Venice in Venice that the others never seem to have perceived."[12] A few months later, he wrote excitedly to a friend:

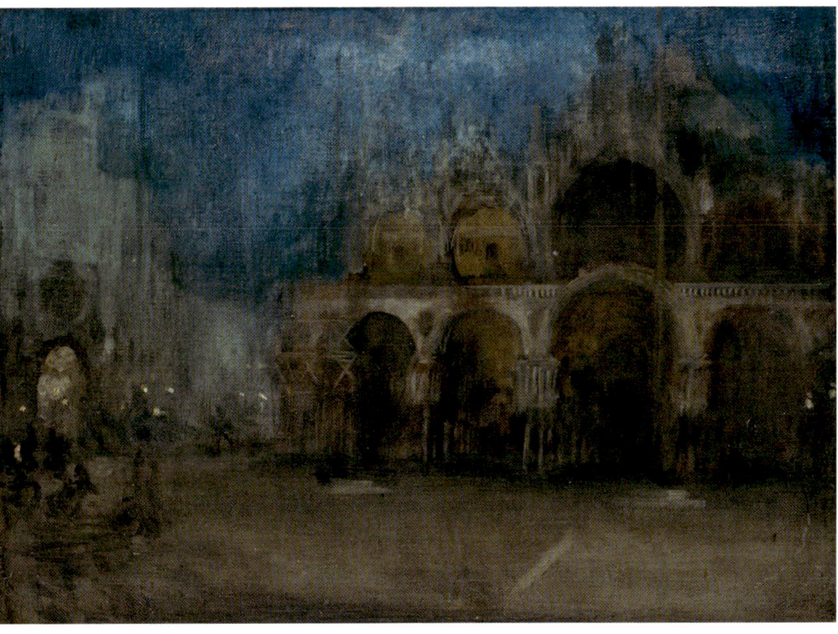

Fig. 4-2
James McNeill Whistler, *Nocturne: Blue and Gold, St. Mark's, Venice,* 1880, oil on canvas, 29 ¹¹⁄₁₆ × 35 ⅝ in., Amgueddfa Cymru—National Museum Wales

> *I can't tell you how intoxicating this place is.... You are perfectly bewildered with the entanglement of beautiful things! You say I will do this and I must do that and I ought to do the other! and if not carefull* [sic]*, it all ends in dizziness and craze!... [I]t is not merely the 'Views of Venice' or the Streets of Venice, or the 'Canals of Venice' such as you have seen brought back by the foolish sketcher—but great pictures that stare you in the face.*[13]

Whistler's initial period of inactivity in Venice in fact transitioned to become one of the most productive stretches in his career. Well aware of the "craze" to see and picture all the "Views of Venice," he aimed for something different. What was novel in Whistler's work was not that he discovered a hidden spot never before painted. Rather he pictured what had been pictured many times before—from the Grand Canal to the humble back alley—but found a new way to show it. His work was not topographical, not a painstaking recording. He was not careful in marking locations or landmarks, and he felt liberated to edit out what he did not like. Whistler released all expectation of verisimilitude in his Venice works, which for some, even his supporters, was difficult to comprehend. As Whistler's friend Walter Richard Sickert lamented, "It worries me, and spoils my pleasure to see the Salute on the Giudecca and San Giorgio on the Zattere. Whistler is great—but so is Venice."[14] After all, pictures of Venice were expected to look like Venice. Whistler redefined that expectation. Rather he promoted a new kind of realism—one that replaced narrative and sentimentality, detail and topographical accuracy with subtlety and gesture, and emphasized aesthetics over content. He offers impressions, not stories. He presents an experience of seeing Venice, not a recording of it.

✲ CAT. 4-3
James McNeill Whistler, *Fruit Stall (Second Venice Set)*, 1879–80, etching and drypoint on paper, 8 15/16 × 5 15/16 in., The Baltimore Museum of Art, The George A. Lucas Collection, purchased with funds from the State of Maryland, Laurence and Stella Bendann Fund, and contributions from individuals, foundations, and corporations throughout the Baltimore community

With an intense disdain for the crowds that gathered at the regular sites, Whistler sometimes retreated indoors to capture views through the windows.[15] But he also made his way to the quieter parts of town to sketch. Others, including Ruskin, had pictured those same back alleys, so the subject was not entirely new. But how Whistler chose to depict these remote places became one key to his innovation.

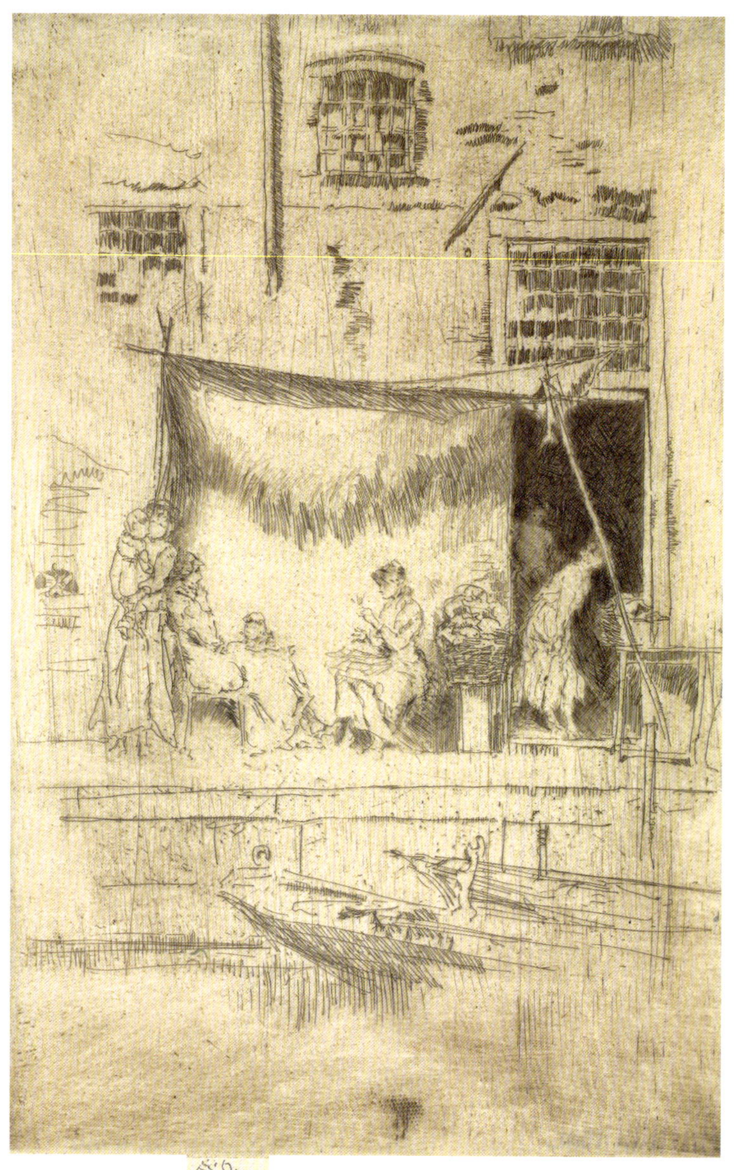

When his collection of Venice etchings and pastels were exhibited at last in London, others saw the innovation too.[16] The artistic virtuosity and technical novelty of these "impressions of nature,"[17] as a critic for the London *Daily News* described them, did not go unnoticed. Viewers were struck both by Whistler's technique and subject. One surprise was his sparing use of line. In a city rich with architectural embellishment, Whistler's work offered little detail. In a work such as *Fruit Stall* (CAT. 4-3), for example, a few vertical and horizontal hatch marks describe the uneven surface of aged plaster walls or shadowy reflections in the water. Perhaps more controversial than his reductive compositions was Whistler's liberal use of inking and toning to achieve unique atmospheric effects in his etchings. For many of his Venice prints, Whistler subtly varied how he inked and worked the plate for each impression, allowing expressive differences to emerge. In two impressions of *Nocturne: Furnace* (CAT. 4-4 and Fig. 4-3), for example, Whistler adjusted the density and emphasis of the ink application in the areas around the

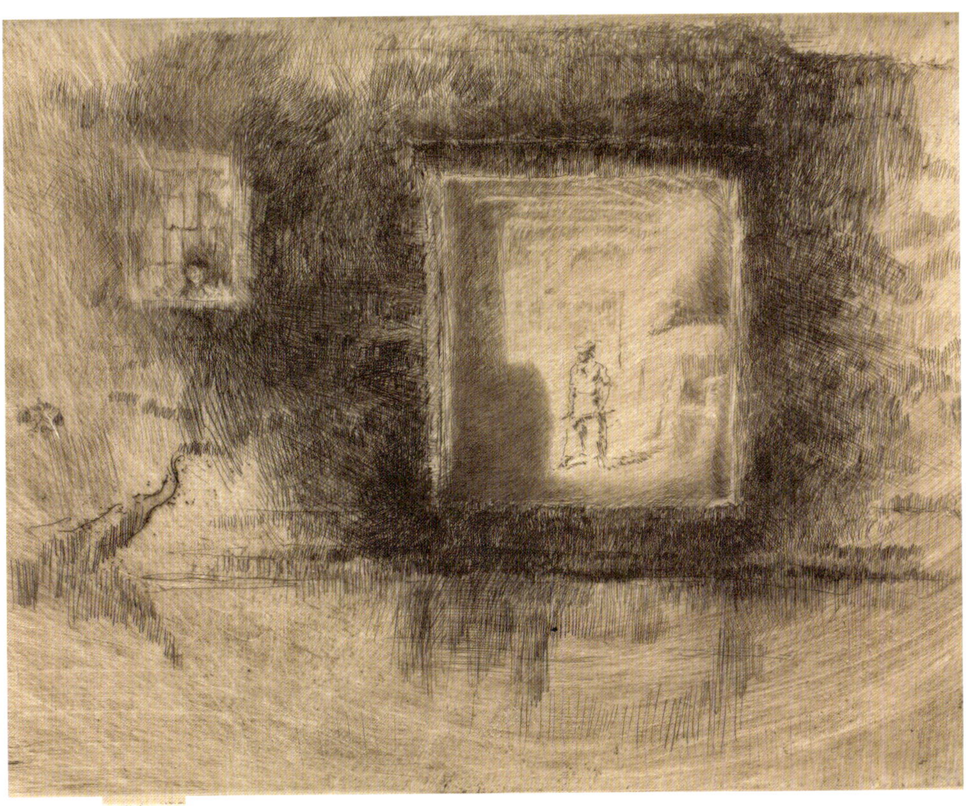

✡ CAT. 4-4
James McNeill Whistler, *Nocturne: Furnace (Second Venice Set)*, 1879–80, etching and drypoint on paper, 6 ¾ × 9 ⅛ in., The Baltimore Museum of Art, The George A. Lucas Collection, purchased with funds from the State of Maryland, Laurence and Stella Bendann Fund, and contributions from individuals, foundations, and corporations throughout the Baltimore community

open door. Though both have darker tones around the top and right edges of the door, in one impression (Baltimore) the wall appears weightier to the left. In that impression, too, broad and sweeping wipe marks are visible across the lower quadrant; evidently Whistler manipulated the ink with a cloth pulled across the plate to achieve this singular outcome. His etchings, each with an individualized approach to wiping and toning on the plate, have been compared with monotypes, or unique impressions that are literally applied each time anew onto a printing plate. As a technique, wiping and toning had been under fire by some conservative critics, including Ruskin, and were derided as amateur solutions to disguise sloppy craftmanship.[18] Nevertheless, Whistler liberally toned his prints, achieving beautiful passages of atmospheric effect, creating unique outcomes for each print and a clear disregard for the status quo.

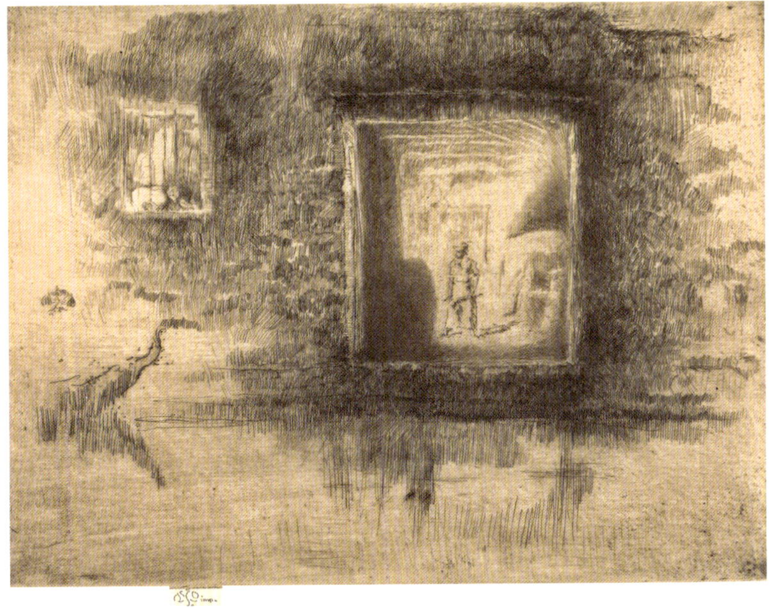

Fig. 4-3
James McNeill Whistler, *Nocturne: Furnace (Second Venice Set)*, 1880, etching and drypoint on paper, 6 ¾ × 9 ⅛ in., National Gallery of Art, Gift of Mr. and Mrs. J. Watson Webb in memory of Mr. and Mrs. H. O. Havemeyer, 1942.15.30

For his Venetian pastels, such as *Canal in Venice (Tobacco Warehouse)* (Fig. 4-4), Whistler again used minimal strokes. Stretches of brown paper were left untouched and visible across his compositions, leaving some to wonder if the artist left the works incomplete. Whistler must have reveled in the opportunity to represent the most favorite Venetian sites of the meticulous Ruskin in this plucky, abbreviated, and unpolished style—a vulgar solution to some, but to others, including the American set that watched him at work, the beginnings of a picture making revolution.[19]

What Whistler had decided to depict also caught notice. "What has been done, and done with cleverness so great as to be almost genius," a reviewer from *The Spectator* explained, "is to sketch the passing, every-day aspect of canal, lagoon and quay....It is not the Venice of a maiden's fancies or a poet's dreams, but the tangible Venice known to tourists."[20] The distinction here between fantasy and reality is one that Whistler appears to acknowledge in his city views. Indeed, for many the imagined and persistently pictured Venice aligned more with romantic fantasy than with any real experience of the city. In poetry, prose, and pictures, Venice was idealized as a city of fairy-tale beauty, complemented by a class of contented if poor Venetians who circulate through the city adding picturesque appeal.

In Julius LeBlanc Stewart's charming *Conversation Vénetienne* (CAT. 4-5), for example, painted a decade after Whistler's time there, two robust and attractive women wrapped in the traditional black shawls of the Venetian working class break for a breezy canal-side chat at sunset. A solo gondolier quietly poles across the empty lagoon behind them. In the distance, church spires on the neighboring island of Murano glow in the light of the setting sun. Here, Stewart offers an imagined view of the Venetians' lives, as if it were a pleasant evening vignette witnessed by a passerby. Yet it was unlikely that a visitor to Venice would have had either such intimate access to or the inclination to engage with real-life Italians. As the tourist traversed the city viewing the sites, real-life Venetians were present in the background, selling flowers, carrying water, stringing beads. In works such as *Venetian Mast* (see p. 31) and *Old Women* (CAT. 4-6), Whistler offers a more realistic vision, addressing not how one might imagine the city, but how one might interact with it. Venetians are pictured, but our access to them is obscured, distanced. Whistler removes the veil of sentiment, instead showing us how it feels to walk through the city, glimpse this way and that, notice one thing or another, and then move on.

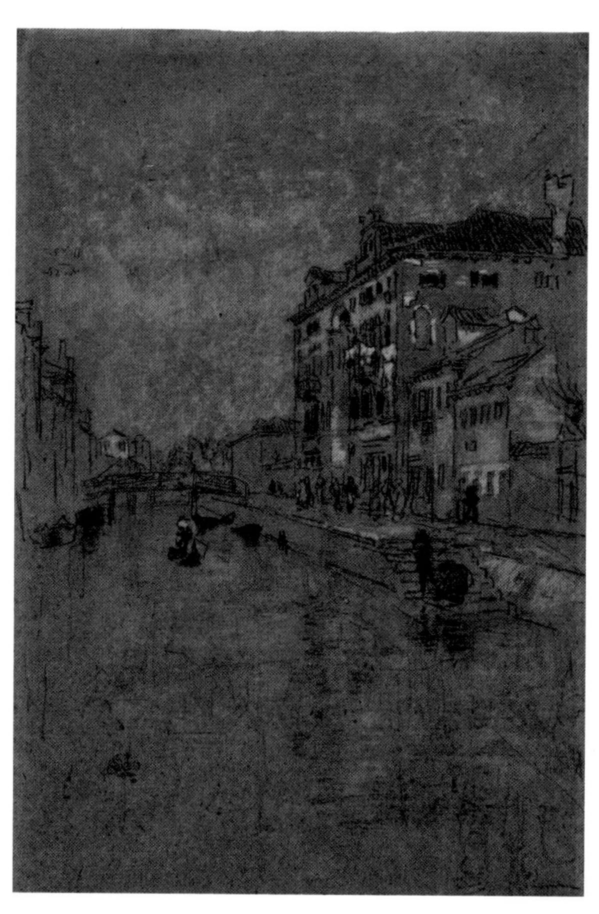

Fig. 4-4
James McNeill Whistler, *Canal in Venice (Tobacco Warehouse)*, 1879–80, pastel and charcoal on paper, 11 11/16 × 8 1/16 in., Hirshhorn Museum and Sculpture Garden, Smithsonian Institution, Washington, DC, Gift of Joseph H. Hirshhorn, 1966, 66.5530

As Whistler retreated from the "dizziness and craze" of Venice, he found his most successful subjects away from the crowds. He shows us doorways and alleys, the shadowy spaces of a humble Venice populated by Venetians—glassblowers and water carriers, beggars, fruit sellers and loiterers, gondoliers, and bead stringers. The city is viewed anecdotally, as in works such as *The Beggars* (CAT. 4-7) and *The Doorway* (CAT. 4-8), which offer darting glimpses through the many tunnellike passageways in the haphazard maze of streets. Indeed, Whistler offers us here recognizable Venetian types—the cloaked man beneath a broad-brimmed hat, women carrying water,

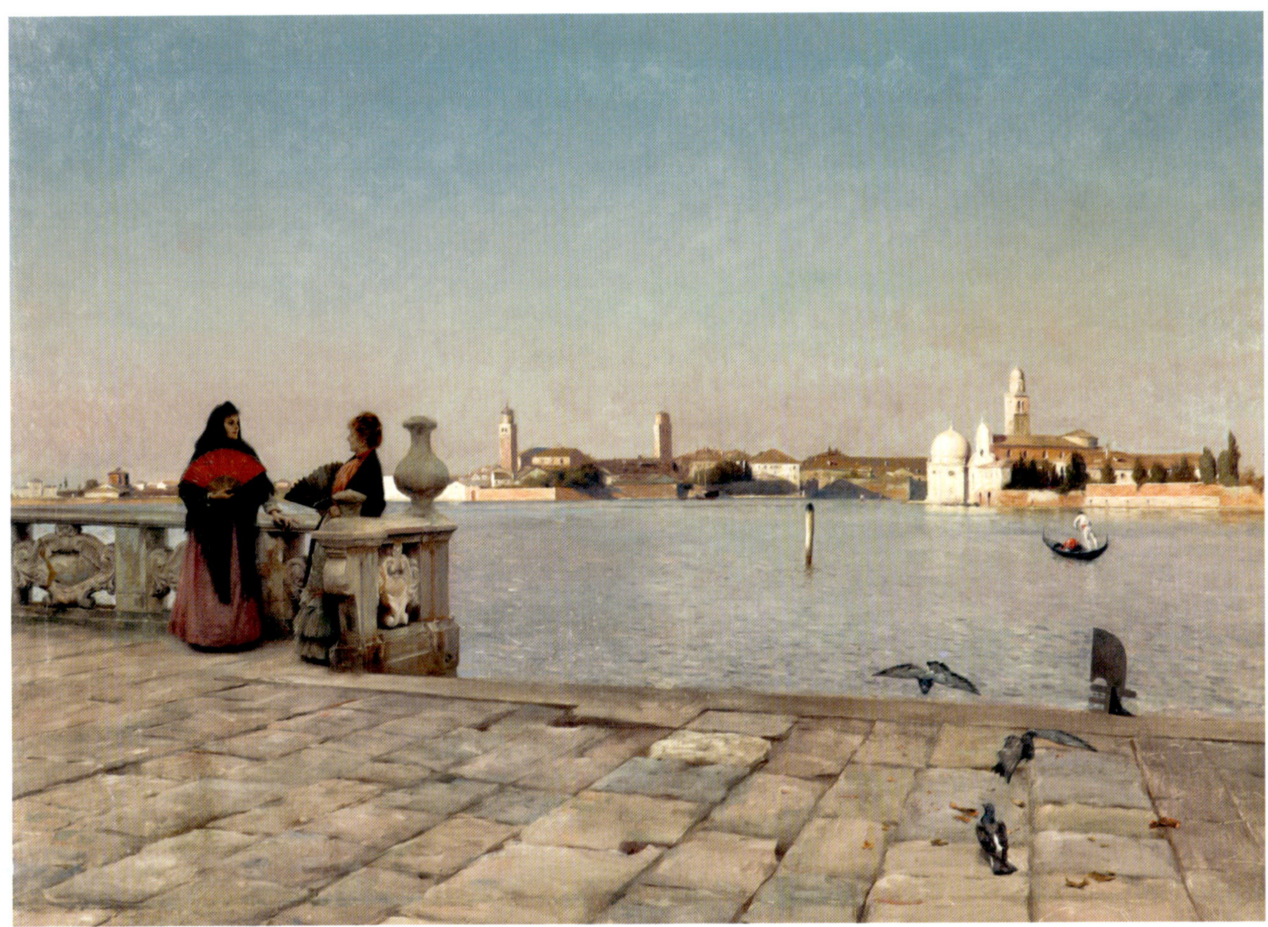

☆ CAT. 4-5
Julius LeBlanc Stewart, *Conversation Vénetienne*, 1891, oil on canvas, 28 ¾ × 39 ¾ in., Private collection

washing clothes, or begging for food. However, these city dwellers dissolve into the darkness while the formal qualities of the pictures—the play of light and shadow—take center stage.

Uncharacteristic, perhaps, for Whistler's Venice work, are the Venetian women situated in the extreme foreground of these two compositions. These figures stand out of the shadows, unmissable and bathed in light. Whistler flirts with narrative here. In *The Doorway*, for example, a young woman bends by a canal, a laundry basket set near her shoeless feet. We see her hesitate before a final step into the water where, presumably, she will wash her clothes. Another woman behind her leans against the wall of the darkened passageway, her form barely visible through the shadow. These are not Stewart's charming ladies in casual chatter at sunset. They perform their work, deflecting the viewer's gaze. In the title of the picture, Whistler reminds us these women, too, are in service to the composition. The exquisitely elaborate doorway—articulated with gestural scrolls, grids, floral carvings, and darting pattern—is the unrivaled subject of the picture. The people here are ancillary. Like a visitor taking in the sights, Whistler encourages us to enjoy the view as we drift slowly by. Similarly, in *The Beggars*, a sympathetic mother and daughter stand starkly visible in the foreground. Their gazes lift directly to the viewer, allowing none of the comfortable distancing that Whistler typically offers. Yet even here Whistler pulls back from emotional content. The figures catch our gaze, but only briefly, bound in silent agreement between the observer and the observed.

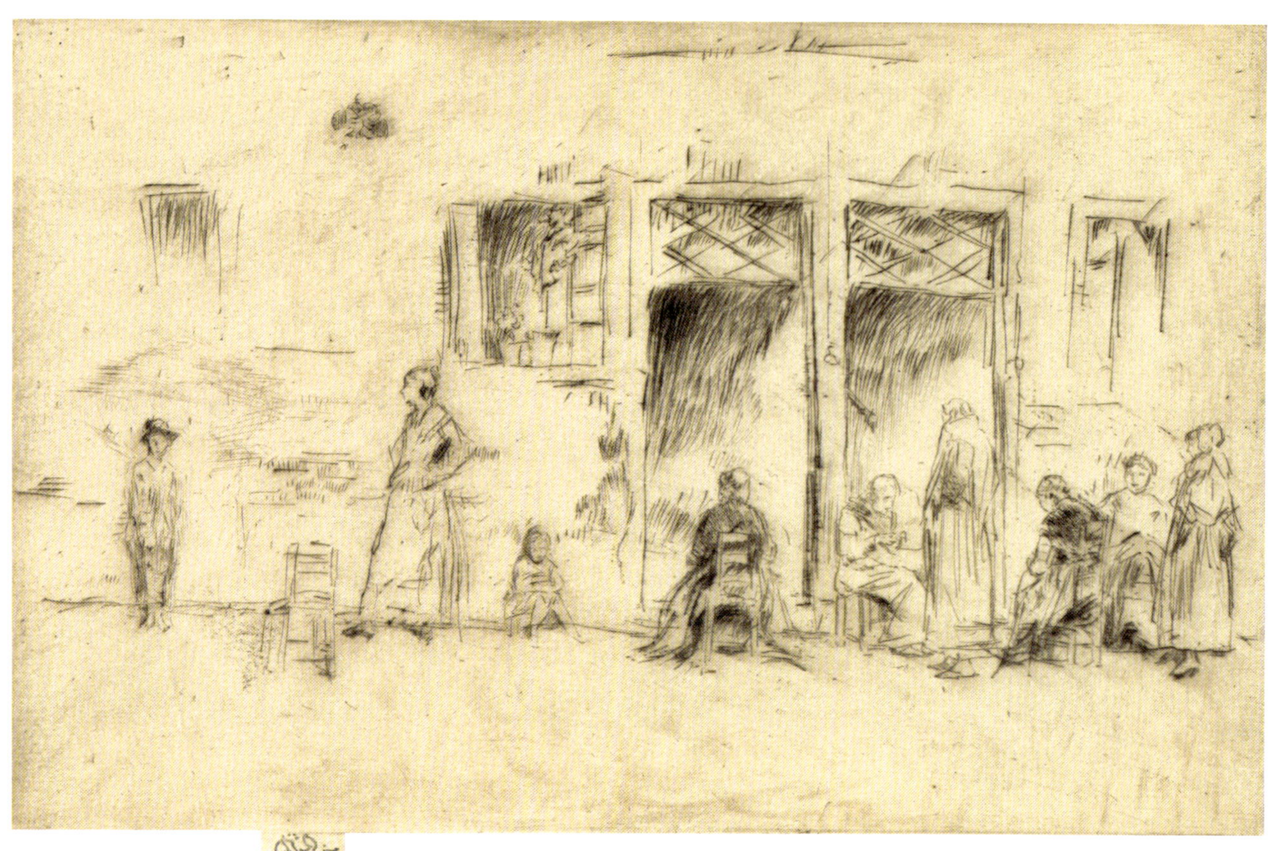

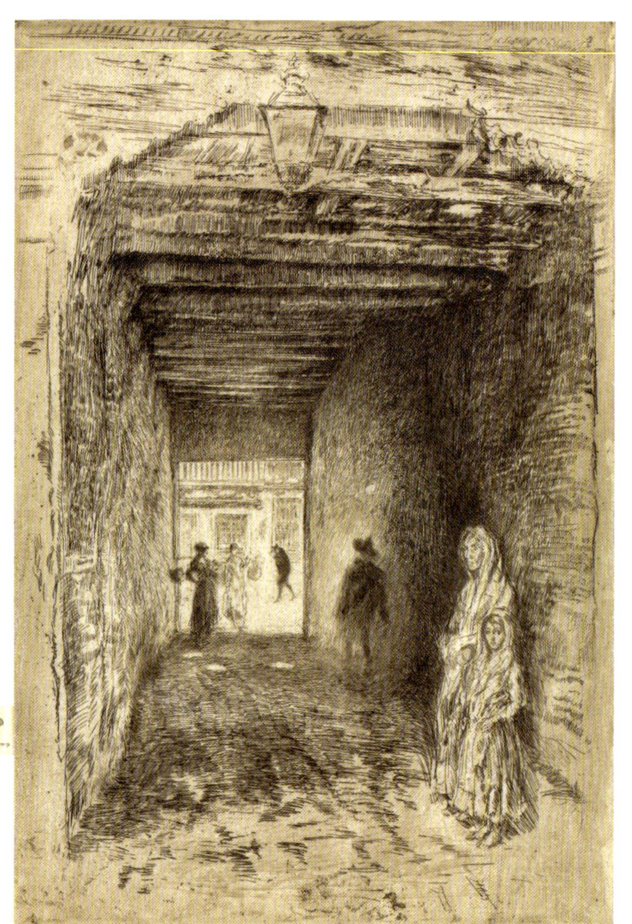

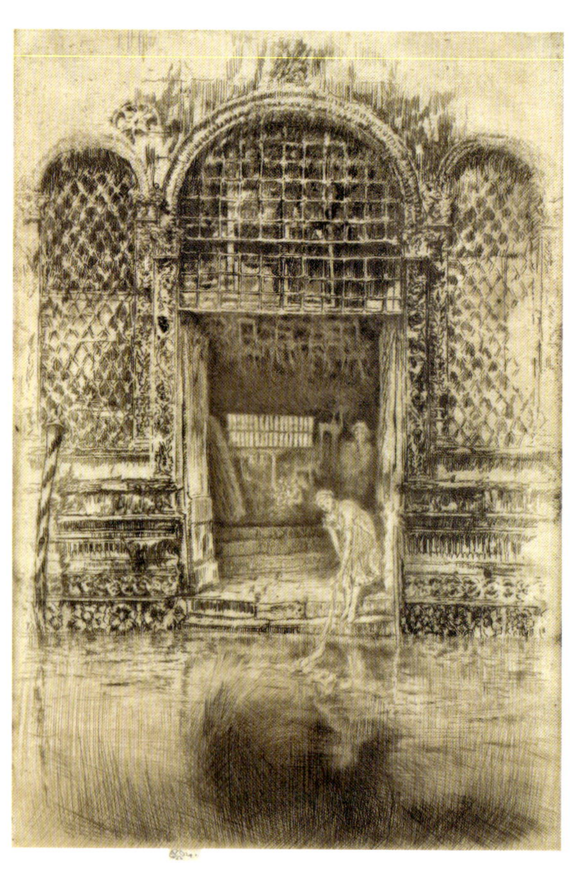

Whistler was not unfamiliar with the choice of working-class people as subjects. Two decades before, he had worked on a series of prints featuring the dockworkers of London. In Venice, however, Whistler appears to accept the challenge of Charles Baudelaire's charge for the modern artist.[21] He views the city not through the eyes of the tourist, but rather as the dispassionate observer, as the man in the crowd seeing not what had been done before, but rather what was in front of him in that moment. He bears witness without emotion.

In the end, Whistler's Venice was about style, not subject. His views are incidental, seen by contemporaries as "rapid sketches of light, of colour, and of aerial distances and architectural effects."[22] What he did in Venice, technically with his prints and pastels, compositionally with his asymmetries and the subversion of subject, and aesthetically with his muted palette, could be and would be applied by other artists in other places. When Whistler's Venetian prints and pastels were shown in New York in the fall of 1883, for example, what struck his American followers was not the Venetian subjects but rather the spare compositions and stylized presentation. The exhibition, artfully titled *Arrangement in Yellow and White,* showed the small pictures simply framed but presented dramatically on crisp white walls accented by yellow trim, flooring, furniture, and flowers.[23] The spare and elegant selection of works and their eccentric installation—the likes of which had never been seen in an American gallery—set "a whole tribe of Americans singing a refrain to Mr. Whistler's song," as art critic Clarence Cook later described it.[24] Whistler's Venetian work offered not something new about Venice, but rather something new about making pictures—and a legacy that would shape the direction of American art for decades to follow.

"FINDING WHAT NO ONE ELSE HAS SOUGHT": SARGENT IN VENICE

In the fall of 1880, John Singer Sargent also drifted from the Grand Canal on what became his first of many visits to Venice since childhood. From his seat in a gondola, he worked on several charming city views. That autumn he also completed more than one sweeping view of the busy streets along the Grand Canal, not unlike those Whistler made the year prior. Yet the bulk of Sargent's Venice work features people, mostly women, walking the streets of Venice or occupied with menial labor in dark and moody interiors.

Like Whistler, Sargent's off-the-beaten-path subjects also caught notice for their originality, first from those in his circle in Venice and later by the press when these works were exhibited in Paris. Not everyone had favorable first impressions. During Sargent's second extended stay in Venice in the summer and fall of 1882, for example, Bostonian Martin Brimmer took note of the "half-finished" pictures he encountered by the young painter at the Palazzo Barbaro, home of Daniel Sargent Curtis and Ariana Wormeley Curtis, where Sargent had been staying. "They are very clever," Brimmer insisted, "but a good deal inspired by the desire of finding what no one else has sought here—unpicturesque subjects, absence of color, absence of sunlight. It seems hardly worthwhile to travel so far for these."[25] The following year in Paris, the *Gazette des Beaux-Arts* expressed wonder at Sargent's choice of banal, commonplace subjects found along "obscure crossroads" or in small, dark rooms. "Where have

✲ CAT. 4-6
James McNeill Whistler, *Old Women*, 1880, drypoint on paper, 5 × 7 15/16 in., Gift of Samuel Putnam Avery, Prints Collection, Miriam and Ira D. Wallach Division of Art, Prints and Photographs, The New York Public Library, Astor, Lenox and Tilden Foundations

✲ CAT. 4-7
James McNeill Whistler, *The Beggars (First Venice Set)*, 1879–80, etching and drypoint on paper, 12 × 8 1/4 in., The Baltimore Museum of Art, The Conrad Collection

✲ CAT. 4-8
James McNeill Whistler, *The Doorway (First Venice Set)*, 1879–80, etching, drypoint, and roulette on paper, 11 9/16 × 8 in., The Baltimore Museum of Art, The Conrad Collection

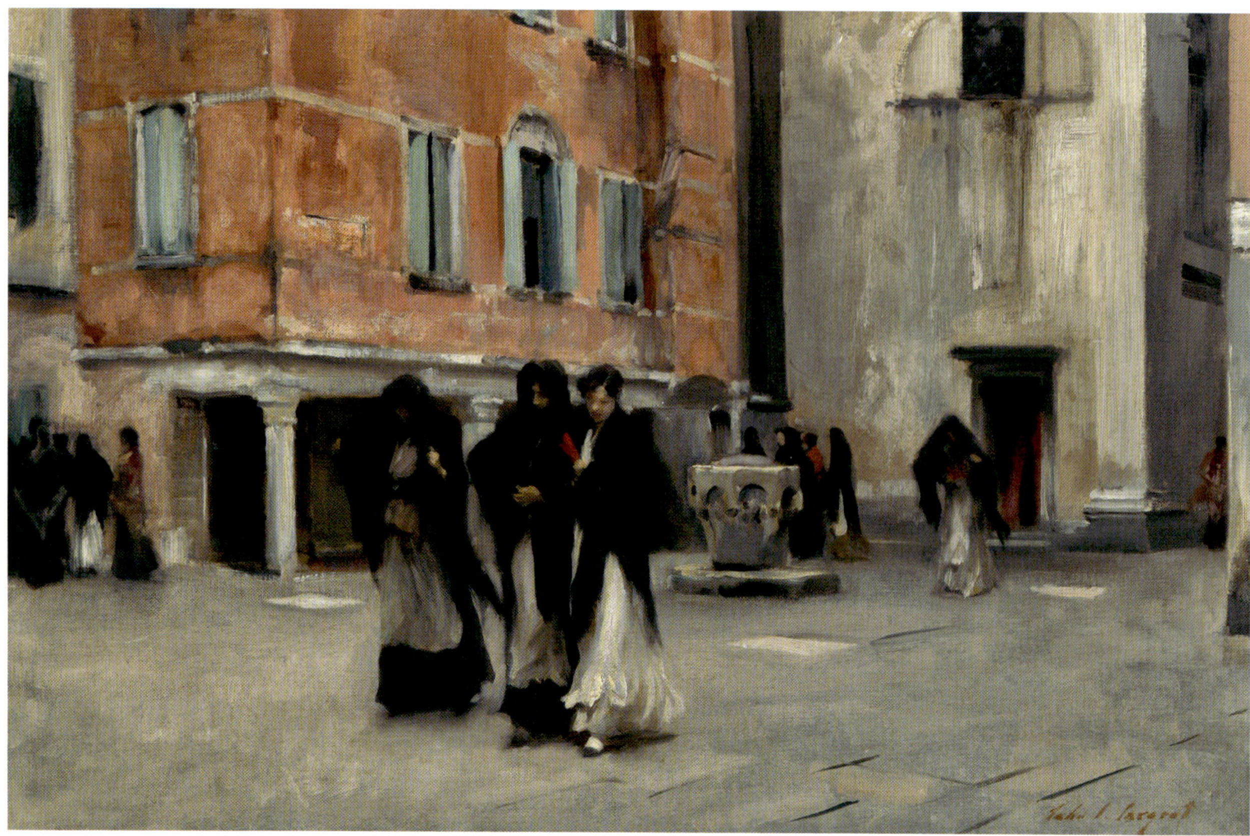

✲ CAT. 4-9
John Singer Sargent, *Leaving Church, Campo San Canciano, Venice*, ca. 1882, oil on canvas, 22 × 33 ½ in., The Collection of Marie and Hugh Halff

Titian's beauties gone?" the review laments. "It is certainly not their descendants that we can scarcely see beneath their unruly hair, draped in their old black shawls, as if shivering with fever? What's the good of going to Italy to collect such impressions?"[26]

Indeed, pictures such as *Leaving Church, Campo San Canciano, Venice* or *A Venetian Interior* (both possibly exhibited in Paris in 1883)[27] might have seemed jarring to an audience accustomed to delightfully quaint representations of Italian privation. Charming and colorfully dressed peasants, depicted among classical ruins or scattered in the countryside, had populated Italian views since the Renaissance. Such cloying imagery could relieve a more privileged audience from grappling with the evident and pervasive poverty in southern Europe. For northern European, British, and American travelers, to go to Italy was to retreat from the harsh realities of the modern world—not to confront them. In Venice, the privileged could escape to a simpler life amid just the right amount of picturesque decay.

By contrast, Sargent's pictures appeared as reminders of the less picturesque aspects of Venetian life—banal, everyday life that to some would seem unworthy of recording. These pictures, such as *Leaving Church* (CAT. 4-9) and *A Venetian Interior* (CAT. 4-10), are darkly toned, chilled by the gray light of winter. Against backdrops of muted ocher, beige, brown, and black, the Venetians here, wrapped in black shawls and their faces in shadow, are not like Stewart's women gossiping at sunset against a brilliant Venetian skyline. But they are also not Whistler's women, whom we might pass without thought in the streets. We notice Sargent's women. They are youthful and confident; they are the central feature of every picture. Despite the *Gazette* reviewer's frustration that they were not the exquisite and reserved "beauties" of Titian's then well-known masterworks, they are also attractive and appealing.

Like many American artists of the nineteenth century, Sargent admired the painters of the Italian Renaissance. As a young artist, only a few years before his 1880 visit, he expressed a fondness for Titian, Michelangelo, and Tintoretto, writing passionately about them in letters. To his cousin, for example, he explained, "I have learned in Venice to admire Tintoretto immensely and to consider him perhaps only second to Michael Angelo and Titian, whose beauties it was his aim to unite."[28] He copied old master paintings in his notebooks, collected pictures of them, and would have had the opportunity to view many works in person throughout his youth on his family's extended travels throughout Europe.[29] In Florence, where he lived in the years preceding his departure for Paris and art school in 1874, he would have seen major examples by all the Italian masters at the Uffizi Gallery, to which countless Americans had made cultural pilgrimages over the course of that century.

Though inspired by the sixteenth-century Italians, Sargent appears to have had other influences in mind when painting in Venice. Time in the Netherlands

✡ CAT. 4-10
John Singer Sargent, *A Venetian Interior*, ca. 1880–82, oil on canvas, 19 1/16 × 23 15/16 in., Sterling and Francine Clark Art Institute, Williamstown, MA

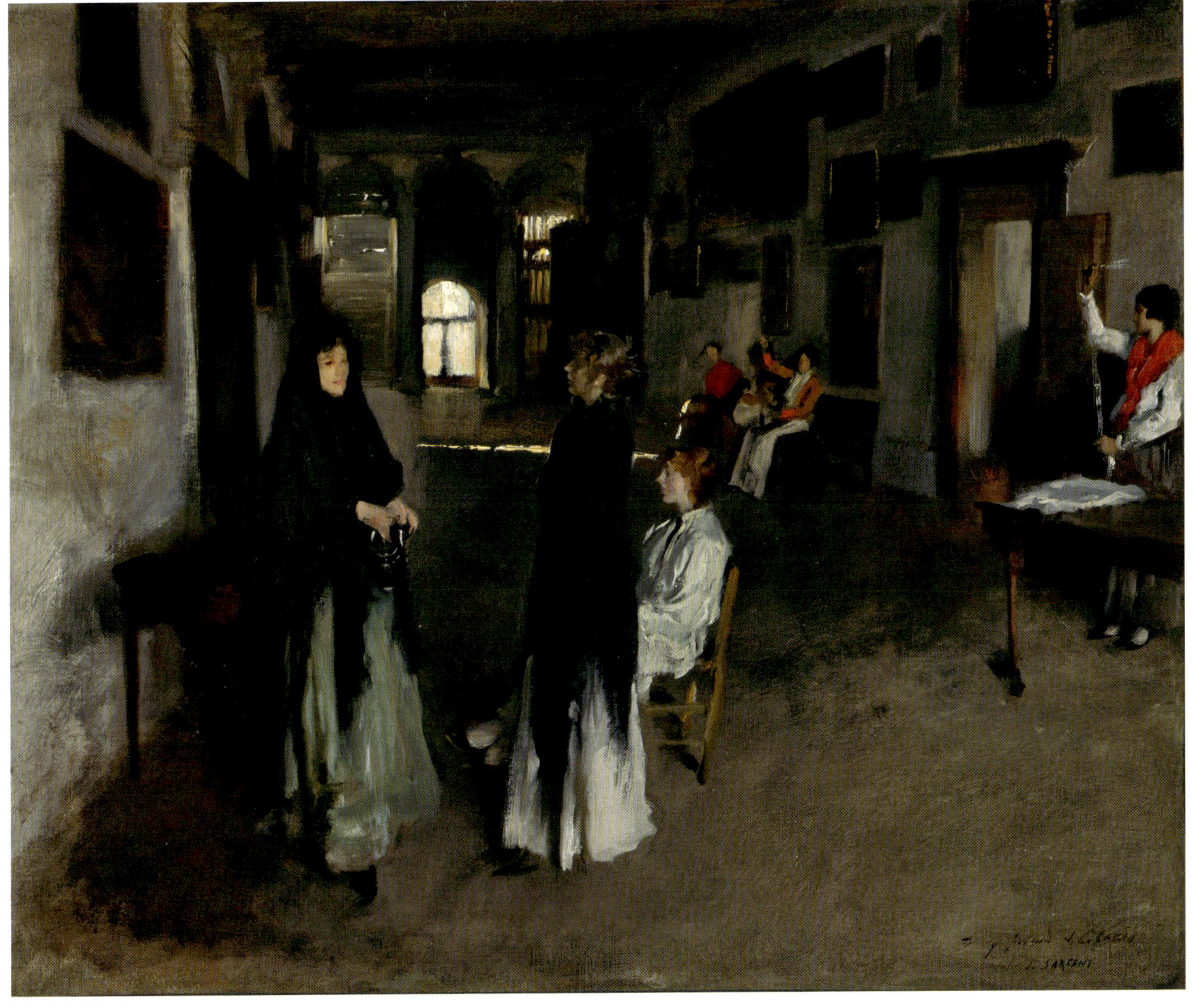

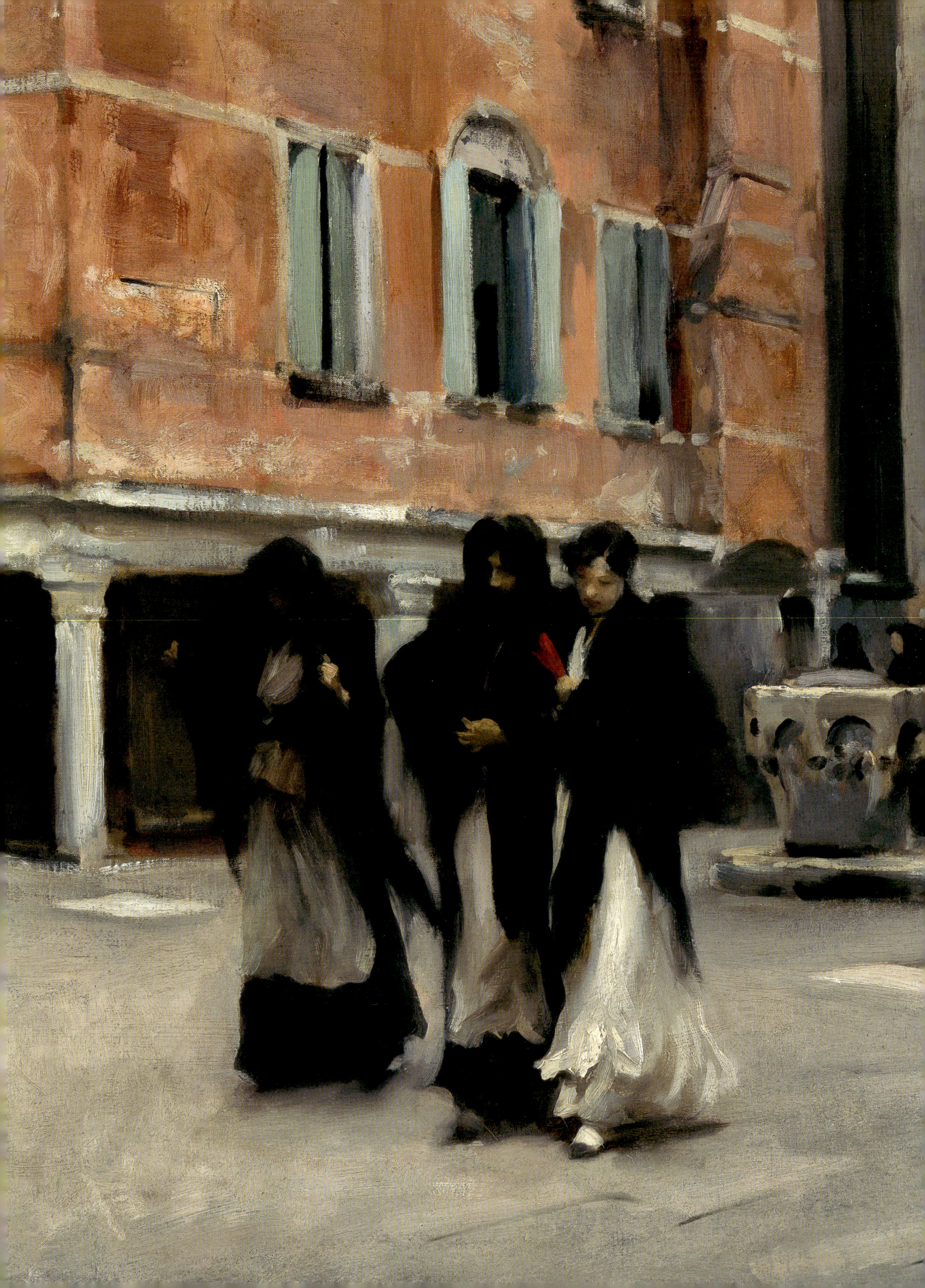

directly before his 1880 visit to Venice, for example, exposed the young artist to the tenebrous works of the Dutch painter Frans Hals, whose dark, brushy, and expressive style appealed to Sargent and others looking to break from strict academic realism.[30] Sargent's pictures are darker than the colorful works that many Americans made in Venice while under the influence of bright, saturated compositions of the Italian old masters. His style loosens in Venice, too, with a vigorous dash of paint to imply the swish of a skirt or the blowing of a shawl in a breeze. Linear precision gives way to impressions and movement.

Though Sargent's works are not made of the colorful palettes and studied lines that so many Americans had admired of the Italian masters, his pictures channel the bravura and confidence of the women pictured in some of the old masters' most famous works. For many nineteenth-century American visitors to European art galleries, the female nudity on display was startling, and Titian's *Venus of Urbino* at the Uffizi was among the more challenging works to confront. As Mark Twain wrote in his tongue-in-cheek description of his encounter with the painting, Venus inspired something more than admiration in impressionable viewers:

> *You enter [the Uffizi], and proceed to that most-visited little gallery that exists in the world—the Tribune—and there, against the wall, without obstructing rag or leaf, you may look your fill upon the foulest, the vilest, the obscenest picture the world possesses—Titian's Venus. It isn't that she is naked and stretched out on a bed—no, it is the attitude of one of her arms and hand... I saw young girls stealing furtive glances at her; I saw young men gazing long and absorbedly at her; I saw aged, infirm men hang upon her charms with a pathetic interest.*[31]

Undoubtedly, Titian's titillating rendering of the goddess of love unnerved some nineteenth-century viewers with her confidence and overt sexuality. Though Sargent's Venetians were not presented as fleshy recumbent nudes, many of his pictures from Venice—which he chose not to exhibit in public at that time—feature attractive women uncommonly at ease under the scrutiny of the male gaze. In pictures such as *Street in Venice* (1882, National Gallery of Art) or *Sulphur Match* (see p. 217), the young women appear to acknowledge their effect on the men in their presence. In the former, the young woman averts her eye and crosses her arms as if in a protective stance, though her gait remains unbroken; she is not unfamiliar with the openness of such exchanges on the city streets. In the latter, the woman is relaxed and enjoying the company of her male companion. She leans back on her chair and looks toward him; an empty wine bottle is discarded by her side. In these unguarded moments, Sargent shows us the humanity of his subjects, if he offers us little else to explain these women and their stories.[32]

Sargent's Venetian women are distinctly of the working class. While some perform activities we expect—stringing beads or passing through the city streets—others appear staged as decorative diversions, such as a curious gathering of women in the grand halls of an old palazzo in *a Venetian Interior*. Perhaps in keeping with representational convention, Sargent's pictures are not about

John Singer Sargent, *Leaving Church, Campo San Canciano, Venice* (detail), ca. 1882; **see p. 154**

the lives of the women he paints but about the place they inhabit. Though he speculates on the social and gendered dynamics Venetian working-class women confronted, his are scenes of the imagination, as much a fiction as his contemporaries' picturesque views of staffage carrying water along the Grand Canal. His pictures are about Venice—the atmosphere, light, and effects of the scenery, and the nameless people who inhabit it. Yet Sargent's is not a picturesque Venice. His is a dusty, dark palazzo or an undistinguished city street. Like Whistler, Sargent shows us places where the visitor might wander but not dwell.

Prospective visitors were undoubtedly aware of the less charming aspects of Venice. For English-speaking readers, the city had been described in entertaining but honest detail by Mark Twain and William Dean Howells in the 1860s, both of whom took note of a place impoverished and depressed, worn by six decades of foreign occupation and a longer period of economic decline.[33] Guidebooks from this moment, too, acknowledged a Venice broken by Austrian rule. "Sky, air and water continue the same," Sir Francis Palgrave wrote in one of the best-selling English-language guidebooks of the region, "but all the actors who peopled the scene are gone." Palgrave carries on with a report from "a resident" who explained that although Venice "is beginning to recover from her depression...it cannot be denied that a large proportion of the rich and fairy patrician palaces are still falling into dilapidation and decay." In addition to the once elegant architecture of the city, he continues, the Venetian aristocracy, too, had suffered "political annihilation" at the hands of the Austrians and the French.[34] Yet even in these accounts intended to prepare the visitor for a deflated Venice—no longer the glittering center of international trade of centuries past—little is mentioned directly about those inhabitants who remained behind. Palgrave relishes enthusiastic detail upon Venice's famous if decaying cultural sights, but the everyday Venetians make rare appearances in his account and, when mentioned, are characterized simply as "poor."[35] Even Twain, who reveled in sharp-tongued character description, when jarred by seeing a man suffering from deformity, efficiently remarked that such sights were "too common in Italy to attract attention."[36] The writers, like the artists, averted their eyes from the less pleasant human elements that could cause emotional discomfort.

Some accounts avoided whitewashing, though these are more difficult to find. Upon his first visit to the city in 1869, for example, Henry James shared his honest impressions in letters to his brother. Repelled by its working-class inhabitants, who were "far too squalid and offensive to the nostrils," James was also disturbed by the "perfectly infernal" mosquitoes that chased him throughout the city.[37] Yet rarely, if ever, did similar observations of this bleaker Venice surface in the typical painted views of the city and its people, making the back-alley scenes by Whistler and Sargent all the more curious to their nineteenth-century audiences.

Working-class Venetians going about their daily activities populate the pictures of Sargent and Whistler, though the images were not realist statements. Rather, though they differed in their approaches—Whistler offers distant views whereas Sargent draws us near—each retains a pleasing aesthetic quality and emotional detachment that distinguishes their work from the socially motivated realism of contemporary artists such as Gustave Courbet, whose unpicturesque renderings of French farm laborers shocked audiences across Europe. Sargent and Whistler also veered from expectation in rendering everyday life. Unlike traditional genre painters, they discard narrative devices. They offer no sentiment, no aid to the viewer seeking emotional connection to the impoverished people they depict, just as Baudelaire's dispassionate observer of modern life retreats into the backdrop.

In a more typical presentation of the same class of Venetian, by contrast, *Venetian Bead Stringers* (Fig. 4-5), painted around 1876 by the well-regarded Austrian painter Cecil van Haanen, pictures an assembly of attractive, trimly dressed women happily engaged in their work. The "laughing, black-eyed, full-lipped, scandal-loving Venetian *donzellas*," as an 1881 reviewer described them, are, "all chattering vigorously over their work as Italian maidens only can laugh and chatter."[38] They are not destitute Venetians but contented workers—alluring, flirty, and unperturbed by observation. In pictures such as Whistler's *Old Women* (see p. 152) or Sargent's *A Venetian Interior* (see p. 155), however, the subjects are more remote and less joyful than van Haanen's "maidens." Clustered in alleys and dark hallways stringing beads and often shown in profile or with their backs to the viewer (CAT. 4-6 detail), these women welcome the outsider's gaze as awkwardly as do the working-class subjects in tense and joyless but commercially popular street photography, such as *Working Women of Venice* by Carlo Naya (Fig. 4-6), pictures that filled nearly every tourist's Venice album.[39] Like the paintings of Whistler and Sargent, these photographs are staged. Also like the paintings, the women in the

Fig. 4-5
Cecil van Haanen, painter; Edmond Ramus, printmaker; *Venetian Bead Stringers*, ca. 1878–80, etching after original painting (unlocated), from *Magazine of Art*, 1887

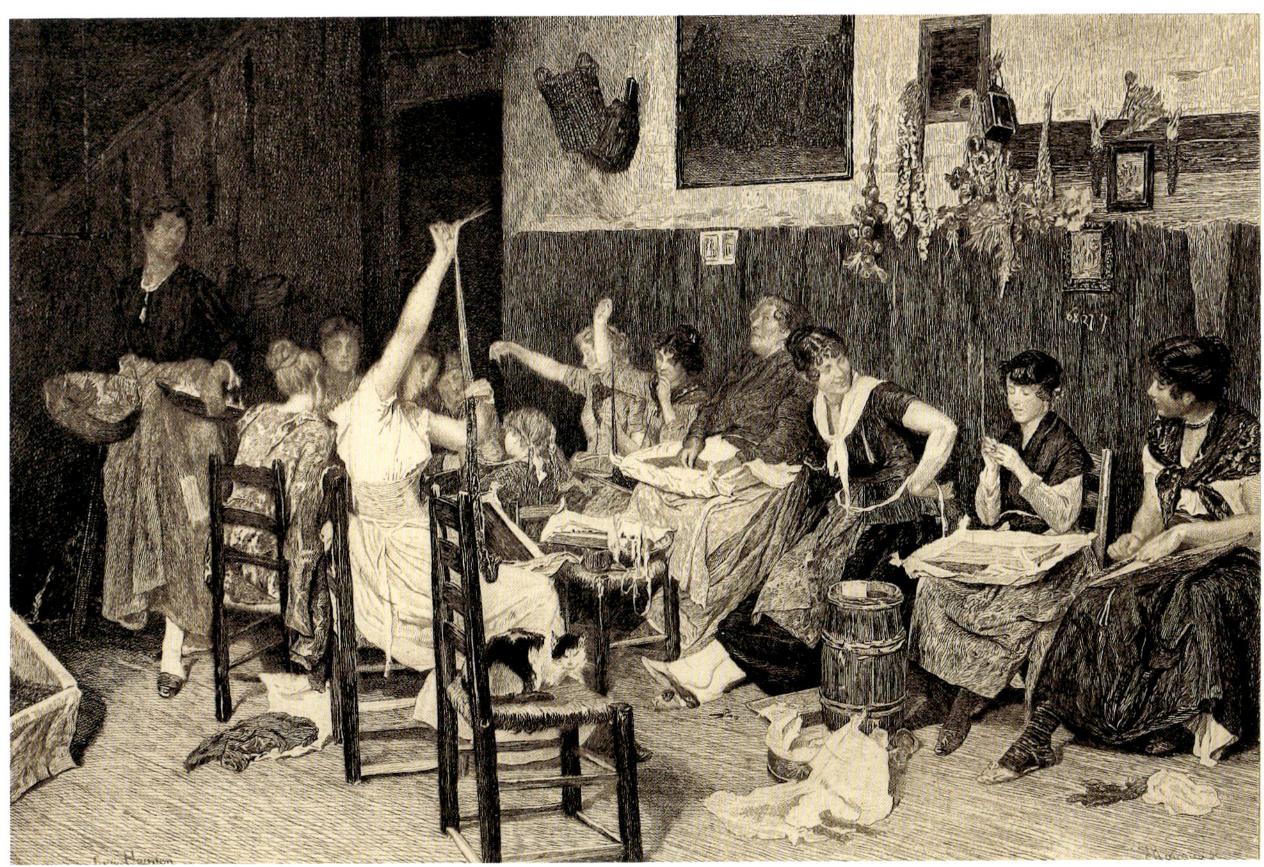

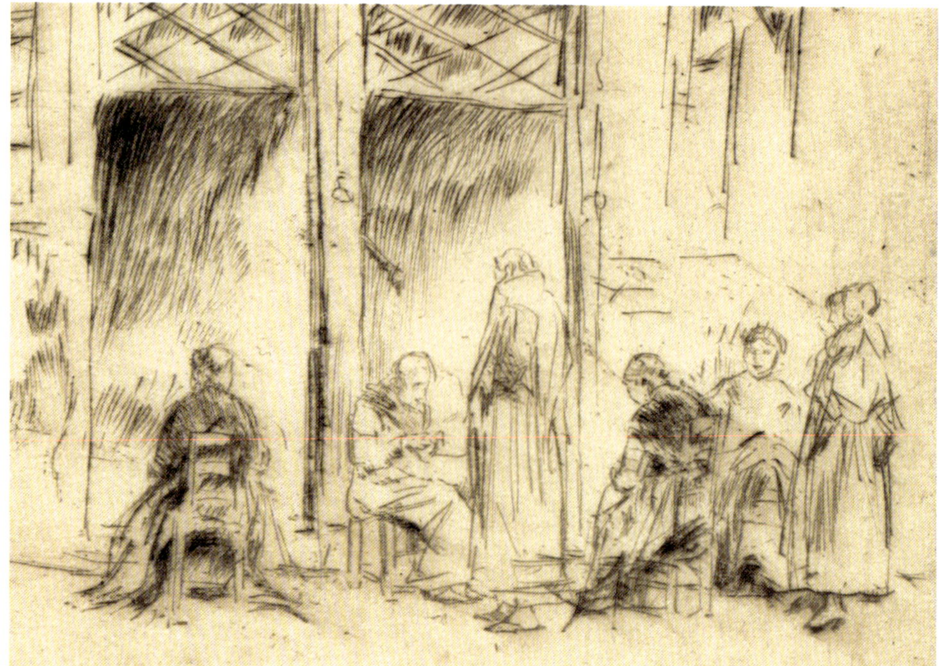

✡ CAT. 4-6
James McNeill Whistler, *Old Women* (detail), 1880; **see p. 152**

Fig. 4-6
Carlo Naya, *Working Women of Venice*, ca. 1857–82, albumen print, Wellesley College, Special Collections

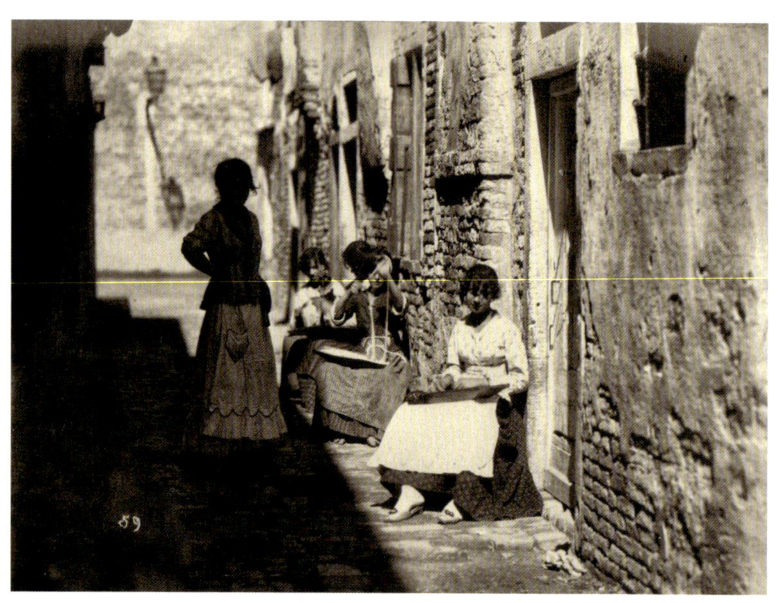

photographs make no show of their work, no efforts to display the colorful and patterned glass beads for which Venice was celebrated (CAT. 4-11). They are not the entertaining "*donzellas*" of van Haanen's picturesque Venice, but the people one might glimpse on the street, in passing, before moving on.

Even though Sargent engaged models rather than people on the street for his Venetian women, Henry James praised him for abandoning the artifice of the traditional painter in Venice. His works, James explained, were "free from that element of humbug which has ever attended most attempts to reproduce the Italian picturesque."[40] Sargent's pictures were not a mere recasting of old and tired themes. According to James, Sargent presents an experience of Venice with which they, as privileged expatriates, were familiar. It was Sargent's host, the Bostonian Daniel Sargent Curtis, after all, who not only lavished money and attention upon the renovation of the dazzling Palazzo Barbaro on the Grand Canal, but also enjoyed wandering among the humbler districts of the city. One friend recalled that Curtis enthusiastically toured him through the "out-of-the way corners that I had not seen before and such that only Venice can show you."[41] Whistler and Sargent similarly veered off the beaten path for their pictures. The authenticity they sought was not in discovering the city's hidden places, but rather in conveying the experience once there. Theirs was the Venice of the foreign observer.

✡ CAT. 4-11
Attributed to Società Veneziana per l'Industria delle Conterie (SVC), Stephen A. Frost & Son, Sample Card with Flameworked Beads, late 19th century–1904, 85 flameworked glass beads mounted to printed card, 13 ½ × 18 in., Illinois State Museum, Gift of Dan Frost

15

S A
F
S

Venice
New York

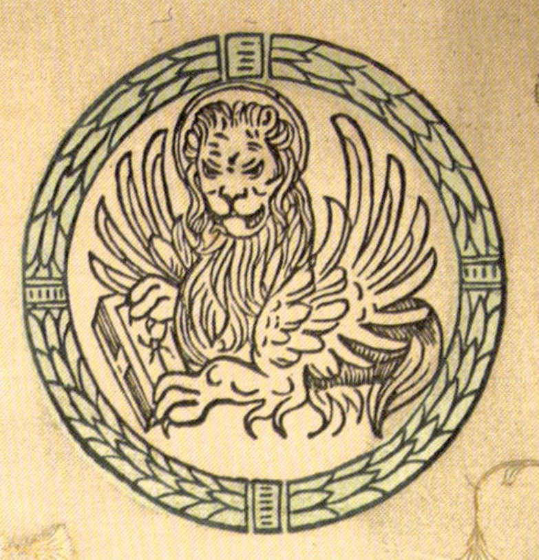

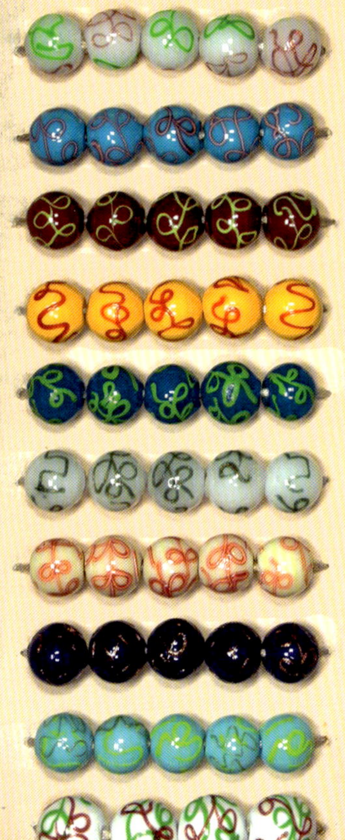

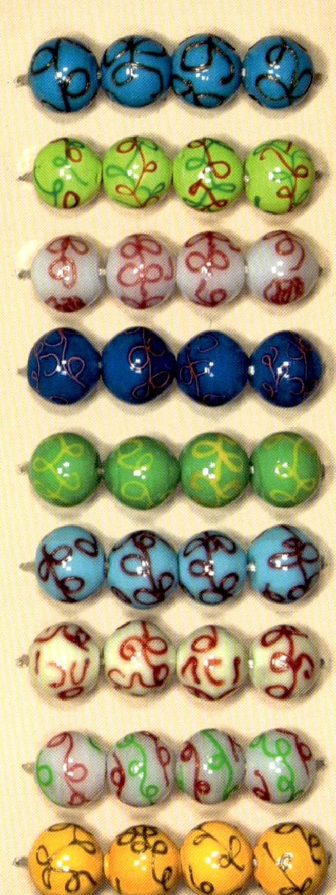

"MORE VENETIAN THAN VENICE ITSELF": BURANO, LACEMAKING, AND SAVING VENICE

While Sargent and Whistler observed Venice, their elite social cohort—a cosmopolitan set of American and British expatriates—lived there. Many of the wealthy Americans who settled in Venice invested emotional and philanthropic collateral in their adopted hometown. In the early 1880s, at the center of the English-speaking social set were the Curtises at the Palazzo Barbaro and the Bronsons—Katharine de Kay and her husband, Arthur—who resided in Ca' Alvisi, just a short gondola ride up the Grand Canal. Katharine de Kay Bronson's parties drew an international crowd and were especially well regarded for the appearance of the occasional celebrity guest, such as an Italian royal or European monarch in exile, but most especially for readings by the English poet Robert Browning, a close friend of the hostess.[42] Also notable was the constant flow of young artists whom she welcomed and supported, among them Sargent, Whistler, and the cluster of American artists gathering in Venice by 1880.

The Bronsons arrived in Venice in 1875, just as the city was reestablishing its cultural and social systems following the departure of the Austrians. A depressed economy surely favored the expatriates, enabling a luxurious lifestyle for far less than it would cost in the United States or Britain.[43] But Bronson, like many in her set, undertook philanthropic projects to address poverty throughout the city. She supported schools, hosted plays by local children, raised funds for charitable causes, and, when called upon, came to the aid of individuals such as Whistler's gondolier, Giovanni, when he had fallen ill.[44]

Bronson also joined a legion of well positioned Italian and expatriate women who led the effort to rebuild a newly independent Venice through the revival of traditional craft industries. Herself a writer, Bronson published in a popular magazine an article on the efforts to reestablish the lacemaking industry, which had been a signature craft of Venice but was suppressed under the Austrians.[45] The essay, which appeared in January 1881, included an account from the Venetian Countess Adriana Marcello detailing the decline of lacemaking, the founding of a new school on the outlying island of Burano, and the revival of the old techniques.[46]

Much of the essay details the establishment of the school and the great success of the revival. Like the fine blown glass produced on nearby Murano, the school's delicate needle lace collars, borders, and cap streamers (CAT. 4-12) became popular grand tour souvenirs, potentially used by the discerning buyer or else treated as art objects for domestic display. The conclusion, however, underscores the moral value of these efforts. With new opportunities for work, the once destitute women of the small island could now afford to buy a "modest

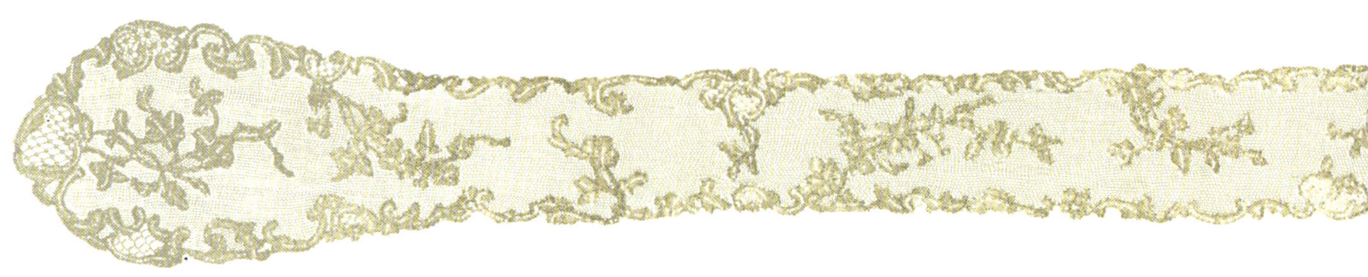

✲ CAT. 4-12
Scuola dei Merletti di Burano, Lace Cap Streamer, late 19th–early 20th century, linen needle lace, 3 9/16 × 42 in., Cooper Hewitt, Smithsonian Design Museum, Gift of an anonymous donor

dwelling," and, even more notably, "Almost all the young men of Burano seek our work-women as wives." Marriage rates had doubled. The number of children born out of wedlock had dropped from twenty-five annually to only two.[47] The moral victory of the lace revival resonated with revival experiments occurring in England as early as 1842 with the development of the Female School of Design in London. Addressing the problem of "idle hands," the introduction of craftwork could provide wholesome and productive activity for middle- and lower-class women and, as reported with the success of the Burano Lace School, assist with poverty and family planning.[48]

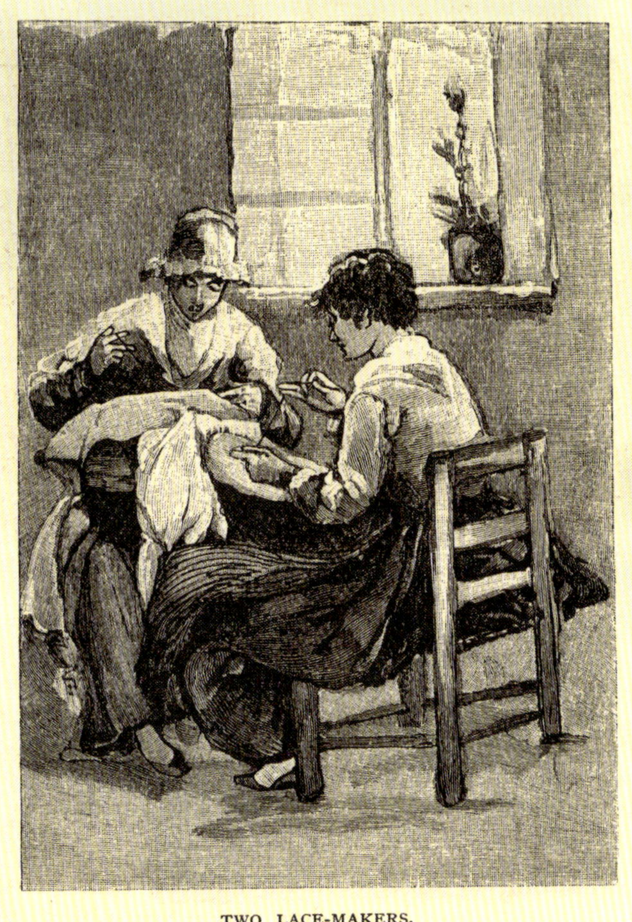

TWO LACE-MAKERS.

Fig. 4-7
Clara, Helen, Henrietta, or Hilda Montalba, *Two Lace-makers*, wood engraving, from *Century Illustrated Monthly Magazine*, January 1882

With a once desperate situation improved through skilled labor, Bronson could encourage her American readers to visit the island to witness the "perfection of the system and its products," and to "pass a Venetian day most agreeably among poor fishermen and their busy wives and daughters on the picturesque island of Burano."[49] To emphasize the charm of a day spent observing the lacemakers of Burano, the article is punctuated with illustrations of the island and its inhabitants. Pictures by the British artists Princess Louise, Marchioness of Lorne (see p. 182), and the Montalba sisters (Fig. 4-7) show industrious, working-class women seated inside by windows contently stitching lace.

These 1881 illustrations prefigure the paintings made a few years later by Robert Frederick Blum, who was among the first Americans to tackle the subject of lacemaking. Blum had overlapped in Venice with both Whistler and Sargent in 1880 and experimented with street compositions such as a bead stringer watercolor, *Bead Stringers, Venice* of 1881 (Fig. 4-8), that critics found resonant with Whistler's Venetian work.[50] In Blum's watercolor from his first visit to Venice, as in Whistler's handling of similar street scenes, the figures are remote and rendered at a distance with little detail. Yet the asymmetry of Blum's composition, and the sweeping passages of ground and wall are reminiscent, too, of Sargent's take on the same bead stringing theme—a correspondence visible especially in works such as Sargent's *The Bead-stringers of Venice* (Fig. 4-9), made sometime from 1880 to 1882.

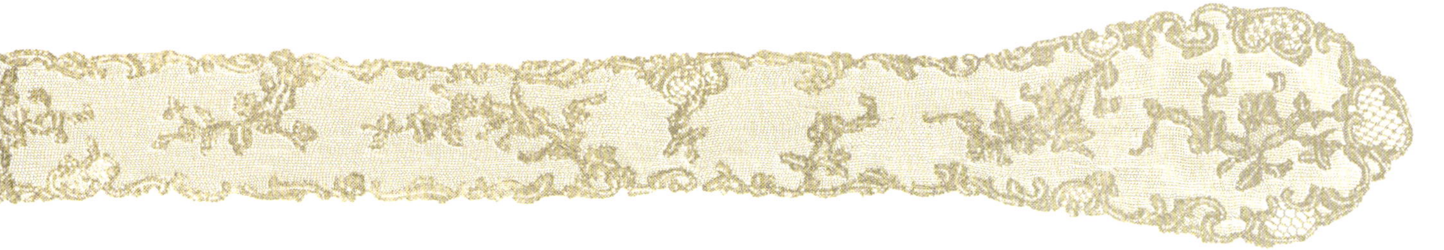

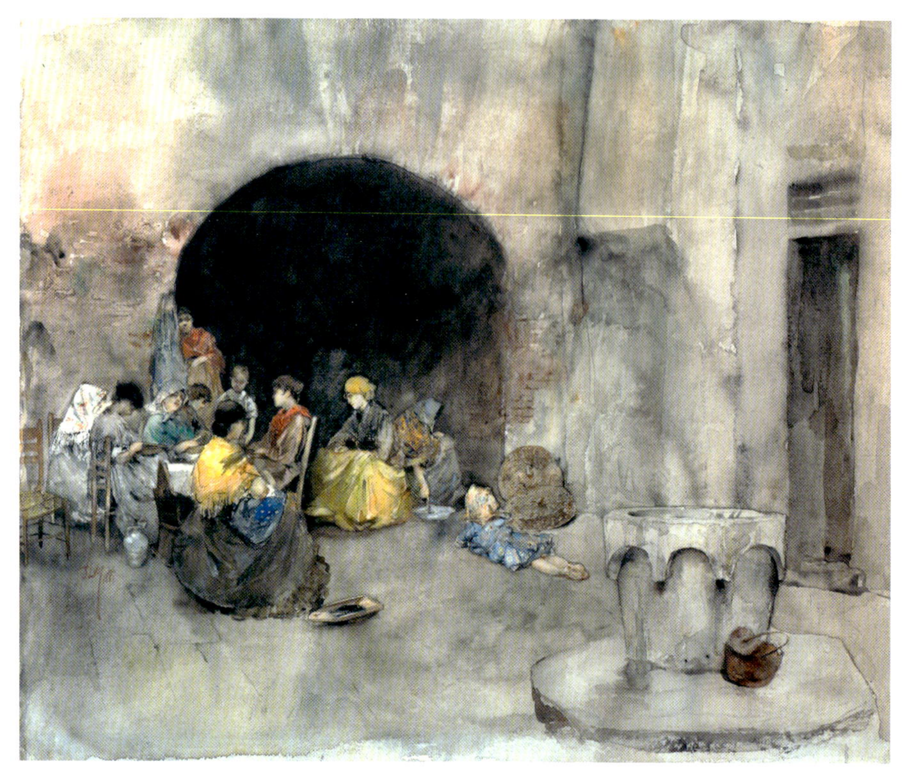

Fig. 4-8
Robert Frederick Blum, *Bead Stringers, Venice*, 1881, watercolor on paper, 18 × 21 ⅞ in., Private collection

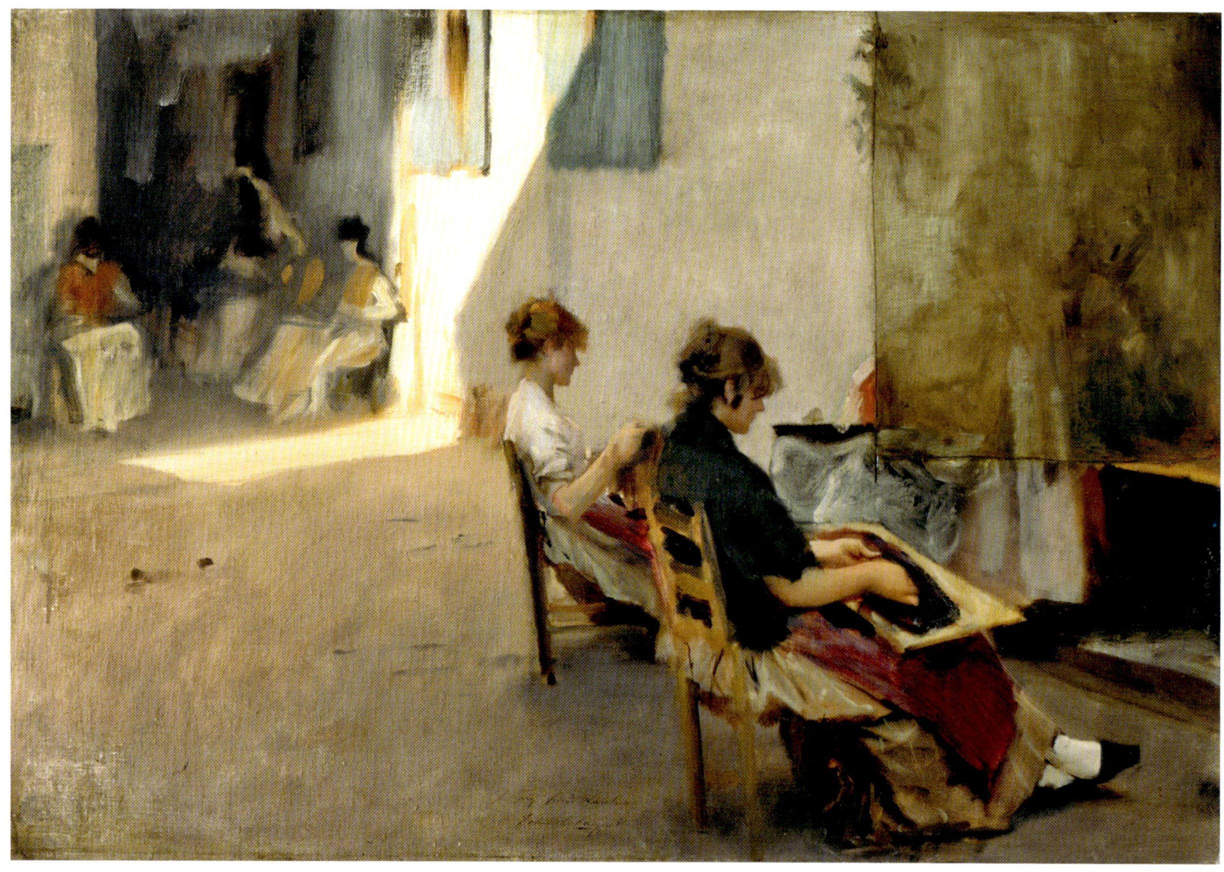

Fig. 4-9
John Singer Sargent, *The Bead-stringers of Venice*, 1880–82, oil on canvas, 22 1/16 × 32 5/16 in., National Gallery of Ireland, Bequeathed, Valentine Lawless, Baron Cloncurry, 1929

Blum's time in Venice with the infamous and revered older artist, Whistler, is well documented in journals, letters, and published accounts such as *With Whistler in Venice* (1908) by their mutual friend, Otto Henry Bacher.[51] By contrast, the young Sargent, just one year older than Blum and likely considered more of a peer than an idol, is not mentioned in these accounts. Yet on more than one occasion Blum and Sargent painted Venice from similar perspectives.[52] Both artists' street scenes of bead stringers from the early 1880s play boldly with asymmetries and unarticulated empty space. Unlike Blum in this instance, Sargent's composition for *The Bead-stringers of Venice* situates the workers in the foreground. Yet the women's identities in these paintings remain equally obscure. Sargent's subjects sit with their backs to the viewer. On one woman's lap, strings are laid out on a board, though what she is doing with these strings is unclear. To her left, her companion appears to be stringing beads, though her "busy hands" are just out of view. A third bead stringer Sargent later cut from the picture before abandoning his work on it altogether.[53] Dressed in livelier colors than her compatriots, this discarded figure was the only one facing the viewer. What is still visible of her body, however, suggests the focal point of this bead stringer would have been her face, unobstructed by the other women, and not her work hidden behind the board on her raised knees. This picture and others painted around 1880 to 1882 by Sargent, Blum, and Whistler share a strategy of deliberate emotional disengagement. The workers and their work made invisible are merely parts of a larger whole.

Back in Venice four years later, however, Blum changed his approach. Directly upon his return in 1885, he settled in Burano for three weeks of sketching and painting at the Burano Lace School.[54] Pictures such as *Venetian Lacemakers* (Fig. 4-10), a small oil with a composition similar to the Montalba sisters' picture of the seated workers, and the etching *Busy Hands* (CAT. 4-13), titled as if to emphasize the happy occupation of these women, suggest that Blum was aware of Bronson's article. Indeed, Blum also published his own illustrations frequently in the same journal.[55] Her essay, the potential appeal of lacemaking among American audiences, and its relative novelty in paintings of Venice may have inspired his turn to this subject.

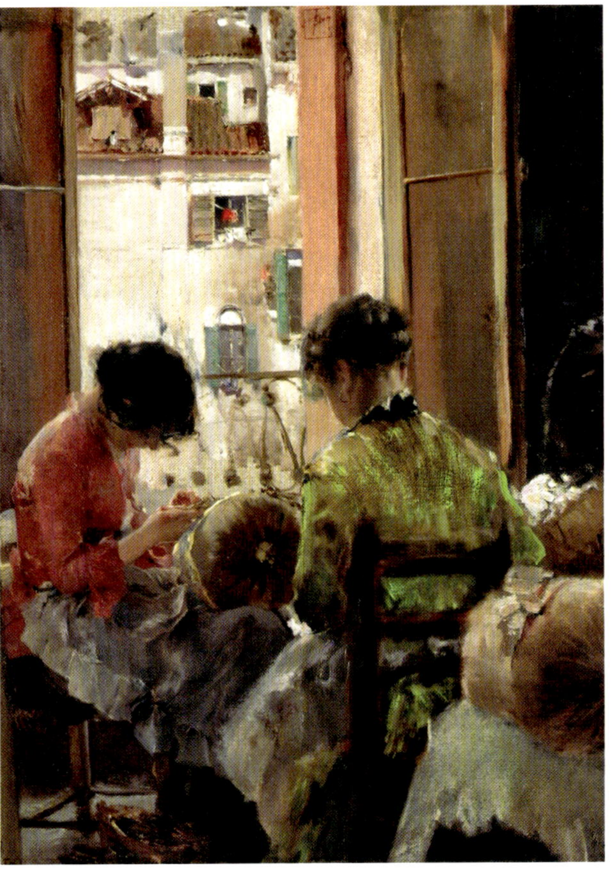

Fig. 4-10
Robert Frederick Blum, *Venetian Lacemakers*, 1885–86, oil on canvas, 16 ⅛ × 12 ¼ in., formerly in the collection of Mr. and Mrs. Raymond J. Horowitz

The most celebrated artwork from Blum's stay on Burano, however, was a large-scale exhibition piece of the Burano lacemakers completed in 1887. *Venetian Lacemakers* (see pp. 192–93) pictures the social and moral outcomes that Bronson mentioned in her article. Here the workers represent the same class of women he had earlier depicted, but they have been elevated from menial to skilled labor, from the street to indoors. Some compositions, such as *Busy Hands* and an 1885 study titled *Venetian Lace-makers* (Fig. 4-11), assemble the women at a table, which gives the appearance of an organized industrial scene, rather than the haphazard

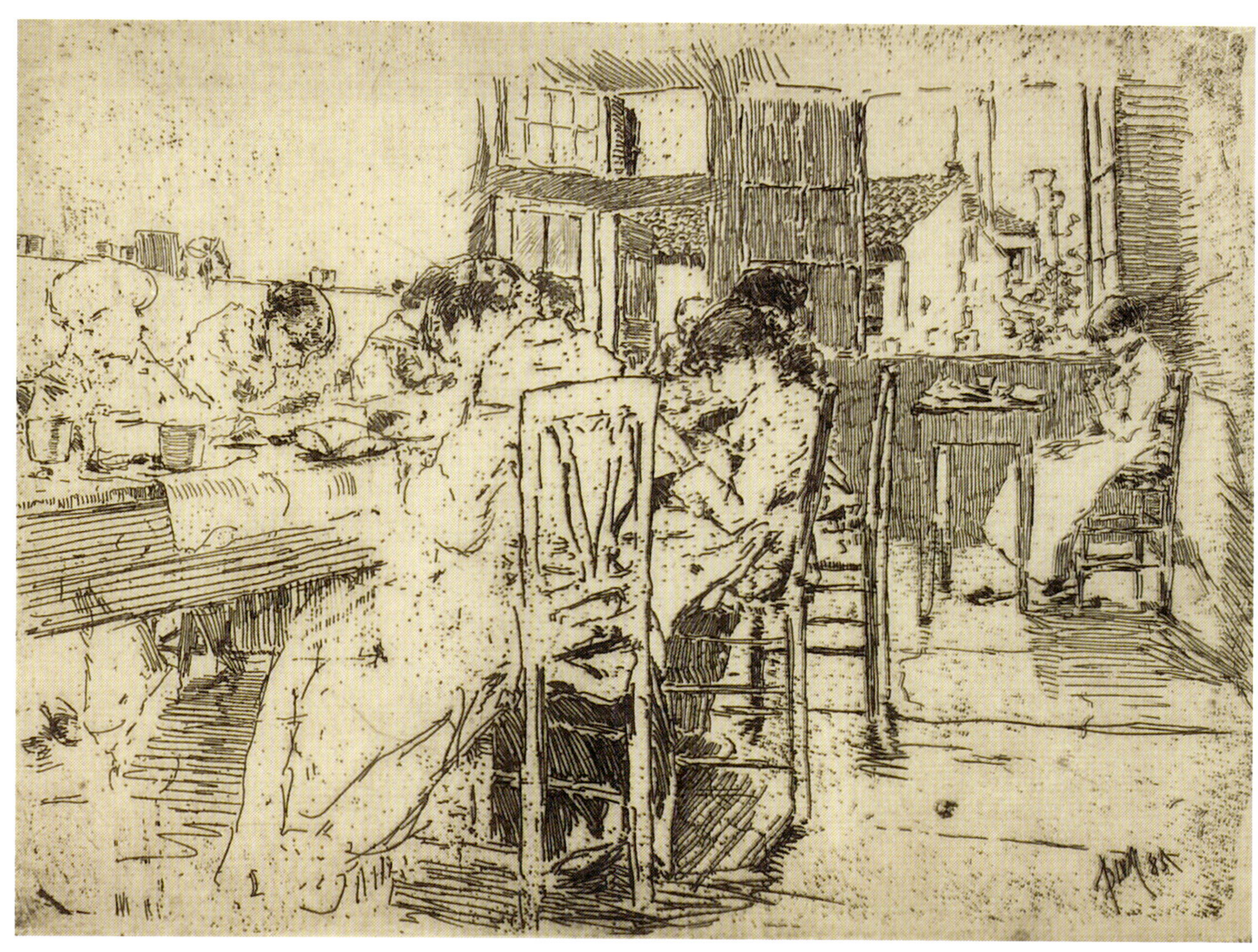

✡ CAT. 4-13

Robert Frederick Blum,
***Busy Hands*, 1885, etching**
on paper, 6 15/16 × 9 11/16 in.,
Cincinnati Art Museum,
Gift of Henrietta Haller

groupings of women in the streets. His exhibition picture from Burano does away with this factorylike setting in favor of an arrangement that highlights the cheerful and social nature of the women and their task.

In the 1887 *Ventian Lacemakers,* Blum's women enjoy conversation and laughs, their *tomboli* (or sewing cushions) resting comfortably in their laps. The clean and brightly painted room offers a safe and guarded space for these women and a cheerful backdrop to their stunning array of colorful dresses—a full embrace of pinks, vermilions, reds, and blues, embroidered patterns, and pretty ribbons. The women, "a brilliant, chattering dozen,"[56] as a review for *Art Amateur* described them, are not the "squalid" Venetians on the streets that Henry James first described, but the happy result of the attention and resources invested in the Burano women.

The painting is picturesque, though undoubtedly also received as an authentic presentation conforming to the wholesome values promoted by patrons such as Bronson, who helped recover this "out-of-the-way corner" of her beloved Venice. As with Sargent's staged renderings of women on the streets of Venice, Blum's 1887 canvas is a work of strategic artifice. When he first started with the theme of lacemaking, it was a fresh subject for American viewers and thus could offer Blum a new approach in a competitive practice. And although the labor portrayed was real and tedious—likely not the perky social gathering Blum describes—Blum did not intend the picture as reportage. Rather it celebrates Burano's social and moral success. Aware that Burano's revival had invested supporters and an uplifting story behind it, Blum adds sentiment and emotion to heighten the picture's impact. His efforts paid off. Blum was commended for

Fig. 4-11
Robert Frederick Blum, *Venetian Lace-makers*, ca. 1885, oil on panel, 14 ⅞ × 18 ⅛ in., Collection of the Arkell Museum at Canajoharie (NY), Gift of Bartlett Arkell, 1936

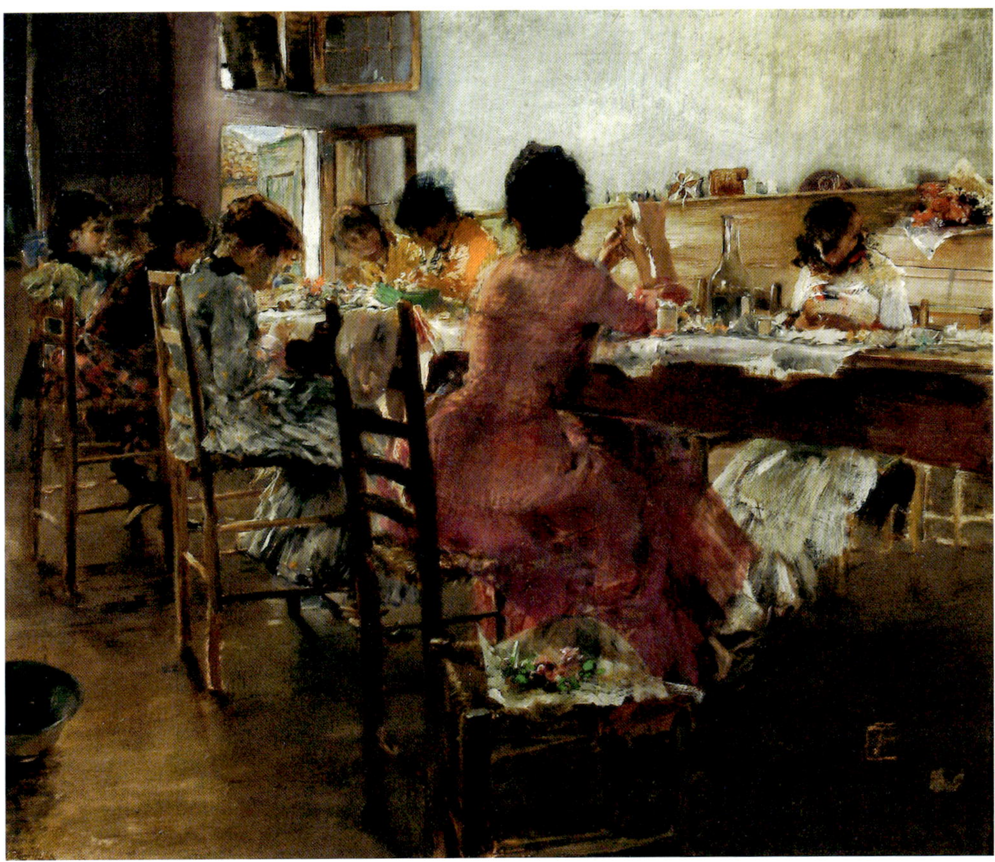

this picture by most who reviewed it, with the women thought by one reviewer to be "not only really, but intensely alive," and by another, "chattering and laughing at their work, look[ing] natural and real."[57]

Bronson urged all visitors to seek out this often-overlooked island for a glance at the real Venice.

> *"Many an enlightened traveler sees nothing beyond the churches and palaces, the pictures and the mysterious water-streets of the most wonderful city of the world. True, this traveler has been made very happy, and ignorant of what is left unseen, goes upon his way in a contented spirit, not knowing that he has lost some of the best of Venice."*[58]

Even the guidebooks suggest a visit there. In Palgrave's *Hand-book for Travellers in Northern Italy,* the author notes that the other islands are "more Venetian than Venice itself, for they convey an accurate idea of what the metropolis herself must have been before she attained her full splendor."[59] When this advice was written in the 1840s, however, Burano and its fellow outlying islands suffered from devastating poverty. Even four decades later, Bronson acknowledged the islanders as "patient and courageous under the heavy hardships of hunger and cold."[60]

In her essay, Bronson makes clear that the competing conditions of Burano's poverty and success coexist—though her view is an optimistic one. Indeed, the relationship that many foreigners had with Venice was full of contradiction. As the painter Francis Hopkinson Smith described it, on the one hand it was "the Venice that bewilders with her glory," and on the other, "where the poorest pauper laughingly shares his scanty crust." For Smith and many Americans, a visit to Venice was a restorative antidote for "this selfish, materialistic, money-getting age."[61] Philanthropic work of Bronson's sort could further assuage the sentimental conscience. For even in the shady alleys, where poverty and misfortune loomed the greatest, where children were "bareheaded, barefooted, and most of them barebacked" and "their mothers and sisters choke up the doorways, stringing beads, making lace, sitting in bunches," the foreigner could be comforted to know that these poor were content with their lives. The working women were happy "listening to a story by some old crone, or breaking out into song, the whole neighborhood joining in the chorus."[62] To accept the cohabitation of poverty and pleasure in Venice could better allow one's enjoyment of it.

In Blum's Burano pictures, these working women are not Whistler's street dwellers nor Sargent's women scarcely seen "beneath their unruly hair, draped in their old black shawls."[63] Blum's women are contented and industrious; they socialize and laugh. They are clean, attractive, well-dressed, and well-fed. Unlike Whistler's and Sargent's emotionally remote renderings of working people of a few years before, Blum's *Venetian Lacemakers* (1887) offers an optimism and sentiment that reflects the philanthropic activities and emotional investments of women like Bronson in the expatriate community.

With this picture Blum asserts his independence from the two artists who, in the six intervening years since their time in Venice, had each become acclaimed for their innovations made there. In his earlier Venetian efforts, Blum was compared with both artists, though especially with Whistler, with one reviewer asserting in 1882 that Blum's Venetian watercolors "are simply and purely tinted Whistler etchings."[64] If, in contrast to Whistler and Sargent, Blum channeled the safer approach of the picturesque with his 1887 *Lacemakers* composition, he also channeled something, too, of the foreigner's ideal experience there. Bronson and Blum shared a vision of Venice—one that highlighted the brighter impressions of a city whose impoverished residents lived in stark contrast to their own comfort, but also a vision that made the case to save that city and elevate the people and their traditions to a higher standard.

By contrast, Whistler and Sargent put aside the emotional framework that foreigners grappled with in Venice. Whistler, like Baudelaire, avoided sentimentality.[65] For him, Venice was an aesthetic place, where "great pictures stare you in the face."[66] The reviewers increasingly understood this of Whistler's Venice work. As time passed, the pastels and etchings were praised not for their Venetian subjects but rather for his daring effects, brevity of style, and for Whistler's innovations in how to display them.[67]

For Sargent, Venice was also a place of observation—not engagement. Yet his presentation of it, perhaps, was closer than either Whistler or Blum to the real experience that most foreign visitors had there. Those who visited only briefly—who viewed the sites, who found themselves charmingly lost in the maze of streets and canals, who observed the crumbling architecture and the impoverished Venetians—were not there long enough to become invested in the recovery of Venice like Bronson and other resident expatriates. The brief, touristic experience was one of romantic expectation, of the accommodating and picturesque experience of poverty and decay that Smith and others had recognized as part of the city's most alluring charm.

If you came to Venice in the 1880s, as Palgrave predicted only a few decades before, you would not arrive a stranger. You came realizing that "almost every feature of importance is already more or less known."[68] Sargent and Whistler chose not to picture these features "of importance," but rather each sought out common people and places. And as they strayed from convention, the skeptics took issue with their work. Yet within short order, both, too, had changed the way Venice was experienced. By the decade's end, Whistler's unconventional back-alley views became understood as models of aesthetic restraint; and Sargent's women, no longer seen as shadowy figures "shivering with fever," had entered the ranks of the picturesque.[69] These women may not have been the descendants of Titian's beauties. But they embodied the kind of gritty beauty that appealed to the late nineteenth-century embrace of life lived with contrast. As Venice's streets increasingly swelled with foreign tourists and painters alike, it was no longer Titian's beauties that people came to see. It was the life on the streets.

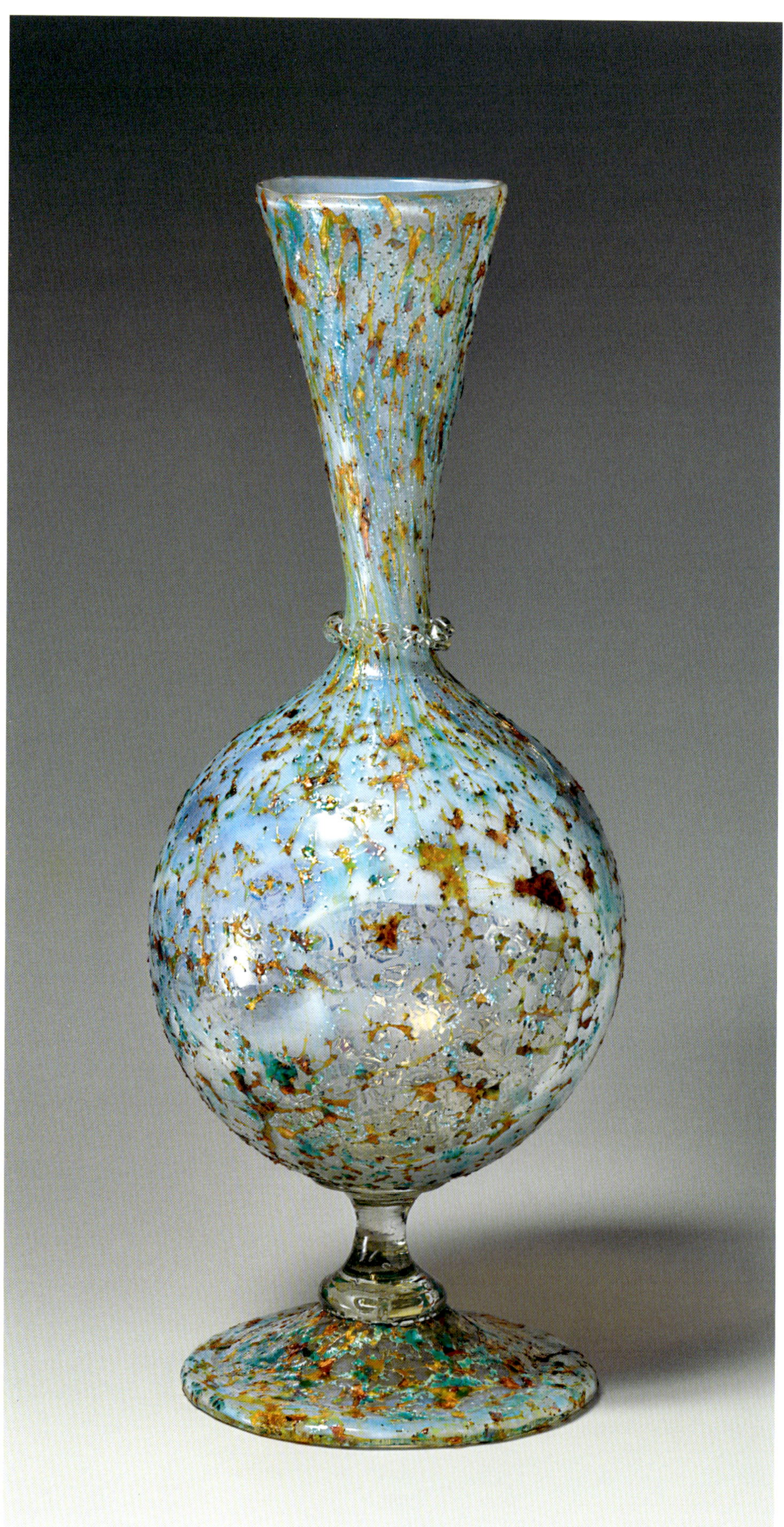

✡ CAT. 4-14
Venice and Murano Glass and Mosaic Company Ltd. (Salviati & Co.), Opalescent Glass Vase with Multicolor Granzioli, ca. 1868–80, blown and applied hot-worked glass, 12 × 4 ⅞ in. diam., The Metropolitan Museum of Art, Gift of James Jackson Jarves, 1881

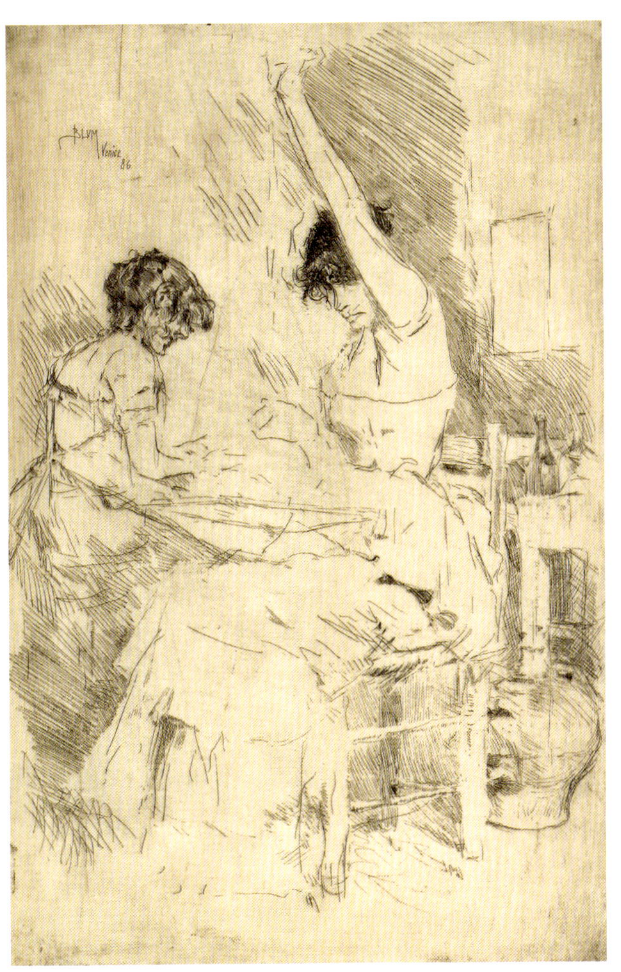

✡ CAT. 4-15
Robert Frederick Blum, *Bead Stringers*, 1886, etching on paper, 12 3/16 × 8 1/16 in., Cincinnati Art Museum, Gift of Henrietta Haller

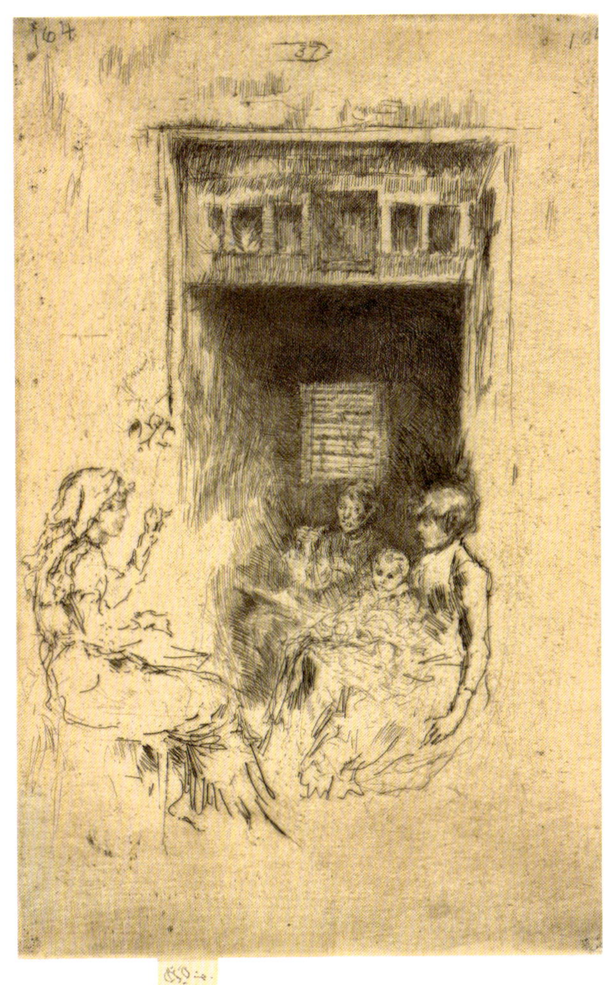

✡ CAT. 4-16
James McNeill Whistler, *Bead Stringers (Second Venice Set)*, 1880, etching and drypoint on paper, 9 1/16 × 6 1/16 in., Gift of Samuel Putnam Avery, Prints Collection, Miriam and Ira D. Wallach Division of Art, Prints and Photographs, The New York Public Library, Astor, Lenox and Tilden Foundations

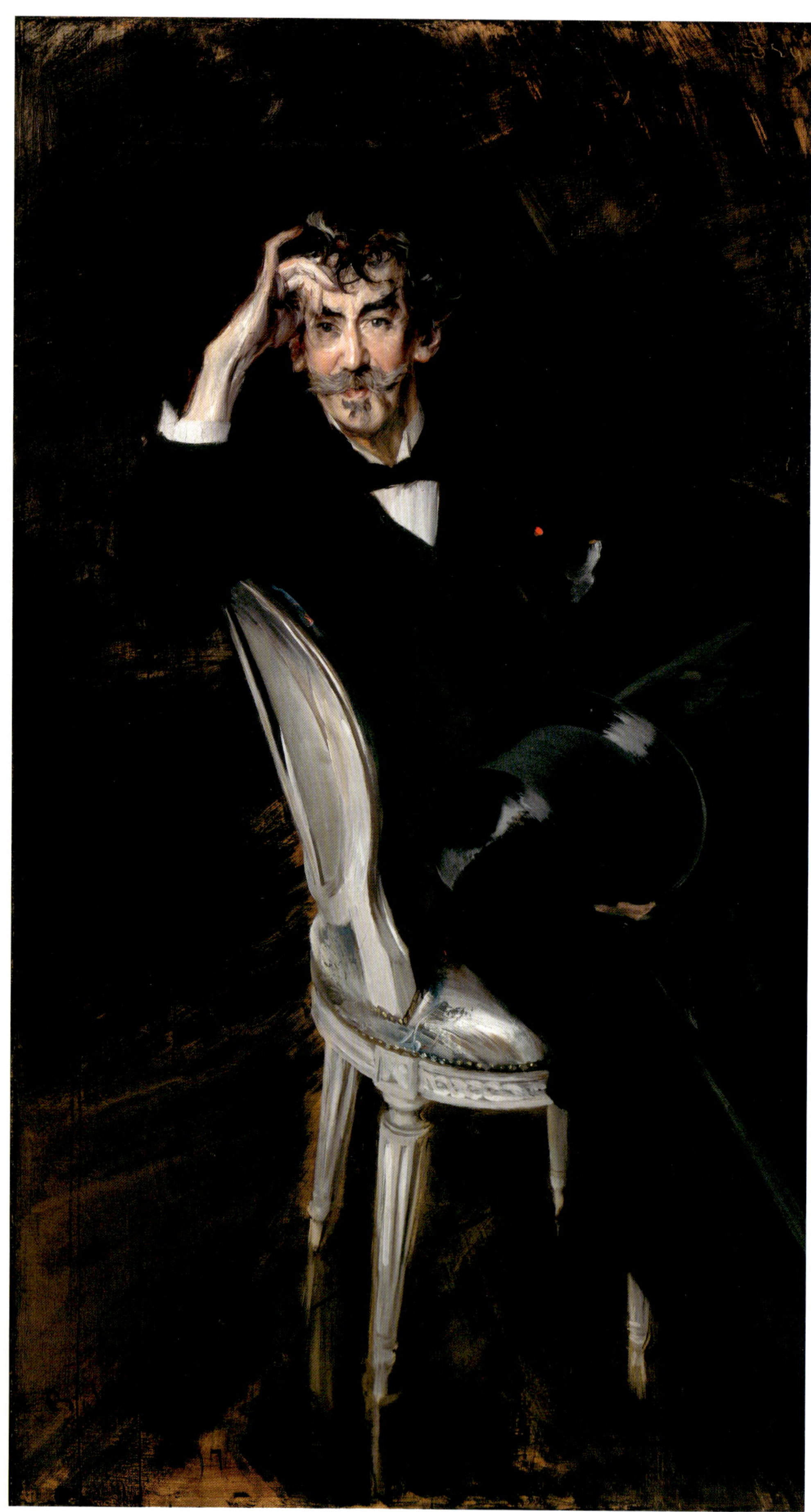

✡ CAT. 4-17
Giovanni Boldini,
Portrait of James McNeill Whistler,
1897, oil on canvas,
67 ¼ × 37 ¼ in.,
Brooklyn Museum,
Gift of A. Augustus Healy

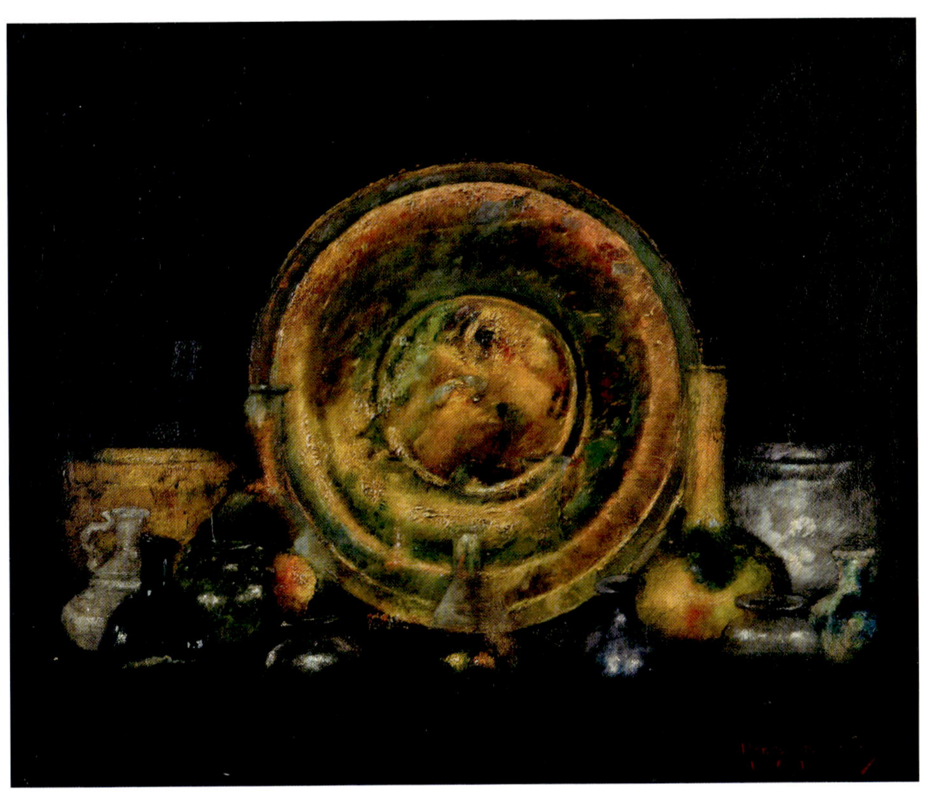

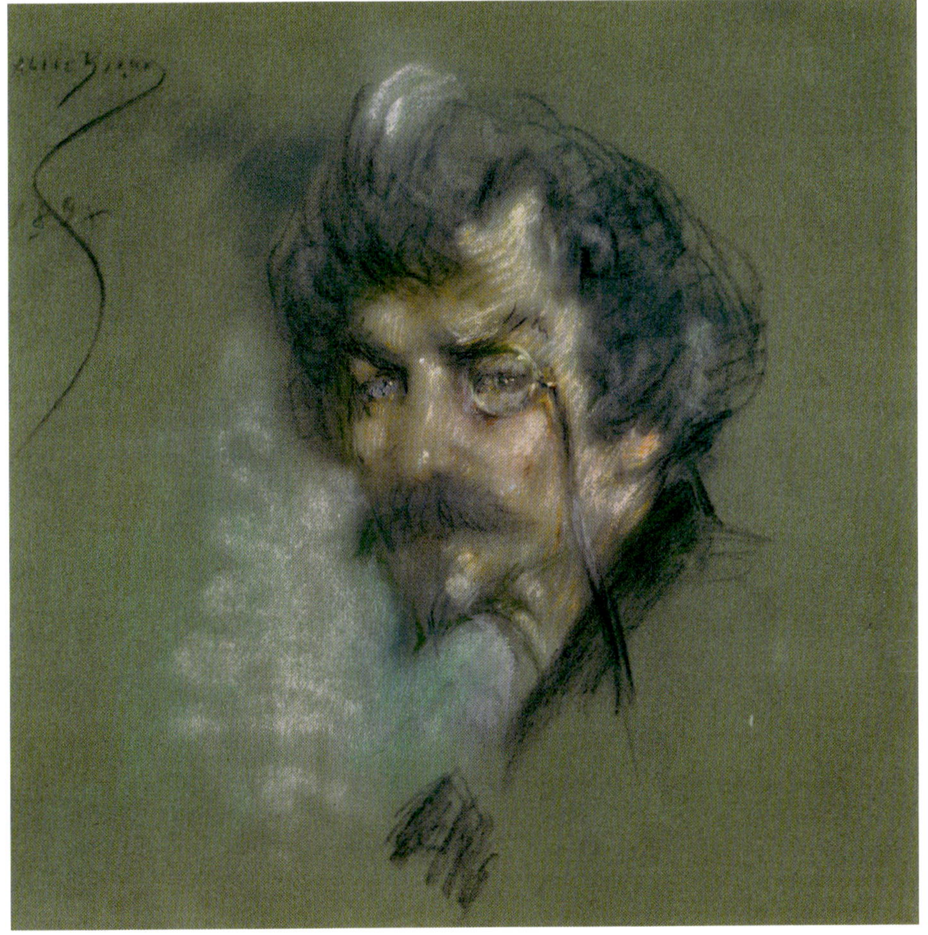

✡ CAT. 4-18
Henry Alexander,
Cyprus Glass, 1894,
oil on canvas,
15 ¾ × 19 in.,
Collection of David Mamet
and Rebecca Pidgeon

✡ CAT. 4-19
Alice Pike Barney,
James McNeill Whistler,
1898, pastel on paper
mounted to paperboard,
19 1⁄16 × 19 3⁄16 in.,
Smithsonian American
Art Museum, Gift of
Laura Dreyfus Barney and
Natalie Clifford Barney
in memory of their mother,
Alice Pike Barney

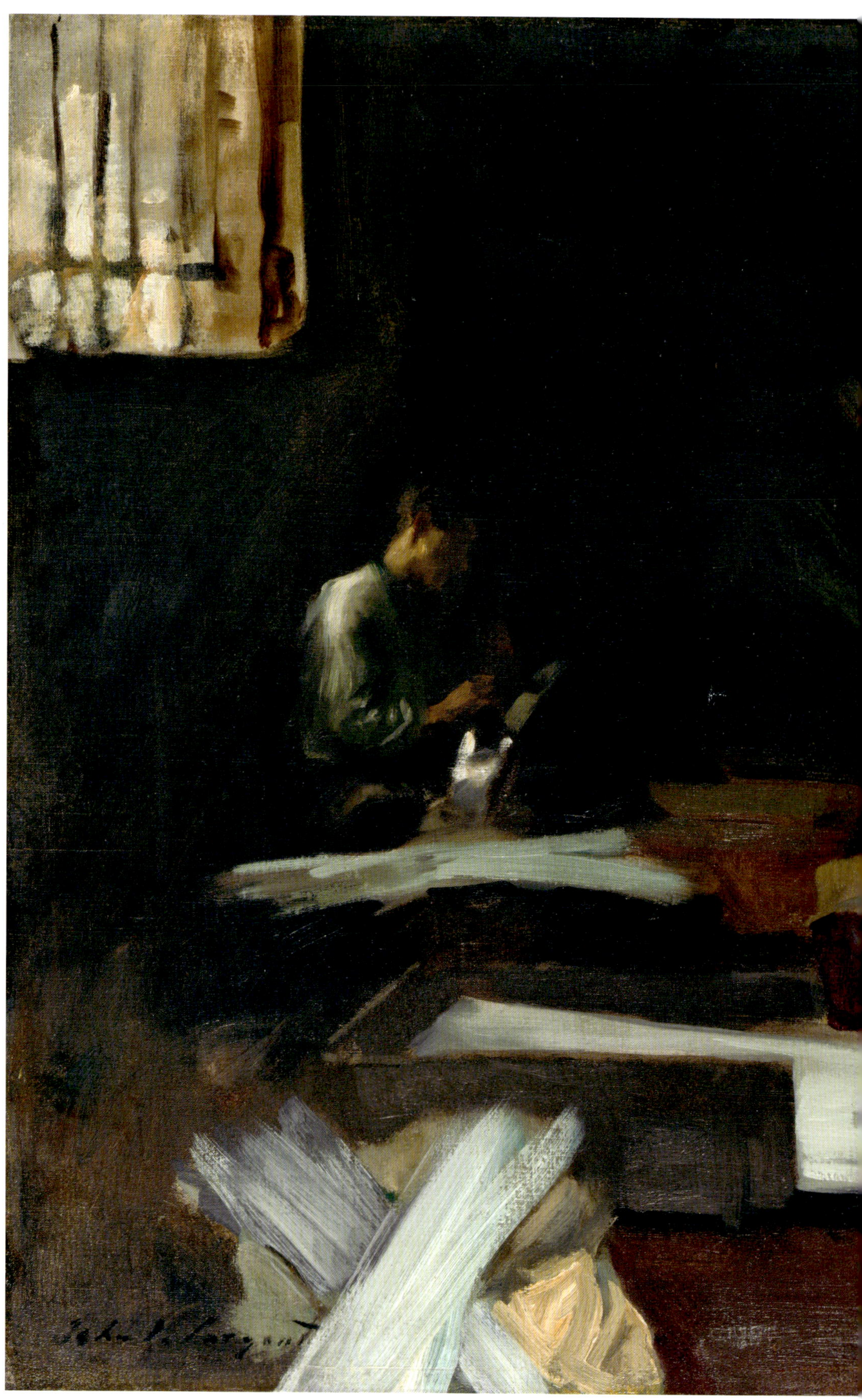

✡ CAT. 4-20

John Singer Sargent, *Venetian Glass Workers*, ca. 1880–82, oil on canvas, 22 ¼ × 33 ¼ in., The Art Institute of Chicago, Mr. and Mrs. Martin A. Ryerson Collection

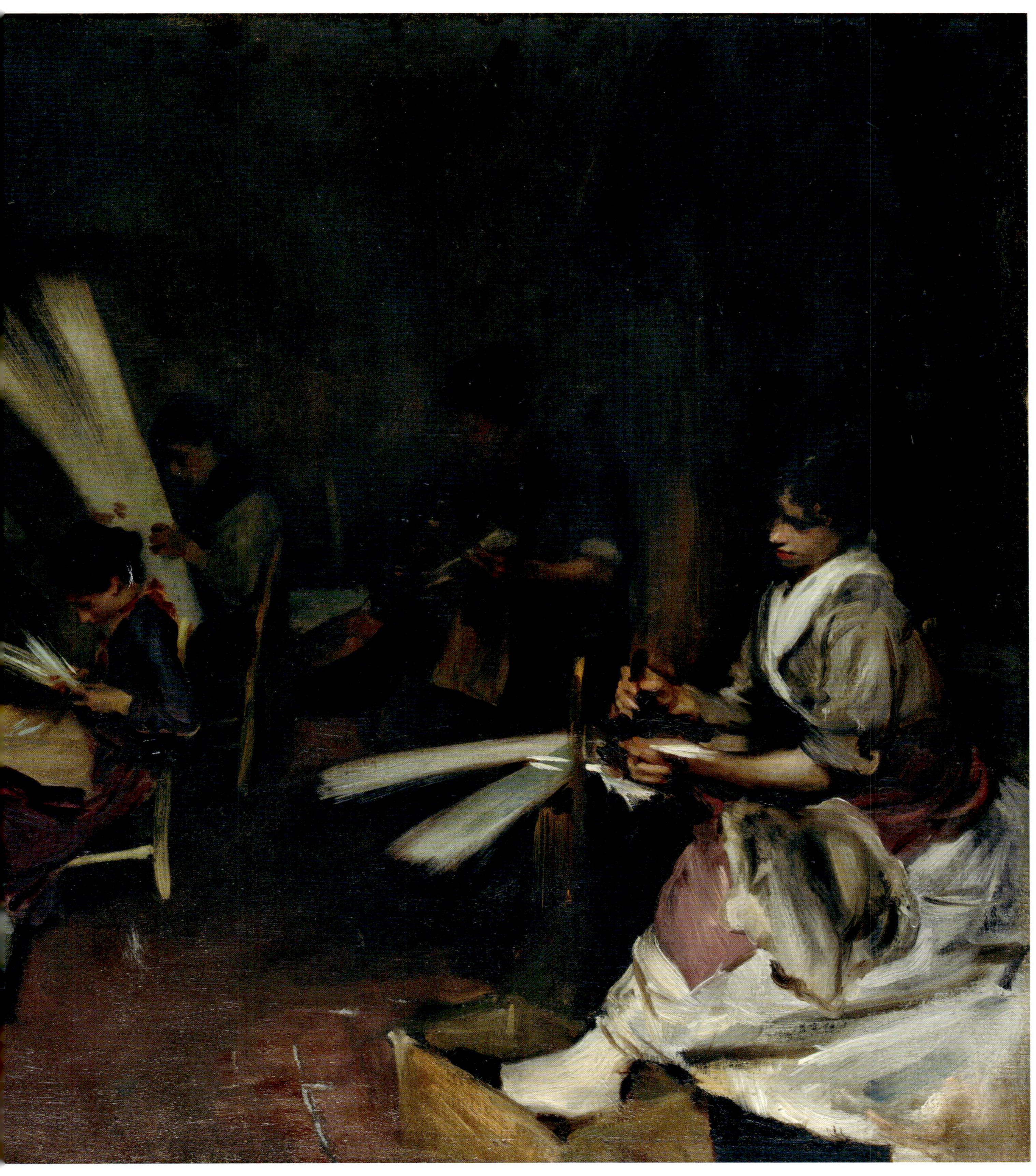

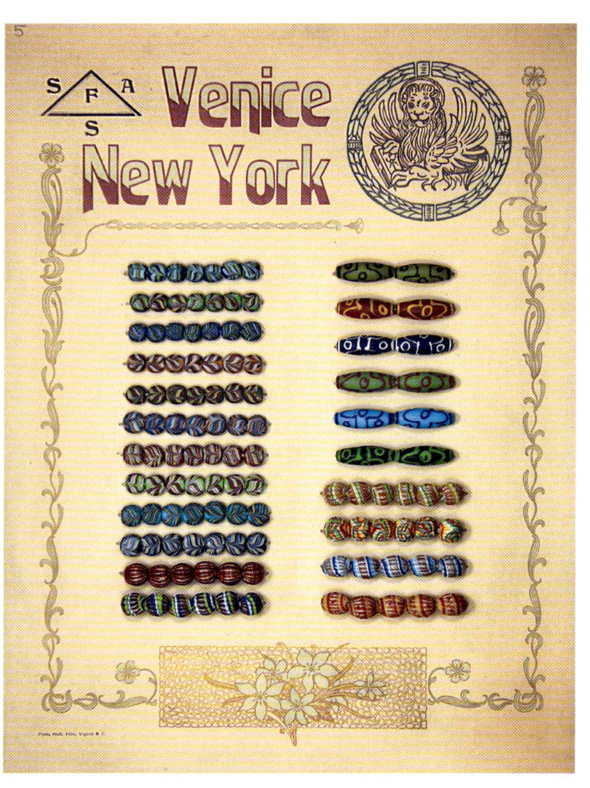
S F A
S
Venice
New York

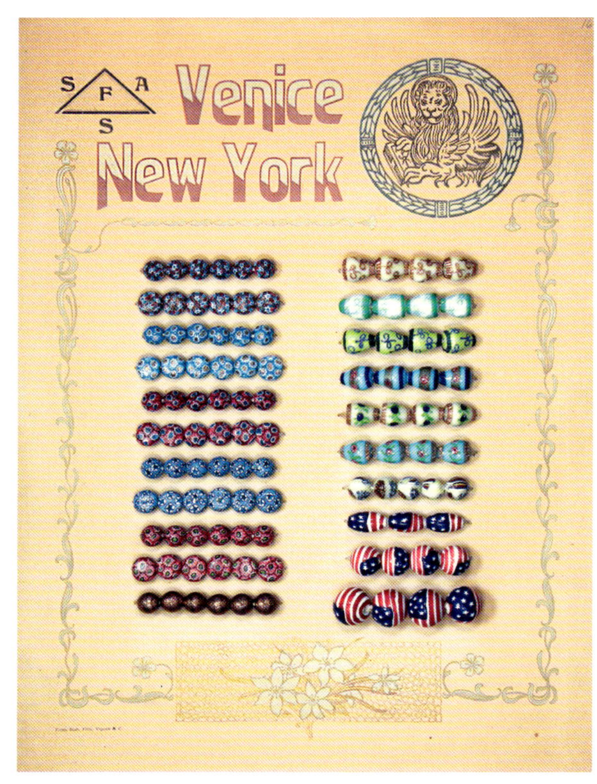
S F A
S
Venice
New York

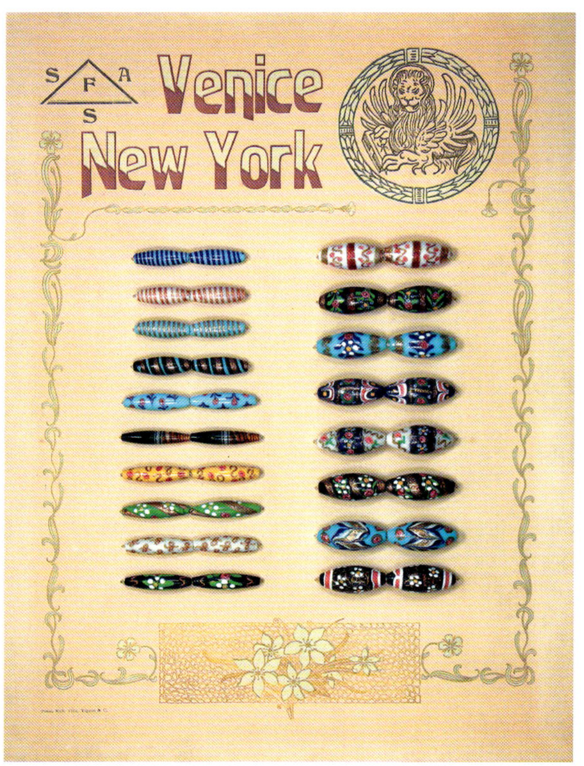
S F A
S
Venice
New York

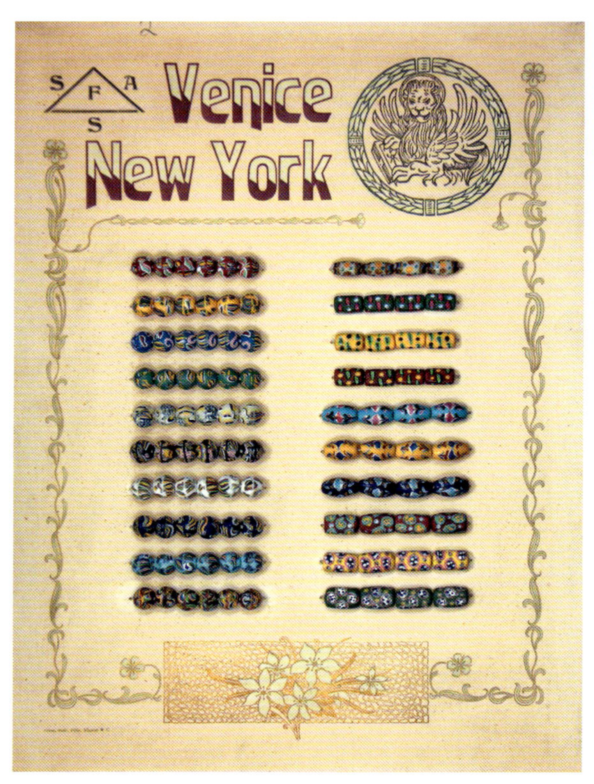
S F A
S
Venice
New York

NOTES

1 Sir Francis Palgrave, *Hand-book for Travellers in Northern Italy* (London: John Murray and Son, 1842), 326, accessed July 22, 2020, https://www.google.com/books/edition/Hand_Book_for_Travellers_in_Northern_Ita/hhFXAAAAcAAJ?hl=en&gbpv=1.

2 On American artists in Venice, see Erica E. Hirshler, "'Gondola Days': American Painters in Venice," in *The Lure of Italy: American Artists and the Italian Experience, 1760–1914*, ed. Theodore E. Stebbins Jr. (New York: Harry N. Abrams, 1992), 112–28; and Margaretta M. Lovell, *A Visitable Past: Views of Venice by American Artists, 1860–1915* (Chicago: University of Chicago Press, 1989). On the influx of Americans in the 1870s and 1880s, one art critic, Julia Cartwright, wrote in 1884, "Within the last few years we have seen the rise of the whole school of English and American artists who owe their inspiration to Venice, and have in great measure formed their style from lessons learned in the lagoons. At no time have painters and etchers been more actively engaged in Venice than they are today." Julia Cartwright, "The Artist in Venice, Part I," *Portfolio* (London) 15 (1884): 17; cited in Richard Ormond, "Modern Life Subjects," in *Sargent and Italy*, ed. Bruce Robertson (Princeton, NJ: Princeton University Press, 2003), 59.

3 Palgrave, *Hand-book for Travellers in Northern Italy*, 328. Palgrave offers quotations and accounts by historians and local residents to convey the destruction of the French and Austrian occupations. Palgrave's account of the evident decay and disrepair is not, however, an indictment. While his description consistently presents a city left behind by the modern world, his account reflects a lingering influence of the romantic sensibilities of the early nineteenth-century elite.

4 Otto H. Bacher, *With Whistler in Venice* (New York: Century, 1908), 29.

5 Ibid, 30.

6 For a comprehensive account of the Ruskin and Whistler trial, see Linda Merrill, *A Pot of Paint: Aesthetics on Trial in* Whistler v. Ruskin (Washington, DC: Smithsonian Institution Press, 1992).

7 Richard Dorment, "Venice," in *James McNeill Whistler*, by Richard Dorment and Margaret F. MacDonald (New York: H. N. Abrams, 1995), 179.

8 In fact, Duveneck's prints of the Riva were mistaken for Whistler's in an 1881 print exhibition hosted by the Society of Painter-Etchers in London. According to Otto Henry Bacher, Whistler wrote a letter to the society to clear up the confusion. See Bacher, *With Whistler in Venice*, 134–43.

9 See *Canaletto, Piazza San Marco*, late 1720s, oil on canvas, Metropolitan Museum of Art, New York, Purchase, Mrs. Charles Wrightsman Gift, 1988, 1988.162.

10 In addition to Frank Duveneck, Whistler overlapped with several Americans in Venice, including John White Alexander, Robert Frederick Blum, John Henry Twachtman, and Theodore Wendel, among others. These artists were inspired by Whistler's advice, and they became somewhat more experimental in Venice than others had been before them. More traditional accounts of Venice can be seen in works by John Linton Chapman, Charles Caryl Coleman, and Joseph Lindon Smith. For more on Americans in Venice, see Lovell, *Visitable Past*.

11 Alastair Grieve remarks on the likelihood of Whistler painting *Nocturne: Blue and Gold, St. Mark's, Venice* as a rebuke of Ruskin. Grieve reports that Whistler encountered one of Ruskin's protégés sketching "a detailed view" of St. Mark's west facade and was inspired to render the basilica, but stripping it of detail and articulation. Grieve speculates that Whistler may have specifically selected some sites because they resembled places that Ruskin described in *The Stones of Venice*. See Alastair Grieve, "The Sites of Whistler's Venice Etchings," *Print Quarterly* 13, no. 1 (March 1996): 24. On Ruskin and his influence of American artists in Venice, see Hirshler, "Gondola Days," 120–21, 389–90.

12 Whistler to Marcus Bourne Huish, 21–26 January 1880, Correspondence of James McNeill Whistler, University of Glasgow Library, MS Whistler LB 3/8, https://www.whistler.arts.gla.ac.uk/correspondence/date/display/?cid=2992&year=1880&month=01&rs=3; cited in Dorment, "Venice," 179. On Whistler in Venice, see also Margaret F. MacDonald, *Palaces in the Night: Whistler in Venice* (Berkeley: University of California Press, 2001).

13 Whistler to Matthew Robinson Elden, 15–30 April 1880, Correspondence of James McNeill Whistler, University of Glasgow Library, MS Whistler E61, https://www.whistler.arts.gla.ac.uk/correspondence/date/display/?cid=12816&year=1880&month=04&rs=3; cited in Marc Simpson, "Venice, Whistler, and the American Others," in *After Whistler: The Artist and His Influence on American Painting*, ed. Linda Merrill (New Haven, CT: Yale University Press, 2003), 33.

14 Osbert Sitwell, ed., *A Free House! Or, the Artist as Craftsman, Being the Writings of Walter Richard Sickert* (London: Macmillan, 1947), 12, 13; cited in Grieve, "Sites of Whistler's Venice Etchings," 20. Grieve also makes the point that for his etchings, Whistler did not bother to render scenes in reverse to account for the reversal in the printing process. Some solved the problem by viewing his etchings in a mirror, so bothered were they by the inaccuracies.

15 See mentions of this practice throughout Bacher's account of Whistler's time in Venice and his comradery with the so-called Duveneck Boys, the young American artists who joined Frank Duveneck in Venice during the summer of 1880. Whistler sketched from the windows of Robert Frederick Blum and Otto Henry Bacher at their lodgings in the Casa Jankowitz. Bacher, *With Whistler in Venice*, 13.

16 Whistler's commission of twelve etchings was exhibited in December 1880 at the Fine Art Society, one year after they had been expected. The society showed Whistler's Venetian pastels in 1881, and in 1883 they exhibited a second set of Venice etchings that he had continued to work on from his London studio. Much has been written about Whistler's work in Venice and the London reception of these works. See, for example, Alastair Grieve, *Whistler's Venice* (New Haven, CT: Yale University Press, 2000); and MacDonald, *Palaces in the Night*.

Clockwise from top left:

Sample bead cards attributed to Società Veneziana per l'Industria delle Conterie (SVC), Stephen A. Frost & Son, late 19th century–1904, 13 ½ × 18 in., Illinois State Museum, Gifts of Dan Frost

✲ CAT. 4-21
Trailed Feather and Eye Beads, 116 mosaic glass and flameworked glass beads mounted to printed card, 1941-0083-XX

✲ CAT. 4-22
Millefiori and Flag Beads, 106 mosaic glass and flameworked glass beads mounted to printed card, 1941-0083-XVI

✲ CAT. 4-23
Marbleized and Millefiori Beads, 100 mosaic glass and flameworked glass beads mounted to printed card, 1941-0083-XXII

✲ CAT. 4-24
Corkscrew and Lace Beads, 36 flameworked glass beads mounted to printed card, 1941-0083-XVII

17 "Mr. Whistler's Venice Pastels," *Daily News* (London), January 31, 1881, 2; reprinted in Robert H. Getscher, *James Abbott McNeill Whistler: Pastels* (New York: George Braziller, 1991), 179.

18 MacDonald, *Palaces in the Night*, 94. MacDonald offers a useful analysis of the technical advances accomplished by Whistler with his Venice work both in pastel and print.

19 Otto Henry Bacher describes Whistler's process for making pastels and etchings in Venice. Of his site selection he explained that Whistler was "very clever" in deciding his pastel subjects. "He generally selected bits of strange architecture, windows, piles, balconies, queer water effects, canal views with boats—very rarely figure subjects—always little artistic views that would not be complete in any other medium." Bacher, *With Whistler in Venice*, 75. For an overview of American artists inspired by Whistler, see Linda Merrill, "Whistler in America," in Merrill, *After Whistler*, 10–31.

20 [Harry Quilter], "Mr. Whistler's 'Venice' at the Fine-Art Society, New Bond Street," *Spectator* 53, December 11, 1880, 1587; quoted in Simpson, "Venice, Whistler, and the American Others," 34.

21 Baudelaire's discussion of modernity and the dispassionate observer, whom he defines as the dandy, was well-known to Whistler. In his 1863 essay, "The Painter of Modern Life," Baudelaire argued that the enduring subjects were found in the moment, in the fashions of the day and the people of the streets. Artists who looked to the past were derivative. Baudelaire's seminal essay emboldened the rising group of impressionist painters and also Whistler, who, by the 1880s, had incorporated many of Baudelaire's concepts into his "Ten O'Clock" lecture. For more on the influence of Baudelaire on Whistler, see Suzanne Singletary, "Manet and Whistler: Baudelairean Voyage," in *Perspectives on Manet*, ed. Therese Dolan (New York: Routledge, 2012), 49–71.

22 "Mr. Whistler's Venice Pastels"; quoted in Getscher, *James Abbott McNeill Whistler: Pastels*, 179.

23 The New York exhibition was a reconstitution of the February 1883 installation at London's Fine Art Society, which also caused a stir. According to David Park Curry, in London, "The walls at the Fine Art Society were covered in white felt fabric to a height of about ten feet, and edged top and bottom with a brilliant yellow ledge and skirting board. The walls were 'picked out,' or detailed, with stenciled yellow lines and butterflies, also in yellow." The pictures were presented in plain, thin white frames that blended with the white walls, and arrangements of daffodils, marguerites, and narcissi set in Asian pottery offered the finishing touches of yellow to define the experience. See David Park Curry, "Total Control: Whistler at an Exhibition," in *James McNeill Whistler: A Reexamination*, ed. Ruth E. Fine, *Studies in the History of Art* 19 (Washington, DC: National Gallery of Art, 1987), 77. On the New York presentation, see Nicolai Cikovsky Jr. with Charles Brock, "Whistler and America," in Dorment and MacDonald, *James McNeill Whistler*, 35.

24 Clarence Cook, remarking on an 1884 exhibition at the Salmagundi Club that drew influence from Whistler's Venetian exhibition. See Clarence Cook, "Two Picture Exhibitions," *Art Amateur* 10, no. 2 (January 1884): 28; cited in Cikovsky, "Whistler and America," 35, 294n61.

25 Martin Brimmer (of the Museum of Fine Arts, Boston) to (artist) Sarah Wyman Whitman, 26 October 1882, Martin Brimmer letters, 1880–96, reel D32, Archives of American Art, Smithsonian Institution; cited in Elizabeth Anne McCauley, "A Sentimental Traveler: Isabella Stewart Gardner in Venice," in *Gondola Days: Isabella Stewart Gardner and the Palazzo Barbaro Circle*, ed. Elizabeth Anne McCauley (Boston: Isabella Stewart Gardner Museum, 2004), 25–27.

26 In French: "Où se cachent les belles du Titien? Ce ne sont certes pas leurs descendantes que nous apercevons à peine sous leur chevelure inculte, drapées dans un vieux châle noir comme si elles grelottaient la fièvre. A quoi bon aller en Italie pour y recueillir de pareilles impressions?" Arthur Baignères, "Première Exposition de la Société Internationale de Peintres et Sculpteurs," *Gazette des Beaux-Arts: Courrier Européen de l'Art et de la Curiosité* 27 (1883): 190. The black shawls, or *zendale*, were, in fact, a part of the typical national dress of Venice. Palgrave noted that this national costume had all but disappeared on the streets during the Austrian occupation. Palgrave, *Handbook for Travellers in Northern Italy*, 326.

27 For a fuller discussion of the Paris exhibition of Sargent's Venice pictures, see Marc Simpson, *Uncanny Spectacle: The Public Career of the Young John Singer Sargent* (New Haven, CT: Yale University Press, 1997), 98.

28 Sargent to Mrs. Austin, Florence, 22 March 1874, transcribed in Evan Charteris, ed., *John Sargent* (New York: Charles Scribner's Sons, 1927), 18; cited in Stephanie L. Herdrich, "John Singer Sargent and Italian Renaissance Art," in Robertson, *Sargent and Italy*, 103, 114n15.

29 Stephanie L. Herdrich, H. Barbara Weinberg, and Marjorie Shelley, *American Drawings and Watercolors in the Metropolitan Museum of Art: John Singer Sargent* (New York: Metropolitan Museum of Art, 2000), 112; and Roberta J. M. Olson, "John Singer Sargent and James Carroll Beckwith, Two Americans in Paris: A Trove of Their Unpublished Drawings," *Master Drawings* 43, no. 4 (Winter 2005): 424–25.

30 On the influences and stylistic approach guiding Sargent on his 1880 trip to Venice, see Ormond, "Modern Life Subjects," 56–57.

31 Mark Twain, *A Tramp Abroad* (Toronto: Belford, 1880), 357; accessed June 25, 2020, https://www.google.com/books/edition/A_Tramp_broad/5t9EAQAAMAAJ?hl=en&gbpv=1.

32 Several contemporary scholars have addressed the sexual nature of Sargent's early Venice work. See, for example, Ormond, "Modern Life Subjects," 75; and Warren Adelson, "Sargent's Life: Routes to Venice," in *Sargent's Venice*, ed. Warren Adelson (New Haven, CT: Yale University Press, 2006), 53–54. For a discussion of how Sargent's contemporary American audiences engaged with these works, and in particular the American stereotyping of Italian ethnic identities, see Jane Dini, "Seeing America's Tangled Threads in Sargent's Street in Venice," in *Republics and Empires: Italian and American Art in Transnational Perspective, 1840–1970*, ed. Melissa Dabakis and Paul Kaplan (Manchester, UK: Manchester University Press, forthcoming 2021).

33 The Venetian Republic fell to the French in 1797, though power was transferred to the Austrians later that year. Venetians gained their independence from Austria in 1866. Mark Twain offers vivid first impressions of a depressed Venice "fallen prey to poverty and neglect, and melancholy decay" from its once elevated position as a "haughty, invincible, magnificent republic." See Mark Twain, *The Innocents Abroad: Or, the New Pilgrims' Progress* (1869; New York: Penguin Books, 1980), 160. Also see William Dean Howells, *Venetian Life* (1866; Boston: Houghton, Mifflin, 1892). Howells was in Venice from 1861 to 1865 as US consul to Italy. The book was released in several editions through the end of the nineteenth century. On the ways Twain, Howells, and Henry James each describe Venice, see William L. Vance, "Seeing Italy: The Realistic Rediscovery by Twain, Howells, and James," in Stebbins, *Lure of Italy*, 94–110.

34 Palgrave, *Hand-book for Travellers in Northern Italy*, 326, 328.

35 Ibid., 372.

36 Twain, *Innocents Abroad*, 147.

37 Henry James to William James, 25 September 1869, published in full in Henry James, *The Letters of Henry James*, ed. Leon Edel, vol. 1, *1843–1875* (Cambridge, MA: Belknap Press, 1974), 142; cited in McCauley, "Sentimental Traveler," 25. Despite these early impressions, James went on to live part time in Venice, becoming one of its greatest champions.

38 "Stringing Pearls at Venice," *Frank Leslie's Illustrated Newspaper* 49, August 28, 1880, 431. Van Haanen completed two versions of this picture: one in 1876 and a second in 1878, after which a print was made.

39 Elizabeth Anne McCauley points out that many of the American expatriates collected pictures such as these. McCauley, "Sentimental Traveler," 27.

40 Henry James, "John S. Sargent," *Harper's New Monthly Magazine* 75, October 1887, 689; cited in Erica E. Hirshler, "John Singer Sargent's Fountain of Youth," in McCauley, *Gondola Days*, 155. On Sargent and James, see also Hugh Honour and John Fleming, *The Venetian Hours of Henry James, Whistler and Sargent* (Boston: Bullfinch Press, 1991).

41 Martin Brimmer to Sarah Wyman Whitman, 26 October 1882, Martin Brimmer letters, 1880–96, reel D32, Archives of American Art, Smithsonian Institution; cited in Alan Chong, "Artistic Life in Venice," in McCauley, *Gondola Days*, 94.

42 In his preface for Katharine de Kay Bronson's 1902 article, "Browning in Venice" (*Cornhill Magazine* 85, February 1902, 145–71), Henry James wrote that Bronson's parties "mingled generations and races." Bronson inspired the character of Mrs. Prest in James's novella *The Aspern Papers* (1888), set in Venice. The Bronson family social activity was organized by Katharine. Arthur Bronson was largely absent during their years in Venice. In 1881 he was hospitalized in Paris, where he died four years later. On Katharine de Kay Bronson and her Venice salons and connections, see Alan Chong, "Introduction: 'Romance and Art and History,'" and McCauley, "Sentimental Traveler," both in McCauley, *Gondola Days*, XII–XV and 8, 12.

43 Daniel Sargent Curtis, for example, wrote in 1879 to his sister of the real estate deals, that a palace in Venice could be acquired for the price of a "new brick box" in Boston. Daniel Sargent Curtis to Mary Curtis, Rome, 9 January 1879, Biblioteca Nazionale Marciana, Venice, Correspondence and two diaries of Daniel and Ariana Curtis; cited in McCauley, "Sentimental Traveler," 13.

44 In a letter to his mother in the spring of 1880, Whistler remarked that Bronson was "the most generous person possible," when recounting this story of his gondolier. James McNeill Whistler to Anna Matilda Whistler, March/May 1880, Correspondence of James McNeill Whistler, University of Glasgow Library; quoted in Chong, "Artistic Life in Venice," 110–11, 126n94. On Bronson's philanthropy, see also McCauley, "Sentimental Traveler," 24–25.

45 Her nom de plume was Catherine Cornaro, the name of the last queen of Cyprus and a subject of Browning's poems.

46 Countess Adriana Marcello, quoted in Catherine Cornaro [Katharine de Kay Bronson], "The Revival of Burano Lace," *Century Illustrated Monthly Magazine* 23, no. 3 (January 1882): 340.

47 Countess Adriana Marcello, quoted in Cornaro [Bronson], "Revival of Burano Lace," 341. For more on the lacemaking revival and Bronson's essay, also see Diana Jocelyn Greenwold's essay in this catalogue, page 182.

48 Anthea Callen, "Sexual Division of Labor in the Arts and Crafts Movement," *Woman's Art Journal* 5, no. 2 (Autumn 1984–Winter 1985): 1–3. A period comparison is the Langdale Linen Industry, founded in 1885, which, as Callen explains, was established to help keep the female population busy within the home and "help stem rural depopulation, [and] stave off increasing urban squalor and unrest," p. 2.

49 Cornaro [Bronson], "Revival of Burano Lace," 343.

50 Bruce Weber, "Robert Frederick Blum (1857–1903) and His Milieu" (PhD diss., The City University of New York, 1985), 120–21. Also acknowledged as an influence on Blum during his early days in Venice is the Spanish painter Mariano José María Bernardo Fortuny y Carbó, known as Mariano Fortuny.

51 Whistler famously adopted the group of young American painters staying at the Casa Jankowitz boardinghouse, among them John White Alexander, Otto Henry Bacher, Robert Frederick Blum, Charles Abel Corwin, George E. Hopkins, Harper Pennington, Julius Rolshoven, and Theodore Wendel. Whistler felt enough at ease with Blum to invite himself (much to the surprise of his young admirer) to set up his easel by the window in the young painter's boardinghouse room to catch the view of the street below. See Otto Henry Bacher's account of this event in Bacher, *With Whistler in Venice*, 11–14.

52 In addition to Venetian street scenes, both painters, for example, painted the passage of mosaic and tile detail of St. Mark's from the same corner of the interior of the basilica. See Sargent, *Pavement of St. Mark's, Venice*, ca. 1880–82, oil on canvas, Private collection; and Blum, *Morning in St. Mark's, Venice*, 1882, watercolor, Cincinnati Art Museum. For further reference to the similar St. Mark's watercolors by Blum and Sargent, see William H. Gerdts, "The International Milieu," in Adelson, *Sargent's Venice*, 174. Gerdts does not assert that Sargent and Blum painted these works at the same time.

53 The canvas was repaired by an acquaintance of Sargent, the Irish nobleman and painter Valentine Lawless. Sargent gave the picture to Lawless upon request.

54 For a solid discussion of Blum in Burano and his lacemaking pictures, see Karen Haas, "Robert Frederick Blum," in Stebbins, *Lure of Italy*, 410–12. Blum also executed a large-scale pastel of his exhibition piece, *Venetian Lace Makers* (1887), which is now in a private collection.

55 Two months prior, for example, Blum illustrated "In the Footsteps of Fortuny and Regnault," *Century Illustrated Monthly Magazine* 23, no. 1 (November 1881): 15–36. Blum was a regular contributor to *Century* (formerly Scribner's) and on his second trip to Venice in 1881 made views on commission, which illustrated a November 1882 article by Henry James. See Henry James, "Venice," *Century Illustrated Monthly Magazine* 25, no. 1 (November 1882): 3–24. Blum was in close correspondence with the magazine's editor, Richard Gilder, Katharine de Kay Bronson's brother-in-law, and may have gained an introduction to her through this connection. Blum may also have met Bronson and her circle—which included the Curtises, Sargent, James, and later Isabella Stewart Gardner—through his associations with Whistler and Duveneck.

56 "The Prize Fund Exhibition," *Art Amateur* 17, no. 1 (June 1887): 9.

57 Mariana Griswold van Rensselaer, "The Third Prize Fund—Exhibition 1," *Independent* (New York), June 2, 1887, 582; and "Fine Arts Society. The American Art Association," *Nation* 44 (May 26, 1887): 457; both cited in Weber, "Robert Frederick Blum and His Milieu," 290.

58 Cornaro [Bronson], "Revival of Burano Lace," 333.

59 Palgrave, *Hand-book for Travellers in Northern Italy*, 371.

60 Cornaro [Bronson], "Revival of Burano Lace," 335.

61 Francis Hopkinson Smith, *Gondola Days* (Boston: Houghton, Mifflin, 1897), preface [n.p.].

62 Smith, *Gondola Days*, 90.

63 Baignères, "Première Exposition de la Société Internationale de Peintres et Sculpteurs," 190.

64 Clarence Cook, "The Art Gallery: The Water-Color Society's Exhibition," *Art Amateur* 6, no. 4 (March 1882): 75; cited in Simpson, "Venice, Whistler, and the American Others," 41.

65 Singletary, "Manet and Whistler," 55.

66 Whistler to Matthew Robinson Elden, April 1880; quoted in Simpson, "Venice, Whistler, and the American Others," 33.

67 Chong, "Artistic Life in Venice," 94.

68 Palgrave, *Hand-book for Travellers in Northern Italy*, 326.

69 For a discussion of the changing reception of Sargent's Venice work from the 1880s, see Simpson, *Uncanny Spectacle*, 97–98.

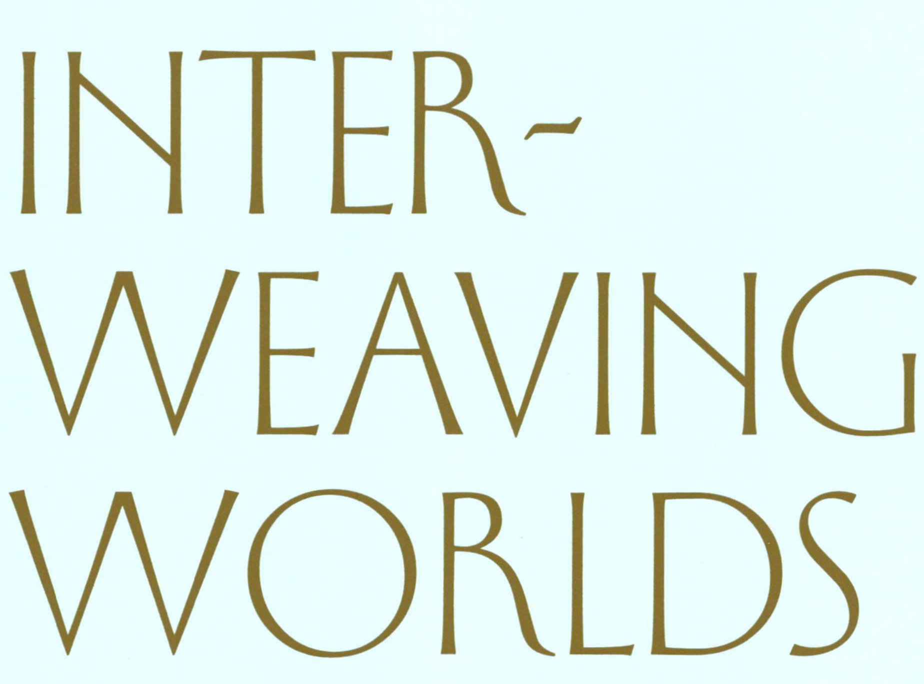

INTER-WEAVING WORLDS

Antique and Revival Lace in Italy and the United States, 1872–1927

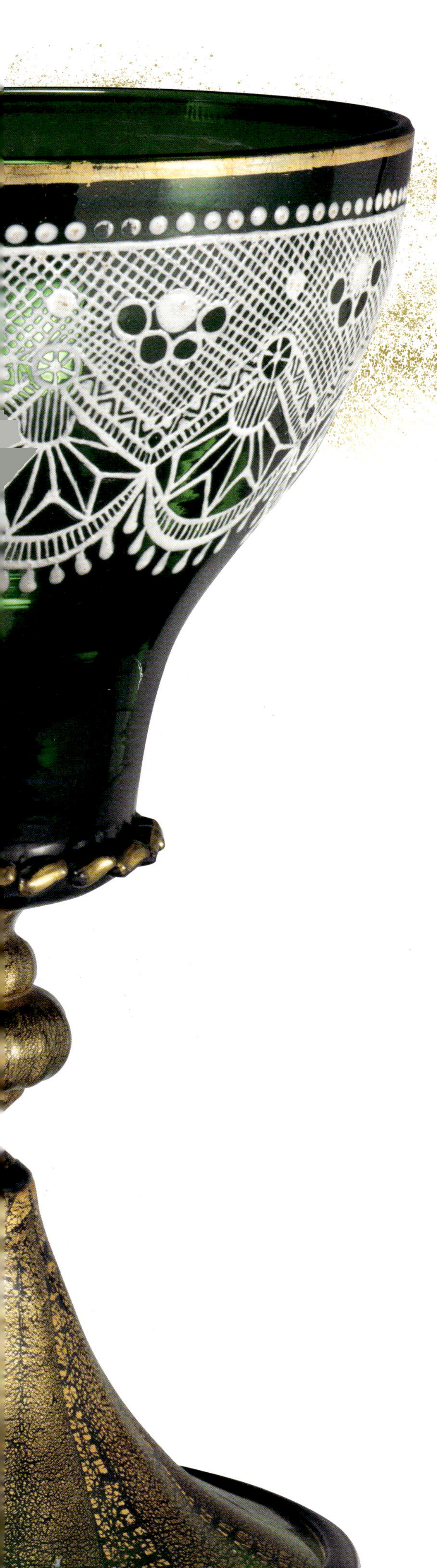

Italian lace was reborn on the Venetian island of Burano in 1872. That year Countess Adriana Marcello and Princess Giovanelli Chigi, with the backing of Italy's Queen Margherita, resurrected the isle's famed seventeenth-century workshops.[1] Lace had an august history in Venice and on Burano, where women used needles to create minute buttonhole stitches that blossomed into intricate patterns. *Punto in aria,* or stitching in air, was supposedly invented in Venice and had long been an extremely precious commodity. Venetian needle lace adorned the cuffs and collars of monarchs and clergy across Europe throughout the sixteenth and seventeenth centuries.[2] In Italy, lace constituted such a potent marker of class that sumptuary laws prohibited women from wearing more than an allotted amount equivalent to their social rank, and sellers measured lace in ounces or carats as if it were a piece of gold or a diamond.[3] The Sun King himself, Louis XIV, commissioned a Burano lace collar for his coronation: the piece took two years to create and cost approximately $20,000 in today's currency.[4] Italian needle lace was so coveted that French and Flemish producers began to create similar types on larger scales so that by the 1860s, lacemaking on Burano was largely moribund.

As the story goes, in 1872 only one remaining craftswoman, Cencia Scarpariola, knew how to create Burano's famed patterns, but she did not have the teaching skills to pass on her craft. Anna Bellorio d'Este, a teacher working at Burano's school for girls, observed the old woman closely, practiced, and began to teach pupils to re-create Scarpariola's techniques. By 1900, the Burano Lace School boasted six hundred students and was producing lace in the vein of Venice's famed antique examples (CAT. 5-1), some even featuring the winged lion of St. Mark, a nod to the iconic symbol of Venice (CAT. 5-2). One American writer noted that the school produced "only the choicest and most beautiful kinds of lace" and helped a generation of women on Burano earn enough income to purchase homes and bolster their dowries.[5] The women of Burano "made the best possible use of the storehouse of beauty Venice possessed in the old Renaissance patterns" and fashioned new objects inspired by antique designs admired in Italy and beyond.[6]

Preceding pages:
Società Anonima per Azioni Salviati & C., Goblet with Lace Design (detail), ca. 1870s;
see p. 43

Like the workshop's Italian supporters, expatriates Katharine de Kay Bronson and Enid Layard contributed to the school on Burano, intending their philanthropy to support their adopted city. Each also added to the growing literature on Italian lace for American audiences. Layard, whose husband was the Murano glass revival financier Sir Austen Henry Layard, translated a treatise on lace production into English. For her part, Bronson published an article in *Century Illustrated Monthly Magazine* that brought the Burano revival industry to US readers in vivid detail.[7] In addition to several photographs of Burano lace, *Century* augmented Bronson's descriptions with a sketch of a young lacemaker seated in front of an open window (Fig. 5-1). Beyond, the Venetian lagoon lies still and quiet. The window's Moorish shape mimics the contour of the young woman's head and shoulders bent over her pillow. Echoing her environment, she pursues her craft—a means of economic independence that is visibly intertwined with symbols of her region's cultural heritage.[8]

Lace was the consummate skilled labor. Traditional lace could only be produced on a small scale and with ample time by trained artists using either a needle or a series of wooden dowels called bobbins. Associated with court culture, the work of lacemaking had, by the late nineteenth century, largely migrated to rural homes and small-scale workshops thanks to the support of a burgeoning group of experts, teachers, and philanthropists. The industries they founded appealed to Arts and Crafts enthusiasts eager to associate products with rural life pursued in concert with the natural world. In Italy, aristocratic families and committed reformers revived lace and embroidery techniques to celebrate a newly formed, unified Italian culture. These industries also provided a means of economic independence for Italians whose agrarian ways of life were disappearing due to dwindling land inheritances and mass migrations northward or to the United States after the Industrial Revolution.[9]

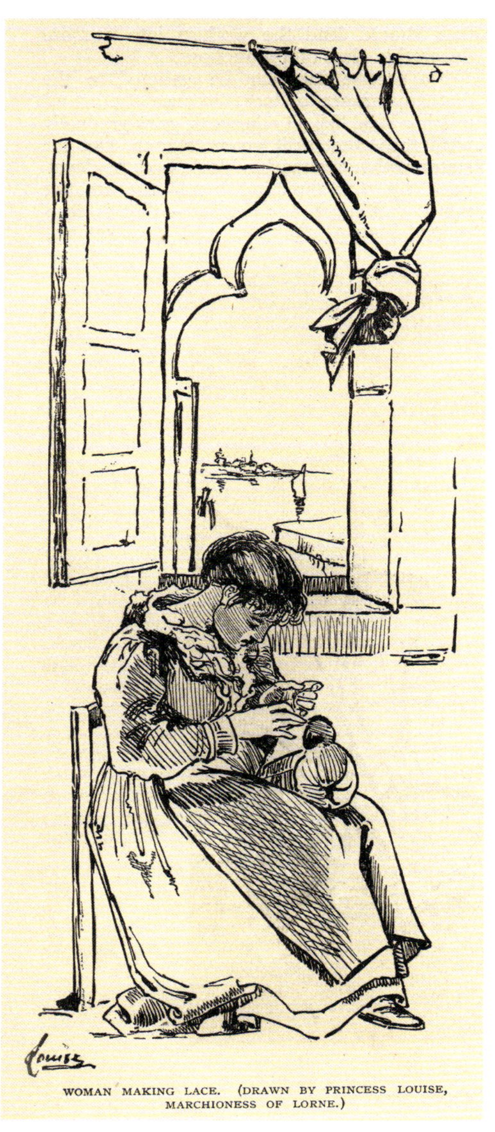
WOMAN MAKING LACE. (DRAWN BY PRINCESS LOUISE, MARCHIONESS OF LORNE.)

Fig. 5-1
Princess Louise, Marchioness of Lorne, *Woman Making Lace*, from Katharine de Kay Bronson, "Revival of Burano Lace," *Century Illustrated Monthly Magazine*, January 1882

The explosion in collecting and reproducing antique Italian lace is a story about nationalism and the long reach of the international Arts and Crafts movement in Italy. Lace revival workshops helped women in disparate regions and communities come together under the umbrella of a shared cultural heritage. These workshops used sixteenth- and seventeenth-century materials and practices as the basis for new works.[10] The objects that Italian and, later, Italian American women created also tell a little-known story about transatlantic ties cemented between American collectors and Italian lace experts who supported the schools and brought them to American shores.[11] Antique lace collecting and revival lace workshops linked women through surprisingly broad networks of exchange that transcended centuries, continents, and class divides. By charting the translation of age-old Italian lace patterns and techniques into new forms and settings, we begin to understand the migration of ideas, cultures, and people between Italy and the United States in new ways. Wealthy Americans traveled to and settled in Italy and transformed its

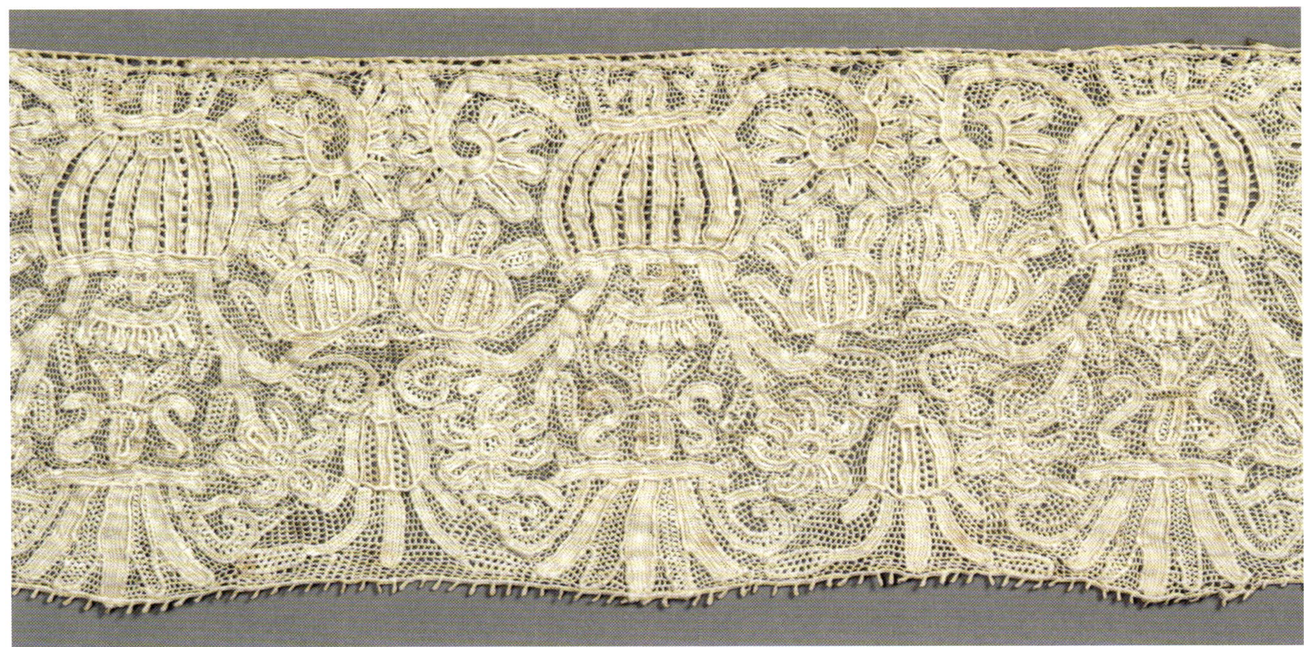

✲ CAT. 5-1
Scuola dei Merletti di Burano, Lace Border (detail), late 19th–early 20th century, linen needle lace, 3 ¹⁄₁₆ × 21 ¼ in., Cooper Hewitt, Smithsonian Design Museum, Bequest of Richard Cranch Greenleaf in memory of his mother, Adeline Emma Greenleaf

institutions, just as many middle- and working-class Italians were immigrating to the United States in unprecedented numbers and altering American culture in durable ways, which lace, both old and new, records and visualizes.[12]

COLLECTING ANTIQUE LACE

Europeans had produced lace since the fifteenth century, but in the nineteenth and early twentieth centuries, the craze for collecting examples from Italy, France, Belgium, and Britain helped preserve an antique art form and encouraged revival industries. The late nineteenth century's financial, political, and social upheavals, combined with debilitating droughts across Europe, forced many landed families off their estates and increased the circulation of luxury goods such as lace on the open market. Shifting political boundaries also loosened the Catholic church's grip on vast holdings, so that ecclesiastical textiles began to appear for sale through dealers such as Jesurum, Lefébure, and Marian Powys in Venice, Paris, and New York.[13] American women living abroad or mindful of international stylistic trends found these meticulously rendered works fascinating and bought with abandon. As historian Rosanna Pavoni has described, Italian material was of particular interest for upper-class American collectors because "Italy was regarded as the depository of a tradition which sprang directly from the master craftsmen of the fifteenth and sixteenth centuries."[14] Renaissance artisanship and its associations with skilled makers and small-scale, guild workshops suited collectors enamored of the Arts and Crafts movement and its emphasis on the handmade.[15]

Every consequential Gilded Age doyenne, it seems, collected lace. Isabella Stewart Gardner, Arabella Huntington, Jane Morgan, and Charlotte Schermerhorn Astor all maintained extensive collections, many of which eventually found their way into public institutions such as the Metropolitan Museum of Art (the Met); the Museum of Fine Arts, Boston; and the United States National Museum (now part of the Smithsonian Institution).[16] The market for these materials was

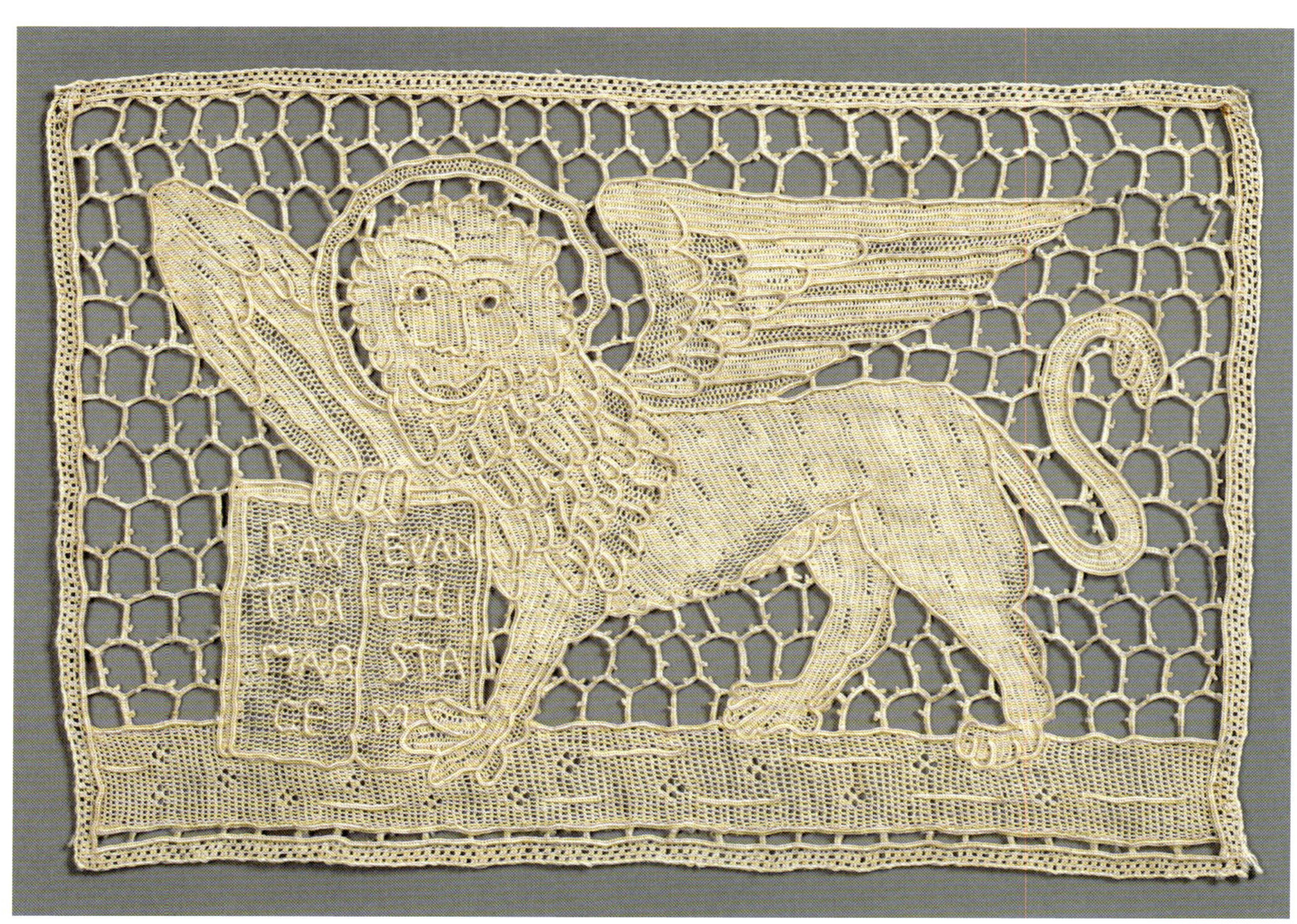

✡ CAT. 5-2

Scuola dei Merletti di Burano, Lace Panel with Lion of St. Mark, 20th century, cotton needle lace, 4 9/16 x 6 5/8 in., Cooper Hewitt, Smithsonian Design Museum, Bequest of Gertrude M. Oppenheimer

cutthroat, with collectors on both sides of the Atlantic vying for fragments and offering tremendous sums of money to secure them. In 1895 writer Maud Howe Elliott declared, "Old lace is now almost priceless; there has been a tremendous run on it. . . . Most of the good old lace has gone to America."[17] The *New York Times* compared Italian laces to fine oil paintings and remarked, "The market price for a flounce of old **Venetian point** is $1,000 a yard. . . . It is so rare that it is registered like a fine old Rembrandt and like the picture the location of a Venetian point flounce is known to collectors and dealers all over the world."[18] Though some women, notably Gardner and Huntington, purchased both paintings and laces, many female collectors focused solely on lace, creating a comparably high-stakes corollary to the male-dominated market for old master paintings.

American women amassed fragments for use as clothing and as household decoration, but also systematically for study and presentation. As *The Queen Lace Book* noted in 1874, "Formerly Lace collections were hidden in presses and cabinets, now they are for public inspection."[19] Wealthy American socialite Rita de Acosta Lydig acquired an admirable collection of antique lace and employed Europe's finest designers to transform her collection into stylish outfits showcasing the latest silhouettes (Fig. 5-2). Lydig owned more than three hundred pairs of shoes by famed shoemaker Pierre Yantorny, many of which he adorned with fragments from her storehouse (Fig. 5-3). Isabella Stewart Gardner spent lavishly on her lace collections, paying prices for some fragments that far exceeded what she spent on Venetian panel paintings.[20] In 1894 Gardner recorded

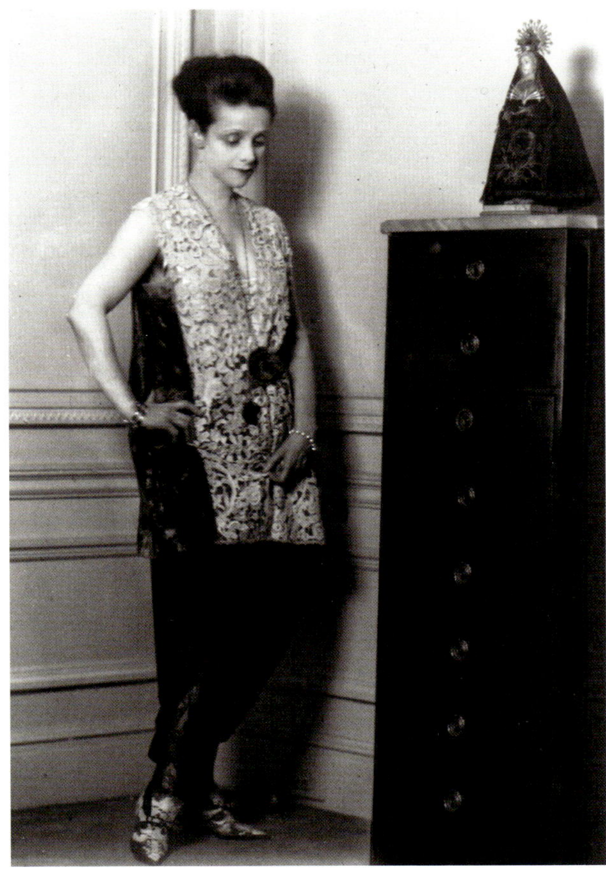

Fig. 5-2
Arnold Genthe, *Portrait photograph of Mrs. Rita Lydig, January 29, 1925*, lantern slide, approx. 5 × 4 in., Library of Congress, Prints and Photographs Division

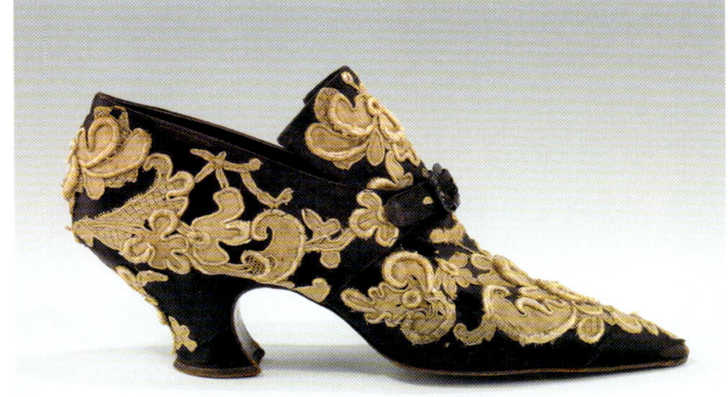

Fig. 5-3
Pierre Yantorny, Evening Shoes, 1914–19, silk, metal, jet, Brooklyn Museum Costume Collection at The Metropolitan Museum of Art, Gift of the Brooklyn Museum, 2009; Gift of Mercedes de Acosta, 1953, 2009. 300.1178a, b

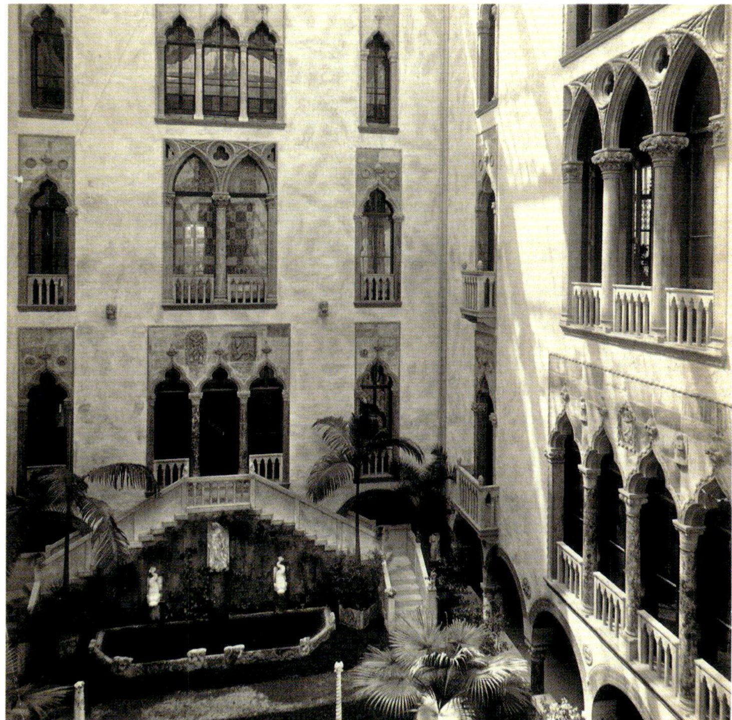

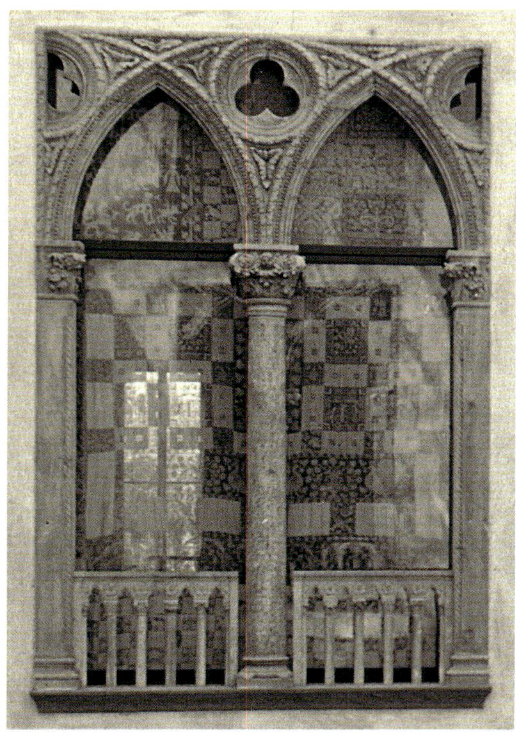

Figs. 5-4a, b
Thomas E. Marr, *Courtyard, Fenway Court*, and window lace detail, 1902, photograph, Isabella Stewart Gardner Museum, Boston

spending a staggering $2,860 for an "old Rosalino point flounce" and $413 for an "old handkerchief and coverlet."[21] She purchased examples from dealers and through connections to fellow Americans in Venice, such as Bronson and her daughter, Edith, the Countess Rucellai.[22] Gardner was the type of educated collector who put together a well-respected group of laces for decorative purposes, but also to display as art objects in her museum. Even as she commissioned seamstresses to combine fragments into curtains that divided the grand second-floor chamber and the central court of her purpose-built museum in Boston (Figs. 5-4a and b), she also featured individual examples in glass cases within the galleries themselves. Like many of her peers, Gardner also collected revival textiles alongside antique materials, acknowledging and celebrating the enlivened interest in leveraging aspects of Italy's past to bolster its present.[23]

LACE AND LACEMAKING ON THE PAGE AND ON THE WALLS

The collection and classification of antique lace fragments gained popularity with elite American collectors through manuals, largely written by women, that helped buyers identify various techniques and regional characteristics. Fanny Bury Palliser's 1865 *History of Lace* weighed the value and rarity of various forms. Reprints of antique pattern books such as Cesare Vecellio's 1591 *Corona delle Nobili et Virtuose Donne* also popularized Renaissance designs among makers and collectors. In 1908 Italian writer Elisa Ricci produced a richly illustrated three-volume guide to Italian laces, *Antiche Trine Italiane,* a work that presents a chronology of forms illustrated with examples from private collections in both Italy and America.[24] In 1920 Metropolitan Museum textile curator Frances Morris and Marian Hague published *Antique Laces of American Collectors,* a publication that detailed the history of European textile collections in the United States in public institutions and private hands.[25] In the United States, associations such as the Needle and Bobbin Club and a journal associated with the group also sprung up to bring together upper-class women with shared interests in fostering antique lace appreciation and supporting the production of contemporary textiles. Lace literature extended knowledge of and interest in the field and connected women between countries.

Americans' interest in lace also peaked thanks to its prominent presentation at the 1893 World's Columbian Exposition in Chicago, a premier venue for art and craft display. Collector, Italian workshop director, and American expatriate Cora Slocomb di Brazzà shepherded Queen Margherita of Italy's prized collection of historic and contemporary textiles to Chicago for the festivities and oversaw their installation in the Woman's Building.[26] The array of finely worked examples celebrated the history of lace from blocky sixteenth-century ***reticella*** to figurative baroque **needle** and **bobbin laces.** On view within hand-carved wooden and wrought iron constructions evoking Renaissance architecture, the displays offered examples "from prehistoric times to the most perfect specimens of the modern school of Burano," positioning lace as the epitome of Italian craftsmanship past and present (Figs. 5-5 and 5-6).[27] As Hubert Howe Bancroft observed, "These are heirlooms descended through many generations, some of them articles the secret of whose manufacture is known only to the royal household, and others samples of varieties which the queen is introducing among the women of Italy, reviving an industrial art that was well nigh lost."[28] The Italian lace displays in Chicago stressed continuity between ancient arts and modern practices with old and new examples on view side by side. Di Brazzà's displays at the exposition developed American tastes for antique and revival examples among a wide range of clientele.

As private collections coalesced and lace went on view at major international expositions, museums across the United States—such as the Smithsonian

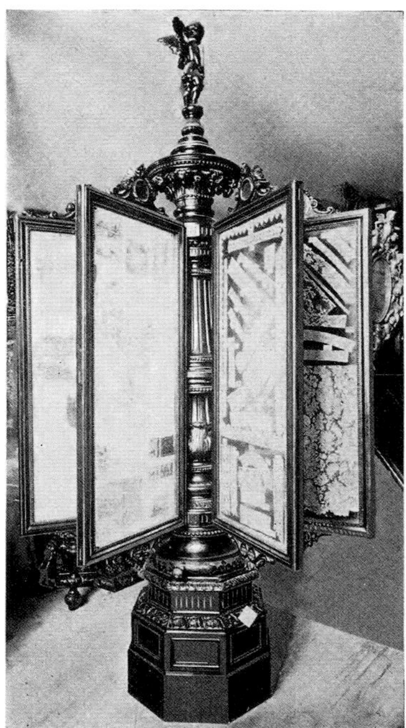

Fig. 5-5
Display of Italian lace at the Chicago World's Fair, from Hubert Howe Bancroft, *The Book of the Fair* (Bancroft, 1893)

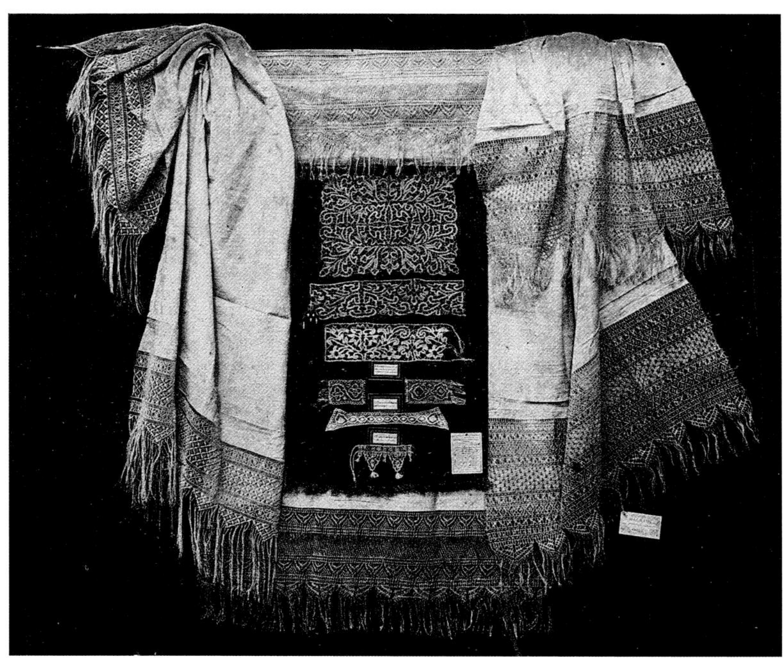

Fig. 5-6
Italian lace display at the Chicago World's Fair, from Maud Howe Elliott, *Art and Handicraft in the Woman's Building of the World's Columbian Exposition, Chicago, 1893* (Goupil, 1893)

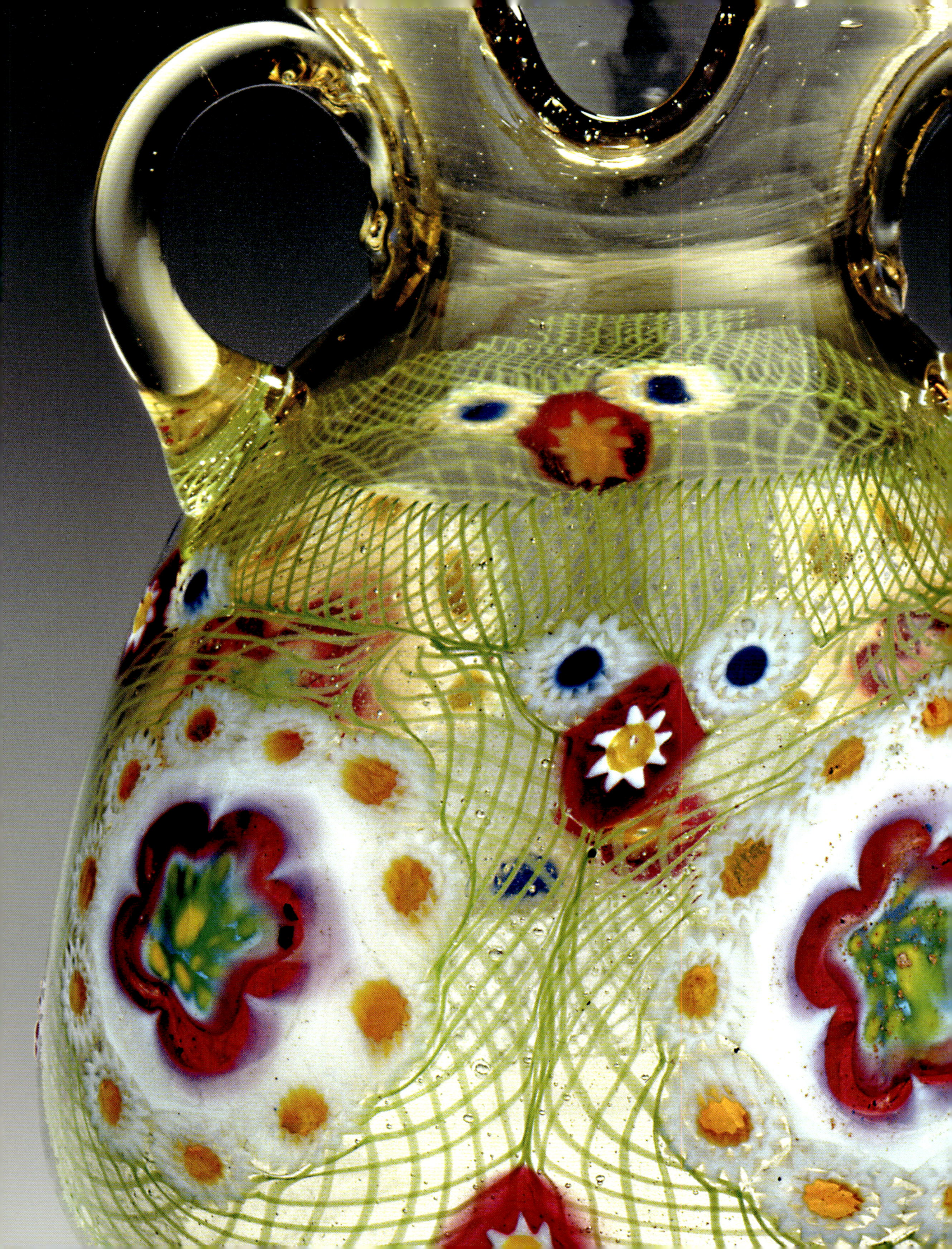

Institution, Art Institute of Chicago, Brooklyn Museum, Corcoran Gallery of Art, Detroit Institute of Arts, de Young Museum, and Minneapolis Institute of Arts—also began receiving donations and exhibiting antique European lace. These institutions understood their role as repositories for the world's great treasures, often donated by a tiny circle of wealthy donors, but also as spaces for working-class men and women to absorb and learn about craftsmanship and to glean inspiration for their own work.[29] The Met received its first major lace collection in 1879 and augmented it at intervals until 1938, by which time its holdings had mushroomed to well over four thousand objects. The Met's list of lace donors reads as a veritable who's who of New York society with names such as Astor, Bliss, de Forest, Harkness, Morgan, and Skyler. In 1921 the Met had two full galleries dedicated exclusively to lace, suggesting the medium's tremendous popularity. True to its founding mission as a space to inspire working-class craftspeople, the museum also welcomed visitors to examine materials up close in the Textile Study Center. As the *Metropolitan Museum of Art Bulletin* declared, "Here one may study the history of lace from its primitive conception in the Coptic network of the early centuries of the Christian era, to the highest perfection of the art in the Venice points; and from this stage one can follow its development in the different countries under varied conditions, each with its marked characteristics, but few attaining the perfection of the early Venetian workers."[30] As lace gained importance in American art institutions, a small group of experts also entered curatorial departments to care for and enlarge the collections. The craze for lace ushered in the first generation of American female museum professionals, women such as Frances Morris at the Met and Sarah Gore Flint Townsend at the Museum of Fine Arts, Boston, both of whom rose through the almost exclusively male ranks to maintain and augment these materials with the help of European experts such as Carolina Amari.[31] Knowledge of antique lace paved the way for women to enter the curatorial profession with an expertise all their own.

AMERICAN ARTISTS DISCOVER THE LACEMAKERS

American artists in Italy looked to the burgeoning revival industries as a picturesque means to visualize labor and small-scale production, specifically in and around Burano and Venice. Like collectors of lace and promoters of revival industries, these painters took a keen interest in the workshops popular among many of their patrons and in the young women who worked in them. Writer F. Mabel Robinson described the Burano Lace School: "When it is filled with pretty lace makers, red or black of head, fair of face, and brilliant of attire, then the lace school with its rows of busy girls is a subject worthy of van Haanen."[32] Though she invoked the Dutch painter Remigius van Haanen rather than an American artist, Robinson recognized in the school a space ripe for artistic attention, filled as it was with young artists clad in bright tones working assiduously on their craft.

Artists from Anders Leonard Zorn to Otto Henry Bacher to Robert Frederick Blum fashioned images of Venetian needlewomen at work in homes and institutions across the city. Blum's 1887 work *Venetian Lacemakers* bursts with

Artisti Barovier, Zanfirico Glass Vase with Floral Murrhines (detail), ca. 1910–13; **see p. 204**

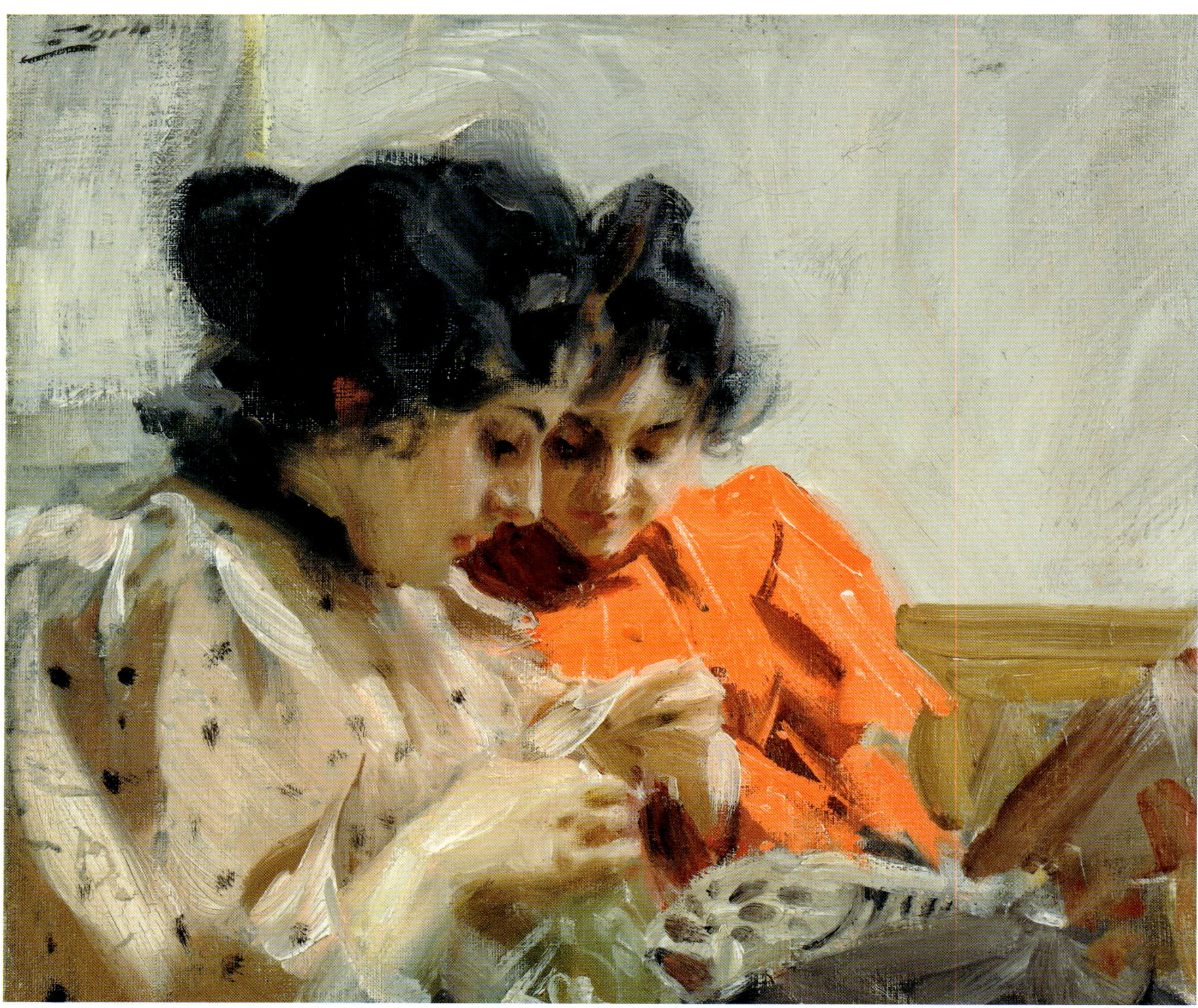

Fig. 5-7
Anders Leonard Zorn, *Lace Making*, 1894, oil on canvas, 16 ½ × 18 ⅞ in., The Zorn Museum, Mora, Sweden

energy (**CAT. 5-3**). Clusters of brightly clothed women congregate by windows in a large, airy room. The needlewomen are immersed in their labor, unaware of the artist and viewer's presence, save a sly look from the worker on the far left, whose smile and cocked head playfully acknowledge her complicity in fashioning the idyllic image of the workplace. An 1894 painting by Swedish artist Anders Zorn similarly expresses the collegial nature of labor in these workshops. *Lace Making* features two young women leaning closely together to inspect a small section of lace (Fig. 5-7). Well-dressed and focused, Zorn's pair upholds the vision of this skill as a refined one that was helpful economically, but also in line with societal conventions of female domesticity that kept women's work confined to the home, ostensibly to save them from degrading industrialized labor and the perceived ills of public life.

Otto Henry Bacher's print *The Lace Makers* is set in the home, where a great deal of revival lace production took place (Fig. 5-8).[33] Like those of his peers, Bacher's scene is similarly idealized. To underscore her economic importance, the lacemaker occupies the composition's focal point, in a room that notably omits a male presence. The children in the foreground appear to be spinning and weaving: activities that mark the transference of tradition from one generation to another and depict a workshop in which all members of the family are engaged. As a friend of James McNeill Whistler and his eventual printer in Venice, Bacher may have happened upon this quiet scene during the pair's explorations of the city, or he could have extrapolated its contours from the plethora of rosy accounts in print that suggested lacemaking could buoy Italian families with needed income and imbue them with a sense of their cultural inheritance.

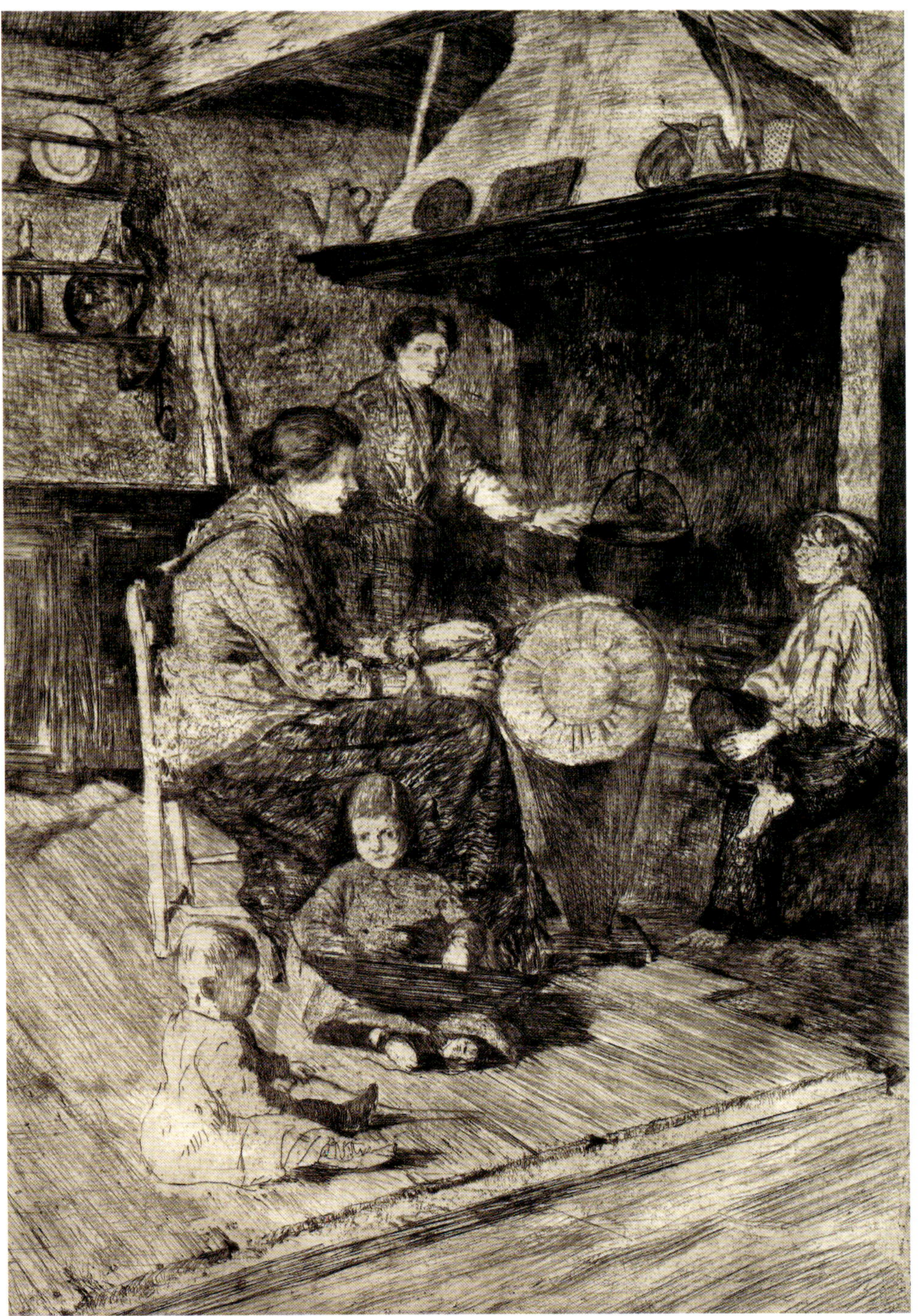

Fig. 5-8
Otto Henry Bacher, *Etchings of Venice: The Lace Makers*, 1880–82, etching on paper, 13 ⅛ × 8 ⅞ in., The Cleveland Museum of Art, Gift of Charles W. Bingham, 1920.18.6

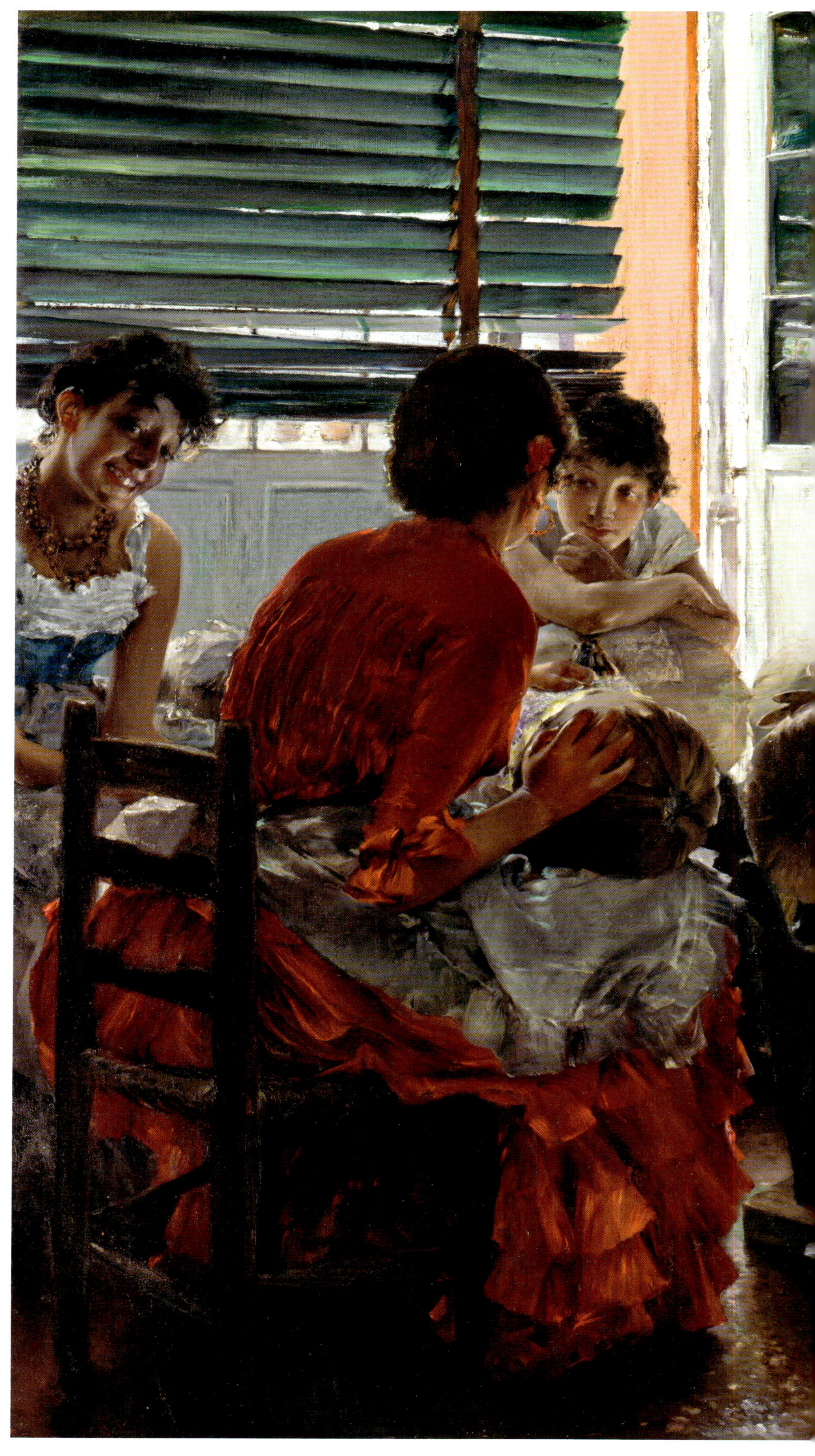

✡ CAT. 5-3
Robert Frederick Blum,
***Venetian Lacemakers*, 1887,**
oil on canvas, 30 ⅛ × 41 ¼ in.,
Cincinnati Art Museum,
Gift of Elizabeth S. Potter

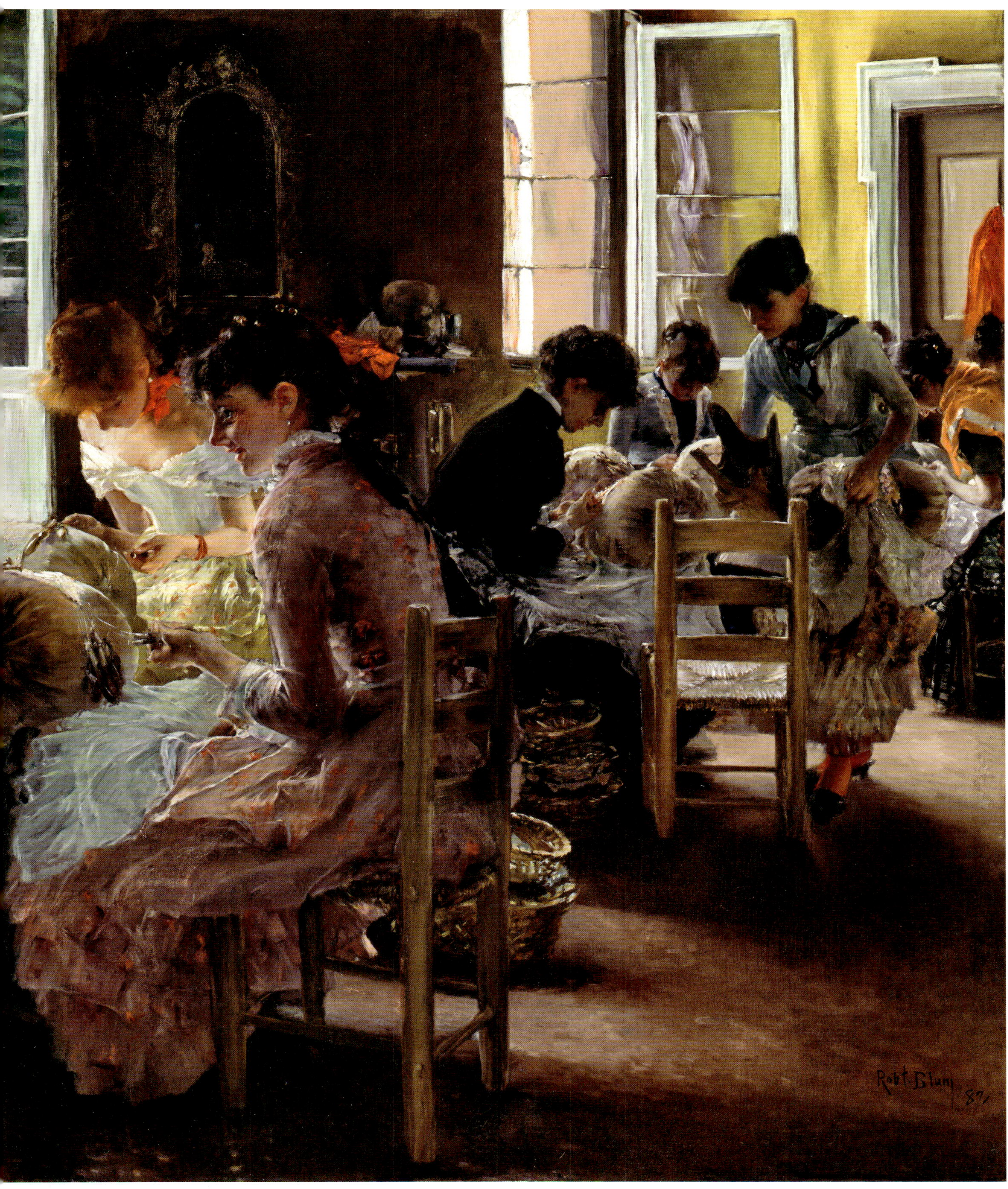
Robt. Blum
87

AMERICAN SUPPORT OF LACE REVIVAL WORKSHOPS

For American women who had settled in Italy, many marrying into landed families and bringing independent fortunes, elevating small-scale, skilled female labor dovetailed with progressive ideals of social uplift and reverence for craft production. Tryphosa Bates-Batcheller lauded her fellow Americans for their support of the women living and working on their estates as follows:

> *Here are three of the most energetic workers in this Society (the Countess Brazzà, the Marchesa di Viti de Marco, the Marchesa di Sorbello), all bearing long and noble Italian names: but we are proud to claim them as American women, who have gone into the Old World, and are not only a credit to the titles that they bear, but an honor to the name of womanhood, for the energy and ability they have shown in advancing the condition of women in the country they have adopted as their own.*[34]

Thanks to the financial backing of American expatriates, small revival projects like the Burano school sprang up across the country, each teaching lace and embroidery techniques to women, often based directly on antique examples.

Cora Slocomb di Brazzà, for instance, teamed up with Italian lace expert Carolina Amari to found institutions that taught women to re-create or reimagine antique needle and bobbin laces into new fashions.[35] Di Brazzà and Amari created a school on di Brazzà's estate in Friuli. By 1905 they had expanded the operation to half a dozen lace schools across the region, employing young women between the ages of fourteen and eighteen. Di Brazzà suggested the labor could serve as a healthful alternative to farming or factory work and might teach morality and cleanliness to rural Italian populations.[36] In 1903 the pair founded the Industrie Femminili Italiane (IFI), a cooperative designed to sell the lacework of its makers. Moreover, the association purchased handmade textiles directly from female producers across Italy. Amari and di Brazzà headquartered the IFI in Rome but also opened outposts in Bologna and Florence. In this way, lacemaking workshops backed by American women spread across Italy to enable women to support their families.

The IFI's tendrils extended not only in Europe, but also across the Atlantic to New York, where millions of Italian immigrants were settling in neighborhoods such as Greenwich Village in Manhattan. With Amari, Florence Colgate and her husband, Gino Speranza, founded the Scuola d'Industrie Italiane in the Richmond Hill Settlement House on MacDougal Street. There they employed young immigrant women to produce copies and adaptations of antique Italian textiles for contemporary American and Italian audiences.[37] Both Colgate and Speranza traveled in Italy and were inspired by projects such as di Brazzà's.[38] Colgate and Speranza's effort to embrace Italian sponsorship for the enterprise in New York also encouraged patrons in the United States to consider the workshop as an extension of an old-world lacemaking revival. Bates-Batcheller wrote, "A branch of the Industrie Femminili in Rome, has been established at Richmond House in MacDougal Street, where these Old World hand-works of women are now to be preserved, renewed, and we surely hope ably supported."[39] While conditions in New York necessitated alterations to

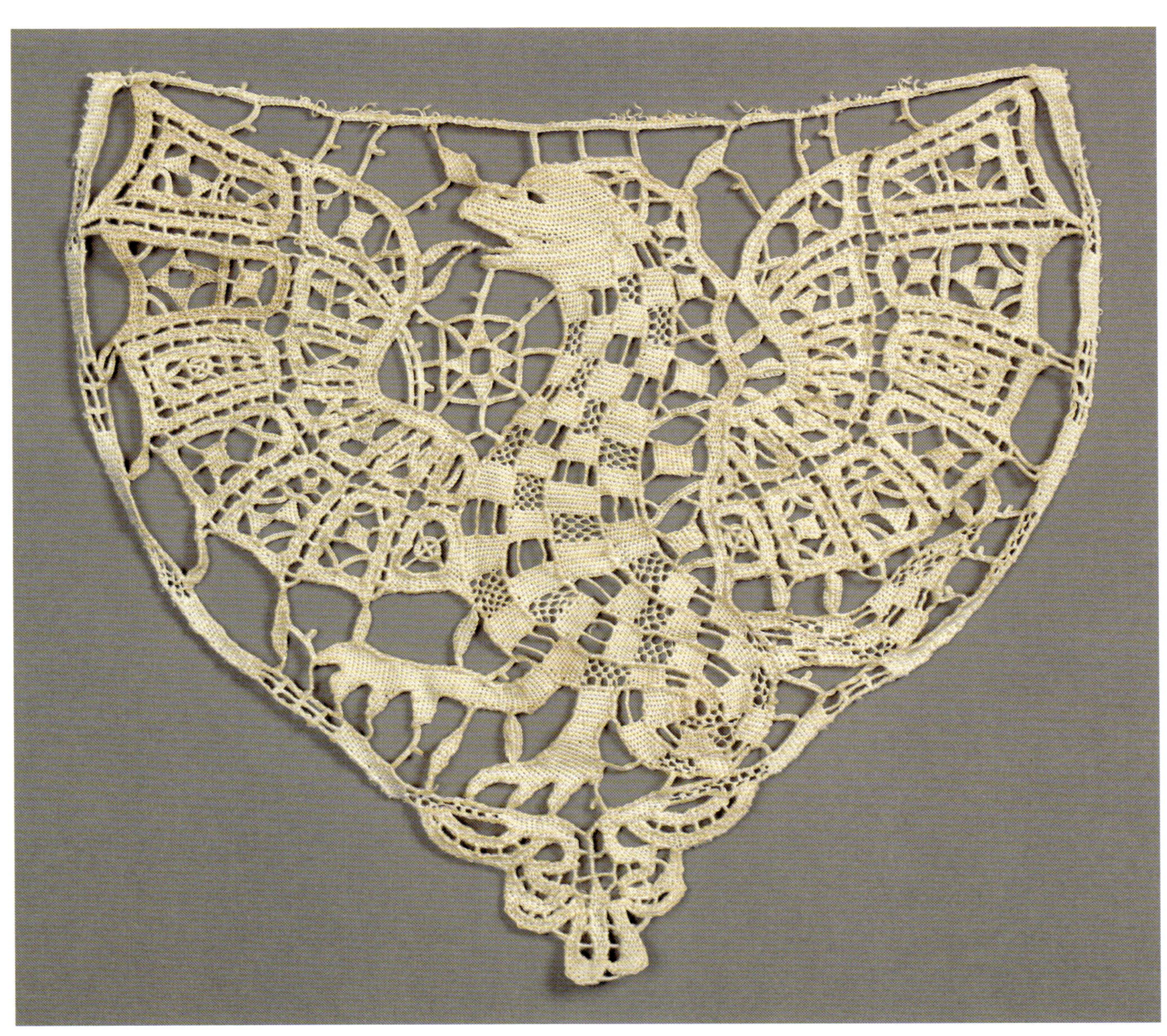

☼ CAT. 5-4
Scuola d'Industrie Italiane, Lace Panel with Dragon, ca. 1920, linen needle lace, 5 ⅜ x 5 ¾ in., Cooper Hewitt, Smithsonian Design Museum, Gift of Marian Hague

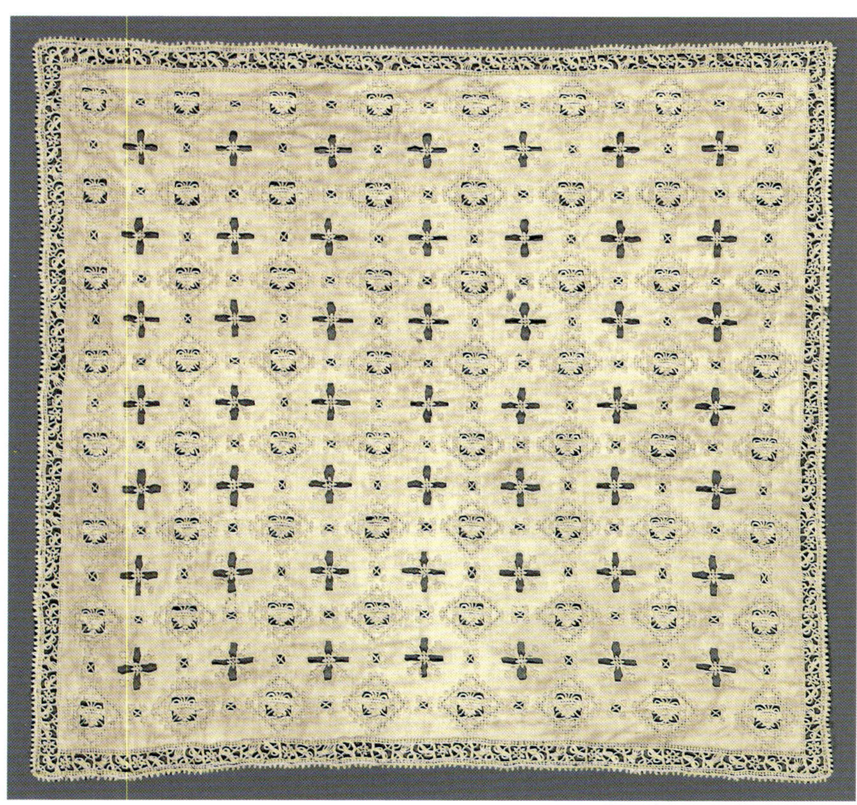

Fig. 5-11
Possibly Spanish, Cover, 16th century, linen, cutwork, 17 × 18 in., The Metropolitan Museum of Art, Anonymous gift, 1879, 79.1.103

Fig. 5-12
Scuola d'Industrie Italiane, Chalice Veil from Altar Set, ca. 1920, linen, plain weave with cutwork and embroidery, 23 ⅛ × 23 ⅛ in., Cooper Hewitt, Smithsonian Design Museum, Gift of Scuola d'Industrie Italiane in New York through Florence Colgate Speranza, 1943-41-1a

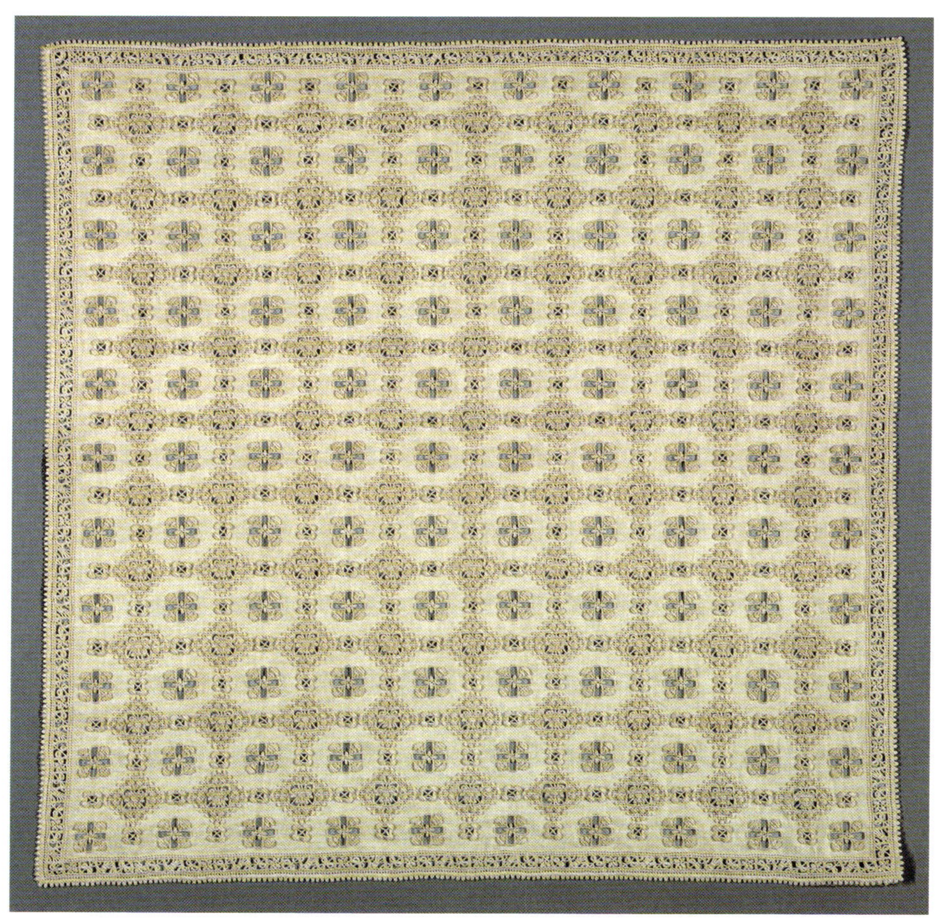

cutwork, drawn work, and *deflected work,* both the original (Fig. 5-11) and the Scuola's reproduction (Fig. 5-12) are made up of alternating rows of Maltese crosses interspersed with tiny baskets enclosed in diamond-shaped shields. Although the Scuola's reproduction is nearly three inches larger than the original, the copy follows the same pattern. The Scuola's designers augmented the textile with attendant items based on sketches (Fig. 5-13) that one of the school's administrators sent from Italy depicting part of an altar set she had seen there. Needleworkers at the Scuola made their burse cover (CAT. 5-5) based on these drawings as well as the Met's original.

The school included this altar set in several of its promotional brochures, often noting the pattern's origin in the Met's collections. One pamphlet boasted that the work constituted "an *exact* reproduction of an example in the Metropolitan Museum of Art."[41] Celebrating their artists' abilities, the Scuola championed the ineffable spirit of Italian artistry that translated antique originals into new objects. As an invitation to the Scuola's Christmas sale read, "Visitors will have an excellent opportunity to see many beautiful pieces varying widely in price from the tiny embroidered glove-purse at 50 cents to the exqui-

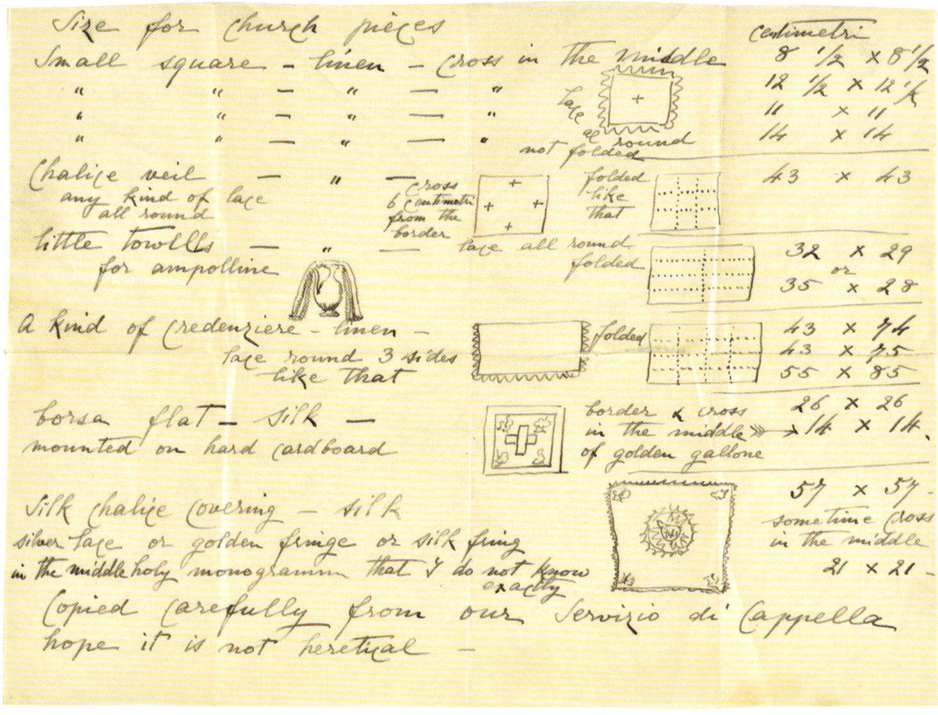
Size for church pieces — Centimetri
Small square - linen - cross in the middle — 8 1/2 x 8 1/2
" " — " — " — 12 1/2 x 12 1/2
" " — " — " — 11 x 11
" " — " — " — lace round, not folded — 14 x 14
Chalice veil — " — cross 6 centimetri from the border — folded like that — 43 x 43
any kind of lace all round
little towlls — " — lace all round, folded — 32 x 29 or 35 x 28
for ampolline
a kind of credenziere - linen - — folded — 43 x 74, 43 x 75, 55 x 85
lace round 3 sides like that
borsa flat - silk - — border & cross in the middle of golden gallone — 26 x 26, 14 x 14.
mounted on hard cardboard
Silk chalice covering - silk — 57 x 57
silver lace or golden fringe or silk fring — sometime cross in the middle
in the middle holy monogramm that I do not know exactly — 21 x 21
Copied carefully from our Servizio di Cappella
hope it is not heretical -

Fig. 5-13
Carolina Amari, sketch, in Helen Pupke to Florence Colgate, June 5, 1909, Gino Speranza Papers, Scuola d'Industrie Italiane, Manuscripts and Archives Division, The New York Public Library

site chalice veil, an exact reproduction of an example in the Metropolitan Museum of Art."[42] Even before this particular textile was completed, the workshop's administrators offered to show it off to its most prominent patrons. In 1911 executive committee member Lathrop Harper wrote to the Morgans suggesting a visit to see the work in progress. "It is really very wonderful," Harper informed Belle Greene, the family's librarian, "and I believe the finest thing in the way of needle work ever produced here. I am sure that it would give her pleasure to know that such beautiful and artistic work is possible under modern

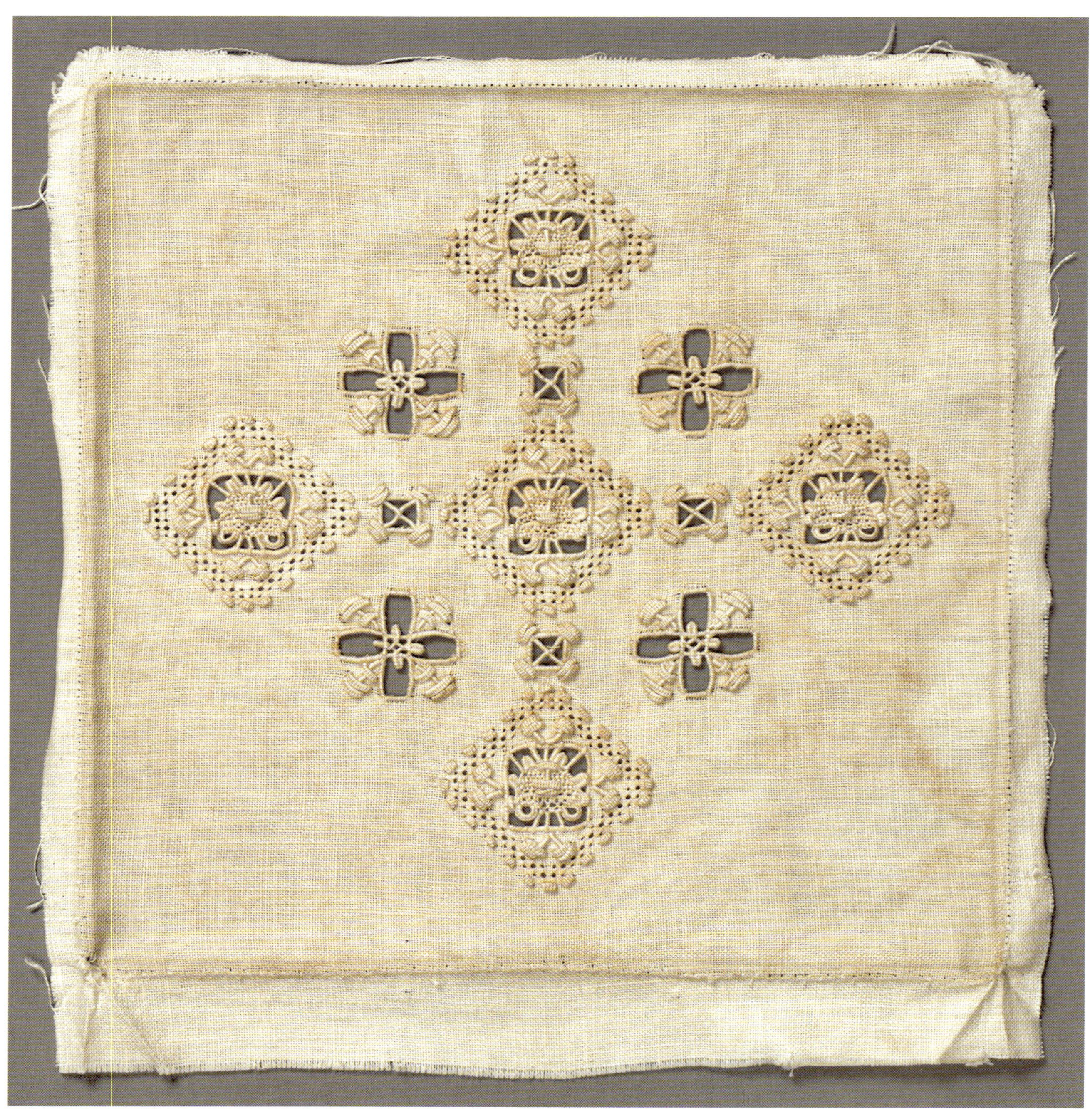

✲ CAT. 5-5

Scuola d'Industrie Italiane, Burse Cover from Altar Set, ca. 1920, linen with cutwork embroidery, 8 ⅛ × 7 11/16 in., Cooper Hewitt, Smithsonian Design Museum, Gift of Scuola d'Industrie Italiane in New York through Florence Colgate Speranza

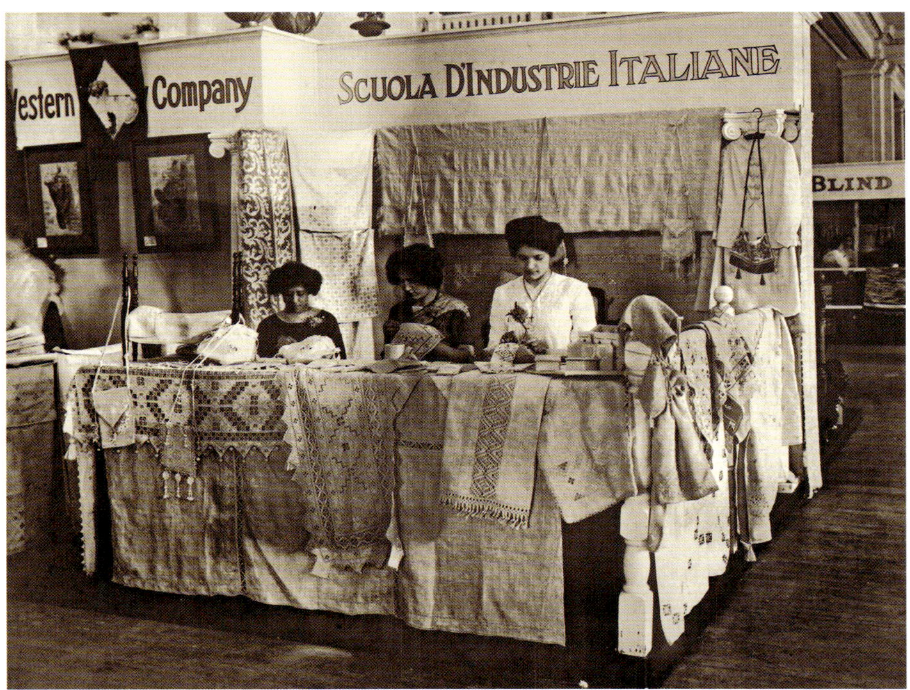

Fig. 5-14
Women Working at a Scuola d'Industrie Italiane Booth, 1905–27, photograph, Cooper Hewitt, Smithsonian Design Museum, Scuola d'Industrie Italiane folder

conditions here. This is quite aside from her coming to purchase it." Although, Harper could not help but add, "of course it is for sale."[43]

The veil, or versions of it, also appeared as part of the workshop's displays across the country. The Scuola featured it in their booth at the Society of Arts and Crafts in Boston and the Architectural League of New York.[44] In one photograph, the veil serves as part of the busy backdrop for three young workers, whose labor appears as much on display as the school's textiles (Fig. 5-14). Just as Harper had invited Mrs. Morgan to the workshop to view the veil while artisans worked to complete it, such displays of women at work stressed the close association between their labor and the objects they created. The last recorded exhibition of the altar set occurred in 1944, when Marian Powys included the work in her exhibition, *A Century of New York Needlework and Decorative Fabrics, 1820–1920,* at the Museum of the City of New York (Fig. 5-15). The installation featured the set as part of a tableau that included other New York workshops such as the Fisk Weavers.[45] In the display, Powys draped the veil over a cup as it might have appeared on an altar and just as a Scuola administrator had sketched it in Italy years earlier. This exhibition, on view more than a decade after the Scuola had closed, recontextualized the workshop's products to celebrate New York industries and the workshop's ties to America rather than the foreign associations of the producers. The veil's context shifted

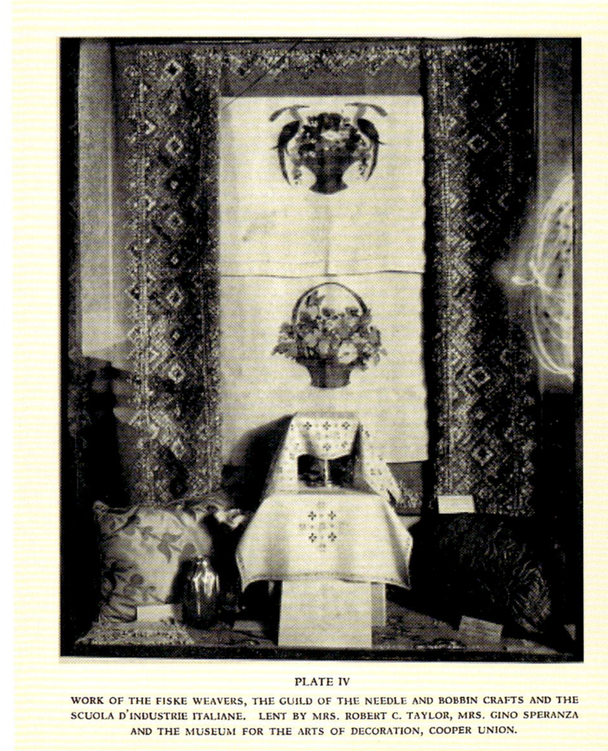
PLATE IV

WORK OF THE FISKE WEAVERS, THE GUILD OF THE NEEDLE AND BOBBIN CRAFTS AND THE SCUOLA D'INDUSTRIE ITALIANE. LENT BY MRS. ROBERT C. TAYLOR, MRS. GINO SPERANZA AND THE MUSEUM FOR THE ARTS OF DECORATION, COOPER UNION.

50

Fig. 5-15
Scuola d'Industrie Italiane Altar Set in the exhibition *A Century of New York Needlework and Decorative Fabrics, 1820–1920*, from *Bulletin of the Needle and Bobbin Club*, 1944, Ratti Textile Center Library Archives, The Metropolitan Museum of Art

to showcase evolving conceptions of Italian Americans as full participants in the shared culture of the United States.

The collection, classification, and exhibition of antique Italian textiles and the revival industries Italian and American women established to resurrect their production fostered transatlantic connections between Europe and the United States and created a robust female-centric economy. The laces solidified national narratives in post-unification Italy and helped bolster the status of immigrant workers in the New World. For Italian Americans such as Scuola workers Millie Mariano, Nettie Muccio, Angelina Pellegrino, and Cora Gindano, the school in New York provided an opportunity both to participate in the modern US economy under the mantle of traditional production and to carve a social and economic space for themselves. In Italy and America, old lace helped middle- and upper-class women affiliate themselves with an idealized version of a storied Italian past while the reproduction of antique patterns applied to new forms offered working-class women a way to engage with traditional modes of production and achieve a measure of economic independence.

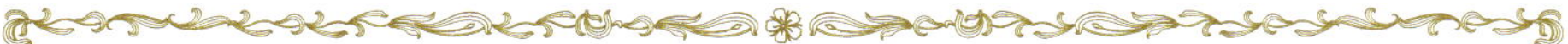

GLOSSARY OF TERMS

Bobbin lace: Lace created with wooden dowels or bobbins wound between one another in sequence.

Cutwork: To create cutwork, an artist excises areas from an existing fabric, reinforces its edges, and then fills it with embroidery or lacework.

Deflected work: Patterns created by the gathering of individual threads in an existing fabric.

Needle lace: Technically embroidery, needle lace is created using buttonhole stitches. Needle lacemakers typically employ a needle to insert stitches between guide threads affixed to a paper pattern.

Punto Burano: Nineteenth-century needlepoint lace created from uneven cotton thread, giving the lace a cloudy appearance. Designs vary from large florals to tiny sprigs.

Reticella: An early form of needle lace, reticella uses buttonhole stitches to fill in portions of space created by withdrawing or bundling warp or weft threads from an existing fabric.

Venetian point: A seventeenth-century textile that features scrolling floral designs, often in relief. Venetian point's delicacy and curvilinear designs are a sharp contrast with earlier, more angular reticella patterns.

Withdrawn (or drawn) work: Like cutwork, withdrawn (or drawn) work is a form of needlework in which individual threads of a base material are removed as part of the overall design.

Definitions for lace terms come from Pat Earnshaw's books *Dictionary of Lace* (Dover, 1999) and *The Identification of Lace* (Shire, 1980).

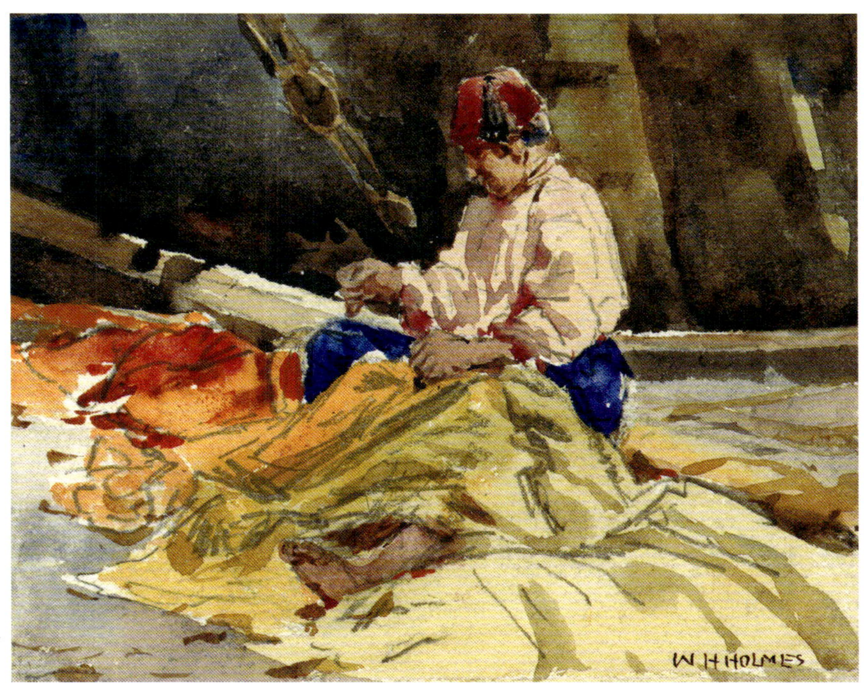

✡ CAT. 5-9
William Henry Holmes, *Venice, Mending Sails*, 1880, watercolor and graphite on paper, 3 ½ × 4 ½ in., National Anthropological Archives, Smithsonian Institution

✡ CAT. 5-10
William Henry Holmes, *Bead Stringer, Venice*, 1880, watercolor and graphite on paper, 4 ½ × 3 ¾ in., National Anthropological Archives, Smithsonian Institution

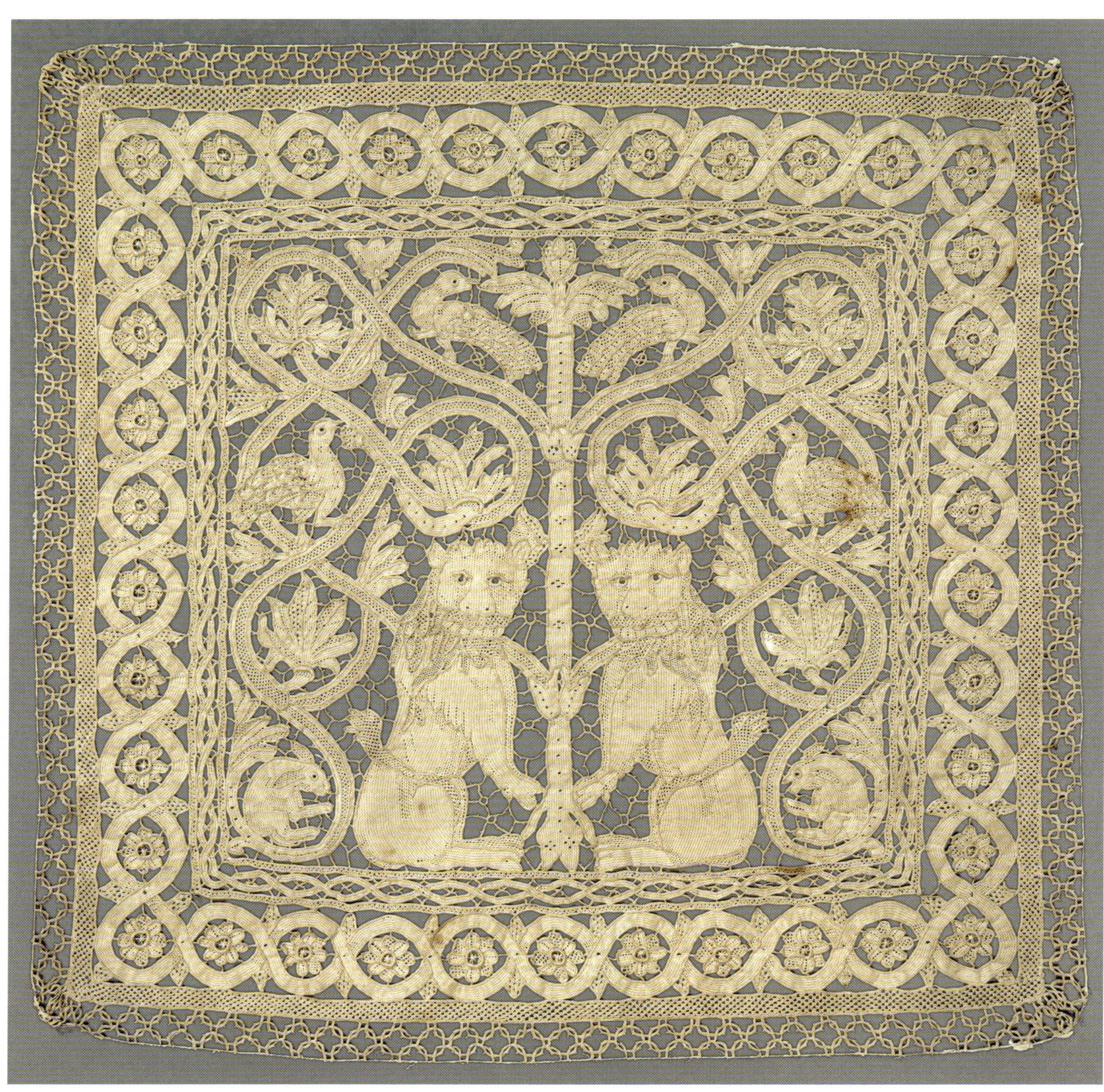

✡ CAT. 5-11
Scuola dei Merletti di Burano, Lace Panel with Lions, late 19th–early 20th century, linen needle lace, 17 × 16 ½ in., Cooper Hewitt, Smithsonian Design Museum, Gift of Charles G. K. Warner and William W. Warner

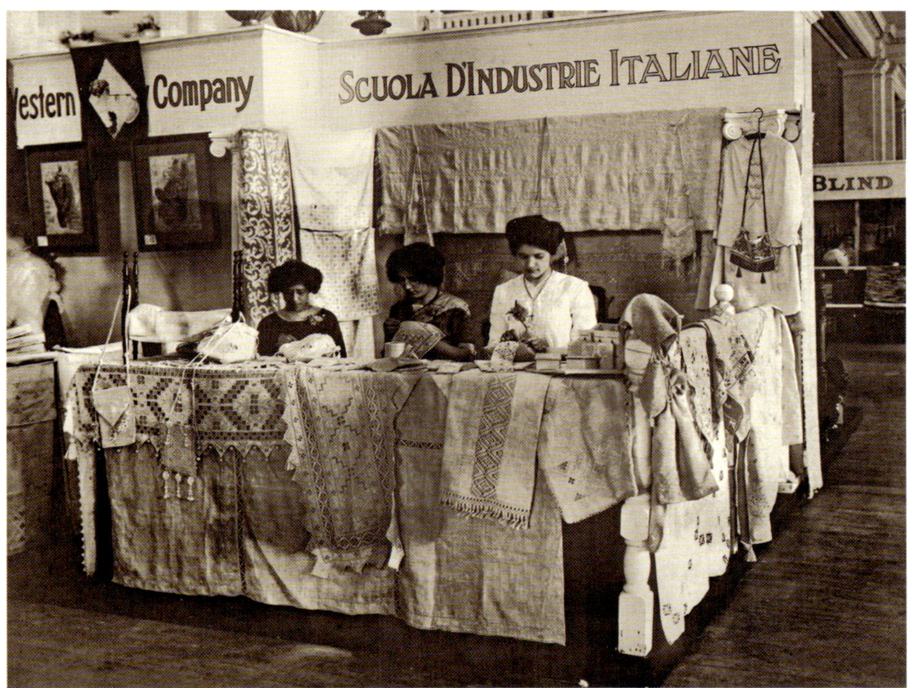

Fig. 5-14
Women Working at a Scuola d'Industrie Italiane Booth, 1905–27, photograph, Cooper Hewitt, Smithsonian Design Museum, Scuola d'Industrie Italiane folder

Fig. 5-15
Scuola d'Industrie Italiane Altar Set in the exhibition *A Century of New York Needlework and Decorative Fabrics, 1820–1920*, from *Bulletin of the Needle and Bobbin Club*, 1944, Ratti Textile Center Library Archives, The Metropolitan Museum of Art

conditions here. This is quite aside from her coming to purchase it." Although, Harper could not help but add, "of course it is for sale."[43]

The veil, or versions of it, also appeared as part of the workshop's displays across the country. The Scuola featured it in their booth at the Society of Arts and Crafts in Boston and the Architectural League of New York.[44] In one photograph, the veil serves as part of the busy backdrop for three young workers, whose labor appears as much on display as the school's textiles (Fig. 5-14). Just as Harper had invited Mrs. Morgan to the workshop to view the veil while artisans worked to complete it, such displays of women at work stressed the close association between their labor and the objects they created. The last recorded exhibition of the altar set occurred in 1944, when Marian Powys included the work in her exhibition, *A Century of New York Needlework and Decorative Fabrics, 1820–1920*, at the Museum of the City of New York (Fig. 5-15). The installation featured the set as part of a tableau that included other New York workshops such as the Fisk Weavers.[45] In the display, Powys draped the veil over a cup as it might have appeared on an altar and just as a Scuola administrator had sketched it in Italy years earlier. This exhibition, on view more than a decade after the Scuola had closed, recontextualized the workshop's products to celebrate New York industries and the workshop's ties to America rather than the foreign associations of the producers. The veil's context shifted

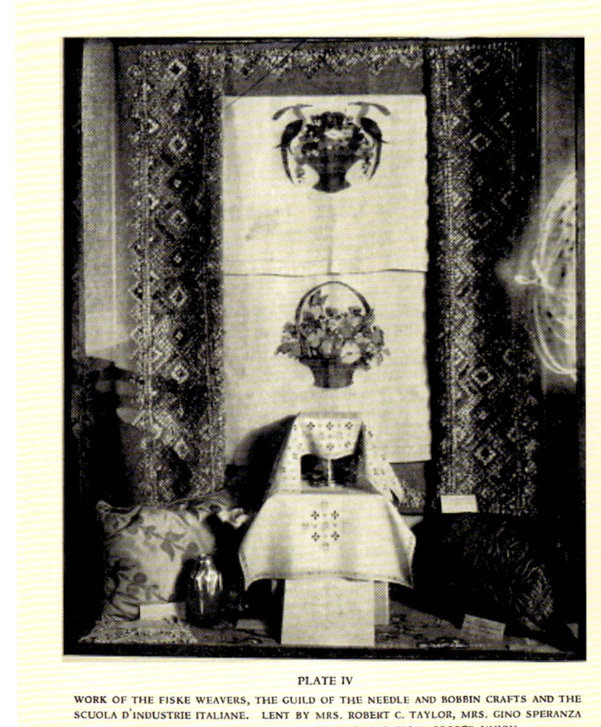
PLATE IV
WORK OF THE FISKE WEAVERS, THE GUILD OF THE NEEDLE AND BOBBIN CRAFTS AND THE SCUOLA D'INDUSTRIE ITALIANE. LENT BY MRS. ROBERT C. TAYLOR, MRS. GINO SPERANZA AND THE MUSEUM FOR THE ARTS OF DECORATION, COOPER UNION.

50

to showcase evolving conceptions of Italian Americans as full participants in the shared culture of the United States.

The collection, classification, and exhibition of antique Italian textiles and the revival industries Italian and American women established to resurrect their production fostered transatlantic connections between Europe and the United States and created a robust female-centric economy. The laces solidified national narratives in post-unification Italy and helped bolster the status of immigrant workers in the New World. For Italian Americans such as Scuola workers Millie Mariano, Nettie Muccio, Angelina Pellegrino, and Cora Gindano, the school in New York provided an opportunity both to participate in the modern US economy under the mantle of traditional production and to carve a social and economic space for themselves. In Italy and America, old lace helped middle- and upper-class women affiliate themselves with an idealized version of a storied Italian past while the reproduction of antique patterns applied to new forms offered working-class women a way to engage with traditional modes of production and achieve a measure of economic independence.

GLOSSARY OF TERMS

Bobbin lace: Lace created with wooden dowels or bobbins wound between one another in sequence.

Cutwork: To create cutwork, an artist excises areas from an existing fabric, reinforces its edges, and then fills it with embroidery or lacework.

Deflected work: Patterns created by the gathering of individual threads in an existing fabric.

Needle lace: Technically embroidery, needle lace is created using buttonhole stitches. Needle lacemakers typically employ a needle to insert stitches between guide threads affixed to a paper pattern.

Punto Burano: Nineteenth-century needlepoint lace created from uneven cotton thread, giving the lace a cloudy appearance. Designs vary from large florals to tiny sprigs.

Reticella: An early form of needle lace, reticella uses buttonhole stitches to fill in portions of space created by withdrawing or bundling warp or weft threads from an existing fabric.

Venetian point: A seventeenth-century textile that features scrolling floral designs, often in relief. Venetian point's delicacy and curvilinear designs are a sharp contrast with earlier, more angular reticella patterns.

Withdrawn (or drawn) work: Like cutwork, withdrawn (or drawn) work is a form of needlework in which individual threads of a base material are removed as part of the overall design.

Definitions for lace terms come from Pat Earnshaw's books *Dictionary of Lace* (Dover, 1999) and *The Identification of Lace* (Shire, 1980).

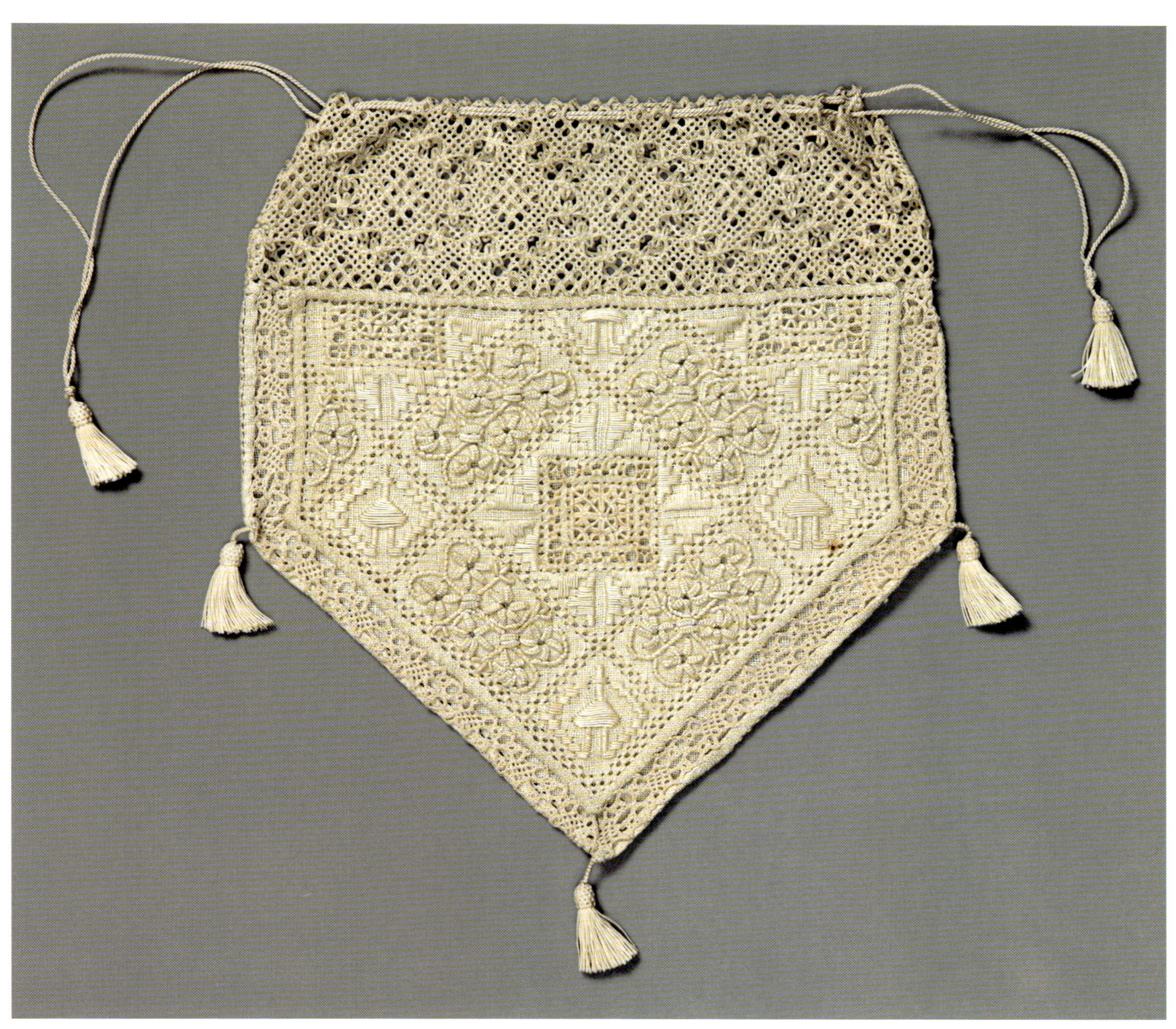

✡ CAT. 5-6
Scuola d'Industrie Italiane, Pouch, ca. 1920, embroidered linen with bobbin lace, 7 ⅞ × 7 5/16 in., Cooper Hewitt, Smithsonian Design Museum, Gift of Marian Hague

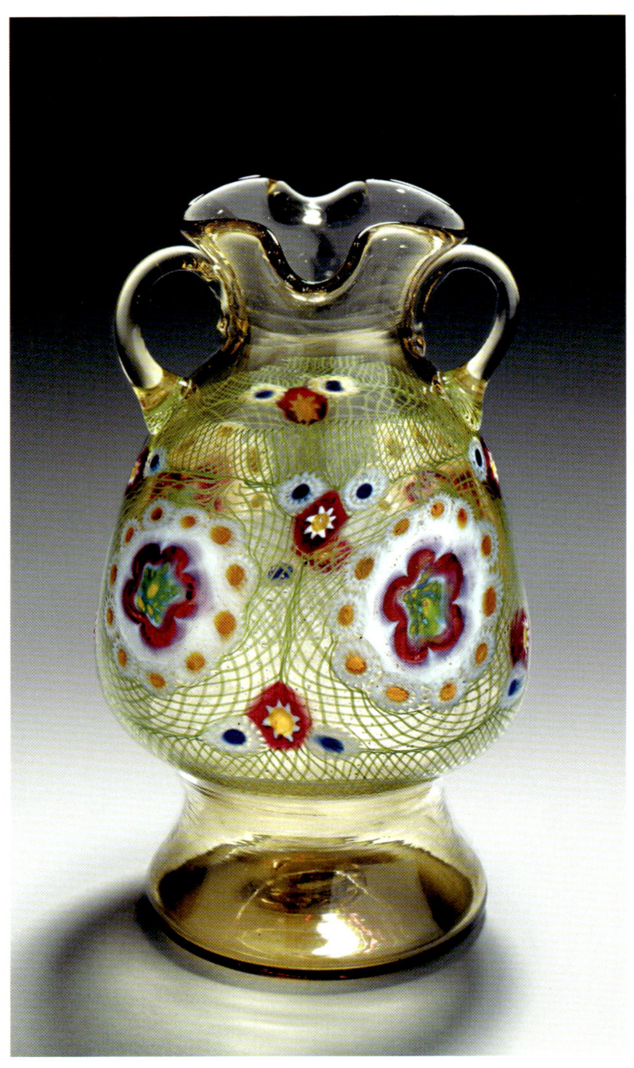

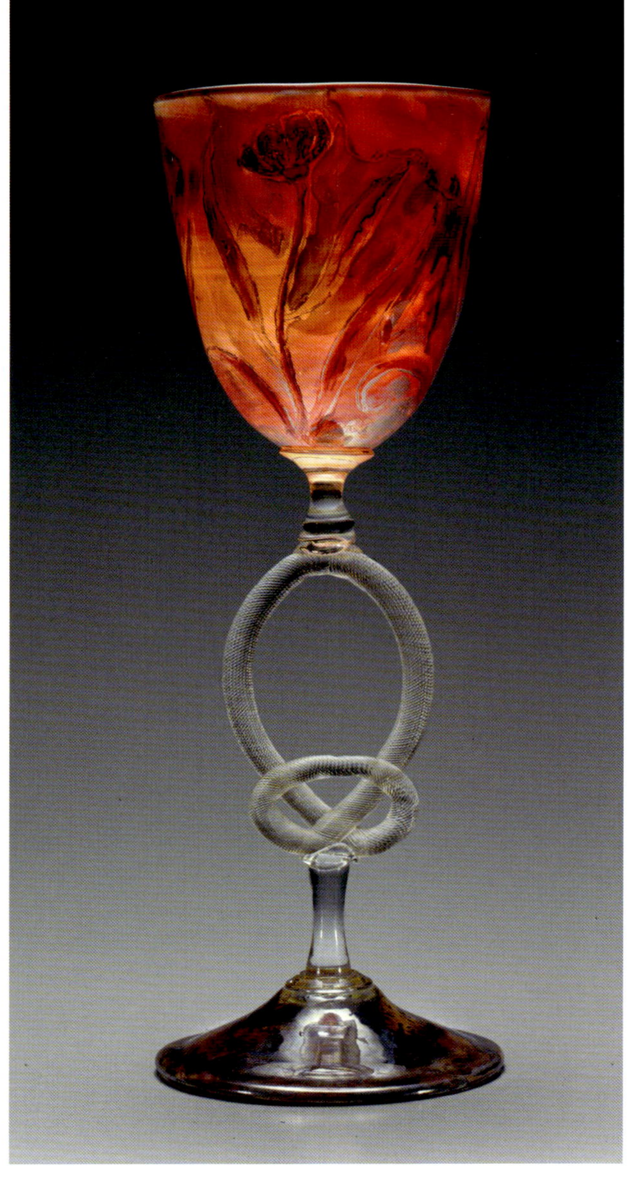

✲ CAT. 5-7
Artisti Barovier, Zanfirico Glass Vase with Floral Murrhines, ca. 1910–13, blown and applied hot-worked glass with mosaic glass inclusions, 7 9/16 × 5 ½ in. diam., Iris & B. Gerald Cantor Center for Visual Arts at Stanford University, Gift of Erede Dr. A. Salviati & Co.

✲ CAT. 5-8
Attributed to Giulio Salviati & C. or Erede Dr. A. Salviati & Co., Floral Goblet with Knotted Stem, ca. 1890–1911, blown and applied hot-worked glass, 8 15/16 × 3 ⅛ in. diam., The Walters Art Museum, Acquired by Henry Walters

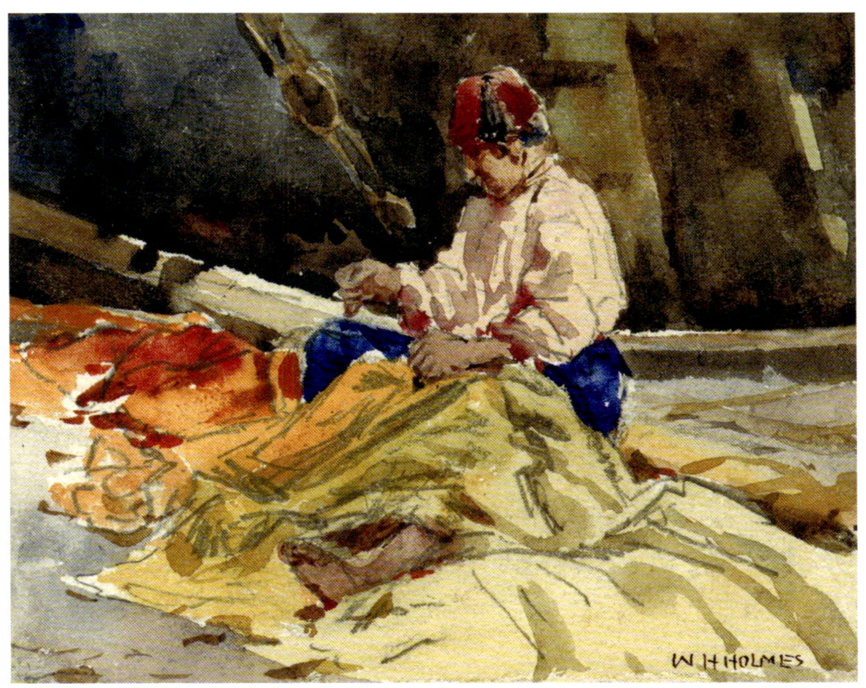

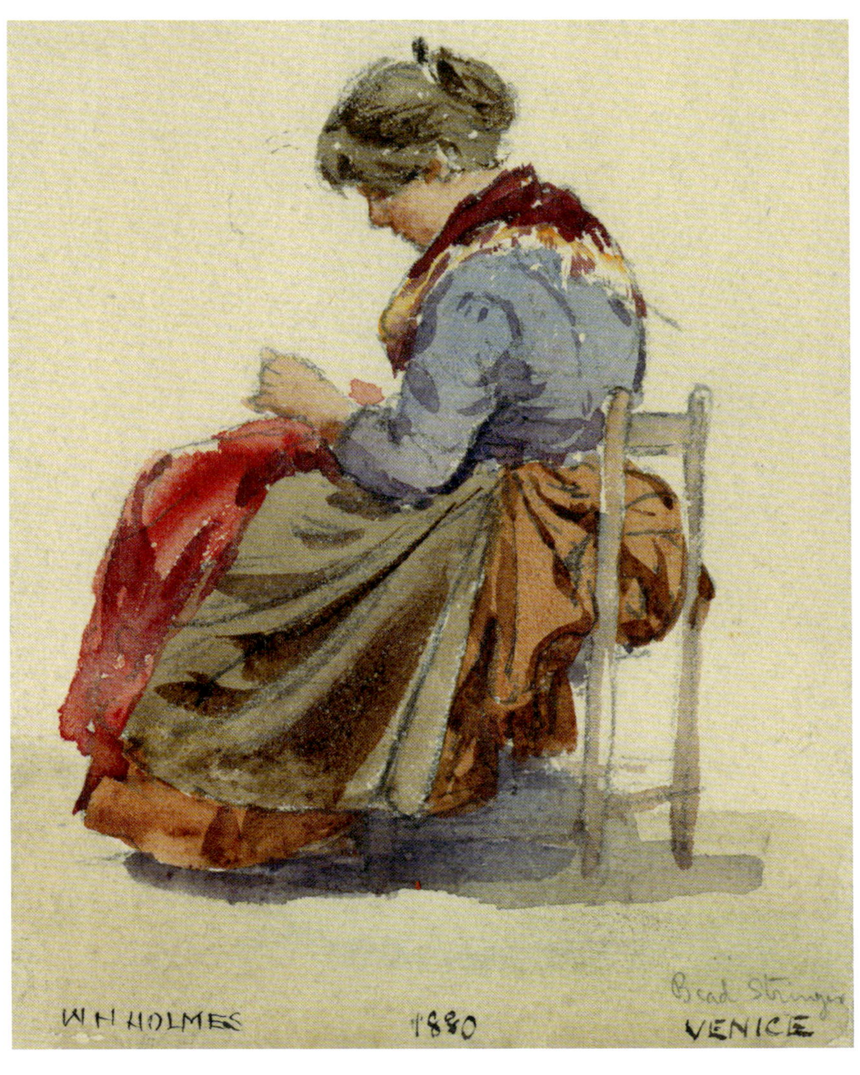

✡ CAT. 5-9
William Henry Holmes, *Venice, Mending Sails*, 1880, watercolor and graphite on paper, 3 ½ × 4 ½ in., National Anthropological Archives, Smithsonian Institution

✡ CAT. 5-10
William Henry Holmes, *Bead Stringer, Venice*, 1880, watercolor and graphite on paper, 4 ½ × 3 ¾ in., National Anthropological Archives, Smithsonian Institution

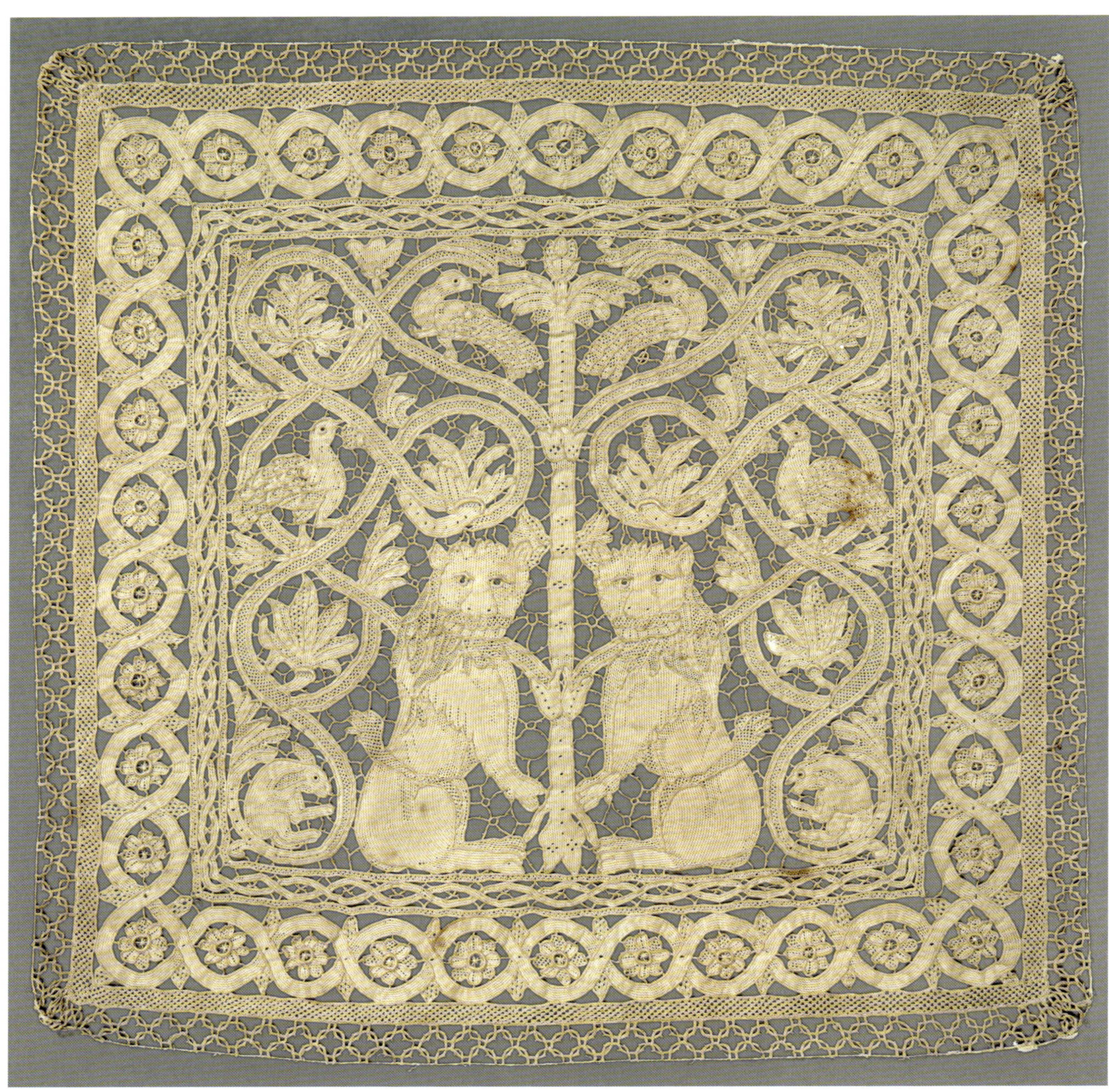

✡ CAT. 5-11
Scuola dei Merletti di Burano, Lace Panel with Lions, late 19th–early 20th century, linen needle lace, 17 × 16 ½ in., Cooper Hewitt, Smithsonian Design Museum, Gift of Charles G. K. Warner and William W. Warner

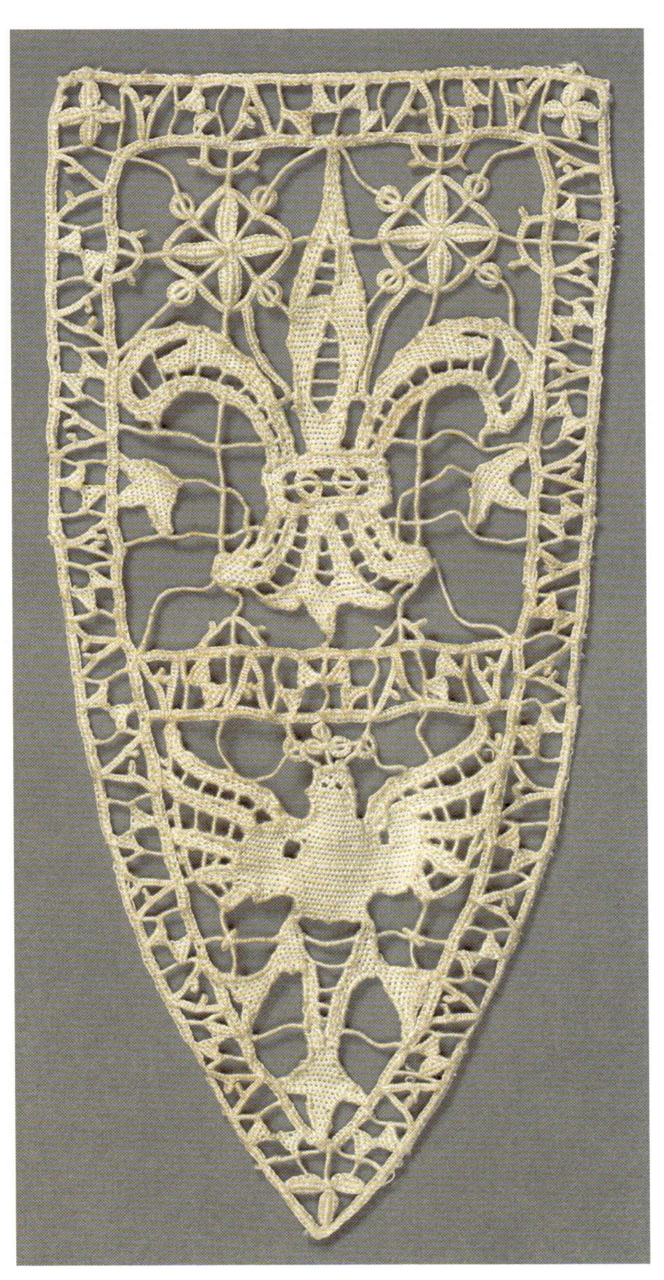

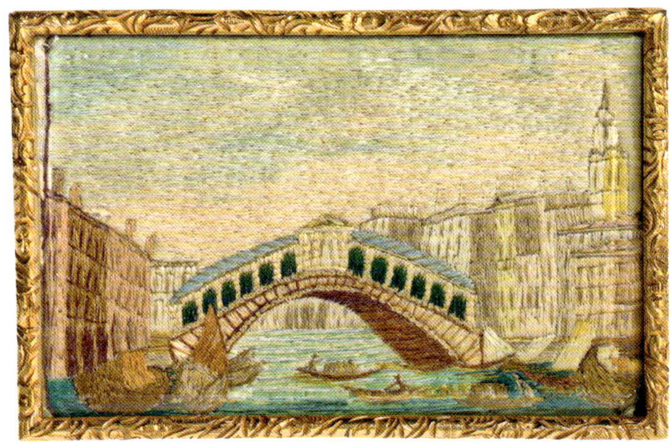

✲ CAT. 5-12
Scuola d'Industrie Italiane, Lace Panel with Fleur-de-Lis, ca. 1920, linen needle lace, 5 ⅞ × 2 ¾ in., Cooper Hewitt, Smithsonian Design Museum, Gift of Marian Hague

✲ CAT. 5-13
Attributed to Scuola di Ricamo, Istituto delle Zitelle, Brooch with Pittura d'Ago (Needle Painting) of the Rialto Bridge, Venice, late 19th century, silk, gold, and glass, 1 ½ × 2 3/16 in., RISD Museum, Bequest of Lyra Brown Nickerson

NOTES

1 Catherine Cornaro [Katharine de Kay Bronson], "The Revival of Burano Lace," *Century Illustrated Monthly Magazine* 23, no. 3 (January 1882): 333–43. For a recent account of Venetian lace industries, see Margaret Plant, *Venice: Fragile City, 1797–1997* (New Haven, CT: Yale University Press, 2002), 179; and Pat Earnshaw, *The Identification of Lace* (Aylesbury, UK: Shire Publications, 1980), 46–48.

2 Earnshaw, *Identification of Lace*, 38.

3 Ann Rosalind Jones, "Labor and Lace: The Crafts of Giacomo Franco's Habiti delle Donne Venetiane," *I Tatti Studies in the Italian Renaissance* 17, no. 2 (Fall 2014): 403, 411.

4 Doretta Davanzo Poli, *Il Merletto Veneziano* (Novara: De Agostini, 1998), 18.

5 Emily Jackson, *A History of Hand-Made Lace* (New York: Charles Scribner's Sons, 1900), 134.

6 F. Mabel Robinson, "The Lace School at Burano," *Magazine of Art* 7 (1884): 258.

7 G. M. Urbani de Gheltof, *A Technical History of the Manufacture of Venetian Laces*, trans. Enid Layard (Venice: Ferd. Ongania, 1882), http://library.si.edu/digital-library/book/technicalhistory00urba; and Cornaro [Bronson], "Revival of Burano Lace." For more recent analyses of American expatriates supporting the Venetian lace revival, see Plant, *Venice: Fragile City*, 179; and Elizabeth Anne McCauley, "A Sentimental Traveler: Isabella Stewart Gardner in Venice," in *Gondola Days: Isabella Stewart Gardner and the Palazzo Barbaro Circle*, ed. Elizabeth Anne McCauley (Boston: Isabella Stewart Gardner Museum, 2004), 25.

8 *Century Illustrated Monthly Magazine* identifies the illustrator of this scene as Princess Louise, Marchioness of Lorne. Louise was a daughter of Queen Victoria. An artist and feminist, her interest in the Royal School, also called the Burano Lace School, is not surprising given the high profile of many of the industry's supporters. For more on the allure of Venice's history for Gilded Age travelers and artists, see Plant, *Venice: Fragile City*, 176–90; Margaretta M. Lovell, *A Visitable Past: Views of Venice by American Artists, 1860–1915* (Chicago: University of Chicago Press, 1989), 1–14; and Alan Chong, "Artistic Life in Venice," in McCauley, *Gondola Days*, 87–128.

9 Aemilia Ars, the Scuola di Sorbello, and the workshops of the Industrie Femminili Italiane are just a few of the revival workshops that emerged at this moment. For more on these workshops, see Gianfranco Tortorelli, *Ricami della Bell'Epoca: La Scuola di Romeyne Robert Ranieri di Sorbello, 1904–1934* (Foligno: Editoriale Umbra, 1996); Daniel Rosenfeld, ed., *European Painting and Sculpture, ca. 1770–1937, in the Museum of Art, Rhode Island School of Design* (Philadelphia: University of Pennsylvania Press, 1991), 160; and Ivana Palomba, *L'Arte Ricamata: Uno Strumento di Emancipazione Femminile nell'Opera di Carolina Amari* (Maniago: Arti Tessili, 2011), 99–143.

10 Eric Hobsbawm introduced the idea of the invention of tradition as a key means by which nineteenth-century European nations coalesced after unification projects. Eric Hobsbawm and Terence Ranger, eds., *The Invention of Tradition* (Cambridge, UK: Cambridge University Press, 1992), 267.

11 For a broad-ranging discussion of lace revival workshops in the United States and their connections to Italy, see Diana Jocelyn Greenwold, "Crafting New Citizens: Immigrant Craft Workshops in American Settlement Houses in New York and Boston, 1900–1945" (PhD diss., University of California, Berkeley, 2016), chap. 2.

12 A large literature exists on late nineteenth-century Italian American immigrants and specifically the place of those women in the United States. Two foundational works are Robert A. Orsi, *The Madonna of 115th Street: Faith and Community in Italian Harlem, 1880–1950* (New Haven, CT: Yale University Press, 1985); and Elizabeth Ewen, *Immigrant Women in the Land of Dollars: Life and Culture on the Lower East Side, 1890–1925* (New York: Monthly Review Press, 1985).

13 Marian Powys opened her Devonshire Lace Shop at 60 Washington Square, New York, in 1916. She later moved the business to West Fifty-Seventh Street. Peter P. Grey, "In These Delicate Constructions . . . ," *American Craft* 41, no. 4 (August/September 1981): 51–55.

14 Rosanna Pavoni, *Reviving the Renaissance: The Use and Abuse of the Past in Nineteenth-Century Italian Art and Decoration* (Cambridge, UK: Cambridge University Press, 1997), 9–10.

15 While the term "Renaissance" applies generally to fifteenth- and sixteenth-century Italy, Americans often employed the term in a broader sense to describe Italian products such as laces made from the fifteenth through eighteenth centuries. Some of the confusion rests in the difficulty of dating authentic laces and later copies of original patterns. For more on the infatuation with the handmade in the late nineteenth-century United States, see T. J. Jackson Lears, *No Place of Grace: Antimodernism and the Transformation of American Culture, 1880–1920* (New York: Pantheon Books, 1981). For more about the Arts and Crafts movement, see Melody Barnett Deusner's essay in this catalogue, pages 60–72.

16 "The Lace Room," *Metropolitan Museum of Art Bulletin* 1, no. 7 (June 1906): 98–100. For more on institutional collecting of antique lace in America, see Greenwold, "Crafting New Citizens."

17 Maud Howe Elliott to her mother, Julia Ward Howe, 10 May 1895, in Maud Howe Elliott, *Three Generations* (Boston: Little, Brown, 1923), 269–70.

18 "Fine Lace Lovers Have Their Club," *New York Times*, December 1, 1918, E-40.

19 *The Queen Lace Book: A Historical and Descriptive Account of the Hand-Made Antique Laces of All Countries* (London: "The Queen" Office, 1874), 37.

20 McCauley, "Sentimental Traveler," 48n113.

21 Isabella Stewart Gardner, "Isabella Stewart Gardner Receipts," October 16, 1894, Isabella Stewart Gardner Museum Archives. Rosalino point likely refers to rosaline or rose point, a type of lace with raised portions used to create floral patterns popular among artists from Venice. Earnshaw, *Dictionary of Lace*, 147.

22 McCauley, "Sentimental Traveler," 25.

23 Ibid.

24 Mrs. Bury Palliser, *History of Lace* (London: Sampson Low, Son, & Marston, 1865); Cesare Vecellio, *Corona delle Nobili et Virtuose Donne* (1591; repr., Venice: F. Ongania, 1891); Elisa Ricci, *Antiche Trine Italiane: Trine a Fuselli* (Bergamo: Istituto Italiano d'Arti Grafiche, 1908); and Elisa Ricci, *Old Italian Lace*, 2 vols. (London: William Heinemann, 1913).

25 Frances Morris and Marian Hague, *Antique Laces of American Collectors* (New York: W. Helburn for the Needle and Bobbin Club, 1920).

26 Benjamin Cummings Truman, *History of the World's Fair: Being a Complete and Authentic Description of the Columbian Exposition from Its Inception* (New York: E. B. Treat, 1893), 222.

27 Eva Marriotti, "Italy," in *Art and Handicraft in the Woman's Building of the World's Columbian Exposition, Chicago, 1893*, ed. Maud Howe Elliott (New York: Goupil, 1893), 230.

28 Hubert Howe Bancroft, *The Book of the Fair: An Historical and Descriptive Presentation of the World's Science, Art, and Industry as Viewed through the Columbian Exposition at Chicago in 1893* (Chicago: Bancroft, 1893), 1:278.

29 For more information on the founding of art institutions in the United States, see Neil Harris, "Museum, Merchandising, and Popular Taste: The Struggle for Influence," in *Cultural Excursions: Marketing Appetites and Cultural Tastes in Modern America* (Chicago: University of Chicago Press, 1990), 56–81.

30 "Lace Room," 98–99.

31 Morris wrote frequently for the Met's bulletin about the collection she oversaw. Frances Morris, "Notes on the Lace Collection," *Metropolitan Museum of Art Bulletin* 3, no. 8 (August 1908): 156–61; Frances Morris, "Rearrangement of the Laces and Textiles," *Metropolitan Museum of Art Bulletin* 12, no. 12 (December 1917): 241, 246–48; Frances Morris, "The Lace Collection," *Metropolitan Museum of Art Bulletin* 20, no. 9 (September 1925): 217–20; Morris, "Laces of Historical Interest," *Metropolitan Museum of Art Bulletin* 20, no. 11 (November 1925): 259–61; Frances Morris, "Historic Laces and Embroideries," *Metropolitan Museum of Art Bulletin* 21, no. 1 (January 1926): 13–16; and Joseph Breck, "Resignation of Miss Frances Morris," *Metropolitan Museum of Art Bulletin* 24, no. 10 (October 1929): 266. Sarah Gore Flint Townsend similarly occupied a key role at the Museum of Fine Arts, Boston, overseeing their collections. For a sample of her stewardship reporting and notes on an exhibition of lace, see Sarah Gore Flint, "Reports of Curators and Others in Charge of Collections: Division of Western Art: Textiles," in Museum of Fine Arts, Boston, *Thirty-Sixth Annual Report for the Year 1911* (Boston: Metcalf, 1912), 115–16.

32 Robinson, "Lace School at Burano," 258. Remigius van Haanen (1812–1894) was a nineteenth-century Dutch painter who worked in Venice. Along with the Austrian painter Ludwig Johann Passini, he is credited with producing the first genre paintings to feature Venetian residents. Rosenfeld, *European Painting and Sculpture*, 160.

33 Otto Henry Bacher traveled with Frank Duveneck to Italy and set up a printing studio there. William H. Gerdts, "The International Milieu," in *Sargent's Venice*, ed. Warren Adelson (New Haven, CT: Yale University Press, 2006), 160.

34 Tryphosa Bates-Batcheller, *Glimpses of Italian Court Life: Happy Days in* Italia Adorata (New York: Doubleday, Page, 1907), 319–20.

35 Palomba, *L'Arte Ricamata*, 121–23.

36 Cora Slocomb di Brazzà, "The Italian Woman in the Country," in *The Congress of Women: Held in the Woman's Building, World's Columbian Exposition, Chicago, U.S.A., 1893*, ed. Mary Kavanaugh Oldham Eagle (Philadelphia: S. I. Bell, 1894), 697–703.

37 Amari's long career in cottage industry textile revivals spanning the Atlantic is relatively under studied. Ivana Palomba provides the most comprehensive treatment of Amari's work in Italy in *L'Arte Ricamata*.

38 Emily Zilber, "'A Delicate Link with Their Far Away Country': The Scuola d'Industrie Italiane (1905–1927) and the Translation of the Nineteenth Century Italian Reproduction Textile Workshop into an American Context" (master's thesis, Bard Graduate Center, 2007), 37.

39 Bates-Batcheller, *Glimpses of Italian Court Life*, 423.

40 Frances Morris, "The Summer Lace Exhibit at the Metropolitan Museum of Art," *Bulletin of the Needle and Bobbin Club* 3, no. 2 (1919): 3–15. The fragment remained in the collections of the Met until 1935, when Speranza requested its return. Mrs. Gino Speranza, "To Mr. Henry F. Davidson, Registrar of the Met," 11 July 1935, Speranza, Gino (Mrs.) 1919–21, 1923, 1935–36, 1941, Sp 3597, Metropolitan Museum of Art Archives.

41 Scuola d'Industrie Italiane, "Catalogue of an Exhibition of Laces and Embroideries Held at the Residence of Mrs. Gino C. Speranza, Fifty East Fifty-Seventh Street, December First MCMX," Gino Speranza Papers, Scuola d'Industrie Italiane, Box 14, Folder 1910, Manuscripts and Archives Division, New York Public Library.

42 "Scuola d'Industrie Italiane Christmas Sale Invitation," Gino Speranza Papers, Scuola d'Industrie Italiane, Box 15, Miscellany, Catalogues, notices of exhibitions, invitations, samples of stationary, etc., Manuscripts and Archives Division, New York Public Library.

43 Lathrop Harper to Belle Greene, 19 September 1911, Morgan Collections Correspondence, ARC 1310: H, Harper, Francis P. & Lathrop C. book dealers, NY, Archives of The Pierpont Morgan Library, New York, NY.

44 Executive Committee Meeting Minutes, March 12, 1914, Gino Speranza Papers, Scuola d'Industrie Italiane Box 14, Folder 1913–15, Manuscripts and Archives Division, New York Public Library.

45 The Fisk Weavers was a workshop founded by Elizabeth Fisk that produced colorful embroidery. Mary LaFollette, *A Partial List of Craftsmen and Handicraft Groups in the United States* (Washington, DC: US Department of Agriculture, Cooperative Extension Service, 1947), 131.

SPARKS OF GENIUS

American Art and the Appeal of Modern Venetian Glass

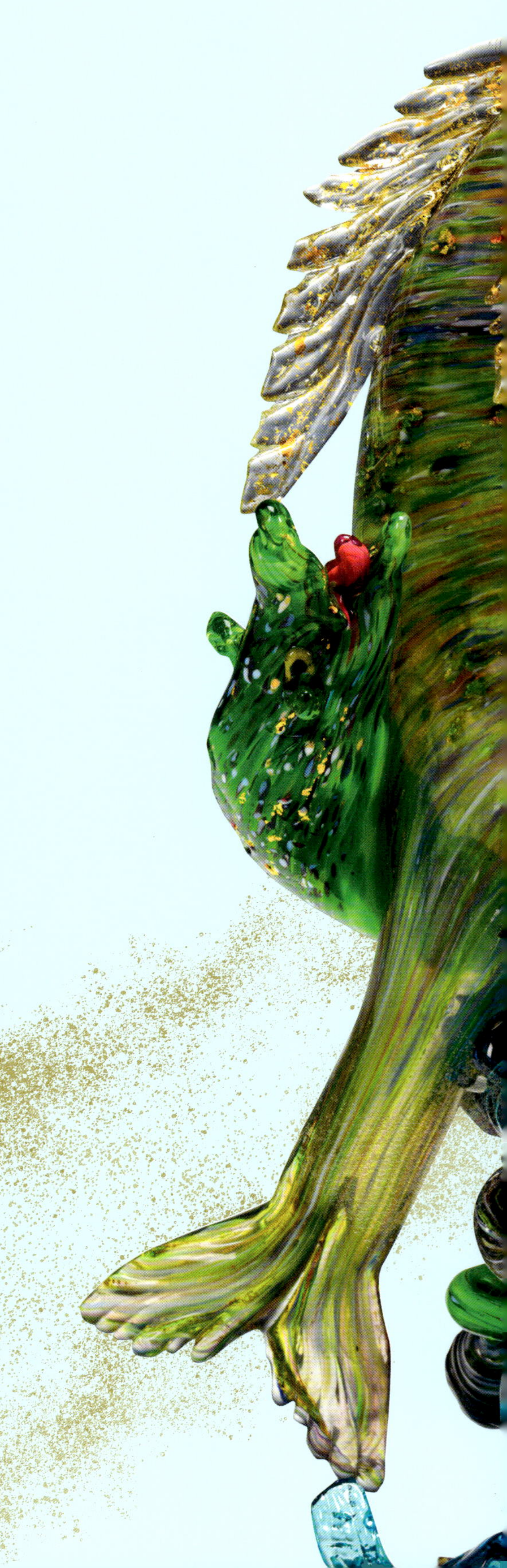

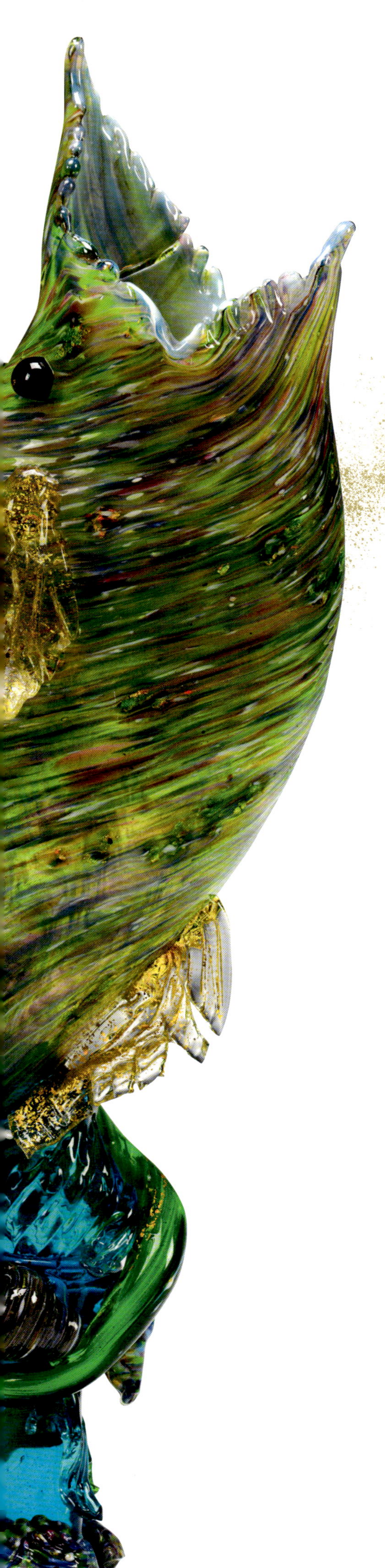

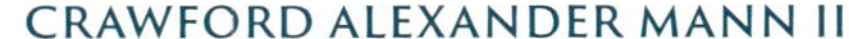

CRAWFORD ALEXANDER MANN III.

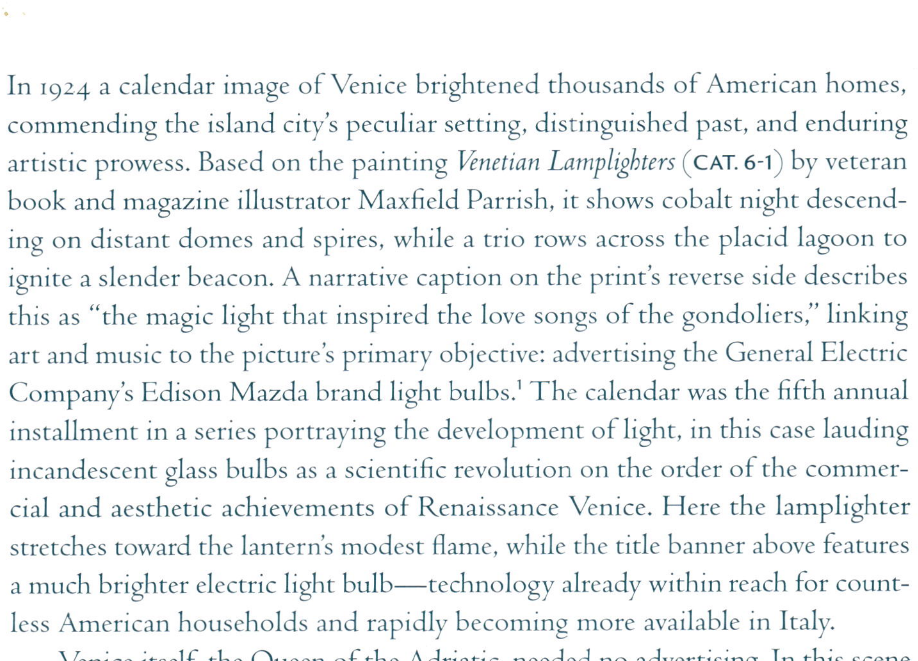

In 1924 a calendar image of Venice brightened thousands of American homes, commending the island city's peculiar setting, distinguished past, and enduring artistic prowess. Based on the painting *Venetian Lamplighters* (CAT. 6-1) by veteran book and magazine illustrator Maxfield Parrish, it shows cobalt night descending on distant domes and spires, while a trio rows across the placid lagoon to ignite a slender beacon. A narrative caption on the print's reverse side describes this as "the magic light that inspired the love songs of the gondoliers," linking art and music to the picture's primary objective: advertising the General Electric Company's Edison Mazda brand light bulbs.[1] The calendar was the fifth annual installment in a series portraying the development of light, in this case lauding incandescent glass bulbs as a scientific revolution on the order of the commercial and aesthetic achievements of Renaissance Venice. Here the lamplighter stretches toward the lantern's modest flame, while the title banner above features a much brighter electric light bulb—technology already within reach for countless American households and rapidly becoming more available in Italy.

Venice itself, the Queen of the Adriatic, needed no advertising. In this scene Parrish and General Electric addressed a broad early twentieth-century American audience who recognized Venice as a site of past greatness and, in contrast to most other European capitals, simultaneously an oven in which new sparks of creativity and competitive spirit were ablaze. This reputation—connecting art and science, past and future—gave Venice a unique appeal within the American cultural imagination of this era, inspiring not only tourism but also purchases of images of Venice (like this calendar) and Venetian-made decorative arts, most notably ornate glassware from the adjacent island of Murano. This essay will explore how the Venetian glass revival of the 1860s to 1910s (when Murano's nearly extinct glassmaking factories rapidly reclaimed the world crown in craftsmanship and design) fueled American enthusiasm for Venice and influenced art, literature, and cultural institutions in the United States. Without attempting to survey the full range of values and symbols associated with Venice in these decades, we

Preceding pages:
Compagnia di Venezia e Murano (CVM), Fish and Eel Vase (detail), ca. 1890; **see p. 222**

examine how Americans' appreciation for Murano glass harmonized these potentially oppositional strains of connoisseurship, synthesizing a respect for history and tradition with a commitment to innovation and modernization.

Parrish's female lamplighter captures this dual appeal. Wearing loose, classical robes, the light-giving maiden is a muse for the arts, an attractive avatar for Venice's picture-worthy waters, skies, architecture, inhabitants, and other sources of visual inspiration. Sailboats crossing nearby suggest that she also acts as a goddess of commerce, illuminating the harbor to aid fishermen and traders. In addition, towering over the lagoon and posed with an upraised arm and light aloft, she becomes a Venetian cousin to New York's Statue of Liberty, a reminder of Italy's recent consolidation into a self-governing constitutional monarchy. In this way, she represents both the past and the future of the floating city in both economics and governance, values shared across the Atlantic. Though the advertisement does not directly reference the glassmaking factories of Murano, those fiery furnaces were key contributors to the former prestige of Venetian art and society and to their renewed prospects, as Americans' glass consumption demonstrates; by the 1920s Murano-made chandeliers, mirrors, mosaics, and sculptural glass vessels sparkled as embellishments and objets d'art in public buildings and homes throughout the United States. The sophistication and mystique of Venetian revival glass and this industry's special contributions to Venice's overall esteem among Americans bear deeper consideration.

WATER, FIRE, AND GLASS: THE NEW VENETIAN GRAND TOUR

Parrish's calendar design contributed to a rich but relatively recent vogue among Americans for images and souvenirs of Venice. The healthy market for such works was the result of changing patterns of tourism, with Venice steadily growing in stature among travelers and art collectors from the United States. During its years of Austrian occupation, between 1797 and its unification with the Kingdom of Italy in 1866, a weak economy made Venice a secondary destination for most Americans. Unlike Rome, Florence, Paris, and London, the island city did not host substantial colonies of foreign artists and was not often chosen for extended stays by expatriates. Describing Venice in 1843 to fellow American painter John Frederick Kensett, Thomas Pritchard Rossiter reported, "It is not...the place to paint original pictures in, unless it be architectural Compositions. Models etc. Are difficult to procure. It therefore is a place essentially for Copies and Sketches."[2] By the late nineteenth century, however, lower prices and faster transportation methods made Great Britain and the Continent more accessible. Steamships, railroads, and a growing hotel industry helped America's refinement-hungry bourgeois class discover Venice, with assistance from an expanding array of tourist guidebooks. The scripted aristocratic grand tour gave way to a variety of possibilities for organizing a visit to Europe, and the *Serenissima*, the most serene city, became attractive to a wider segment of the American population. As a result, appetite grew for artwork associated with Venice, but the nature of the city's appeal changed.

Though some American artists of this era expressed their interest in Venice through enduring patterns (architectural studies and old master copies, as Rossiter had earlier described), many adopted a reduced visual language and embraced it as a space for experimentation. Forsaking the tradition of *veduta* paintings and prints (stone-by-stone recordings of the city's churches, palaces, and squares), newer generations discarded documentary detail in favor of pastiche and poetry. By the 1880s, American artists could trust that their audiences recognized the open lagoons, narrow canals, and Gothic facades from travel writing and an abundance of images already in circulation, including fine art, old prints, magazines, and book illustrations. "Venice has been painted and described many thousands of times," stated American writer Henry James, "and of all the cities of the world is the easiest to visit without going there."[3] This foundation empowered Thomas Moran, better known today for his views of the American West, to create scores of watercolors and oil paintings of Venice following his first of many stays there in May of 1886. "Venice is an inexhaustible mine of pictorial treasures for the artist," he wrote, "and of dreamy remembrance to those who have been fortunate enough to visit it."[4] Inspired by Joseph Mallord William Turner's brilliantly colored celebrations of the city's water and sky, Moran crafted majestic scenes like *A View of Venice* (CAT. 6-2), a contrived vista of the entrance of the Grand Canal. His miniature landmarks on the horizon are the same employed in Parrish's *Venetian Lamplighters*, including the domes of the church of Santa Maria della Salute at the picture's center. Moran also makes adjustments to the architecture so that other favorite sights, such as the Bridge of Sighs, are inaccurately visible from afar.[5] The vast, open sky, inscribed with calligraphic, cloudy wisps, occupies the full upper half of his canvas, and Venetian architecture functions primarily as a pedestal for this dynamic atmosphere. Most likely neither Moran's seascape nor Parrish's advertisement were made in Italy; though travel and firsthand sketching informed these Americans' work, the artists were free to evoke Venice as a dreamy constellation of visual cues, as seen here, without purporting to offer a studious window into a precise site or widely shared grand tour experience.

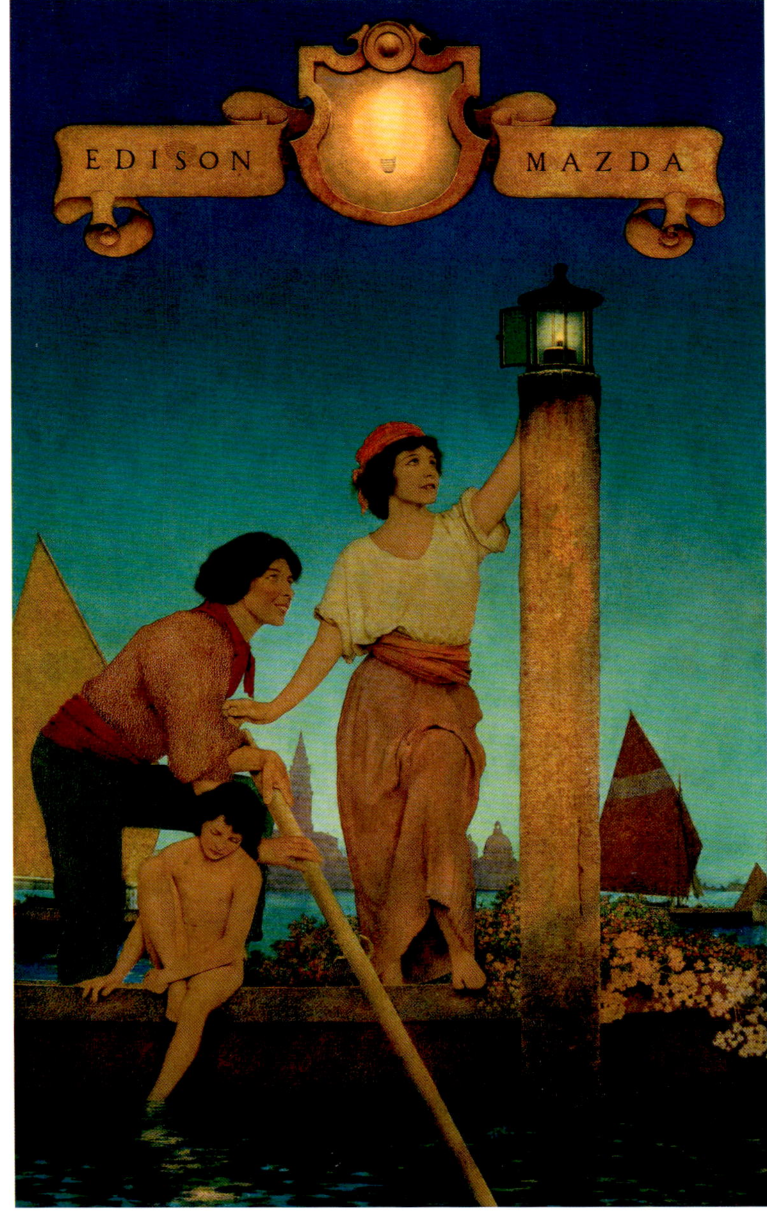

✲ CAT. 6-1
Maxfield Parrish, *Venetian Lamplighters*, 1922, oil on panel, 28 ¾ × 18 ¾ in., National Museum of American Illustration, Newport, RI, and American Illustrators Gallery, New York, NY

With minimal reliance on famous landmarks, artists adopted alternative signifiers of a Venetian setting, particularly water, fire, and glass. Water—the

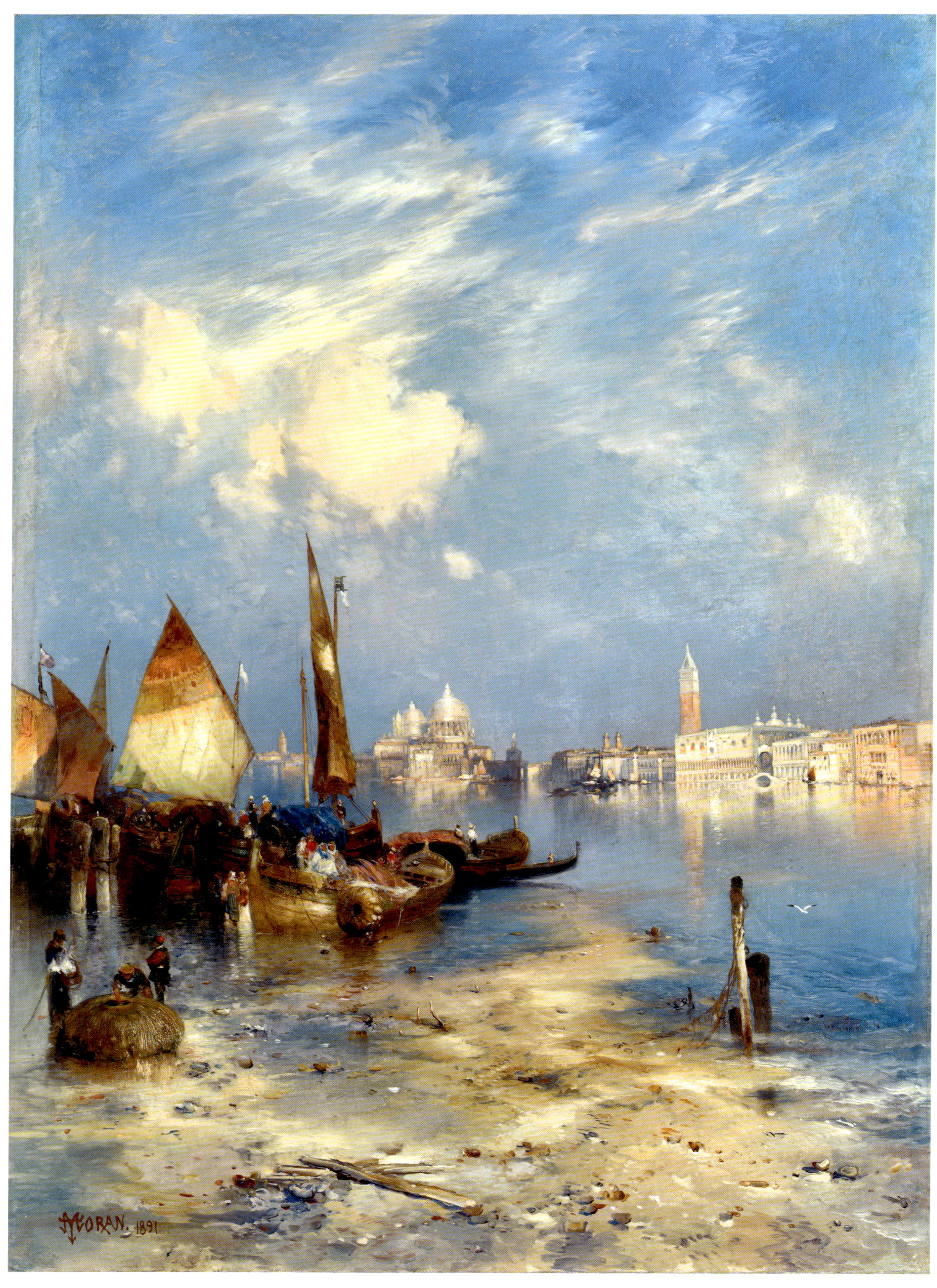
MORAN. 1891

wide lagoon—and the sensation of a gondola ride structure both Moran's and Parrish's pictures, with tiny towers on the horizon as accessories to this uniquely Venetian experience. Parrish also plays with fire, both through its role in the history of illumination (his subject) and by creating a lantern-lit nocturne, a frequent choice for late nineteenth-century painters of Venice. Night scenes offered unusual representational challenges, such as the reflections of Carnevale lanterns dancing on the water, or heavy mists transforming gas street lamps into bright pulsing spheres. James McNeill Whistler was not the inventor of this genre, but the extreme simplification of his night paintings and nocturne prints of Venice had particular renown and influence. "If Whistler was sent into the world for any purpose that no one else could fulfil [*sic*] it was to make a Venetian Nocturne," concluded an American critic in 1925, writing almost a half century after Whistler's brief but fruitful 1879 to 1880 sojourn there.[6] The provocative possibilities of this problem of nighttime light and water are captured in *Murano* (CAT. 6-3), a painting that Hermann Dudley Murphy probably executed *en plein air* from the Fondamenta Nove looking northward across the lagoon. Channeling Whistler, whom he openly admired, Murphy presents a sheet of nearly solid blue, with only a thin brown line and a few bright dots suggesting the form of an island through the hazy darkness. Are these glowing lights, as in Parrish's ode to electricity, more than a painterly exercise, perhaps functioning as symbols of progress and ingenuity? Well-read viewers of Murphy's work and also those who had visited Venice might associate the specks of faraway fire on Murano with the ever-burning furnaces of its glass factories, speaking to fresh creative activity

✲ CAT. 6-2
Thomas Moran, *A View of Venice*, 1891, oil on canvas, 35 ⅛ × 25 ¼ in., Smithsonian American Art Museum, Transfer from the US Department of the Interior, National Park Service

✲ CAT. 6-3
Hermann Dudley Murphy, *Murano*, 1907, oil on canvas, 19 ¾ × 30 ½ in., Collection of Lisa and Michael Sandman

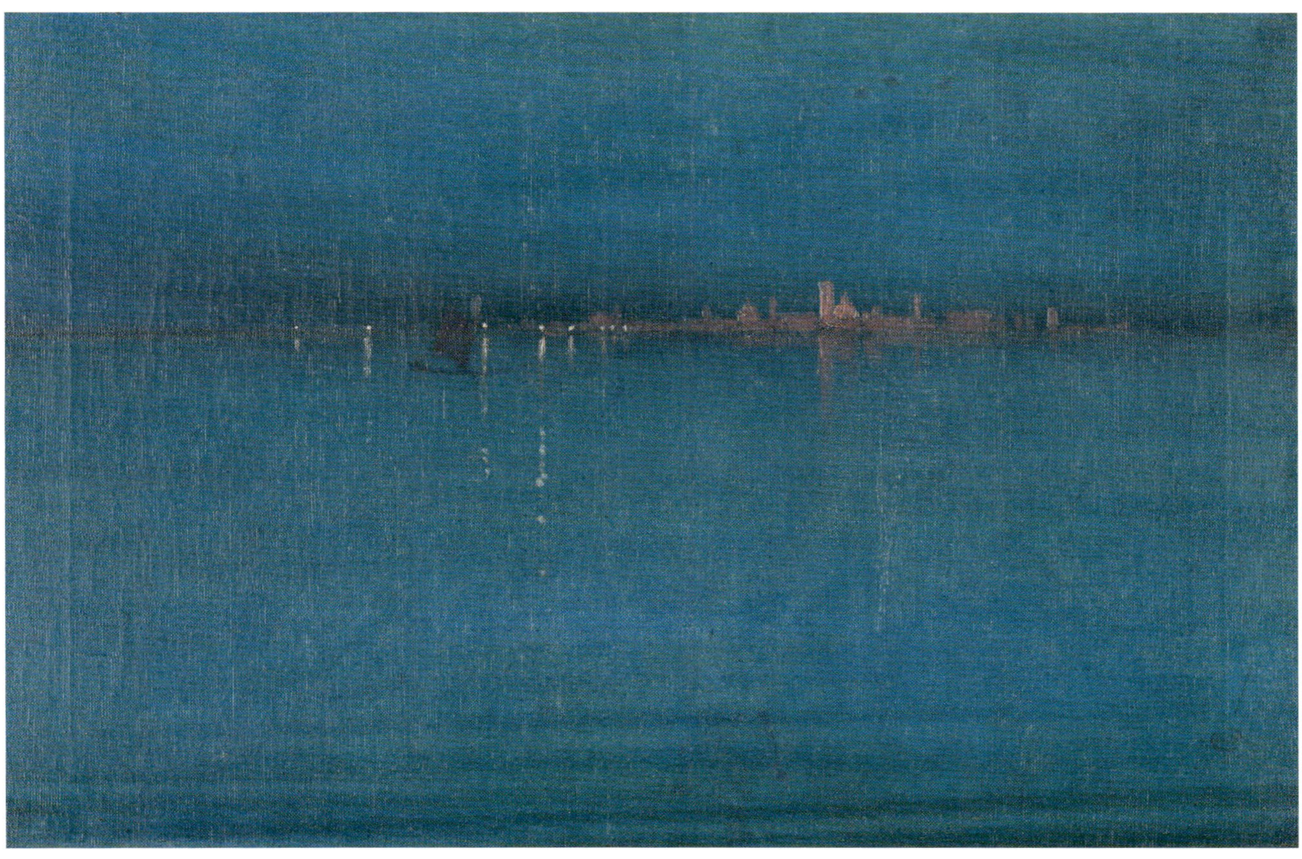

and cultural capital. In this way, though void of detail, Murphy's nocturne links contemporary trends in painting (learned from Whistler and the French impressionists) with the glass industry, thereby offering a provocatively modern alternative to the grand tour *veduta* tradition.

Nocturnal intrigue and references to glass also subtly reinforce the Venetian setting of genre subjects, updating another category of grand tour art that remained popular into the early twentieth century. A fine example is John Singer Sargent's *The Sulphur Match* (CAT. 6-4), a shadowy evening episode that revises and perpetuates the alluring stereotype of Venice as the Mediterranean's leading den of vice. Here a swarthy man draped in a fur-lined cloak (a traditional Venetian *tabarro*) lights his cigarette, while beside him a young woman rocks back in her wooden chair, mouth open in laughter. Her white dress and red shawl emphasize the couple's warm skin tones and black hair, while a straw-covered flask and broken wine glass rest on the floor nearby, casualties of the evening. Are we witness to an innocent spark of romance in a neighborhood café, or is this a dangerous scene of intoxication and seduction, as the overturned bottle, shards of glass, and chair's precarious angle may hint? Tobacco and wine enhance this invitation to sensual indulgence, precursors to improprieties that Sargent could safely suggest among working-class Italians but not among Americans of his own social standing.[7] Although this blue-collar romance is staged, orchestrated by the artist with hired models, Sargent may have witnessed such an incident or envisioned it through published accounts by earlier visitors to the city. Notably, the male figure in this painting matches the affectionate description of the *lazzagnon*, or dandy-loafer, in William Dean Howells's *Venetian Life*, a compendium of anecdotes from his tenure in Venice as consul from 1861 to 1865.[8] Sargent confirms the character of this local barfly through precise doubling between the *lazzagnon* and the wine bottle, akin with their dark colors and a crest of brown at their respective necks. The discarded bottle and shattered glass on the floor also make reference to the glass factories of Murano, relatively quiet in Howells's day but flourishing by the time of this picture's creation in 1882. Sargent's fantasy, with just a tiny flame on the tip of the smoker's match, romantically recalls the dreary decades of Venice's pre-Risorgimento recession, while perhaps also alluding to Murano's new fires.

In the context of American homes, such Venetian images—whether landscapes or figures—nurtured an alternative mode of showcasing grand tour collections that privileged imagination over education. Murano glass and related bric-a-brac could be displayed in conversation with views of Venice or other distant realms for greater impact. In some cases such décor referenced one's travels and collecting abroad, but by the 1870s the availability of pictures and sophisticated craft products from overseas allowed consumers to bring specimens of Venice into their living rooms without crossing the Atlantic.[9] Still lifes and domestic scenes, such as Walter Launt Palmer's painting *Interior at 6 Elk Street (Residence of the Reverend Frank L. Norton)* (see p. 64) record this trend. Here a representation of the Bridge of Sighs hangs on the right, perhaps adding context to the nearby table of fine crystal. In such an artfully arranged parlor, visitors and residents were free to fabricate their own ideas connecting these enticing trophies. Similarly, in

✡ CAT. 6-4
John Singer Sargent, *The Sulphur Match*, 1882, oil on canvas, 23 × 16 ¼ in., The Collection of Marie and Hugh Halff

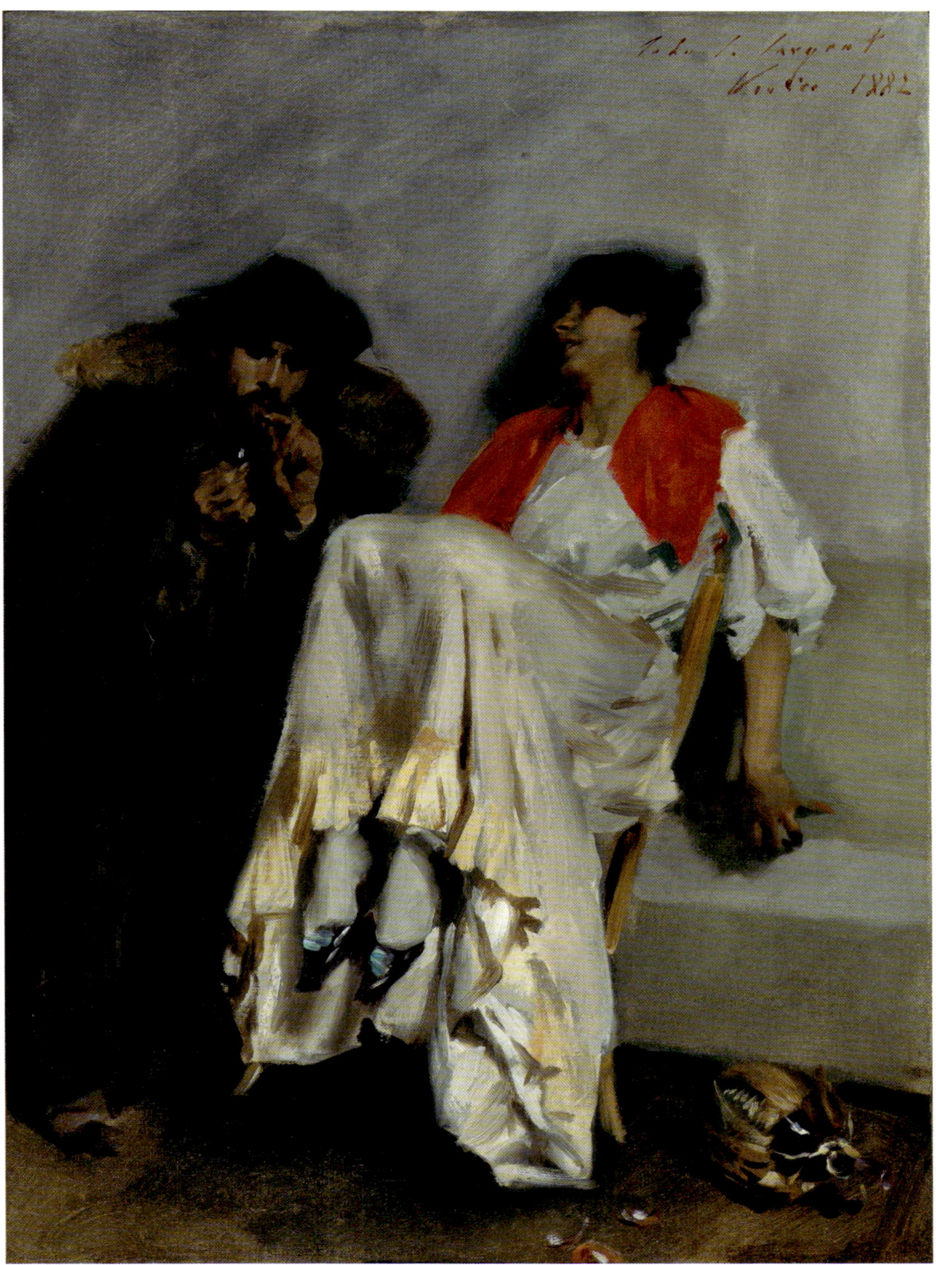

Edith Wharton's 1903 short story "A Venetian Night's Entertainment," a young Bostonian embarks on his grand tour with particular eagerness for Venice, inspired by childhood recollections of his elders' travel souvenirs, including Murano glass and a print depicting St. Mark's Square. The print became "the spring-board of fancy, the first step of a cloud-ladder leading to a land of dreams," coupled with "a slender Venice glass, gold-powdered as with lily-pollen or the dust of sunbeams, that, standing in the corner cabinet betwixt two Lowestoft caddies, seemed, among its lifeless neighbours, to palpitate like an impaled butterfly."[10] Pictures and glassware work in tandem to arouse the young man's curiosity about a city that will be both familiar and exotic. The story featured illustrations by Maxfield Parrish, and though these did not include a rendering of the corner cabinet and its dazzling contents, Wharton's words prepared him to create other views of Venice, like the later calendar, calculated to fuel fantasies and a desire for travel. Whereas an eighteenth-century-style grand tour display of pictures and souvenirs might pedantically reflect its owner's past adventures, the modern bric-a-brac cabinet with Venetian images and objects might also be purely aspirational. A loose combination of glitter and water could stimulate the senses in preparation for a firsthand taste of Venice and its art treasures.

FROM FIASCO TO PHOENIX: THE MAGIC OF GLASSBLOWING

While cabinets of glassware contributed to generalized evocations of Venice's charms, firsthand viewing of glass production heightened many Americans' appreciation for the island city as a site for contemporary art making. The glass revival, as promoted by Antonio Salviati and other early advocates, centered on deliberately ornate and technically challenging blown vessels whose creation was spectacular to witness. Salviati opened his first workshop dedicated to *vetri artistici*, high-end decorative glassware, in 1867, and soon Murano boasted multiple competing studios designing sophisticated yet consumer-friendly cups, bottles, and vases. By 1884 Salviati reportedly had seventy employees, and half of Murano's population of four thousand had jobs across its revitalized glass industry.[11] The factories welcomed audiences (customers), and the local newspaper provided routine accounts of princes, politicians, and a variety of illustrious visitors. In the summer of 1879, these reports recount a party of fifty Americans who toured its museum, churches, and glass studios, a group that may have included painters then residing in Venice like Frank Duveneck and Ralph Wormeley Curtis.[12] Though St. Mark's Basilica and the Doge's Palace remained the most lauded attractions, the furnaces soon became a popular itinerary item, supplementing guidebooks' familiar lists of historic sites.

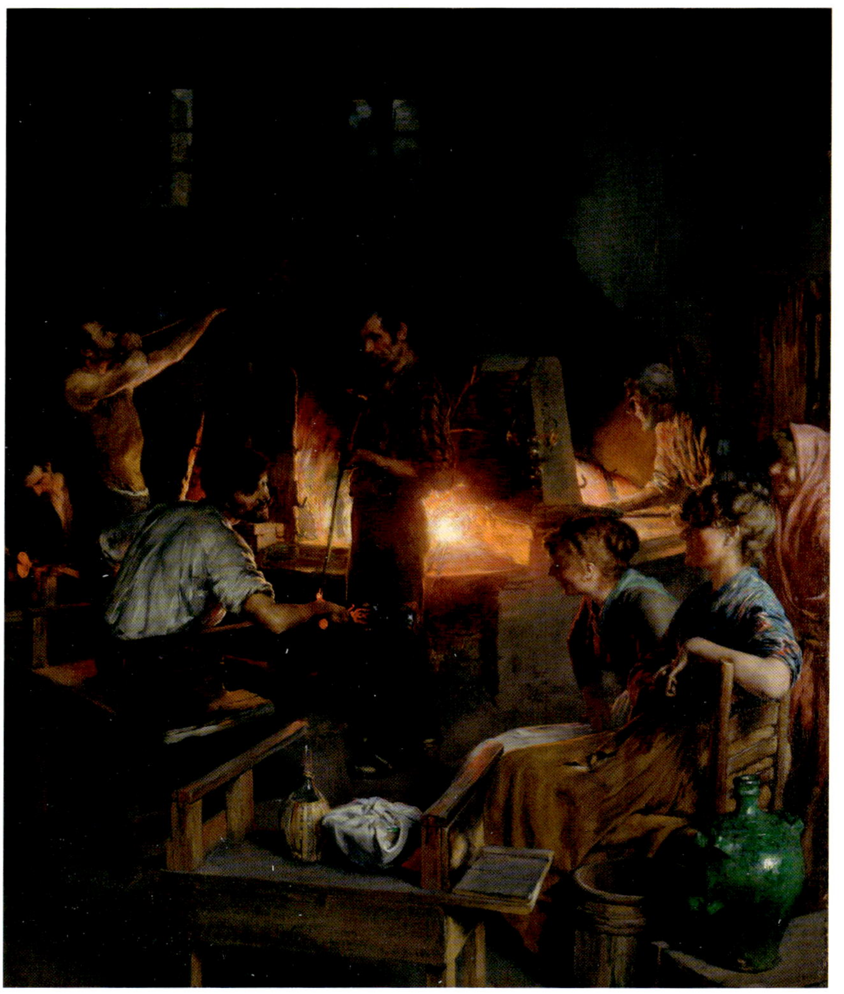

Fig. 6-1
Charles Frederic Ulrich, *Glass Blowers of Murano*, 1886, oil on wood, 26 ⅛ × 21 ⅛ in., The Metropolitan Museum of Art, Gift of Several Gentlemen, 1886, 86.13

Charles Frederic Ulrich's 1886 painting *Glass Blowers of Murano* (Fig. 6-1) narrates this new favorite tourist experience to provide an up-to-date image of the energy and optimism of the glass revival.[13] In the center of the smoky room, the fiery aperture blazes white-hot, a cave of creation illuminating the faces and partially exposed bodies of five heroic workmen, each at a different stage in the making of a typical Venetian revival goblet. The seated man in the foreground holds a pontil attached to the base of the nearly complete cup, with bowl formed and virtuoso embellishment of the stem underway. He balances his rod on the arm of the bench to maintain the symmetry of the still-molten vessel, while his coworker standing above applies additional decorative elements, building a confection of interlaced rods that glow orange like a magical rune. Soon the critical moment will arrive when the entire piece must be delicately detached from the rod and slowly cooled in an annealing kiln, resulting in a goblet much like this example (CAT. 6-5). Such fanciful and fragile cups, replicas of or riffs on Venetian Renaissance designs, became a staple of any Murano glass collection. The techniques involved—blowing a thin bowl and then constructing an intricate, sculptural, hot-worked stem or handles—held bravura appeal in their level of detail and in the difficulty of achieving symmetry, a feat entrancing to observe. Perhaps to emphasize this cup's complexity, Ulrich paints a straw-covered wine bottle, a typical Italian *fiasco*, resting on a bench in the foreground, with the leg and shoe of the central figure in the striped shirt drawing a line between it and the more elegant production in progress.

Standard visual tropes of the sublime heighten the picture's drama. Using strong light/dark contrasts, perhaps suggested by Jacopo Tintoretto and other Venetian old master painters of religious miracles, Ulrich brings mystery and magic to his subject. Period travel writers create similar tension, as in this anonymous 1869 account:

> *I spent hours in the work-room of Murano, fascinated, despite the blinding heat, by the fairy forms and rainbow hues evolved before my eyes; by the intense, grave, silent enthusiasm of the workmen, which extends itself even to the small children admitted to watch the proceedings; by the impossibility of quitting the scene of labor until the piece in hand could be secured from failure by completion.*[14]

Despite frequent articles in popular journals that decoded the process in layman's terms, it seemed more like sorcery than science to many. The American writer and theologian Lyman Abbott made this comparison in the essay "Glass-Blowing as a Fine Art" from 1871:

> *The modern necromancer drops a little carefully selected sand into his crucible, waves his wand over it, and draws forth such a variety of objects, both of use and beauty, as puts to the blush the fabled achievements of the Oriental magicians. Dishes for our table, vases for our flowers, ornaments of all kinds for our mantel . . . these are among the products of the necromantic art which we call glassmaking.*[15]

Blowing glass was thus a combination of scientific and manual mysteries, and tourists could marvel as the craftsmen solved riddles of chemistry and physics, then performed impossible feats of dexterity to conjure a variety of shapes and designs.

Ulrich directly includes a lesson in spectatorship to further inspire reverence for his subjects. As the glassblowers work their magic, a trio of young women exchange flirtatious glances with the mustachioed, seated figure. His smiling response while manipulating this delicate object shows a nonchalant ease with his trade. The giggling women, presumably local maidens, take his skills for

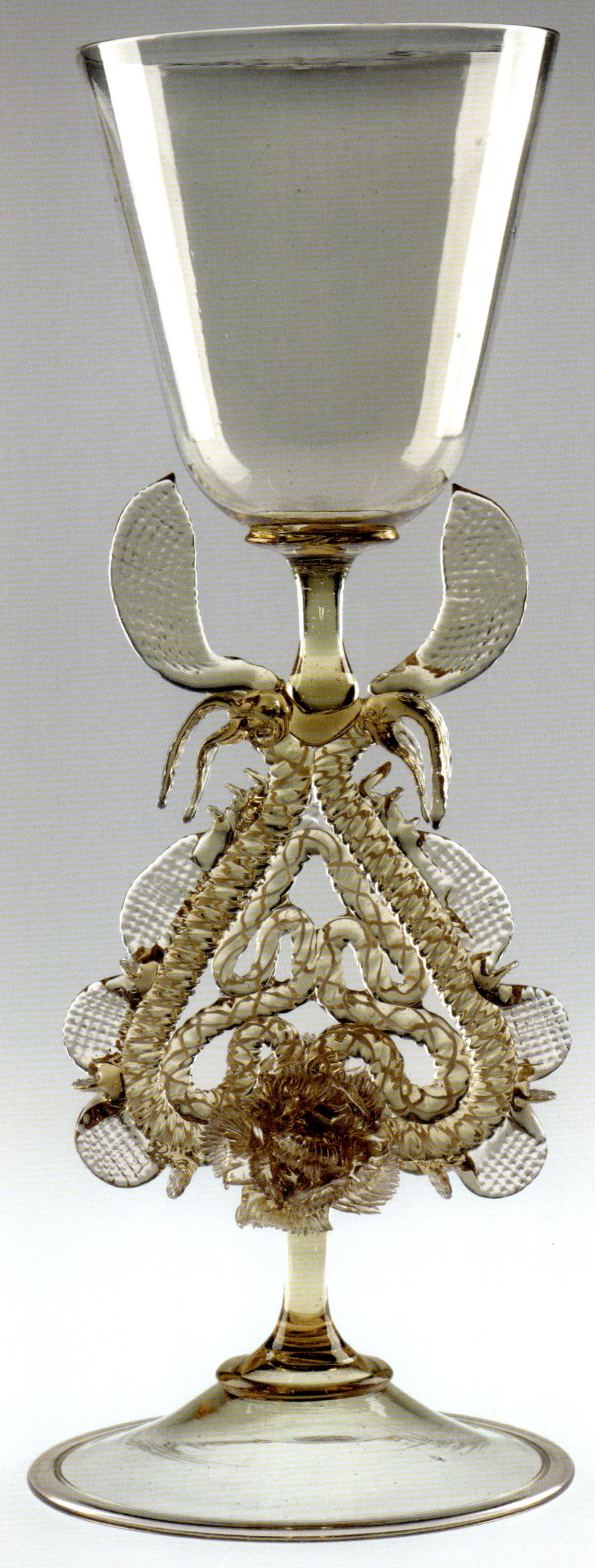

granted, thereby encouraging more serious (American) viewers of the painting to look instead at the goblet and appreciate the glassmakers' craftsmanship and creativity. If Sargent's *lazzagnon* barfly embodies the danger and decadence of the past, Ulrich offers a new face and direction for Venice: a future of productivity and talent. "The glass-blower of Murano is no mere mechanic or artisan," announced Antonio Salviati's son, Giulio, in an 1889 lecture. "He is in every respect a true artist, an artist endowed with the perception of beauty and genius, who invents and creates daily new forms and colors. The glass is to him what the chisel is to the sculptor, the brush to the painter."[16] Whistler likewise included a fuzzy cluster of spectators on the far left in his print *Murano—Glass Furnace* (CAT. 6-6). Here a dozen workers faintly emerge through the hazy hatching, some standing around the central ovens while others sit hunched over benches. The scene is the same as in Ulrich's painting (possibly at the same factory), but Whistler gives only outlines of the craftsmen, suggesting how thick clouds of smoke from the furnaces might partially obscure a tourist's view and heighten the sense of mystery and wonder. The heat and fumes were unpleasant, forcing visitors to choose between fascination and comfort as they elected how much of the demonstration to attend. These notorious conditions might account for the print's sparse and frenzied character, given that Whistler was known to incise his Venetian plates directly from life.[17] Nonetheless, the printmaker's priorities are evident through the composition and selective detail of this sketchy scene, in which the most fully realized figures are the cluster of spectators (which may include a self-portrait) and the seated glassblower in the center, Whistler's fellow artist.

✡ CAT. 6-5
Attributed to Salviati Dott. Antonio, Replica of a Seventeenth-Century Goblet with Knotted Stem, ca. 1870s–80s, blown and applied hot-worked glass, 11 ⅞ × 4 $^{7}/_{16}$ in. diam., RISD Museum, Gift of Mrs. Frank Mauran and John O. Ames

✡ CAT. 6-6
James McNeill Whistler, *Murano—Glass Furnace*, 1879–80, drypoint on paper, 6 ¼ × 9 ¼ in., Gift of Samuel Putnam Avery, Prints Collection, Miriam and Ira D. Wallach Division of Art, Prints and Photographs, The New York Public Library, Astor, Lenox and Tilden Foundations

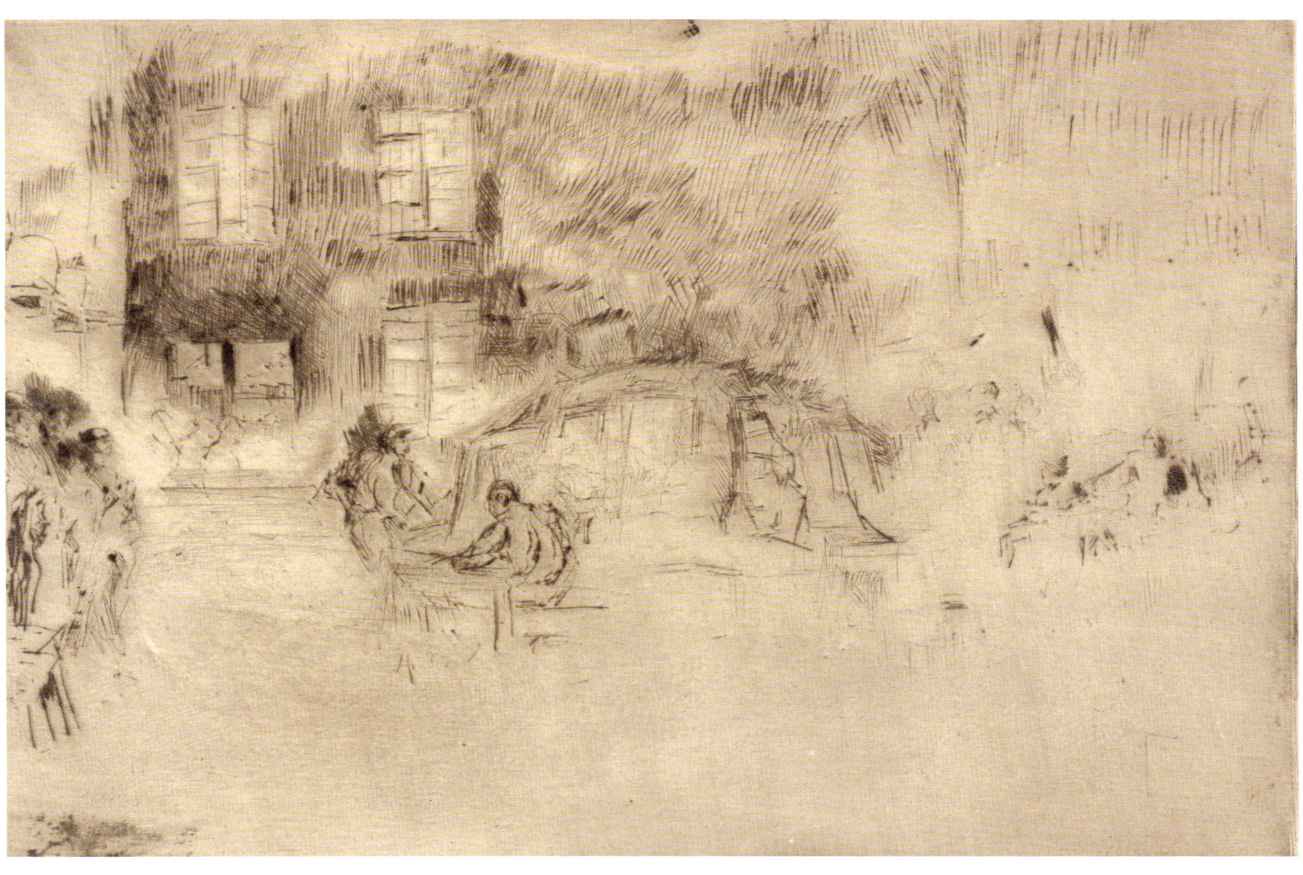

✡ CAT. 6-7
Compagnia di Venezia e Murano (CVM), Fish and Eel Vase, ca. 1890, blown and applied hot-worked glass, 12 × 4 ¼ × 5 ¼ in., Smithsonian American Art Museum, Gift of John Gellatly

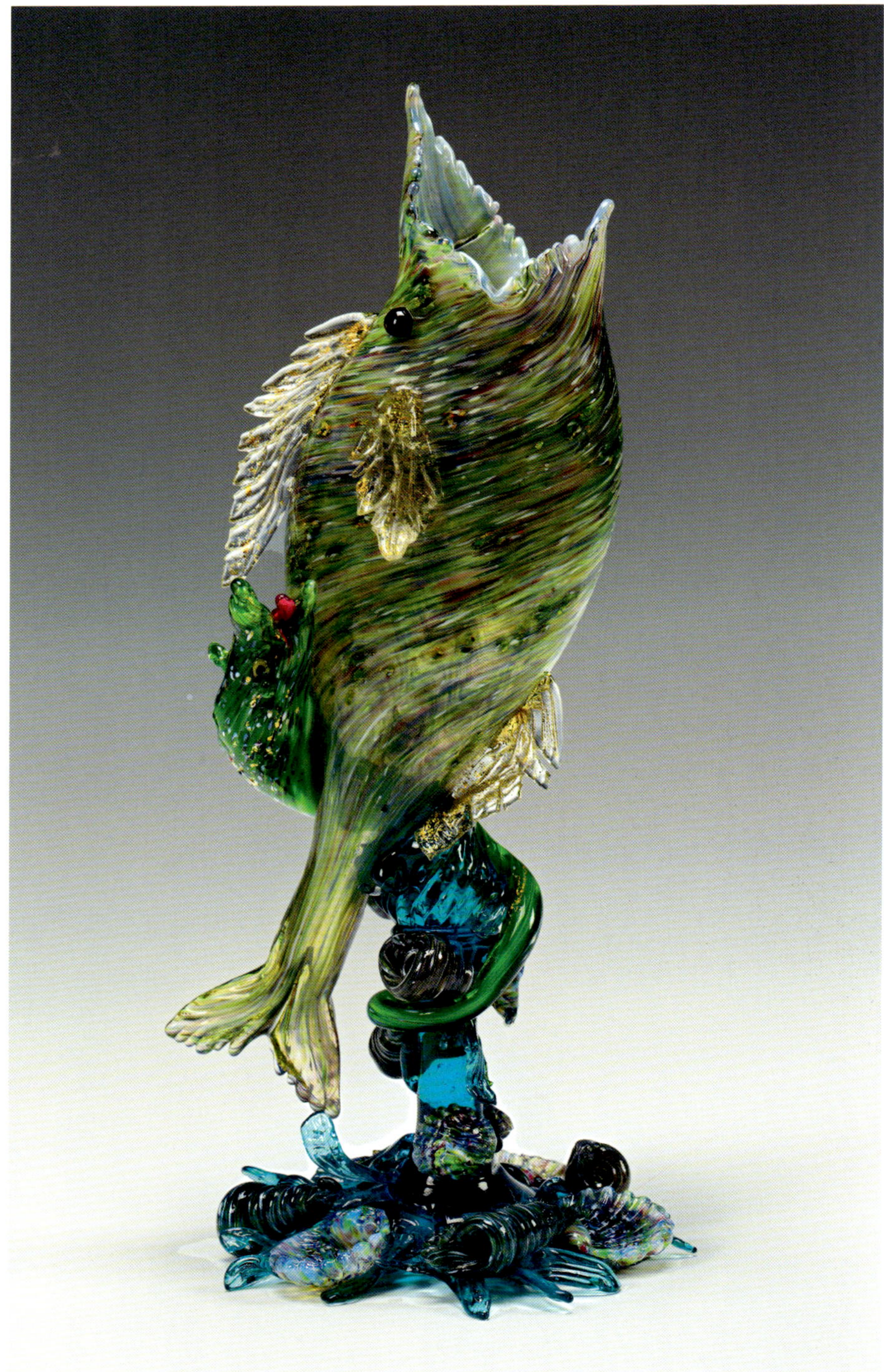

While Whistler's drypoint constructs a visceral sense of the glassmaking process, Ulrich's heroic presentation remains focused on the glowing chalice in progress. In his painting, the laughing women and the glass maestri are a team of midwives and doctors who assist at the birth of a golden treasure. This orchestration of the scene reinforces praise by period historians and tastemakers. "Venetian glass is unlike all other glass," proclaimed art critic and glass collector James Jackson Jarves in a widely read magazine in 1882. "Its highest merit and greatest value consist in its virtually being incapable of being used for other purposes than to administer to the human craving for beauty, perfection, the supreme aesthetic ideal of the moment."[18] These *vetri artistici* or *cristallo* productions included elaborate goblets and some pieces, such as the vase in the shape of a fish from the Smithsonian American Art Museum's Gellatly Collection (CAT. 6-7), in which a playful combination of flameworked elements completely departs from familiar vessel forms. Here the rainbow-striated fish leaps upward, supported by an open-mouthed green eel and a base of glass shells and curling waves. The complexity and whimsy of such designs surprised and delighted viewers, despite their potential impracticality; as lauded by Jarves, suitability for everyday use was of secondary importance, superseded by aesthetic appeal—the delivery of intellectual and sensual pleasure. According to some critics, the prowess of their makers alone could qualify Venetian revival glassware as worthy of acquisition by public museums: "The amount of dexterity and skill in manipulation required to produce works so minute and delicate in their details must always place specimens of this glass among the most valuable artistic treasures a nation can possess."[19] Americans thus marveled at the revival of the Venetian glass industry not only for its rapid resurgence in manufacturing volume, but also for its new heights of aesthetic excellence. Artists' depictions and firsthand accounts by tourists reinforced consumers' respect for the intricacy and singularity of these creations.

By celebrating the beauty of glass and the spectacle of its fabrication, Ulrich's *Glass Blowers of Murano* ultimately garnered accolades of its own. The picture received top honors in New York in 1886 at the American Art Association's Second Prize Fund Exhibition of contemporary paintings, prompting its immediate purchase and donation to the Metropolitan Museum of Art as the "Gift of Several Gentlemen." The group of subscribers funding this $2,000 prize included prominent art collectors who themselves owned Venetian paintings and glass, such as William T. Evans, William T. Walters, Henry G. Marquand, and Edward C. Moore.[20] Among these knowledgeable connoisseurs, both Marquand and Moore later made substantial gifts of glass and antiquities to the museum, thereby complementing Ulrich's painting of glass production with thousands of ancient specimens and fragments in this medium.[21] The Met promptly hung Ulrich's painting in its Western galleries, a home in which it could play a double role: it became both an exemplar of multifigure painting with compelling action and dark/light visual dynamism, as well as a tribute to a another branch of artistry. Well-traveled viewers might be able to use this picture to demonstrate their understanding of the chemistry, tools, and actions of glassmaking, while others could simply marvel at the fiery performance. By 1890, the image reached an even wider audience with its publication as a photogravure (see p. 32) by the Parisian art gallery Goupil & Co. in a luxury, folio-size book praising contemporary American artists.[22] The acclaim for Ulrich's painting and its instant acquisition by the Met demonstrate the enormous success and impact of the Venetian glass revival. Within two decades, Murano's struggling glass industry had expanded from the humdrum manufacture of beads and bottles to world leadership in this art form, as acclaimed on the walls of a major North American museum.

TO EMBODY THE PAST: THE COLORFUL HISTORY OF VENICE AND MURANO

In the eyes of American artists, collectors, and museumgoers, the genius of Venetian revival glassware lay not only in its creators' skill, but in the close relationships between these objects and antique works. The "revival" of Venetian glass in the second half of the nineteenth century was both a return to robust activity by a local industry that had nearly ceased operation, as well as a dedication to revered earlier models and motifs. This generation of glassmakers studied a library of examples from Venice's museums and churches and earned praise for understanding and carrying on the spirit of their ancestors. "The authorities in antique glass maintain that Salviati can to-day give you all the wonders and all the beauties of the once lost 'art of glass' of the sixteenth century,"[23] reported American tourist Mary Sherwood in 1872. The collecting of Murano glass, as well as its depiction within other artworks, offered both a surrogate for a modern-day transatlantic voyage and a fantasy of time travel to historical moments when Venice enjoyed heights of material decadence and refined taste. The history of the United States, by contrast, included no cycles of power and decline, and no North American city had the abundance and density of historical architecture found on this cluster of Italian islands. Revival-style glass thus fascinated American audiences by offering opportunities to touch and potentially possess the luxuries enjoyed by the doges and princes of earlier times, giving imaginative access to a world exalted in history and literature for its sensual adventures.

Venetian revival glass provided an ideal starting point for consideration of the city's history through its studious fidelity to antique models. While many artistic and architectural trends of the nineteenth century, such as the Gothic Revival, adapted general forms and elements from the past, Venetian glassmakers were especially literal in their references, creating exact copies of earlier masterworks. A report commissioned for the US Census Office in 1884 noted the centrality of historically inspired designs within new output: "the recent very successful revival of the manufacture of Venetian glass at Murano...promises to restore to that city the world-wide celebrity of its former days of glass-making." After listing a dozen color formulas and decorative techniques famous in Renaissance-era glassware, it concludes, "all of these products of the elder Venetian glass houses are reproduced with wonderful fidelity in the modern Venetian glass of the Venice and Murano Glass and Mosaic Company."[24] The report notes in particular "the remarkable enameling of the famous tasse of St. Mark's," citing a Byzantine drinking cup in the Treasury of St. Mark's Basilica, made of deep purple transparent glass, fitted with metal handles, and painted with floral patterns and classical vignettes.[25] Many esteemed this piece, known as the *San Marco Bowl*, because it was the oldest article of glass in the Treasury.[26] Replicas, such as this example from the Corning Museum of Glass (**CAT. 6-8**), became a routine presence at displays of Venetian glass at world's fairs, from Paris's Exposition Universelle of 1878 to the Louisiana Purchase Exposition held in St. Louis in 1904.[27] These joined modern copies of other antiques, such as the *Guggenheim Cup* (see p. 115), the *Disch-Sangiorgi Cantharus* (see p. 132), the *Chalice of Emperor Romanos II* (see p. 131), and the *Campanile Cup* (see p. 126), to establish a canon of highlights in the history of glassmaking, allowing American collectors to demonstrate their knowledge of this field, just as one might invest in a painted copy of a famous work by Titian. The original *San Marco Bowl* was not for sale, but well-made replicas placed its visual and tactile pleasures within reach of an audience with no lineage of their own in this branch of art.

The pleasures of owning a specimen of skillfully made glass, whether antique or modern, are summarized in Charles Caryl Coleman's painting *Interior with Lute Player* (CAT. 6-9). Using an exquisitely detailed and precise style, Coleman depicts a young man in Renaissance costume who has exchanged his musical instrument for silent appreciation of a stemmed tazza of transparent dark blue glass. He stands in a busy world of patterned fabrics and surfaces, including his embroidered doublet, the medieval fresco on the wall, and the gilt ewer, painted casket, and gold plate on the floor. The elegant curves of the cup surpass this visual cacophony and invite appreciation both with one's eyes and fingertips, following the lute player's example. His careful hold confirms that the glass is empty and emphasizes its very light weight more so than the pleasures of drinking wine. Creating such delicate trophies with a use of minimal materials demonstrated the maker's skill. This quality—a hallmark of antique blown works from Murano—was the primary goal of artists during the nineteenth-century revival. "The airy nothings of patrician Venice table-ware in the Middle Ages, are ours, now," reported Constance Cary Harrison in an 1881 home decorating manual, citing the ability of contemporary craftsmen to match the thinness of their ancestors' handiwork.[28] These fragile articles demanded extra caution and protection: "It requires consummate

✡ CAT. 6-8

Compagnia di Venezia e Murano (CVM), Replica of a Byzantine Glass Bowl (*San Marco Bowl*), ca. 1878, blown, enameled, and gilded glass, with gilded bronze handles, 4 1/16 × 7 5/8 × 4 15/16 in., The Corning Museum of Glass

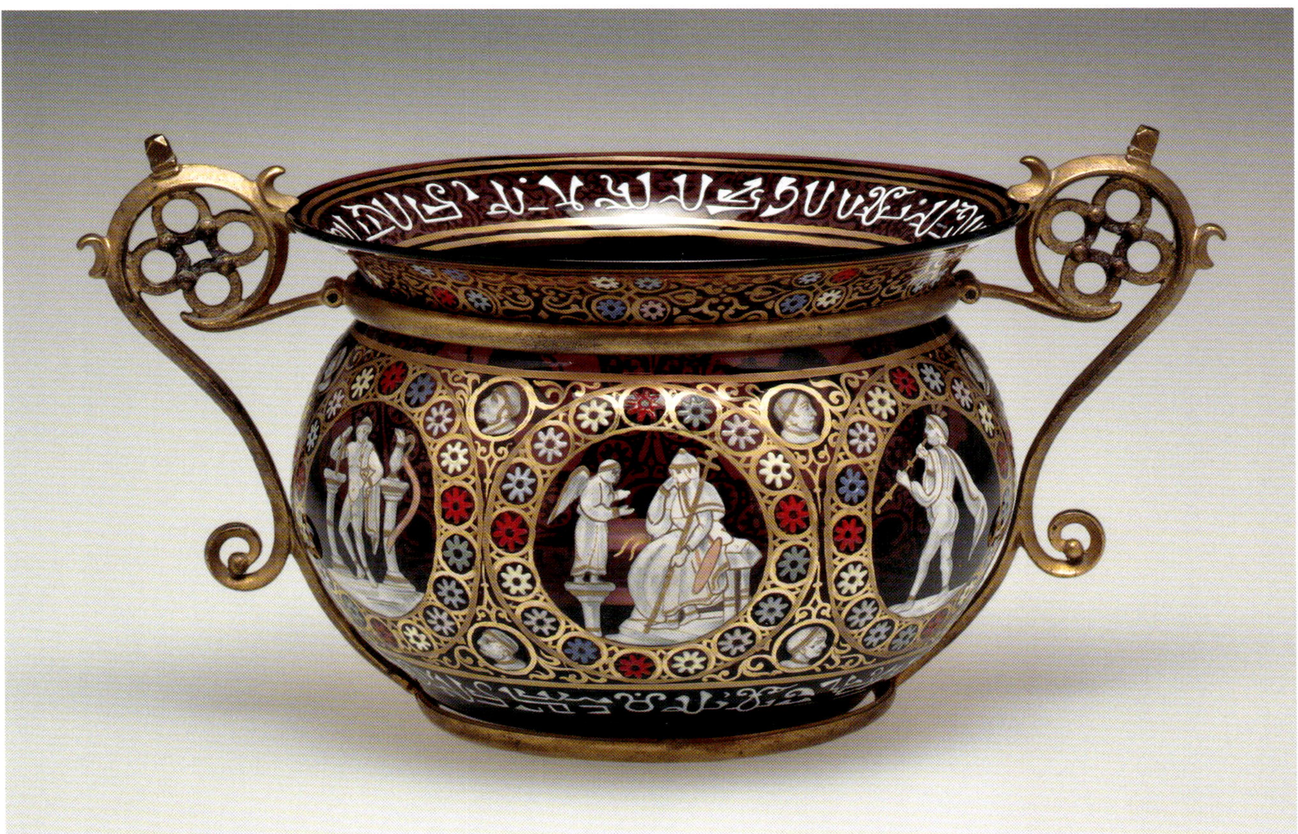

care to preserve its daintiness intact," advised Jarves, "The slightest mishap may crush it as easily as a butterfly's wing or a bright bubble of the air."[29] The cup in Coleman's painting conveys this delicacy with its transparent blown bowl and its stem adorned with *alette*, symmetrical lacey studded wings. Thus, just as Ulrich's *Glass Blowers of Murano* shows esteem for the glassmaking process, this picture provides a lesson in multiple modes of glass connoisseurship.

By filling this decadent interior with historical objects and props, Coleman also complicates the scene with temporal ambiguity. His small blue goblet is unmistakably Venetian by virtue of its rich color and its intricate stem design, copied or interpreted from sixteenth-century shapes. This genealogy poses the question: Is the lute player here admiring its workmanship, or is he trying to deduce its age? Is this a three-hundred-year-old antique, or is it an expert replica from Salviati's recently reopened and prizewinning furnaces? The historicist character of revival glass made age difficult for American collectors to confirm without expert guidance. For a piece with no famous precedent, like Coleman's little cup, dating required close examination of form, coloration, clarity, condition, and any flaws or imperfections. Wear and tear did not necessarily weaken the appeal of older objects, just as ruined temples and castles spurred the imaginations of travelers elsewhere on the grand tour. Likewise, modern replicas sometimes offered experience of a famous fragment in its original, pristine state, but in other cases Murano artists created deliberate blemishes or an appearance of aging to gratify those that preferred an antiquated or archaeological aesthetic. Many appreciated both, including American glass enthusiast John Gellatly, whose collection contained genuine antique Roman-era oil and perfume bottles (CAT. 6-10), as well as a large replica antique skyphos made in the nineteenth century (CAT. 6-11) with similar swirling, multicolored, marbled patterns. Like Gellatly, Coleman also collected Italian glass, as well as ancient Egyptian, Roman, and Western Asian fragments. He likely owned this blue goblet, but given the documented diversity of his holdings, its exact age is impossible to guess from this painting alone.[30] On Murano, craftsmen openly consulted antique examples, and their goals were not to make replicas as forgeries (though revival wares were sometimes mistaken as antiques by careless consumers or later hawked on the secondary market with inaccurate dating by unscrupulous sellers).[31] In the eyes of most American consumers, genuine antiques and exquisite replicas appealed on the same terms, and if the glass were well crafted, indecipherable dating might heighten one's reverence.

In the hands and homes of American collectors, the historical references of Venetian revival glass often achieved greater impact through display in conversation with other antiques. Coleman's painting illustrates this effect: although the tazza is the center of attention for both the musician and viewers, the assortment of objects elsewhere in the scene adds layers of meaning. Like the glass goblet, the scattered antiques are also from the artist's personal collection, which he deployed throughout the 1870s and 1880s in fancy pictures featuring costumed models and in a series of large-scale, still life paintings (see p. 73).[32] As recounted by a visitor who was writing an article for a decorating journal in 1884, Coleman's entire studio—in Rome at that time—served as a personal

✲ CAT. 6-9
Charles Caryl Coleman, *Interior with Lute Player*, 1875, oil on canvas, 12 ¾ × 8 ¼ in., McGuigan Collection

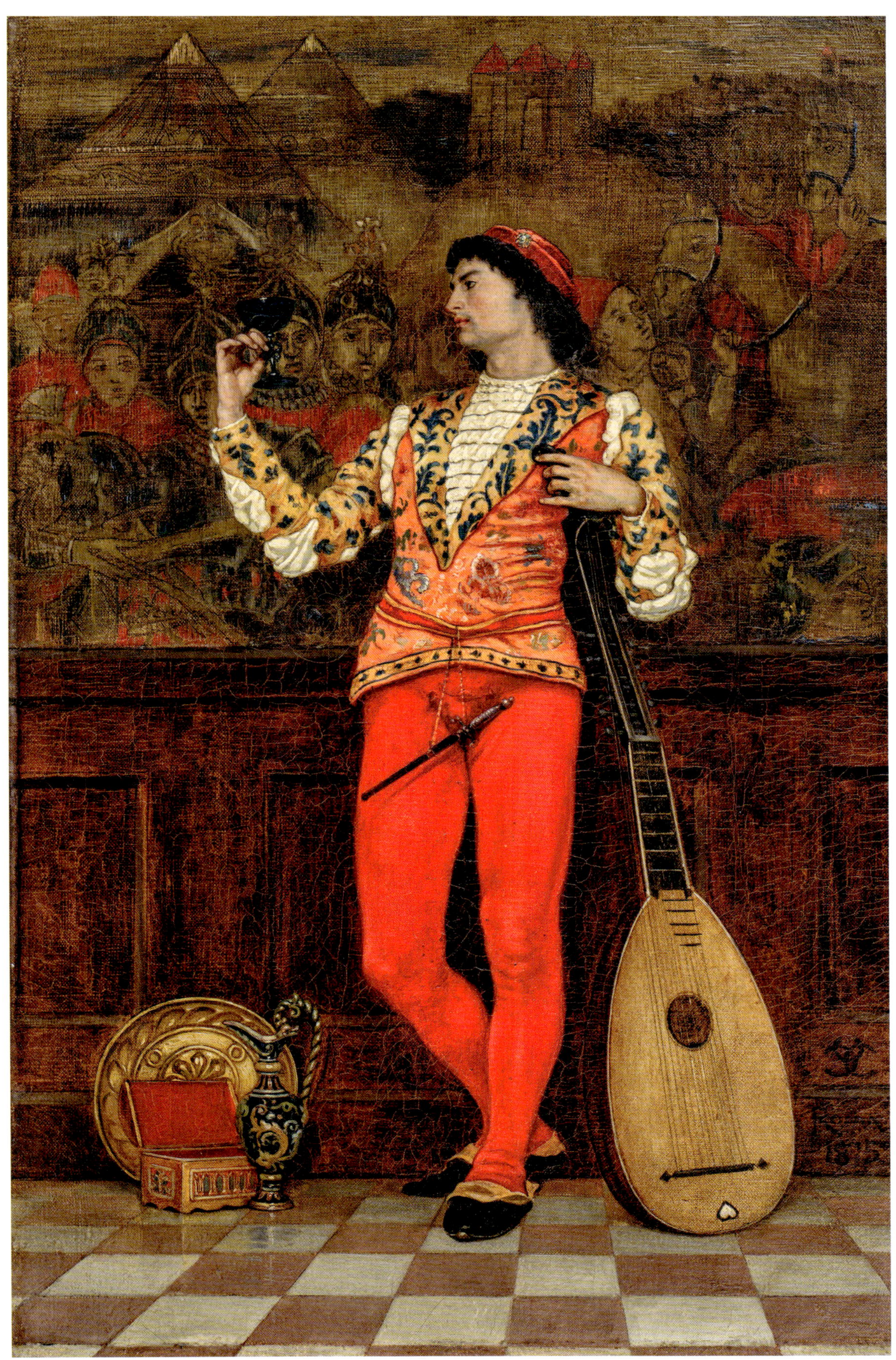

✲ CAT. 6-10
Ancient Mediterranean Flasks, sixth century BCE–fourth century CE, glass (various techniques), 2 ½ to 4 ½ in. tall, Smithsonian American Art Museum, Gifts of John Gellatly

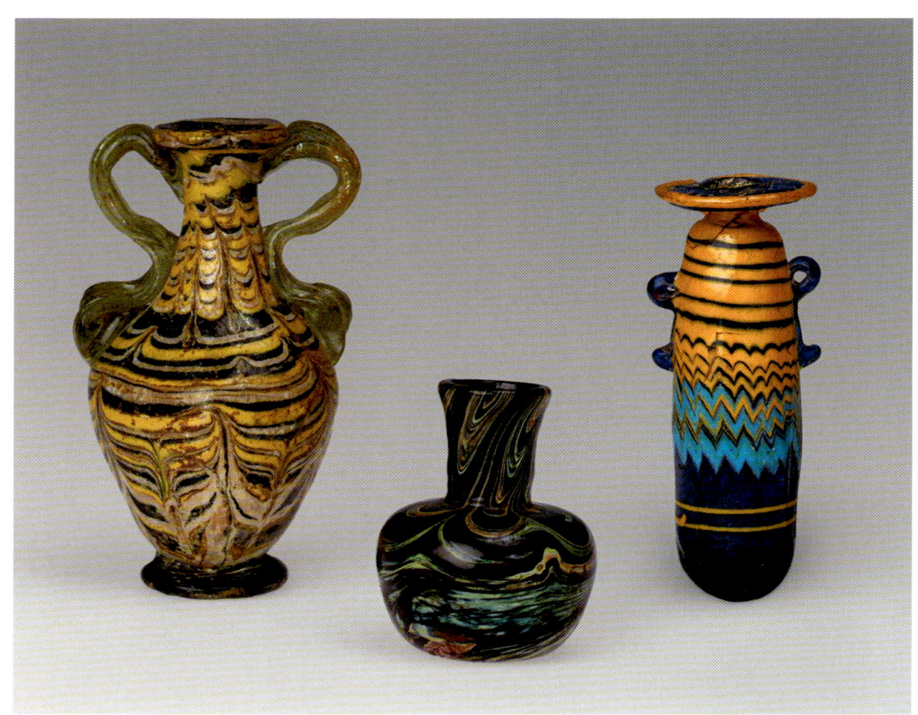

✲ CAT. 6-11
Venice and Murano Glass and Mosaic Company Ltd. (Salviati & Co.), Ancient Roman–Style Skyphos (Two-Handled Wine Cup), ca. 1870s, cast, polished, and applied glass, 3 ⅝ × 10 ¼ × 5 ⅝ in., Smithsonian American Art Museum, Gift of John Gellatly

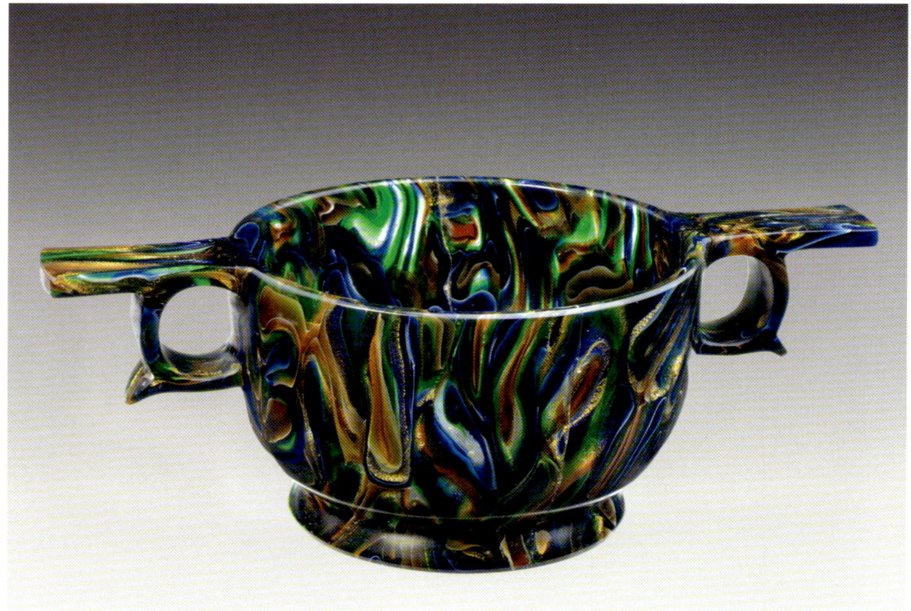

museum or cabinet of curiosities, featuring "Venetian glasses three hundred years old" and "a lute that Romeo might have played."[33] This immersive bric-a-brac display offered a buffet for the senses, and the reporter enumerates literary and historical references brought to mind by the eccentric décor. Viewers of *Interior with Lute Player* can build similar associations with the musical instrument suggesting romance and courtship, perhaps the world of Shakespearean lovers like Lorenzo and Jessica from *The Merchant of Venice* or Romeo and Juliet from nearby Verona. Fine glassware like this tazza would be appropriate for raising a toast at a feast or wedding, and period journals often mention the

Renaissance-era custom of breaking a fancy goblet at an especially elegant dinner, thereby commemorating an evening among esteemed guests and demonstrating the host's indifference to expense.[34] American connoisseurs would have gasped at the notion of deliberately destroying any of these treasures, no doubt preferring to protect and display them as prized ensembles with links to old-world artistry and opulence.

Venetian glass also held appeal through its associations with darker chapters of the city's history and its reputation for intrigue and violence. In Coleman's painting, the dagger adds an element of danger; perhaps this is the "poison-bearing poniard" cited in the published description of Coleman's Rome studio?[35] Tales of Venetian treachery, tyranny, and political intrigue routinely titillated US audiences, particularly when contemplated with an ocean of distance and centuries of time between them and the unhappy events. William Shakespeare's *Othello*, for example, was a theater favorite for this generation and also a popular subject in period artwork.[36] For a mass-produced plaster statuette illustrating this play, titled with the quote *"Ha! I Like Not That"* (CAT. 6-12), John Rogers chose the pivotal scene in which the vile Iago, on the far left, plants the seeds of murderous jealousy in the titular character, whose wife, Desdemona, appears to receive inappropriate attentions from a rival. Exalting in an abundance of accessories, the parlor sculpture delights the eyes, fingers, and imagination with swords, ceramics, feathers, brocades, leather, and lace, despite knowledge of the story's tragic end. Murano glassware likewise had deadly associations, notably a myth that the thinnest and finest glass goblets could detect poison. "The cup would break into shivers if any envenomed beverage were poured into it," reported Murray's guidebook and other commentaries.[37] In an 1876 magazine short story, an American traveler to Murano hears this legend amid a sales pitch for an allegedly rare sixteenth-century cup, said to be "the sole remaining relic of an art long lost." These bold claims lead readers to suspect that the tourist has been duped by a salesman's hyperbole, but after the buyer's return to the United States, use of the cup reveals by chance that his wife is a serial poisoner, thereby saving him from near mariticide.[38] Through such legends, Murano contributed to "a sense of pervasive wickedness" distinctive to the literary reputation of Venice, with luxury glass at the center of a volatile world of pleasures and threats.[39] An 1859 newspaper article summarized this favorite perception of the island city: "What dark intrigues, what mysterious adventures, what unimagined crimes have taken place in these gorgeous but now silent palaces, these noiseless gondolas! What tales could those deep canals tell, had they voices!"[40]

Aided by these melodramatic associations, combinations of medieval and Renaissance décor, costumes, artwork, and glass blurred lines between past and present, truth and fiction, in paintings, on stage, and in the homes of art collectors. Is Coleman's *Interior with Lute Player* an illustration of an anecdote from the fifteenth century, or is it a contemporary theatrical scene, with a Shakespearean actor in costume and surrounded by props? In the nineteenth century, the orchestration of *tableaux vivants* was a favorite parlor game, restaging well-known antique statues and old master paintings to delight friends and guests. In Italy the proximity of

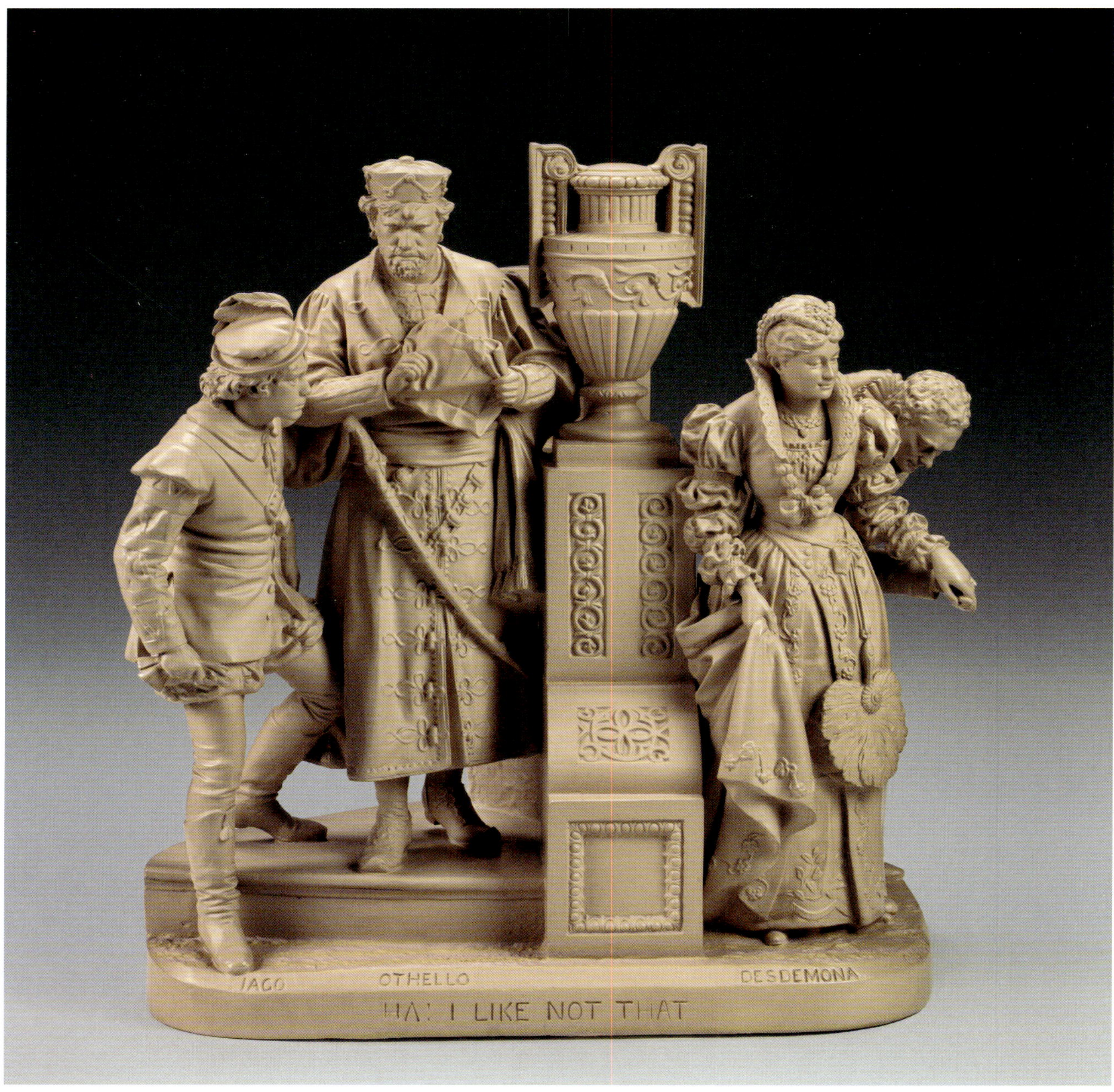

✡ CAT. 6-12
John Rogers, *"Ha! I Like Not That,"* 1882, painted plaster, 22 × 20 ¾ × 14 ⅜ in., Smithsonian American Art Museum, Gift of John Rogers and Son

museums and art collections encouraged this practice, and several leaders of Venice's Anglo-American expatriate community were fond of hosting parties centered around such performances.[41] Artists generally served as participants and designers, based on their expected knowledge of the piece to be mimicked and their assumed instincts for all questions of aesthetics. For example, in 1883 Ariana Curtis recounted in a letter that Frank Duveneck had organized an evening of living pictures, himself dressing as a Venetian *bravo* (a hired assassin) and performing a mock murder.[42] Though the subjects for nineteenth-century *tableaux vivants* were not exclusively local Venetian works of art, accounts show a preponderance of Italian scenes and characters in these programs.

The same circles of artists and collectors also restaged Venetian history and art beyond the island city to share their favorite fantasies of its beauty and sensuality among peers. Notable instances include William Merritt Chase's organization of *tableaux vivants* in New York in the 1890s, while, for a costumed artist's ball in Boston in 1889, Isabella Stewart Gardner dressed as a "grand Venetian dame" from the age of Paolo Veronese, an indication of her appreciation for historical art and a statement of her present-day wealth and power.[43] Coleman himself meanwhile remained in Italy, where for a portrait photograph made around 1924 at the Villa Narcissus, his home on the island of Capri, he wore the costume of a Venetian senator, thereby continuing to demonstrate a passion for the past (Fig. 6-2).[44] Americans found that dressing in historical costume and owning antiques and historical replicas had educational benefits and nurtured their own creativity. Armed with scholarly books, novels, and art, they imaginatively explored the sea-skirted city of Venice and its illustrious, decadent, and sometimes dangerous heritage.

YOUNG ITALY AND MURANO GLASS: AMERICA'S HOPES FOR MODERN VENICE

While the Venetian glass revival enjoyed esteem around the globe for its aesthetic excellence, technical ambitions, and historical connections, it held additional appeal in the United States in political terms. By the time of the Risorgimento, Italy had already long been an inspiration and cultural reference point in other lands. Symbolizing prestige, stability, authority, and virtue, its classical architecture provided models for grand civic buildings, churches, and homes in the growing nation across the Atlantic. Increasingly in the nineteenth century, Americans embraced this visual language not only in public architecture and statuary, but also in the domestic sphere, using pictures, furniture, and decorative arts to express values and moral aspirations.[45] Within this aesthetic tradition, they admired and collected Italian artworks, including Murano glass, as embodiments of the legendary artistic genius of the Mediterranean, enduring talents manifest over countless generations. However, this changed in the second half of the nineteenth century, when the rapid redefinition of Italy's society and economy replaced the "myth of Italy"—romantic conceptions of its storied past—with a new identity, playing a robust role in current world politics, commerce, and culture.[46] In particular, the city of Venice became a favored site within Italy for making and exhibiting contemporary art, nurturing expectations of future creativity and industry. This shift occurred quickly; already at Boston's 1883 Foreign Exhibition, the organizers lauded displays of Italian wares, including Murano glass, as evidence that Italy's new republican government would improve the nation's productivity and artistic prowess. "So complete a transformation from the anarchy of a few decades ago could scarcely have been hoped for by the most enthusiastic of her admirers," the exhibition's catalogue reported. It concluded, "She [Italy] has had, and doubtless will have, many a hard struggle before she succeeds in liberating her entire people from

Fig. 6-2
Morgan Heiskell, *Charles Caryl Coleman Wearing the Costume of a Venetian Senator*, from "Charles Caryl Coleman," *American Magazine of Art*, September 1924

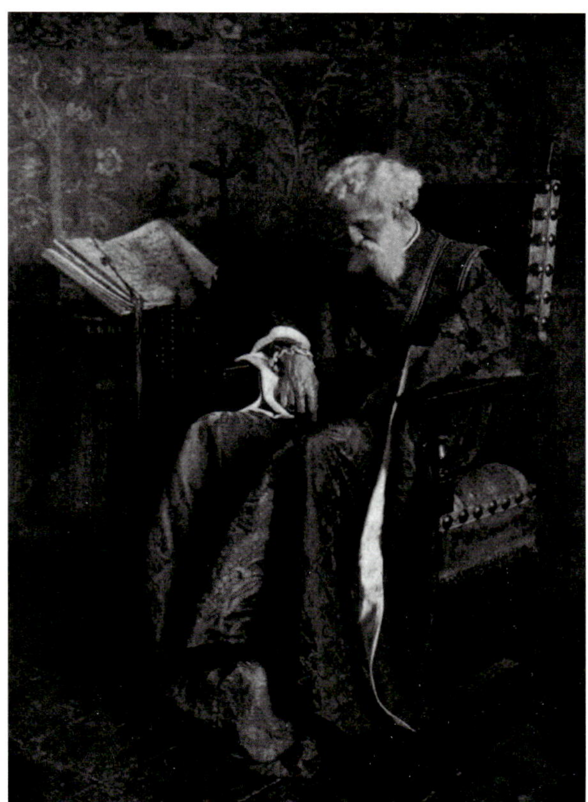

moral and intellectual bondage."[47] Such accolades encouraged collecting of Venetian revival glass to support the recent achievements of the Risorgimento. This patronage updated the two nations' kinship, so that in the minds of Americans the New World now served as a model for the Old. The United States could be both teacher and student to modern Venice, learning from the city's artistic heritage and specialized skills in fields like glassmaking, while also providing an example for virtuous governance and social equality.

Confidence in the city's prospects emerges as a theme in period art, subtly illustrating these new connections between the ingenuity of Venetian citizens and their ambitions for affluence. Visiting artists from the United States began to break from Ruskinian traditions of mourning Venice's faded splendor, creating instead images of promise and progress. The transformation assumes a heroic scale in Frank Duveneck's *Water Carriers, Venice* (CAT. 6-13), a panorama of working-class Venetians traversing the Riva degli Schiavoni waterfront. Although this busy embankment is lined with hotels and adjacent to St. Mark's Square, the painting includes no foreign tourists, only native fishermen and families proudly performing their quotidian chores. The dragging shoulder of the young girl on the far right demonstrates the contributions of all ages to Venice's pending prosperity. This picture celebrates diligence, in contrast with the leisurely flirtation and intoxication of the characters in Sargent's *Sulphur Match*. It also differs from more sentimental and sanitized European genre scenes, where appeal sometimes depended primarily on exotic costumes or unfamiliar, outmoded customs of the countryside. In this work, the figures are full-length, individualized, humanized, and in one case, returning our gaze. Duveneck thus offers rich studies in character, as seen in *Glass Blowers of Murano*, painted by his associate Ulrich. With such works, American artists recognized the picturesque appeal of their anonymous blue-collar subjects but used staging and details to add grandeur to these glimpses of everyday life in modern Venice.

Hopes for Venice to reclaim its pride and productivity depended especially on rekindling the native genius of its young people, unlocking the talents of future generations. Amid calls for Italian unification in the mid-nineteenth century, depictions of Italian children garnered political symbolism in foreigners' eyes, a reputation recognized by the Franco-Swiss painter Louis Léopold Robert, Americans James Edward Freeman and John Gadsby Chapman, and certain other specialists in images of Italian peasants. These expatriates were firsthand witnesses to the emergence of Giuseppe Mazzini's Giovane Italia (Young Italy) resistance movement, instrumental in the Risorgimento's early years, and their artworks capitalized on the international sympathy Mazzini, Giuseppe Garibaldi, and their fellow patriots inspired.[48] Duveneck's *Water Carriers* continues these themes in a Venetian setting, especially through the two boys on the balustrade, whose grimy, bare feet add rustic charm and a suggestion of authenticity to this orchestrated studio composition. The elegant domes of the churches of San Giorgio Maggiore and Santa Maria della Salute frame the pair to create a sharp contrast between the economic struggles of the present and the city's seventeenth-century success.[49] Their contemplative poses invite speculation: Will Venice regain its cultural leadership within these boys' lifetime?

Across the lagoon on Murano, Americans saw proficiency with glass as a uniquely local instinct, a bond with the past and a resource for recovery. According to an 1886 article, "There seems to have been something in those old workmen at Murano—there seems to be something in their descendants of today: an esthetic feeling, as well as a mechanical skill, born in brain and fingers, and transmitted hereditarily."[50] Such praise encouraged tourists in Venice to admire young glassmakers as the descendants of revered old master painters: "In her manufactures the art-idea which once found expression from the pencils of Titian, Paul Veronese, Tintoretto and Palma Vecchio, in mural decoration, now finds form in the scarcely less ambitious work of artisans," advised a New York style columnist in 1894.[51] For most American consumers (with the exception of Isabella Stewart Gardner), acquiring a genuine painting by Titian was not possible, but Venetian revival glass was both a respectable alternative and an investment in Italy's future. These romantic links across generations propose bold thoughts for the black-soled boy looking across the water in Duveneck's painting. Is he meditating on the majesty of his home city, newly self-governing once more, or is he dreaming of how he might improve it? Duveneck's sensitive studies of Venetian youth in this painting, in sketchbooks, and in finished drawings like *Gypsy Boy* (CAT. 6-14) amplifed Americans' romantic admiration for the beneficiaries of the revolutionary efforts of the Giovane Italia movement and other leaders in the recent and successful quest for liberty. Such artworks suggest that young Italians' pride, intellect, physical beauty, and perhaps artistic gifts, as captured on a single face, are the seeds for achievement on a national level.

Anecdotes from the island city's artistic past reinforced American appreciation for the potential of modern Venice to make remarkable new accomplishments in the arts. The lives of Italy's great bygone artists were popular subject matter for painters and writers in this period, introducing Duveneck and his audiences to the humble boyhoods of Giotto, Michelangelo Buonarroti, and neoclassical sculptor Antonio Canova, who began and ended his career in Venice.[52] Guidebooks directed tourists to Canova's works on display in the city's museums, to the Ca' Farsetti where he trained as a boy, to the house where he died in 1822, and to his grand pyramidal memorial in the Basilica of Santa Maria Gloriosa dei Frari.[53] Meanwhile, the legend of the discovery of his talent became a popular children's story: while serving in the kitchen of a ducal Venetian household, the ten-year-old purportedly sculpted an impressively lifelike table centerpiece of a lion that surprised his elders and launched his distinguished career.[54] In American painter Pinckney Marcius-Simons's interpretation of this anecdote, *The Child Canova Modeling a Lion out of Butter* (CAT. 6-15), the swarthy Italian lad—another iteration of this recurring ideal of Italian youth and promise—confidently crafts his first chef d'oeuvre, which some accounts specify as a winged Lion of St. Mark, a symbol of Venice. Other household staff watch in astonishment, and an assortment of antique kitchenware completes the scene, suggesting the variety of materials, forms, and textures that had trained the young sculptor's hands. Like Duveneck's *Water Carriers,* this picture offers an optimistic American view of the common people of Italy and their creative potential. Furthermore, the painting reminds its audiences that young Canova's

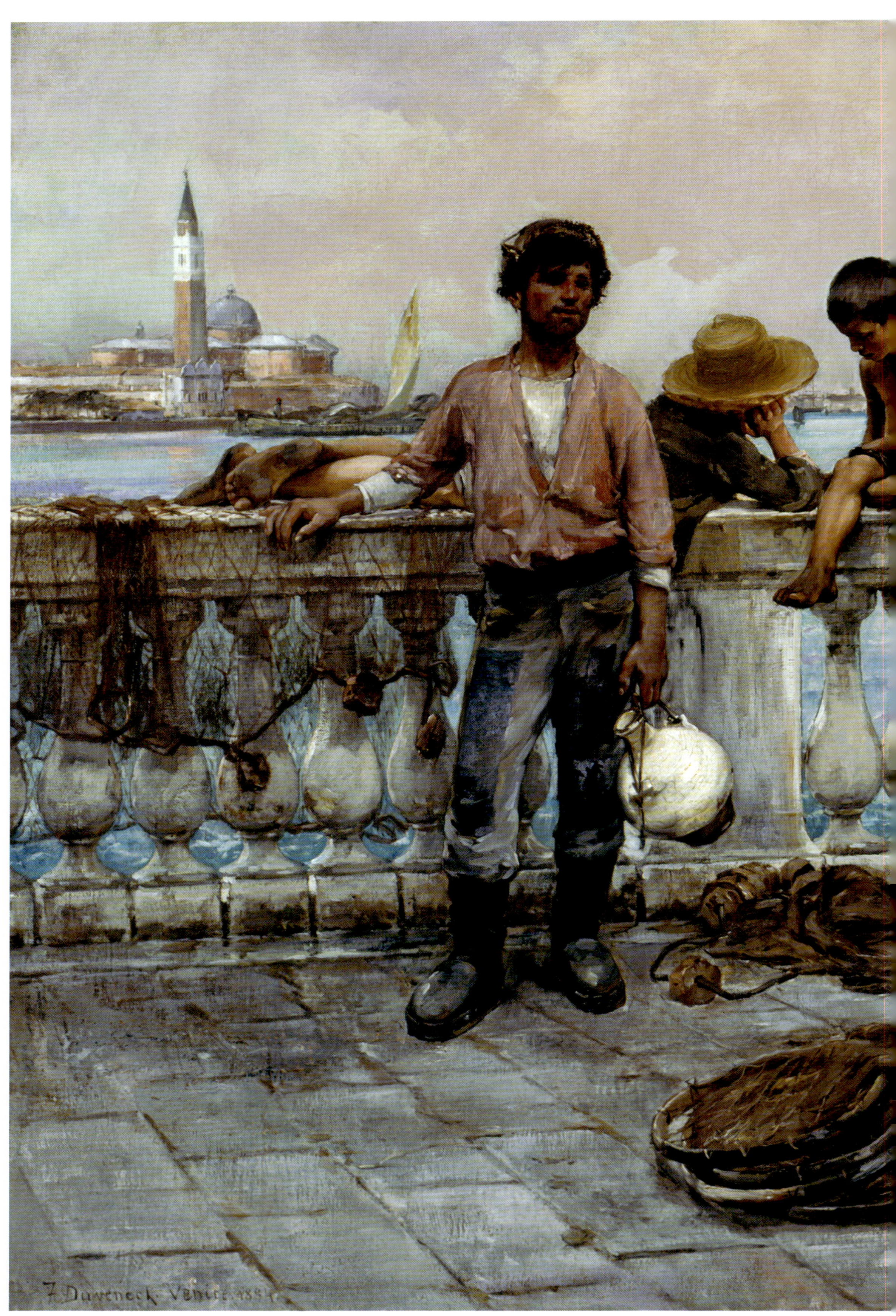

✡ CAT. 6-13
Frank Duveneck, *Water Carriers, Venice*, 1884, oil on canvas, 48 ⅜ × 73 ⅛ in., Smithsonian American Art Museum, Bequest of Reverend F. Ward Denys

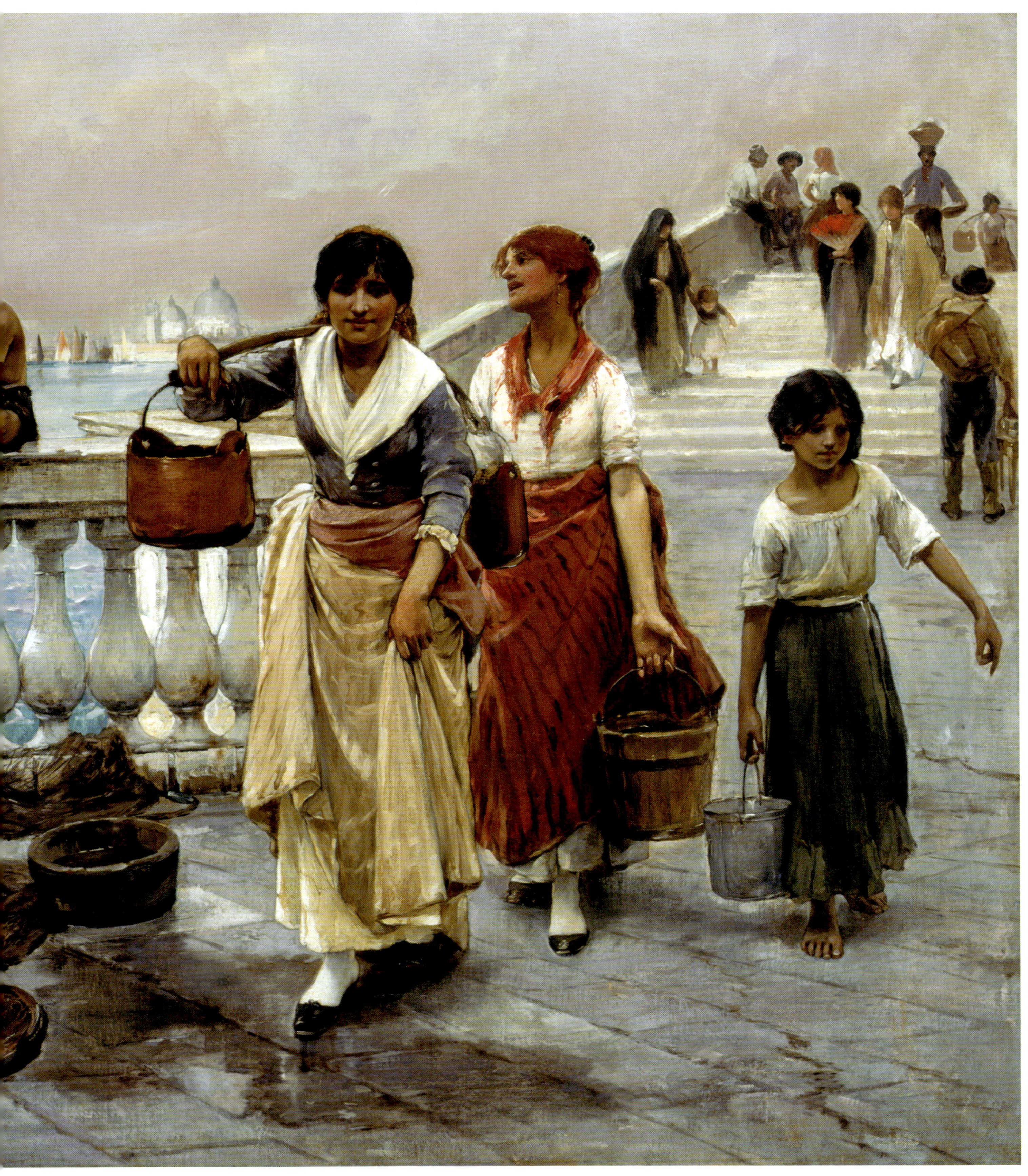

✡ CAT. 6-14
Frank Duveneck, *Gypsy Boy*, 1885, pastel on paper, 17 ½ × 13 ¾ in., Collection of Jane Joel Knox, promised gift to the Virginia Museum of Fine Arts, in loving memory of Irving Joel

✡ CAT. 6-15
Pinckney Marcius-Simons, *The Child Canova Modeling a Lion out of Butter*, ca. 1885, oil on canvas, 23 ¾ × 29 in., Chrysler Museum of Art, Norfolk, VA, Gift of the Mowbray Arch Society

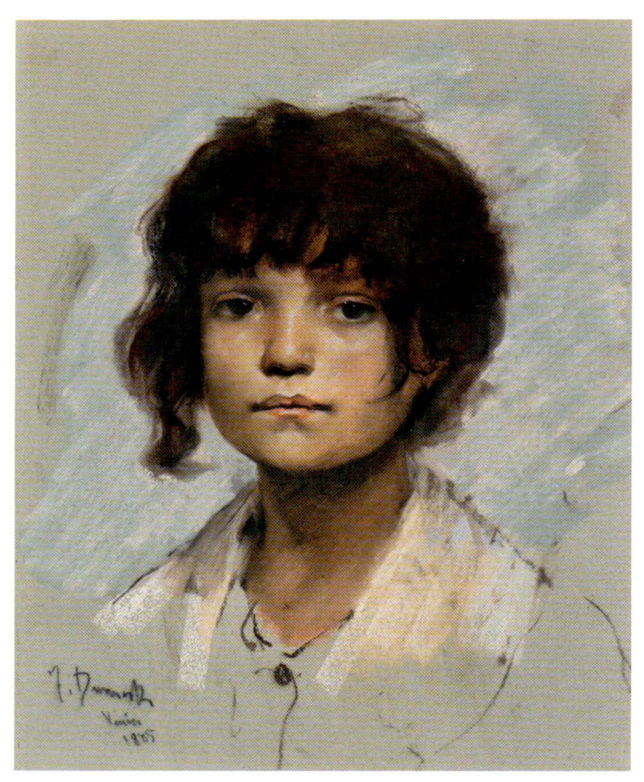

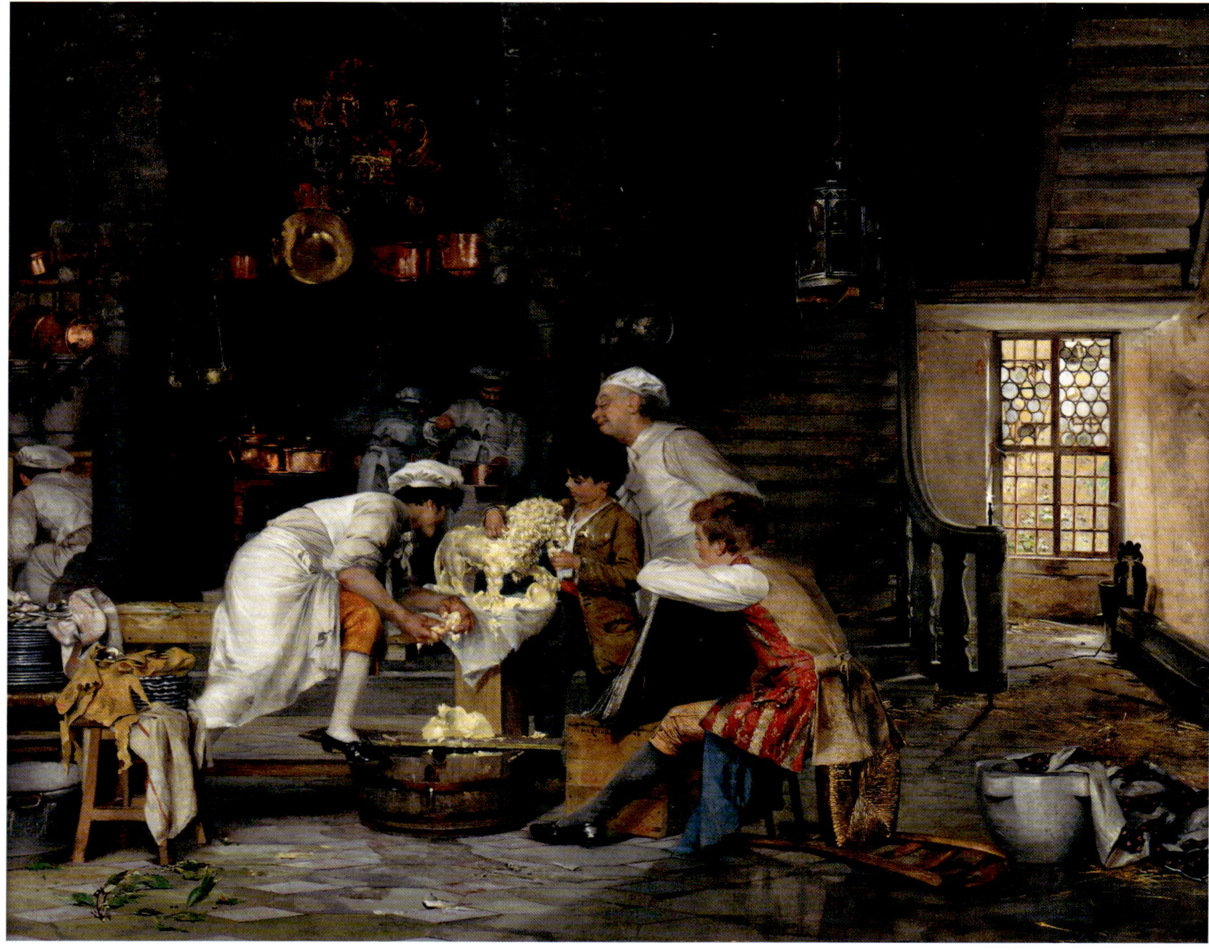

transition from kitchen helper to master artist depended on patronage—with Gilded Age American collectors and consumers encouraged to become sponsors and supporters, taking on roles once held by European nobility. The recipe for cultural achievements, it argues, is a combination of stimulating surroundings, civic patronage, and an egalitarian society in which movement among classes is possible and welcome.

American political values likewise guide the presentation of the Murano glass industry in the 1901 novel *Marietta: A Maid of Venice* by best-selling American historical fiction writer Francis Marion Crawford.[55] Set in the Renaissance, it tells the story of a prodigy glassblower named Zorzi, who has immigrated to Italy from Dalmatia in eastern Europe and become an assistant to the wealthy maestro Angelo Beroviero. However, Zorzi's ambitions are stymied by protectionist laws that forbid foreigners from learning these skills and potentially disrupting the native Venetians' monopoly on the production of luxury glass. By the novel's end, Zorzi's artistic genius and honest character win the respect of his master, and, more importantly, the heart of Beroviero's daughter, Marietta. Despite the schemes of malevolent pirates, princes, courtesans, and rival artisans, the glassmaker from abroad receives permission to wed his sweetheart, fully integrate into Venetian society, and enjoy the professional esteem of managing his own furnace-workshop. This plot thus hinges largely on a critique of inequalities in the social structure of Renaissance Venice. The book's Venetian patricians are mostly indolent spendthrifts, while the maestro Beroviero is hot-tempered and lacking empathy, and his son is a greedy scoundrel. (Meanwhile the heroine Marietta is intelligent and nurturing, and Crawford implies that she might succeed as a glassblower, were women allowed to learn the trade.) Such tales of old-world injustice and treachery conformed to Americans' perception of the United States as an industrious and morally grounded meritocracy. In this way, the book joined James Fenimore Cooper's *The Bravo* and other works that reproached the monarchies of Europe.[56] Nineteenth-century novels and poems about Venice routinely include scheming nobles and hired assassins as characters, as well as episodes of imprisonment, typically prompted by a false denunciation. Meanwhile tourists shuddered to imagine confinement in the notorious Piombi prison within the Doge's Palace, so-named because its lead roof trapped summer heat and offered little insulation in winter, amplifying the miseries of incarceration. Howells concludes his 1865 commentary in *Venetian Life* with a summary of the past decadence, corruption, and cowardice of city leaders, but after living there during the bleak years of Austrian occupation, he is ready to forgive the republic's litany of misdeeds if a new government can bring American-style "Liberty" to the city's full populace.[57] Crawford's hero Zorzi manages to avoid the Piombi prison, but the writer made no efforts to veil his disdain of Italian rulers in *Salve Venetia: Gleanings from Venetian History*, calling its early modern oligarchy "the most unscrupulous, skeptical, suspicious, and thoroughly immoral organisation that ever was devised by man."[58] Like American artists of his generation, he distrusted Europe's privileged classes but felt sympathy and respect for the general population of Venice and expected audiences to share these sentiments.[59]

While dramatizing Venice's flaws, Crawford's novel *Marietta* also flatters Murano as a place of ambition and cutting-edge experimentation, where artisans tested and expanded the capabilities of their medium. Beroviero and Zorzi use a scientific trial-and-error process seeking a formula for a richer red color, taking notes and guarding this research from other glassmakers. Just as Venice's early dominance in this field resulted in part from its mastery of exceptionally clear transparent glass and attempted monopoly over chemical compounds, the Venetian glass revival sought both to recover and preserve famous historic practices and to develop new colors and visual effects. As reported by foreign visitors in the 1860s, Salviati encouraged creativity in his workmen, allowing them two hours per day for "original attempts" and "producing new designs," so that their sweat resulted in more than "servile copies."[60] This custom distinguished the Murano furnaces from the oppressive monotony of other industrial labor, including conditions in the allied bottle and sheet glass factories in the United States. Salviati calculated that this freedom and autonomy would foster a happier workforce and potentially also generate lucrative discoveries or fresh forms and themes, and American observers applauded this endeavor. The emphasis on creativity, individuality, and artistic freedom offered economic benefits to the Venetian glassmakers, but in American eyes, such practices aligned the operations of the glass furnaces with wider cultural values.

As Americans followed the success of the Venetian glass revival, watching its contributions to the restoration of wealth and civic pride through tradition and technology, many also studied Venice as a living textbook for nurturing glassmaking at home. American producers of glass saw the displays at the Metropolitan Museum of Art and at world's fairs as both an inspiration and a gauntlet. Some collectors of Venetian glass were active in American enterprises that competed with Murano for prestige in the luxury goods market, including Louis Comfort Tiffany and his firm's chief silver designer, Edward C. Moore.[61] Tiffany's enterprise found visual models in Italian glassware, as well as marketing and profit strategies among the practices of its European competitors. Meanwhile another American glass pioneer, Julian de Cordova, looked to his personal collection of modern Venetian glass in devising new patterns for the Union Glass Company in Somerville, Massachusetts, which he owned. This inspiration is evident in his "Venetian" series (CATS. 6-16, 6-17), in which cups and pitchers bear gold leaf decoration, mimicking Murano's famous *aventurine* technique of producing glittery gold dust qualities within molten glass. This series also used serpentine applied handles, in subtle reference to the ornaments and flourishes of more complex Venetian revival specimens, such as this vase with sculptural flame-worked creatures embellishing its handle and stem (CAT. 6-18).[62] In his letter donating a selection of Union Glass products to the growing representations of American scientific and industrial prowess at the Smithsonian Institution, de Cordova patriotically requested that the objects' display labels state their national origin by announcing "that all in the case is purely American progress in the manufacture of Art Glass designed by an American, executed in an American factory from Glass made from American discovery."[63] De Cordova thus learned from Venetian traditions, then sought to ignite similar sparks of

✲ CAT. 6-16

Union Glass Company, Venetian-Style Twin-Handled Vase, 1894–1910, mold-blown, tooled, and applied glass with gold leaf, 12 ⅝ × 5 11/16 × 4 ⅛ in., The Corning Museum of Glass

✲ CAT. 6-17

Union Glass Company, Venetian-Style Creamer with "Snake" Handle, 1894–1910, blown and applied glass with gold leaf, 5 ¾ × 4 ⅛ × 2 ⅞ in., The Corning Museum of Glass

✲ CAT. 6-18

Venice and Murano Glass and Mosaic Company Ltd. (Salviati & Co.) or Fratelli Barovier, Vase with Dolphin and Serpent, ca. 1870s–90s, blown and applied hot-worked glass, 15 ½ × 6 in. diam., RISD Museum, Gift of Mrs. Frank Mauran and John O. Ames

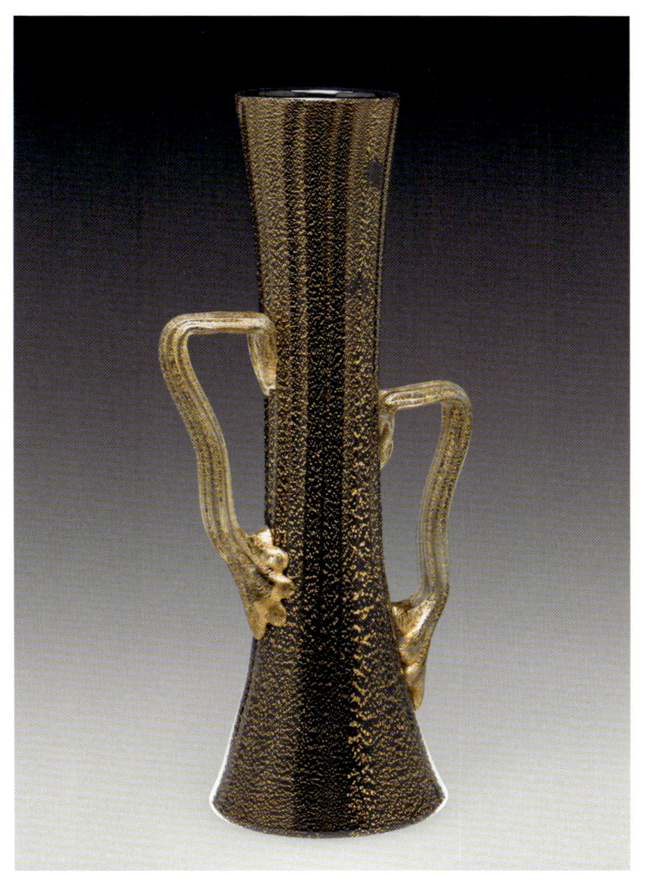
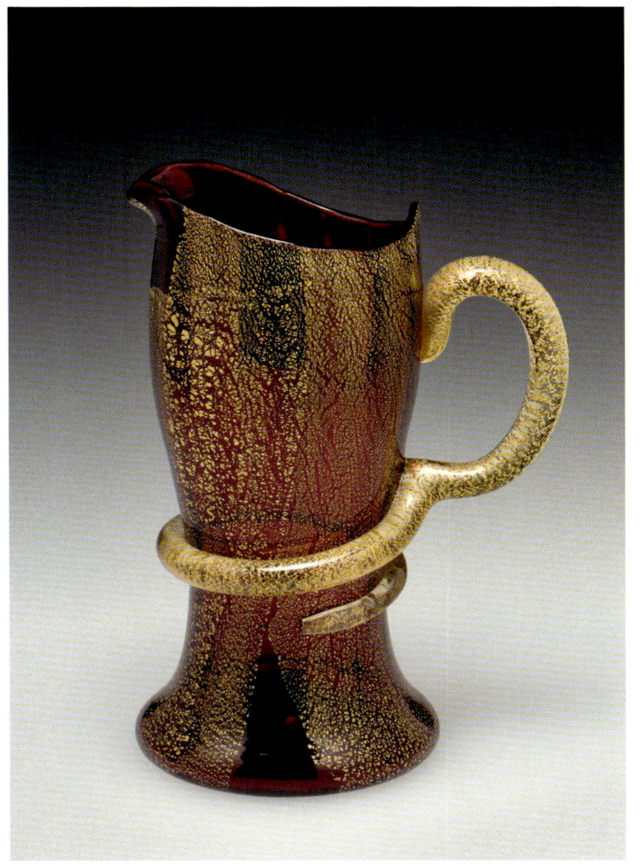
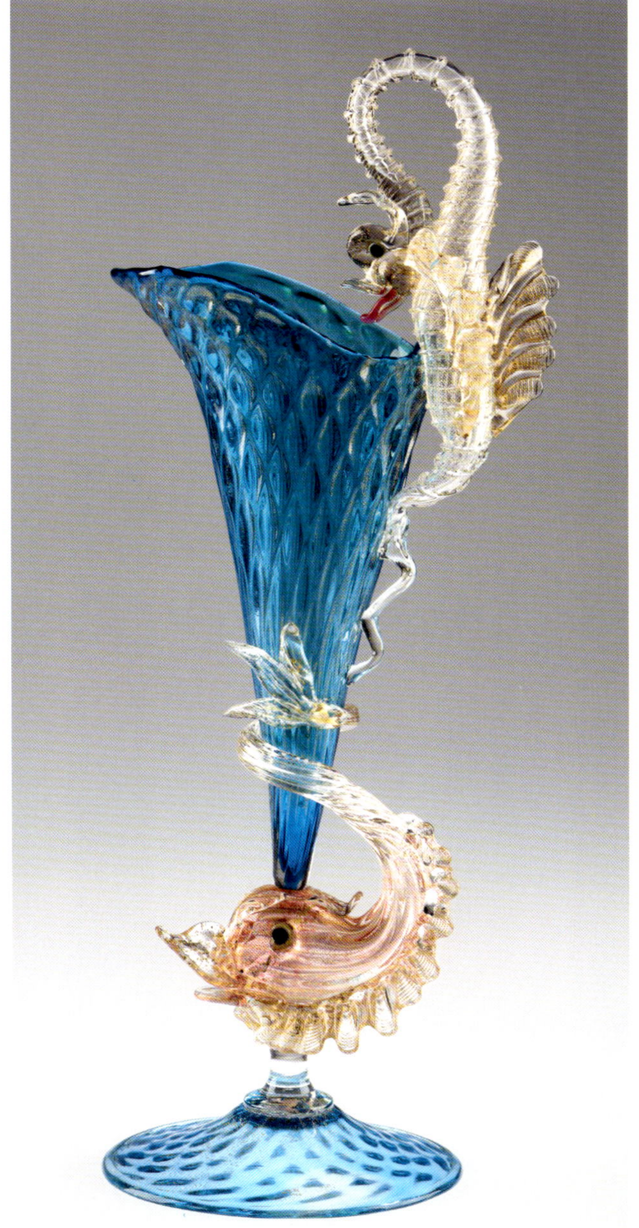

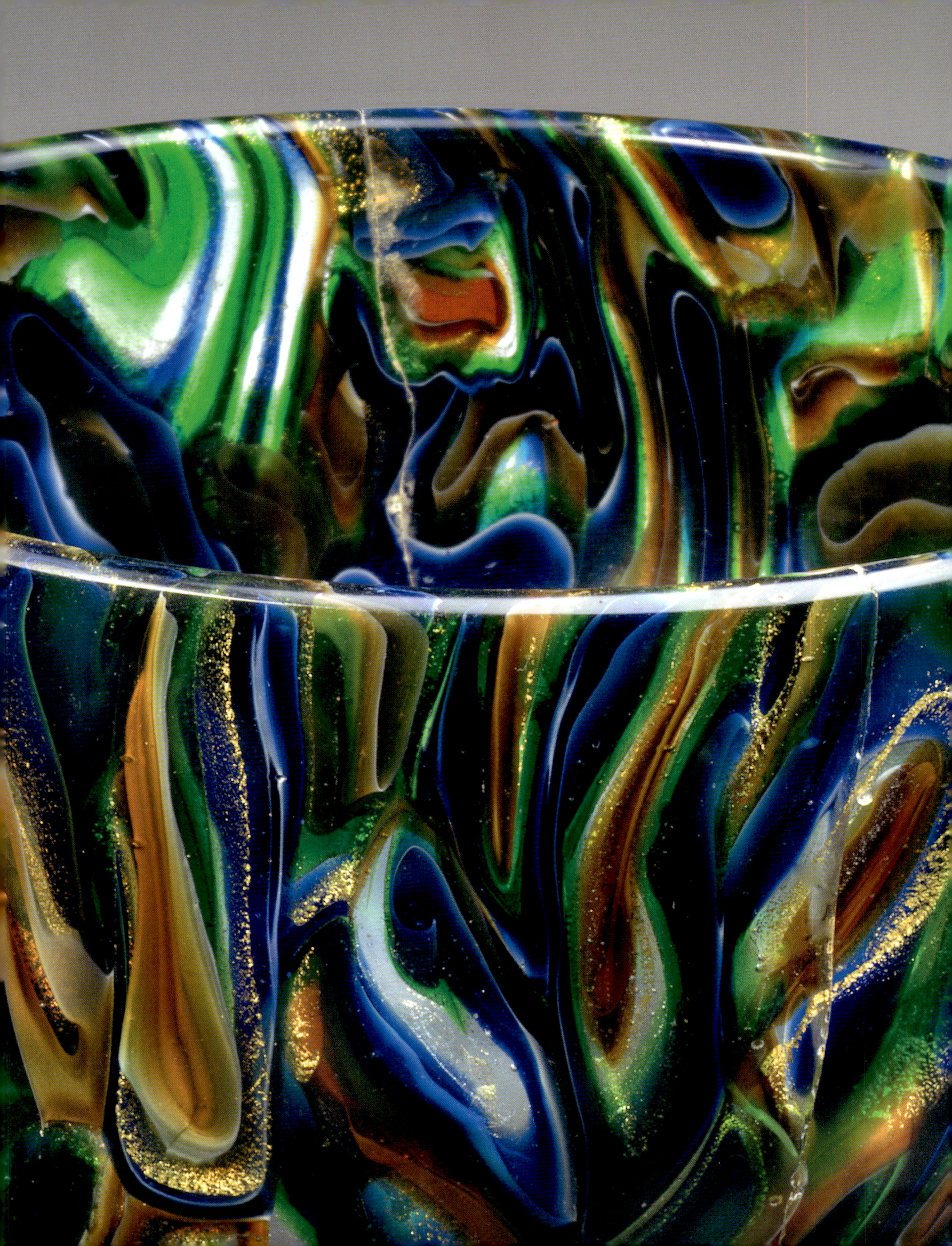

genius in his own factories in Massachusetts. Union Glass's hybrid "Venetian" wares allowed American consumers to express their appreciation for the genius of Venice while making patriotic purchases in support of their own nation's pursuit of excellence in art and design. This rivalry was healthy, and patronage of Murano's glassworks and enthusiasm for Venice's cultural revitalization did not dampen artistic and manufacturing ambitions in the United States.

BURN THE GONDOLAS: REVIVAL GLASS AND THE AVANT-GARDE

Within three decades of its integration into the Italian nation, a cascade of changes and improvements ushered a liberated Venice into a prosperous future. Some of these developments threatened to alter the city's cherished historical fabric and weaken its tourist appeal. Meanwhile, new technologies and stylistic trends triggered a critical reevaluation of Venetian glass on both sides of the Atlantic. Civic investments in infrastructure led the way, with channels in the lagoons deepened to host increased shipping traffic. Expansions to the Arsenale prepared the city to reenter the shipbuilding industry, and a bridge between Murano and Venice was proposed, raising alarm on the smaller island that a loss of autonomy might be coming.[64] City leaders also increased investment in the arts. In 1887 Venice announced itself to the world as a reborn center of creativity with its own Esposizione Nazionale Artistica, a fine arts fair reportedly showcasing more than one thousand paintings and statues. Its opening, featuring illuminated festivities and King Umberto I in attendance, received international press attention, and its success inspired the launch of the Biennale series in 1895.[65] "Venice will be a Mecca for art lovers," reported one American reviewer at the first Biennale, noting the show's rigorous standards and contemporary focus: "No works are to be admitted that are not really original and select."[66] The island of Murano asserted its artistic reputation at the first Biennale by sponsoring one of its top prizes, with a value of 2,500 lire, which was awarded to James McNeill Whistler for *Symphony in White No. 2: The Little White Girl* (a triumphal redemption for a painting scorned by critics at its 1864 debut). America's leading artists continued to receive recognition at subsequent Biennali and soon occupied dedicated rooms within the show. Exhibitors at the second Biennale in 1897 included Sargent, Coleman, Julius LeBlanc Stewart, John White Alexander, Ralph Curtis, Elihu Vedder, and several others. Although Whistler's work was not shown that year, he and Sargent were appointed to represent the United States on the exhibition's committee of celebrity patrons in 1897 and again in 1899. Among America's leading artists, these two held especially strong reputations for work that challenged conventions and forged new directions, fitting the profile of the show and Venice's self-branding as a modern city.

Glassmaking joined fine art within these increasing international artistic exchanges taking place in Venice. Although formal exhibitions of glass were not included in the earliest Biennali, Murano held concurrent expositions of contemporary glassware as satellite projects. As they had done for fairs abroad, the glassmakers pushed their skills to the limit with experimental and virtuoso works.[67] Among the most innovative were the members of the Barovier family (descendants of the maestro who inspired Crawford's *Marietta*), who explored art nouveau trends

Venice and Murano Glass and Mosaic Company Ltd. (Salviati & Co.), Ancient Roman–Style Skyphos (Two-Handled Wine Cup) (detail), ca. 1870s; **see p. 228**

from Paris, Vienna, and Milan.[68] Hallmarks of the Artisti Barovier company's glassware became smooth profiles, simplified forms, and use of mosaic glass and murrhines to make patterns and pictorial compositions. Such designs replaced historically inspired gilding, enamel painting, and bravura sculptural flourishes as guiding aesthetic features. Like revival-style creations, these were often difficult to execute and impossible to duplicate, commanding admiration as singular pieces of fine art. A goblet from the Gellatly Collection (CAT. 6-19) has hallmarks of 1910s or '20s Barovier makership: a bowl composed of clear transparent blocks, each lined in dark purple, and selectively punctuated with mosaic glass tesserae depicting green rosettes and white flowers.[69] As the most contemporary design within its owner's diverse glass collection, it illustrates the breadth of American tastes, wherein

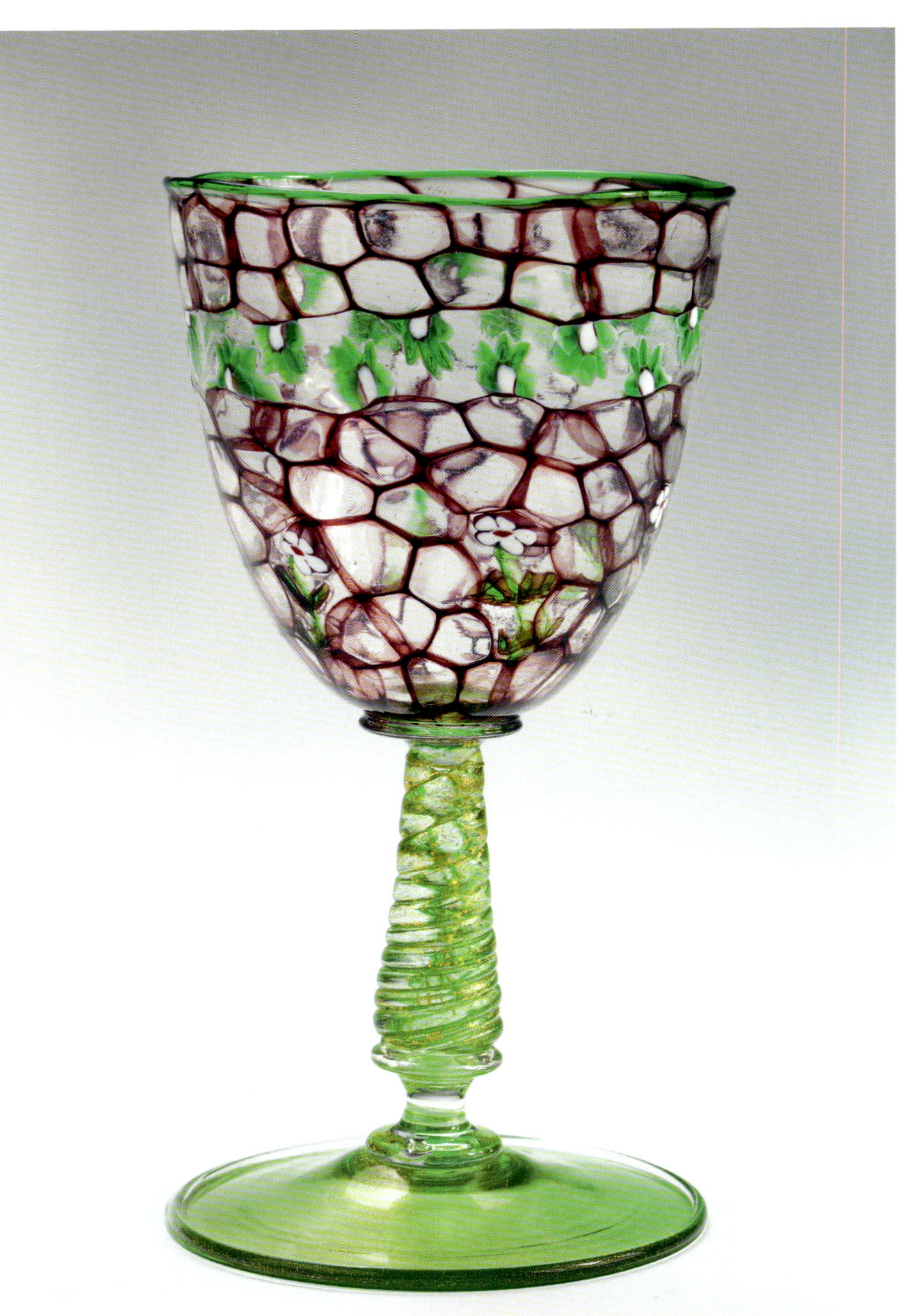

✲ CAT. 6-19
Artisti Barovier, Mosaic Glass Goblet, ca. 1914–28, blown and applied hot-worked glass with mosaic glass inclusions, 6 ⅝ × 3 ¼ in. diam., Smithsonian American Art Museum, Gift of John Gellatly

appreciation for the streamlined designs of the early twentieth century did not preclude admiration for the sculptural complexity and historical fidelity of 1870s forms.

The success and diversification of glassmaking operations on Murano opened new channels for direct collaboration between the furnaces and artists who specialized in other media. Painters had long contributed to large-scale architectural mosaic projects, including Antonio Ermolao Paoletti, a professor at Venice's Accademia di Belle Arti, who provided designs for many projects executed by Erede Dr. A. Salviati & Co., including decoration of the chapel and art museum at Stanford University (see p. 123). Using the firm's inventory of more than seventeen thousand colors of glass tesserae, technicians re-created Paoletti's painted cartoons to the dimensions and level of detail demanded by each commission. In the late 1890s, the character of these cross-media collaborations on Murano became less mimetic and more experimental. Around 1899 American painter Maurice Brazil Prendergast made a small mosaic set in plaster during an eighteen-month Venetian sojourn, *Fiesta Grand Canal, Venice* (CAT. 6-20), translating one of his watercolor paintings into sparkling shades of blue, green, and gold. His subject was a nighttime flotilla of lantern-bearing gondolas, with smaller tiles near the top to create perspectival recession. Irregular block shapes add fuzzy ambiguity to the nocturnal spectacle, and the result is remarkably similar in visual character to Prendergast's distinctive, divisionist painting style, which likewise builds images with discrete dots and dabs of color. In the oil painting *Ponte della Paglia* (CAT. 6-21), from the same Venetian visit, the artist uses this technique to portray the rainbow of parasols and dresses among the crowds on the Riva degli Schiavoni, as viewed from the piano nobile balcony of the Doge's Palace. Both this painting and the Grand Canal mosaic celebrate the crowds and merriment of Venice's public spaces, but the glass panel gains extra visual charm through its uneven, shimmering surface, which multiplies and reflects light just as the lagoon's waters do. Prendergast's correspondence does not reveal the circumstances around his creation of this unusual project. Was the American artist

✲ CAT. 6-20

Maurice Brazil Prendergast, *Fiesta Grand Canal, Venice*, ca. 1899, glass and ceramic mosaic tiles in plaster, 11 × 23 in., Williams College Museum of Art, Bequest of Mrs. Charles Prendergast

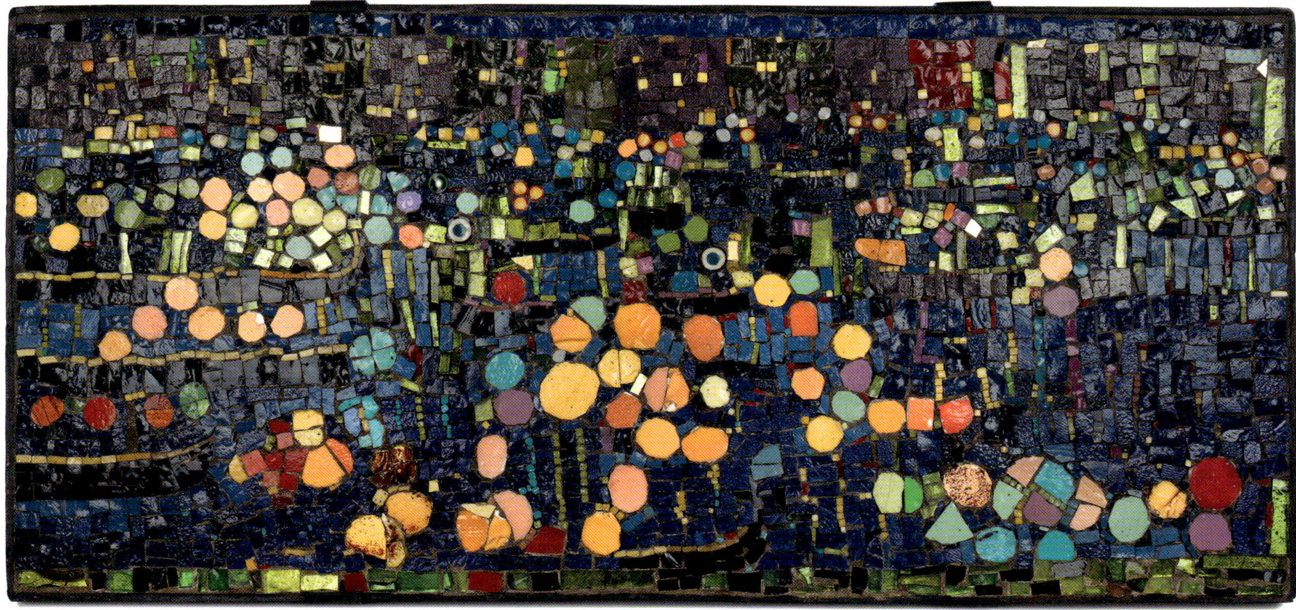

✲ CAT. 6-21

Maurice Brazil Prendergast, *Ponte della Paglia*, ca. 1898, reworked 1922, oil on canvas, 27 ⁷⁄₈ × 23 ⅛ in., The Phillips Collection, Acquired 1922

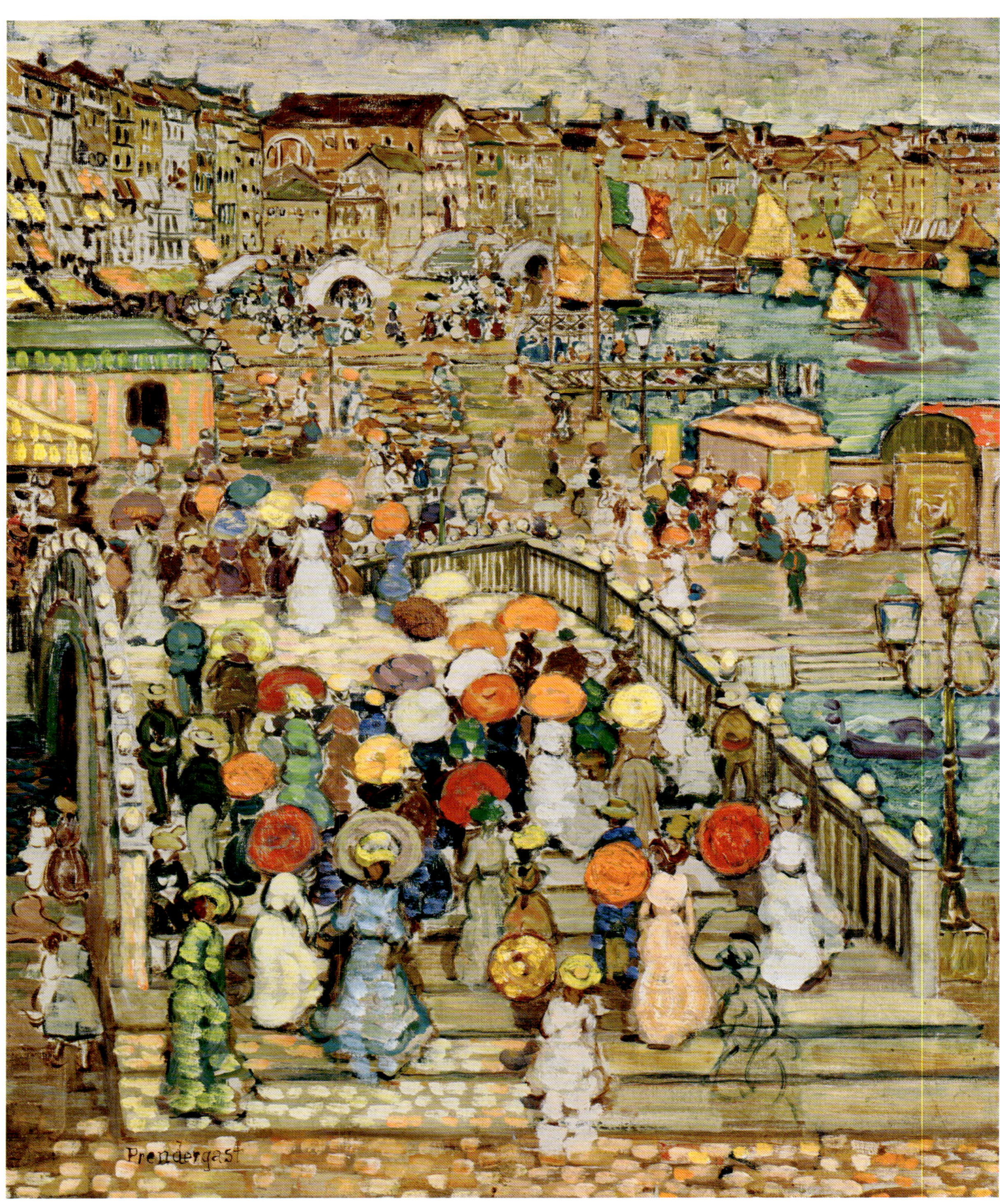

independently using scraps from a Venetian mosaic factory, or was this made with full access to Salviati's library of colored tiles, perhaps with Italian assistants helping to arrange and combine the pieces? The mosaic remained in the artist's possession and provides an unusual testament to experimentation, and perhaps collaboration, across cultures and media. It also anticipates the acclaimed collaborations that occurred a decade later between the master glassmakers of the Artisti Barovier studio and the avant-garde painters Vittorio Zecchin and Teodoro Wolf-Ferrari, who composed richly colored fused mosaic glass plaques with canes and tesserae patterns echoing design motifs of the Vienna secession.[70] Like Prendergast with his glittering nocturne, these Italian artists utilized the physical properties of these materials for visual effects that paintings could not achieve. Their works, both on canvas and in glass, were declined for exhibition at the Venice Biennale and exhibited instead at the Ca' Pesaro, a forum for Venice's youngest artists and most experimental projects. Through such connections, Murano's glassmakers were active in conversations about avant-garde art of their moment, balancing creative freedom with reverence for the past.

This reputation for both historical fidelity and experimentation continued across the ocean, where thousands of Americans encountered Venetian glass in Chicago at the 1893 World's Columbian Exposition. In addition to Italy's national pavilion, where the firm Dott. Antonio Salviati & C. contributed a display, the Venice and Murano Company (Salviati's chief rival) opened its own building among individual and corporate exhibitors. Operating a furnace with a staff of twenty glassblowers and fifty assistants, this pavilion brought the magic of Murano to the shores of Lake Michigan.[71] Some visitors received trinkets as souvenir gifts, including Luigi Moretti's glass cane slice murrhine depicting Christopher Columbus (CAT. 6-22), a marvel of miniature portraiture less than an inch wide, made through careful construction of an image in glass rods, fused into a tube and then cut into disks.[72] These tokens acknowledged the occasion of the fair—the four hundredth anniversary of Columbus's voyage—while honoring the Italian-born navigator for his ambition and leadership, sometimes in defiance of authority, a history-changing ancestor for both nations. Dazzled reporters lauded the recent achievements of Murano in political terms: "But with the pulsating vigor of the 'New Italy' came a revival of long-neglected arts and industries, among them that of glassmaking. The Venetian workmen of today, in their wonderful coloring and intricacy of design, display the artistic skill which anticipates for their city a return of its former lustre."[73] In their eyes, the furnaces of Murano were also torches leading a city and a nation toward a bright future in which the arts served as a foundation for a just and prosperous society.

Elsewhere at the World's Columbian Exposition, Venice was at the center of a contest between technology and nostalgia within a debate about watercraft. Well in advance of the fair's opening, newspapers announced that twenty Venetian gondolas and sixty pilots would be available to conduct attendees across the

✲ CAT. 6-22
Compagnia di Venezia e Murano (CVM), Glass Cane Slice with Portrait of Christopher Columbus, 1892, mosaic glass, 1/8 × 13/16 in. diam., The Corning Museum of Glass, Gift of Mrs. Giusy Moretti

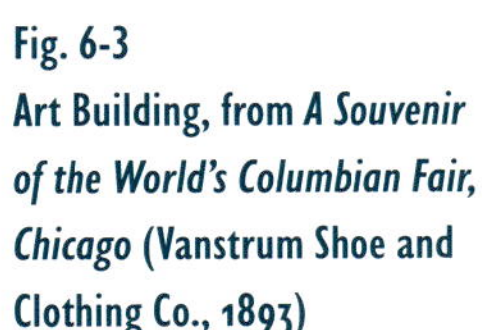

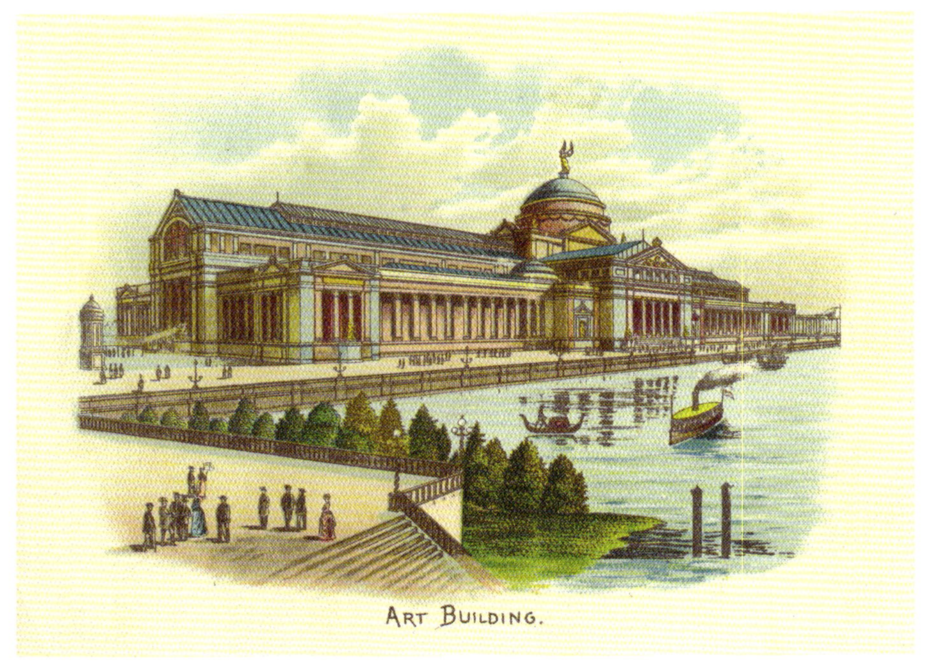

Fig. 6-3
Art Building, from *A Souvenir of the World's Columbian Fair, Chicago* (Vanstrum Shoe and Clothing Co., 1893)

✡ CAT. 6-23
Winslow Homer, *The Fountains at Night, World's Columbian Exposition*, 1893, oil on canvas, 16 3/8 × 25 1/8 in., Bowdoin College Museum of Art, Brunswick, Maine, Bequest of Mrs. Charles Savage Homer Jr.

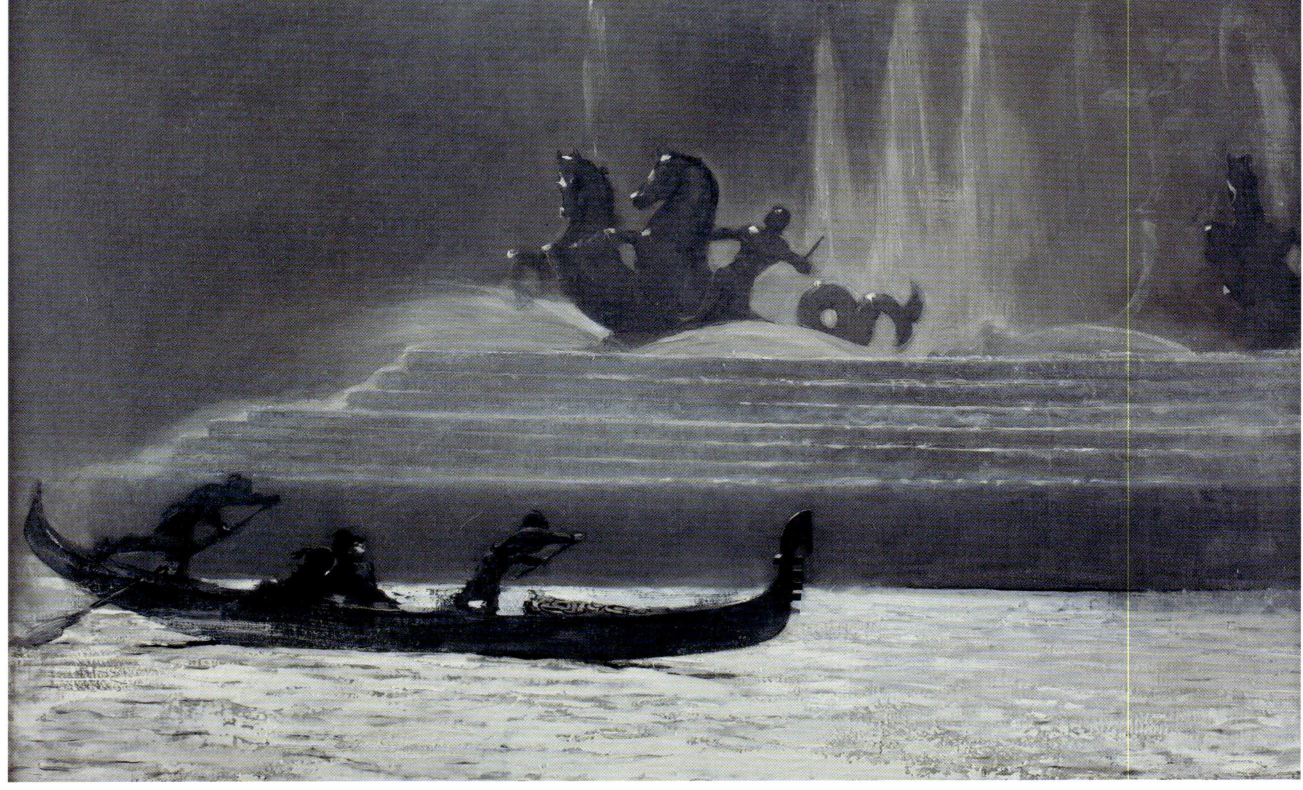

central lagoon and grant a domestic taste of this famous foreign experience.[74] Painter Francis Hopkinson Smith, a master of canal views, reported encountering in Chicago gondoliers he knew from routine sojourns in Italy. "For the instant I am in Venice again," he wrote in *Scribner's Magazine,* fantasizing that the recently constructed classical architecture of the fair was actually centuries old. He continued regarding the gondolas: "No other craft that floats could so perfectly harmonize with these surroundings; none so dainty, so graceful, so dignified."[75] Illustrations in souvenir books show the gondolas as exotic jewels, joining the fair's palatial, white-columned exhibition halls to bring the grand tour to the United States (Fig. 6-3). Though the gondolas presented a picturesque appearance, others preferred the speed and efficiency of motorboat ferries for crossing the fair's artificial lake. The book of photographs, *Picturesque World's Fair,* described the choice:

> *It was a clever suggestion which resulted in bringing from Venice real gondolas and real gondoliers in all their finery, but, oddly enough, it had the effect, probably, of soon making the gondola a thing of the past even in the old European city. The boat was picturesque, but it was slow and clumsy, and the electric launch glided past or around it at will, swifter, noiseless, more graceful, and above all, more comfortable.*[76]

This problem may have inspired Winslow Homer's consideration of the Chicago gondolas in his painting *The Fountains at Night, World's Columbian Exposition* (**CAT. 6-23**). Skimming over the surface of the pond with no trace of a wake, propelled by the strength of two shadowy gondoliers bent forward in exertion, his silhouetted craft suggests grace and speed, like a black dart sweeping across the moonlit pond. Behind are statues of two fish-tailed seahorses, appearing to splash through the fountain in pursuit, but neither these mythological beasts nor any mechanical watercraft here threaten the slender vessel.

Identical rivalries played out in Venice itself, as visitors and artists questioned whether modernization would require the Queen of the Seas to renounce her picturesque past. American consul Franklin R. Grist observed in 1886 that gondolas were becoming an endangered species in their natural habitat due to a lack of work, limited licenses, hotels with private gondola service, and, of course, motorboats. "The march of progress now threatens the peculiar institution, the classic types of Venetian life, the gondola and the gondolier," he reported.[77] Travel writer Anna Fuller noted in 1896 that when gondolas were no longer seaworthy, they were often burned as fuel for the glass factories. "The poor old things must be glad to breathe their dying breath into those exquisite flasks and vases," she speculates poetically.[78] Mitigating the potential wistfulness of seeing a beautiful vessel pass out of service, she suggests it will be reincarnated as an equally prestigious glass vessel. Gondola and boat designs were in fact favorites of the Murano craftsmen, adapted to serve as ornamental salt cellars, condiment dishes, or tureens, depending on size. Oft repeated was a pitcher or nef in the shape of a boat, such as this example from the Museum of the City of New York (**CAT. 6-24**),

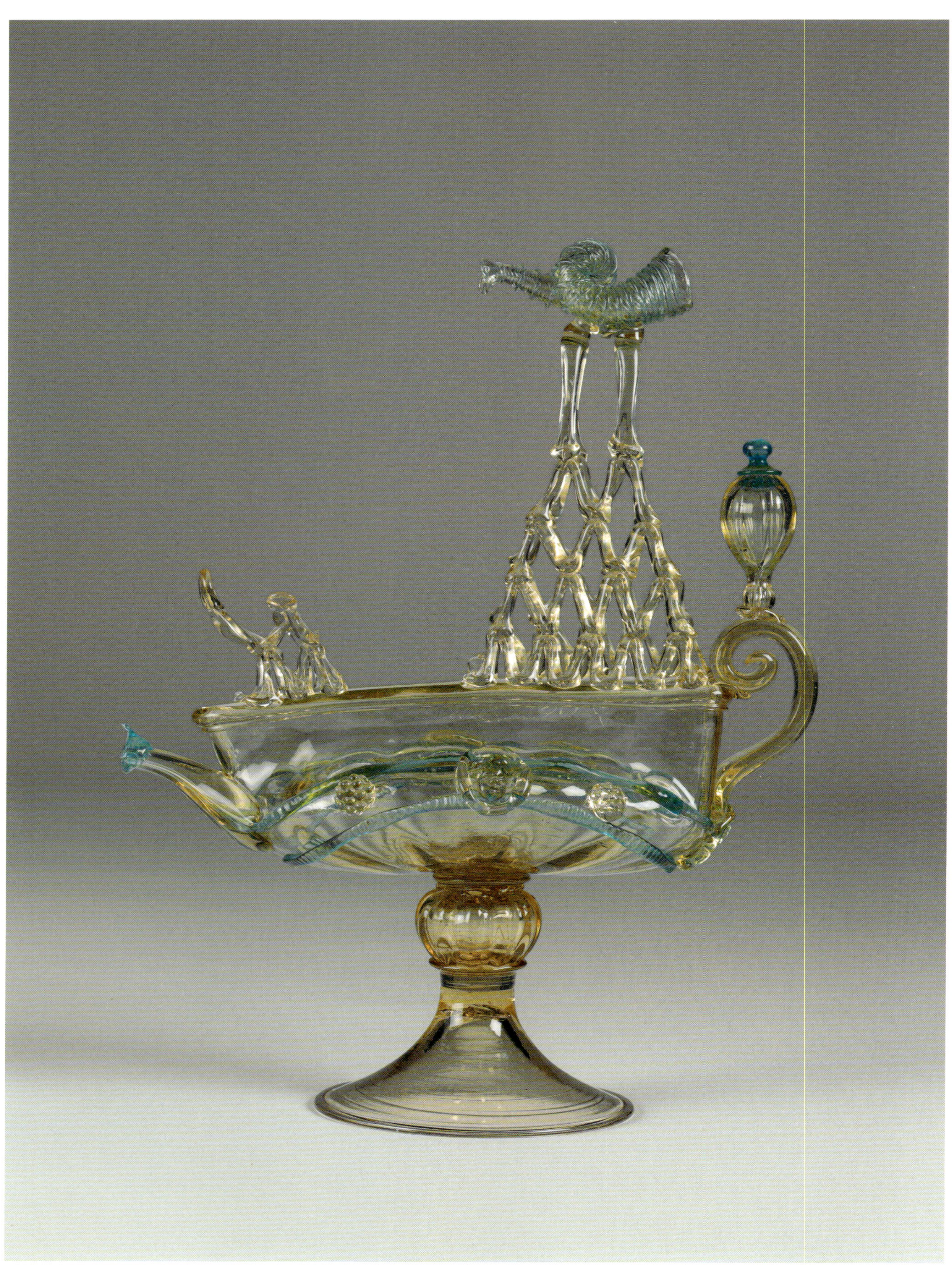

✲ CAT. 6-24
Venice and Murano Glass and Mosaic Company Ltd. (Salviati & Co.) or Fratelli Barovier, Replica of a Sixteenth-Century Nef (Ewer) in the Form of a Boat, ca. 1870s, blown and applied hot-worked glass, 12 ¼ × 9 ¼ × 4 ¼ in., Museum of the City of New York, Gift of Harry Harkness Flagler

✲ CAT. 6-25
Arthur Beecher Carles, *Venetian Gondolas*, ca. 1909, oil on canvas, 25 × 24 ⅛ in., The Estate of Robert and Linda Wueste

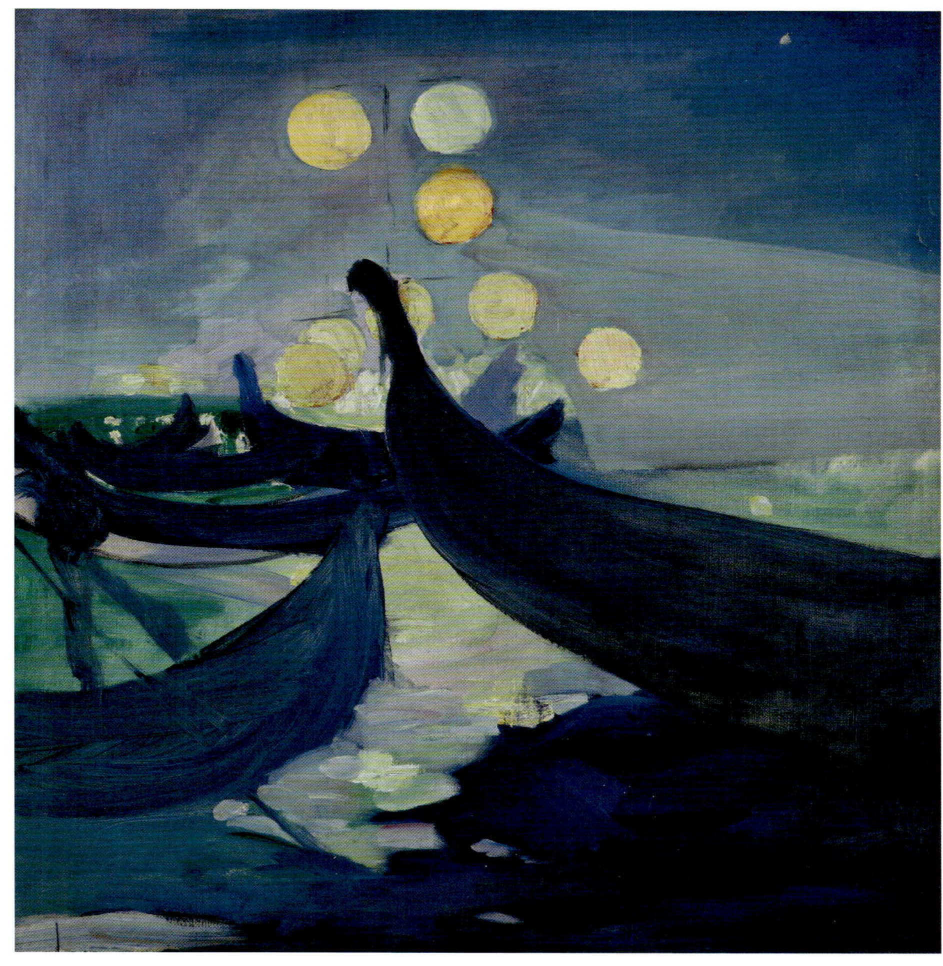

with a net of delicate, flame-worked glass riggings and the prow as its spout. Collectors treasured such creations' virtuoso workmanship, nautical themes, and historical references, revising a Venetian Renaissance-era form (patented in 1521 by female glassmaker Armenia Vivarini).[79] As artworks and tourists' accounts show, gondolas, decorative luxury glassware, and other signature elements of Venice's artistic history were coming to hold more appeal for foreign visitors than Italians. The boats remained popular subjects for American painters into the early 1900s, from Thomas Moran (who purchased and imported an antique gondola) to younger artists like Prendergast and Arthur Beecher Carles.[80] Painted around 1909, *Venetian Gondolas* (CAT. 6-25) is one of several evocations by Carles of lights, shapes, and shadows on the lagoon, presenting a cluster of pointed hulls against a constellation of moonlike lanterns. With radical simplification, he updates the genre of Venetian nocturne painting, challenging conventional artistic styles with an evocative homage to an increasingly obsolete feature of the local scenery.

In the early twentieth century, historic preservation and restoration remained civic priorities in Venice, but industry and technology emerged as new sources of artistic inspiration. As the Biennale gained momentum as a showplace for contemporary art, some Italian artists found their world-famous symbols and traditions restrictive, and they rejected the historicist principles that had fueled much of the glass revival and other branches of late nineteenth-century Venetian art making. On July 8, 1910, the futurists, led by poet Filippo Tommaso Marinetti, dramatically denounced the veneration of earlier artistic styles and all allegiance to the past, strategically choosing Venice as the focal point of their attack. From atop the clock tower, they showered crowds in St. Mark's Square with hundreds of thousands of leaflets printed with their manifesto, "Contro Venezia Passatista" (Against Traditionalist Venice), proclaiming disgust at the city's slavish reverence to history and its pandering to foreign tourists. "Burn the gondolas," they commanded, "and erect up to the sky the rigid geometry of large metallic bridges and manufactories with waving hairs of smoke." Repeating commitments to technology and efficiency, they proposed eliminating the beloved visual charms of the grand tour and its artists: "May the dazzling reign of divine Electrical Light at

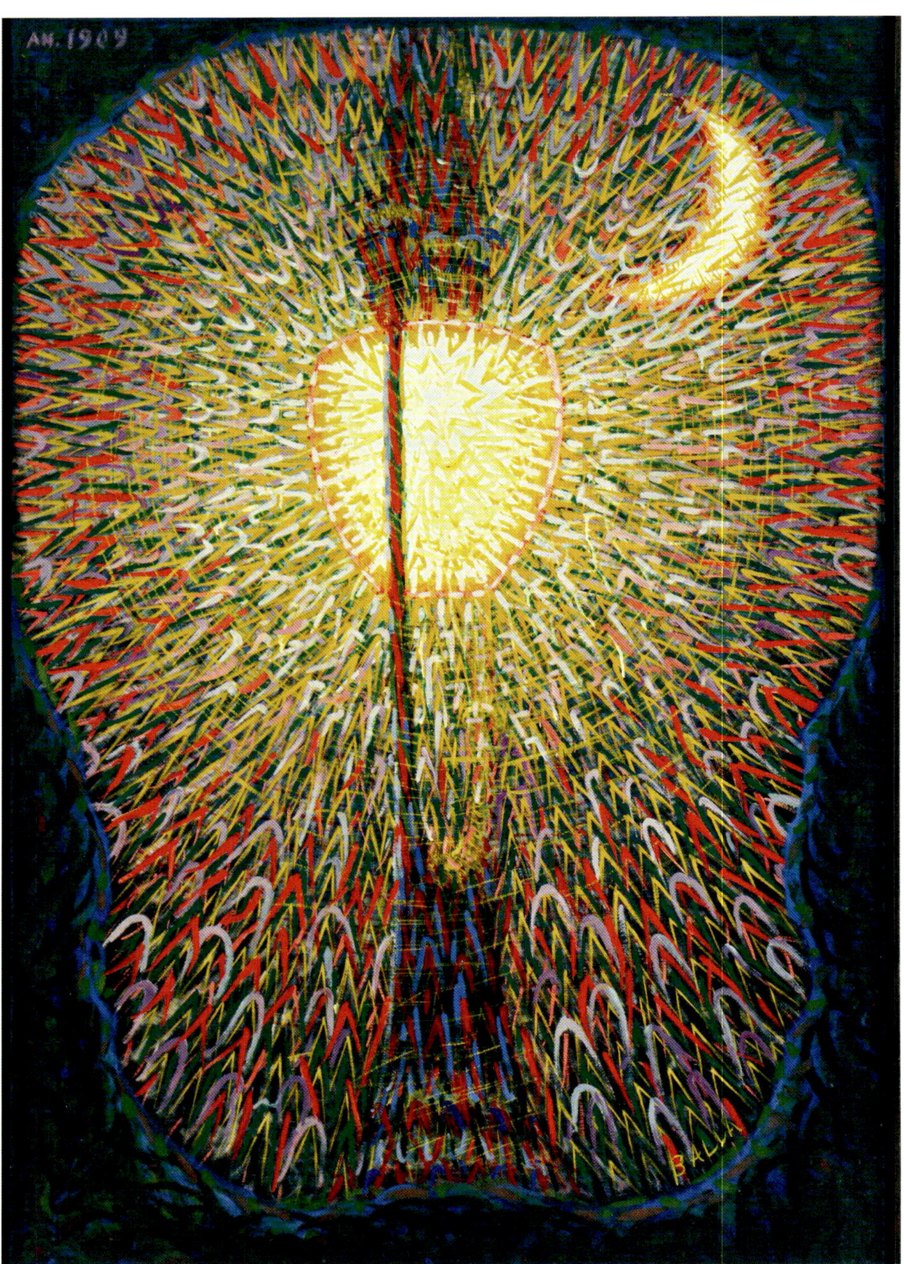

Fig. 6-4
Giacomo Balla, *Street Light*, ca. 1910–11 (dated on painting 1909), oil on canvas, 68 3/4 × 45 1/4 in., Museum of Modern Art, Hillman Periodicals Fund, 7.1954

last free Venice from her venal furnished rooms of moonshine," Marinetti implored.[81] In Venice such praise of artificial light over natural was practically a declaration of war; at the time the islands lagged behind Paris, New York, and numerous other cities in the race for municipal electrification, but many artists, particularly those with expertise in moonlit scenes, expressed concern about this change.[82] The futurists, meanwhile, had already stated their ambitions to "kill the moonlight," a proposition that Giacomo Balla translated into paint with *Street Light* (Fig. 6-4).[83] In this simple yet iconoclastic image, an incandescent arc lamp shoots darts of light across a large, inky canvas, forming a colorful cartouche that partially veils the crescent moon. Whereas Maxfield Parrish's *Venetian Lamplighters* presents electricity as a beautiful scientific blessing in harmony with the past, Balla's image of artificial radiance demands an aggressive and violent change in

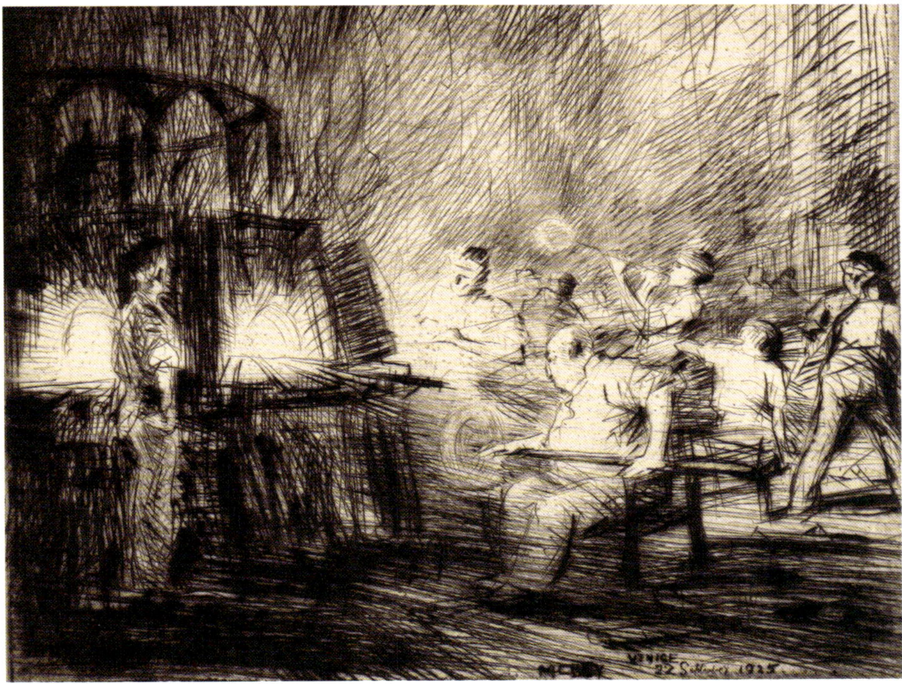

✲ CAT. 6-26
James McBey, *Glass Blowers, Murano*, 1925, printed 1930, drypoint on paper, 5 × 6 in., Gift of Mrs. James McBey, Prints Collection, Miriam and Ira D. Wallach Division of Art, Prints and Photographs, The New York Public Library, Astor, Lenox and Tilden Foundations

which outmoded paradigms must be vanquished. The futurists' inversion of aesthetic hierarchies and hostility toward history—presented through artworks, incendiary rhetoric, and attention-grabbing stunts—earned outrage, derision, or dismissal among many foreign critics. They had support, however, among some Venetian artists, notably Wolf-Ferrari and his Ca' Pesaro circle, who were collaborating with Artisti Barovier on glass projects in these years.[84] In sympathy with their futurist friends, this set of artists helped usher the arts of Venice, both painting and glassmaking, beyond commended historicist playbooks, enriching and diversifying the cultural identity of the city.

The First World War soon disrupted the futurists' aesthetic campaigns, glassmaking activities on Murano, and American tourism to Europe, thereby derailing Venice's growing significance as an international center for the avant-garde. Nonetheless, the pilgrimage to Murano—for both its history and spectacle—continues in 1925 in James McBey's drypoint *Glass Blowers, Murano* (CAT. 6-26).

The factory is active, with a dozen workers exhaling into raised pipes or perched on benches to shape half-molten bubbles. Sharp lines of light and heat shoot from the blazing furnace to pierce their outlined forms, manifesting the power and energy of the fire, much as Balla had done with his street lamp. Movement and speed are also made visible by the seated figure in the foreground (reportedly the maestro Giovanni Seguso, from a long-renowned Murano clan), whose artwork-in-progress dissolves into a spinning circle.[85] By building the scene with frenetic hatching, McBey suggests that his work with needle and plate is a practice of nonstop physical action like that of the glassblowers, who cannot pause until each piece is completed. Despite its expressive and modern style, no visual clues in this picture convey its date; the fundamental tools, steps, and techniques of this medium were the same in McBey's day as a half century earlier, when Whistler, Sargent, and other Americans visited the studios of Murano, and as they were in the High Renaissance, the golden era of Venetian prestige and power, as recalled in guidebooks and in novels like *Marietta*. In depicting this dramatic, mysterious, and timeless craft practice with movement and force, McBey successfully celebrates both the past and the future of Venetian glassmaking with the creative fires burning brightly, as distinguished art traditions evolve and thrive.

CONCLUSION

The elegance, history, politics, and charms of Venice and its glassware—as captured in art, literature, around the Biennale, and at the World's Columbian Exposition—are visually fused in Maxfield Parrish's painting *A Venetian Night's Entertainment* (CAT. 6-27), published in 1903 as the title illustration for Edith Wharton's magazine short story. It depicts the first moments in Venice for the young American traveler Tony Bracknell, who had been beguiled in childhood by his uncle's Venetian prints and a corner cabinet of dazzling *cristallo*.[86] The young man, wearing a tricornered hat and with pale or powdered hair, is a perfect Bostonian type seemingly plucked from a painting by John Singleton Copley or another American master. Seated in a lantern-illuminated loggia, he is surrounded by a swarm of festively attired musicians, revelers, and servers, setting the nocturnal pageantry of St. Mark's Square into motion. The youth reaches out to grasp a slender, clear transparent wineglass as he is seduced into conversation and intrigue by an Italian dandy in a lace collar and cuffs and a plumed hat. In the story's plot, innocent Tony has just arrived in Venice as the first stop on a grand tour and is immediately immersed in the magic and chaos of the Carnevale. The wily Italian is a con man, calling himself Count Rialto, who befriends the youth and engages a team of coconspirators to entrap Tony in a web of romantic intrigue designed to fleece him. Under the influences of wine, music, and the general decadence of Venice, Tony is happy in his ignorance of the scheme, indulging in a fantasy that confirms all of his boyhood dreams of Italian luxuries and adventures. Parrish presents this growing confusion of the senses through a lute player, large lanterns improbably floating amid the sea of heads, and an array of glasses and bottles that sparkle in the moonlight. The delicate cups and their alcoholic contents suggest both refinement and temptation, sophisticated counterparts to the wine flasks in Sargent's Venetian tavern scenes. As in Coleman's *Interior with Lute Player*, the architecture, music, costumes, wine, and glassware in this image invite connoisseurial admiration. However, readers of Wharton's story discover that Venice is a mix of reality and illusion, genuine treasures and copies or fakes. In contrast with the delicate and transparent glass at the center of Parrish's illustration, we find a masked figure in the upper left, a playful or perhaps sinister presence. The American visitor—naive and virtuous—wants to relish this spectacle, but does he have the skills to evaluate age, materials, and workmanship of the artworks around him, as well as the moral character of their makers and purveyors?

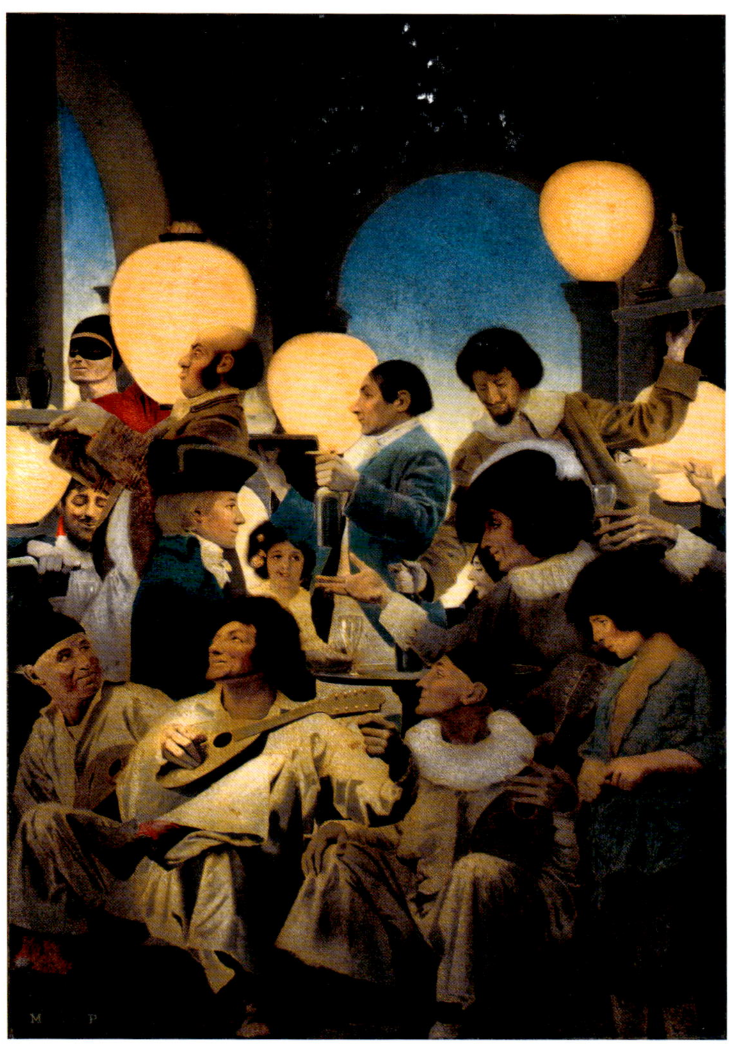

✡ CAT. 6-27
Maxfield Parrish, *A Venetian Night's Entertainment*, 1903, oil on paper on panel, 17 ⅞ × 12 ⅜ in., Lucas Museum of Narrative Art

Such questions continue to confront today's tourists and art collectors traveling to Venice. Before its fashion, food, and fine wine became symbols of cultural prestige in the United States, Italy's history and artistic traditions distinguished it from other nations in the American imagination. "Italy is a land of artists, as we all know: art is in the very air," proclaimed an American ladies' magazine in 1886, as Venice regained its allure in Americans' eyes.[87] In the late nineteenth century, the Venetian glass revival popularized both ancient and modern Venetian glassware around the globe, prompting Murano's exports to become cherished in homes and museums in the United States, alongside paintings and prints celebrating the beauty of Venice's setting, monuments, and people. However, the reception of these extravagant and colorful treasures in America is more than a tale of grand tour souvenir hunting by dilettante antiquarians. The revival occurred within a period of political, economic, and social transition for Italy as a whole, and particularly for Venice, as familiar archetypes of gloom and picturesque decay were replaced by an increasingly developed and cosmopolitan city not strictly beholden to the past. Examining the ongoing but evolving appeal of Italy, critic Leslie A. Fiedler characterizes it as "a distorting mirror," a familiar world that confronts introspective Americans with both a reflection and a caricature.[88] As the United States clarified its identity and ambitions in the wake of the Civil War, the rise and fall of the Republic of Venice and the recent rebirth of glassmaking on Murano provided valuable object lessons. Admiring and collecting glass helped American artists, aesthetes, and museum professionals express a range of domestic social and political priorities and to nurture innovation, creativity, and appreciation for beauty—sparks of American genius—in future generations.

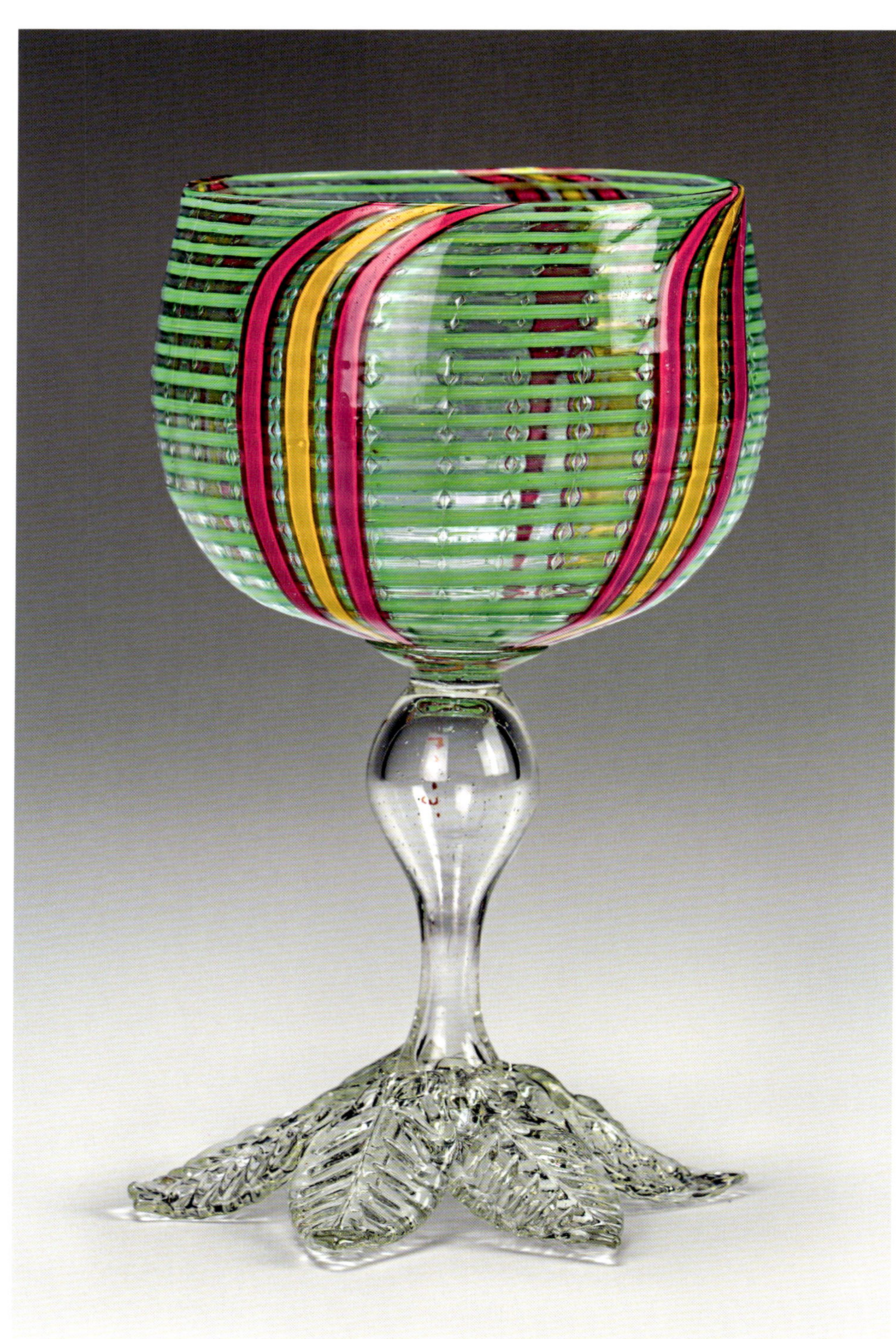

✡ CAT. 6-28
Unidentified, Murano, Goblet with Striped Bowl, ca. 1890s–1910s, blown, enameled, and applied hot-worked glass, 6 × 3 5/8 in. diam., Smithsonian American Art Museum, Gift of John Gellatly

✲ CAT. 6-29
Unidentified, Murano, Fragment of a Footed Bowl with Medici Family Arms, ca. 1513–34, mold-blown, gilded, and enameled glass, 4 ⅜ × 11 ½ in. diam., Smithsonian American Art Museum, Gift of John Gellatly

✲ CAT. 6-30
Unidentified, probably Murano, Byzantine-Style Mosaic Necklace with Christ and Twelve Apostles, ca. 1870s–1910s, gold with glass and shell inlay, 9 ¼ × 16 × ¼ in. (variable), Smithsonian American Art Museum, Gift of John Gellatly

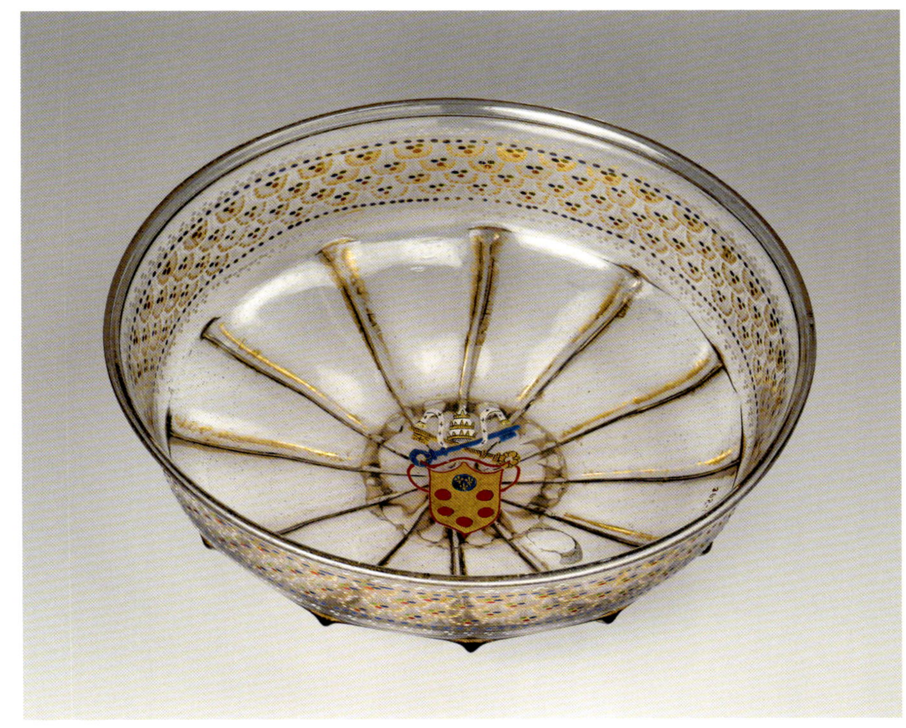

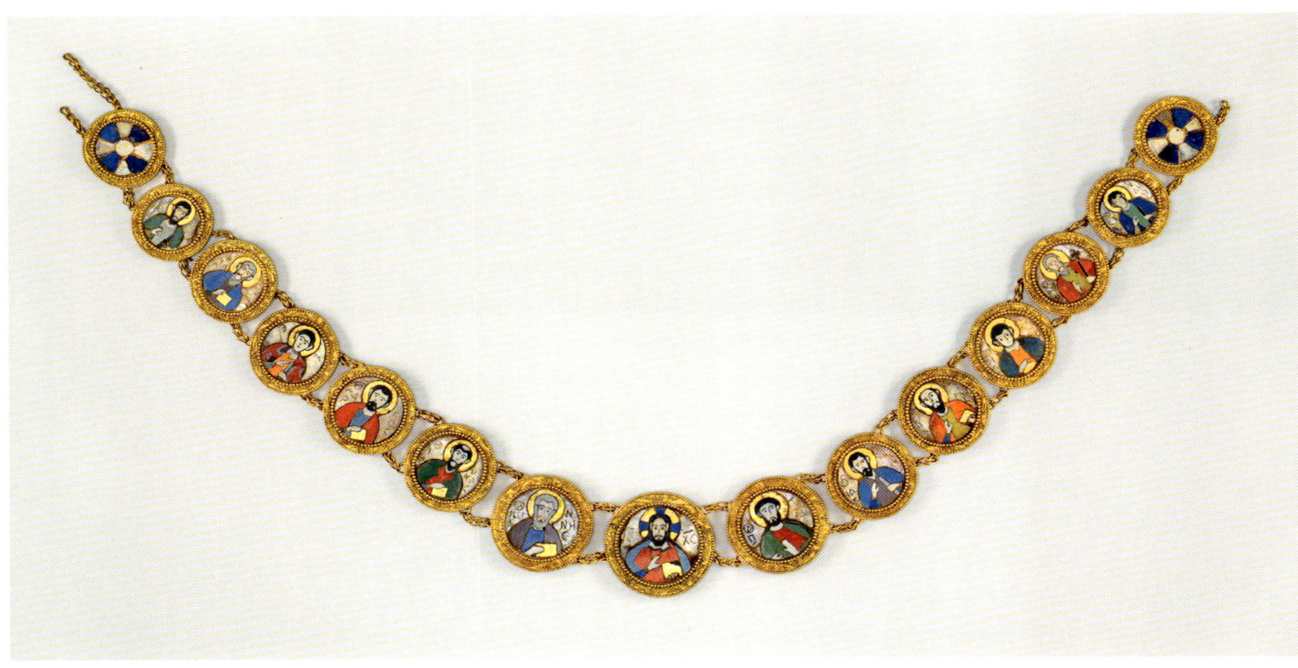

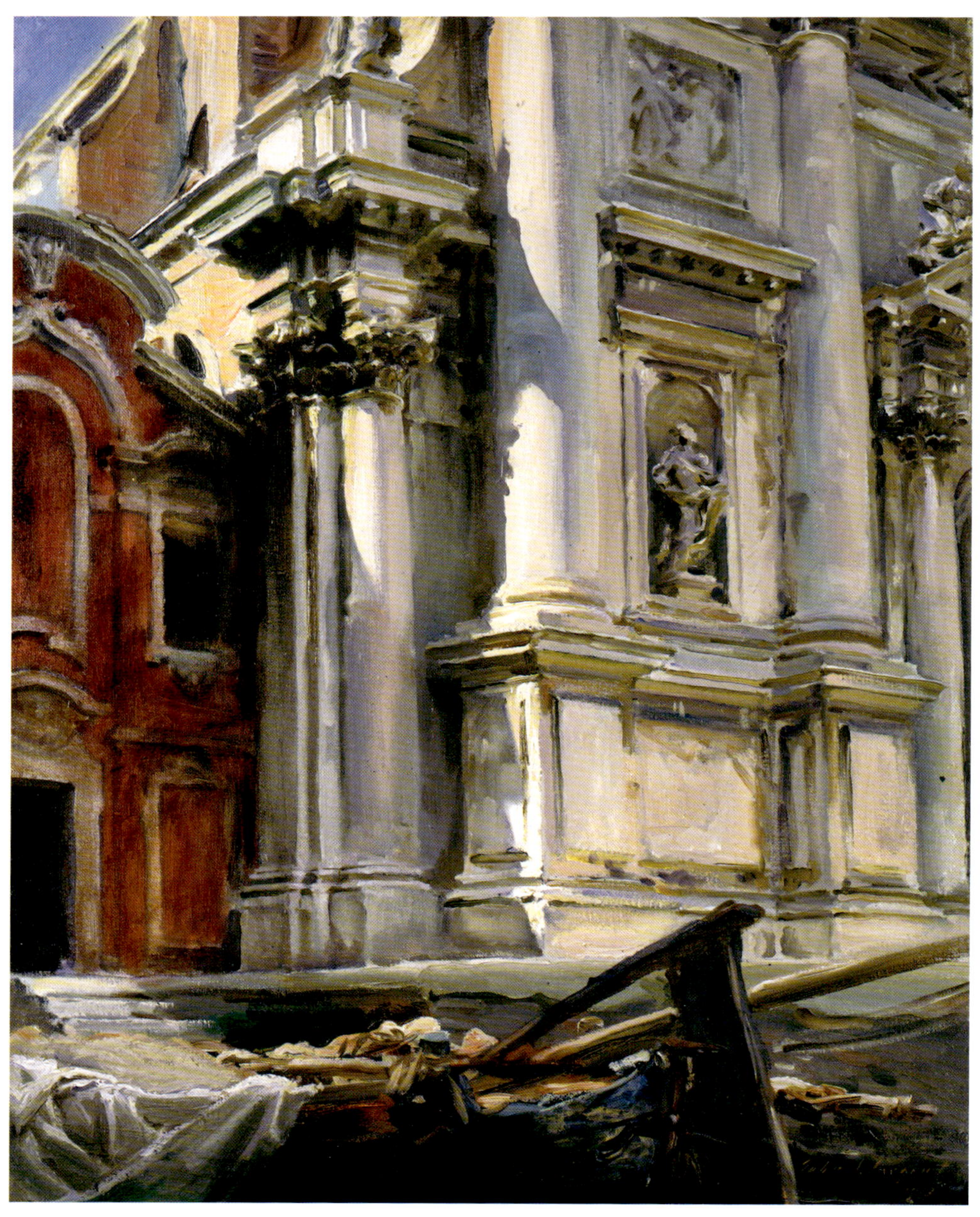

✡ CAT. 6-31
John Singer Sargent,
Corner of the Church of San Stae, 1913,
oil on canvas,
28 ½ × 22 in.,
Private collection

✡ CAT. 6-32
Frank Duveneck,
Bridge of Sighs, Venice,
1885, etching on paper, 12 × 9 ⅝ in.,
Smithsonian American Art Museum,
Museum purchase

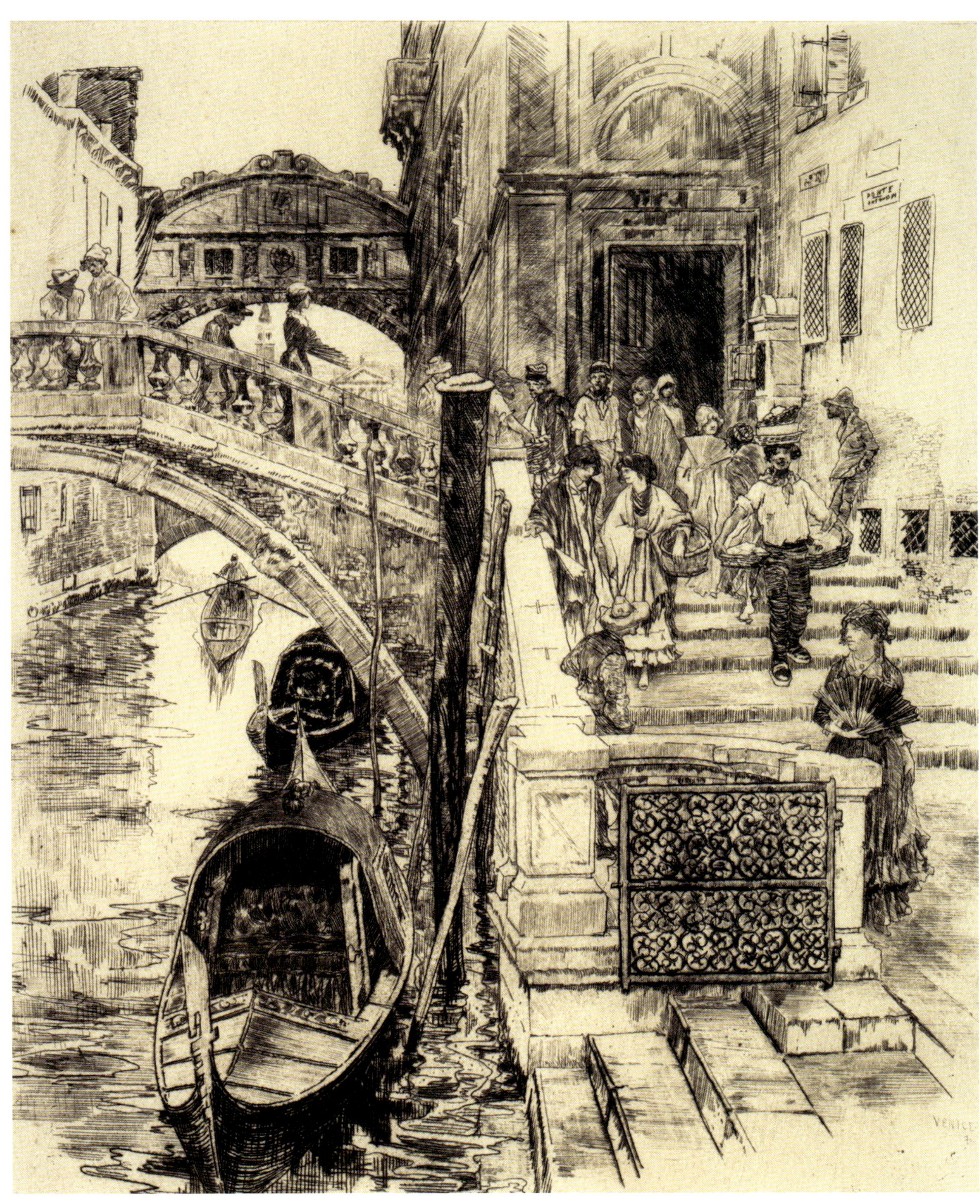
VENICE

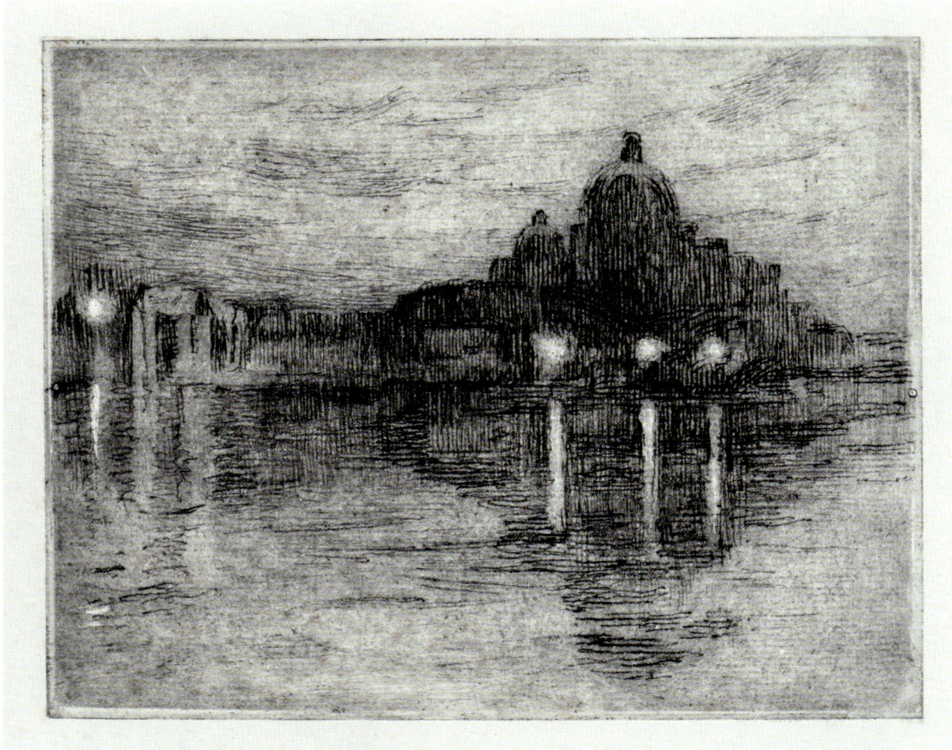

✡ CAT. 6-33
Ellen Day Hale, *First Night in Venice*, 1890, soft-ground etching and aquatint on paper, 6 × 7 ⅜ in., The National Museum of Women in the Arts, Gift of Wallace and Wilhelmina Holladay

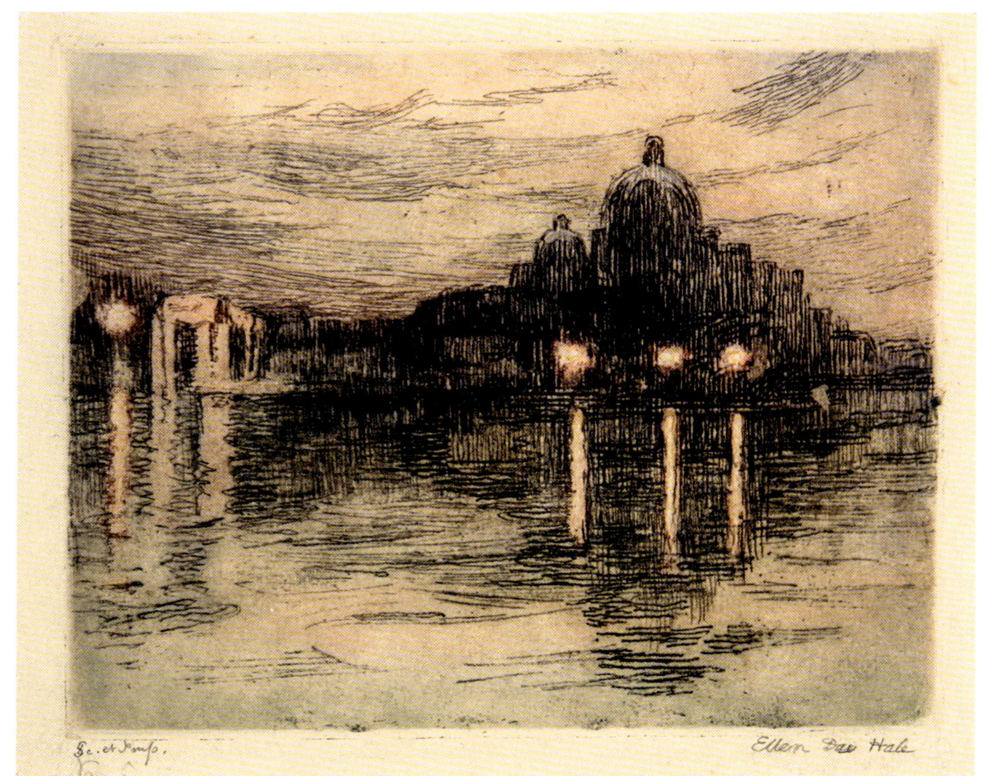

✡ CAT. 6-34
Ellen Day Hale, *First Night in Venice*, 1890, soft-ground etching and aquatint with *à la poupée* color inking on paper, 6 × 7 ⅜ in., The National Museum of Women in the Arts, Gift of Wallace and Wilhelmina Holladay

☼ CAT. 6-35
Andrew Kay Womrath, designer; Yoshijiro Urushibara, printer; *Venice by Day*, ca. 1920s, color woodblock print on paper, 6 ⅜ × 9 ⅞ in., Collection of Darrel C. Karl

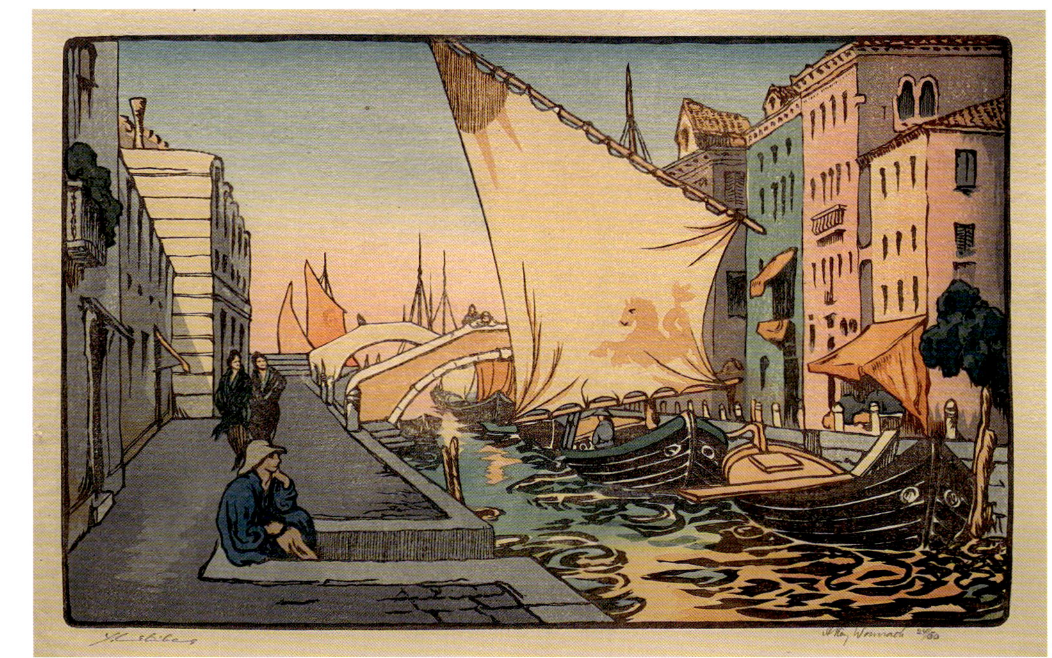

☼ CAT. 6-36
Andrew Kay Womrath, designer; Yoshijiro Urushibara, printer; *Venice by Night*, ca. 1920s, color woodblock print on paper, 6 ⅜ × 9 ⅞ in., Collection of Darrel C. Karl

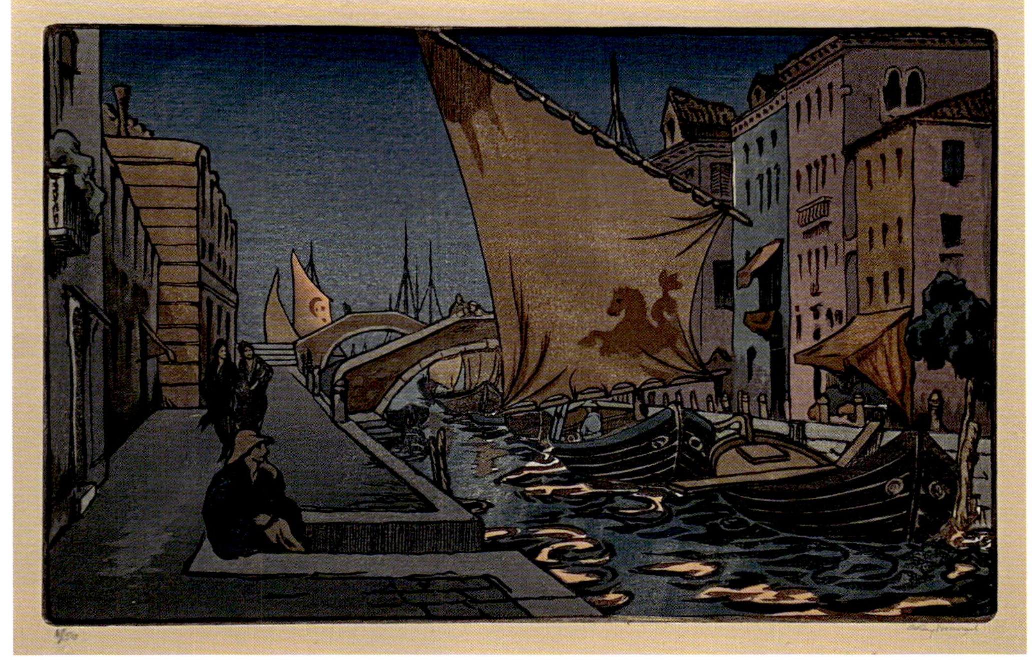

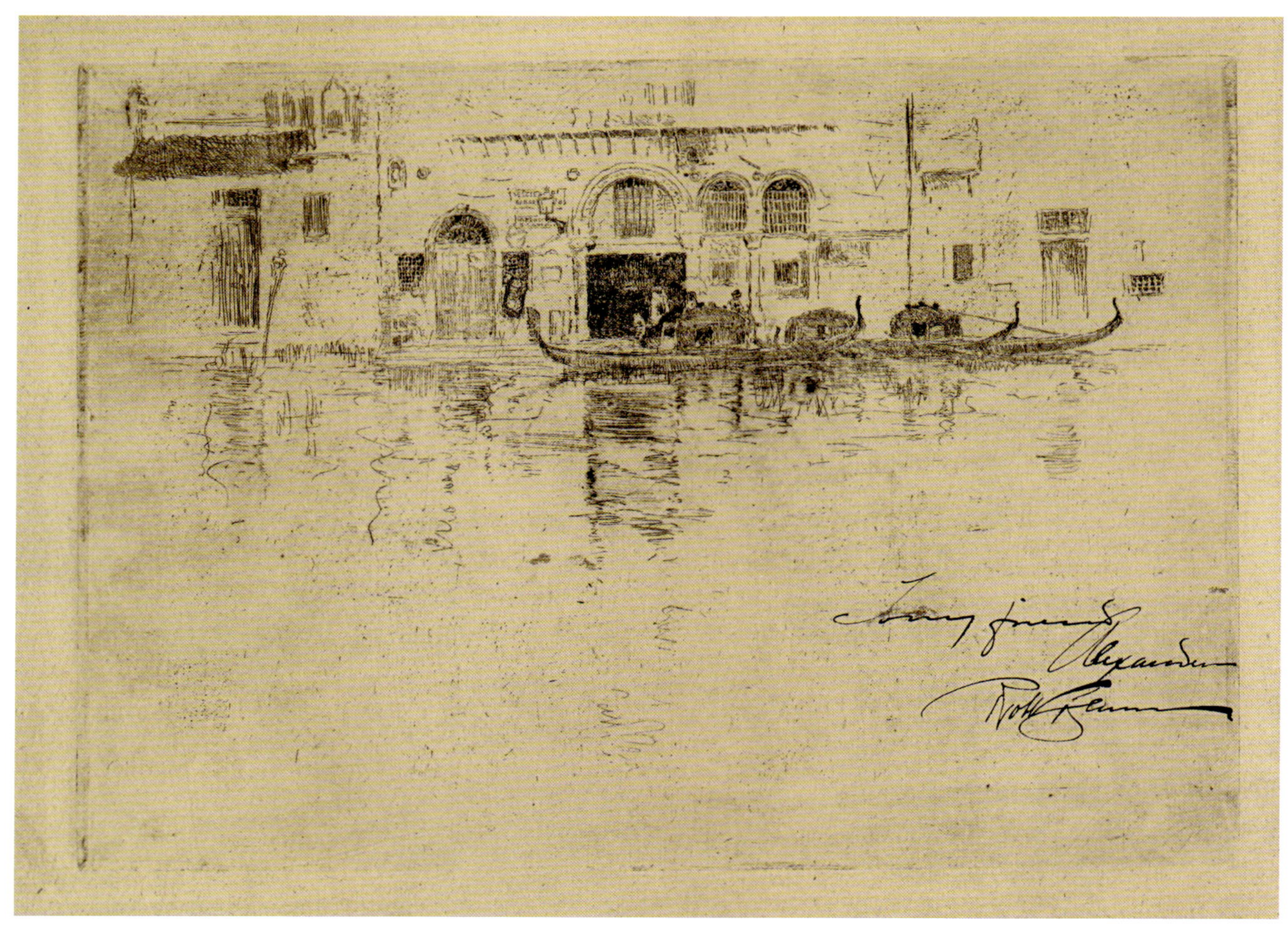

✲ CAT. 6-37

Robert Frederick Blum, *Venetian Doorway and Gondolas*, ca. 1880, etching and drypoint on paper, 5 ¼ × 7 1/16 in., Collection of Mary Anne Goley

NOTES

1 The painting and its description circulated in calendar form and also appeared printed in color in *General Electric Review: A Monthly Magazine for Engineers* 27, no. 1 (January 1924): 2–3.

2 Thomas Pritchard Rossiter to John Frederick Kensett, Venice, 27 August 1843, collection of Thomas B. Brumbaugh; transcribed in Thomas B. Brumbaugh, "A Venice Letter from Thomas P. Rossiter to John F. Kensett—1843," *American Art Journal* 5, no. 1 (May 1973): 76.

3 Henry James, "Venice," *Century Magazine* 25, no. 1 (November 1882): 3. Johann Wolfgang von Goethe had written virtually the same in his diary more than a century prior: "So much has been said and written about Venice already that I do not want to describe it too minutely," he noted on arrival in Venice on September 29, 1786. Goethe, *Italian Journey [1786–1788]*, trans. W. H. Auden and Elizabeth Mayer (London: Penguin, 1970), 77.

4 Moran to fine prints dealer Christian Klackner, quoted in Klackner's pamphlet *"The Gate of Venice" Etched by Thomas Moran, N. A.* (1888), Print Collection of the New York Public Library; cited in Margaretta M. Lovell, *Venice: The American View, 1860–1920* (San Francisco: Fine Arts Museums of San Francisco, 1984), 66.

5 Lovell, *Venice*, 66–67.

6 Royal Cortissoz, "Venice as a Painting-Ground," in *Personalities in Art* (New York: Charles Scribner's Sons, 1925), 118. Stephanie Mayer Heydt's essay in this volume provides further discussion of the innovative character of Whistler's depictions of Venice, pages 144–53.

7 Richard Ormond and Elaine Kilmurray, *John Singer Sargent: Figures and Landscapes, 1874–1882* (New Haven, CT: Yale University Press, 2006), 313–15.

8 William Dean Howells, *Venetian Life* (New York: Hurd & Houghton, 1866), 301–3.

9 See Alice Cooney Frelinghuysen, "Aesthetic Forms in Ceramic and Glass," in *In Pursuit of Beauty: Americans and the Aesthetic Movement*, by Doreen Bolger Burke et al. (New York: Metropolitan Museum of Art, 1986), 236–46.

10 Edith Wharton, "A Venetian Night's Entertainment," *Scribner's Magazine* 34, no. 6 (December 1903): 642.

11 Joseph Dame Weeks, *Report on the Manufacture of Glass* (Washington, DC: Government Printing Office, 1884), 76.

12 "I Viaggiatori Americani," *Voce di Murano*, July 30, 1879, 58.

13 See Doreen Bolger Burke, "Charles Ulrich," in *American Paintings in the Metropolitan Museum of Art* (New York: Metropolitan Museum of Art, 1980), 3:316–18.

14 "Blowing a Wine-Glass," *Manufacturer and Builder* 1, no. 6 (June 1869): 169.

15 Lyman Abbott, "Glass-Blowing as a Fine Art," *Harper's New Monthly Magazine* 42, no. 249 (February 1871): 337.

16 Originally delivered at the Society of Arts in London, Giulio Salviati's lecture was published in various British and American periodicals, including "Venetian Glass," *American Architect and Building News* 26, no. 708 (July 20, 1889): 29.

17 Early critics found the subject unrecognizable: "Vaguely one discerns some oblong things, and some bristly things, of unfamiliar character," wrote a reviewer for the *Daily News* (London), February 20, 1883; quoted in entry for *Murano—Glass Furnace*, in *James McNeill Whistler: The Etchings, A Catalogue Raisonné*, University of Glasgow, accessed January 29, 2021, https://etchings.arts.gla.ac.uk/catalogue/place/display/?catno=K217&rs=1&pid=ItMurano.

18 James Jackson Jarves, "Ancient and Modern Venetian Glass of Murano," *Harper's New Monthly Magazine* 64, no. 380 (January 1882): 187.

19 Madeline Anne Wallace-Dunlop, *Glass in the Old World* (New York: Scribner & Welford, 1882): 147.

20 For further discussion of this group and early patronage at the Metropolitan Museum of Art, see Wendell D. Garrett, "The First Score for American Paintings and Sculpture, 1870–1890," *Metropolitan Museum Journal* 3 (1970): 307–35.

21 Moore was director of the silver division and a chief designer for Tiffany & Co., and his personal collection, bequeathed to the Metropolitan Museum in 1892, included a vast assortment of ancient Mediterranean and East Asian glass, ceramics, and metalwork. See "The Edward C. Moore Collection," *Collector* 3, no. 13 (May 1, 1892): 199–201. See also Medill Higgins Harvey, ed., *Collecting Inspiration: Edward C. Moore at Tiffany & Co.* (New York: Metropolitan Museum of Art, 2021).

22 George William Sheldon, *Recent Ideals of American Art* (New York: D. Appleton, 1888–90), ill. opp. 28.

23 Mary Elizabeth Wilson Sherwood, "Venice," *Galaxy* 14, no. 5 (November 1872): 671.

24 Weeks, *Report on the Manufacture of Glass*, 70.

25 Ibid.

26 See Katharine Reynolds Brown, "21. Gilded and Painted Glass Bowl," in *The Treasury of San Marco, Venice*, ed. David Buckton, Christopher Entwistle, and Margaret Lyttelton (Milan: Olivetti, 1984), 180–83.

27 William Phipps Blake, "Notable Arts and Objects at the Paris Exposition," *Independent* (Boston), October 31, 1878, 3; and "All'Esposizione Mondiale di Saint Louis le Dite Muranesi Toso Francesco-Borella," *Voce di Murano*, February 29, 1904, 12.

28 Constance Cary Harrison, *Woman's Handiwork in Modern Homes* (New York: Charles Scribner's Sons, 1881), 229.

29 Jarves, "Ancient and Modern Venetian Glass of Murano," 186.

30 In conjunction with the 1893 World's Columbian Exposition, Coleman loaned around two thousand pieces for exhibition at the Art Institute of Chicago. See "C. C. Coleman," *Chicago Tribune*, February 21, 1893, 6. In 1895 Coleman sold his glass collection, and after passing through the hands of Thomas E. H. Curtis (1852–1915), much was acquired by Edward Drummond Libbey

(1854–1925) and then donated to the Toledo Museum of Art. Russell Sturgis, "The Coleman Collection of Antique Glass," *Century: A Popular Quarterly* 48, no. 4 (August 1894): 554–58; and Gisela M. A. Richter, "The Curtis Collection of Ancient Glass," *Art in America: An Illustrated Magazine* 2, no. 1 (December 1913): 72–87.

31 See Rosa Barovier, "Roman Glassware in the Museum of Murano and the Muranese Revival of the Nineteenth Century," *Journal of Glass Studies* 16 (1974): 111–19; and Jutta-Annette Page, Lisa Pilosi, and Mark T. Wypyski, "Ancient Mosaic Glass or Modern Reproductions?" *Journal of Glass Studies* 43 (2001): 115–39.

32 See David Park Curry, "The Painting over the Table," *Source Notes in the History of Art* 24, no. 2 (Winter 2005): 60–69; and Adrienne Baxter Bell, "Utopian Pastiche: The Still Life Paintings of Charles Caryl Coleman," in *A Seamless Web: Transatlantic Art in the Nineteenth Century*, ed. Cheryll L. May and Marian Wardle (Newcastle, UK: Cambridge Scholars, 2014), 147–62.

33 "A Roman Studio," *Decorator and Furnisher* 5, no. 3 (December 1884): 86–87. See also Bell, "Utopian Pastiche," 152–55. For discussion of bric-a-brac collections in a wider context, see Christopher P. Monkhouse, "Bric-A-Brac at the Pedestal Fund Art Loan Exhibition," in *In Support of Liberty: European Paintings at the 1883 Pedestal Fund Art Loan Exhibition*, ed. Maureen C. O'Brien (Southampton, NY: Parrish Art Museum, 1986), 87–94.

34 Descriptions of this custom can be found in Jarves, "Ancient and Modern Venetian Glass of Murano," 185; and "Glass and Its History," *Frank Leslie's Popular Monthly* 10, no. 3 (September 1880): 359.

35 "Roman Studio," 86–87.

36 On the popularity of *Othello* with American audiences of the late nineteenth century and its associations with Venice, see Paul H. D. Kaplan, "Contraband Guides: Twain and His Contemporaries on the Black Presence in Venice," *The Massachusetts Review* 44, no. 1/2 (Spring–Summer 2003): 182–202.

37 Palgrave, *Hand-book for Travellers in Northern Italy* (London: John Murray and Son, 1842), 371. See also Harrison, *Women's Handiwork*, 229.

38 Brander Matthews, "Venetian Glass: A Romance of Two Cities," *Aldine* 8, no. 4 (1876): 116, 119–121.

39 Margaretta Markle Lovell, "A Visitable Past: Views of Venice by American Artists, 1860–1915" (PhD diss., Yale University, 1980), 40.

40 "Venice," *North American and United States Gazette*, July 25, 1859, 196.

41 These included American Katharine de Kay Bronson (1834–1901), a patron of the Burano lace revival, and Lady Enid Layard (1843–1912), whose husband, Sir Austen Henry Layard (1817–1894), was a chief advocate for the Murano glass industry and investor in Salviati's glassmaking enterprises. Rosella Mamoli Zorzi reconstructs *tableaux vivants* performed in Venice from period letters in several articles, including "Art in the Museums and Art in the Homes: Tableaux Vivants in Isabella Stewart Gardner's Time," *Annali di Ca' Foscari* 41, no. 1–2 (2002): 63–89; and "Pageants of Nineteenth-Century American Queens," in *Pageants and Processions: Images and Idiom as Spectacle*, ed. Herman du Toit (Newcastle, UK: Cambridge Scholars, 2009), 199–215. See also Alice Cazzola, "Les Tableaux Vivants à Venise au Tournant du XXe Siècle: L'Histoire d'un Passe-Temps Mondain Retracée dans le Journal de Lady Layard," *RACAR: Revue d'art Canadienne / Canadian Art Review* 44, no. 2 (2019): 110–27.

42 Ariana Curtis to Mary Curtis, 27 October 1883, Venice, Palazzo Barbaro, manuscript in the Biblioteca Nazionale Marciana, Venice; quoted in Rosella Mamoli Zorzi, ed., *Henry James: Letters from the Palazzo Barbaro* (London: Pushkin Press, 1998), 172.

43 Mamoli Zorzi, "Art in the Museums," 63–66, 79.

44 "Charles Caryl Coleman," *Magazine of Art* 15, no. 9 (September 1924): 467. See also Adrienne Baxter Bell, "Echoes of the East, Echoes of the Past: Charles Caryl Coleman's *Azaleas and Apple Blossoms*," in *Locating American Art: Finding Art's Meaning in Museums, Colonial Period to the Present*, ed. Cynthia Fowler (Burlington, VT: Ashgate, 2016), 38–39.

45 Though nuanced and critiqued by later scholars, Howard R. Marraro's writings are the essential starting point for considering American knowledge of Italian history and culture and how this may have influenced the domestic politics and foreign relations of the United States in the mid-nineteenth century. See Marraro, "Interpretation of Italy and Italians in Eighteenth Century America," *Italica* 25, no. 1 (March 1948): 59–81; and Marraro, *American Opinion on the Unification of Italy, 1846–1861* (New York: AMS Press, 1969). See also Luca Codignola, "The Civil War: The View from Italy," *Reviews in American History* 3, no. 4 (December 1975): 457–61.

For a survey of earlier reception of antique styles of art, architecture, and furniture in the United States, see Wendy A. Cooper, *Classical Taste in America, 1800–1840* (Baltimore: Baltimore Museum of Art, 1993), especially chapter five, "American Heroes: Classical Style: Public and Domestic Virtue," 236–68. A deeper discussion of these themes, connecting fine art and literature, is William L. Vance, *America's Rome*, vol. 1, *Classical and Contemporary Rome* (New Haven, CT: Yale University Press, 1989).

46 See Joseph Luzzi, *Romantic Europe and the Ghost of Italy* (New Haven, CT: Yale University Press, 2008).

47 C. B. Norton, *Official Catalogue, Foreign Exhibition, Boston, 1883* (Boston: George Coolidge, 1883), 34.

48 Most interpretative commentary on Italian peasant genre painting concentrates on pre-Risorgimento Rome-based artists and southern Italian subjects, but Venetian iterations of these themes multiply in the latter half of the nineteenth century, corresponding to its growing popularity as a destination for tourists and artists. For interpretations of key works for this context, see Olivier Bonfait, ed., *Le Peuple de Rome: Représentations et Imaginaire de Napoléon à l'Unité Italienne* (Montreuil, France: Gourcuff-Gradenigo, 2013); Pierre Gassier, *Léopold Robert* (Neuchâtel: Ides et Calendes, 1983); and John F. McGuigan Jr. and Mary K. McGuigan, *James E. Freeman, 1808–1884: An American Painter in Italy* (Utica, NY: Munson-Williams-Proctor Arts Institute, 2009).

49 On Duveneck's working practices, see Elizabeth A. Simmons, "Discovering Frank Duveneck's Drawings," in *Frank Duveneck: American Master*, ed. Julie Aronson (Cincinnati, OH: Cincinnati Art Museum, 2020), 126–28.

50 Emily J. Mackintosh, "Venetian Glass and Murano," *Peterson's Magazine* 90, no. 3 (September 1886), 216.

51 Sarah Anne Brock Putnam, "Venetian Art Glass," *Decorator and Furnisher* 23, no. 5 (February 1894): 170.

52 See Ernst Kris and Otto Kurz, *Legend, Myth, and Magic in the Image of the Artist: A Historical Experiment* (New Haven, CT: Yale University Press, 1979), 8–60; and Frances Haskell, "The Old Masters in Nineteenth-Century French Painting," *Art Quarterly* 34, no. 1 (1971): 55–85.

53 By the 1870s, some guidebooks even illustrated Canova's tomb. See *A Week in Venice: A Complete Guide-book to the City and its Environs*, 3rd ed. (Venice: Colombo Coen and Son, 1875), 34.

54 The lengthiest elaboration of this tale is Frédéric Kœnig (Just-Jean-Étienne Roy), *Le Lion de Beurre de Canova, ou, Le Premier Chef-d'Œuvre de ce Grand Artiste* (Tours, France: Alfred Mame et Fils, 1867). Some studious historians, such as Edward Everett Hale, acknowledged that this tale might be apocryphal or embellished but nonetheless included it in their biographies of Canova. Hale, ed., *Lights of Two Centuries* (New York: A. S. Barnes, 1887), 39–40.

55 Francis Marion Crawford, *Marietta: A Maid of Venice* (New York: Macmillan, 1901).

56 As a nominal republic for much of its history, Venice served as a unique opportunity for comparison of models of government, prompting self-scrutiny by American readers. See Joy S. Kasson, *Artistic Voyagers: Europe and the American Imagination in the Works of Irving, Allston, Cole, Cooper, and Hawthorne* (Westport, CT: Greenwood Press, 1982), esp. "James Fenimore Cooper: History and Society," 137–64.

57 Howells, *Venetian Life*, 352–59.

58 Francis Marion Crawford, *Salve Venetia: Gleanings from Venetian History* (New York: Macmillan, 1905), 2:2.

59 Regina Soria suggests that Crawford may have personally experienced social inequality in Italian society as a foreigner, despite his birth and long residence in Italy and his linguistic fluency (his father, neoclassical sculptor Thomas Crawford, was an American expatriate). Soria, "Rome in F. Marion Crawford's Novels," *Italica* 33, no. 4 (December 1956): 284–85. See also John Pilkington Jr., "F. Marion Crawford: Italy in Fiction," *American Quarterly* 6, no. 1 (Spring 1954): 59–65; and Van Wyck Brooks, "Marion Crawford," in *The Dream of Arcadia: American Writers and Artists in Italy, 1760–1915* (New York: E. P. Dutton, 1958).

60 "Modern Venetian Glass and Enamel Mosaics," *Cornhill Magazine* 19, no. 112 (April 1869): 466.

61 See Alice Cooney Frelinghuysen, "Louis Comfort Tiffany at the Metropolitan Museum," *Metropolitan Museum of Art Bulletin* 56, no. 1 (Summer 1998): 53–61; Elizabeth L. Kerr Fish, "Edward C. Moore and Tiffany Islamic-Style Silver, c. 1867–1889," *Studies in the Decorative Arts* 6, no. 2 (Spring–Summer 1999): 42–48; and Harvey, ed., *Collecting Inspiration*.

62 Kelly Ann Conway, "Art Glass of Union Glass Company, Somerville, Massachusetts (1893–1927)" (master's thesis, Cooper-Hewitt, National Design Museum and Parsons School of Design, 2005), 31–34.

63 These remain in the collection of the National Museum of American History as examples of artistry, ingenuity, technology, and invention. Julian de Cordova to Richard Rathbun, assistant secretary of the Smithsonian Institution, 2 January 1905, NMAH archives, 43908. The author is grateful to Bonnie Campbell Lilienfeld, assistant director of curatorial affairs and curator of ceramics and glass at the National Museum of American History, for photocopies of de Cordova correspondence from the NMAH files.

64 "Ponte da Venezia a Murano e Campalto," *Voce di Murano*, February 29, 1880, 16.

65 "Current Foreign Topics," *New York Times*, May 3, 1887, 1.

66 "Trans-Atlantic Topics," *Nebraska State Journal*, February 4, 1895, 4.

67 On the presence of glassmaking around the earliest Venice Biennali, see Attilia Dorigato, "Il Vetro Soffiato di Murano alle Esposizioni di Ca' Pesaro," in *Venezia: Gli Anni di Ca' Pesaro, 1908–1920*, ed. Chiara Alessandri, Giandomenico Romanelli, and Flavia Scotton (Milan: Gabriele Mazzotta, 1987), 239–40; and Giovanni Sarpellon, "L'arte, il Vetro, e la Biennale," in *Venezia e la Biennale: I Percorsi del Gusto*, ed. Jean Clair and Giandomenico Romanelli (Milan: Fabbri, 1995): 139–43.

68 In Italy this became known as the "Stile Floreale," given its enthusiasm for flower motifs, or "Stile Liberty" (Liberty Style), in reference to London's Liberty department store, a renowned promoter of this movement. See Rosa Barovier Mentasti and Cristina Tonini, "Venetian Glass between Art Nouveau, Secession and Deco," in *Study Days on Venetian Glass: The Origins of Modern Glass Art in Venice and Europe, about 1900* (Venice: Istituto Veneto di Scienze, Lettere ed Arti, 2017), 33–64.

69 See Marina Barovier, ed., *The Art of the Barovier: Glassmakers in Murano, 1866–1972* (Venice: Arsenale, 1993); and Rosa Barovier Mentasti, "Datazione ed Attribuzione delle Murrine Veneziane, 1910–1925," in *Murrine e Millefiori nel Vetro di Murano dal 1830 al 1930*, ed. Aldo Bova, Rossella Junck, and Puccio Migliaccio (Venice: Galleria Rossella Junck, 1998), 9–14.

70 See Attilia Dorigato, "Il Vetro a Murrine e gli Artisti del '900," in Bova, Junck, and Migliaccio, *Murrine e Millefiori nel Vetro di Murano*, 15–19; and Stefania Portinari, "A Springtime of the Arts, Venice, 1900s," in *Study Days on Venetian Glass*, 1–19.

71 "Murano Art Glass Exhibit," *Chicago Tribune*, April 16, 1893, 2.

72 "Esposizione di Chicago," *Voce di Murano*, February 28, 1893, 10.

73 Roy C. Garver, "Mosaic Works: The Venetian Glass Exhibit at the World's Fair," *Streator* (IL) *Free Press*, April 14, 1893, 7.

74 Stuart Charles Wade, ed., *Rand, McNally & Co.'s Handbook of the World's Columbian Exposition* (Chicago: Rand, McNally, 1893), 166.

75 Francis Hopkinson Smith, "The Picturesque Side," *Scribner's Magazine* 14, no. 5 (November 1893), 602.

76 *Picturesque World's Fair: Fine Art Series* 1, no. 2 (February 17, 1894): 25.

77 Franklin R. Grist, "Venice, Report of Vice-Consul Grist," January 26, 1886, *Index to the Executive Documents of the House of Representatives for the First Session of the Forty-Ninth Congress, 1885–'86* (Washington, DC: Government Printing Office, 1886), 293–94.

78 Anna Fuller, *A Venetian June* (New York and London: G. P. Putnam's Sons, 1896), 220.

79 On Vivarini, see Patricia Fortini Brown, *Private Lives in Renaissance Venice: Art, Architecture, and the Family* (New Haven, CT: Yale University Press, 2004), 147–48; and Cristina Tonini, "A Margine di una Natura Morta di Giuseppe Recco: Proposte di Datazione di Alcuni Soffiati Veneziani," in *Il Vetro in Età Protostorica in Italia: XVI Giornate Nazionali di Studio sul Vetro*, ed. Silvia Ciappi, Annamaria Larese, and Marina Uboldi (Milan: Centro Culturale Mediolanense Studium, 2014), 172.

80 For further account of Moran's gondola, see Erica Hirshler, "Thomas Moran," in *The Lure of Italy: American Artists and the Italian Experience, 1860–1914* (Boston: Museum of Fine Arts, Boston, 1992), 420.

81 Marinetti's provocation received wide press in the United States, with excerpts from the manifesto provided to shock and amuse generally unsympathetic American readers. Quoted here from the translation printed in "Venetian Lagoons A-Boil," *St. Louis Post-Dispatch*, July 16, 1910, 4. For a recent scholarly translation of the full manifesto, see Willard Bohn, *The Other Futurism: Futurist Activity in Venice, Padua, and Verona* (Toronto: University of Toronto Press, 2004), 8–10.

82 Gaslights had been introduced to St. Mark's Square in 1843, and there were reportedly protests at the installation of the first electric streetlamps in the mid-1880s, though the city did not have wide access to electric current until the construction of its first electric power plant on the mainland in 1921. R. J. B. Bosworth, *Italian Venice: A History* (New Haven, CT: Yale University Press, 2014), 10. On further connections between art and electrification, see See Hollis Clayson, "La Ville Lumière and Its Lights," in *Electric Paris*, by Margarita Karasoulas and Hollis Clayson (Greenwich, CT: Bruce Museum, 2017), 16; and Wolfgang Schivelbusch, "A Flood of Light," in *Disenchanted Night: The Industrialization of Light in the Nineteenth Century*, trans. Angela Davies (Berkeley: University of California Press, 1995), 114–27.

83 Marinetti published the manifesto "Tuons le Claire de Lune!" first in French in 1909, then in Italian ("Uccidiamo il Chiaro di Luna!") in 1911.

84 Bohn, *Other Futurism*, 10, 17.

85 Giovanni Seguso (1853–1931). Martin Hardie and Charles Carter, *The Etchings and Dry Points from 1924 by James McBey (1883–1959)* (Aberdeen, UK: Aberdeen Art Gallery, 1962), cat. no. 243.

86 Wharton, "Venetian Night's Entertainment," 641–51.

87 Mackintosh, "Venetian Glass and Murano," 216.

88 Leslie A. Fiedler, "Italian Pilgrimage: The Discovery of America," in *An End to Innocence: Essays on Culture and Politics* (Boston: Beacon Press, 1955), 93.

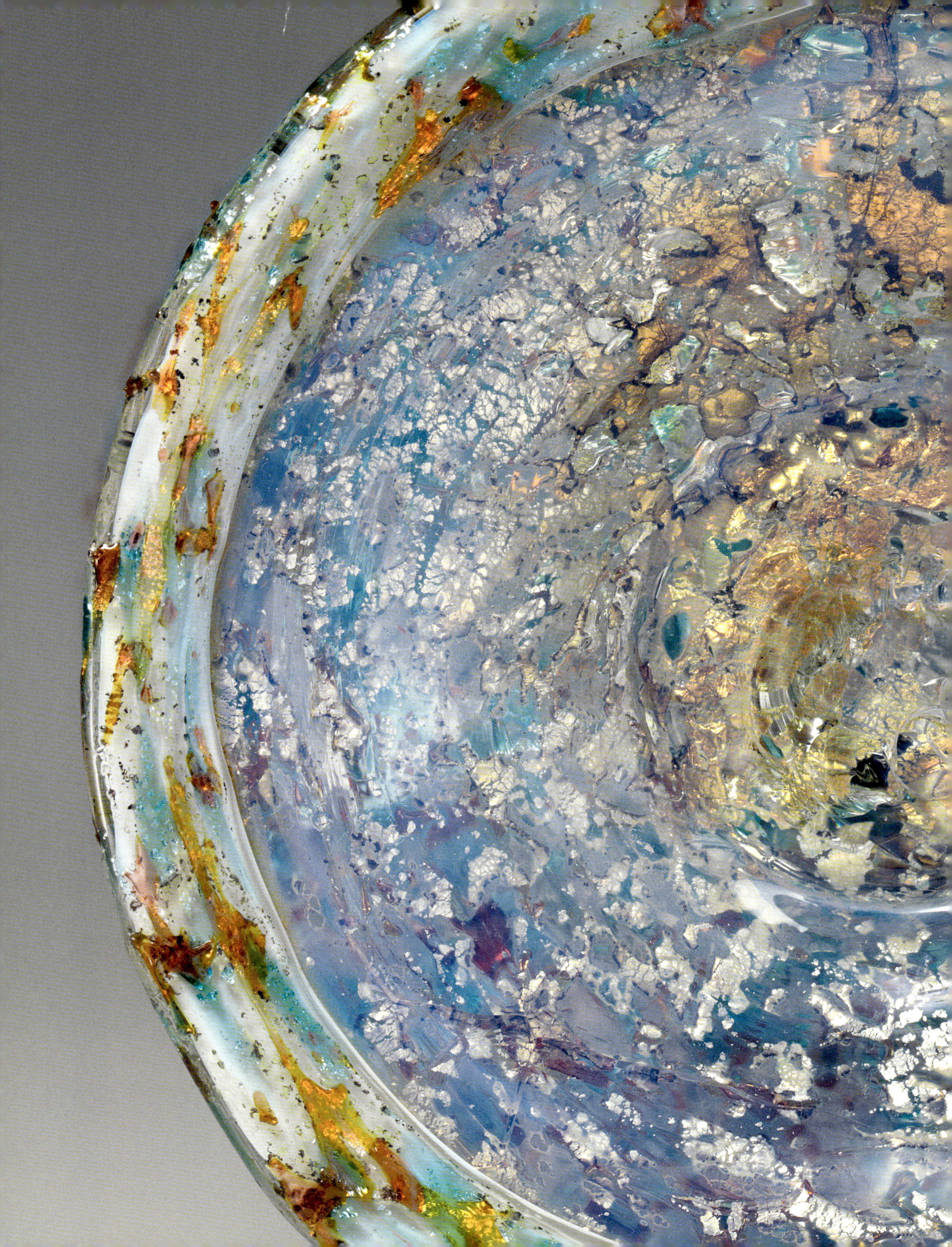

Biographies

BRITTANY EMENS STRUPP
CRAWFORD ALEXANDER MANN III.

These brief biographies of artists, critics, and collectors provide additional information and anecdotes about the exhibition's protagonists. They include the creators and past owners of many objects illustrated in this book, some famous and others less well-known. This is not a comprehensive list of the many figures who contributed to the popularity of Venice and of Murano glass in the United States in the late nineteenth century, but it can serve as a basis for further research. A selected bibliography is provided for each individual, and CAPITALIZED NAMES *within each biography indicate those who have a separate entry.*

HENRY ALEXANDER

b. San Francisco, CA, 1860; *d.* New York City, 1894

✡ ARTIST

Henry Alexander's family emigrated from eastern Europe to the young state of California. He began taking classes at the California School of Design when he was about thirteen years old; then in 1877, at age seventeen, he traveled to Germany to study at the Royal Academy of Fine Arts in Munich. There he quickly mastered the precise academic style and muted tones characteristic of the Munich school, which he subsequently applied in a series of highly detailed and tightly rendered interior genre scenes and still lifes. While abroad, Alexander visited Paris with artist CHARLES FREDERIC ULRICH and allegedly saw Venice as well.

Upon his return to the United States in 1883, Alexander worked as a professional painter, based first in San Francisco and later in New York City, where he became recognized for depictions of individuals within elaborate interiors. Collectors in New York, San Francisco, Boston, Chicago, and Philadelphia sought Alexander's work. He exhibited with some regularity as

Venice and Murano Glass and Mosaic Company Ltd. (Salviati & Co.), Opalescent Glass Vase with Multicolor Granzioli (detail), ca. 1868–80; **see p. 170**

early as 1879 in Munich, followed by critically praised showings at the National Academy of Design in 1892, where he submitted a painting of ancient Roman glass; the 1893 World's Columbian Exposition in Chicago; and the California State Fair in 1894, where he won a gold medal. Despite these honors, his success was fleeting and the artist took his own life in 1894.

Compounding the tragedy, Alexander's legacy was nearly lost in the devastating fire that followed the 1906 San Francisco earthquake. His family, intending to stage a posthumous retrospective for the artist later that year, had amassed a large collection of his work in a warehouse that was completely destroyed. What little information survives has been pieced together through accounts from his friends and contemporaries like Ulrich and WILLIAM MERRITT CHASE, obituaries, and about thirty surviving paintings.

References

Burke, Doreen Bolger. "Henry Alexander, 1860–1894." In *American Paintings in the Metropolitan Museum of Art*, edited by Kathleen Luhrs, 370–72. Vol. 3, *A Catalogue of Works by Artists Born between 1846 and 1864*. New York: Metropolitan Museum of Art, 1980.

Gordon, Lois K. Typescript of "Henry Alexander: San Francisco's First Native-Born Artist." 1978. Archives of American Art, Smithsonian Institution.

Karlstrom, Paul J. "The Short, Hard, and Tragic Life of Henry Alexander." *Smithsonian* 12 (March 1982): 108–17.

"Misfortune Leads to Death." *San Francisco Examiner*, May 16, 1894.

"Suicide of an Artist: End of Henry Alexander at New York." *San Francisco Chronicle*, May 16, 1894.

Wilson, Raymond L. "Henry Alexander: Chronicler of Commerce." *Archives of American Art Journal* 20, no. 2 (1980): 10–13.

WILLIAM AMES

b. Providence, RI, 1842; *d.* Providence, RI, 1914

✡ COLLECTOR

Brevet Brigadier General William Ames distinguished himself as a commander for the Union army during the American Civil War and became a prominent public figure in his native Rhode Island. His father Samuel Ames (1806–1865), a state supreme court chief justice, encouraged Ames to attend Brown University. He was enrolled from 1858 to 1861 but left before graduating to join the Second Regiment, Rhode Island Volunteer Infantry. He fought first at Bull Run, then Yorktown, Williamsburg, Fort Sumter, and Fort Pulaski, among others. For his service, Ames was honored by the state of Rhode Island and the nation with the highest testimonials and the rank of brevet brigadier general of volunteers.

As a civilian, Ames worked in the banking and insurance industries and in various capacities for the state for nearly twenty-five years. He is perhaps best known for his leadership on the committee organizing the design and construction of the Rhode Island State House, a grand Beaux-Arts building designed by the firm McKim, Mead & White and completed in 1904. He stayed on the commission and supervised the arrangement and installation of artworks that decorated the building's interior as well.

Ames supported many institutions across the state, including the Rhode Island Hospital and the Rhode Island School of Design Museum, where he regularly participated as a member of various committees. At some point in time, Ames acquired an extensive collection of nineteenth-century Venetian glass containing nearly every principal type and form available. After his death, his children Harriette Fletcher (Mrs. Frank L. Mauran, 1875–1952) and John O. Ames (1872–1936) donated Ames's collection to the museum. Their gift, which included approximately two hundred pieces of Venetian glass, was likely determined by their father's engagement with the institution and offered a valuable complement to the museum's strong collection of English lead glass.

References

Bicknell, Thomas Williams. "General William Ames." In *The History of the State of Rhode Island and Providence Plantations*, 4:246–49. New York: American Historical Society, 1920.

"Brunonians Far and Near: General William Ames." *Brown Alumni Monthly* 14, no. 9 (April 1914): 249.

Rowe, Louis Earle. "The Ames Collection of Venetian Glass." *Bulletin of the Rhode Island School of Design* 2, no. 4 (October 1914): 30–32.

Samuel Putnam Avery

b. New York City, 1822; *d.* New York City, 1904

✡ COLLECTOR

Following early success as a printmaker and illustrator, Samuel Avery changed careers to become a leading art dealer, a respected collector, and ultimately a transformative philanthropist for the cultural life of New York City. The death of his father in a cholera epidemic led Avery at age ten to train in copper engraving and work for the American Bank Note Company. By the 1840s he had mastered wood engraving and was producing commercial illustrations for newspapers, books, and magazines, including *Harper's Monthly* and *The Crayon*, one of America's earliest journals dedicated to contemporary fine art. He began to attend auctions and make modest personal art purchases, leading to friendships with artists and with wealthy collectors, to whom he offered advice.

In the 1860s Avery developed a partnership with Baltimore collector William T. Walters (1820–1894) for importing and reselling fine paintings from Europe, often with transactions arranged by their mutual friend, Paris-based connoisseur **GEORGE A. LUCAS**. Avery opened his first showroom in 1864, and between 1871 and 1882 he made annual trips to Europe to buy and commission work from leading contemporary artists in France, Germany, and the Low Countries. In 1885 he retired, and the business passed to his son Samuel P. Avery Jr. (1847–1920). Through clients like Walters, William H. Vanderbilt (1821–1885), and John Taylor Johnston (1820–1893), Avery built some of the most esteemed art collections in the United States in the late nineteenth century, many of which were later donated to civic museums.

As Avery's reputation for connoisseurship grew, he occupied many arts leadership roles. In 1867 he served as commissioner for the American Art Department at the Exposition Universelle in Paris, selecting works of art to represent the United States at this prestigious international forum. This may have been his introduction to the work of **JAMES MCNEILL WHISTLER**, who lobbied for his work's inclusion through Avery's friend Lucas. Soon after, at the instigation of his much wealthier collector friends, Avery became a founding board member of the Metropolitan Museum of Art. He also served as a trustee of the New York Public Library, on the boards of the Grolier Club and Union League Club, and on the commission overseeing the construction of the Statue of Liberty in New York Harbor. These and other advisory roles earned him a reputation for philanthropy that was modest in monetary terms but vast in expertise.

Avery's personal collecting also earned respect, though his spending power was significantly less than that of his elite clients. Based on his knowledge of printmaking, he assembled a deep collection of nineteenth-century etchings and lithographs, including many rare impressions and early states. Most were by French artists, but he also purchased prints by Americans like Mary Cassatt (1844–1926) and Whistler. In 1900 he donated the collection—17,775 works by 978 artists—to found the prints department at the New York Public Library. This followed his large gift in 1890 of art and architectural treatises to Columbia University in memory of his prematurely deceased son Henry (1852–1890), a distinguished young architect. Avery also received acclaim for his own collections of bronzes, medals, East Asian porcelain, and rare book bindings. —CAM

References

Beaufort, Madeleine F., Herbert L. Kleinfield, and Jeanne K. Welcher, eds. *The Diaries, 1871–1882, of Samuel P. Avery, Art Dealer.* New York: Arno Press, 1979.

Goodman, Ted, and Angela Giral. "Samuel Putnam Avery and the Founding of the Avery Library, Columbia University." *Art Documentation: Journal of the Art Libraries Society of North America* 16, no. 2 (Fall 1997): 6–8.

Sturgis, Russell. "Samuel Putnam Avery." *Columbia University Quarterly* 6 (December 1904): 14–23.

Wood, Louisa Ruby. "Samuel Putnam Avery as a Collector of Drawings: A Complete Checklist from the New York Public Library's Print Collection." *Biblion: The Bulletin of the New York Public Library* 9, nos. 1/2 (2001): 104–47.

Otto Henry Bacher

b. Cleveland, OH, 1856; *d.* Bronxville, NY, 1909

☆ARTIST

Otto Henry Bacher spent a decade in Europe studying and building friendships with other prolific American artists, including **JAMES MCNEILL WHISTLER** and fellow Ohioan **FRANK DUVENECK**. Bacher set off in 1878 to study at the Royal Academy of Fine Arts in Munich, before meeting Duveneck and joining the colony of American painters he had established nearby in Polling, Bavaria. From 1880 to 1882, Bacher accompanied this group of students—the "Duveneck Boys," as they came to be known—to Italy, where they spent winters in Florence and summers in Venice.

Bacher resided at the Casa Jankowitz on the Riva degli Schiavoni with Duveneck and his students, where they all shared studio space and occasionally collaborated. Whistler, who was on his first and only trip to Venice during this time, stayed here as well. Bacher and Whistler formed a friendship—as the younger and less experienced artist, Bacher welcomed critiques from Whistler, who, in turn, described Bacher as "one of his favourite pupils." Bacher was already a proficient etcher and owned a collection of old master etchings and an etching press, which Whistler used to print part of his "Venice Sets." Prints produced in Bacher's style were referred to among the Whistler and Duveneck circles as "Bachertypes."

In London in 1881, Bacher exhibited seventeen etchings, many of Venice, with the Society of Painter-Etchers and Engravers. That same year, Bacher exhibited a set of his Venetian etchings at the Society of American Artists in New York City. Then, as Whistler did with his "First Venice Set," Bacher printed his own series of twelve Venetian etchings in a bound, limited edition portfolio in 1882. He received favorable reviews of these prints, and Venice remained a significant subject of his painted and graphic work throughout the 1880s.

In 1886 Bacher returned to Venice and lived at the Palazzo Contarini degli Scrigni on the Grand Canal with artists **ROBERT FREDERICK BLUM** and **CHARLES FREDERIC ULRICH**, where all three captured scenes of lacemakers at work. Bacher spent the remainder of his career in the United States after 1887. He wrote an autobiographical account of his first Venetian sojourn titled *With Whistler in Venice* (1908), offering a colorful sketch of his activities there with Whistler, Duveneck, and their circles.

References

Andrew, William W. *Otto H. Bacher*. Madison, WI: Education Industries, 1981.

Bacher, Otto H. *With Whistler in Venice*. New York: Century, 1908.

Otto Bacher papers, 1873–1938. Archives of American Art, Smithsonian Institution.

Alice Pike Barney

b. Cincinnati, OH, 1857; *d.* Los Angeles, CA, 1931

☆ARTIST, PATRON

Patron of the arts and civic leader Alice Pike Barney was also an accomplished portraitist. Her interest in the arts began when she accompanied her father Samuel Napthali Pike (1822–1872), a successful distiller of whiskey and Cincinnati arts patron, on cultural outings as a child. After her father's death, Barney traveled through Italy and other parts of Europe with her mother, Ursula Muellion "Ellen" Miller Pike (1822–1908). These travels fueled Barney's love of art and encouraged her to start her collection, which began with a few paintings and two marble busts of herself and her father.

Barney first enrolled in art classes in Cincinnati under the tutelage of Elizabeth Nourse (1859–1938), then matured into a painter of expressive portraits while living in Europe from 1886 to 1888. She attended women's classes at the Académie Julian in Paris in 1888 before joining the atelier of Charles Auguste Émile Durand (1837–1917), a French artist and teacher known as Carolus-Duran. With his encouragement, she submitted to the Paris Salon her first major painting, which was accepted in 1889.

Barney's plans to continue her studies in France ended abruptly when her husband, Albert Clifford Barney (1848–1902), relocated their family to Washington, DC, in late 1888. She continued painting and earned a reputation in Washington as "an artist, not a dilettante...[who] strives to do something worth while." Barney returned to Paris briefly in 1896, resuming her studies with Carolus-Duran. Her portrait of her daughter Natalie Clifford Barney (1876–1972) was accepted to the Salon that year and was illustrated in its prestigious *Catalogue Illustré*. She traveled back to the United States the following year.

In 1898 Barney received a letter from her friend John White Alexander (1856–1915) urging her to study with JAMES MCNEILL WHISTLER in Paris at the Académie Carmen. She followed Alexander's advice, but, like many of her peers, she became discouraged by Whistler's general absenteeism. When he finally materialized in class, he advised her not to be "too clever" in her painting. Barney and Whistler quickly formed a friendship, meeting often to discuss art and critique Barney's work. Her portrait of Whistler done the year of their meeting is left intentionally unfinished at Whistler's request (see p. 173).

Back in the United States, Barney described life in Washington as: "Small talk and lots to eat, an infinite series of teas and dinners. Art? There is none!" Hoping to transform the arts scene, Barney established a salon in 1901 to gather artists, collectors, and intellectuals. In 1903 she built Studio House, modeled after ISABELLA STEWART GARDNER's museum-residence, where Barney lived above a series of galleries, reception rooms, and studio space dedicated to the Washington arts community. A testament to the preeminent artistic influence in her life, Studio House boasted a Whistler-inspired room hand-stenciled after his Peacock Room (1876–77). Ultimately, Barney became one of the foremost cultural leaders of Washington, and her impact has been compared to that of Duncan Phillips (1886–1966) and William Wilson Corcoran (1798–1888). Her grave marker in Dayton, Ohio, states simply: "The Talented One."

References

"Can It Be Washington Has No Artistic Instinct!" *Washington Times*, February 2, 1902.

Kling, Jean L. "Alice Pike Barney: Bringing Culture to the Capital." *Washington History* 2, no. 1 (Spring 1990): 68–89.

——. *Alice Pike Barney: Her Life and Art*. Washington, DC: National Museum of American Art in association with Smithsonian Institution Press, 1994.

Rodriguez, Suzanne. *Wild Heart: A Life; Natalie Clifford Barney and the Decadence of Literary Paris*. New York: HarperCollins, 2002.

ROBERT FREDERICK BLUM

b. Cincinnati, OH, 1857; *d.* New York City, 1903

✫ ARTIST

Among his extensive travels, Robert Frederick Blum spent considerable time learning from and working with fellow American artists in Venice. Through paintings and etchings, he recorded iconic views of the city as well as Venetian women at work. His formal art education began in 1874 at FRANK DUVENECK's nightly drawing classes at the Ohio Mechanics Institute. He stayed for a year, then became a student at the Pennsylvania Academy of the Fine Arts for nine months. Not long after, in 1879, he moved to New York City and began work as an illustrator for *Scribner's Monthly*. Through this role he visited Europe for the first time, traveling with art department director Alexander Drake (1843–1916). Together they toured London, Paris, Genoa, Pisa, and Rome, before arriving in Venice in May 1880.

In Venice Blum found his former teacher, Duveneck, as well as WILLIAM MERRITT CHASE and JAMES MCNEILL WHISTLER. Whistler was living alongside the "Duveneck Boys" at the Casa Jankowitz, and Blum became his neighbor. The elder artist instructed Blum in the principles of Japanese design and the use of pastels, a medium in which Whistler excelled. The two artists sometimes worked side by side, capturing views from the Casa Jankowitz or around Venice. Writing home on June 27, 1880, Blum expresses admiration for an artist who would have a lasting influence on his career: "Whistler is here, and I know him well, and he is very busy making an etching from my window and he seems very much interested in me and though I am sometimes dissatisfied with my work he always encourages me. He is a nice man."

After a few months, Blum left Venice in August 1880 but returned the following year, spending the summer and early fall working again at the Casa Jankowitz. In November 1882, he published a series of illustrations made during this second stay for an article on Venice written by Henry James (1843–1916) for *Century Illustrated Monthly Magazine*. Blum visited Italy again in June 1885, remaining in Venice for a year and a half. There he shared a studio with Duveneck, working with him once again, as well as with CHARLES FREDERIC ULRICH and OTTO HENRY BACHER, among others.

Encouraged by both Whistler and Duveneck to look for subject matter off the beaten path, together with his interest in depicting women at work, Blum ventured to the nearby island of Burano to visit the lacemakers at the Scuola dei Merletti (School of Lace). His *Venetian Lacemakers* (1887) won a bronze medal at the Exposition Universelle in Paris, and his images of working-class women engaged in local craft, including lacemaking and bead stringing, became popular among American audiences as well.

References

Birnbaum, Martin. *Robert Frederick Blum*. New York: Berlin Photographic Company, 1913.

Boyle, Richard J. *Robert F. Blum, 1857–1903: A Retrospective Exhibition*. Cincinnati, OH: Cincinnati Art Museum, 1966.

James, Henry. "Venice." *Century Illustrated Monthly Magazine* 25, no. 1 (November 1882): 3–24.

Merrill, Linda, ed. *After Whistler: The Artist and His Influence on American Painting*. New Haven, CT: Yale University Press, 2003.

Weber, Bruce. "Robert Frederick Blum (1857–1903) and His Milieu." PhD diss., City University of New York, 1985.

Arthur Beecher Carles

b. Philadelphia, PA, 1882; *d.* Philadelphia, PA, 1952

✡ ARTIST

Arthur Beecher Carles studied at the Pennsylvania Academy of the Fine Arts in his native city between 1900 and 1907. The award of two Cresson Traveling Scholarships allowed him to go abroad, first to Europe for the summer and then on an extended trip for several years that included study in Paris. Around 1909 Carles met and befriended siblings Gertrude (1874–1946) and Leo Stein (1872–1947), becoming familiar with their collections of avant-garde European art, which included work by Henri Matisse (1869–1954), Paul Cézanne (1839–1906), and Pablo Picasso (1881–1973), each of whom would influence his work. After his return to the United States in 1910, Carles's painting style evolved rapidly as he began to build form with intense, vibrant colors and bravura brushwork, constructing dynamic compositions that bordered on complete abstraction.

While overseas, Carles visited Rome in April 1909 to copy Raphael's *Transfiguration* (1516–20) at the Vatican. He most likely visited Venice around the same time. An undated photograph shows Carles standing on a dock in Venice among gondolas, much like those shown in his own *Venetian Gondolas* (see p. 249). One of several works depicting Venice and Venetian subjects by Carles, it reflects his transitional style wherein the subject matter is still recognizable but simplified and painted using an exaggerated palette. Most of these works, however, remain unlocated and are largely remembered through exhibition records alone.

References

Gardiner, Henry G. "Arthur B. Carles: A Critical and Biographical Study." *Philadelphia Museum of Art Bulletin* 64, nos. 302–3 (January–June 1970): 134–35, 139–89.

Wolanin, Barbara Ann Boese. *Arthur B. Carles: Painting with Color*. Philadelphia: Pennsylvania Academy of the Fine Arts, 1984.

———. "Arthur B. Carles, 1882–1952: Philadelphia Modernist." PhD diss., University of Wisconsin–Madison, 1981.

William Merritt Chase

b. Williamsburg, IN, 1849; *d.* New York City, 1916

✡ ARTIST, TEACHER

William Merritt Chase first visited Venice in spring 1877 for nine months to paint and study the city's old masters; then he returned years later to teach. He first arrived in the company of FRANK DUVENECK, his classmate from the Royal Academy of Fine Arts in Munich. They stayed in lodging on the Grand Canal near the Church of San Trovaso and the Gallerie dell'Accademia di Venezia.

Chase suffered ill health and severely depleted finances while in Venice but copied the old masters as planned. He also completed an ambitious still life of the fish market, a series of architectural studies, and *In the Baptistry of St. Mark's, Venice* (see p. 133). These works highlight Chase's attention to unexpected views and details of common scenes while showcasing his technical skill in capturing a wide range of textures. In addition to painting, Chase spent much of his time collecting fine and decorative arts, even acquiring a pet monkey, Jocko, whose antics kept him and his traveling companions amused.

Chase was back in New York City by way of Munich in 1878. Over the next decade, he returned to the continent five times, visiting France, England, the Netherlands, and Spain, often as a teacher, but he did not return to Italy until June 1907. He brought with him forty art students, and they toured Rome, Milan, Florence (where the class was based), and Venice, where Chase spent much of his own time. A brief visit in 1910 followed, succeeded by a longer, seven-week stay with students in 1913—his last summer in Europe before his death. During this final trip, he spent his time painting from his hotel balcony and searching for a studio where he could work on his then-famous fish still lifes. Overall, Chase completed at least twenty known Venetian paintings, comprising generally small, loosely brushed architectural scenes, interiors, and still lifes, but many remain unlocated.

References

Gallati, Barbara Dayer. *William Merritt Chase.* New York: Harry N. Abrams; Washington, DC: National Museum of American Art, Smithsonian Institution, 1995.

Hirshler, Erica E. *William Merritt Chase.* Boston: Museum of Fine Arts, Boston, 2016.

Pisano, Ronald. *The Complete Catalogue of Known and Documented Work by William Merritt Chase (1849–1916).* 4 vols. New Haven, CT: Yale University Press, 2006–10.

Roof, Katherine Metcalf. *The Life and Art of William Merritt Chase.* New York: Hacker Art Books, 1975.

Smithgall, Elsa, Erica E. Hirshler, Katherine M. Bourguignon, Giovanna Ginex, and John Davis. *William Merritt Chase: A Modern Master.* Washington, DC: Phillips Collection; New Haven, CT: Yale University Press, 2016.

Charles Caryl Coleman

b. Buffalo, NY, 1840; *d.* Capri, Italy, 1928

✡ ARTIST

Expatriate Charles Caryl Coleman first traveled abroad in 1856 at age sixteen. He likely developed his early interest in painting from his father, John Hull Coleman (1813–possibly 1887), who sold artists' supplies, and from his uncle, an art auctioneer. He studied landscape painting as a teenager in Buffalo, New York, with local artists, then moved to Paris, where he trained with leading French academic artist Thomas Couture (1815–1879). He visited Florence in 1860, returned to Paris, then traveled back to the United States in 1862 to fight in the American Civil War as part of Buffalo's Company K, One Hundredth Regiment. Lieutenant Coleman was honorably discharged around August 1863 after a fellow officer mistakenly fired a revolver and hit Coleman in the jaw. While recovering in New York City, he maintained a studio and exhibited some of his work.

After the war, Coleman was eager to return to Italy. In 1866 he left America permanently, living in Rome for nearly twenty years before moving in 1886 to the island of Capri, where he established his home and studio at the Villa Narcissus. During this time, Coleman visited Venice on several occasions, as evidenced by inscriptions on drawings of the city dated September 1871, May 1873, and July 1875. Many of the paintings he exhibited at the National Academy of Design in New York between 1877 and 1894 depict Venetian subjects. Both directly observed and imagined, they include views of St. Mark's Basilica as well as interior genre scenes and still lifes that incorporate contemporary Venetian glass from Murano.

Also an avid collector, Coleman's penchant for bric-a-brac is reflected in his paintings, which bring together objects from disparate times and places, many acquired during his travels. Ancient glass objects and Venetian glass vessels mingle with antique tapestries, Japanese fans, and floral sprigs (see p. 73). While his paintings were widely exhibited at home and abroad, Americans, enthusiastic for his romantic interpretations of Italy's elusive past and poetic present, were the primary purchasers of his work.

References

Bell, Adrienne Baxter. "Echoes of the East, Echoes of the Past: Charles Caryl Coleman's *Azaleas and Apple Blossoms.*" In *Locating American Art: Finding Art's Meaning in Museums, Colonial Period to the Present,* edited by Cynthia Fowler, 33–45. Burlington, VT: Ashgate Publishing, 2016.

———. "Utopian Pastiche: The Still Life Paintings of Charles Caryl Coleman." In *A Seamless Web: Transatlantic Art in the Nineteenth Century,* edited by Cheryll L. May and Marian Wardle, 147–62. Newcastle upon Tyne: Cambridge Scholars Publishing, 2014.

"C. C. Coleman's Capri Paintings at His Studio." *Evening World* (New York), June 10, 1916.

"Charles Caryl Coleman." *American Magazine of Art* 15, no. 9 (September 1924): 466–67.

Sturgis, Russell. "The Coleman Collection of Antique Glass." *Century Illustrated Monthly Magazine* 48, no. 4 (August 1894): 554–58.

Kenyon Cox

b. Warren, OH, 1856; *d.* New York City, 1919

✡ ARTIST, TEACHER

A skilled and supremely disciplined artist, Kenyon Cox sought to better himself through diverse techniques and comprehensive knowledge of international arts philosophies. He studied at the McMicken School of Drawing and Design in Cincinnati (where he met ROBERT FREDERICK BLUM and FRANK DUVENECK), the Pennsylvania Academy of the Fine Arts in Philadelphia, and in Paris at the École des Beaux-Arts, the Académie Julian, and in the atelier of Carolus-Duran.

Cox traveled to Italy in late summer and fall of 1878 as a student, and his experience did much to establish his belief in the timeless beauty and superiority of Italian art. Among the many cities he visited across central and northern Italy, Venice most strongly captured the artist's interest. Writing to his mother, Helen Finney Cox (1828–1911), in September 1878, Cox noted: "The city is just a dream of color and beauty.... There is everywhere... violet and pink and pale yellow fire." Over the course of about a month and a half, his longest stay in any one Italian city, Cox attempted to reproduce Venice's unique light in paint and photography, but he was frequently unsatisfied with the results. Although he finished few paintings, his first Paris Salon entry was of a young Venetian woman, painted around 1878, now lost.

The impact of this trip was long-lasting and, as his art matured, Cox became increasingly captivated by traditional artistic standards in the face of modernism, consistently modeling his art on classical Greco-Roman practice and the Venetian Renaissance. Based on his reputation as a painter and his related interest in the Venetian old masters, Cox accepted a commission from Bowdoin College in April 1893 to paint an allegorical lunette honoring Venice. He traveled there again in the summer of 1893 with his wife, painter LOUISE HOWLAND KING COX, "to get the atmosphere" of the city in preparation for painting the mural. It was completed one year later in April 1894 and sent to Bowdoin in early May for mounting. Cox depicts Venice enthroned and flanked by figures representing Mercury (or Commerce) and Painting, accompanied by the Lion of St. Mark, an iconic symbol of the city (see p. 44). Just one element of a four-part allegorical cycle decorating McKim, Mead & White's Walker Art Building, Cox's lunette was joined by panels celebrating other significant cities of the Renaissance and classical antiquity, including Florence, Rome, and Athens by Abbott Handerson Thayer (1849–1921), Elihu Vedder (1836–1923), and John La Farge (1835–1910), respectively.

Cox's public mural cycles received high praise and included major commissions for the Library of Congress in Washington, DC, in 1896 and 1897, and for the Liberal Arts Building at the 1893 World's Columbian Exposition in Chicago, executed together with his wife.

References

Morgan, H. Wayne, ed. *An Artist of the American Renaissance: The Letters of Kenyon Cox, 1883–1919*. Kent, OH: Kent State University Press, 1995.

Morgan, H. Wayne. *Kenyon Cox, 1856–1919: A Life in American Art*. Kent, OH: Kent State University Press, 1994.

Van Hook, Bailey. *Angels of Art: Women and Art in American Society, 1876–1914*. University Park: Pennsylvania State University Press, 1996.

West, Richard V. *The Walker Art Building Murals*. Occasional Papers 1. Brunswick, ME: Bowdoin College Museum of Art, 1972.

Louise Howland King Cox

b. San Francisco, CA, 1865; *d.* Windham, CT, 1945

✡ ARTIST

Despite numerous medals and prizes, the reputation of Louise Howland King Cox is frequently overshadowed by that of her husband, painter KENYON COX. In 1881, at age sixteen, the precocious Cox left her home in San Francisco for New York City and the National Academy of Design, taking the first steps in her career as a painter of children's portraits and idealized pictures of women. She soon grew restless with the Academy's relative conservatism and transitioned to the newer, more "enlightened" Art Students League in 1883 at age eighteen. There she met Kenyon, and after a lengthy courtship (described by one biographer as a "four-volume Victorian novel"), the two were engaged in January 1892 and married that June.

On June 10, 1893, Louise and Kenyon departed for a honeymoon in Europe. The Coxes traveled first to Paris, then Milan and Verona, and on to Venice. Immediately enamored, they stayed in Venice for nearly a month. Some of Cox's later paintings feature Venetian glass objects of the type she may have seen for sale during this trip. After her husband's death, Cox returned to Italy in the early 1920s and purchased a home near Florence, where she lived for about two years before returning to the United States.

References

Cox, Louise Howland King, and Richard Murray. "Louise Cox at the Art Students League: A Memoir." *Archives of American Art Journal* 27, no. 1 (1987): 12–20.

Kenyon and Louise Cox papers, 1876–1977. Archives of American Art, Smithsonian Institution.

Morgan, H. Wayne, ed. *An Artist of the American Renaissance: The Letters of Kenyon Cox, 1883–1919*. Kent, OH: Kent State University Press, 1995.

"Mrs. Kenyon Cox, Portrait Painter: Artist's Widow, Recipient of Many Prizes, Dies—Known for Work with Children." *New York Times*, December 12, 1945, 26.

Ralph Wormeley Curtis

b. Boston, MA, 1854; *d.* Beaulieu-sur-Mer, France, 1922

✡ ARTIST

Ralph Wormeley Curtis was encouraged to pursue art from an early age by his father, Daniel Sargent Curtis (1825–1908), and his aunt, Anne Sargent Gage (née Nancy Brown, 1794–1876), both of whom drew and painted in watercolor. After graduating from Harvard University, where he cofounded and contributed illustrations to the *Harvard Lampoon*, Curtis enrolled at the Académie Julian in 1878 before taking classes with Carolus-Duran in Paris. There he first met JOHN SINGER SARGENT, a distant relative, and they began a lifelong friendship. The pair frequently traveled together in their student days and likely sketched together in Venice from 1880 to 1882. Curtis also spent time sketching and painting alongside FRANK DUVENECK in Venice during the summer of 1878. He later joined the "Duveneck Boys" there in the fall of 1880.

Meanwhile, Curtis's family expatriated from Boston to Italy, renting quarters at the Palazzo Barbaro on the Grand Canal in 1877 and purchasing the property in 1885. The Curtis residence became an artistic salon, a gathering place for cultural luminaries such as Duveneck, Sargent, Henry James, Edith Wharton (1862–1937), ISABELLA STEWART GARDNER, and JAMES MCNEILL WHISTLER. Curtis's family connections opened doors for many artists visiting the Palazzo Barbaro, and he introduced his parents to Whistler, Sargent, and Duveneck personally. If Sargent and Whistler crossed paths in Venice, it was most likely through the Curtis family. Sargent often lodged with them when visiting Venice and painted an informal portrait of the family within the palazzo's salon in 1899.

Curtis was influenced by each of these artists—Whistler, Sargent, and Duveneck—but his family wealth allowed him the freedom to develop his style and interests independently without having to worry about the "taste" of patrons or critics. Now often recalled as a handsome and charismatic gentleman artist, Curtis produced paintings that were well respected in his day and that offer candid, if somewhat glamorous, views of Venice at the turn of the century. He was known for his genre scenes, impressionist landscapes, and city views, especially of Venice, which he exhibited regularly at the Paris Salon beginning in 1881. While he did not rely on the sale of his artwork to make a living, he did sell his paintings with some regularity and to noted collectors, including Gardner.

References

McCauley, Elizabeth Anne, ed. *Gondola Days: Isabella Stewart Gardner and the Palazzo Barbaro Circle*. Boston: Isabella Stewart Gardner Museum, 2004.

Zorzi, Rosella Mamoli. "Henry James in a 'Venetian' Diary." *Henry James Review* 11, no. 2 (Spring 1990): 101–14.

———. *Ralph W. Curtis, Un Pittore Americano a Venezia: Biografia*. Venice: Supernova, 2019.

Maria Oakey Dewing

b. New York City, 1845; *d.* New York City, 1927

✡ ARTIST

Before pursuing painting full-time, Maria Oakey Dewing established herself as an illustrator and author of etiquette and housekeeping literature. She helped illustrate a series of articles in *Scribner's Monthly* written by art critic Clarence Chatham Cook (1828–1900), who later published them as the immensely popular book on house décor, *The House Beautiful* (1878). Dewing portrayed elegant women within artfully decorated interiors to visualize the principles of aestheticism—a late nineteenth-century movement that favored beauty for beauty's sake over narrative and didacticism in art—for the middle classes (see p. 68). Dewing's own illustrated publications included *Attic to Cellar: A Book for Young Housekeepers* (1879), *Beauty in Dress* (1881), and *Beauty in the Household* (1882). She built a reputation for expertise in décor and interior design but nonetheless made painting her primary profession by the late 1870s. In a 1921 interview with the critic Royal Cortissoz (1869–1948), Dewing recalled fellow aesthete Oscar Wilde (1854–1900) once asking her, "Why don't you go into decoration and wipe them all out?" Her response: "Because I must paint pictures or die."

Dewing studied at the Cooper Union School of Design for Women and the National Academy of Design in New York in the 1860s. Trained first in figure painting, she shifted focus to flowers in the 1880s, shortly after her marriage to artist THOMAS WILMER DEWING and the birth of her daughter. She adopted what was considered a more appropriate, feminine subject for a wife and mother and so she could better attend to her new domestic duties. Possible study with John La Farge may also have encouraged her to specialize in this genre. WILLIAM MERRITT CHASE admiringly referred to these works as her "impeccable flowers," and her skill as a painter was broadly recognized by artists, collectors, and at world's fairs where she was awarded medals of merit in 1893, 1901, and 1907. Dewing's paintings were collected by Smithsonian benefactors Edith (m. 1886) and JOHN GELLATLY and Charles Lang Freer (1856–1919). Despite her successes, she expressed a desire to accomplish more, writing in 1927, "I have hardly touched any achievement. I dreamed of groups and figures in big landscapes and I still see them."

References

Burns, Sarah, and John Davis. "Beauty, Vision, and Modernity." In *American Art to 1900: A Documentary History*, edited by Sarah Burns and John Davis, 941–1020. Berkeley: University of California Press, 2009.

Dewing, Maria Oakey. "Flower Painters and What the Flower Offers to Art." *Art and Progress* 6, no. 8 (June 1915): 255–62.

Hobbs, Susan A. "Maria Oakey Dewing's Flowers and Figures." *Magazine Antiques* (January 2004): 152–59.

Martin, Jennifer A. "The Rediscovery of Maria Oakey Dewing." *Feminist Art Journal* (Summer 1976): 24–27, 44.

Stott, Annette. "Floral Femininity: A Pictorial Definition." *American Art* 6, no. 2 (Spring 1992): 60–77.

Thomas Wilmer Dewing

b. Boston, MA, 1851; *d.* New York City, 1938

✡ ARTIST, TEACHER

Thomas Wilmer Dewing was introduced to the art world as a lithography shop apprentice, a position he took on when his father died and the family's paper manufacturing company in Boston fell on hard times. By seventeen he showed a marked talent as a lithographer, and by 1872, Dewing listed his profession as "artist" in the Boston City Directories. Very few of his lithographs have survived, but Dewing worked regularly in this medium for at least a decade before he began painting.

By 1874 Dewing secured a working space and was attending lectures in the Studio Building in Boston before traveling to Europe. He attended the Académie Julian in Paris in 1876 and became acquainted with WILLIAM MERRITT CHASE and WALTER GAY. While abroad it is possible that Dewing studied alongside FRANK DUVENECK at the Royal Academy of Fine Arts in Munich. After returning to Boston, Dewing taught at the new School of the Museum of Fine Arts briefly before moving permanently to New York City in 1880.

In New York he aligned himself with the progressive Society of American Artists, which also included Duveneck, JAMES MCNEILL WHISTLER, and LOUISE HOWLAND KING COX. In 1881 Dewing began teaching composition at the Art Students League. There he reconnected with Chase, who taught the portrait class, and met his wife, MARIA OAKEY DEWING.

By the late 1880s, Dewing had formed the basic style and subject matter for which he became known—elegant, refined women executed in a limited range of colors and set in quiet interiors or outside amid nature. Inspired in part by Dutch seventeenth-century painter Johannes Vermeer (1632–1675) and Whistler, Dewing used his brush and palette to soften, even blur, the figures, ascribing them an ethereal quality. While it is unlikely that he ever traveled to Venice, on several occasions Dewing painted Venetian glass objects from the collection of friend and artist Dwight William Tryon (1849–1925). Dewing became a favorite artist of collectors JOHN GELLATLY and Charles Lang Freer, both of whom made transformative donations to the Smithsonian Institution.

References

Bolz, Diane M. "The Timeless Women of Thomas Wilmer Dewing." *Smithsonian* 27, no. 7 (October 1996): 34.

Hobbs, Susan. *Thomas Wilmer Dewing: Beauty into Art. A Catalogue Raisonné.* New Haven, CT: Yale University Press, 2018.

——. "Thomas Wilmer Dewing: The Early Years, 1851–1885." *American Art Journal* 13, no. 2 (Spring 1981): 4–35.

Pyne, Kathleen. "Aesthetic Strategies in the 'Age of Pain': Thomas Dewing and the Art of Life." In *Art and the Higher Life: Painting and Evolutionary Thought in Late Nineteenth-Century America,* 135–218. Austin: University of Texas Press, 1996.

FRANK DUVENECK

b. Covington, KY, 1848; *d.* Cincinnati, OH, 1919

✡ ARTIST, TEACHER

Frank Duveneck forged connections among many American artists in Venice while capturing romanticized views of the city in his etchings and paintings. He trained at the Royal Academy of Fine Arts in Munich before opening his own atelier, where he gained an enthusiastic following. In Germany, Duveneck became close with one of the country's premier portraitists, Franz von Lenbach (1836–1904), who recognized Duveneck's talent and encouraged him to go to Venice to study the old masters. Duveneck went for the first time in 1873, until a cholera outbreak forced him to return to the United States, then visited again in 1877 with WILLIAM MERRITT CHASE for a nine-month stay. In 1879 he returned for a third time, remaining in Italy for two years in the company of his students, who were nicknamed the "Duveneck Boys" and included ROBERT FREDERICK BLUM and RALPH WORMELEY CURTIS. The group spent winters in Florence and summers in Venice. Duveneck lodged at the Casa Jankowitz with OTTO HENRY BACHER and JAMES MCNEILL WHISTLER. He also met JOHN SINGER SARGENT around this time. His exposure to Sargent's and Whistler's work influenced him to break away from the traditional academic style he learned in Munich and develop his so-called "Italian style," marked by a brightly colored palette, less dense pigment, and a tendency toward smoothness and polish with less obvious brushwork.

Working alongside Whistler and under the technical guidance of Bacher, who owned a printing press, Duveneck also developed his skills as a graphic artist, ultimately completing an impressive thirty-two plates, mostly of Venetian subjects (see pp. 146, 257). Because he pulled prints from the same press as Whistler and often selected similar subject matter, period critics favorably compared the artists' etchings. In 1881 Whistler's brother-in-law mistook Duveneck's etchings for Whistler's, causing a scandal and enraging the elder artist. While Whistler influenced his interest in copperplate etching and some of his color schemes, Duveneck's broader stylistic transformation to a more brilliant palette in his Venetian marines was indebted to Sargent.

Around the same time, Duveneck produced a realist series of Italy's architecture, countryside, and people. He focused on the working classes engaged in their daily labor, featuring peasants, water carriers, shopgirls, and gondoliers (see pp. 234–35). Duveneck went to Venice for the last time between 1882 and 1885, but the artist did not produce much work during his final visit.

References

Duveneck, Josephine Whitney. *Frank Duveneck: Painter-Teacher.* San Francisco: John Howell-Books, 1970.

Exhibition of the Work of Frank Duveneck. Cincinnati, OH: Cincinnati Art Museum, 1936.

Neuhaus, Robert. *Unsuspected Genius: The Art and Life of Frank Duveneck.* San Francisco: Bedford Press, 1987.

WILLIAM THOMAS EVANS

b. Cloughjordan, Ireland, 1843; *d.* Glen Ridge, NJ, 1918

✡ COLLECTOR

William Thomas Evans was considered a trailblazer among American collectors in his day. Beginning in 1900, Evans turned his attention from European to American art and effectively built two distinct collections of American paintings over the next two decades, bolstering the market value of this work in the process. In 1915 he donated more than 150 works of art by more than a hundred American artists to dramatically expand the fledgling collection of American art at the Smithsonian Institution. This unrestricted gift permitted future substitutions and additions, allowing the collection to grow and adapt over time.

Evans sought to collect works from across the field, ranging from KENYON COX and LOUISE HOWLAND KING COX to ROBERT FREDERICK BLUM and WINSLOW HOMER. While Evans was focused on American subjects, many paintings in his collection represented scenes of prominent European destinations, including at least ten paintings of Venice by Blum, William Gedney Bunce (1840–1916), and Samuel Colman (1832–1920). Evans may have accompanied his family to Europe in the 1890s, when they left the United States to avoid scandal after his daughter's elopement, but he was not known as an avid traveler.

Evans earned his fortune as the president of Mills and Gibb, a dry goods business, but he supplemented this income with bold investments in art and real estate. Between 1891 and 1915, he bought and sold two mansions and hundreds of paintings, both to build his collection and later to avoid public bankruptcy. In part, his financial troubles were the result of fraudulent use of company funds to purchase art for his collection, which he then sold to dealers and museums. The scandal was considered so egregious that by about 1915 creditors threatened to reclaim gifts of art already made to museums. In a turn of events that changed Evans's legacy dramatically, he used his private fortune to guarantee his creditors at Mills and Gibb against loss. The company was ultimately reorganized without Evans at the helm, and the lawsuits threatening the museum collections were dropped.

References

William T. Evans letters, 1842–1969. Archives of American Art, Smithsonian Institution.

Kirby, Thomas E., William A. Coffin, and Charles DeKay. *Catalogue of American Paintings Belonging to William T. Evans.* New York: J. J. Little, 1900.

"Memorial to Wm. T. Evans." *American Magazine of Art* 12, no. 1 (January 1921): 33–34.

Truettner, William H. "William T. Evans, Collector of American Paintings." *American Art Journal* 3, no. 2 (Autumn 1971): 50–79.

ISABELLA STEWART GARDNER

b. New York City, 1840; *d.* Boston, MA, 1924

☆ COLLECTOR, PATRON

Isabella Stewart Gardner assembled an impressive collection with examples of European, Asian, and American paintings, sculptures, tapestries, rare books, and decorative arts. She began her collection of Italian work with books written by medieval poet-philosopher Dante Alighieri (1265–1321). Her interest in Venice was likely sparked by a meeting with Henry James during an 1879 tour of London and Paris. James, who first visited Venice in 1869 under the influence of John Ruskin (1819–1900), lived in the city and later wrote about it in his novels. He imparted some of his enthusiasm and knowledge to Gardner, who purchased Ruskin's *Stones of Venice* (1851–53) by 1882, around the same time she purchased her first artwork featuring a Venetian view.

She made her first trip to Venice in May of 1883, staying at the Hotel Europa on the Grand Canal. Gardner and her husband, John L. "Jack" Gardner (1837–1898), subsequently became frequent visitors to Venice, making nine trips between 1884 and 1897. The family of artist RALPH WORMELEY CURTIS cultivated Gardner's interest in the city, introducing her to the sights and shops and inviting her to the elegant Palazzo Barbaro, where they socialized with artists, writers, and other cultural luminaries.

By the late 1880s, Gardner was visiting Venice with the intent to build her collection, and in 1891 a bequest of $1.75 million from her father increased her collecting momentum. Among her art acquisitions, she bought Venetian glass and a substantial amount of lace. An 1892 *Boston Globe* article details one of her visits, which included leading friends "to Murano for a view of the famous glass and mosaic factories, the museum of old glass, etc."

Despite Jack's death in 1898, Gardner proceeded with their plan to bring Venice to Boston in the form of a new museum, and the Isabella Stewart Gardner Museum opened its doors to the public in 1903. The Venetian Gothic architecture of the Palazzo Barbaro, which she later purchased, in part inspired the building's design, and it incorporated actual balconies from the Ca' d'Oro, another Grand Canal palazzo. When Gardner died, she left her museum "for the education and enjoyment of the public forever." Her will provided a large operating endowment but stipulated that no art be bought or sold, and nothing in the galleries move from its original placement. Her view of Venice is still on display in Boston today.

References

Lucey, Donna M. *Sargent's Women: Four Lives Behind the Canvas.* New York: W. W. Norton, 2017.

McCauley, Elizabeth Anne, ed. *Gondola Days: Isabella Stewart Gardner and the Palazzo Barbaro Circle.* Boston: Isabella Stewart Gardner Museum, 2004.

"Mr. and Mrs. 'Jack' Gardner." *Boston Globe*, October 30, 1892.

Shand-Tucci, Douglass. *The Art of Scandal: The Life and Times of Isabella Stewart Gardner.* New York: HarperCollins, 1997.

Tharp, Louise Hall. *Mrs. Jack: A Biography of Isabella Stewart Gardner.* Boston: Isabella Stewart Gardner Museum, 1965.

WALTER GAY

b. Hingham, MA, 1856; *d.* Dammarie-lès-Lys, France, 1937

✡ ARTIST

Walter Gay was born into an affluent family in New England. He spent a year herding cattle on his uncle's Nebraska ranch before pursuing painting in Boston. He began his career with genre scenes and still lifes until another uncle, landscape painter Winckworth Allan Gay (1821–1910), and artist William Morris Hunt encouraged him to go to Europe. He traveled abroad for the first time in 1876 to study in the atelier of Léon Bonnat (1833–1922) in Paris, where he realistically portrayed France's peasant class. After three years abroad, Gay decided to stay in France and made his professional debut at the Paris Salon in 1879.

In 1889 Gay married Matilda Travers (1855–1943), the daughter of a New York City investor. Her wealth ensured him the financial freedom to paint as he wished, without having to rely on commissions or align with academic tastes. They enjoyed traveling and toured Europe for up to two months each summer. Their favorite destination outside of France was Venice, but Gay painted little during these vacations. He did, however, complete three bright and detailed studies of highly ornamented interiors from the city—the small chinoiserie room in the Museo Civico (now Museo Correr), the library of the Palazzo Querini Stampalia, and the salon of the Palazzo Barbaro (see p. 75), a space also documented by JOHN SINGER SARGENT. Because these works omitted figures, the artist called them "portraits of rooms."

Gay's paintings were met with critical success at the Paris Salons, world's fairs, and other major exhibitions in Europe throughout his career. He received numerous awards for his paintings, and the Museum of Fine Arts, Boston, and the Metropolitan Museum of Art hired him as a purchasing consultant. While his early work was well respected, he is best remembered for his charming interiors.

References

Gallatin, Albert E. "Mr. Walter Gay's Interiors." *Art and Progress* 4, no. 9 (July 1913): 1023–27.

Rieder, William. *A Charmed Couple: The Art and Life of Walter and Matilda Gay.* New York: Harry N. Abrams, 2000.

Taube, Isabel L. *Impressions of Interiors: Gilded Age Paintings by Walter Gay.* Pittsburgh, PA: Frick Art and Historical Center; London: D Giles, 2012.

JOHN GELLATLY

b. New York City, 1853; *d.* New York City, 1931

✡ COLLECTOR, PATRON

John Gellatly built a vast art collection with the intent of donating the full ensemble to a museum. His collecting practices sought to prove his belief that the contemporary artists of the United States were "in sympathy with the great masters who preceded them." He began by assembling large groups of paintings by single American artists, including THOMAS WILMER DEWING and Albert Pinkham Ryder (1847–1917). He then bought works from across different cultures, including European, Asian, and ancient art, in order to draw parallels between American art and what he considered to be the esteemed art of the past. An eccentric miniature made by Gellatly's English butler and later curator of his collection, Ralph Seymour (active 1920s), demonstrates how Gellatly may have paired such works within his home and gallery spaces to emphasize affinities between them (see p. 61).

Gellatly began collecting in earnest when he married Edith Rogers (m. 1886), a socialite, avid collector, and painter of still lifes. Her wealth and interests encouraged Gellatly to devote himself to cultural pursuits, and the couple built an art collection together, which they housed in a private gallery behind their New York City brownstone. When Edith died in 1913, Gellatly continued to purchase artworks. In 1928 he sold his house, relocated his collection to rented quarters, and moved into the Hotel Buckingham in New York to keep funds available for further art acquisitions. The following year, Gellatly made a generous gift of more than 1,500 artworks to the Smithsonian Institution, establishing himself as one of its most important early patrons.

In IRVING RAMSAY WILES's portrait of Gellatly (see p. 82), he is presented as the consummate collector in a white suit, which, according to Wiles and others who knew Gellatly, he wore "no matter what the weather, or time of year." This ostentatious attire recalls the affected clothing of WILLIAM MERRITT CHASE, whom Gellatly admired and supported as a patron. Wiles initiated the portrait after viewing Gellatly's collection at his home in New York, expressing his desire to paint a portrait to accompany the collection to the Smithsonian. The official portrait was not considered "finished" by the artist; Gellatly passed away before it was completed, so it was purposefully left in an abbreviated state for sentimental reasons.

References

Beggs, Thomas M. *Catalog of American and European Paintings in the Gellatly Collection.* 4th ed. Washington, DC: National Collection of Fine Arts, Smithsonian Institution, 1954.

Conroy, Sarah Booth. "The Wily Old Collector." *Washington Post,* June 18, 1978, H1–H2.

Gardner, Paul V. "Archaeological Highlights in the John Gellatly Collection." *Archaeology* 7, no. 2 (June 1954): 66–73.

ELLEN DAY HALE

b. Worcester, MA, 1855; *d.* Brookline, MA, 1940

✡ ARTIST

Ellen Day Hale was born into a family with a remarkable social and intellectual reputation dating back to the Revolutionary era. Two of her great-aunts were Harriet Beecher Stowe (1811–1896), author of *Uncle Tom's Cabin* (1852), and Catharine Esther Beecher (1800–1878), a noted advocate of education and women's rights, and Hale was a distant relative of suffragist Susan B. Anthony (1820–1906). This network of remarkable women helped to inspire the artist's progressive outlook.

Hale lived abroad from 1881 to 1883, visiting England, France, Belgium, the Netherlands, and Italy, and studying in Paris at the Académie Julian and in the atelier of Carolus-Duran. On arrival in Venice in September 1881, she promptly wrote to her father that Venice was the "goal of my desires." Unlike previous correspondence outlining her meals and itinerary, her letters about Venice were enthusiastic and impassioned. She detailed everything, including the glory of St. Mark's Basilica, which she described as "beautiful" and "the strangest place [she] ever was in." Over the course of her trip, Hale followed *Baedeker's Northern Italy* guidebook (1867–68), visiting the Rialto Bridge, Santa Maria della Salute, Gallerie dell'Accademia di Venezia, Doge's Palace, and Scuola di San Rocco.

Hale visited Venice again in 1895 with her life partner and traveling companion, artist Gabrielle de Veaux Clements (1858–1948), staying in the Hotel Aurora, located on the Riva degli Schiavoni near the Casa Jankowitz, where JAMES MCNEILL WHISTLER and the circle of FRANK DUVENECK once lodged. The position offered Hale and Clements a clear view of Santa Maria della Salute and the island of San Giorgio. Hale occasionally sketched from her room, and these drawings were later transferred to etchings, a skill she learned through Clements. Working in this medium, Hale documented her extensive travels through the United States, Europe, and the Middle East. She depicted Santa Maria della Salute and other familiar sights on her third trip to Venice in 1921, again staying with Clements at the Hotel Aurora.

During her lifetime, Hale exhibited at the Pennsylvania Academy of the Fine Arts, where she attended classes, the Paris Salons, and the World's Columbian Exposition in Chicago (1893).

References

Earenfight, Phillip, ed. *Inked Impressions: Ellen Day Hale and the Painter-Etcher Movement.* Carlisle, PA: Trout Gallery, Dickinson College, 2007.

Ellen Day Hale, 1855–1940. New York: Richard York Gallery, 1981.

Fitzpatrick, Tracy. "Ellen Day Hale: Painting the Self, Fashioning Identity." *Woman's Art Journal* 31, no. 1 (Spring/Summer 2010): 28–34.

Hirshler, Erica E. *A Studio of Her Own: Women Artists in Boston, 1870–1940.* Boston: Museum of Fine Arts, Boston, 2001.

Hoppin, Martha J. "Women Artists in Boston, 1870–1900: The Pupils of William Morris Hunt." *American Art Journal* 13, no. 1 (Winter 1981): 17–46.

Hermann Herzog

b. Bremen, Germany, 1831; *d.* Philadelphia, PA, 1932

✡ ARTIST

Hermann Herzog was best known in Europe and the United States for his landscapes in the romantic tradition, following the formula of broad, richly colored views of mountains and dramatic weather effects, which he regularly exhibited at the Pennsylvania Academy of the Fine Arts. He likely arrived in America from Germany for the first time in the early 1860s. He settled in Philadelphia and became a naturalized citizen in 1876. Over time Herzog explored the United States in full, venturing first up the Hudson River in 1871, then moving progressively westward, and eventually painting pictures of Yosemite beginning in 1873.

Herzog traveled frequently, often alone, and while the diversity and drama of the American landscape provided him with plenty of subject matter, he also spent time in Europe, including at least one trip to Venice, where his son, Lewis Herzog (1868–1943), held a studio. While his journeys are not well-documented, he painted at least fourteen highly detailed Venetian subjects (see p. 51) according to his carefully recorded paintings journal, suggesting a prolonged stay or repeat visits.

Herzog became an early investor in the Pennsylvania Railroad, and this income gave him freedom to travel within the United States and abroad. Not reliant on the sale of his paintings, he chose later in life to maintain ownership of much of his work. In 1929 Herzog reported, "I have not sold a painting for years. I still go on painting, but my children are financially comfortable, so they do not want me to sell any of my work, and I don't want to either. I like to see it around." Painting as he pleased during much of his one-hundred-year lifetime, Herzog completed more than 1,200 pictures reflecting his international explorations.

References

Lewis, Donald S., Jr. *American Paintings of Herman Herzog.* Chadds Ford, PA: Brandywine River Museum, 1992.

Staley, Thomas H. *Herman Herzog: On the Waccasassa.* Gainesville, FL: Storter Childs, 2013.

William Henry Holmes

b. Cadiz, OH, 1846; *d.* Royal Oak, MI, 1933

✡ ARTIST-SCIENTIST, CURATOR

William Henry Holmes led a remarkably varied life as a geologist, archaeologist, artist, and curator before becoming the first director of the Smithsonian Institution's new unit, the National Gallery of Art, now the Smithsonian American Art Museum, in 1920. With little formal training before 1872 and no college degree, at age twenty-five Holmes supplemented his independent scientific learning with art lessons in Washington, DC. He practiced by sketching from museum taxidermic animal specimens, and when Smithsonian staff spotted his talent, they hired him on the spot as a scientific illustrator, with lodging provided in one of the Smithsonian Castle's towers. In 1872 he joined Ferdinand Hayden (1829–1887) and his team for the US Geological Survey to explore the region of northwestern Wyoming, which later became Yellowstone National Park, and Colorado. Like landscape artist THOMAS MORAN, who joined the expedition in 1871, Holmes worked to convey the grandeur of western scenery and its geographical features.

Holmes traveled abroad in June 1879 and spent the next year and a half examining collections in European museums and galleries and sketching in Rome, Naples, Venice, and other Italian cities. In each destination he focused his attention on the local people, recording their daily activities and appearances (see p. 205). His stay in Venice coincided with that of JAMES MCNEILL WHISTLER, though there is no evidence the two artists spent time together. In the winter of 1879, he traveled on to Munich to work with the colony of American artists surrounding FRANK DUVENECK. Holmes returned to the United States in August 1880 and exhibited the drawings and watercolors he completed while abroad, including several small watercolors of Venetians at work, at the Corcoran Gallery of Art and the Cosmos Club in Washington, DC, where he was a founding member. For the next sixty years, Holmes held roles in all parts of the Smithsonian, with special interest in archaeology, geology, and fine art. During his career as an artist-scientist, he served as both head curator of anthropology and director of the Bureau of American Ethnography before transitioning to the

National Gallery of Art. Holmes was buried alongside his wife, and their unassuming marker reads: "They gave to art and science."

References

Hough, Walter. "William Henry Holmes." *American Anthropologist,* n.s., 35, no. 4 (October–December 1933): 752–64.

Meltzer, David J., and Robert C. Dunnell, eds. *The Archaeology of William Henry Holmes.* Washington, DC: Smithsonian Institution Press, 1992.

Nelson, Clifford M. "William Henry Holmes: Beginning a Career in Art and Science." *Records of the Columbia Historical Society, Washington, D.C.* 50 (1980): 252–78.

Swanton, John R. "Biographical Memoir of William Henry Holmes, 1846–1933." *National Academy of Sciences* 17, no. 10 (1935): 223–52.

Tozzer, Alfred M. "William Henry Holmes (1846–1933)." *Proceedings of the American Academy of Arts and Sciences* 69, no. 13 (February 1935): 514–15.

"William Henry Holmes (1846–1933): Renaissance Man." Smithsonian Institution Archives. Accessed November 25, 2019. https://siarchives.si.edu/history/artists/william-henry-holmes.

WINSLOW HOMER

b. Boston, MA, 1836; *d.* Prouts Neck, ME, 1910

✡ ARTIST

Winslow Homer was raised in Cambridge, Massachusetts, and his artistic education began with a two-year apprenticeship to Boston lithographer John Henry Bufford (1810–1870). Homer worked as a freelance illustrator before moving to New York City in 1859 at the age of twenty-three to establish himself as a commercial printmaker and increase his opportunities for commissions from publishers. In the spring of 1861, he briefly studied oil painting with Frederick Rondel (1826–1892) while in New York, then traveled to Virginia that fall as an artist-correspondent for *Harper's Weekly* to cover the front lines of the American Civil War.

Homer's first trip abroad came after the war, in 1866, when he spent ten months studying in Paris, as well as at the Cernay-la-Ville artists' colony and in Picardy. Years later he went abroad once more, this time to England from 1881 to 1882, staying near Tynemouth in Cullercoats. There Homer's subjects and style evolved dramatically as he was inspired by the local fishing community and their relationship with nature. The following summer he settled permanently in Prouts Neck on the coast of Maine. From there, he made hunting, fishing, and sketching trips in the eastern United States and the Caribbean.

Homer never traveled to Italy, but he experienced some of the history and grandeur of Venice in 1893 when visiting the World's Columbian Exposition in Chicago. In a painted souvenir of this visit, he depicted the architectural showpiece of the exposition, the Court of Honor and its re-created Venetian canals and lagoons, complete with gondolas and gondoliers.

References

Cikovsky, Nicolai, Jr. *Winslow Homer.* Library of American Art. New York: Harry N. Abrams; Washington, DC: National Museum of American Art, Smithsonian Institution, 1990.

Cikovsky, Nicolai, Jr., and Franklin Kelly. *Winslow Homer.* New Haven, CT: Yale University Press, 1995.

Downes, William Howe. *The Life and Works of Winslow Homer.* Boston: Houghton Mifflin, 1911.

Lovell, Margaretta M. "Picturing 'A City for a Single Summer': Paintings of the World's Columbian Exposition." *Art Bulletin* 78, no. 1 (March 1996): 40–55.

Nemerov, Alexander. "Winslow Homer's Dream." In *Night Vision: Nocturnes in American Art, 1860–1960,* edited by Joachim Homann, 151–55. Brunswick, ME: Bowdoin College Museum of Art, 2015.

BERTHA EVELYN JAQUES

b. Covington, OH, 1863; *d.* Chicago, IL, 1941

✡ ARTIST

Born in a village in Ohio, Bertha Evelyn Jaques (née Clausen) became a leader in American printmaking and a founder and longtime officer of the Chicago Society of Etchers (est. 1909–10). Over the course of her career, she gave countless talks and demonstrations around the country on printmaking. In her own work, she focused on prints of plant life and cityscapes.

Jaques and her husband made Chicago their home after the devastating successive deaths of their three children. There she attended the 1893 World's Columbian Exposition, where she encountered etchings by renowned French art instructor Maxime Lalanne (1827–1886), JAMES MCNEILL WHISTLER, and Swedish impressionist Anders Leonard Zorn (1860–1920), among others. Soon after, she used Lalanne's *Treatise on Etching* (1880) to learn the basics of the medium. She located a printing press in Milwaukee, had it transported to Chicago, and her husband, a surgeon, fashioned her etching tools from medical instruments. By 1903 she was exhibiting her work professionally. Chicago lore claims Jaques owned the only printing press in the city and, according to an article in *Art Digest*, "the first etching ever made in Chicago was printed, with the artist, Mrs. Jaques, zealously heaving at the press."

Jaques's earliest prints are views of Chicago and Europe, created not for the market but as personal souvenirs. She made her first trip abroad around 1910, visiting Italy—including Venice—England, the Netherlands, Spain, and Sweden. Later journeys farther afield also took her to Japan and Egypt. By 1911 Jaques had pulled her first prints of Venice, among them scenes of a shipyard at Chioggia where she recorded fishermen drying their nets. Additional prints of fish markets, canals, and the city's architecture followed each year from 1913 to 1916.

References

De Vecsey, Esther. *Bertha E. Jaques (1863–1941): An American Printmaker—A Retrospective*. Houston, TX: Gerhard Wurzer Gallery, 1982.

Duncan, Virginia Hope. "Bertha E. Jaques." *Prints* 3, no. 2 (January 1933): 26–34.

"Etchings Win Bertha Jaques High Honor." *Chicago Tribune*, June 23, 1929.

"A Leader Retires." *Art Digest* 12 (October 15, 1939): 25.

Lovely, Deborah, and James O. Pierce. *Bertha E. Jaques: An Exhibition of Prints and Drawings, December 1983*. Oakbrook Terrace, IL: Lovely Fine Arts, 1983.

"Mrs. Jaques Dies." *Art Digest* 15, no. 14 (April 15, 1941): 20.

Patterson, Joby. *Bertha E. Jaques and the Chicago Society of Etchers*. Madison, NJ: Fairleigh Dickinson University Press, 2002.

JAMES JACKSON JARVES

b. Boston, MA, 1818; *d.* Tarasp, Switzerland, 1888

✡ COLLECTOR, SCHOLAR, CRITIC

James Jackson Jarves credited his interest in glass and collecting to his father, Deming Jarves (1790–1869), who founded the Boston and Sandwich Glass Company in 1825 and was known as the "Father of American Glass." Jarves recalled in his book *Art Thoughts: The Experiences and Observations of an American Amateur in Europe* (1869) that as a boy he collected "as soon as [he was] promoted to the dignity of pockets." His ambitious collecting practices, however, nearly drove him to bankruptcy as an adult. Yet this never deterred him, and Jarves acquired Italian works of art and glass that would be included in major museum collections in the United States.

After entrepreneurial adventures in California, Mexico, South America, and the islands of Hawai'i, Jarves settled in Europe. His collection of Venetian glass was largely acquired between 1878 and 1881, while he was living in Italy. Early on, Jarves had ideas for converting his father's firm to a Venetian-style glass production company, preferring beautiful and nonutilitarian approaches over the pressed glass for which the Sandwich factory was known. This was never realized, and Jarves focused instead on his own collection. Jarves sought to profit from his collecting, but he also wrote about the value of educational public institutions like art museums and encouraged European works of art to be added to their collections. Ultimately, Yale University Art Gallery acquired his extensive holdings of old master Italian paintings, and he donated nearly three hundred examples of Venetian glass from the sixteenth to the nineteenth centuries to the Metropolitan Museum of Art in his father's memory.

Jarves lived in Florence for more than thirty years altogether, frequently contributing articles on European life to *Harper's Monthly Magazine* and later publishing many of his essays on art and travel as books, including *Art-Hints: Architecture, Sculpture, and Painting* (1855) and *Italian Rambles: Studies of Life and Manners in New and Old Italy* (1883).

References

Glasscock, Ann Marie. "James Jackson Jarves: Collecting Venetian Glass for America." *Revista de História da Arte* 3 (2015): 45–57.

Hollister, Paul. "The Remarkable Glass Gift of James Jackson Jarves, a Collector in a Hurry." *Acorn: Journal of the Sandwich Glass Museum, the Sandwich Historical Society* 5 (1994): 5–18.

Rudoe, Judy. "'Reproductions of the Christian Glass of the Catacombs': James Jackson Jarves and the Revival of the Art of Glass in Venice." *Metropolitan Museum Journal* 37 (2002): 305–14.

Sizer, Theodore. "James Jackson Jarves: A Forgotten New Englander." *New England Quarterly* 6, no. 2 (June 1933): 328–52.

Steegmuller, Francis. *The Two Lives of James Jackson Jarves*. New Haven, CT: Yale University Press, 1951.

Walter Franklin Lansil

b. Bangor, ME, 1846; *d.* Boston, MA, 1925

✡ ARTIST

In 1884 Walter Franklin Lansil sold more than a hundred of his paintings and sketches in order to travel to Europe and study the old masters. He sailed for Paris from Boston that summer and enrolled at the Académie Julian, then used France as a base for further travels to Belgium, the Netherlands, Germany, and Italy. He was in Paris when he arranged a trip to Venice with his brother, Wilbur Lansil (1855–1897), also an artist, arriving first in Turin in February 1885, then quickly traveling on to their destination.

Lansil described his early morning arrival in detail in his 1914 memoir, *A Trip to Venice*, expressing disappointment with the cold and damp winter climate: "We were now in Venice, not indeed the charming Venice that we expected to see painted by artists and praised by poets...but a dark and dreary dismal city." However, after a lengthy gondola ride across the Grand Canal to his lodging, misted over and subtly lit by the early morning sun, and settling into his hotel, an old palazzo near the Santa Maria della Salute, Lansil had begun to appreciate the romance of Venice's past. Visits to sites like the Piazzetta, St. Mark's Basilica, Doge's Palace, Public Gardens, and Murano's glass factories—which produced "the finest glass-ware in the world," according to Lansil—inspired him to create work that earned him mention as "the celebrated Venetian painter" in the *New York Times* in 1897.

In his memoir, Lansil repeatedly noted the history and "past glory" of Venice. The many varied fishing boats, for example, once the pride of Venice, were increasingly departing for the nearby town of Chioggia after the advent of motorized watercraft. For Lansil, these sailboats embodied the city's romantic past. He described their painted sails and brilliant colors reflected in the Adriatic waters and believed the costumes worn by fishermen to be largely forgotten cultural treasures. Lansil hoped to convey the grandeur of Venice and re-create its maritime traditions through his work. He stayed for nearly a year, painting scenes of the Grand Canal and the lagoon, along with some cityscapes and a few portraits. Upon his return home, he continued to paint Venetian subjects for an eager American audience for nearly forty years.

References

Lansil, Walter. Two handwritten drafts of Lansil's memoir "A Trip to Venice," 1914. Archives of American Art, Smithsonian Institution.

Scollans, Carol G. J. *The Allure of Venice: Paintings by Walter Franklin Lansil.* Portsmouth, NH: Blue Tree, 2018.

George Aloysius Lucas

b. Baltimore, MD, 1824; *d.* Paris, France, 1909

✡ COLLECTOR, PATRON

As a connoisseur, dealer, and patron, George A. Lucas was a key figure in the transatlantic art world of the late nineteenth century. His father, Fielding Lucas Jr. (1781–1854), operated a successful Baltimore paper supply and publishing firm, best known for its high-quality maps and its *Progressive Drawing Book* (1827), one of the first art instruction manuals produced in the United States. The elder Lucas was also a founder and early vice president of the Maryland Institute for the Promotion of the Mechanic Arts (established in 1826, and now the Maryland Institute College of Art). George Lucas studied engineering at the United States Military Academy at West Point and worked briefly in the railroad industry in his twenties, then moved to Paris in 1857 and built a new career at the center of its dynamic international arts community.

In Paris Lucas followed the latest exhibitions of contemporary European art, then leveraged this knowledge to become an art buyer for wealthy Americans seeking to amass choice collections of fine European paintings. His clients included William Henry Vanderbilt, William Wilson Corcoran, SAMUEL PUTNAM AVERY, and father-and-son collectors William T. and HENRY WALTERS (fellow Baltimoreans). His most conspicuous and high-value dealings involved well-regarded contemporary French artists, including landscape painters of the Barbizon School like Jean-Baptiste-Camille Corot (1796–1875), academic figure painters like Alexandre Cabanel (1823–1889), and specialists in bronze sculpture like Antoine-Louis Barye (1795–1875). He also purchased eighteenth- and early nineteenth-century European art but exhibited minimal interest in the French impressionists and other more experimental Parisian artists of his day, exercising his eye for quality and market value within well-established codes of taste.

Lucas's recommendations and purchases often hinged on personal friendships with artists, and he nurtured many younger painters, including Americans visiting or studying in the French capital, with loans and assistance in acquiring supplies and organizing exhibitions. His American circle included Mary Cassatt, **WALTER GAY**, and **JAMES MCNEILL WHISTLER**, whose elder brother George had been a friend and coworker during Lucas's pre-Paris engineering career. Although Lucas's mild-mannered and somewhat reclusive personality differed from Whistler's flamboyant and often hot-headed temperament, they were steady friends from the 1850s until 1886, when Lucas severed ties with Whistler to express disapproval of the artist's acrimonious separation from his long-term mistress and model Maud Franklin (1857–ca. 1941). Despite these personal differences, Lucas later developed an appreciation for the merits in Whistler's artwork and gathered an extensive collection of the artist's prints and ephemera, possibly with the intent of writing a book about his former friend. Inspiration for collecting Whistler and other printmakers may have come from Avery, who was building an encyclopedic collection of nineteenth-century prints, with Lucas serving as his chief art buyer. Lucas also acquired Asian ceramics, art books, and paintings, many received as gifts from the artists he supported.

Unlike his adventurous American friends, Lucas disliked travel and rarely left Paris. His scant explorations of Europe during five decades abroad included a week in Venice in July 1887 to see its churches, museums, and the Esposizione Nazionale Artistica (a forerunner to the Venice Biennale). Though he never returned to the United States, he directed that his personal art collection benefit his hometown of Baltimore through its donation to the Maryland Institute. Later transferred to the Baltimore Museum of Art, the vast ensemble encompasses three hundred paintings, 140 bronzes, and almost nineteen thousand works on paper, including 180 prints by Whistler. —CAM

References

Lucas, William Fielding, Jr. *Exhibition of Paintings, Bronzes, and Porcelains from the George A. Lucas Collection*. Baltimore: Maryland Institute for the Promotion of the Mechanical Arts, 1911.

Mahey, John A. "The Letters of James McNeill Whistler to George A. Lucas." *Art Bulletin* 49, no. 3 (September 1967): 247–57.

Mazaroff, Stanley. *A Paris Life, a Baltimore Treasure: The Remarkable Lives of George A. Lucas and His Art Collection*. Baltimore: Johns Hopkins University Press, 2018.

Randall, Lilian M. C., ed. *The Diary of George A. Lucas: An American Art Agent in Paris, 1857–1909*. 2 vols. Princeton, NJ: Princeton University Press, 1979.

PINCKNEY MARCIUS-SIMONS

b. New York City, 1865; *d.* Bayreuth, Bavaria (now Germany), 1909

✡ ARTIST

Pinckney Marcius-Simons began art lessons in Paris at age twelve with the leading French academic painters of the 1870s, studying as a teenager with Jean-Léon Gérôme (1824–1904), Édouard Detaille (1848–1912), and Jehan Georges Vibert (1840–1902). His youthful works followed the manner and subjects of his teachers, especially Vibert, comprised of highly detailed, sometimes humorous, historical scenes of aristocratic pageantry and of enjoyment of the arts. He first exhibited at the Paris Salon in 1882, and a subsequent sale to French industrialist and influential art collector Camille Groult (1832–1908) attracted critical attention and special praise for his bold use of colors, in the manner of English Romantic landscape painter J. M. W. Turner (1775–1851).

Following a severe illness at around age twenty, Marcius-Simons's artistic style took a mystical turn. Henceforth his skill in rendering details of historical architecture and costumes contributed to fantasy scenes; he painted his dreams and illustrated anecdotes from mythology, poetry, and theater. He shared this enthusiasm for spiritual and literary themes with members of the Ordre de la Rose + Croix, a mystical society that included painters Jean Delville (1867–1953) and Fernand Khnopff (1858–1921), composer Erik Satie (1866–1925), and other artists, poets, and intellectuals. The group organized a series of exhibitions in Paris in the 1890s, and Marcius-Simons exhibited in four of these Salons (as the only American participant). Harmonious combinations of visual art and music, as developed in the operas of German composer Richard Wagner (1813–1883), were of special interest to the members of the Rose + Croix, and this became a chief motivation in Marcius-Simons's later work. He created what he called "tone paintings" to propose and illustrate a theory of systematic correlations between colors and sounds, often depicting episodes from Wagner operas and Shakespeare plays. His *Parsifal* series and other works appeared in solo exhibitions in Boston, Providence, New York, Chicago, and Washington, DC, sometimes accompanied by music recitals to enhance the understanding of his theories.

Marcius-Simons received wide notice for his radiant colors and his challenges to established boundaries within the arts, but many critics, particularly in the United States, found his works' imaginative character excessive, confusing, or distasteful. Nonetheless, prominent American collectors acquired his pictures, including **HENRY WALTERS**, **GEORGE A. LUCAS**, **SAMUEL PUTNAM AVERY**, and US President Theodore Roosevelt (1858–1919). In 1904 Roosevelt wrote to Marcius-Simons praising his paintings: "When I look at them, I feel a lift in my soul; I feel my imagination stirred." Meanwhile, the artist expanded his practice to include set design and was working for the renowned Bayreuth festival of Wagner operas at the time of his death. —CAM

References

Eldredge, Charles C. "Pinckney Marcius-Simons." In *American Imagination and Symbolist Painting*, 157. New York: Grey Art Gallery, 1979.

Greene, Vivien. *Mystical Symbolism: The Salon de la Rose + Croix in Paris, 1892–1897*. New York: Guggenheim Museum Publications, 2017.

Marcius-Simons, Pinckney. *The Parsifal Tone Pictures*. New York: M. Knoedler, 1904.

"Obituary: P. Marcius-Simons." *American Art News* 7, no. 34 (August 14, 1909): 2.

Slavkin, Mary. "Statistically Speaking: Central Exhibitors at the Salons of the Rose + Croix." *Nineteenth-Century Art Worldwide* 14, no. 3 (Autumn 2015), http://www.19thc-artworldwide.org/autumn15/slavkin-on-central-exhibitors-at-the-salons-of-the-rose-croix.

Waterbury, Jennie Bullard. "Paris Letter." *Brooklyn Life*, October 13, 1894, 14.

James McBey

b. Aberdeenshire, Scotland, 1883;
d. Tangier, Morocco, 1959
✡ ARTIST

Born in Scotland, James McBey spent most of his life between studios and homes in Tangier, London, New York City, and Philadelphia. A frequent traveler, he first visited Venice from 1924 to 1925 at age forty-two, renting a palazzo overlooking the Grand Canal. Little of McBey's time in Venice is recorded, but his traveling companion, artist Martin Hardie (1875–1952), described McBey passing entire days sketching in all weather conditions, spending "hours at the end of the Rialto or at a table under the colonnade of the Chioggia Café in the Piazzetta," followed by nightly gondola rides working by candlelight. McBey used these sketches to create etchings of the city. To eliminate the need to reverse his sketches prior to printing, McBey used an automobile mirror affixed to the easel, with his back to the scene, efficiently capturing the image directly on the etching plate.

In 1926 he published three sets of etchings depicting Venice, each capturing the light and atmosphere of the city at different times of day. They were exhibited in London that spring with high praise and commercial success; critics compared his printmaking skills to those of Dutch artist Albrecht Dürer (1471–1528) and other old masters.

McBey visited the United States in 1929, meeting and marrying American artist Marguerite Huntsberry Loeb (1905–1999) in 1931. He became a US citizen in 1942. After World War II, the couple left New York to live primarily at the estate McBey had purchased ten years prior in Morocco, making trips back to the States from time to time.

References

Hardie, Martin, Charles Carter, and Malcolm C. Salaman. *The Etchings and Dry-Points of James McBey (1883–1959)*. San Francisco: Alan Wolfsy Fine Arts, 1997.

McBey, James. *The Early Life of James McBey: An Autobiography, 1883–1911*. Edited by Nicolas Barker. Oxford: Oxford University Press, 1977.

McNiff, Philip J., Marguerite McBey, and Sinclair Hitchings. *James McBey: A Portrait of the Artist*. Boston: Boston Public Library, 1985.

Thomas Moran

b. Bolton, England, 1837; *d.* Santa Barbara, CA, 1926

✡ ARTIST

At seven years old, Thomas Moran emigrated from England to Philadelphia. He established himself as a painter of the American West after joining Ferdinand Hayden's 1871 US Geological Survey expedition to Yellowstone as an artist-surveyor, a position also held by WILLIAM HENRY HOLMES, who joined the survey in 1872 after viewing Moran's *Grand Canyon of the Yellowstone* (1872). Later in his career, Moran also became a painter of Venice, completing more than a hundred views of the city before his death.

For the first time since childhood, Moran returned to Europe in 1861 to study the old masters. On a subsequent trip in 1866, funded by the sale of sixty-four of his artworks, he saw Venice. He stayed at the Grand Hotel situated at the mouth of the Grand Canal in May and June of that year, following in the footsteps of earlier artists to paint the city's most popular sites. During this first stay, he worked on preparatory sketches and watercolor studies that would provide source material for the rest of his career. He revisited Venice in the summer of 1890, bringing home more sketches as well as an elegantly carved gondola, allegedly once owned by poets Robert and Elizabeth Browning, which he used for inspiration and entertainment in Hook Pond near his home in East Hampton, New York. Moran completed most of his Venetian paintings after his second trip. This subject far outnumbers any others he depicted, including his popular scenes of the Rocky Mountains, and he returned to it throughout his career.

Moran frequently exhibited his Venetian works in the United States and abroad. His submissions to exhibitions at the National Academy of Design in New York between 1887 and 1900 were typically Venetian subjects, and he painted at least one scene of Venice annually, often even more, for the next twenty years. Moran's Venetian views reached an even wider audience when one of his works was reproduced in an 1898 calendar by the Brown and Bigelow firm, which circulated to more than twenty-two million readers.

References

Anderson, Nancy K. *Thomas Moran.* New Haven, CT: Yale University Press, 1997.

Beddington, Charles. *Venice: Canaletto and His Rivals.* London: National Gallery, 2010.

Braff, Phyllis. *Thomas Moran: A Search for the Scenic; His Landscape Paintings of the American West, East Hampton, and Venice.* East Hampton, NY: Guild Hall Museum, 1980.

Moran, Thomas, and Ruth B. Moran. *Venice.* East Hampton, NY: Studio, 1934.

Hermann Dudley Murphy

b. Marlborough, MA, 1867; *d.* Lexington, MA, 1945

✡ ARTIST, FRAMEMAKER

Venice was of interest to Hermann Dudley Murphy long before he traveled abroad. In remembering his earliest work, Murphy wrote, "I had an old steel engraving of San Giorgio Maggiore from an oil by an old American artist who had painted in Venice, and that I copied laboriously, in water color, spending a great deal of time upon it.... That was my first painting and my first sale." Murphy had planned to join his father's shoe business after college, but instead, with his father's blessing, turned his attention to art. After completing formal training at the School of the Museum of Fine Arts, Boston, he worked as an illustrator in the city for about a year. Some of his earliest known drawings—copies after JAMES MCNEILL WHISTLER, whom Murphy later met and continued to emulate—were made on assignment for *American Art Illustrated.*

In 1891 Murphy moved to Paris to study for the next five years at the Académie Julian and the École des Beaux-Arts. He also befriended Whistler, who taught him, among other things, the relationship of a painting to its frame. Upon his return to Boston in 1897, Murphy applied these lessons and the carving and gilding skills he acquired in Paris to open the Carrig-Rohane frame shop with Charles Prendergast (1863–1948), brother of MAURICE PRENDERGAST. By 1907 Murphy was considered "the leading frame manufacturer in Boston, that is, of high-priced frames." He operated the shop until 1917.

Murphy traveled abroad again from around 1907 to 1908, visiting Italy for nearly a year and spending five of those months in Venice. Dozens of paintings resulted from this trip, many completed long after he returned home, as evidenced by exhibition records that list paintings with relevant titles dated after 1908. Some of these early paintings were included in a 1909 exhibition at the Toledo Museum of Art at the same time images of Venice by **THOMAS MORAN** were being shown there.

References

"Artist-Craftsman: Herman Dudley Murphy, Boston Painter." *Boston Daily Globe*, December 11, 1904.

Dickerson, James Spencer. "Hermann Dudley Murphy: Painter—Craftsman." *Sketch Book* 6, no. 6 (November 1907): 302–6.

"Fine Paintings: Exhibit of Compositions by Herman Dudley Murphy." *Hartford Courant*, May 21, 1907, 4.

Kvam, Elizabeth Daily, and Sandra Leff. *Hermann Dudley Murphy, 1867–1945: Boston Painter at Home and Abroad.* New York: Graham Gallery, 1985.

M. K. "Hermann Dudley Murphy." *Brush and Pencil* 5, no. 2 (November 1899): 49–57.

Hermann Dudley Murphy papers, circa 1878–1982. Archives of American Art, Smithsonian Institution.

WALTER LAUNT PALMER

b. Albany, NY, 1854; *d.* Albany, NY, 1932

✡ ARTIST

Walter Launt Palmer, son of sculptor Erastus Dow Palmer (1817–1904), embarked on his first European sojourn in 1873 with his family, visiting Scotland, France, Germany, and Italy. On one of many subsequent trips abroad, Palmer trained in the atelier of Carolus-Duran in Paris, where he met fellow student **JOHN SINGER SARGENT**. When Palmer and his family traveled again in 1874, he saw Venice for the first time. Captivated by the city, Palmer gave up his New York City space in the Tenth Street Studio Building, which he shared with his mentor, landscape artist Frederic Edwin Church (1826–1900), and returned for a third, extended European trip in 1881, staying in Venice for two months.

Palmer spent much of his time in Venice with **WILLIAM MERRITT CHASE**, **FRANK DUVENECK**, and **ROBERT FREDERICK BLUM**. During his stay, Palmer changed focus from elaborate interiors of upper-class homes to scenes of the city and its environs. He focused on landmarks near St. Mark's Square, Grand Canal, and San Giorgio Maggiore, working in multiple media and developing his talents as a master colorist. His depictions of Venice quickly gained a following in the United States, helping to establish his professional reputation.

Overall, Palmer painted more than one hundred Venetian scenes. Meticulous notes, sketches, and photographs allowed him to produce faithful representations of the city long after he returned to Albany in 1882. They were exhibited widely and especially popular around New York State, where they were displayed at the National Academy of Design, commissioned by prominent collectors, and featured in solo exhibitions. In the mid-1880s, Palmer began working on a new series of American landscapes in winter, scenes he painted along with his Venetian work until his death.

References

Mann, Maybelle. *Walter Launt Palmer: Poetic Reality*. Exton, PA: Schiffer Publishing, 1984.

Walter Launt Palmer Collection, 1873–1959. Albany Institute of History and Art Library, New York.

"W. L. Palmer, 78, Famous Painter, Art Critic, Dies." *Chicago Daily Tribune*, April 17, 1932, 16.

MAXFIELD PARRISH

b. Philadelphia, PA, 1870; *d.* Plainfield, NH, 1966

✡ ARTIST

As the son of painter-etcher Stephen Parrish (1846–1938), Maxfield Parrish was encouraged to pursue art from an early age. Parrish considered his father his most influential teacher, and the two traveled and studied alongside one another in the United States and Europe, including a two-year trip beginning in 1884 to England, northern Italy, and France. In 1888 Parrish began his formal arts education, initially enrolling in the architecture program at Haverford College before transferring to the Pennsylvania Academy of the Fine Arts in 1892 to focus on painting.

While Parrish was at the Academy, a representative for Harper and Brothers noticed his preparatory illustrations for murals and invited him to submit artwork for publication. Between 1895 and 1900, Parrish won multiple commissions for covers of their periodicals, including *Harper's Bazaar, Harper's Weekly*, and *Harper's Monthly Magazine*. This success captured the attention of author Edith Wharton, who commissioned Parrish to illustrate her book *Italian Villas and Their Gardens* (1904), which brought him to Europe again for three months in 1903. Later that year, *Scribner's Magazine*, at Wharton's behest, invited Parrish to create the frontispiece for her short story, "A Venetian Night's Entertainment" (1903) (see p. 253).

Parrish also adapted his repertoire of fantasy subjects and foreign, often European, locales for advertising purposes. In 1917, when General Electric commissioned Parrish to create a series of paintings advertising their Edison Mazda Lamps, he drew on this material for an annual calendar with lithographs illustrating the history of light. He worked on the project until 1924, and while the company dictated most of the images, Parrish submitted his own concept for the final two paintings, which included *Venetian Lamplighters* (see p. 213). Painted in 1922, the year Venice first implemented electricity, the image commemorates its gaslit past as it transitioned into a modern city.

References

Cutler, Laurence. *Maxfield Parrish*. London: Bison Books, 1993.

Cutler, Laurence, and Judy Goffman Cutler. *Maxfield Parrish*. San Diego, CA: Thunder Bay Press, 2001.

——. *Maxfield Parrish and the American Imagists*. Edison, NJ: Chartwell Books, 2007.

Gilbert-Smith, Alma. *Maxfield Parrish: The Masterworks*. Berkeley, CA: Ten Speed Press, 2001.

Ludwig, Coy. *Maxfield Parrish*. New York: Watson-Guptill, 1973.

Wagner, Margaret E. *Maxfield Parrish and the Illustrators of the Golden Age*. San Francisco: Pomegranate, 2000.

Wharton, Edith. *Italian Villas and Their Gardens*. New York: Century, 1904.

Yount, Sylvia. *Maxfield Parrish: 1870–1966*. New York: Harry N. Abrams, 1999.

MAURICE BRAZIL PRENDERGAST

b. St. John's, Canada, 1858; *d.* New York City, 1924

☆ ARTIST

Raised in Boston, Maurice Prendergast left for Paris in 1891 to study at the Académie Colarossi and Académie Julian. He later spent eighteen months in Italy from 1898 to 1899 and became immediately and profoundly taken with Venice. As friend and artist Charles Hovey Pepper (1864–1950) described, "He soaked up Venice. Then saturated, he worked."

Prendergast stayed on Giudecca and spent at least six months studying the city's architecture and art collections. Though impressed by its monuments—the High Renaissance decorative mural cycles by Vittore Carpaccio (ca. 1465–ca. 1526) and the mosaics in St. Mark's Basilica—it was the daily life of Venice that most captured his attention. He painted crowds of locals and visitors traversing bridges, narrow alleys, and expansive squares in all weather conditions and framed these scenes against fragmented views of recognizable sites.

Prendergast sought to represent the newly unified Italy in an appropriately modern, impressionistic style that he adapted to make his own. Marked by the fixed repetition of tesserae-like shapes and colors, his style is suggestive of glass mosaics, a medium he used on at least one occasion in Venice (see p. 243). In late 1899, while he was still in the city, Prendergast's work was displayed to critical acclaim in his first solo show in the United States, and it was then later shown alongside paintings by his friend and fellow Bostonian HERMANN DUDLEY MURPHY in exhibitions in Boston and Chicago. Over the next ten years, Prendergast's work was seen in cities across the United States, including New York, Philadelphia, and Cincinnati. He returned to Venice from 1911 to 1912 for his second and last trip to Europe, this time focusing on capturing the bridges of Venice and the effects of rain on the city's iconic architecture.

Prendergast produced more than fifty watercolors, oil paintings, and monotypes during his two Venetian sojourns. These works contributed to his commercial success and recognition as an American modernist and garnered the attention and patronage of prominent collectors, including a young Duncan Phillips, the critic and patron who helped to establish America's first museum of modern art.

References

Clark, Carol, Nancy Mowll Mathews, and Gwendolyn Owens. *Maurice Brazil Prendergast, Charles Prendergast: A Catalogue Raisonné.* Munich: Prestel; Williamstown, MA: Williams College Museum of Art, 1990.

Glavin, Ellen. "Maurice Prendergast's Second Visit to Venice: Disaster or New Impulse?" *Archives of American Art Journal* 42, nos. 1–2 (2002): 17–25.

Mathews, Nancy Mowll, with Elizabeth Kennedy. *Prendergast in Italy.* New York: Merrell; Williamstown, MA: Williams College Museum of Art; Chicago: Terra Foundation for American Art, 2009.

Pepper, Charles Hovey. "Is Drawing to Disappear in Artistic Individuality? A Sketch of the Work of Maurice Prendergast." *World To-Day* 19, no. 1 (July 1910): 716–19.

Wattenmaker, Richard J. *Maurice Prendergast.* New York: Harry N. Abrams; Washington, DC: National Museum of American Art, Smithsonian Institution, 1994.

Mabel Pugh

b. Morrisville, NC, 1891; *d.* Raleigh, NC, 1986

✲ ARTIST, TEACHER

Mabel Pugh attended the Peace Institute in Raleigh, North Carolina, one of the oldest institutions of higher education for women in the United States. After receiving her art diploma in 1913, she went to New York City to study at the Art Students League for two years, then to the Pennsylvania Academy of the Fine Arts from 1916 to 1921. Through a prestigious Cresson Traveling Scholarship awarded in 1919, Pugh spent time in France and Switzerland and toured major cities and monuments throughout the Italian peninsula during the summer of 1921.

With journal entries and sketches, Pugh carefully annotated what she aptly titled "Art Aspects of Trip Abroad." In the subsection "Masterpieces of Art," she listed places and works of art of interest in Venice, including St. Mark's Basilica, the "Venetian Lace Factory," and "interesting glass works." While Pugh was only in the city for a few days, the experience inspired her to complete at least one oil painting, *Near the Rialto* (location unknown, 1921).

Pugh sketched freely and often while abroad, creating hundreds of small preliminary drawings and watercolors. She traced some of these images onto onionskin paper, working out areas of light and dark to create linoleum block prints. In the years following her return to North Carolina in 1923, she made work based on her tour and completed more than a dozen prints of Italian subjects (see pp. 52, 53). She exhibited this Italian set in 1926 at the Museum of Fine Arts, Houston, where records indicate they were also available for purchase.

Pugh moved to New York for a few years after visiting Europe and began to publish illustrations for *McCall's* and *Ladies' Home Journal*, establishing herself as a professional artist there. She continued to publish her work after returning home to Morrisville in the 1930s and became the town's first female author when she wrote and illustrated the children's book *Little Carolina Bluebonnet* (1933). Pugh went abroad again in 1935 through a grant from the Louis Comfort Tiffany Foundation, visiting the British Isles, the Netherlands, Germany, Switzerland, and France. In 1936 she returned to teach at her alma mater (now William Peace University) and served as head of the art department until her retirement in 1960.

Reference

Mabel Pugh papers, 1907–1975. Archives of American Art, Smithsonian Institution.

John Rogers

b. Salem, MA, 1829; *d.* New Canaan, CT, 1904

✲ ARTIST

John Rogers was educated in the graphic arts at Boston's English High School, the first public high school in the United States. His parents discouraged him from pursuing art any further, so Rogers began a career in civil engineering. He spent eight years experimenting in clay while working as a railroad mechanic before seeking formal training as a sculptor.

When the depression of 1857 interrupted his career on the railroad, Rogers traveled abroad. He arrived first in Paris in 1858, studying with Antoine Laurent Dantan (1798–1878) for two months, then went to Rome to learn from English sculptor Benjamin Edward Spence (1822–1866). From there he visited Florence, Pisa, Genoa, and Turin over another four months. He returned home to the United States in spring 1859.

Rogers created highly popular statues illustrating scenes from family life and the literature of William Shakespeare (1564–1616) and Henry Wadsworth Longfellow (1807–1882), including works set in Venice—such as Shakespeare's *Othello* (1604) and *The Merchant of Venice* (1605). His work was mass-produced and could be found in many middle-class American homes; he sold almost eighty thousand "Rogers groups," many for about fifteen dollars, before the turn of the century.

References

Bleier, Paul, and Meta Bleier. *John Rogers Statuary*. Atglen, PA: Schiffer Publishing, 2001.

Craven, Wayne. *Sculpture in America*. Newark: University of Delaware Press, 1984.

Orcutt, Kimberly. *John Rogers: American Stories*. New York: New-York Historical Society, 2010.

Wallace, David H. *John Rogers: The People's Sculptor*. Middletown, CT: Wesleyan University Press, 1967.

Ernest David Roth

b. Stuttgart, Germany, 1879; *d.* Cambridge, NY, 1964

✡ ARTIST

When he was five years old, Ernest David Roth's family immigrated to the United States from Germany and settled in New York City. By age thirteen, Roth was working as an errand boy for an art print shop, where he encountered works by old masters and contemporary printmakers like **JAMES MCNEILL WHISTLER** and had access to an extensive library. Between 1900 and 1903, Roth attended evening classes in painting and etching at the National Academy of Design. He became a naturalized citizen in 1905, then departed for Europe for three years, living and working primarily in Florence and Venice. He explored the architecture of Italy in depth through painting and etching and created his earliest extant graphic depictions of Venice during this time. Two of his prints were shown at the 1907 Venice Biennale, the sales of which helped him continue his travels in Italy as well as to Paris and Constantinople. Roth went back to New York to exhibit his etchings, but later returned to Italy and France to collect more material for a new set of prints.

After about 1910, Roth was an increasingly prominent member of the American etching community and was active in numerous artists' and etchers' societies. He exhibited at the National Academy of Design and Pennsylvania Academy of the Fine Arts, where he also received training, by 1911. Roth received his first solo exhibition, comprising eighty prints, through Frederick Keppel & Co. in New York in the spring of 1914. Around the same time, in 1915, he received first prize for his Venetian etchings from the Chicago Society of Etchers exhibition. Later that year more recognition followed, when eight etchings of Venice were sent to the Panama–Pacific International Exposition held in San Francisco. Its jury of senior artists, including **FRANK DUVENECK** and Joseph Pennell (1857–1926), who also made etchings of Venice, presented Roth with a silver medal for etching and a bronze medal for painting. The Uffizi Galleries in Florence acquired twelve of his etchings for the museum's collection, and Roth continued to exhibit regularly from that point on.

After World War I, in 1924, he visited Italy again for about a year, which may have included a final visit to Venice, and produced some of his most successful prints of the city. The subject remained central to his painting and printmaking output through the late 1920s. In the 1930s, Roth became interested in the architecture of lower Manhattan, especially the juxtaposition between the aging waterfront and new skyscrapers. His New York studio served as a rendezvous for etchers until he moved to Redding, Connecticut, soon after the onset of World War II.

References

Denker, Eric. *Reflections and Undercurrents: Ernest Roth and Printmaking in Venice, 1900–1940*. Carlisle, PA: Trout Gallery, Dickinson College, 2012.

Hall, Elton W. "The Etchings of Ernest Roth and André Smith." In *Aspects of American Printmaking, 1800–1950*, edited by James O'Gorman, 177–204. Syracuse, NY: Syracuse University Press, 1988.

Antonio Salviati

b. Vicenza, Austrian Empire (now Italy), 1816;
d. Venice, Italy, 1890
✡ GLASS MANUFACTURER

Antonio Salviati was a lawyer before he played an integral role in reestablishing Murano as a center of Italian glassworking. He revived the tradition by forming a small firm to assist with the restoration of mosaics. Over time his business evolved into multiple companies that employed numerous highly skilled workers to produce elaborate mosaics and blown glass in quantities designed for export.

Disappointed by the poor condition of St. Mark's Basilica in Venice and the lack of raw materials available to repair its mosaics, Salviati founded the firm Salviati Dott. Antonio fu Bartolomeo in 1859 to manufacture colored smalti (glass tesserae for mosaics) and provide skilled workers for their installation. The firm received a fifteen-year contract for the restoration of the old mosaics and the creation of new ones, where necessary.

Salviati recruited two experts to lead design and operations at his new factory: Lorenzo Radi (1803–1874), an innovative Muranese glassmaker, and Enrico Podio (active 1860–1870), a mosaicist from Rome recently established in Venice. Together Salviati, Radi, and Podio revived and taught traditional glassmaking skills and adapted them to modern processes. Soon they had more than two hundred workers crafting mosaics and ornamental glass.

Just three years after its founding, the firm's mosaics received the Grand Medal of Honour at the International Exhibition in London, beating out the celebrated workshops of the Vatican and imperial Russia. Employing highly skilled and inventive artists, the Salviati firm took on new projects beyond St. Mark's, including mosaic programs for modern churches and public edifices like London's South Kensington Museum (now the Victoria and Albert Museum), executed between 1862 and 1865.

By 1864 Salviati obtained financial backing from English partners to launch a full-scale revival of the ancient traditions of Venetian glassmaking, including blown glass. Reflecting the new collaboration, the company's name changed to Società Anonima per Azioni Salviati & C. Over the next decades, it grew, splintered, and reconstituted itself under different names as glassmaking evolved on Murano and as Salviati's unique luxury goods found an international clientele through his showrooms and displays at world's fairs. After Salviati's death in 1890, its principal leaders included his sons, Giulio Salviati (1843–1898) and Silvio Salviati (active 1890s–1920), astute business manager Maurizio Camerino (1859–1931), and esteemed Venetian academic painter Antonio Ermolao Paoletti (1834–1912), who supplied designs for many of the firm's later pictorial mosaics, including those commissioned by JANE ELIZABETH LATHROP STANFORD for Stanford University's art museum and memorial chapel.

References

Barr, Sheldon. *Venetian Glass: Confections in Glass, 1855–1914*. New York: Harry N. Abrams, 1998.

Bova, Aldo, Attilia Dorigato, Puccio Migliaccio, and Vladimira Rusca. *Vetri Artistici: Antonio Salviati, 1866–1877*. Venice: Marsillo, 2008.

Bova, Aldo, Claudio Gianolla, and Rossella Junck. *Dragons, Serpents, and Sea Monsters in 19th Century Murano Glass*. Venice: Galleria Junck and Gianolla, 1997.

Liefkes, Reino. "Antonio Salviati and the Nineteenth-Century Renaissance of Venetian Glass." *Burlington Magazine* 136, no. 1094 (May 1994): 283–90.

Mentasti, Rosa Barovier. *Exquisite Glass Ornaments: The Nineteenth-Century Murano Glass Revival in the de Boos-Smith Collection*. Venice: Marsillo, 2010.

John Singer Sargent

b. Florence, Italy, 1856; *d.* London, England, 1925
✡ ARTIST

In 1854 John Singer Sargent's parents left Philadelphia to live an itinerant lifestyle abroad. Born in Italy, he became intimately familiar with its landscape and culture. Sargent continued to live a peripatetic European existence as an adult, frequently returning to Italy, and, while he never stayed long, Venice became a favored destination and subject.

Sargent visited Venice for the first time in February 1874 at age eighteen after enrolling at the Accademia de Belle Arti in Florence for his first formal art training. While there, his family explored the city from their quarters on the Grand Canal. He spent time studying artworks throughout the city, showing special interest in sixteenth-century Venetian painter Jacopo Tintoretto (ca. 1518–1594). He returned six years later in September 1880 as an accomplished artist after receiving further training from leading French portraitist Carolus-Duran in Paris. He stayed with family, this time at the Hotel d'Italie on the Campo San Moisè, before relocating to rooms on St. Mark's Square, beside the clock tower. Later he took a studio on an upper floor of the elegant Palazzo Rezzonico on the Grand Canal, where JAMES MCNEILL WHISTLER held a work space the previous year.

Although Sargent was lodging in the heart of the city, steps away from St. Mark's Basilica, the Doge's Palace, and the Grand Canal, few of his paintings from the 1880s depict these prominent sites. Instead, Sargent concentrated on painting narrow side streets and squares and the people who occupied them, along with watercolors of truncated architectural views. Sargent stayed in Venice for about a year before returning to Paris, but he made the trip again in 1882 for a four-month visit. This time he resided at the Palazzo Barbaro, the adopted residence of his distant relatives, the family of RALPH WORMELEY CURTIS. Sargent and Whistler probably crossed paths in Venice through the Curtis family, perhaps at the Palazzo Barbaro.

Sargent lodged with the Curtis family again in 1898 and painted their portrait. Around this time, he shifted the focus of his work to canal and architectural views under varying conditions of light. Venice became a base for his later rambles in the Italian and Austrian Alps within the region of Tyrol, but Sargent's European travels abruptly ended with the outbreak of World War I, and he returned home to London, his permanent residence since 1886.

References

Adelson, Warren, ed. *Sargent's Venice*. New Haven, CT: Yale University Press, 2006.

Ormond, Richard, and Elaine Kilmurray. *John Singer Sargent, Complete Paintings*. Vol. 1, *The Early Portraits*. New Haven, CT: Yale University Press, 1998.

———. *John Singer Sargent, Complete Paintings*. Vol. 6, *Venetian Figures and Landscapes, 1898–1913*. New Haven, CT: Yale University Press, 2009.

Robertson, Bruce, ed. *Sargent and Italy*. Princeton, NJ: Princeton University Press, 2003.

FRANCIS HOPKINSON SMITH

b. Baltimore, MD, 1838; *d.* New York City, 1915

✡ ARTIST

An author, engineer, and painter, Francis Hopkinson "Hop" Smith pursued a career that reflects the group of artists, scientists, and statesmen from whom he descended, which includes a signer of the Declaration of Independence. Although Smith was interested in art from an early age, a collapse in his family's fortunes precluded college and obliged him to follow a more practical career path. Smith worked as an engineer, and in 1862 he established his own firm in New York City. Specializing in submarine masonry, the company worked on many government projects, including the design and construction of the seawall and foundation for the Statue of Liberty.

Smith was drawn to art throughout his life and turned his full attention to painting at the age of fifty, briefly studying drawing with Alfred Jacob Miller (1810–1874). Smith exhibited his first picture in 1865 with the American Society of Painters in Water Colors. He became a regular exhibitor and began to sell his work, earning the attention of important collectors, including John Jacob Astor (1822–1890), Charles Havemeyer (1867–1898), and William Thompson Walters. Smith became a leading member of the respected Tile Club, a weekly arts society known, among other things, for painting ceramic tiles, forging connections with painters and illustrators like WINSLOW HOMER and WILLIAM MERRITT CHASE.

Smith first went to Europe in 1882, visiting the Netherlands and Italy and carefully capturing what he saw through painting and writing. He traveled for the rest of his life, spending almost every summer in Venice from the late 1880s into the 1910s, and began to write in earnest about his travels in 1886. One of his most colorful illustrated articles, which appeared in an 1891 *Scribner's Magazine*, described his former gondolier and their relationship. He wrote, "In Venice my gondola is always my home, and my gondolier always my best friend."

Illustrated accounts of his journeys are published in works like *Venice of To-Day* (1895; also published as *Gondola Days*), which includes an image of the Palazzo Barbaro, a site he captured at the request of ISABELLA STEWART GARDNER when she resided there in 1894. The romantic quality of his writing extends from travel sketches to short stories and novels, conveying a passion for Venice through a variety of art forms.

References

Carbone, Teresa. *Summers Abroad: The European Watercolors of Francis Hopkinson Smith.* New York: Jordan-Volpe Gallery, 1985.

De Marchi, Agnese. *Between Pen and Palette: Images of Venice in the Work of F. Hopkinson Smith.* Washington, DC: Academica Press, 2018.

Fuller-Walker. "Francis Hopkinson Smith." *Aldine* 9, no. 6 (1878): 195–98.

JANE ELIZABETH LATHROP STANFORD

b. Albany, NY, 1828; *d.* Honolulu, HI, 1905

✡ COLLECTOR

Jane Elizabeth Lathrop Stanford briefly attended the Albany Female Academy but was primarily educated at home. She married Leland Stanford (1824–1893) in 1850. Her husband followed his brothers to Sacramento to profit from the California Gold Rush, and she joined them in 1855, after her father died. Her husband was very successful in California as cofounder and president of the Central Pacific Railroad and president of the Southern Pacific Railroad. He later served a term as governor from 1862 to 1863 and US senator from 1885 to 1893. Jane and Leland Stanford's only child, Leland DeWitt Stanford Jr. (1868–1884), was born when she was thirty-nine.

Leland Jr. took an early interest in art and classical archaeology, actively collecting objects and relics from their travels, which he carefully catalogued and displayed in their home in San Francisco. Encouraging his curiosity, the Stanfords went on traditional grand tours through Europe, first in 1880 and again in 1883. On their first trip, Leland Jr. and his mother traveled to Rome, Naples, Pompeii, Milan, and Venice, among other popular destinations. Their second sojourn followed a similar trajectory but was cut short in Florence in March 1884, when Leland Jr. contracted typhoid fever and passed away. His death marked a turning point for the Stanfords, who channeled their grief into the creation of the Leland Stanford Junior University, founded in 1885 and opened October 1, 1891.

After Leland Sr.'s death in 1893, the family's extensive assets were frozen while the estate was settled. Stanford took financial control, using her personal income to keep the young university solvent and to establish an art museum and chapel on campus. The Leland Stanford Jr. Museum was erected in 1894 as an institution dedicated to art and archaeology. Stanford attempted to incorporate her son's tastes, but her own interests are present in the collection as well, reflected in acquisitions of work by Albert Bierstadt (1830–1902) and local San Francisco artists.

Stanford hired Erede Dr. A. Salviati & Co., a Murano-based firm specializing in mosaics and glassmaking, to carry out her vision for the museum and chapel. Both structures feature extensive mosaic decoration, and the museum benefited from three large gifts from the firm, amounting to approximately 450 examples of late nineteenth- and early twentieth-century Venetian blown glass. The Stanfords' relationship with the Salviati firm and its director Maurizio Camerino began in Venice in the early 1880s, when the Stanfords patronized the firm's showroom for art glassware and visited St. Mark's Basilica, where they were profoundly impressed by the mosaic restoration taking place—a project begun by ANTONIO SALVIATI in 1859.

Until her untimely death, Stanford was described as the driving force behind the university. She served as founder, financial overseer, curator, and director, and on the building committee for its museum and chapel. By 1905 she had built the largest privately owned museum building in the world.

References

Barr, Sheldon. "Venetian Glass at Stanford University." *Magazine Antiques* 162, no. 3 (September 2002): 112–21.

Nagel, Gunther W. *Jane Stanford: Her Life and Letters.* Stanford, CA: Stanford Alumni Association, 1975.

Osborne, Carol M. *Venetian Glass of the 1890s: Salviati at Stanford University.* London: Philip Wilson Publishers in association with the Iris & B. Gerald Cantor Center for Visual Arts at Stanford University, 2002.

Osborne, Carol M., Paul Venable Turner, and Anita Ventura Mozley. *Museum Builders in the West: The Stanfords as Collectors and Patrons of Art, 1870–1906.* Stanford, CA: Stanford University Museum of Art, 1986.

Julius LeBlanc Stewart

b. Philadelphia, PA, 1855; *d.* Paris, France, 1919

✡ ARTIST

Born in Philadelphia, Julius LeBlanc Stewart was living in Paris, immersed in an artistic and lavish expatriate lifestyle by the time he was ten years old. His father, sugar millionaire William Hood Stewart (1820–1897), built his fortune in Cuba through enslaved labor and the exploitation of Black and Indigenous populations in the Caribbean and invested much of his substantial income in art. He was an early patron of painter Mariano Fortuny y Madrazo (1871–1949), other Spanish moderns, and the artists of the French Barbizon school. As a teenager, Stewart took classes at the École des Beaux-Arts and trained privately with both Spanish and French masters. He gained early and ongoing recognition, exhibiting regularly at the Paris Salon after 1878.

Stewart's wealth allowed him to develop an individual style, without regard for patron or market demands, and depict subjects of his choosing, which he occasionally painted on an ambitious scale. Widely known as the "Parisian from Philadelphia," Stewart became famous for his highly publicized paintings of Paris's elite society, including business moguls, aristocrats, artists, and actors, many of whom were his personal friends.

The date of Stewart's first trip to Venice is unknown, but he likely began visiting in the late 1880s and certainly did in 1890, when he arrived with *New York Herald* publisher James Gordon Bennett Jr. (1841–1918). In Venice, Stewart adopted a new group of American friends, including artists **ROBERT FREDERICK BLUM**, **FRANCIS HOPKINSON SMITH**, and **CHARLES FREDERIC ULRICH**. While his society paintings were popular, Stewart sent at least ten paintings of Venice to the Paris Salon between 1908 and 1912. He painted Venetian subjects, including a series of genre scenes and landscape views, in the 1890s and throughout the first decade of the twentieth century, reflecting his increasing visits to the city.

References

Hiesinger, Ulrich W. *Julius LeBlanc Stewart: American Painter of the Belle Époque*. New York: Vance Jordan Fine Art, 1998.

Thompson, D. Dodge. "Julius L. Stewart, a 'Parisian from Philadelphia.'" *Magazine Antiques* 130, no. 5 (November 1986): 1046–58.

Charles Frederic Ulrich

b. New York City, 1858; *d.* Berlin, Germany, 1908

✡ ARTIST

The son of a German émigré photographer and painter, Charles Frederic Ulrich began his formal studies in 1873 at the National Academy of Design in New York before leaving for Europe in 1875. There, Ulrich enrolled at the Royal Academy of Fine Arts in Munich, where **FRANK DUVENECK** and **WILLIAM MERRITT CHASE** had trained earlier. He met Duveneck around 1876 through Duveneck's student John Henry Twachtman (1853–1902).

In 1879 Ulrich went back to New York City for five years, working steadily and gaining recognition through the National Academy of Design and the Society of American Artists. In the 1880s, he earned critical and commercial success for his genre scenes of the working class. Both Chase and Duveneck painted portraits of Ulrich, and Duveneck submitted his as a diploma piece to the National Academy of Design in 1882. Ulrich returned to Europe with Chase and **ROBERT FREDERICK BLUM** in 1884, intending to stay for several years. Ulrich frequently traveled with his artist friends; Chase and Blum in particular accompanied him regularly throughout the 1880s, and Blum accompanied Ulrich to Venice in 1885. Ulrich established a residence there the following year and remained in Europe for most of his career.

In Venice, Ulrich and Blum stayed at the Palazzo Contarini degli Scrigni on the Grand Canal in the San Trovaso quarter. Accounts from Blum and Duveneck provide details about their group's activities in the city over the next several years. Influenced by the international Arts and Crafts movement, Ulrich often painted laborers absorbed in the creative process, like his prize-winning *Glass Blowers of Murano* (see p. 218).

Ulrich was likely still residing in Venice in 1890 when he sent a painting to the Royal Academy of Arts in London, listing the city as his address. Ulrich later settled permanently in Berlin. His paintings of Venetian subjects were sought after by prominent collectors, such as **WILLIAM THOMAS EVANS**, a Smithsonian benefactor, and can be found in museums in Europe and the United States.

References

"C. F. Ulrich Dead." *New York Times*, May 21, 1908, 7.

Meislin, Andrea Popowich. "Charles Frederick Ulrich in New York, 1882 to 1884." MA thesis, University of Arizona, 1996.

Shapiro, Emily Dana. "'An Art Unknown to the Delicate Hand': Labor and Gender in Charles F. Ulrich's *An Amateur Etcher*." In "Machine Crafted: The Image of the Artisan in American Genre Painting, 1877–1908," 56–89. PhD diss., Stanford University, 2003.

Weber, Bruce. "Robert Frederick Blum (1857–1903) and His Milieu." PhD diss., City University of New York, 1985.

HENRY WALTERS

b. Baltimore, MD, 1848; *d.* New York City, 1931

✫ COLLECTOR

Henry Walters's father, William Thompson Walters, instilled in his son a passion for travel, art, and collecting. The elder Walters earned his fortune through the wine and liquor business and then expanded his interests into banking and transportation. He founded the Safe Deposit Company of Baltimore, the predecessor of the Mercantile Bank, and later, after various mergers, took control of the powerful Atlantic Coast Line Railroad.

In 1861, with major business interests in the North and South, the elder Walters took his family to Europe at the start of the American Civil War. Using art collecting as a means of edification for his son, he brought Henry to galleries and museums in Paris and required him to write thoughtful essays on what he saw. Upon his father's death in 1894, Walters inherited an estate valued at $4.5 million, which included the management of the Atlantic Coast Line Railroad and the art collection. William Walters had collected mostly fine art, particularly old master and nineteenth-century European paintings, with advice and assistance from New York art dealer SAMUEL P. AVERY and Paris-based connoisseur GEORGE A. LUCAS. His son had wider interests, and he continued to acquire paintings through Lucas while also avidly buying decorative arts and antiques. By 1899 Henry Walters's art interests largely superseded his involvement in the business, and the initial collection grew from approximately three thousand objects to more than twenty-two thousand.

In 1911 Walters acquired about thirty pieces of glass produced in Murano, some still bearing labels from ANTONIO SALVIATI's firms. Walters's first trip to Italy was in 1873, when he spent five months in Europe, visiting France, England, Belgium, and Switzerland as well. During Walters's next trip abroad, undertaken in 1879, he kept a thirty-six-page notebook of his itinerary and observations, recording in Venice particular admiration for the interiors of St. Mark's Basilica and Santa Maria della Salute.

In 1903 Walters returned aboard his yacht, the *Narada*, and he developed friendships with two other visitors from the United States, architect William Adams Delano (1874–1960) and collector Cornelius Vanderbilt III (1873–1942). Together the men toured the Venetian antique shops. Delano had recently graduated from the École des Beaux-Arts in Paris with a degree in architecture, and Walters invited him to design a museum for his collection.

The vision of an Italian palazzo-like structure came to fruition, and in 1909 Walters began welcoming the public to his new gallery building, which housed a vast collection of manuscripts; arms and armor; and Islamic, Russian, and ancient Middle Eastern art; in addition to Venetian glass objets d'art. When Walters died in 1931, he left the museum in its entirety and an endowment to the mayor and city council of Baltimore, "for the benefit of the public." It opened under the city's management in 1934. Since then, the museum has expanded to include a range of works from across a broad arc of time, geography, and culture.

References

Johnston, William R. *William and Henry Walters: The Reticent Collectors*. Baltimore: Johns Hopkins University Press in association with the Walters Art Gallery, 1999.

Mazaroff, Stanley. *Henry Walters and Bernard Berenson: Collector and Connoisseur*. Baltimore: Johns Hopkins University Press, 2010.

Herman Armour Webster

b. New York City, 1878; *d.* Paris, France, 1970

✡ ARTIST

Herman Armour Webster attended St. Paul's School in Concord, New Hampshire, where he met William M. Ivins Jr. (1881–1961), a longtime friend and ally who would become the first curator of prints at the Metropolitan Museum of Art. Webster produced his earliest etchings as illustrations for *The Yale Record* at Yale University, where he attended the Sheffield Scientific School. He traveled to Paris for the first time after graduation, arriving in 1900, just in time to visit the Exposition Universelle. There he studied with art nouveau painter and graphic artist Alphonse Mucha (1860–1939). The following spring, he took the recently completed Trans-Siberian Railway to Vladivostok, traveling on to Japan and China, and then returned to Chicago around 1902. He worked briefly as an illustrator for the *Chicago Record-Herald* before traveling to Paris again in 1904 to study at the Académie Julian.

While at the Académie, Webster developed his skill as a printmaker with the help of fellow student Donald Shaw MacLaughlan (1876–1938). His early etchings record the quotidian side streets and antique buildings of Paris and the Gothic towns of northern France and Spain. Webster stayed abroad, making France his primary residence for the rest of his life.

By 1915 Webster temporarily abandoned his art to enlist in the American Ambulance Corps in support of the Allied forces in World War I. He served through 1917, until exposure to militarized gas severely impaired his vision. For his service to the nation of France, he received the Croix de Guerre, was made a Chevalier de la Légion d'Honneur, and, in 1956, his rank was elevated to officer.

By the time of his twenty-fifth Yale class reunion, Webster's eyesight was just beginning to return to its previous state. Having to give up the detailed work of etching, Webster turned to watercolor and ink wash painting for about a decade. While working in Venice after the war, he produced watercolors and drawings of the city's architecture. He continued to make, sell, and exhibit his art regularly through the 1930s until the beginning of World War II, wherein he again served as a decorated soldier.

In 1946 Webster wrote to a friend that his etching skills had suffered from lack of use over the years, but he continued to sketch and paint watercolors. By then, however, his dealers in New York City and Chicago, which had shown his work since 1905, had gone out of business, and he struggled to find new representation.

References

Mather, Frank Jewett, Jr. "The Etchings of Herman A. Webster." *Art and Progress* 2, no. 10 (August 1911): 283–86.

Shapiro, Jerome B. *Herman Armour Webster: American Artist, French Patriot.* New York: Glandulae Press, 2018.

T. S. "Prints by Herman Webster." *Bulletin of the Associates in Fine Arts at Yale University* 8, no. 3 (June 1938): 73.

Herman Armour Webster papers, 1900–1974. Archives of American Art, Smithsonian Institution.

James Abbott McNeill Whistler

b. Lowell, MA, 1834; *d.* London, England, 1903

✡ ARTIST, TEACHER

James Abbott McNeill Whistler was raised in St. Petersburg, Russia, where his father served as an engineer for the construction of a railroad line to Moscow. During this time, Whistler and his mother spent about a year with relatives in London, where Francis Seymour Haden (1818–1910), his brother-in-law from marriage to Whistler's half sister, encouraged his artistic inclination, buying him art supplies and introducing him to collectors and artists. After his father's death in 1849, the family returned to the United States, and in 1851 he attended the US Military Academy at West Point before working for the drawing unit of the US Coast and Geodetic Survey. He eventually pursued a career as an artist, first in Paris, then, following rejection at the Salon of 1859, in London.

In 1877 after a successful but financially devastating libel lawsuit against John Ruskin—who had accused the artist of "flinging a pot of paint in the public's face"—Whistler was bankrupt, estranged from his patrons, and emotionally drained. A fortuitous commission from the Fine Art Society of London for a set of twelve etchings of Venice encouraged him to visit the city he had long planned to see. Hoping to mend his reputation and bank balance, Whistler departed

London in September 1879 for his first and only visit to Venice. The terms of the commission stated a December 1879 delivery date for the etchings, but Whistler encountered bitter cold and wet weather upon his arrival that hindered his work. By spring, however, conditions improved, prompting his more optimistic reflection that Venice existed especially for artists.

Whistler first stayed at the Palazzo Rezzonico, where JOHN SINGER SARGENT would stay the next year. They likely crossed paths at the Palazzo Barbaro through RALPH WORMELEY CURTIS. By winter Whistler had moved to modest rooms near the Church of the Frari. As the weather warmed, FRANK DUVENECK and his group of Munich school–trained American artists, including OTTO HENRY BACHER and ROBERT FREDERICK BLUM, descended upon the city and drew Whistler into their circle. Whistler again changed living quarters, joining the "Duveneck Boys" at the Casa Jankowitz. There his room overlooked San Giorgio, the Doge's Palace, and Santa Maria della Salute, which he sketched from his window. When he returned to London in November 1880, his fourteen-month stay had yielded at least fifty etchings, more than ninety pastel drawings, and three oil paintings.

The commissioned etchings were delivered eleven months late and became known as Whistler's "First Venice Set." They were exhibited at the Fine Art Society of London in December 1880 in a small room lined with maroon cloth, an installation designed by the artist himself. A second exhibition comprising fifty-three pastels of Venice followed in January 1881, also at the Fine Art Society. A third show featuring twenty-one Venetian etchings was held at the Society in 1883, and, in 1886, London gallery Dowdeswell & Dowdeswell's exhibited *A Set of Twenty-Six Etchings*. Known as his "Second Venice Set," it included twenty-one Venetian and five English subjects printed in an edition of thirty. These works firmly established Whistler's dominance in the medium of etching, and his vision of Venice influenced artists for generations to come.

Though Whistler never returned to Venice, his works were later exhibited at some of its earliest biennial International Art Exhibitions. At the first Venice Biennale in 1895, his *Symphony in White, No. 2: The Little White Girl* (1864, Tate Britain) received the Comune di Murano prize, and he was one of two American members, Sargent being the other, of the exhibition's honorary Comitato di Patrocinio (Patronage Committee) in 1897 and 1899.

References

Bacher, Otto H. *With Whistler in Venice*. New York: Century, 1908.

Dorment, Richard, and Margaret F. MacDonald. *James McNeill Whistler*. London: Tate Gallery Publications, 1994.

Grieve, Alastair. *Whistler's Venice*. New Haven, CT: Yale University Press, 2000.

Pennell, Elizabeth Robins, and Joseph Pennell. *The Life of James McNeill Whistler*. London: W. Heinemann, 1908.

Simpson, Marc. *Like Breath on Glass: Whistler, Inness, and the Art of Painting Softly*. Williamstown, MA: Clark Art Institute, 2008.

IRVING RAMSAY WILES

b. Utica, NY, 1861; *d.* Peconic, NY, 1948

✡ ARTIST

At age eighteen, Irving Ramsay Wiles began teaching art in western New York State, working alongside his father, painter Lemuel Maynard Wiles (1826–1905), near the town of Perry on Silver Lake. In 1879, at his father's recommendation, he left home to study with Carroll Beckwith (1852–1917), THOMAS WILMER DEWING, and WILLIAM MERRITT CHASE at the newly formed Art Students League in New York City. Founded in 1875, the League was known for its progressive curriculum, in contrast to the staid program of the National Academy of Design. Wiles, having grown up focusing on landscape painting, quickly transitioned to a style more au courant as he became closer with Chase, developing the bravado brushwork that would become the hallmark of his painting.

In the fall of 1882, Wiles left New York for Paris, enrolling first at the Académie Julian and later in the private atelier of Carolus-Duran. While abroad, Wiles made an abbreviated tour of Europe with his father in 1883; a watercolor of two Venetian women and an ink sketch of the Ponte della Paglia document his visit to Venice during this trip. He returned in 1909, when his portrait of Miss Julia Marlowe (1901, National Gallery of Art) was exhibited at the eighth Venice Biennale.

Wiles rose to fame as a painter of society portraits and of young women at their leisure, which provided the artist with a steady income from the 1890s into the 1920s. His portrait of collector JOHN GELLATLY (see p. 82), however, was initiated by the artist in 1930, when commissions were in steep decline due to changing artistic tastes and the Great Depression. Although Wiles likely needed money during this time, he offered to paint Gellatly without charge. After viewing Gellatly's collection, which included work by Wiles's former instructor Dewing and examples of ancient and contemporary glass, and hearing of the collector's plans to donate it in full to the Smithsonian Institution, Wiles felt that a full-length portrait of the donor should accompany the collection.

References

Fleming, Geoffrey K. *Irving Ramsey Wiles, N.A.: Portraits and Pictures, 1899–1948*. Southold, NY: Southold Historical Society in association with Hudson Hills Press, 2011.

Paul, William D., Jr. *The Art of Irving Ramsey Wiles (1861–1948)*. St. Joseph, MO: Albrecht Gallery Museum of Art, 1971.

Reynolds, Gary A. *Irving R. Wiles*. New York: National Academy of Design, 1988.

ANDREW KAY WOMRATH

b. Philadelphia, PA, 1874; *d.* Biot, France, 1953

✲ ARTIST

The artist, who went by Kay Womrath, spent the early twentieth century working mostly in Europe. He first traveled abroad around 1890, arriving in London before visiting Scotland and France. In London he befriended leaders of the Arts and Crafts movement, such as Anglo-Welsh painter, printmaker, and designer Frank Brangwyn (1867–1956). Womrath then went to Paris, where he worked as an illustrator and designed bookplates. His engravings and drawings were regularly published in *The Savoy, Saint-Nicholas, La Revue du Touring-Club de France,* and *The Studio,* among other popular periodicals.

Amid his travels, Womrath met expatriate Japanese printmaker Yoshijirō "Mokuchu" Urushibara (1888–1953), possibly through Brangwyn. Urushibara had come to London in 1910 to demonstrate color woodcut printing at the Japan-British Exhibition and afterward became a preparator for the Asian art collection at the British Museum. He established himself as a woodcut artist within London's printmaking circles and by 1918 began working with Brangwyn and other artists on collaborative projects that utilized Urushibara's specialized knowledge of traditional Japanese printmaking techniques.

Through Urushibara, Womrath learned *mokuhanga,* a multicolor, water-based ink woodblock printing method. Urushibara translated several of Womrath's works into color woodblock prints, and the pair partnered at least once on a Venetian scene, a view looking south down the Rio de la Fornace in Dorsoduro, printed as both day and night views (see p. 259). These two prints, in addition to at least five others depicting the Venetian cityscape and fishing boats, suggest that Womrath and Urushibara visited Venice within their travels around Europe. In the 1920s Womrath and his wife settled in Biot, a village in the south of France, and he redecorated the house there with a Venetian-themed motif. At the onset of the Second World War, Urushibara moved back to Japan, while the Womraths relocated temporarily to Las Cruces, New Mexico, then returned to Biot at the war's end.

References

Chapman, Hilary, and Libby Horner. *Yoshijirō Urushibara: A Japanese Printmaker in London: A Catalogue Raisonné*. Leiden: Brill, 2017.

Fielding, Mantle. *Mantle Fielding's Dictionary of American Painters, Sculptors and Engravers*. Poughkeepsie, NY: Apollo, 1983.

Horner, Libby. "Brangwyn and the Japanese Connection." *Journal of the Decorative Arts Society* 26 (2002): 72–83.

Exhibition Checklist

I. American Art

173 **Henry Alexander**
1860–1894

Cyprus Glass, 1894
oil on canvas
15 ¾ × 19 in. (40 × 48.3 cm)
Collection of David Mamet and Rebecca Pidgeon

173 **Alice Pike Barney**
1857–1931

James McNeill Whistler, 1898
pastel on paper mounted to paperboard
19 1/16 × 19 3/16 in. (48.4 × 48.7 cm)
Smithsonian American Art Museum, Gift of Laura Dreyfus Barney and Natalie Clifford Barney in memory of their mother, Alice Pike Barney, 1951.14.110

171 **Robert Frederick Blum**
1857–1903

Bead Stringers, 1886
etching on paper
image:
12 3/16 × 8 1/16 in. (31 × 20.4 cm);
sheet:
15 ¼ × 10 7/16 in. (38.8 × 26.5 cm)
Cincinnati Art Museum, Gift of Henrietta Haller, 1905.57a

166 **Robert Frederick Blum**
1857–1903

Busy Hands, 1885
etching on paper
image:
6 15/16 × 9 11/16 in. (17.6 × 24.6 cm)
sheet:
12 5/16 × 14 13/16 (31.3 × 37.6 cm)
Cincinnati Art Museum, Gift of Henrietta Haller, 1905.47

49 **Robert Frederick Blum**
1857–1903

Canal in Venice, San Trovaso Quarter, ca. 1885
oil on canvas
34 × 23 ⅛ in. (86.5 × 58.6 cm)
Smithsonian American Art Museum, Gift of William T. Evans, 1909.7.7

260 **Robert Frederick Blum**
1857–1903

Venetian Doorway and Gondolas, ca. 1880
etching and drypoint on paper
5 ¼ × 7 1/16 in. (13.3 × 18 cm)
Collection of Mary Anne Goley

192 **Robert Frederick Blum**
1857–1903

Venetian Lacemakers, 1887
oil on canvas
30 ⅛ × 41 ¼ in. (76.5 × 104.8 cm)
Cincinnati Art Museum, Gift of Elizabeth S. Potter, 1905.8

172 **Giovanni Boldini**
1842–1931

Portrait of James McNeill Whistler, 1897
oil on canvas
67 ¼ × 37 ¼ in. (170.8 × 94.6 cm)
Brooklyn Museum, Gift of A. Augustus Healy, 09.849

249 **Arthur Beecher Carles**
1882–1952

Venetian Gondolas, ca. 1909
oil on canvas
25 × 24 ⅛ in. (63.5 × 61.3 cm)
The Estate of Robert and Linda Wueste

133 **William Merritt Chase**
1849–1916

In the Baptistry of St. Mark's, Venice, 1878
oil on canvas
33 ½ × 43 ½ in. (85.1 × 110.5 cm)
North Carolina Museum of Art, Raleigh, Gift of Marcia Bishopric Gest in memory of Joseph Henry Gest and Henry Gest Jr., 2016.13

227 **Charles Caryl Coleman**
1840–1928

Interior with Lute Player, 1875
oil on canvas
12 ¾ × 8 ¼ in. (32.4 × 21 cm)
McGuigan Collection

73 **Charles Caryl Coleman**
1840–1928

Still Life with Peach Blossoms, 1877
oil on canvas
71 ½ × 25 ¼ in. (181.6 × 64.1 cm)
Art Bridges, AB.2016.1

137 **Charles Caryl Coleman**
1840–1928

The Bronze Horses of San Marco, Venice, 1876
oil on canvas
40 ¼ × 32 ½ in. (102.2 × 82.6 cm)
Minneapolis Institute of Art, Gift of the Regis Collection, 79.13

44 **Kenyon Cox**
1856–1919

Study for *Venice*, 1894
oil and graphite on canvas
29 ⅝ × 59 ⅝ in. (75.3 × 151.5 cm)
Bowdoin College Museum of Art, Brunswick, Maine, Gift of Colonel Leonard Cox, Mrs. Caroline Cox Lansing, and Mr. Allyn Cox, 1959.3.1

40 **Louise Howland King Cox**
1865–1945

May Flowers, 1911
oil on canvas
24 ⅛ × 20 ⅛ in. (61.2 × 51 cm)
Smithsonian American Art Museum, Gift of William T. Evans, 1911.6.1

68 **Maria Oakey Dewing**
1845–1927

Henry Marsh, engraver
1826–1912

An Every-day Mantel-piece, Simply Treated, 1878
Plate 45 in Clarence Cook, *The House Beautiful* (New York: Scribner, Armstrong, 1878)
wood engraving on paper
image:
4 15/16 × 3 ½ in. (12.5 × 8.9 cm)
sheet:
9 ⅝ × 7 ⅛ in. (24.4 × 18.1 cm)
Private collection

257 **Frank Duveneck**
1848–1919

Bridge of Sighs, Venice, 1885
etching on paper
image:
12 × 9 ⅝ in. (30.4 × 24.4 cm)
sheet:
15 ½ × 11 ¼ in. (39.4 × 28.6 cm)
Smithsonian American Art Museum, Museum purchase, 1972.70

236 **Frank Duveneck**
1848–1919

Gypsy Boy, 1885
pastel on paper
17 ½ × 13 ¾ in. (44.5 × 34.9 cm)
Collection of Jane Joel Knox, promised gift to the Virginia Museum of Fine Arts, in loving memory of Irving Joel

146 **Frank Duveneck**
1848–1919

Riva degli Schiavoni, No. 2, 1880
etching on paper
image:
13 ¼ × 8 ⅝ in. (33.6 × 22 cm)
sheet:
19 ⅝ × 12 in. (49.8 × 30.5 cm)
Smithsonian American Art Museum, Museum purchase, 1978.14

234 **Frank Duveneck**
1848–1919

Water Carriers, Venice, 1884
oil on canvas
48 ⅜ × 73 ⅛ in. (122.8 × 185.7 cm)
Smithsonian American Art Museum, Bequest of Reverend F. Ward Denys, 1943.11.1

75 **Walter Gay**
1856–1937

Interior of Palazzo Barbaro, Venice, 1902
oil on canvas
35 ⅝ × 39 ½ in. (90.5 × 100.3 cm)
Museum of Fine Arts, Boston, The Hayden Collection—Charles Henry Hayden Fund, 11.1537

258 **Ellen Day Hale**
1855–1940

First Night in Venice, 1890
soft-ground etching and
aquatint on paper
image: 6 × 7 3/8 in. (15.2 × 18.7 cm)
sheet: 8 × 10 in. (20.3 × 25.4 cm)
The National Museum of Women in the Arts, Gift of Wallace and Wilhelmina Holladay, 1986.99.1

258 **Ellen Day Hale**
1855–1940

First Night in Venice, 1890
soft-ground etching and
aquatint with *à la poupée*
color inking on paper
image: 6 × 7 3/8 in. (15.2 × 18.7 cm)
sheet: 7 1/2 × 9 3/4 in.
(19.1 × 24.8 cm)
The National Museum of Women in the Arts, Gift of Wallace and Wilhelmina Holladay, 1986.99.2

51 **Hermann Herzog**
1831–1932

Along the Grand Canal, Venice,
ca. 1890s
oil on canvas
23 1/2 × 30 1/2 in. (59.7 × 77.5 cm)
Woodmere Art Museum,
Bequest of Charles Knox Smith

205 William Henry Holmes
1846–1933

Bead Stringer, Venice, 1880
watercolor and graphite on paper
4 1/2 × 3 3/4 in. (11.4 × 9.5 cm)
National Anthropological Archives, Smithsonian Institution, MS2011-19.2

205 **William Henry Holmes**
1846–1933

Venice, Mending Sails, 1880
watercolor and graphite on paper
3 1/2 × 4 1/2 in. (8.9 × 11.4 cm)
National Anthropological Archives, Smithsonian Institution, MS2011-19.3

246 **Winslow Homer**
1836–1910

The Fountains at Night, World's Columbian Exposition, 1893
oil on canvas
16 3/8 × 25 1/8 in. (41.6 × 63.8 cm)
Bowdoin College Museum of Art, Brunswick, Maine, Bequest of Mrs. Charles Savage Homer Jr., 1938.2

94 **Bertha Evelyn Jaques**
1863–1941

April Shower, Venice, 1914
etching on paper
image:
5 1/4 × 7 7/8 in. (13.4 × 20.1 cm)
sheet:
7 5/8 × 10 1/2 in. (19.4 × 26.7 cm)
Smithsonian American Art Museum, Gift of Chicago Society of Etchers, 1935.13.490

50 **Walter Franklin Lansil**
1846–1925

The Coming Storm, 1908
oil on canvas
22 × 29 in. (55.9 × 73.7 cm)
Fry Fine Art Gallery

236 **Pinckney Marcius-Simons**
1865–1909

The Child Canova Modeling a Lion out of Butter, ca. 1885
oil on canvas
23 3/4 × 29 in. (60.3 × 73.7 cm)
Chrysler Museum of Art, Norfolk, VA, Gift of the Mowbray Arch Society, 2014.14

251 **James McBey**
1883–1959

Glass Blowers, Murano, 1925,
printed 1930
drypoint on paper
image: 5 × 6 in. (12.7 × 15.2 cm)
sheet: 7 1/16 × 10 1/4 (18 × 26 cm)
Gift of Mrs. James McBey, Prints Collection, Miriam and Ira D. Wallach Division of Art, Prints and Photographs, The New York Public Library, Astor, Lenox and Tilden Foundations, 95504

214 **Thomas Moran**
1837–1926

A View of Venice, 1891
oil on canvas
35 1/8 × 25 1/4 in. (89.2 × 64.1 cm)
Smithsonian American Art Museum, Transfer from the US Department of the Interior, National Park Service, 1968.120.1

215 **Hermann Dudley Murphy**
1867–1945

Murano, 1907
oil on canvas
19 3/4 × 30 1/2 in. (50.2 × 77.5 cm)
Collection of Lisa and Michael Sandman

64 **Walter Launt Palmer**
1854–1932

Interior at 6 Elk Street (Residence of the Reverend Frank L. Norton),
1885
oil on canvas
22 1/2 × 26 1/2 in. (57.2 × 67.3 cm)
Albany Institute of History & Art purchase, 1968.72

35 **WALTER LAUNT PALMER**
1854–1932

Interior San Marco, 1902
gouache on composition board
24 × 17 in. (61 × 43.2 cm)
Albany Institute of History & Art, Bequest of J. Townsend Lansing, 1920.7.1

54 **WALTER LAUNT PALMER**
1854–1932

Wing and Wing, 1890
oil on canvas
18 × 27 in. (45.7 × 68.6 cm)
Private collection

253 **MAXFIELD PARRISH**
1870–1966

A Venetian Night's Entertainment, 1903
oil on paper on panel
17 7/8 × 12 3/8 in. (43.4 × 31.4 cm)
Lucas Museum of Narrative Art, 2018.269

213 **MAXFIELD PARRISH**
1870–1966

Venetian Lamplighters, 1922
oil on panel
28 3/4 × 18 3/4 in. (73 × 47.6 cm)
National Museum of American Illustration, Newport, RI, and American Illustrators Gallery, New York, NY

243 **MAURICE BRAZIL PRENDERGAST**
1858–1924

Fiesta Grand Canal, Venice, ca. 1899
glass and ceramic mosaic tiles in plaster
11 × 23 in. (27.9 × 58.4 cm)
Williams College Museum of Art, Bequest of Mrs. Charles Prendergast, 95.4.79

244 **MAURICE BRAZIL PRENDERGAST**
1858–1924

Ponte della Paglia, ca. 1898, reworked 1922
oil on canvas
27 7/8 × 23 1/8 in. (70.8 × 58.7 cm)
The Phillips Collection, Acquired 1922, 1610

53 **MABEL PUGH**
1891–1986

Near the Rialto, Venice, ca. 1923–26
linoleum cut on paper
image:
9 1/2 × 7 3/8 in. (24 × 18.7 cm)
sheet:
13 × 8 5/8 in. (33 × 21.9 cm)
Smithsonian American Art Museum, Transfer from the North Carolina Museum of Art (Gift of the artist, 1977), 2020.4.11

52 **MABEL PUGH**
1891–1986

St. Mark's, Venice, ca. 1923–26
linoleum cut on paper
image:
5 1/4 × 4 1/8 in. (13.3 × 10.5 cm)
sheet:
7 1/2 × 4 7/8 in. (19.1 × 12.4 cm)
Smithsonian American Art Museum, Transfer from the North Carolina Museum of Art (Gift of the artist, 1977), 2020.4.12

230 **JOHN ROGERS**
1829–1904

"Ha! I Like Not That," 1882
painted plaster
22 × 20 3/4 × 14 3/8 in.
(55.8 × 52.6 × 36.5 cm)
Smithsonian American Art Museum, Gift of John Rogers and Son, 1882.1.4

94 **ERNEST DAVID ROTH**
1879–1964

A Quiet Canal, 1905
etching on paper
image:
4 1/2 × 9 1/8 in. (11.3 × 23.2 cm)
sheet:
7 3/4 × 12 5/8 in. (19.7 × 32.1 cm)
Smithsonian American Art Museum, Gift of Mr. and Mrs. Harry Katz, 1971.386

155 **JOHN SINGER SARGENT**
1856–1925

A Venetian Interior, ca. 1880–82
oil on canvas
19 1/16 × 23 15/16 in. (48.4 × 60.8 cm)
Sterling and Francine Clark Art Institute, Williamstown, MA, 1955.580

30 **JOHN SINGER SARGENT**
1856–1925

A Venetian Woman, 1882
oil on canvas
93 3/4 × 52 3/8 in. (238.2 × 133 cm)
Cincinnati Art Museum, The Edwin and Virginia Irwin Memorial, 1972.37

256 **JOHN SINGER SARGENT**
1856–1925

Corner of the Church of San Stae, 1913
oil on canvas
28 1/2 × 22 in. (72.4 × 55.9 cm)
Private collection

154 **JOHN SINGER SARGENT**
1856–1925

Leaving Church, Campo San Canciano, Venice, ca. 1882
oil on canvas
22 × 33 1/2 in. (55.9 × 85.1 cm)
The Collection of Marie and Hugh Halff

217 **JOHN SINGER SARGENT**
1856–1925

The Sulphur Match, 1882
oil on canvas
23 × 16 ¼ in. (58.4 × 41.3 cm)
The Collection of
Marie and Hugh Halff

174 **JOHN SINGER SARGENT**
1856–1925

Venetian Glass Workers, ca. 1880–82
oil on canvas
22 ¼ × 33 ¼ in. (56.5 × 84.5 cm)
The Art Institute of Chicago,
Mr. and Mrs. Martin A. Ryerson
Collection, 1933.1217

48 **FRANCIS HOPKINSON SMITH**
1838–1915

On the Way to the Public Garden,
ca. 1895
opaque watercolor and pastel over
graphite on paper
14 ½ × 24 ½ in. (36.8 × 62.2 cm)
Smithsonian American Art Museum,
Gift of Laura Dreyfus Barney and
Natalie Clifford Barney in memory
of their mother, Alice Pike Barney,
1957.13.22

151 **JULIUS LEBLANC STEWART**
1855–1919

Conversation Vénetienne, 1891
oil on canvas
28 ¾ × 39 ¾ in. (73 × 101 cm)
Private collection

76 **JULIUS LEBLANC STEWART**
1855–1919

Venetian Market Scene (Sotoportego del Magazen), 1907
oil on canvas
21 ½ × 28 ¾ in. (54.6 × 73 cm)
Michael and Jean Antonello Family
Foundation

32 **CHARLES FREDERIC ULRICH**
1858–1908

GOUPIL & CO., printer
1850–1887

Glass Blowers, 1887, printed 1890
Plate opp. pg. 28 in George William
Sheldon, *Recent Ideals in American Art*
(New York: D. Appleton, 1890)
photogravure on paper
image:
10 15/16 × 8 ¾ in. (27.8 × 22.2 cm)
sheet:
16 3/16 × 11 9/16 in. (41.1 × 29.4 cm)
Private collection

134 **HERMAN ARMOUR WEBSTER**
1878–1970

To the Caffetteria—Capuccino's Time, Venice Zattere, 1935
carbon pencil on paper
5 ¼ × 7 in. (13.3 × 17.8 cm)
Smithsonian American Art Museum,
Gift of Moune G. H. Webster,
1973.124.21

171 **JAMES MCNEILL WHISTLER**
1834–1903

Bead Stringers (Second Venice Set),
1880
etching and drypoint on paper
9 1/16 × 6 1/16 in. (23.5 × 15.1 cm)
Gift of Samuel Putnam Avery,
Prints Collection, Miriam and
Ira D. Wallach Division of Art,
Prints and Photographs, The
New York Public Library, Astor,
Lenox and Tilden Foundations,
108711

148 **JAMES MCNEILL WHISTLER**
1834–1903

Fruit Stall (Second Venice Set),
1879–80
etching and drypoint on paper
8 15/16 × 5 15/16 in. (23 × 15.1 cm)
The Baltimore Museum of Art,
The George A. Lucas Collection,
purchased with funds from the State
of Maryland, Laurence and Stella
Bendann Fund, and contributions
from individuals, foundations,
and corporations throughout the
Baltimore community, 1996.48.12298

221 **JAMES MCNEILL WHISTLER**
1834–1903

Murano—Glass Furnace, 1879–80
drypoint on paper
6 ¼ × 9 ¼ in. (16.2 × 23.4 cm)
Gift of Samuel Putnam Avery,
Prints Collection, Miriam and
Ira D. Wallach Division of Art,
Prints and Photographs, The
New York Public Library, Astor,
Lenox and Tilden Foundations,
108730

149 **JAMES MCNEILL WHISTLER**
1834–1903

Nocturne: Furnace (Second Venice Set), 1879–80
etching and drypoint on paper
6 ¾ × 9 1/8 in. (17.1 × 23.1 cm)
The Baltimore Museum of Art,
The George A. Lucas Collection,
purchased with funds from the State
of Maryland, Laurence and Stella
Bendann Fund, and contributions
from individuals, foundations,
and corporations throughout the
Baltimore community, 1996.48.18102

152 **James McNeill Whistler**
1834–1903

Old Women, 1880
drypoint on paper
5 × 7 15/16 in. (12.5 × 20 cm)
Gift of Samuel Putnam Avery, Prints Collection, Miriam and Ira D. Wallach Division of Art, Prints and Photographs, The New York Public Library, Astor, Lenox and Tilden Foundations, 108734

152 **James McNeill Whistler**
1834–1903

The Beggars (First Venice Set), 1879–80
etching and drypoint on paper
12 × 8 1/4 in. (30.5 × 21 cm)
The Baltimore Museum of Art, The Conrad Collection, 1932.17.16

152 **James McNeill Whistler**
1834–1903

The Doorway (First Venice Set), 1879–80
etching, drypoint, and roulette on paper
11 9/16 × 8 in. (29.4 × 20.3 cm)
The Baltimore Museum of Art, The Conrad Collection, 1932.17.13

135 **James McNeill Whistler**
1834–1903

The Piazzetta (First Venice Set), 1879–80
etching and drypoint on paper
10 1/16 × 7 1/16 in. (25.5 × 17.9cm)
The Baltimore Museum of Art, Garrett Collection, 1946.112.5965

144 **James McNeill Whistler**
1834–1903

The Riva, No. 2 (Second Venice Set), 1879–80
etching and drypoint on paper
8 7/16 × 11 7/8 in. (21.5 × 30.2 cm)
The Baltimore Museum of Art, The George A. Lucas Collection, purchased with funds from the State of Maryland, Laurence and Stella Bendann Fund, and contributions from individuals, foundations, and corporations throughout the Baltimore community, 1996.48.12313

31 **James McNeill Whistler**
1834–1903

The Venetian Mast (First Venice Set), 1879–80
etching and drypoint on paper
13 7/16 × 6 7/16 in. (34.1 × 16.4 cm)
The Baltimore Museum of Art, Garrett Collection, 1946.112.5970

82 **Irving Ramsay Wiles**
1861–1948

John Gellatly, 1930–32
oil on canvas
79 × 38 3/8 in. (200.8 × 97.6 cm)
Smithsonian American Art Museum, Gift of the artist, 1932.6.1

259 **Andrew Kay Womrath**
1874–1953

Yoshijiro Urushibara, printer
1888–1953

Venice by Day, ca. 1920s
color woodblock print on paper
image:
6 3/8 × 9 7/8 in. (16.2 × 25.1 cm)
sheet:
8 × 11 1/4 in. (20.3 × 28.6 cm)
Collection of Darrel C. Karl

259 **Andrew Kay Womrath**
1874–1953

Yoshijiro Urushibara, printer
1888–1953

Venice by Night, ca. 1920s
color woodblock print on paper
image:
6 3/8 × 9 7/8 in. (16.2 × 25.1 cm)
sheet:
7 7/8 × 11 5/8 in. (20 × 29.5 cm)
Collection of Darrel C. Karl

II. Glass Vessels

228 **Unidentified**
ancient Mediterranean

Alabastron (Oil or Perfume Flask), 6th–5th century BCE
core-formed and applied glass
4 1/16 × 1 5/8 × 1 3/8 in.
(10.3 × 4.1 × 3.5 cm)
Smithsonian American Art Museum, Gift of John Gellatly, 1929.8.157.27

62 **Unidentified**
ancient Mediterranean

Ewer, 6th–5th century BCE
core-formed and applied hot-worked glass
2 5/8 × 1 1/2 × 1 3/4 in.
(6.7 × 3.8 × 4.4 cm)
Smithsonian American Art Museum, Gift of John Gellatly, 1929.8.147.3

228 **Unidentified**
ancient Mediterranean

Amphoriskos (Two-Handled Flask), 3rd–1st century BCE
core-formed and applied hot-worked glass
4 1/2 × 2 1/2 × 2 3/8 in.
(11.4 × 6.4 × 6 cm)
Smithsonian American Art Museum, Gift of John Gellatly, 1929.8.157.32

112 **UNIDENTIFIED**
Roman Empire

Mosaic Glass Bowl,
1st century BCE–1st century CE
slumped, polished, and applied mosaic glass
5 1/8 × 6 3/4 in. diam. (13 × 17.2 cm)
Smithsonian American Art Museum, Gift of John Gellatly, 1929.8.147.5

42 **UNIDENTIFIED**
Roman Empire

Mosaic Glass Patella Cup,
1st century BCE–2nd century CE
slumped, polished, and applied mosaic glass
1 1/2 × 3 5/8 in. diam. (3.9 × 9.2 cm)
Smithsonian American Art Museum, Gift of John Gellatly, 1929.8.147.13

62 **UNIDENTIFIED**
Roman Empire

Goblet, 1st century CE
blown, hot-worked, lathe-cut, and applied glass
4 7/8 × 3 3/8 in. diam. (12.4 × 8.6 cm)
Smithsonian American Art Museum, Gift of John Gellatly, 1929.8.174.3

228 **UNIDENTIFIED**
Roman Empire

Flask, 1st–4th century CE
blown and hot-worked glass
2 1/2 × 1 7/8 in. diam. (6.4 × 4.8 cm)
Smithsonian American Art Museum, Gift of John Gellatly, 1929.8.174.5

62 **UNIDENTIFIED**
Roman Empire

Aryballos (Oil Flask),
1st–4th century CE
blown and applied hot-worked glass
3 1/4 × 2 1/4 in. diam. (8.3 × 5.7 cm)
Smithsonian American Art Museum, Gift of John Gellatly, 1929.8.157.19

62 **UNIDENTIFIED**
Roman Empire

Flask, 1st–4th century CE
blown and applied hot-worked glass
3 3/8 × 3 1/8 in. diam. (8.6 × 7.9 cm)
Smithsonian American Art Museum, Gift of John Gellatly, 1929.8.157.8

62 **UNIDENTIFIED**
Roman Empire

Aryballos (Oil Flask),
1st–4th century CE
blown and applied hot-worked glass
3 5/8 × 3 1/2 × 3 5/8 in.
(9.2 × 8.9 × 9.2 cm)
Smithsonian American Art Museum, Gift of John Gellatly, 1929.8.170.23

255 **UNIDENTIFIED**
Murano, Venice, Italy

Fragment of a Footed Bowl with Medici Family Arms, ca. 1513–34
mold-blown, gilded, and enameled glass
4 3/8 × 11 1/2 in. diam. (11.1 × 29.2 cm)
Smithsonian American Art Museum, Gift of John Gellatly, 1929.8.305

110 **ATTRIBUTED TO LEOPOLDO BEARZOTTI,** enamelist
active 1868–1880

SOCIETÀ ANONIMA PER AZIONI SALVIATI & C., manufacturer,
Murano, Venice, Italy
active 1866–1872

Renaissance-Style Dish with Christ and Four Evangelists,
ca. 1870s
blown, enameled, and gilded glass
2 3/4 × 18 5/8 in. diam. (7 × 47.3 cm)
The Metropolitan Museum of Art, Gift of James Jackson Jarves, 1881, 81.8.39

131 **ATTRIBUTED TO LEOPOLDO BEARZOTTI,** enamelist
active 1868–1880

SOCIETÀ ANONIMA PER AZIONI SALVIATI & C., manufacturer,
Murano, Venice, Italy
active 1866–1872

Replica in Glass of a Byzantine Chalice (*Chalice of Emperor Romanos II*), ca. 1870
blown, enameled, and gilded glass
8 3/16 × 6 5/16 in. diam.
(20.8 × 16.1 cm)
The Walters Art Museum, Acquired by Henry Walters, 1911, 47.356

43 **ATTRIBUTED TO LEOPOLDO BEARZOTTI,** enamelist
active 1868–1880

SOCIETÀ ANONIMA PER AZIONI SALVIATI & C., manufacturer,
Murano, Venice, Italy
active 1866–1872

Goblet with Lace Design, ca. 1870s
blown, enameled, and gilded glass
7 3/4 × 4 7/8 in. diam.
(19.7 × 12.4 cm)
The Metropolitan Museum of Art, Gift of James Jackson Jarves, 1881, 81.8.221

109 **SOCIETÀ ANONIMA PER AZIONI SALVIATI & C.,** manufacturer,
Murano, Venice, Italy
active 1866–1872

Fenicio Goblet with Swans and Initial "S" Stem, ca. 1870
blown and applied hot-worked glass
12 5/8 × 5 1/8 in. diam. (32.1 × 13 cm)
Smithsonian American Art Museum, Gift of John Gellatly, 1929.8.469.6

115 **Possibly Isidoro Seguso**
1858–1897
or

Giuseppe Barovier
1853–1942

Venice and Murano Glass and Mosaic Company Ltd. (Salviati & Co.), manufacturer, Murano, Venice, Italy
active 1872–1877

Replica of a Seventeenth-Century Lidded Pokal (*Guggenheim Cup*), ca. 1876–1880s
blown and applied hot-worked glass
26 × 6 in. diam. (66 × 15.2 cm)
Museum of the City of New York, Gift of the Estate of Miss Agnes Miles Carpenter, 55.172.2A, 55.172.3B

170 **Attributed to Giuseppe Barovier**
1853–1942

Venice and Murano Glass and Mosaic Company Ltd. (Salviati & Co.), manufacturer, Murano, Venice, Italy
active 1872–1877

Opalescent Glass Vase with Multicolor Granzioli, ca. 1868–80
blown and applied hot-worked glass
12 × 4 7/8 in. diam. (30.5 × 12.4 cm)
The Metropolitan Museum of Art, Gift of James Jackson Jarves, 1881, 81.8.125

248 **Venice and Murano Glass and Mosaic Company Ltd. (Salviati & Co.)**, manufacturer, Murano, Venice, Italy
active 1872–1877
or

Fratelli Barovier, manufacturer, Murano, Venice, Italy
active 1878–1895

Replica of a Sixteenth-Century Nef (Ewer) in the Form of a Boat, ca. 1870s
blown and applied hot-worked glass
12 1/4 × 9 1/4 × 4 1/4 in.
(31.1 × 23.5 × 10.8 cm)
Museum of the City of New York, Gift of Harry Harkness Flagler, 1949.49.166.23

33 **Venice and Murano Glass and Mosaic Company Ltd. (Salviati & Co.)**, manufacturer, Murano, Venice, Italy
active 1872–1877
or

Fratelli Barovier, manufacturer, Murano, Venice, Italy
active 1878–1895

Opalescent Glass Lidded Pokal with Serpent Stem, ca. 1870s–90s
blown and applied hot-worked glass
14 × 4 3/16 in. diam. (35.7 × 12.2 cm)
RISD Museum, Gift of Mrs. Frank Mauran and John O. Ames, 14.208

239 **Venice and Murano Glass and Mosaic Company Ltd. (Salviati & Co.)**, manufacturer, Murano, Venice, Italy
active 1872–1877
or

Fratelli Barovier, manufacturer, Murano, Venice, Italy
active 1878–1895

Vase with Dolphin and Serpent, ca. 1870s–90s
blown and applied hot-worked glass
15 1/2 × 6 in. diam. (39.4 × 15.2 cm)
RISD Museum, Gift of Mrs. Frank Mauran and John O. Ames, 14.376

113 **Attributed to Giuseppe Barovier**
1853–1942
or

Benvenuto Barovier
1855–1932

Venice and Murano Glass and Mosaic Company Ltd. (Salviati & Co.), manufacturer, Murano, Venice, Italy
active 1872–1877

Lidded Mosaic Glass Urn with Silver Leaf Design, ca. 1880
blown and applied hot-worked glass
11 3/4 × 7 1/4 in. diam.
(29.8 × 18.4 cm)
The Metropolitan Museum of Art, Gift of James Jackson Jarves, 1881, 81.8.213a, b

228 **Attributed to Vincenzo Moretti**
1835–1901

Venice and Murano Glass and Mosaic Company Ltd. (Salviati & Co.), manufacturer, Murano, Venice, Italy
active 1872–1877

Ancient Roman–Style Skyphos (Two-Handled Wine Cup), ca. 1870s
cast, polished, and applied glass
3 5/8 × 10 1/4 × 5 5/8 in.
(9.2 × 26 × 14.3 cm)
Smithsonian American Art Museum, Gift of John Gellatly, 1929.8.147.27

42 **Vincenzo Moretti**
1835–1901

Venice and Murano Glass and Mosaic Company Ltd. (Salviati & Co.), manufacturer,
Murano, Venice, Italy
active 1872–1877
or

Compagnia di Venezia e Murano (CVM), manufacturer,
Murano, Venice, Italy
active 1877–1919

Ancient Roman–Style Mosaic Glass Bowl, ca. 1875–80
hot-worked and slumped mosaic glass with applied glass rim
1 7/8 × 6 13/16 in. diam. (4.8 × 17.3 cm)
The Walters Art Museum, Acquired by Henry Walters, 47.298

118 **Vincenzo Moretti**
1835–1901

Venice and Murano Glass and Mosaic Company Ltd. (Salviati & Co.), manufacturer,
Murano, Venice, Italy
active 1872–1877
or

Compagnia di Venezia e Murano (CVM), manufacturer,
Murano, Venice, Italy
active 1877–1919

Ancient Roman–Style Striped Glass Bowl, ca. 1875–80
hot-worked and slumped glass with applied glass rim
1 1/16 × 4 3/4 in. diam. (2.7 × 12 cm)
Toledo Museum of Art, Gift of Edward Drummond Libbey, 1923.1490

136 **Vincenzo Moretti**
1835–1901

Venice and Murano Glass and Mosaic Company Ltd. (Salviati & Co.), manufacturer,
Murano, Venice, Italy
active 1872–1877
or

Compagnia di Venezia e Murano (CVM), manufacturer,
Murano, Venice, Italy
active 1877–1919

Ancient Roman–Style Mosaic Glass Bowl, ca. 1875–80
hot-worked and slumped mosaic glass with applied glass rim
2 × 5 3/4 in. diam. (5 × 14.7 cm)
Toledo Museum of Art, Purchased with funds from the Libbey Endowment, Gift of Edward Drummond Libbey, 1977.12

225 **Vincenzo Moretti**
1835–1901

Compagnia di Venezia e Murano (CVM), manufacturer,
Murano, Venice, Italy
active 1877–1919

Replica of a Byzantine Glass Bowl (*San Marco Bowl*), *ca.* 1878
blown, enameled, and gilded glass, with gilded bronze handles
4 1/16 × 7 5/8 × 4 15/16 in.
(10.3 × 19.3 × 12.5 cm)
The Corning Museum of Glass, 59.3.36

92 **Compagnia di Venezia e Murano (CVM)**, manufacturer,
Murano, Venice, Italy
active 1877–1919

Kuttrolf-Style Vase, ca. 1880s–90s
blown and applied hot-worked glass
13 3/8 × 5 1/4 in. diam. (34 × 13.3 cm)
Smithsonian American Art Museum, Gift of John Gellatly, 1929.8.469.4

41 **Attributed to Compagnia di Venezia e Murano (CVM)**, manufacturer,
Murano, Venice, Italy
active 1877–1919

Vase with Dolphins and Flowers, ca. 1880s–90s
blown and applied hot-worked glass
20 1/2 × 8 1/8 in. diam.
(52.1 × 20.6 cm)
Smithsonian American Art Museum, Gift of John Gellatly, 1929.8.469.1

222 **Attributed to Vittorio Zanetti**
active 1870s–1890s

Compagnia di Venezia e Murano (CVM), manufacturer,
Murano, Venice, Italy
active 1877–1919

Fish and Eel Vase, ca. 1890
blown and applied hot-worked glass
12 × 4 1/4 × 5 1/4 in.
(30.5 × 10.8 × 13.3 cm)
Smithsonian American Art Museum, Gift of John Gellatly, 1929.8.469.2

116 **Fratelli Barovier**, manufacturer,
Murano, Venice, Italy
active 1878–1895
or

Compagnia di Venezia e Murano (CVM), manufacturer,
Murano, Venice, Italy
active 1877–1919

Ewer with Serpent Handle, ca. 1870s–90s
blown, gilded, enameled, and applied hot-worked glass
9 11/16 × 4 in. diam. (24.6 × 10.2 cm)
RISD Museum, Gift of Mrs. Frank Mauran and John O. Ames 14.362

70 **Attributed to Giuseppe Barovier**
1853–1942
or
Benvenuto Barovier
1855–1932
Salviati Dott. Antonio, manufacturer, Murano, Venice, Italy
active 1877–1890

Conical Goblet with Entwined Serpents Stem, ca. 1880s
blown and applied hot-worked glass
12 3/8 × 6 3/8 in. diam.
(31.4 × 16.2 cm)
Smithsonian American Art Museum, Gift of John Gellatly, 1929.8.469.7

92 **Attributed to Giuseppe Barovier**
1853–1942
or
Benvenuto Barovier
1855–1932
Salviati Dott. Antonio, manufacturer, Murano, Venice, Italy
active 1877–1890

Goblet with Thorny Stem,
ca. 1870–90s
blown and applied hot-worked glass
11 × 5 in. diam. (27.9 × 12.7 cm)
Museum of the City of New York, Gift of the Estate of Miss Agnes Miles Carpenter, 1955, 55.172.6

220 **Attributed to Salviati Dott. Antonio,** manufacturer, Murano, Venice, Italy
active 1877–1890

Replica of a Seventeenth-Century Goblet with Knotted Stem,
ca. 1870s–80s
blown and applied hot-worked glass
11 7/8 × 4 7/16 in. diam.
(30.2 × 11.3 cm)
RISD Museum, Gift of Mrs. Frank Mauran and John O. Ames, 14.294

91 **Unidentified**
Murano, Venice, Italy

Seventeenth Century–Style Goblet with Undulating Bowl,
ca. 1870s–90s
blown and applied hot-worked glass
7 5/8 × 4 3/8 in. diam. (19.4 × 11.3 cm)
RISD Museum, Gift of Mrs. Frank Mauran and John O. Ames, 14.248

105 **Attributed to Compagnia di Venezia e Murano (CVM)**, manufacturer, Murano, Venice, Italy
active 1877–1919

Seventeenth Century–Style Long-Stemmed Goblet, ca. 1900
blown and applied hot-worked glass
11 × 5 in. diam. (27.9 × 12.7 cm)
Museum of the City of New York, Gift of the Estate of Miss Agnes Miles Carpenter, 1955, 55.172.9

132 **Compagnia di Venezia e Murano (CVM)**, manufacturer, Murano, Venice, Italy
active 1877–1919
or
Salviati Dott. Antonio, manufacturer, Murano, Venice, Italy
active 1877–1890

Replica of an Ancient Roman Diatreta or Cage Cup (*Disch-Sangiorgi Cantharus*),
ca. 1880s–90s
blown, gilded, and applied hot-worked glass
7 × 6 3/16 in. diam. (17.8 × 15.7 cm)
RISD Museum, Gift of Mrs. Frank Mauran and John O. Ames, 14.252

102 **Artisti Barovier**, manufacturer, Murano, Venice, Italy
active 1895–1919

Chalcedony Glass Urn,
ca. 1890–1904
blown and applied hot-worked glass
6 × 5 7/8 × 5 5/16 in.
(15.2 × 14.9 × 13.5 cm)
Iris & B. Gerald Cantor Center for Visual Arts at Stanford University, Gift of Erede Dr. A. Salviati & Co., JLS.11064

93 **Attributed to Compagnia di Venezia e Murano (CVM)**, manufacturer, Murano, Venice, Italy
active 1877–1919

Flame Glass Amphora,
ca. 1890–1913
blown and applied hot-worked glass
7 3/8 × 3 1/2 in. diam. (18.8 × 8.8 cm)
Iris & B. Gerald Cantor Center for Visual Arts at Stanford University, Gift of Erede Dr. A. Salviati & Co., JLS.11073

128 **Artisti Barovier**, manufacturer, Murano, Venice, Italy
active 1895–1919
or
Compagnia di Venezia e Murano (CVM), manufacturer, Murano, Venice, Italy
active 1877–1919

Smelze Glass Vase, ca. 1890–1904
blown and applied hot-worked glass
9 3/4 × 3 3/4 in. diam. (23.3 × 11.5 cm)
Iris & B. Gerald Cantor Center for Visual Arts at Stanford University, Gift of Erede Dr. A. Salviati & Co., JLS.11201

204 **Attributed to Giuseppe Barovier**
1853–1942

Artisti Barovier, manufacturer,
Murano, Venice, Italy
active 1895–1919

Zanfirico Glass Vase with Floral Murrhines, ca. 1910–13
blown and applied hot-worked glass with mosaic glass inclusions
7 9⁄16 × 5 ½ in. diam. (19.3 × 13.9 cm)
Iris & B. Gerald Cantor Center for Visual Arts at Stanford University, Gift of Erede Dr. A. Salviati & Co., JLS.11103

90 **Fratelli Toso**, manufacturer,
Murano, Venice, Italy
active 1854–1980

Mosaic Glass Amphora,
ca. 1880s–90s
blown and applied hot-worked, acid-etched glass
6 5⁄16 × 3 ⅛ in. diam. (15.9 × 7.9 cm)
RISD Museum, Gift of Mrs. Frank Mauran and John O. Ames, 14.355

39 **Attributed to Fratelli Toso**, manufacturer,
Murano, Venice, Italy
active 1854–1980

Goblet with Twisted Floral Stem,
ca. 1900–1903
blown, gilded, enameled, and applied hot-worked glass
7 ⅞ × 3 ⅜ in. diam. (20.2 × 8.6 cm)
RISD Museum, Gift of Mrs. Frank Mauran and John O. Ames, 14.364

126 **Francesco Toso Borella**,
enamelist
1846–1905
or

Vittorio Toso Borella,
enamelist, or workshop
1878–1915

Compagnia di Venezia e Murano (CVM), manufacturer,
Murano, Venice, Italy
active 1877–1919

Replica of a Renaissance Goblet (*Campanile Cup*), ca. 1903–12
blown, enameled, and gilded glass
5 ⅝ × 4 ⅛ in. diam. (14.2 × 10.5 cm)
The Corning Museum of Glass, 2006.3.70

Francesco Toso Borella,
enamelist
1846–1905
or

Vittorio Toso Borella,
enamelist, or workshop
1878–1915

Compagnia di Venezia e Murano (CVM), manufacturer,
Murano, Venice, Italy
active 1877–1919

Replica of a Renaissance Goblet (*Campanile Cup*), ca. 1903–12
blown, enameled, and gilded glass
5 9⁄16 × 4 1⁄16 in. diam.
(14.2 × 10.3 cm)
Iris & B. Gerald Cantor Center for Visual Arts at Stanford University, Gift of Erede Dr. A. Salviati & Co., JLS.11274
(not illustrated)

Francesco Toso Borella,
enamelist
1846–1905
or

Vittorio Toso Borella,
enamelist, or workshop
1878–1915

Compagnia di Venezia e Murano (CVM), manufacturer,
Murano, Venice, Italy
active 1877–1919

Replica of a Renaissance Goblet (*Campanile Cup*), ca. 1903–12
blown, enameled, and gilded glass
5 9⁄16 × 4 in. diam. (14.1 × 10.2 cm)
Promised gift to the Chrysler Museum of Art, Norfolk, VA
(not illustrated)

239 **Union Glass Company**,
manufacturer, Somerville, MA
active 1851–1927

Venetian-Style Twin-Handled Vase, 1894–1910
mold-blown, tooled, and applied glass with gold leaf
12 ⅝ × 5 11⁄16 × 4 ⅛ in.
(32 × 14.5 × 10.4 cm)
The Corning Museum of Glass, 2008.4.128

239 **Union Glass Company**,
manufacturer, Somerville, MA
active 1851–1927

Venetian-Style Creamer with "Snake" Handle, 1894–1910
blown and applied glass with gold leaf
5 ¾ × 4 ⅛ × 2 ⅞ in.
(14.6 × 10.5 × 7.4 cm)
The Corning Museum of Glass, 2008.4.114

204 **ATTRIBUTED TO GIULIO SALVIATI & C.**, manufacturer, Murano, Venice, Italy
active 1896–1903
or
EREDE DR. A. SALVIATI & CO., manufacturer, Murano, Venice, Italy
active 1903–1920

Floral Goblet with Knotted Stem, ca. 1890–1911
blown and applied hot-worked glass
8 15/16 × 3 1/8 in. diam. (22.7 × 7.9 cm)
The Walters Art Museum, Acquired by Henry Walters, 47.327

254 **UNIDENTIFIED**
Murano, Venice, Italy

Goblet with Striped Bowl, ca. 1890s–1910s
blown, enameled, and applied hot-worked glass
6 × 3 5/8 in. diam. (15.2 × 9.2 cm)
Smithsonian American Art Museum, Gift of John Gellatly, 1929.8.469.8

242 **ATTRIBUTED TO ERCOLE BAROVIER**
1889–1974
or
NICOLÒ BAROVIER
1886–1953

ARTISTI BAROVIER, manufacturer, Murano, Venice, Italy
active 1895–1919

Mosaic Glass Goblet, ca. 1914–28
blown and applied hot-worked glass, with mosaic glass inclusions
6 5/8 × 3 1/4 in. diam. (16.8 × 8.3 cm)
Smithsonian American Art Museum, Gift of John Gellatly, 1929.8.469.9

III. MOSAICS, LACE, AND OTHER WORKS OF ART

52 **POSSIBLY STUDIO DEL MOSAICO VATICANO**, Rome, Italy, founded 1727

Micromosaic with Lion of St. Mark, ca. 1860–84
glass micromosaic
2 3/4 × 4 × 11/16 in.
(7 × 10.2 × 1.7 cm)
Iris & B. Gerald Cantor Center for Visual Arts at Stanford University, Stanford Family Collections, JLS.17610

255 **UNIDENTIFIED**
probably Murano, Venice, Italy

Byzantine-Style Mosaic Necklace with Christ and Twelve Apostles, ca. 1870s–1910s
gold with glass and shell inlay
9 1/4 × 16 × 1/4 in. (variable)
(23.5 × 40.6 × 0.6 cm)
Smithsonian American Art Museum, Gift of John Gellatly, 1929.8.247

130 **LUIGI TADDEI**
1824–1874

St. Mark's Body Venerated by the Doge, 1871
glass mosaic tiles
16 × 32 in. (40.6 × 81.3 cm)
Collection of Vincent and Kako Crisci

106 **ENRICO PODIO**
active 1860s–70s

SALVIATI DOTT. ANTONIO FU BARTOLOMEO, manufacturer, Murano, Venice, Italy
active 1859–1866

Portrait of Abraham Lincoln, 1866
glass mosaic tiles
22 3/4 × 20 1/4 in. (57.8 × 51.4 cm)
US Senate Collection, 39.00001.000

245 **LUIGI MORETTI**
1867–1946

COMPAGNIA DI VENEZIA E MURANO (CVM), manufacturer, Murano, Venice, Italy
active 1877–1919

Glass Cane Slice with Portrait of Christopher Columbus, 1892
mosaic glass
1/8 × 13/16 in. diam. (0.25 × 2.06 cm)
The Corning Museum of Glass, Gift of Mrs. Giusy Moretti, 99.3.94

125 **EREDE DR. A. SALVIATI & CO.**, manufacturer, Murano, Venice, Italy
active 1903–1920

Portrait of Theodore Roosevelt, ca. 1904
glass mosaic tiles and cement
24 5/8 × 19 1/8 in. (62.5 × 48.5 cm)
The Corning Museum of Glass, 2007.3.70

125 **DOTT. ANTONIO SALVIATI & C.**, manufacturer, Murano, Venice, Italy
active 1896–1903
or
EREDE DR. A. SALVIATI & CO., manufacturer, Murano, Venice, Italy
active 1903–1920

Portrait of Jane Lathrop Stanford, ca. 1902
glass mosaic tiles
21 1/2 × 16 5/8 in. (54.6 × 42.2 cm)
Iris & B. Gerald Cantor Center for Visual Arts at Stanford University, Gift of Erede Dr. A. Salviati & Co., JLS.11462

123 **Attributed to Antonio Ermolao Paoletti**
1834–1912

Erede Dr. A. Salviati & Co., manufacturer, Murano, Venice, Italy
active 1903–1920

Study for *David* Mosaic in Stanford Memorial Chapel, ca. 1903–5
oil on canvas
21 ½ × 16 ½ in. (54.6 × 41.9 cm)
Stanford University Libraries, Department of Special Collections, Stanford Mosaic Collection (SC0187)

127 **Erede Dr. A. Salviati & Co.**, manufacturer, Murano, Venice, Italy
active 1903–1920

Fragment from Stanford Memorial Church Mosaic Cycle, ca. 1903–5
glass mosaic tiles and cement on sandstone with gold foil
11 7⁄16 × 9 ½ × 2 15⁄16 in. (29 × 24.1 × 7.5 cm)
The Corning Museum of Glass, Gift of Sheldon Barr and Thomas Gardner, 2017.3.13

207 **Attributed to Scuola di Ricamo, Istituto delle Zitelle**, Venice, Italy
active 1880s–early 1900s

Brooch with Pittura d'Ago (Needle Painting) of the Rialto Bridge, Venice, late 19th century
silk, gold, and glass
1 ½ × 2 3⁄16 in. (3.8 × 5.6 cm)
RISD Museum, Bequest of Lyra Brown Nickerson, 16.602

183 **Scuola dei Merletti di Burano**, Burano, Venice, Italy
active 1872–1970

Lace Border, late 19th–early 20th century
linen needle lace
21 ¼ × 3 1⁄16 in. (54 × 7.8 cm)
Cooper Hewitt, Smithsonian Design Museum, Bequest of Richard Cranch Greenleaf in memory of his mother, Adeline Emma Greenleaf, 1962-50-223

162 **Scuola dei Merletti di Burano**, Burano, Venice, Italy
active 1872–1970

Lace Cap Streamer, late 19th–early 20th century
linen needle lace
42 × 3 9⁄16 in. (106.7 × 9 cm)
Cooper Hewitt, Smithsonian Design Museum, Gift of an anonymous donor, 1967-46-8

206 **Scuola dei Merletti di Burano**, Burano, Venice, Italy
active 1872–1970

Lace Panel with Lions, late 19th–early 20th century
linen needle lace
17 × 16 ½ in. (43.2 × 41.9 cm)
Cooper Hewitt, Smithsonian Design Museum, Gift of Charles G. K. Warner and William W. Warner, 1971-83-2

184 **Scuola dei Merletti di Burano**, Burano, Venice, Italy
active 1872–1970

Lace Panel with Lion of St. Mark, 20th century
cotton needle lace
4 9⁄16 × 6 5⁄8 in. (11.6 × 16.8 cm)
Cooper Hewitt, Smithsonian Design Museum, Bequest of Gertrude M. Oppenheimer, 1981-28-460

37 **Attributed to Società Veneziana per l'Industria delle Conterie (SVC)**, Murano, Venice, Italy
active 1898–1993

Stephen A. Frost & Son, New York, NY
active 1848–1937

Sample Card with Flameworked Beads, late 19th century–1904
107 flameworked glass beads mounted to printed card
13 ½ × 18 in. (34.3 × 45.7 cm)
Illinois State Museum, Gift of Dan Frost, 1941-0083-XIII

161 **Attributed to Società Veneziana per l'Industria delle Conterie (SVC)**, Murano, Venice, Italy
active 1898–1993

Stephen A. Frost & Son, New York, NY
active 1848–1937

Sample Card with Flameworked Beads, late 19th century–1904
85 flameworked glass beads mounted to printed card
13 ½ × 18 in. (34.3 × 45.7 cm)
Illinois State Museum, Gift of Dan Frost, 1941-0083-XV

176 **Attributed to Società Veneziana per l'Industria delle Conterie (SVC)**, Murano, Venice, Italy
active 1898–1993

Stephen A. Frost & Son, New York, NY
active 1848–1937

Sample Card with Millefiori and Flag Beads, late 19th century–1904
106 mosaic glass and flameworked glass beads mounted to printed card
13 ½ × 18 in. (34.3 × 45.7 cm)
Illinois State Museum, Gift of Dan Frost, 1941-0083-XVI

176 **Attributed to Società Veneziana per l'Industria delle Conterie (SVC)**, Murano, Venice, Italy
active 1898–1993

Stephen A. Frost & Son, New York, NY
active 1848–1937

Sample Card with Corkscrew and Lace Beads, late 19th century–1904
36 flameworked glass beads mounted to printed card
13 ½ × 18 in. (34.3 × 45.7 cm)
Illinois State Museum, Gift of Dan Frost, 1941-0083-XVII

176 **Attributed to Società Veneziana per l'Industria delle Conterie (SVC)**, Murano, Venice, Italy
active 1898–1993

Stephen A. Frost & Son, New York, NY
active 1848–1937

Sample Card with Trailed Feather and Eye Beads, late 19th century–1904
116 mosaic glass and flameworked glass beads mounted to printed card
13 ½ × 18 in. (34.3 × 45.7 cm)
Illinois State Museum, Gift of Dan Frost, 1941-0083-XX

176 **Attributed to Società Veneziana per l'Industria delle Conterie (SVC)**, Murano, Venice, Italy
active 1898–1993

Stephen A. Frost & Son, New York, NY
active 1848–1937

Sample Card with Marbleized and Millefiori Beads, late 19th century–1904
100 mosaic glass and flameworked glass beads mounted to printed card
13 ½ × 18 in. (34.3 × 45.7 cm)
Illinois State Museum, Gift of Dan Frost, 1941-0083-XXII

207 **Scuola d'Industrie Italiane**, New York, NY
active 1905–1927

Lace Panel with Fleur-de-Lis, ca. 1920
linen needle lace
5 ⅞ × 2 ¾ in. (14.9 × 7 cm)
Cooper Hewitt, Smithsonian Design Museum, Gift of Marian Hague, 1938-48-7-b

197 **Scuola d'Industrie Italiane**, New York, NY
active 1905–1927

Lace Panel with Dragon, ca. 1920
linen needle lace
5 ⅜ × 5 ¾ in. (13.7 × 14.6 cm)
Cooper Hewitt, Smithsonian Design Museum, Gift of Marian Hague, 1938-48-7-a

200 **Scuola d'Industrie Italiane**, New York, NY
active 1905–1927

Burse Cover, ca. 1920
linen with cutwork embroidery
8 ⅛ × 7 11/16 in. (20.7 × 19.5 cm)
Cooper Hewitt, Smithsonian Design Museum, Gift of Scuola d' Industrie Italiane in New York through Florence Colgate Speranza, 1943-41-1-c

203 **Scuola d'Industrie Italiane**, New York, NY
active 1905–1927

Pouch, ca. 1920
embroidered linen with bobbin lace
7 ⅞ × 7 5/16 in. (20 × 18.5 cm)
with tassels:
9 ¼ × 9 ½ in. (23.5 × 24.1 cm)
Cooper Hewitt, Smithsonian Design Museum, Gift of Marian Hague, 1942-7-22

83 **Follower of Francesco Guardi**

Canal in Venice, 18th century
oil on canvas
3 1/16 × 4 5/16 in (7.8 × 11 cm)
Smithsonian American Art Museum, Gift of John Gellatly, 1929.6.50

M. Grieve Company, New York, NY
active 1906–1955

Sixteenth-Century Venetian-Style Frame, ca. 1924
gilded and painted wood frame
5 ⅞ × 7 ⅛ × ¾ in.
(14.9 × 18.1 × 1.9 cm)
Smithsonian American Art Museum, Gift of John Gellatly (1929)

61 **Ralph Seymour**
active 1920s

Miniature Diorama of John Gellatly Collection, ca. 1924–29
wood, fabric, glass, and other materials
11 ⅞ × 12 ¼ × 6 in. (open)
(30.2 × 32.4 × 15.2 cm)
Smithsonian American Art Museum, Gift of John Gellatly, 1929.8.530

Selected Bibliography

Archives

Archives of American Art, Smithsonian Institution, Washington, DC.

Biblioteca Nazionale Marciana, Venice.

British Library, London.

Freer Gallery of Art and Arthur M. Sackler Gallery Archives, Smithsonian Institution, Washington, DC.

Isabella Stewart Gardner Museum Archives, Boston.

Archives and Special Collections, Glasgow University Library, Glasgow.

The Juliette K. and Leonard S. Rakow Research Library of the Corning Museum of Glass, Corning, New York.

Special Collections and University Archives, Stanford University, Stanford, California.

Periodicals, 1800 to 1945

The Aldine. New York, 1876.

The American Architect and Building News. New York, July 1889.

American Journal of Pharmacy. Philadelphia, May 1871 and February 1877.

The American Magazine of Art. New York, January 1921.

American Mechanics' Magazine. New York, September 1825.

Appletons' Journal. New York, December 1869, March 1874, April–May 1875, and January 1876.

The Art Amateur. New York, March 1882, January 1884, June 1887, February 1888, and May 1890.

Art Journal. New York, 1866, August 1870, and 1880.

Art and Progress. Washington, DC, August 1911.

Art in America: An Illustrated Magazine. New York, December 1913.

Art World. New York, December 1917.

Arthur's Home Magazine. Philadelphia, July 1882.

Brown Alumni Monthly. Providence, RI, April 1914.

Brush and Pencil. Chicago, November 1899.

Bulletin of the Needle and Bobbin Club. New York, 1919.

Bulletin of the Rhode Island School of Design. Providence, RI, October 1914.

The Catholic World. New York, September 1899.

The Century Illustrated Monthly Magazine. New York, November 1881, January 1882, November 1882, August 1894, and May 1907.

The Churchman. New York, May 1886.

The Collector. New York, May 1892.

The Cornhill Magazine. London, April 1869.

The Crayon. New York, August 1855.

The Decorator and Furnisher. New York, December 1884 and February 1894.

Frank Leslie's Popular Monthly. New York, September 1880.

Gazette des Beaux-Arts: Courrier Européen de l'Art et de la Curiosité. Paris, 1883.

Harper's Bazaar. New York, August 1872.

Harper's New Monthly Magazine. New York, May 1869, February 1871, January 1882, October 1887, and June–November 1889.

The Independent. London, October 31, 1878.

The Ladies' Repository: A Monthly Periodical, Devoted to Literature and Religion. Cincinnati, June 1871.

Literary World. Boston, December 1872.

Magazine of Art. New York and London, 1884, April 1890.

The Manufacturer and Builder. New York, June 1869.

The Metropolitan Museum of Art Bulletin. New York, June 1906, August 1908, December 1917, September 1925, November 1925, and January 1926.

Le Monde Illustré. Paris, December 29, 1883.

The Nation. New York, May 1887.

New York Herald. New York, August 16, 1875.

New York Herald Tribune. New York, May 30, 1929.

New York Times. New York, December 6, 1800, December 7, 1880, August 7, 1881, March 9, 1898, May 21, 1908, December 1, 1918, and December 12, 1945.

The North American Review. New York, January 1893.

North American and United States Gazette. Philadelphia, July 25, 1859.

The Outlook. New York, February 1909.

Peterson's Magazine. Philadelphia, September 1886.

Scribner's Magazine. New York, December 1891, November 1892, November 1893, and December 1903.

Scribner's Monthly. New York, April 1876 and July 1879.

La Voce di Murano. Venice, 1875–1904.

Primary Literature

Arnold, Matthew. *Culture and Anarchy: An Essay in Political and Social Criticism*. 2nd ed. New York: Macmillan, 1875.

Bacher, Otto Henry. *With Whistler in Venice*. New York: Century, 1908.

Baedeker, Karl. *Northern Italy, Leghorn, Florence and Ancona, and the Island of Corsica. Handbook for Travellers*. Coblenz: Karl Baedeker, 1868.

Bancroft, Hubert Howe. *The Book of the Fair: An Historical and Descriptive Presentation of the World's Science, Art, and Industry, as Viewed through the Columbian Exposition at Chicago in 1893*. Chicago: Bancroft, 1893.

Bates-Batcheller, Tryphosa. *Glimpses of Italian Court Life: Happy Days in Italia Adorata*. 4th ed. New York: Doubleday Page, 1907.

The Bay of San Francisco: The Metropolis of the Pacific Coast and Its Suburban Cities; A History. 2 vols. Chicago: Lewis Publishing, 1892.

Burty, Philippe. *Chefs-d'Oeuvre des Arts Industriels*. Paris: Paul Ducrocq, 1866.

Church, Ella Rodman. *How to Furnish a Home*. New York: D. Appleton, 1881.

Cook, Clarence. *The House Beautiful: Essays on Beds and Tables, Stools and Candlesticks*. New York: Scribner, Armstrong, 1878.

Cortissoz, Royal. *Personalities in Art*. New York: Charles Scribner's Sons, 1925.

Crawford, Francis Marion. *Salve Venetia: Gleanings from Venetian History*. New York: Macmillan, 1905.

——. *Marietta: A Maid of Venice*. New York: Macmillan, 1901.

Dewing, Maria Oakey. *Beauty in the Household*. New York: Harper and Brothers, 1882.

Eastlake, Charles Locke. *Hints on Household Taste*. London: Longmans, Green, 1868.

Edel, Leon, ed. *Henry James: Letters*. Vol. 1, *1843–1875*. Cambridge, MA: Belknap Press, 1974.

Edis, Robert William. *Decoration and Furniture of Town Houses*. New York: Scribner and Welford, 1881.

Elliott, Maud Howe, ed. *Art and Handicraft in the Woman's Building of the World's Columbian Exposition, Chicago, 1893*. New York: Boussod, Valadon, 1893.

Harrison, Constance Cary. *Bric-a-Brac Stories*. New York: Charles Scribner's Sons, 1885.

——. *Woman's Handiwork in Modern Homes*. New York: Charles Scribner's Sons, 1881.

Howells, William Dean. *Venetian Life*. New York: Hurd and Houghton, 1866.

Hubbard, Elbert. *Little Journeys to the Homes of Eminent Artists*. New York: G. P. Putnam's Sons, 1907.

Jackson, Emily. *A History of Hand-Made Lace: Dealing with the Origin of Lace, the Growth of the Great Lace Centres, the Mode of Manufacture, the Methods of Distinguishing and the Care of Various Kinds of Lace*. New York: Charles Scribner's Sons, 1900.

James, Henry, and Joseph Pennell. *Italian Hours.* Boston: Houghton Mifflin, 1909.

Jarves, James Jackson. *Art Thoughts: The Experiences and Observations of an American Amateur in Europe.* New York: Hurd and Houghton, 1870.

———. *Art-Hints: Architecture, Sculpture, and Painting.* London: Sampson Low, Son, 1855.

———. *The Art-Idea: Part Second of Confessions of an Inquirer.* New York: Hurd and Houghton, 1864.

———. *Italian Rambles: Studies of Life and Manners in New and Old Italy.* London: Sampson Low, Marston, Searle, and Rivington, 1883.

Layard, Austen Henry. *Paper on Mosaic Decoration: Read at a Meeting of the Royal Institute of British Architects.* London: Venice and Murano Glass & Mosaic, 1869.

Lucas, Edward Verrall, and Harry Morley. *A Wanderer in Venice.* New York: Macmillan, 1914.

Morris, Frances, and Marian Hague. *Antique Laces of American Collectors.* New York: Needle and Bobbin Club and William Helburn, 1920.

Nesbitt, Alexander. *Catalogue of the Collection of Glass Formed by Felix Slade, Esq., F.S.A.* London: Wertheimer, Lea, 1871.

———. *A Descriptive Catalogue of the Glass Vessels in the South Kensington Museum.* London: Chapman and Hall, 1878.

Norton, C. B. *Official Catalogue, Foreign Exhibition, Boston, 1883.* Boston: George Coolidge, 1883.

Palgrave, Francis. *Hand-Book for Travellers in Northern Italy: States of Sardinia, Lombardy and Venice, Parma and Piacenza, Modena, Lucca, Massa-Carrara, and Tuscany, as Far as the Val d'Arno.* London: John Murray and Son, 1842.

Palliser, Fanny Bury, Mrs. *History of Lace.* London: Sampson Low, Son and Marston, 1865.

Pellatt, Apsley. *Curiosities of Glass Making: With Details of the Processes and Productions of Ancient and Modern Ornamental Glass Manufacture.* London: David Bogue, 1849.

Pennell, Elizabeth Robins, and Joseph Pennell. *The Life of James McNeill Whistler.* London: William Heinemann, 1908.

Ricci, Elisa. *Antiche Trine Italiane: Trine a Fuselli.* Bergamo: Istituto Italiano d'Arti Grafiche, 1908.

———. *Old Italian Lace.* 2 vols. London: William Heinemann, 1913.

Ruskin, John. *The Stones of Venice.* 3 vols. London: Smith, Elder, 1851–53.

Sauzay, Alexandre. *La Verrerie depuis les Temps les Plus Reculés jusqu'à Nos Jours.* Paris: L. Hachette, 1869.

———. *Wonders of Glass-Making in All Ages.* New York: Charles Scribner's Sons, 1885.

Sherwood, Mary Elizabeth Wilson. *Here and There and Everywhere: Reminiscences.* Chicago: Herbert S. Stone, 1898.

Singleton, Esther, ed. *Venice as Seen and Described by Famous Writers.* New York: Dodd, Mead, 1905.

Smith, Francis Hopkinson. *Gondola Days.* Boston: Houghton Mifflin, 1897.

Spofford, Harriet Prescott. *Art Decoration Applied to Furniture.* New York: Harper and Brothers, 1877.

Truman, Benjamin Cummings. *History of the World's Fair: Being a Complete and Authentic Description of the Columbian Exposition from Its Inception.* New York: E. B. Treat, 1893.

Twain, Mark. *The Innocents Abroad; Or, The New Pilgrim's Progress.* Hartford, CT: American Publishing Company, 1869.

———. *A Tramp Abroad.* Toronto: Belford, 1880.

Wallace-Dunlop, Madeline A. *Glass in the Old World.* New York: Scribner and Welford, 1882.

Waters, Clara Erskine Clement. *Venice: The Queen of the Adriatic.* Boston: Dana Estes, 1893.

Weeks, Joseph D. *Report on the Manufacture of Glass.* Washington, DC: Department of the Interior Census Office, 1884.

Wharton, Edith. *Italian Villas and Their Gardens.* New York: Century, 1904.

Wheeler, Candace. *Household Art.* New York: Harper and Brothers, 1893.

Whistler, James McNeill. *Mr. Whistler's Ten O'Clock,* originally delivered in 1885. London: Chatto and Windus, 1888.

Zanetti, D. Vincenzo. *Guida di Murano e delle Celebri Sue Fornaci Vetrarie.* Venice: Gaetano Longo, 1880.

———. *Monografia della Vetraria Veneziana e Muranese.* Venice: Antonelli, 1874.

———. *Il Museo di Murano.* Venice: Giuseppe Cecchini, 1873.

———. *La Scuola di Disegno pegli Artieri in Murano: Notizie di Vincenzo Zanetti.* Venice: Tipografia Municipale di Gaetano Longo, 1871.

Secondary Literature

Adelson, Warren, et al. *Sargent's Venice.* New Haven, CT: Yale University Press, 2006.

Adler, Kathleen, Erica E. Hirshler, and H. Barbara Weinberg. *Americans in Paris 1860–1900.* London: National Gallery, 2006.

Alessandri, Chiara, Giandomenico Romanelli, and Flavia Scotton, eds. *Venezia: Gli Anni di Ca' Pesaro, 1908–1920.* Milan: Mazzotta, 1987.

Alloway, Lawrence. *The Venice Biennale 1895–1968; From Salon to Goldfish Bowl.* Greenwich, CT: New York Graphic Society, 1968.

Anderson, Nancy K. *Thomas Moran.* New Haven, CT: Yale University Press, 1997.

Angelilli, Claire Ellen, et al. *Inked Impressions: Ellen Day Hale and the Painter-Etcher Movement.* Carlisle, PA: Trout Gallery, Dickinson College, 2007.

Armstrong, Isobel. *Victorian Glassworlds: Glass Culture and the Imagination, 1830–1880.* Oxford: Oxford University Press, 2008.

Bardazzi, Francesca, and Carlo Sisi, eds. *Americans in Florence: Sargent and the American Impressionists.* Venice: Marsilio, 2012.

Barovier, Marina, ed. *Art of the Barovier: Glassmakers in Murano, 1866–1972.* Venice: Arsenale, 1993.

Barovier, Rosa. "Roman Glassware in the Museum of Murano and the Muranese Revival of the Nineteenth Century." Corning Museum of Glass, *Journal of Glass Studies* 16 (1974): 111–19.

Barr, Sheldon. "An Extraordinary Gift: The Salviati-Camerino Collection at Stanford." *VETRI: Italian Glass News* (Spring 2002): 4–5.

——. "Venetian Art Nouveau Glass." *Magazine Antiques* 157, no. 2 (February 2000): 314–23.

——. "Venetian Glass at Stanford University." *Magazine Antiques* 162, no. 3 (September 2002): 112–21.

——. *Venetian Glass Mosaics 1860–1917.* Woodbridge, UK: Antique Collectors' Club, 2008.

Barr, Sheldon, and John Bigelow Taylor. *Venetian Glass: Confections in Glass, 1855–1914.* New York: Harry N. Abrams, 1998.

Bell, Adrienne Baxter. "Charles Caryl Coleman on Capri." *Magazine Antiques* 165, no. 5 (November 2005): 138–47.

——. "Echoes of the East, Echoes of the Past: Charles Caryl Coleman's *Azaleas and Apple Blossoms.*" In *Locating American Art: Finding Art's Meaning in Museums, Colonial Period to the Present,* edited by Cynthia Fowler, 33–45. Burlington, VT: Ashgate, 2016.

——. "Utopian Pastiche: The Still Life Paintings of Charles Caryl Coleman." In *A Seamless Web: Transatlantic Art in the Nineteenth Century,* edited by Cheryll L. May and Marian Wardle, 147–62. Newcastle: Cambridge Scholars, 2014.

Bellavitis, Anna. *Perle e Impiraperle: Un Lavoro di Donne a Venezia tra '800 e '900.* Venice: Arsenale, 1990.

Black, Jeremy. *Italy and the Grand Tour.* New Haven, CT: Yale University Press, 2003.

Bova, Aldo, et al. *Murrine and Millefiori in Murano Glass from 1830 to 1930.* Venice: Galleria Rossella Junck, 1998.

Bova, Aldo, Attilia Dorigato, and Puccio Migliaccio. *Vetri Artistici: Antonio Salviati, 1866–1877.* Vol. 2, *Museo del Vetro di Murano.* Corpus delle Collezioni del Vetro Post-Classico nel Veneto. Venice: Marsilio, 2008.

Bova, Aldo, Claudio Gianolla, Rosella Junck, Rosa Barovier Mentasti, and Andrea Morucchio. *Dragons, Serpents, and Sea Monsters in 19th Century Murano Glass.* Venice: Galleria Junck and Gianolla, 1997.

Bova, Aldo, Rossella Junck, and Puccio Migliaccio, eds. *The Colours of Murano in the XIX Century.* Venice: Arsenale, 1999.

Brettell, Richard R., and Caroline B. Brettell. *Painters and Peasants in the Nineteenth Century.* New York: Rizzoli, 1983.

Brooks, Julian. *The Lure of Italy: Artists' Views.* Los Angeles: J. Paul Getty Museum, 2017.

Brooks, Van Wyck. *The Dream of Arcadia: American Writers and Artists in Italy, 1760–1915.* New York: Dutton, 1958.

Buonomo, Leonardo. *Backward Glances: Exploring Italy, Reinterpreting America (1831–1866).* Madison, NJ: Fairleigh Dickinson University Press, 1996.

Burke, Doreen Bolger, et al. *In Pursuit of Beauty: Americans and the Aesthetic Movement.* New York: Metropolitan Museum of Art, 1986.

Burns, Sarah. *Inventing the Modern Artist: Art and Culture in Gilded Age America.* New Haven, CT: Yale University Press, 1996.

Carbone, Teresa. *Summers Abroad: The European Watercolors of Francis Hopkinson Smith.* New York: Jordan-Volpe Gallery, 1985.

Carroll, B. Harvey, Jr., and Jamey D. Allen. "Bead Making at Murano and Venice." *Beads: Journal of the Society of Bead Researchers* 16 (2004): 17–37.

Carter, Morris. *Isabella Stewart Gardner and Fenway Court.* 3rd ed. Boston: Trustees, Isabella Stewart Gardner Museum, 1972.

Casanova, Lucia Bellodi, et al. *La Scuola dei Merletti di Burano.* Burano: Consorzio Merletti, 1981.

Clair, Jean, and Giandomenico Romanelli. *Venezia e la Biennale: I Percorsi del Gusto.* Milan: Fabbri, 1995.

Conway, Kelly Ann. "Art Glass of Union Glass Company, Somerville, Massachusetts, 1893–1927." MA thesis, Cooper-Hewitt, National Design Museum, Smithsonian Institution, and Parsons School of Design, 2005.

Curry, David Park. *James McNeill Whistler: Uneasy Pieces.* Richmond: Virginia Museum of Fine Arts; New York: Quantuck Lane Press, 2004.

———. "The Painting over the Table." In "Problems in Connoisseurship," special issue, *Notes in the History of Art* 24, no. 2 (Winter 2005): 60–69.

De Marchi, Agnese. *Between Pen and Palette: Images of Venice in the Work of F. Hopkinson Smith.* Washington, DC: Academica Press, 2018.

Denker, Eric. *Reflections and Undercurrents: Ernest Roth and Printmaking in Venice, 1900–1940.* Carlisle, PA: Trout Gallery, Dickinson College; Seattle: University of Washington Press, 2012.

———. *Whistler and His Circle in Venice.* London: Merrell; Washington, DC: Corcoran Gallery of Art; Freer Gallery of Art, Smithsonian Institution, 2003.

Deusner, Melody Barnett. *Aesthetic Painting in Britain and America: Collectors, Art Worlds, Networks.* London: Paul Mellon Centre for Studies in British Art, 2020.

Dorment, Richard, and Margaret F. MacDonald. *James McNeill Whistler.* New York: Harry N. Abrams, 1995.

Elbern, Victor H. "A Group of Pseudo-Ancient Glass Vessels from Italy." *Journal of Glass Studies* 10 (1968): 171–75.

Gardner, Albert Ten Eyck. "The History of a Collection." *Metropolitan Museum of Art Bulletin*, n.s., 5, no. 8 (April 1947): 215–20.

Gerdts, William H. "John Singer Sargent and His American Contemporaries in Venice." *Antiques & Fine Art* 7, no. 4 (2007): 274–81.

Getscher, Robert H. *James Abbott McNeill Whistler: Pastels.* New York: G. Braziller, 1991.

———. "Whistler and Venice." PhD diss., Case Western Reserve University, 1970.

Glasscock, Ann Marie. "James Jackson Jarves: Collecting Venetian Glass for America." *Revista de História da Arte* 3 (2015): 45–57.

Glavin, Ellen. "Maurice Prendergast's Second Visit to Venice: Disaster or New Impulse?" *Archives of American Art Journal* 42, nos. 1–2 (2002): 17–25.

Goldfarb, Hilliard T., Erica E. Hirshler, and T. J. Jackson Lears. *Sargent: The Late Landscapes.* Boston: Isabella Stewart Gardner Museum, 1999.

Greenwold, Diana Jocelyn. "Crafting New Citizens: Immigrant Craft Workshops in American Settlement Houses in New York and Boston, 1900–1945. " PhD diss., University of California, Berkeley, 2016.

Grieve, Alastair. "The Sites of Whistler's Venice Etchings." *Print Quarterly* 13, no. 1 (March 1996): 20–39.

———. *Whistler's Venice.* New Haven, CT: Yale University Press, 2000.

Halsby, Julian. *Venice: The Artist's Vision; A Guide to British and American Painters.* London: Unicorn Press, 1990.

Harden, Donald B. "Study and Research on Ancient Glass: Past and Future." *Journal of Glass Studies* 26 (1984): 9–24.

Harvey, Medill Higgins. *Collecting Inspiration: Edward C. Moore at Tiffany & Co.* New York: Metropolitan Museum of Art, 2021.

Herdrich, Stephanie L., H. Barbara Weinberg, and Marjorie Shelley. *American Drawings and Watercolors in the Metropolitan Museum of Art: John Singer Sargent.* New York: Metropolitan Museum of Art, 2000.

Hewison, Robert. *Ruskin and Venice.* New York: Thames and Hudson, 1978.

Hird, Frank. "Venetian Beads." *Beads: Journal of the Society of Bead Researchers* 10 (1999): 57–62.

Hirshler, Erica E. *William Merritt Chase.* Boston: MFA Publications, 2016.

Hirshler, Erica E., and Theresa A. Carbone. *John Singer Sargent Watercolors.* Boston: MFA Publications, 2013.

Hirshler, Erica E., Janet L. Comey, and Ellen E. Roberts. *A Studio of Her Own: Women Artists in Boston, 1870–1940.* Boston: MFA Publications, 2001.

Hollister, Paul. "Muranese Millefiori Revival of the Nineteenth Century." In "International Glass Conference: June 6–12, 1982." Special issue, *Journal of Glass Studies* 25 (1983): 201–6.

———. "The Remarkable Glass Gift of James Jackson Jarves, a Collector in a Hurry." *Acorn: Journal of the Sandwich Glass Museum* 5 (1994): 5–18.

Honour, Hugh, and John Fleming. *The Venetian Hours of Henry James, Whistler and Sargent.* Boston: Little, Brown, 1991.

Huntington, David C. *The Quest for Unity: American Art between World's Fairs, 1876–1893.* Detroit: Detroit Institute of Arts, 1983.

Isabella Stewart Gardner Museum. *Cultural Leadership in America: Art Matronage and Patronage*. Boston: Isabella Stewart Gardner Museum, 1997.

Jaffe, Irma B., ed. *The Italian Presence in American Art, 1860–1920*. New York: Fordham University Press, 1992.

Johnston, William R. *William and Henry Walters, The Reticent Collectors*. Baltimore, MD: Johns Hopkins University Press; Walters Art Gallery, 1999.

Kaplan, Paul H. D. "Contraband Guides: Twain and His Contemporaries on the Black Presence in Venice." *Massachusetts Review* 44, nos. 1–2 (Spring/Summer 2003): 182–202.

Karklins, Karlis. "Dominique Bussolin on the Glass Bead Industry of Murano and Venice (1847)." *Beads: Journal of the Society of Bead Researchers* 2 (1990): 69–84.

Kasson, Joy S. *Artistic Voyagers: Europe and the American Imagination in the Works of Irving, Allston, Cole, Cooper, and Hawthorne*. Westport, CT: Greenwood Press, 1982.

Kilmurray, Elaine, and Richard Ormond. *Sargent e l'Italia*. Ferrara: Ferrara Arte, 2002.

Koch, Michael. "Antonio Salviati and the Nineteenth-Century Renaissance of Venetian Glass." *Burlington Magazine* 136, no. 1094 (May 1994): 283–90.

———. "Minton, Elkington and Salviati: Acquisitions Made by the Bayerisches Nationalmuseum at the Vienna Exhibition of 1873." *Journal of the Decorative Arts Society, 1850 to the Present*, no. 16 (1992): 62–75.

Lochnan, Katharine A. *Whistler and His Circle: Etchings and Lithographs from the Collection of the Art Gallery of Ontario*. Toronto, Canada: Art Gallery of Ontario, 1986.

Lovell, Margaretta M. *Venice: The American View 1860–1920*. San Francisco: Fine Arts Museums of San Francisco, 1984.

———. *A Visitable Past: Views of Venice by American Artists, 1860–1915*. Chicago: University of Chicago Press, 1989.

———. "A Visitable Past: Views of Venice by American Artists, 1860–1915." PhD diss., Yale University, 1980.

Luzzi, Joseph. *Romantic Europe and the Ghost of Italy*. New Haven, CT: Yale University Press, 2008.

MacDonald, Margaret F. *Palaces in the Night: Whistler in Venice*. Berkeley: University of California Press, 2001.

Macleod, Dianne Sachko. *Enchanted Lives, Enchanted Objects: American Women Collectors and the Making of Culture, 1800–1940*. Berkeley: University of California Press, 2008.

Mariacher, Giovanni. *Antonio Salviati e la Rinascita Ottocentesca del Vetro Artistico Veneziano*. Venice: Museo Civico di Palazzo Chiericati, 1982.

Marraro, Howard R. *American Opinion on the Unification of Italy, 1846–1861*. New York: AMS Press, 1969.

Mathews, Nancy Mowll, and Elizabeth Kennedy. *Prendergast in Italy*. New York: Merrell; Williamstown, MA: Williams College Museum of Art; Chicago: Terra Foundation for American Art, 2009.

McCarthy, Kathleen D. *Women's Culture: American Philanthropy and Art, 1830–1930*. Chicago: University of Chicago Press, 1991.

McCauley, Elizabeth Anne, et al. *Gondola Days: Isabella Stewart Gardner and the Palazzo Barbaro Circle*. Boston: Isabella Stewart Gardner Museum, 2004.

McClaugherty, Martha Crabill. "Household Art: Creating the Artistic Home, 1868–1893." *Winterthur Portfolio* 18, no. 1 (Spring 1983): 1–26.

McClelland, Donald. *Paintings by Edwin Scott from the Alice Pike Barney Memorial Collection, Smithsonian Institution*. Washington, DC: Smithsonian Institution, 1970.

McCray, Patrick. *Glassmaking in Renaissance Venice: The Fragile Craft*. Brookfield, VT: Ashgate, 1999.

McNab, Jessie. "A Species of Creation." *Metropolitan Museum of Art Bulletin* 19, no. 3 (November 1960): 90–99.

McTavish, David. *Canadian Artists in Venice, 1830–1930; 18 February–1 April 1984*. Kingston, Canada: Agnes Etherington Art Centre, Queen's University, 1984.

Mentasti, Rosa Barovier. *Exquisite Glass Ornaments: The Nineteenth-Century Murano Glass Revival in the de Boos-Smith Collection*. Venice: Marsilio, 2010.

———. "Roman Glassware in the Museum of Murano and the Muranese Revival of the Nineteenth Century." *Journal of Glass Studies* 16 (1974): 111–19.

———. "La Vetraria Veneziana Moderna dal 1895 al 1920." *Journal of Glass Studies* 19 (1977): 147–59.

———. *Vetri di Murano dell'800*. Venice: Alfieri Editori, 1978.

Mentasti, Rosa Barovier, and Cristina Tonini, eds. *Atti / Istituto Veneto di Scienze, Lettere ed Arti, Classe di Scienze Fisiche, Matematiche e Naturali* 174, no. 1 (2016): 1–207.

———, eds. *Study Days on Venetian Glass: The Birth of the Great Museum; The Glassworks Collections between the Renaissance and Revival*. Venice: Istituto Veneto di Scienze, Lettere, ed Arti, 2016.

Merrill, Linda, ed. *After Whistler: The Artist and His Influence on American Painting*. New Haven, CT: Yale University Press, 2003.

———. *A Pot of Paint: Aesthetics on Trial in Whistler v. Ruskin*. Washington, DC: Smithsonian Institution Press, 1992.

Nagel, Gunther. *Jane Stanford: Her Life and Letters*. Stanford, CA: Stanford Alumni Association, 1975.

Neuhaus, Robert. *Unsuspected Genius: The Art and Life of Frank Duveneck*. San Francisco: Bedford Press, 1987.

Ninni, Irene. "*L'Impiraressa*: The Venetian Bead Stringer." Translated by Lucy Segatti. *Beads: Journal of the Society of Bead Researchers* 3 (1991): 73–82.

Nonnenberg, Sheryl Nese. "Women's Culture in the West: The Philanthropy and Art Patronage of Jane Stanford and Alma Spreckels." MA thesis, Stanford University, 2000.

Norwich, John Julius. *A History of Venice*. New York: Vintage Books, 1989.

O'Brien, Maureen C., ed. *In Support of Liberty: European Paintings at the 1883 Pedestal Fund Art Loan Exhibition*. Southampton, NY: Parrish Art Museum, 1986.

Olson, Roberta J. M., ed. *Ottocento: Romanticism and Revolution in 19th-Century Italian Painting*. New York: American Federation of Arts, 1992.

O'Neill, Michael, Mark Sandy, and Sarah Wootton, eds. *Venice and the Cultural Imagination: "This Strange Dream Upon the Water."* London: Pickering and Chatto, 2012.

Ormond, Richard, and Elaine Kilmurray. *John Singer Sargent: The Early Portraits*. Vol. 1 of *Complete Paintings*. New Haven, CT: Yale University Press, 1998.

———. *John Singer Sargent: Figures and Landscapes, 1874–1882*. Vol. 4 of *Complete Paintings*. New Haven, CT: Yale University Press, 2006.

———. *John Singer Sargent: Venetian Figures and Landscapes, 1898–1913*. Vol. 6 of *Complete Paintings*. New Haven, CT: Yale University Press, 2009.

———. *Sargent: Portraits of Artists and Friends*. London: National Portrait Gallery Publications, 2015.

Osborne, Carol Margot. *Venetian Glass of the 1890s: Salviati at Stanford University*. London: Philip Wilson, 2002.

Osborne, Carol Margot, Paul Venable Turner, and Anita Ventura Mozley. *Museum Builders in the West: The Stanfords as Collectors and Patrons of Art, 1870–1906*. Stanford, CA: Stanford University Museum of Art, 1986.

Page, Jutta-Annette, Lisa Pilosi, and Mark T. Wypyski. "Ancient Mosaic Glass or Modern Reproductions?" *Journal of Glass Studies* 43 (2001): 115–39.

Pavanello, Giuseppe, and Giandomenico Romanelli, eds. *Venezia nell'Ottocento: Immagini e Mito*. Milan: Electa, 1983.

Pavoni, Rosanna. *Reviving the Renaissance: The Use and Abuse of the Past in Nineteenth-Century Italian Art and Decoration*. Cambridge, UK: Cambridge University Press, 1997.

Perrot, Paul N. *Three Great Centuries of Venetian Glass: A Special Exhibition, 1958*. Corning, NY: Corning Museum of Glass, 1958.

Pilkington, John, Jr. "F. Marion Crawford: Italy in Fiction." *American Quarterly* 6, no. 1 (Spring 1954): 59–65.

Pine-Coffin, R. S. *Bibliography of British and American Travel in Italy to 1860*. Florence: Olschki, 1974.

Plant, Margaret. *Venice: Fragile City, 1797–1997*. New Haven, CT: Yale University Press, 2002.

Poli, Doretta Davanzo. *Arts and Crafts in Venice*. Cologne: Könemann, 1999.

———. *Il Merletto Veneziano*. Novara: Istituto Geografico De Agostini, 1998.

Pratt, Frances. *Murano Glass in the Twentieth Century*. St. Petersburg, FL: Museum of Fine Arts, 1983.

Quick, Michael. *An American Painter Abroad: Frank Duveneck's European Years*. Cincinnati: Cincinnati Art Museum, 1987.

Redford, Bruce. *Venice and the Grand Tour*. New Haven, CT: Yale University Press, 1996.

Richardson, E. P., and Otto Wittmann. *Travelers in Arcadia: American Artists in Italy, 1830–1875*. Detroit: Detroit Institute of Arts, 1951.

Ritter, Dorothea. *Venice in Old Photographs 1841–1920*. Boston: Bulfinch Press, 1994.

Robertson, Bruce, ed. *Sargent and Italy*. Princeton, NJ: Princeton University Press, 2003.

Rudoe, Judy. "'Reproductions of the Christian Glass of the Catacombs': James Jackson Jarves and the Revival of the Art of Glass in Venice." *Metropolitan Museum Journal* 37 (2002): 305–14.

Sarpellon, Giovanni. *Miniature Masterpieces: Mosaic Glass 1838–1924*. New York: Prestel, 1995.

———. *Salviati: Il Suo Vetro e I Suoi Uomini 1859–1987*. Venice: Stamperia di Venezia, 1989.

———. *Venetian Murrine and Beads*. Venice: Fondazione Musei Civici di Venezia, 2018.

Schwander, Martin, ed. *Venice: From Canaletto and Turner to Monet.* Ostfildern, Germany: Hatje Cantz, 2008.

Sciama, Lidia D., and Joanne B. Eicher, eds. *Beads and Bead Makers: Gender, Material Culture, and Meaning.* Cross-Cultural Perspectives on Women. New York: Berg, 1998.

Scollans, Carol G. J. *The Allure of Venice: Paintings by Walter Franklin Lansil.* Portsmouth, NH: Blue Tree, 2018.

Simpson, Marc, and Wanda M. Corn. *Like Breath on Glass: Whistler, Inness, and the Art of Painting Softly.* Williamstown, MA: Sterling and Francine Clark Art Institute, 2008.

Simpson, Marc, Richard Ormond, and H. Barbara Weinberg. *Uncanny Spectacle: The Public Career of the Young John Singer Sargent.* New Haven, CT: Yale University Press, 1997.

Sizer, Theodore. "James Jackson Jarves: A Forgotten New Englander." *New England Quarterly* 6, no. 2 (June 1933): 328–52.

Smithgall, Elsa, et al. *William Merritt Chase: A Modern Master.* New Haven, CT: Yale University Press, 2016.

Soria, Regina. *Visions of Italy.* New York: Borghi, 1988.

Stebbins, Theodore E., and William H. Gerdts, eds. *The Lure of Italy: American Artists and the Italian Experience, 1760–1914.* Boston: Museum of Fine Arts, 1992.

Steegmuller, Francis. *The Two Lives of James Jackson Jarves.* New Haven, CT: Yale University Press, 1951.

Tait, Hugh. "Felix Slade (1790–1868)." *Glass Circle Journal* 8 (1996): 70–87.

———, ed. *Five Thousand Years of Glass.* London: British Museum, 1991.

———. *The Golden Age of Venetian Glass.* London: British Museum, 1979.

Tharp, Louise Hall. *Mrs. Jack: A Biography of Isabella Stewart Gardner.* Boston: Little, Brown, 1965.

Tolman, R. P. *Catalog of the American and European Paintings in the Gellatly Collection.* Washington, DC: Smithsonian Institution, 1945.

Truettner, William H. "William T. Evans, Collector of American Paintings." *American Art Journal* 3, no. 2 (Autumn 1971): 50–79.

Van Hook, Bailey. *Angels of Art: Women and Art in American Society, 1876–1914.* University Park: Pennsylvania State University Press, 1996.

Wright, Nathalia. *American Novelists in Italy: The Discoverers, Allston to James.* Philadelphia: University of Pennsylvania Press, 1965.

Zecchin, Paolo. "Il Muranese Lorenzo Radi, Un Pioniere Quasi Dimenticato." *Rivista della Stazione Sperimentale del Vetro* 39, no. 3 (2009): 11–22.

———. "La Vetreria Salviati a Murano: Cronaca dei Primi Passi." *Journal of Glass Studies* 49 (2007): 191–205.

Zecchin, Sandro, and Vettore Zaniol. *La Cristalleria "Franchetti" a Murano.* Saonara: Il Prato, 2011.

Zilber, Emily. *"'A Delicate Link with Their Far Away Country': The Scuola d'Industrie Italiane (1905–1927) and the Translation of the Nineteenth Century Italian Reproduction Textile Workshop in an American Context. "* MA thesis, The Bard Graduate Center, 2007.

Zorzi, Rosella Mamoli. "'Foresti' in Venice in the Second Half of the 19th Century: Their Passion for Paintings, Brocades, and Glass." *Atti dell'Istituto Veneto di Scienze, Lettere ed Arti* 174 (2016): 1–43.

———, ed. *Henry James: Letters from the Palazzo Barbaro.* London: Pushkin Press, 1998.

———, ed. *Henry James: Letters to Isabella Stewart Gardner.* London: Pushkin Press, 2009.

———. "Pageants of Nineteenth-Century American Queens." In *Pageants and Processions: Images and Idiom as Spectacle,* edited by Herman du Toit, 199–215. Newcastle: Cambridge Scholars, 2009.

———. *Ralph W. Curtis, Un Pittore Americano a Venezia: Biografia.* Venice: Supernova, 2019.

Zukowski, Karen. *Creating the Artful Home: The Aesthetic Movement.* Layton, UT: Gibbs Smith, 2006.

Index

Page numbers in *italics* indicate illustrations.

B

C

D

E

F

G

H

T

U

V

W

Y

Z

Image Credits

JACKET

Back cover: Photo by Mildred Baldwin

FRONT MATTER

pp. 4–5: Photo by Mildred Baldwin

p. 6: Photo by Susan Goines

p. 8: Image copyright © The Metropolitan Museum of Art. Image source: Art Resource, NY

p. 13: © Maxfield Parrish Family, LLC / Licensed by VAGA at Artists Rights Society (ARS), NY. Image © 2018 Christie's Images Limited

pp. 14–15: Photo by Mindy Barrett

p. 17: Photo by Susan Goines

pp. 24–25: Birds' Eye View of Venice, *The Century Illustrated Monthly Magazine*, vol. 25, no 1 (November 1882), p. 22

INTRODUCTION

p. 32: Photo by Mindy Barrett

pp. 40, 41: Photos by Mildred Baldwin

p. 42 (bottom): Photo by Mindy Barrett

p. 43: Image copyright © The Metropolitan Museum of Art. Image source: Art Resource, NY

p. 44 (top): Courtesy of the Library of Congress, Prints and Photographs Division, LC-DIG-stereo-1s07025

pp. 48, 49: Photos by Mildred Baldwin

p. 51: Photo by Rick Echelmeyer

pp. 52 (bottom), 53: Photo by Mindy Barrett

pp. 54–55: Photo by Douglas Eng

MURANO GLASS AND ITS COLLECTORS IN AESTHETIC AMERICA

pp. 58–59: Photo by Gene Young

p. 61: Photo by Mildred Baldwin

p. 62: Photo by Mindy Barrett

p. 65: Charles Locke Eastlake, *Hints on Household Taste* (London: Longmans, Green, 1869), 2nd edition, plate 34 (incorrectly numbered 36), facing p. 227. Courtesy of the Getty Research Institute, via Archive.org

p. 66: Harriet Prescott Spofford, *Art Decoration Applied to Furniture* (New York: Harper and Brothers, 1877), p. 193

p. 67: Image copyright © The Metropolitan Museum of Art. Image source: Art Resource, NY

p. 68: Clarence Cook, *The House Beautiful* (New York: Scribner, Armstrong, 1878), plate 45, p. 125. Private collection. Photo by Mindy Barrett

p. 69: Clarence Cook, *The House Beautiful* (New York: Scribner, Armstrong, 1878), plate 37, p. 99. Photo by Mindy Barrett

p. 70: Photo by Mildred Baldwin

p. 71: *Harper's New Monthly Magazine*, vol. 64, no. 380 (January 1882), p. 178

p. 75: Photograph © 2021 Museum of Fine Arts, Boston

p. 78: From Carol M. Osborne, *Venetian Glass of the 1890s: Salviati at Stanford University* (London: Philip Wilson, 2002), p. 31

p. 80 (left): W. H. Schieffelin & Co (New York), *General Prices Current of Foreign and Domestic Drugs, Medicines, Chemicals*, 1876, p. 124. Courtesy of the US National Library of Medicine, via Archive.org

p. 80 (right): *Good Furniture* vol. 7, no. 1 (January 1919), p. 34. Courtesy of the University of California, via HathiTrust

p. 82: Photo by Michael Fischer

p. 83: Photo by Mildred Baldwin

pp. 85, 88–89: Courtesy of the Smithsonian Institution Archives, Image # 2002-10669

p. 87: Courtesy of Debra Force Fine Art

p. 92 (left): Photo by Mildred Baldwin

p. 94 (top): Photo by Lea Christiano

p. 94 (bottom): Photo by Mindy Barrett

VENETIAN MOSAICS AND GLASS IN THE UNITED STATES

pp. 98-99: Photo by Gene Young

p. 108: Giovanni Sabbatini, Giuseppe Carraro, and Eusebio Fiorioli, eds., *L'Italia alla Esposizione Universale di Parigi nel 1867: Rassegna Critica, Descrittiva, Illustrata* (Florence: Le Monnier, 1868), p. 308. Courtesy of Bayerische Staatsbibliothek

p. 109: Photo by Gene Young

p. 110: Image copyright © The Metropolitan Museum of Art. Image source: Art Resource, NY

p. 111: Alexander Nesbitt, *Catalogue of the Collection of Glass Formed by Felix Slade* (London: Wertheimer, Lea, 1871), unnumbered plate between pages 104 and 105. Courtesy of the Asiatic Society of Mumbai, via Archive.org

p. 112: Photo by Mildred Baldwin

p. 113: Image copyright © The Metropolitan Museum of Art. Image source: Art Resource, NY

p. 130: Photo: Matt Flynn © Smithsonian Institution

p. 134: Photo by Lea Christiano

p. 138: Photo: Matt Flynn © Smithsonian Institution

WHERE HAVE TITIAN'S BEAUTIES GONE?

pp. 142–44: Photo by Gene Young

p. 145: Courtesy of the Trustees of Sir John Soane's Museum. Photo © Sir John Soane's Museum, London

p. 146: Photo by Mindy Barrett

p. 147: © Amgueddfa Genedlaethol Cymru / © National Museum of Wales

p. 151: Photo by Susan Goines

p. 155: Image courtesy of Sterling and Francine Clark Art Institute, clarkart.edu

p. 159: *The Magazine of Art*, vol. 10 (1887), frontispiece. Courtesy of the University of Toronto, Robarts Library, via Archive.org

p. 160: Wellesley College, Special Collections, Venezia Album, Browning Collection H170, p. 54

p. 163: *The Century Magazine*, vol. 23, no. 3 (January 1882), p. 340

p. 164 (top): Courtesy of Menconi + Schoelkopf

p. 165: From Theodore E. Stebbins, *The Lure of Italy: American Artists and the Italian Experience, 1760–1914* (Boston: Museum of Fine Arts, 1992), p. 411

p. 170: Image copyright © The Metropolitan Museum of Art. Image source: Art Resource, NY

p. 173 (top): Photo by Susan Goines

p. 173 (bottom): Photo by Gene Young

pp. 174–75: Photo Credit: The Art Institute of Chicago / Art Resource, NY

INTERWEAVING WORLDS

pp. 180–81: Image copyright © The Metropolitan Museum of Art. Image source: Art Resource, NY

p. 182: *The Century Magazine*, vol. 23, no. 3 (January 1882), p. 336

p. 185 (left): Courtesy of the Library of Congress, Prints & Photographs Division, Arnold Genthe Collection, LC-G4085- 0365

p. 185 (right): Image copyright © The Metropolitan Museum of Art. Image source: Art Resource, NY

p. 187 (left): Hubert Howe Bancroft, *The Book of the Fair* (Chicago: Bancroft, 1893), vol. 2, p. 272. Courtesy of the Smithsonian Libraries

p. 187 (right): Maud Howe Elliott, *Art and Handicraft in the Woman's Building of the World's Columbian Exposition, Chicago, 1893* (New York: Goupil & Co., 1893), p. 18. Courtesy of the Smithsonian Libraries

p. 196 (both): Elisa Ricci, *Antiche Trine Italiane: Trine ad Ago* (Bergamo: Istituto Italiano d'Arte Grafiche, 1908). Courtesy of the Getty Research Institute, via Archive.org

p. 198 (top): Image copyright © The Metropolitan Museum of Art. Image source: Art Resource, NY

p. 199: MssCol 2844, Gino Speranza Papers, Scuola d'Industrie Italiane, Box 14, Folder 1909, Manuscripts and Archives Division, The New York Public Library

p. 201 (bottom): Plate 4 in "A Century of New York Needlework and Cecorative Fabrics," *The Bulletin of the Needle and Bobbin Club*, vol. 28, 1944. Courtesy of the University of Arizona, On-Line Digital Archive of Documents on Weaving and Related Topics

SPARKS OF GENIUS

pp. 210–11: Photo by Mildred Baldwin

p. 213: © Maxfield Parrish Family, LLC / Licensed by VAGA at Artists Rights Society (ARS), NY

p. 214: Photo by Mildred Baldwin

p. 218: Image copyright © The Metropolitan Museum of Art. Image source: Art Resource, NY

p. 222: Photo by Mildred Baldwin

p. 228 (top): Photo by Mindy Barrett

p. 228 (bottom): Photo by Gene Young

p. 230: Photo by Mildred Baldwin

p. 231: Photograph by Morgan Heiskell, *The American Magazine of Art*, vol. 15, no. 9 (September 1924), p. 467. Courtesy of the University of Virginia, via HathiTrust

pp. 234–35: Photo by Gene Young

p. 236 (top): Photo: Travis Fullerton, © Virginia Museum of Fine Arts

p. 240: Photo by Gene Young

p. 242: Photo by Mildred Baldwin

p. 249: Photo by Susan Goines

p. 250: © 2021 Estate of Giacomo Balla / Artists Rights Society (ARS), New York / SIAE, Rome. Digital Image © The Museum of Modern Art / Licensed by SCALA / Art Resource, NY

p. 253: © Maxfield Parrish Family, LLC / Licensed by VAGA at Artists Rights Society (ARS), NY. Image © 2018 Christie's Images Limited

p. 254: Photo by Mildred Baldwin

pp. 255 (both), 257, 260: Photos by Mindy Barrett

p. 264: Image copyright © The Metropolitan Museum of Art. Image source: Art Resource, NY

Acknowledgments

Glassmaking requires teamwork, and the most complex examples of Venetian revival glass featured in this project result from collaboration among multiple glassblowers or gaffers, plus designers, experts in flameworking, enamel decorators, gilders, and countless assistants. There are also the chemists who mix colors, the technicians who maintain furnaces, and those who describe and market finished glassware in showrooms, with support from entrepreneurs and financiers. Likewise, this exhibition and catalogue bear witness to the skills, dedication, and generosity of many organizations and individuals.

The genesis of this project is the remarkable glass collection of the Chrysler Museum of Art in Norfolk, VA, and the artists and educators who run its Perry Glass Studio. During my tenure as the Chrysler's Joan and Macon Brock Curator of American Art, friends and former colleagues planted the seeds for a show juxtaposing Venetian glass with American paintings, prints, and watercolors. Glass expertise from Kelly Conway and Diane C. Wright has been the map for this voyage, with further guidance from Lloyd DeWitt, Seth Feman, Jeff Harrison, Susan Leidy, Mark Lewis, and Cheryl Little. Many artists have shaped my understanding of the material properties of glass through demos, classes, exhibits, and conversations at the Chrysler and beyond, especially Charlotte Potter Kasic, Hannah Kirkpatrick, Beth Lipman, Matthew Day Perez, Robin and Julia Rogers, and Norwood Viviano. The ensemble of glass scholars, makers, and collectors who live in and visit Norfolk define it as an American Murano, and I dedicate this project to four inspiring friends from the Chrysler community who I deeply wish were alive to celebrate it with me today: Macon Brock, Richard and Leah Waitzer, and Amy Brandt.

Information and research are the raw materials of an exhibition, like grains of sand to be melted and fused into molten glass. My research is deeply indebted to another American Murano, the Corning Museum of Glass, for the opportunity to be a David Whitehouse Scholar-in-Residence there in 2019. For collections access, guidance in Corning's Rakow Research Library, and targeted feedback, I thank Stephen Brucker, Regan Brumagen, William Gudenrath, Elizabeth Hylen, Katherine Larson, Christopher Maxwell, Alexandra Ruggiero, Susie J. Silbert, Mikki Smith, Karol Wight, and all of their colleagues. I am also grateful to the North Caroliniana Society for an Archie K. Davis Fellowship, which funded research at the Wilson Special Collections Library at the University of North Carolina, Chapel Hill, with particular assistance from Jason Tomberlin. Finally, access to the museums and archives of Venice was essential to this project, and I thank the Terra Foundation for American Art for an International Curatorial Travel Grant to facilitate these inquiries. In Venice, hospitality and advice from David Landau, Federica Marangoni, Giovanni Sarpellon, Pierpaolo Seguso, Chiara Squarcina, Mauro Stocco,

Gražina Subelytė, Patricia Curtis Viganò, Jerome Zeiseniss, Rosella Mamoli Zorzi, and the staff of the Biblioteca Nazionale Marciana made this research a success.

A Smithsonian Scholarly Studies Award facilitated additional travel and access to museums, libraries, archives, and private collections around the United States. Countless colleagues and friends in the field of American art, in museums, universities, and galleries, gave advice and opened doors during these studies, and many assisted in locating key artworks and research materials. I thank Warren Adelson, Michael Altman, Nicole Amoroso, Robyn Asleson, Aaron Bastian, Eric Baumgartner, Katherine Baumgartner, Adrienne Baxter Bell, William T. Billeck, Abigail Bisbee, Lydia Blackmore, Jennifer Blancato, Katherine Blood, Graham C. Boettcher, Mark Brock, Mel Buchanan, Timothy Anglin Burgard, Laurie E. Burgess, Jason T. Busch, Sarah Cash, Fern Cohen, Hersh Cohen, Michele Cohen, Thomas Colville, Katelyn D. Crawford, Brandy Culp, David Park Curry, Bethany Dobson, Alexandra Eliopoulos, Stuart P. Feld, Debra Force, Kathleen A. Foster, Thomas Gardner, Christine Gervais, James Glisson, John Stuart Gordon, Chloe Heins, Dot Hendler, Marissa Hershon, Frederick D. Hill, Jennifer Krieger, Betty Krulik, Shelley Langdale, Bonnie Campbell Lilienfeld, Mary Lublin, Anna O. Marley, Katherine Martin, Leo Mazow, Justin McCann, Susan E. Menconi, Thomas Michie, Erin Monroe, Christopher Oliver, Elizabeth Oustinoff, Lauren Palmor, Theresa Papanikolas, Molly Phelps, Tyler Prince, Susan J. Rawles, Richard Rossello, William Keyse Rudolph, Jillian Russo, Daisy Hill Saunders, Andrew Schoelkopf, Jonah Siegel, Nathaniel Silver, Jonathan Spies, Gail Stavitsky, Michael Taylor, Tom Veilleux, Stefanie Walker, Meredith Ward, Eric Widing, Debra G. Wieder, Tessa Wild, Elizabeth Dospěl Williams, and Kathy Wong. Most valuable of all has been the work of past scholars of the American grand tour to Venice, named abundantly in this book's notes and bibliography, with Eric Denker, Erica Hirshler, Margaretta M. Lovell, Richard Ormond, and Rosella Mamoli Zorzi deserving highest praise. In comparison, I am a novice on this subject in terms of knowledge, but I dare to boast that our esteem and love for these artworks is equal.

This exhibition concept benefitted immensely from critique by patient and wise audiences during several lectures and workshops. At the Smithsonian American Art Museum's Research and Scholars Center, Amelia Goerlitz and Stacy Weiland facilitated my first presentation of this idea as a lunchbag seminar, where it received comments from fellows and from colleagues at the Smithsonian American Art Museum (SAAM), the National Portrait Gallery, and the Archives of American Art. I also thank the University of Delaware Department of Art History, particularly Professors Lawrence Nees and Wendy Bellion, for the invitation to speak about the Venetian grand tour for the 2019 Wayne Craven Lecture in American Art, where faculty and students helpfully challenged its methods and premises. The Historic Charleston Foundation in Charleston, SC, also permitted me to share this project with its informed community of decorative arts collectors and enthusiasts, and I thank Lauren Northup and Julius A. Dargan for their hospitality during that visit.

SAAM's support of my research on American artists in Italy long predates my curatorial work on its staff, and I am fortunate to name this museum as a formative influence on my training through a Terra Foundation for American Art Predoctoral Fellowship, with William H. Truettner and Cynthia Mills co-advising my studies. They join Alexander Nemerov, Timothy Barringer, Judith Colton, Edward Cooke, Michael Hatt, John F. Kasson, Joy S. Kasson, Jonathan D. Katz, Mary Pardo, and other advisers who have shaped my art historical research and writing skills. For curatorial mentorship I am indebted to Jan Howard, Julia Marciari-Alexander, Emily J. Peters, and Angus Trumble, all of whom will recognize in this project echoes of research pursued under their supervision.

As the furnaces heated and this exhibition gathered momentum, my fellow curators at SAAM have been steady and invaluable allies, and I thank them for encouraging exploration of a topic that, when first presented, may have seemed outside this museum's areas of strength. Virginia Mecklenburg helped frame guiding questions, and E. Carmen Ramos gave generous feedback on catalogue manuscript drafts. Eleanor Jones Harvey and Karen Lemmey were essential thought partners through their expertise in nineteenth-century paintings and sculpture. Meanwhile Saisha Grayson,

Melissa Ho, John Jacob, Sarah Newman, and Leslie Umberger helped this project synchronize with wider museum programs and goals. At our sister museum, the Renwick Gallery, Nora Atkinson and Mary Savig have been extraordinary advocates. They have articulated how this show's checklist dovetails with the Renwick's rich holdings in contemporary glass and demonstrated how many of the innovations of the Venetian glass revival remain alive today in the field of American craft.

This show has itself benefitted incalculably from the work of assistants and interns, particularly the dedicated research and management work of Brittany Strupp, who contributed not only expertise in American art of the late nineteenth century, but also an enthusiasm for these artworks that inspired our whole team. Its scale could not have been accomplished without subsequent expert curatorial assistance from Maria R. Eipert, as well as Laura Augustin, Anne Hyland, and Stacy Mince, with managerial support from Tae Edell and Jean Lavery. Roberta Geier provided volunteer research, and Helena Black and Kathleen Maher made valuable contributions during internships coordinated by Judith Houston Holloman. The American Art and Portrait Gallery Library was a daily resource, and I am deeply indebted to Anne Evenhaugen, Patricia L. Reid, Alexandra Reigle, and all Smithsonian Libraries staff and volunteers.

Across the museum a wider team of staff have translated these ideas into a beautiful exhibition and book. With the confidence and grace of a master glassblower, Director Stephanie Stebich breathed life into this ambitious show and its international tour, despite the COVID-19 pandemic that upended every facet of our museum's operations. This leadership, along with Deputy Director David Voyles's astute supervision of the budget, preserved our fragile project and our team's spirits. Doug Wilde and Kelly DeFilippis provided financial oversight, with Krista Duncan reviewing and processing purchase orders to guarantee that the right tools were in hand at every step of this endeavor. The Development department, led by Donna Rim, helped meet the funding needs, providing the fuel for our furnaces. Elizabeth Daoust, Christie Davis, and Kate Earnest contributed to appeals and grant applications with unique insights. Laura Baptiste, Amy Fox, Katie Hondorf, Amy Hutchins, Howard Kaplan, Sara Snyder, and Alex Tyson have handled publicity, marketing, and media while adapting to new communications platforms and strategies. Previews, the opening, and other special events have been organized by Chavon Jones and Mary Beth Maggio, and Andrew Rondinone, with Kayleigh Bryant-Greenwell and Gloria Kenyon creating the show's lecture series and Carol Wilson leading the Education department in its related offerings. Thanks to their work, we can welcome a global audience to experience the exhibition both virtually and in person.

The fragility of these glass artworks and the challenges of their installation exposes the skills and courage of other colleagues. Collections managers James Concha, Claire Denny, Lily Sehn, and Denise Wamaling assisted with the study of hundreds of works in storage, helping craft a foundation for the checklist within SAAM's holdings. Conservators Leah Bright, Amber Kerr, Gwen Manthey, Catherine Maynor, and Ariel O'Connor then prepared the finest of these for display and travel, with research by intern Sarah Montonchaikul building knowledge of understudied works. In the Registrars department, Cassandra Belliston, Annie Farrar, and Jennifer Lee, with leadership from Melissa Kroning and Lynn Putney, organized arrangements with tour venues and managed an equally complex list of loans, with Christopher Kirages and Matthew Bacon coordinating shipping. David Gleeson's Exhibitions team has united these treasures in the galleries, with Adam Rice coordinating production, and Eunice Park Kim and Grace Lopez creating the design and graphic identity. I marvel at their sensitivity to the character and history of these artworks, and also at the meticulous work of Nick Primo and Caleb Plattner in executing these plans by preparing the walls, casework, and countless other dimensions of an exceptionally complicated installation. Thanks to matting, framing, and mounts by Thomas Irion and Martin Kotler, and with Scott Rosenfeld's lighting expertise, the magic of each work of art is magnified by this presentation. Joanna Marsh, Carlos Parada, and Anne Showalter managed interpretative strategies and produced the introductory video. From beginning to end, scheduling coordination by Erin J. Bryan kept all these tasks in motion.

The catalogue is a work of art in its own right, thanks to the insight and editing of Tiffany Farrell, whose appreciation for detail is beautifully suited to the intricacies of these glass masterpieces and the twists and turns of their story. Publications director Theresa Slowik provided crucial wisdom on the book's structure and managed its copublication with Princeton University Press, working with Michelle Komie and Ali Parrington. SAAM's designers Karen Siatras and Denise Arnot embraced the colors and playfulness of Venetian glass in crafting this book's elegant layout. Aubrey Vinson coordinated hundreds of images and permissions, with Mildred Baldwin, Mindy Barrett, and Riche Sorensen managing photography; thanks to them, many of these artworks appear here in print for the first time. The authors who have contributed to this catalogue deserve extraordinary respect not only for the knowledge and perspectives they bring to this subject, but also for perseverance in navigating the challenges of research, writing, and editing amid telework, library closures, and the professional and personal challenges faced during the pandemic and its lockdowns. Beyond the content of their essays, Sheldon Barr, Melody Deusner, Diana Greenwold, and Stephanie Heydt have consulted on the checklist of this exhibition, and many of the finest works presented here are the direct results of their suggestions. The words on these pages convey only a fraction of the brilliance each brings to this overall project. Finally, Rosemary Hammack, Magda Nakassis, and Julianna White have provided editing and fact-checking, and I accept full responsibility for all errors and omissions that remain within these pages.

Organizing loans depended on the generosity of dozens of institutions and colleagues, many of whom welcomed me into their study rooms, archives, and libraries for research and firsthand viewing. In addition to some already named, the success of this show is a tribute to assistance from Tammis K. Groft and W. Douglas McCombs, Albany Institute of History & Art; Paul R. Provost and Ashley Holland, Art Bridges; James Rondeau and Sarah Kelly Oehler, Art Institute of Chicago; Christopher Bedford, Andaleeb Badiee Banta, Morgan Dowty, Joanna Karlgaard, and Asma Naeem, Baltimore Museum of Art; Anne Collins Goodyear, Frank H. Goodyear, Joachim Homann, and Laura Latman, Bowdoin College Museum of Art; Anne Pasternak, Jane Dini, Margarita Karasoulas, and Shea Spiller, Brooklyn Museum; Susan Dackerman, Aleesa Pitchamarn Alexander, Patrick R. Crowley, Shanna Dickson, and Susan Roberts-Manganelli, Iris & B. Gerald Cantor Center for Visual Arts at Stanford University; Erik Neil, Devon Dargan, Carolyn Swan Needell, Melanie Neil, and Corey Piper, Chrysler Museum of Art; Cameron Kitchin, Julie Aronson, Anne Buening, and Kristin Spangenberg, Cincinnati Art Museum; Olivier Meslay, Esther Bell, Kristie Couser, and Kathleen Morris, Clark Art Institute; John Davis, Caitlin Condell, Crystal Ferrer, Laura Fravel, Emily Orr, and Kimberly Randall, Cooper Hewitt, Smithsonian Design Museum; Mindy Taylor, Fry Fine Art; Cinnamon Catlin-Legutko and Brooke Morgan, Illinois State Museum; Sandra Jackson-Dumont and Jillian Griffith, Lucas Museum of Narrative Art; Max Hollein, Stephanie L. Herdrich, Iris Moon, Lisa Pilosi, and Sylvia Yount, Metropolitan Museum of Art; Katie Luber and Robert Cozzolino, Minneapolis Institute of Art; Matthew Teitelbaum and Erica Hirshler, Museum of Fine Arts, Boston; Whitney Donhauser, Leslie Gerhauser, and Matt Heffernan, Museum of the City of New York; Judy Goffman Cutler and Sara Bliss Cohen, National Museum of American Illustration; Susan Fisher Sterling, Catherine Bade, and Virginia Treanor, National Museum of Women in the Arts; Anthony W. Marx, David Christie, and Madeleine Viljoen, New York Public Library; Valerie Hillings, John W. Coffey, and Maggie Gregory, North Carolina Museum of Art; Dorothy Kosinski, Michele De Shazo, Elsa Smithgall, and Trish Waters, Phillips Collection; John W. Smith, Emily Banas, Tara Emsley, Sionan Guenther, Maureen O'Brien, and Elizabeth Williams, RISD Museum; Kirk Johnson and Katherine Crowe, Smithsonian National Museum of Natural History; Robert G. Trujillo and Gurudarshan Khalsa, Stanford University Libraries; Adam M. Levine and Diane C. Wright, Toledo Museum of Art; Theresa Malanum and Alexander Lourie, US Senate Commission on Art; Julia Marciari-Alexander, Gregory Bailey, and Jo Briggs, Walters Art Museum; Pamela Franks and Kevin Murphy, Williams College Museum of Art; and William Valerio and Rachel McCay, Woodmere Art Museum.

The private lenders to this exhibition deserve special thanks for permitting their treasures to be featured in this show and for assistance with image gathering for publication in this book. These lenders have also generously shared from their knowledge of the works and from their personal research, with contributions that deserve recognition here. I thank Vincent and Kako Crisci, Mary Anne Goley, Darrel C. Karl, Jane Joel Knox, David Mamet and Rebecca Pidgeon, and *sopratutto* John F. McGuigan Jr. and Mary K. McGuigan, who have significantly amplified my appreciation for American artists in Italy through their friendship and their ongoing scholarship.

As I cede pride in this exhibition's creation to all named here, I look forward to sharing it with visitors in Washington, DC, and at its two tour venues. At the Amon Carter Museum of American Art, I praise the work of Andrew Walker, Margaret Adler, Heather Creamer, Alessandra Guzman, Spencer Wigmore, and their colleagues as they prepare this project for a vibrant presentation in Fort Worth, TX. *Grazie* also to Gabriella Belli, director of the Fondazione Musei Civici di Venezia, and Elisabetta Barisoni, head of the Ca' Pesaro Galleria Internazionale d'Arte Moderna, for their enthusiasm. It is an honor to partner with them so that these interconnected objects and stories can be reassembled in Venice, near the sites of creation for many, where this incomparable context may spark ideas for future research and international collaboration.

Countless great monuments in Venice testify to the city's resilience through the pandemics of past centuries, and all named above deserve extra respect for their contributions and the sacrifices made while weathering the emotional hurricanes of 2020–2021. My small share of this work could not have succeeded without encouragement from family and friends, in particular Ben Cook, Richard Escobedo, Eli Feiman, Kenneth Hill, Josh Holshauser, Rob James, Andrew Ly, Joe Madura, Nathaniel Phillips, Davis Richardson, Andrew Rondinone, Grant Salley, Tom Saunders, and Mike Stratmoen. In addition to my parents, Linda Weathersby and Lex Mann, I owe special thanks to my cousin Kendall Scales Glade, who traveled with me on my first visit to Italy, and to our late grandparents, Sally Ann and Ace Mann, who made that adventure possible.

CAM

SARGENT, WHISTLER & VENETIAN GLASS

American Artists and the Magic of Murano

Published in conjunction with the exhibition of the same name, on view at the Smithsonian American Art Museum, Washington, DC, October 8, 2021 to May 8, 2022. Also traveling to the Amon Carter Museum of American Art, Fort Worth, TX, June 25 to September 11, 2022; and the Ca' Pesaro Galleria Internazionale d'Arte Moderna, Venice, Italy, October 15, 2022 to January 8, 2023.

© 2021 Smithsonian American Art Museum

All rights reserved. No part of this book may be reproduced or used in any forms or by any means—graphic, electronic, or mechanical, including photocopying, recording, taping, or information storage and retrieval systems—without written permission of the Smithsonian American Art Museum.

Produced by the Publications Office, Smithsonian American Art Museum, Washington, DC, AmericanArt.si.edu

Theresa J. Slowik, Chief of Publications
Tiffany D. Farrell, Senior Editor
Julianna C. White, Editor
Karen Siatras, Senior Designer
Denise Arnot, Designer
Aubrey Vinson, Permissions Coordinator
Rosemary Hammack, Proofreader
Magda Nakassis, Proofreader
Kate Mertes, Indexer

Published by the Smithsonian American Art Museum in association with Princeton University Press, Princeton and Oxford, press.princeton.edu

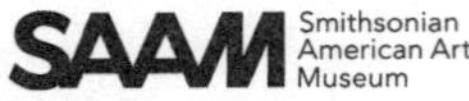

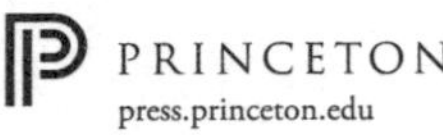

The Smithsonian American Art Museum is home to one of the largest collections of American art in the world. Its holdings—more than 43,000 works—tell the story of America through the visual arts and represent the most inclusive collection of American art of any museum today.

It is the nation's first federal art collection, predating the 1846 founding of the Smithsonian Institution. The Museum celebrates the exceptional creativity of the nation's artists, whose insights into history, society, and the individual reveal the essence of the American experience.

For more information, write to:
Publications Office
Smithsonian American Art Museum
MRC 970, PO Box 37012
Washington, DC 20013-7012

DETAIL CAPTIONS

Cover: John Singer Sargent, *A Venetian Woman* (detail), 1882; see p. 30

Title page: Venice and Murano Glass and Mosaic Company Ltd. (Salviati & Co.) or Fratelli Barovier, Vase with Dolphin and Serpent (detail), ca. 1870s–90s; see p. 239

pp. 4–5: Francis Hopkinson Smith, *On the Way to the Public Garden* (detail), ca. 1895; see p. 48

p. 6: Julius LeBlanc Stewart, *Conversation Vénetienne* (detail), 1891; see p. 151

p. 7: Charles Caryl Coleman, *Still Life with Peach Blossoms* (detail), 1877; see p. 73

p. 8: Venice and Murano Glass and Mosaic Company Ltd. (Salviati & Co.), Lidded Mosaic Glass Urn with Silver Leaf Design (detail), ca. 1880; see p. 113

p. 9: Pinckney Marcius-Simons, *The Child Canova Modeling a Lion out of Butter* (detail), ca. 1885; see p. 236

p. 11: Maurice Brazil Prendergast, *Fiesta Grand Canal, Venice* (detail), ca. 1899; see p. 243

p. 12: Venice and Murano Glass and Mosaic Company Ltd. (Salviati & Co.) or Compagnia di Venezia e Murano (CVM), Ancient Roman–Style Mosaic Glass Bowl (detail), ca. 1875–80; see p. 136

p. 13: Maxfield Parrish, *A Venetian Night's Entertainment* (detail), 1903; see p. 253

Contents: Unidentified, probably Murano, Byzantine-Style Mosaic Necklace with Christ and Twelve Apostles (detail), ca. 1870s–1910s; see p. 255

opp. Lenders page: Arthur Beecher Carles, *Venetian Gondolas* (detail), ca. 1909; see p. 249

opp. Ambassador's Welcome: Charles Caryl Coleman, *The Bronze Horses of San Marco, Venice* (detail), 1876; see p. 137

opp. Director's Foreword: Fratelli Toso, Mosaic Glass Amphora (detail), ca. 1880s–90s; see p. 90

pp. 24–25: *Bird's-Eye View of Venice,* from Henry James Jr., "Venice" in *Century Illustrated Monthly Magazine,* November 1882

p. 26: Giovanni Boldini, *Portrait of James McNeill Whistler* (detail), 1897; see p. 172

p. 27: John Singer Sargent, *The Sulphur Match* (detail), 1882; see p. 217

Back cover: Attributed to Compagnia di Venezia e Murano (CVM), Vase with Dolphins and Flowers (detail), ca. 1880s–90s; see p. 41

LIBRARY OF CONGRESS CATALOGING-IN-PUBLICATION DATA

NAMES:
Mann, Crawford Alexander, III, editor. | Barr, Sheldon. Venetian mosaics and glass in the United States, 1860–1917. | Deusner, Melody Barnett. Murano glass and its collectors in aesthetic America. | Greenwold, Diana. Interweaving worlds. | Heydt, Stephanie Mayer. Where have Titian's beauties gone?

TITLE:
Sargent, Whistler, and Venetian glass: American artists and the magic of Murano | edited by Crawford Alexander Mann III; contributions by Sheldon Barr, Melody Barnett Deusner, Diana Jocelyn Greenwold, Stephanie Mayer Heydt, and Crawford Alexander Mann III.

DESCRIPTION:
Washington, DC: Smithsonian American Art Museum (2021) | Includes bibliographical references and index.

IDENTIFIERS:
LCCN 2021016688
ISBN 9780691222677 (hardcover)

SUBJECTS:
LCSH: Glass art—Italy—Murano—Exhibitions. | Lace and lace making—Italy—Burano—Exhibitions. | Aesthetics, American—Exhibitions. | Glass art—Collectors and collecting—United States—Exhibitions. | Painting, American—19th century—Exhibitions. | Painting, American—20th century—Exhibitions. | Venice (Italy)—In art—Exhibitions.

CLASSIFICATION:
LCC NK5152.M85 S265 2021
DDC 748.0945—dc23

LC record available at https://lccn.loc.gov/2021016688

Typeset in Centaur MT Pro, Trajan Pro, Gill Sans Nova Condensed, and Beata.

Printed in Italy by EBS Editoriale Bortolazzi Stei on GardaMatt Art 170 gsm and Munken Lynx 130 gsm paper.